ENGLISH WORKSHOP

THIRD COURS

D1305350

HOLT, RINEHART AND WINSTON

Harcourt Brace & Company

Austin • New York • Orlando • Chicago • Atlanta
San Francisco • Boston • Dallas • Toronto • London

T   6 018 09

TABLE OF CONTENTS

PREWRITING: FINDING IDEAS FOR WRITING

Writing actually begins when you think up ideas, not when you pick up your pencil. Your experiences, observations, feelings, and opinions are rich sources of topics and ideas. The following prewriting techniques can help you find and explore ideas.

WRITER'S JOURNAL

Use a *writer's journal* to record experiences, observations, feelings, opinions, ideas, and questions. Your journal might be a notebook, a blank book, or a special folder. Write in it daily, and date your entries.

- Use your imagination; write down dreams, daydreams, parts of songs, and stories.
- Collect poems, articles, quotations, and cartoons. When you include something, tell why you like it or what it reminds you of.
- Don't worry about spelling, grammar, or neatness. Just keep track of your ideas.

FREEWRITING

When you *freewrite*, you write whatever comes to mind. You don't worry about what you are saying or how you are saying it. Freewriting can help you to relax about writing. It can also give you some ideas for later writing.

- Use a timer, and write for three to five minutes.
- Begin with a word or topic that is important to you. Write whatever the word or topic makes you think of. Don't worry about grammar, spelling, or punctuation. Just write!
- If you get stuck, copy the same word or phrase until you think of something else.

EXERCISE 1   Using Prewriting Techniques

Plan a paragraph about something that you have learned through experience. It might be a fact, a skill, or a new way of thinking. To find and develop your ideas, write a page for your writer's journal. Combine two prewriting techniques by freewriting in your journal for three to five minutes.

PREWRITING: BRAINSTORMING AND CLUSTERING

BRAINSTORMING

When you *brainstorm*, you free your mind to come up with ideas in response to a word. You can brainstorm alone, with a partner, or in a group.

- Write a word or subject on a sheet of paper. Then list every idea about the word or subject that comes into your mind. If you are brainstorming with a partner or group, one person should record all the ideas.
- Do not stop to judge the ideas. You can do that later.
- Keep going until you have no more ideas.

CLUSTERING

Clustering is also called webbing or making connections. When you cluster, you use a series of circles and connecting lines. This process helps you break a large subject into its smaller parts.

- Write your subject in the center of a sheet of paper. Circle it.
- Around the subject, write all the related ideas that occur to you. Circle the ideas, and draw lines to connect them to the original subject.
- Let your mind wander. Add new ideas to the original subject and to its related ideas. Keep writing, circling, and connecting until your paper is filled.

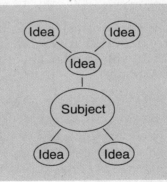

EXERCISE 2 Brainstorming and Clustering

With a partner, choose one of the subjects below. Work together to brainstorm a list of related ideas or subjects. Then, working alone, choose one of the ideas, and use it as the subject of a cluster. When your cluster diagram is finished, meet with your partner to compare and contrast your clusters.

dangerous jobs   sports heroes   comedy

government   hobbies   modern life

PREWRITING: ASKING QUESTIONS

ASKING THE *5W-HOW?* QUESTIONS

One way to collect information about a subject is by asking the *5W-How? questions: Who? What? Where? When? Why?* and *How?* Not every question applies to every subject. Sometimes you won't need all of the questions. You may also use some of the questions more than once. Here is an example of the way you might use the questions to gather information about the woman known as Typhoid Mary.

- *Who?*   Who was Typhoid Mary?
- *What?*   What did she do to spread typhoid?
- *Where?*   Where did she live and work?
- *When?*   When did this happen?
- *Why?*   Why did she spread the disease? Why wasn't she cured?
- *How?*   How was she finally stopped from spreading typhoid?

ASKING "WHAT IF?" QUESTIONS

Asking **"What if?"** questions can help you generate a variety of ideas for creative writing. You explore what might follow if something occurred.

- *What if some historical moment had been different?* (What if President Kennedy had not been assassinated? What if the wheel hadn't been invented?)
- *What if something amazing happened to a common person?* (What if a street musician won a million-dollar lottery? What if a teenager suddenly became middle-aged?)
- *What if a character had special powers or abilities?* (What if I woke up with the ability to read people's minds? What if a young girl could instantly transport herself to other places?)

EXERCISE 3   Using the *5W-How?* Questions

You are writing a report about one of the subjects below. On your own paper, make a list of the *5W-How?* questions that you can use to explore the subject.

the Carnegie Hero Fund	trampolines	mummies
the Vietnam Veterans Memorial	Seattle	Hawaii

EXERCISE 4   Using "What if?" Questions

Working with a partner, choose two of the following items. Then work together to write five "What if?" questions for each of the two items. Write your questions on the lines below.

1. a rocket ship
2. an inflatable boat
3. a small gold charm
4. tap water

5. rain
6. elections
7. the latest fashions
8. telephones

Item 1 _____

_____

_____

_____

_____

_____

_____

Item 2 _____

_____

_____

_____

_____

_____

_____

PREWRITING: ARRANGING IDEAS

After you have gathered ideas, you need to spend some time arranging, or ordering, them. There are four common ways to order ideas.

ARRANGING IDEAS		
Type of Order	Definition	Examples
Chronological	Narration: order that presents events as they happen in time	Story, narrative poem, explanation of a process, drama, history, biography
Spatial	Description: order that describes objects according to location	Descriptions (near to far, outside to inside, left to right, top to bottom)
Importance	Evaluation: order that gives details from least to most important or the reverse	Persuasion, description, explanations, evaluation
Logical	Classification: order that relates items and groups	Definitions, classifications

EXERCISE 5   Arranging Ideas

On your own paper, identify the method of organization that would be best for each of the following writing situations. Be prepared to explain your choice of order.

1. You are writing a report on Guatemala and are describing the Mayan city of Tikal.
2. You want to give three reasons why your school should get a new gymnasium.
3. You want to discuss the differences between high school basketball and professional basketball.
4. You want to explain how to make a pizza.

WRITING A FIRST DRAFT

At some point, you have to stop gathering information and start writing a first draft. People take different approaches to drafting. Some write quickly, while others work more slowly and carefully. Some people work from rough notes, while others use a detailed outline. As you write your first draft, you might try these suggestions.

- Use your prewriting plans as a guide.
- Write freely, and focus on expressing your ideas clearly.
- You may discover new ideas as you write. Include these new ideas in your draft.
- Don't worry about catching or correcting errors in grammar, usage, or mechanics while you are drafting. You will be able to focus on these aspects later.

Here is a first draft of a paragraph about the silk industry. Notice how the writer has inserted questions and notes. They will remind the writer to return to prewriting to gather more information before the final draft. Also, notice that the writing still needs more polishing. The polishing comes later.

> Silk is a natural fiber that is spun by the silkworm [Latin name?] as it spins it ~~cocoon~~ cocoon. Each silkworm cocoon is actually one single fiber. [how long?] To harvest the silk, the cocoons are first washed and heated. Then they are unwound and several [how many] fibers are spun together to make a single thread. Then the thread is dyed. This process was discovered by the Chinese about 2600 B.C. ~~and~~ For years, they kept the secret inside China. ~~In fact a law prevented anyone from telling~~

EXERCISE 6 Writing a First Draft

Using what you've learned about arranging ideas in chronological order, draft a narrative about how to do some simple process. For example, you might explain how to cover and decorate a textbook, or how to make your locker look truly unique. Just be sure it's a process you know how to do. Write your first draft on your own paper. Include specific details that will help readers identify the steps you followed and the order in which you performed them. When you have finished, share your first draft with other students.

EVALUATING AND REVISING

EVALUATING

Evaluating is the first step in improving a draft. To *evaluate* is to look for the strengths and weaknesses of your paper. A good way to identify strengths and weaknesses is to use a checklist or set of standards. Below are four examples of standards for good writing.

- The writing is interesting and holds a reader's attention.
- The main ideas are clear and supported with details.
- There are no unrelated ideas, and any unfamiliar terms are explained.
- The details are arranged in a sensible order, and the connections among them are clear.

Professional writers evaluate their own work, but they also ask for other opinions. They get valuable feedback from their peers, or equals. You can ask your peers, or classmates, to help you evaluate your work. Here are some tips that can help you evaluate your own writing or that of a peer.

Self-Evaluation	Peer Evaluation
1. Set your draft aside for a while to give yourself a fresh eye the next time you read it.	1. Provide encouragement by telling your classmate what parts are particularly good.
2. Read your draft several times: once for content, once for organization, and once for style.	2. Make specific suggestions for improvement.
3. Read your draft aloud, and listen to yourself. You may notice things that you missed during a silent reading.	3. Focus on content and organization. Errors in mechanics, including spelling, can be caught during proofreading.
	4. Be sensitive to the writer's feelings. Ask helpful questions.

EXERCISE 7   Practicing Peer Evaluation

Practice your peer-evaluation skills by evaluating the paragraph below with a partner. Use the standards for good writing listed at the top of the previous page. Write your evaluation on your own paper, beginning with a comment about what's good about the paragraph. Then write suggestions that would help a writer improve the paragraph.

1   One of the most famous lighthouse keepers of all times was a

2   young woman, Ida Lewis. The Lewis family moved to Lime Rock

3   lighthouse in 1857. Mr. Lewis was supposed to keep the lamps lit all

4   night. Soon after they arrived, he had a stroke, and his daughter Ida

5   took over the work. She was the oldest of four children. Three

6   soldiers were in a boat and Ida rescued one of them. Then she saved

7   three men and a sheep. Her sister was sick, and Ida became sick. In

8   1869, during a blizzard, she saved two men from drowning. A

9   newspaper learned about this rescue and the earlier ones. Ida Lewis

10   became famous, but she remained a lighthouse keeper. In fact, the

11   governor made her job official.

For Better or For Worse®   **by Lynn Johnston**

For Better or For Worse copyright 1986 Lynn Johnston Prod. Reprinted with permission of Universal Press Syndicate. All rights reserved.

REVISING

When you *revise*, you make changes in your draft to correct weaknesses found when evaluating. Use the following techniques to make changes when you revise.

REVISION TECHNIQUES	
Technique	**Example**
1. **Add.** Add new information: words, phrases, sentences, even paragraphs.	Navajo weavers use dyes made *berries, roots, and flowers taken from* of plants.
2. **Cut.** Take out unrelated or repeated ideas, words, or details.	Navajo rugs are quite beautiful ⊙ and nice to look at.
3. **Replace.** Replace weak or awkward words with more precise, vivid language.	Chokecherries are used to make preserves with a *soft red* nice color.
4. **Reorder.** Move information for variety and clarity.	Cream, brown, and black are some of the natural colors of the wool used in Navajo rugs and also gray.

EXERCISE 8   Evaluating and Revising a Piece of Writing

Read the narrative you wrote for Exercise 6. Then use the standards on page 7 to evaluate your first draft. Next, revise your draft, using the techniques described above. Make your changes by hand, directly on your paper. Finally, rewrite the narrative on your own paper, and incorporate the revisions.

PROOFREADING AND PUBLISHING

PROOFREADING

When you *proofread,* you read carefully for mistakes in grammar, spelling, capitalization, and punctuation. It's easier to spot such mistakes if you put your writing away for a while before looking at it. Peer proofreading is also useful. Exchange papers with a partner, and look for errors in each other's papers. Use the following guidelines when you proofread.

Guidelines for Proofreading

- Is every sentence a complete sentence instead of a fragment or a run-on?
- Does every sentence begin with a capital letter? Are all proper nouns capitalized?
- Does every sentence end with an appropriate punctuation mark? Are other punctuation marks used correctly?
- Do the verbs agree in number with their subjects?
- Are the verb forms and tenses used correctly?
- Are the subject and object forms of personal pronouns used correctly?
- Does every pronoun agree with its antecedent in gender and in number? Are the pronoun references clear?
- Are all the words spelled correctly?

Symbols for Revising and Proofreading

≡	South america	Capitalize a letter.
℮	to to school	Take out a word, letter, or punctuation mark.
∪	twon	Change the order of words or letters.
∧	the city Dallas	Insert a word, letter, or punctuation mark.
#	saltmarsh	Insert a space.

EXERCISE 9   Proofreading a Paragraph

Proofread the paragraph below. Use proofreading symbols to mark the ten errors in the paragraph.

[1] The japanese architect Tange Kenzo hasan international

reputation. [2] Kenzo's creations in his his own coutry include the

town hall in Kawaga the Atami Gardens Hotel, and a cathedral in

Tokyo. [3] Later, he branched out overseas and he developed a

reputation in Europe and the Middle east. [4] However, Kenzo did

not not stop working in his own country. [5] he also desinged

important civic buildings for both Tokyo and Yokohama..

PUBLISHING

The final step of writing is *publishing* your work, or sharing it with readers. There are a number of ways you can publish.

- Invite friends and classmates to read what you have written.
- Submit your work to a school or community newspaper. Your opinion on a local issue could become a letter to the editor.
- Enter a writing contest. Your teacher or counselor can probably give you information about such contests. Many contests award prizes.
- Find out which magazines publish student stories, poems, essays, and articles. Most magazines have special guidelines for the submission of work. A copy of the magazine or a guide to writers' markets will explain these guidelines. Look in the reference section of your library.
- Keep a portfolio of your best work. Provide a special folder, notebook, or envelope for the final copies.

Guidelines for Manuscript Form

1. Use only one side of a sheet of paper.
2. Write in blue or black ink, type your paper, or use a word processor. If you type, double-space the lines.
3. Leave one-inch margins at the top, sides, and bottom of each page.
4. Indent the first line of each paragraph.
5. Follow your teacher's instructions for placing your name, the date, and the title of the paper.
6. Keep your pages neat and clean. Use correction fluid if needed, but be sure that it is barely noticeable to the reader.

EXERCISE 10   Finding Ideas for Publishing

Read the following descriptions of types of writing. On the lines after each description, list one or two publishing ideas for the piece.

1. a science fiction story _____

   _____

2. an essay on the effects of television advertising aimed at young

   children _____

   _____

3. a review of a free open-air concert held in your city last weekend _____

   _____

4. an article about how to keep a photographic journal _____

   _____

EXERCISE 11   Preparing a Final Copy

Proofread and correct the draft that you revised for Exercise 8 on page 9. Then prepare a clean, final copy of the paper, using the manuscript guidelines above. Meet with a group of classmates, and take turns reading your work aloud. Finally, discuss ways that each of you might publish your writing.

MAIN IDEAS AND TOPIC SENTENCES

Most paragraphs have one *main idea*. This main idea, which tells what the paragraph is about, is usually expressed in a single sentence called the *topic sentence*. A topic sentence can help you keep your focus as you write or read a paragraph. A topic sentence can also suggest how you should order details in a paragraph.

A topic sentence can appear anywhere in a paragraph, but it often appears as the first or second sentence. In the following paragraph, the topic sentence comes at the beginning. It tells the reader what to expect in the rest of the paragraph.

> Grains of pollen are very tiny and come in a variety of shapes. One grain of pollen can be as minuscule as 1/5000 inch or as big as 1/125 inch, which is still extremely small. Some grains of pollen are shaped like footballs. Others are round. Pine pollen appears to have a tiny ear on each side of the grain.

Not all paragraphs have topic sentences, however. For example, a paragraph that relates a sequence of events or actions may not have a topic sentence or even a single main idea. The following paragraph has no topic sentence, but it does relate a sequence of events.

> The girl trudged across the rocky terrain. The wind sneaked through the edges of her fur-lined hood and mittens. By the time she found a campsite, it was nearly dark. She gathered firewood and set up a grill. While the fish she had just caught was cooking, she built a lean-to. After hiking all day, she was almost too tired to worry about the shelter, but it looked as if the storm would arrive before morning.

EXERCISE 1   Identifying Main Ideas and Topic Sentences

On your own paper, write the main idea of each paragraph in your own words. If the paragraph has a topic sentence, underline it.

1. Seagaia is Japan's attempt to recreate a tropical paradise. Seagaia is an indoor beach that can accommodate as many as ten thousand people. In this controlled environment, rain never spoils the family vacation. The roof can be closed when it's raining and opened when the sun is shining. The ocean that washes the 280-foot-long shoreline is perfectly clean, salt-free, and temperature-controlled. A computer ensures that surfers get perfect waves to

ride several times a day. But this perfect beach provides more than water. Artificial breezes ruffle the leaves of plastic palm trees. And a mechanically produced chorus of birds serenades the contented Japanese beachgoers.

2. Before he was appointed to the U.S. Supreme Court, Thurgood Marshall worked effectively as the chief attorney for the National Association for the Advancement of Colored People (NAACP). He travelled throughout the country, fighting within the legal system. And he overcame many social and legal obstacles to improve social opportunities for African Americans. His main accomplishment was in the area of school desegregation, where he was the lead attorney in the *Brown vs. Board of Education of Topeka* case, in which the U.S. Supreme Court finally prohibited racially segregated schools.

3. Even though drive-in theaters may not be as popular today as they were in the 1950s, they are still around. At the height of their popularity, more than 4,000 drive-in theaters dotted the American landscape. However, attendance at drive-ins dropped drastically during the 1970s and 1980s. This change probably resulted from the growing popularity of television and the introduction of home videos. Many drive-in owners were forced to close their theaters. By 1993, only 870 theaters remained in operation. Most of these theaters are able to make a profit, however, by opening on Friday and Saturday evenings only and by showing wholesome movies that appeal to parents who want an inexpensive evening out with their children.

4. Carlos looked up and saw the beach ahead. Without much effort, he leaped out of the water. Two seconds later, he crossed the line. He heard the spectators cheering as he squirmed into his bike shorts and T-shirt and fastened his helmet. Carlos completed the ride around the lake in record-breaking time. After quickly changing clothes, Carlos stretched his legs to prepare for the long run ahead. He had a three-minute lead over his nearest competitor when he dashed to the road to begin the final leg of the triathlon.

UNITY

A paragraph has *unity* when all the sentences work together to express or support one main idea. Sentences can work as a unit in one of three ways.

(1) All Sentences Relate to the Main Idea Stated in the Topic Sentence. In the following paragraph, the topic sentence tells the main idea. Each of the supporting sentences provides details related to that idea.

> Idioms are colorful expressions that add interest and, occasionally, a touch of humor to our everyday language. *Chewing the fat, biting someone's head off,* and *raining cats and dogs* are examples of idioms that create lively and somewhat humorous mental images. Such expressions are more interesting than simple, direct statements. *Taking the plunge,* for example, seems much more daring and adventurous than *trying to do something.*

(2) All Sentences Relate to an Implied Main Idea. The following paragraph doesn't have a topic sentence. Each sentence, however, helps support an implied main idea: Producing electrical power causes problems.

> Hydroelectric plants do not pollute the air or water, but the dams destroy wildlife habitats. Nuclear energy plants do not produce smog, but there is no proven safe way to store nuclear waste. Burning wood or coal produces smoke and depletes natural resources. It seems that if we are to have electrical power, we must make some hard decisions.

(3) All Sentences Relate to a Sequence of Events. The following paragraph does not have a clearly stated main idea. But each detail is part of a sequence that begins when the character faces an emergency situation.

> Thick smoke seeped under the door of the room. Neka began to cough. Realizing what was happening, she went to the door. It felt warm to her touch. Then she went over to the window and looked down twenty stories. Fire apparatus and emergency vehicles filled the street below. Neka tried to recall what she had read about surviving a fire in a high-rise building. After a few moments, she went into the bathroom. She soaked a towel in water and stuffed it under the door. Then she soaked a face cloth and held it to her mouth and nose.

EXERCISE 2   Identifying Sentences That Destroy Unity

In each paragraph below, find the sentence that doesn't support the main idea of the paragraph. Draw a line through that sentence.

1. Paintings that appear on the walls of buildings are called murals. Many artists, however, prefer to paint on canvas. Murals often tell a story. The subjects of these stories vary according to the inspiration and intention of the artist. Murals are often in clear view of all passersby and can be appreciated by a vast audience. Because these paintings reach so many people, some Hispanic and African American artists, among others, have used this art form to protest social conditions.

2. Lugging her two heavy suitcases, Dee got off the train. She stood for a moment on the platform and looked around. The escalator that would take her to the main concourse was straight ahead. The train station had recently been renovated. At the top of the escalator, Dee spotted Uncle Carter. She waved. He waved back and moved toward her, taking the bags from her hands. After giving her a quick hug and a peck on the cheek, he said, "Follow me, Dee. We're going home."

3. A traffic light should be installed at the intersection of Central Street and Liberty Square Road. Although the $150,000 cost will mean an increase in property taxes, the light is necessary for three reasons. The town spends more money for things that are less vital. First, the light will keep traffic flowing smoothly at that busy intersection. Second, a light will allow pedestrians to cross safely. The third, and most important reason for installing the light is that it will help prevent accidents.

4. Lamont knelt in the on-deck circle, waiting, worrying, hoping that Rodríguez would not strike out. "Ball four!" the umpire called. Rodríguez walked to first base. Lamont stood up slowly and took a couple of practice swings. "I think I'm going to be sick," he thought as he walked to the batter's box. "Relax. Stay cool," he muttered to himself softly. "So what if you don't get a hit? Lots of players don't get a hit their first time at bat." But Lamont couldn't relax. He was anything but cool. Sweat ran down his face and neck. Everyone was watching—his parents, his three brothers, his grandfather, thirty-one thousand spectators. The stadium held thirty-five thousand people. "Please let me get a hit," he whispered softly.

COHERENCE

A paragraph in which all the ideas are sensibly arranged and clearly connected has *coherence*. You can create coherent paragraphs if you pay attention to two things: (1) the order in which you arrange your ideas, and (2) the connections you make between ideas.

ORDER OF IDEAS

Arrange, or order, your ideas in the paragraph in a way that makes sense to the reader. Often, the subject you're writing about will suggest the most sensible order of ideas.

Chronological Order. When you write about a series of actions or events, it makes sense to arrange them according to the order in which they happened.

Spatial Order. Writers sometimes order details according to how they are spaced—nearest to farthest, left to right, or any other reasonable arrangement.

Order of Importance. Sometimes one detail or piece of information is more important than another. Then the writer may arrange ideas by order of importance, perhaps starting or ending with the most important information.

Logical Order. It may make sense to group or arrange ideas together to show how they are related. For example, a writer might use logical order in a paper about the differences between football and soccer.

EXERCISE 3 Choosing an Order of Ideas

On your own paper, identify which order of ideas would make the most sense for each topic below: *chronological order, spatial order, order of importance,* or *logical order*. For some topics, more than one order might work.

1. kinds of healthful snack foods
2. making a barometer with a glass jar
3. the view from your bedroom window
4. deciding who to vote for in school elections
5. three characteristics of a great action video game

CONNECTIONS BETWEEN IDEAS

Besides ordering ideas in a paragraph in a sensible way, you need to show how the ideas are connected. You can show connections by (1) making *direct references* to something else in the paragraph or (2) using words that make a *transition*, or bridge, from one idea to another.

Direct References. Direct references link ideas by (1) referring to a noun or pronoun used earlier, (2) repeating a word, or (3) using a word or phrase that means the same thing as one used earlier.

Transitional Words and Phrases. Transitional words and phrases connect ideas and show *how* the ideas are connected. They include conjunctions and prepositions that show chronological or spatial order.

Comparing Ideas	also, and, another, moreover, similarly, too
Contrasting Ideas	although, but, however, in spite of, instead, nevertheless, on the other hand, still, yet
Showing Cause and Effect	as a result, because, consequently, for, since, so, so that, therefore
Showing Time	after, at last, at once, before, eventually, finally, first, meanwhile, next, then, thereafter, when
Showing Place	above, along, around, before, behind, down, here, in, inside, into, next to, over, there, under, up
Showing Importance	first, last, mainly, more important, then, to begin with

EXERCISE 4   Identifying Direct References and Transitions

On your own paper, make two lists of the connections in the paragraph below: one list of direct references and one list of transitions.

The otter glided effortlessly down the icy river, looking for food. All at once, he dove into the water. When the otter came up again, he held a squirming sunfish in his mouth. The otter flung the fish on a patch of ice and quickly hoisted himself up next to the flopping creature. With his nose, he began playing with the fish. As he pushed it slowly along the ice, it slid and skidded over the slippery surface. Eventually, the otter tired of the game and ate his unlucky prey.

USING DESCRIPTION

One strategy writers use to develop a paragraph is description. You use *description* to tell what something is like or what it looks like. You look at the individual features of whatever you are describing. In a description, you'll use sensory details to support your main idea. *Sensory details* are pieces of information that a writer observes through any of the five senses—sight, hearing, touch, taste, and smell. And you'll often use spatial order to organize those details. Notice how the following paragraph uses sensory details and spatial order to describe an old library building.

It has been thirty-five years since my first visit to the West End Library, but I remember it as if it happened yesterday. When I close my eyes, I am once again walking up those wide, concrete steps, holding tightly to the wrought-iron handrails. French lilacs grew tall and bushy on one side of the stairway, perfuming the air in early spring. A willow tree grew on the other side. At the top of the stairs was a flagstone landing. Light gray marble benches curved around either side of the landing. They flanked the huge oak double doors that led to the inside of the building. Those benches stayed cool all the time, making me shiver whenever I sat on them, even on hot summer days. The entrance doors opened out, and I had to step up over a high marble threshold to get inside. Once inside, the first thing I noticed was the darkness, and the second thing was the librarian's desk. The huge desk was located about twenty feet from the front door in the center of the room. Piles of books always sat on top of the desk, beside it, in front of it, and behind it. Even now, I can hear Mrs. Morrison whispering, "Watch where you step, Joanie. These books cost money, you know!"

EXERCISE 5 Using Description as a Strategy

Choose one of the subjects below. On your own paper, list the features that will help describe the subject you have chosen. Try to focus on sensory details. After you run out of ideas, arrange the details in spatial order.

1. the strangest place you've ever seen
2. your classroom first thing in the morning, before the teacher arrives
3. a crowd of people watching a parade or other public event
4. a well-known actor during a performance
5. your favorite shoes

USING EVALUATION

When you use *evaluation,* you attempt to determine the value of a subject. You make a judgment about it. For example, you are evaluating when you say that all high school students should do volunteer work in the community.

Once you tell your readers your evaluation, or statement of opinion, you also need to give them some reasons to support it. One way to organize your reasons is by order of importance. You might begin with your most important reason. Or you might begin with your least important reason and conclude with your most important.

EVALUATION	There are many good reasons why the entertainment committee should select the Back Roads to play at
REASON	our class fund-raiser dance. First, the Back Roads is the most popular local band around. A large crowd means we will sell a lot of tickets and make a lot of
REASON	money. In addition, the band is fun to listen to. They play original music and the most popular dance music.
REASON	Finally, the Back Roads will play for free. All the band members are Crawford High School graduates and are willing to donate their time.

EXERCISE 6   Using Evaluation as a Strategy

Choose two of the three subjects below, and evaluate them. On your own paper, write at least one sentence stating your evaluation of, or opinion about, each subject. Then list two or three reasons to support each judgment.

EX   1. Music Videos
   Evaluation: Music videos should be phased out.
   Reasons: (1) Viewers don't have to use their own imagination while listening to the words and music of a song. (2) Music videos often have nothing to do with the songs.

1. a book you've recently read (Would you recommend it to someone else? Why or why not?)
2. after-school jobs (Should the number of hours that high school students work be limited?)
3. sports safety equipment, such as bicycle helmets (Should individuals have the right to decide whether or not to wear protective gear, or should wearing protective gear be the law?)

USING NARRATION

What happened when you moved to a new town? How did you meet your best friend? What caused you to quit the baseball team? When you answer these questions, you use *narration*.

Narration looks at changes over a period of time. Since narration looks at events and actions in time, you will usually use chronological order to arrange ideas and information. You can use narration to tell a story or relate an incident (what happened at last night's baseball game), to explain a process (how to build a campfire), or to explain causes and effects (the effects of water pollution).

Telling a Story.   One way to develop a narrative paragraph is to tell a story—to tell what happened. The story may be true, or it may be imaginary (fiction). In the following paragraph, the writer tells a story to explain how the car got dented.

> Kelsey had never driven in the snow before and did not realize how slippery the roads could become. Everyone on the highway was driving quite slowly, but Kelsey felt she could have walked faster than the big yellow snowplow in front of her. As soon as she pulled left to pass, in the rear view mirror she saw a giant truck coming up fast. It couldn't seem to slow down, and it bumped her car. Kelsey tried to stay on the slippery road, but the car spun around two times and then slid into the median strip. Fortunately, there were no trees or overpasses in her path, and she was not hurt.

Explaining a Process.   Another way to develop a narrative paragraph is to explain a process—to tell how something works or how to do something. In explaining a process, the writer uses narration to look at a subject as it changes over time. In the following paragraph, the writer explains how to prepare falafel.

> Combine chickpeas, eggs, bread crumbs, herbs, spices, and oil in a large bowl. Use a wooden spoon or your hands to mix the ingredients until the eggs have been totally incorporated and the mixture sticks together. Then moisten your hands with cold water. Break off a small piece of the mixture—about two tablespoons—and hold it in the palm of one hand. Place the other hand over the mixture, and roll it until it forms a patty. Then you fry the patties.

Explaining Cause and Effect.   To explain what caused something or what the effects of something are, you have to look at the way things have changed over the course of time. The following paragraph looks at the effects of cutting and peeling onions.

CAUSE EFFECT	A woman sliced an onion in half with a sharp kitchen knife. Immediately, molecules from the cut onion were released into the air. The onion molecules drifted up into the woman's face and came in contact with the watery fluid in
EFFECT	her eyes. The onion's molecules combined with the salty water in the woman's eyes and changed into sulfuric acid. At
EFFECT	that moment, the woman's eyes started stinging, and tears began to trickle down her face.

EXERCISE 7   Identifying Narrative Paragraphs

In a magazine, newspaper, or book, find a paragraph that uses the strategy of narration. On your own paper, identify the source (the name of the magazine, newspaper, or book). Below the source, identify the topic of the paragraph, and list the supporting details. Then tell whether narration is being used to tell a story, to explain a process, or to explain causes and effects.

EXERCISE 8   Using Narration as a Strategy

Following the instructions for using narration, develop the items below. Write your lists on your own paper.

1. Select one of the subjects below, and list at least three actions that took place.
    a. the time I got on the wrong bus after a concert (Make up the actions.)
    b. how the Underground Railroad operated (Check in an encyclopedia or a history book.)
2. Select one of the subjects below, and list at least four steps in the process.
    a. how to make popcorn (If you don't know how, ask someone.)
    b. how to wash clothes (If you don't know how to do laundry, this is a good time to learn.)
3. Select one of the subjects below, and list at least three causes or effects.
    a. arriving home two hours after your curfew (Identify the causes.)
    b. the bombing of Pearl Harbor on December 7, 1941 (List the effects. You may need to check some newspapers or magazines or to talk to someone who is an expert in this area.)

USING CLASSIFICATION

What are the major differences between schools in Japan and schools in the United States? To answer this question, you need to look at one subject as it relates to other subjects in a group. You need to *classify.* When you use **classification** to develop a paragraph, you may divide a subject into its parts (the parts of a guitar), define it (what is freedom?), or compare and contrast it (road bikes and mountain bikes).

Dividing.   You may need to look at the parts of a subject in order to explain it. For example, to explain the structure of the government of the United States, you may have to divide it into its executive, legislative, and judicial branches. The following paragraph uses the strategy of dividing to explain the separate layers of growth in a rain forest.

> The Amazon rain forest has three distinct layers of growth. The top layer, known as the *canopy,* is exposed to bright sunlight. The trees and plants that make up the lush green canopy grow up to a height of 130 feet. The middle layer of the forest, which grows to about 80 feet, is known as the *understory.* The plants and vines in this layer of growth compete with each other for the scant rays of sunshine that manage to penetrate the thick canopy above. The *forest floor* is the bottom layer of the forest. It is seldom, if ever, touched by direct sunlight. Hardly anything grows on the forest floor.

Defining.   To define a subject, first identify the large class or group it belongs to. Then tell what makes the subject different from other members of that group. In the following paragraph, the first sentence defines *honey.* The other sentences give examples to explain what honey is and to tell how it is different from other sugary substances.

> Honey is a sticky, sugary substance. Produced by honey-making bees, it is twenty-five percent sweeter than sugar. Honey also contains forty percent more calories than sugar. The flavor and aroma of honey come from the flower nectar used to produce it. Honeybees will gather nectar from any and all of the flowers in their nectar-gathering area. But the honey's essential flavor comes from the flower that supplies the majority of the nectar. For example, nectar that is gathered in an area near an orange grove will most likely produce a honey that tastes like citrus blossoms.

Comparing and Contrasting.   Comparing and contrasting are closely related to dividing and defining. For example, the paragraph about the rain forest divides the subject of the rain forest into three layers and looks at the differences (contrasts) among those layers. You can look at subjects by comparing them (telling how they are alike), contrasting them (telling how they are different), or by both comparing and contrasting them. The following paragraph contrasts board games and video games.

> Many board games require a minimum of two players. Video games, on the other hand, can be played alone and most often are. Because board games are played by at least two people, they promote lively and sometimes humorous discussion. People playing video games often don't speak to anyone for long stretches of time. The electronic bleeping and humming of the computer may be the only noises that break the silence. Board games require strategy and patience as players decide how to proceed. But video games require quick reflexes and excellent hand-eye coordination.

EXERCISE 9   Using Classification as a Strategy

Follow the directions below that tell which classification strategy to use to develop each main idea below. Work in a group with two other classmates. Choose one member of your group as the recorder, and then work together to list ideas. After you finish your lists, discuss the strategies. Which one was the most difficult to use? the easiest? How did the strategies help you stay focused on your subject?

Main Idea	Classification Strategy
1. Whatever your ability, there is a type of athletic activity that will suit you.	Look at the subject of athletics by dividing it into types; then list details for each type to support this main idea.
2. White blood cells help in the healing process.	Look at the subject of white blood cells by defining it. Identify the larger group to which these cells belong, and then list some features that make them different from other blood cells.
3. If you like one movie an actor starred in, will you also like another movie in which the actor stars?	Compare and contrast two movies starring the same actor by listing likenesses and differences.

PLANNING A COMPOSITION

Writing a composition, like writing a single paragraph, requires planning. Before you begin to write, you need to complete these steps.

- Choose a topic, and decide on your main idea.
- Gather information related to your topic and main idea.
- Organize the information in a way that will make sense to readers.

You can organize your ideas by making an early plan or a formal outline.

THE EARLY PLAN

To create an *early plan*, or rough outline, sort your ideas or facts into groups, and then arrange the groups in order.

GROUPING.   After you have gathered details on your topic, group the details that have something in common. Write a heading for each group to show how the details in that group are related. (Details that don't fit into any group may be useful later. For now, put them in a separate list.)

ORDERING.   Next, order the details within each group, and order the groups themselves. There are several ways to order, or arrange, ideas.

Chronological (time) *order* presents events in the order that they happen in time.

Spatial order presents details according to where they are located.

Order of importance presents details from most important to least important, or vice versa.

Classification presents your topic in logical order by defining it, or by comparing and contrasting it with something else.

THE FORMAL OUTLINE

A *formal outline* is a highly structured, clearly labeled writing plan. It divides a subject into main headings and subheadings that are labeled with letters and numbers. There are two kinds of formal outlines. A *topic outline* states ideas in words or brief phrases. A *sentence outline* states ideas in complete sentences. A sample topic outline appears at the top of the next page.

Title: Neighbors Helping Neighbors
Main Idea Statement: Although natural disasters such as hurricanes and floods cause widespread destruction, they also tend to bring out the best in people.

I.   Hurricane Rita

    A.   Description of storms
    B.   Devastation and destruction
    C.   Areas affected
    D.   Examples of how people helped each other

II. Flooding of New Orleans

    A.   Events leading up to the flood
    B.   Areas affected
    C.   Immediate effects of the flood
    D.   What people did to help each other
        1.   Volunteering at clinics and hospitals
        2.   Organizing relief programs

EXERCISE 1   Creating an Early Plan

Below are some notes for a composition about the ways in which a major invention helped to modernize America. Work with a partner to organize the notes into two separate groups. On your own paper, write a heading for each group to show what the notes in that group have in common. Finally, arrange the notes within each group in a sensible order.

airmail—faster communication

the airplane revolutionized warfare

1945—airplanes used to track hurricanes

airplanes are useful in agriculture to distribute pesticides, weed-killers, and fertilizers

1919—first use of airplanes to drop water to fight wildfires

1932—Amelia Earhart, first woman to fly solo across the Atlantic Ocean

1903—Orville and Wilbur Wright—first successful flight of an airplane

1927—Charles Lindbergh, Spirit of St. Louis, first nonstop flight from New York to Paris

1918—World War I, interest in air travel grows

EXERCISE 2   Creating a Formal Outline

Using the early plan you made for Exercise 1, create a formal outline on your own paper. You can use a topic or a sentence outline. Add a title and a main idea statement.

WRITING INTRODUCTIONS

A composition begins with an *introduction.* The introduction has three important functions.

1. **CATCHING THE READERS' INTEREST.**   The introduction should make readers want to continue reading. It should arouse readers' interest or curiosity.

2. **SETTING THE TONE.**   The introduction should also set the composition's *tone*—its general feeling. For example, the tone might be serious and formal or humorous and lighthearted.

3. **PRESENTING THE THESIS.**   Most importantly, the introduction should tell readers what the composition will be about. In other words, it should present a *thesis statement*—a sentence or two that announces the composition's main idea. Often, but not always, the thesis statement comes at the end of the introduction.

NOTE   The body of a composition contains paragraphs that support the main idea expressed in your thesis. In supporting the main idea, these paragraphs should all work together to achieve **unity** and **coherence.** For more about these two elements, see pages 15–18.

TECHNIQUES FOR WRITING INTRODUCTIONS

Writers use a variety of techniques to grab their readers' attention in the introduction. Here are five.

- **Begin with an example or an anecdote.**   An example or an anecdote (a short, interesting, or humorous incident) draws readers in with concrete, vivid details. These details not only spark the readers' interest but also can include important aspects of the topic.

> "Stop the car!" she shouted. The taxi driver was so startled that she stopped right there on the roadway. The woman leapt from the car and ran to the side of the road. The driver looked to see what the trouble was, but there was no emergency. The woman was a newspaper photographer looking for that perfect photo opportunity.

- **Begin by stating a startling fact or by adopting an unusual position on a topic.**   A curious reader will keep reading. A surprising fact or an unexpected opinion can startle readers and arouse their curiosity.

> Imagine a place where the temperature rises above freezing only two months of the year. Imagine a place cut off from the rest of the world by frozen rivers and seas. Who could tolerate the isolation and harsh conditions of this Arctic land? The Inuit people of Canada's Northwest Territories can. They have survived in this remote area of the world for centuries.

- **Use an appropriate quotation.**   Writers can use someone else's words in an introduction if these words are interesting and make an important point. Quotations from experts, authors, or someone mentioned in the composition can add interest to the topic.

  > "Brains, not brawn," my father always said to me. Sometimes brawn is necessary, but most of the time my father's words are good advice. It certainly would have helped me to have heeded this advice when I met the class bully.

- **Give some background information.**   Providing background details can help readers understand the thesis, help them recall what they already know about a topic, or simply build interest.

  > Throughout their history, Mexicans have always valued the humble egg. Ancient Mayans believed that babies who were fed eggs during a special ceremony would acquire wisdom. Eggs later came to symbolize wealth and prosperity and were used to show religious devotion. Today, modern Mexicans value eggs as food and prepare them in a variety of delicious ways.

- **Begin with a simple statement of your thesis.**   A writer often states the thesis plainly, without fuss or fanfare. This technique immediately focuses readers' attention on the composition's main idea.

  > The typical American family rarely, if ever, has the time to eat dinner together. Dad works two jobs and gets a bite to eat on the road. Mom barely gets in the door and has to rush off to a committee meeting at the town hall. The children can't stick around for a lengthy family dinner because of soccer practice, gymnastics practice, the basketball game, or a study group.

EXERCISE 3   Identifying Types of Introductions

On the line after each of the following paragraphs, write the technique used in the attention-getting introduction.

1.   You sit down at your computer, carefully placing your fingers on the keyboard. You take a deep breath, flex your fingers, and begin. The sounds of rock-and-roll music fill your room. It is only your fifth lesson, but you are playing the piano like Elton John. Well, that might be a slight exaggeration, but, thanks to the latest in computer technology, you are making progress.

2.   Great-Granddad called me over and said, "Let me tell you about the most tremendous experience of my life." He pulled me up on his lap and told me the story of his meeting President John F. Kennedy.

---

3.   The surge of creative achievement by African Americans in the 1920s was known as the Harlem Renaissance. This cultural movement was marked by the celebrated poetry of such writers as Langston Hughes, Countee Cullen, and Claude McKay.

---

4.   Did you know that the average lead pencil can draw a line that is thirty-five miles long? The estimated number of English words that a pencil can write is fifty thousand. I try to remember this fact when I sit down to write a composition.

EXERCISE 4   Writing an Introduction to a Composition

Work with a partner to draft an introduction to a composition based on the formal outline you created for Exercise 2. Use one of the techniques for writing introductions discussed in this lesson. Write your introduction on your own paper.

Calvin and Hobbes   by Bill Watterson

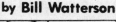

Calvin & Hobbes copyright 1986 Watterson. Reprinted with permission of Universal Press Syndicate. All rights reserved.

WRITING CONCLUSIONS

The *conclusion* is the last part of a composition. The conclusion should leave readers feeling satisfied that the composition is complete. To achieve this sense of completion, a conclusion must reinforce the main idea while bringing the composition to a definite close.

TECHNIQUES FOR WRITING CONCLUSIONS

Here are six ways to write conclusions.

- **Restate the main idea.** The most direct way to end your composition is to restate the thesis *in different words*. Try to find a newer, stronger wording. The following conclusion restates in different words the idea that professional photographers are always on the lookout for the perfect photograph.

  > The picture taken by the photographer in the middle of the road won first prize in a national photography contest. Was that opportunity worth stopping traffic for? Most professional photographers would answer yes. And most would agree that they would do just about anything for a perfect photo.

- **Summarize your major points.** Emphasize the major points of your composition by summarizing them in the conclusion.

  > The most important piece of advice to hikers, then, is to be prepared. Make sure you have warm clothing and enough food and water to last at least twenty-four hours should you get stranded. Travel with others, and always tell someone where you are headed and when you will return. These precautions can help ensure a safe and happy adventure.

- **Close with a final idea or example.** You can reinforce, or pull together, your main points by using a final example. Below, the writer of an essay about the time demands on families leaves readers with one last thought.

  > It is unlikely that American families will slow down. Finding the time to have even one meal together a week might seem impossible. But the Martínez family of Ash Creek has made the time. "Sunday evening, no matter what is going on, we eat together," says Mr. Martínez. "We use that time to catch up on everything that is happening in our busy lives. It's an important time for all of us—a small family reunion once a week."

- **Make a final comment on the topic.** Give a sense of completeness to your composition by ending with one final comment on your topic. You can provide a thoughtful observation, give a personal reaction, or project a vision of the future. In the following conclusion, the writer tells her thoughts on current immigration policies in the United States.

  > The United States, which once welcomed millions of immigrants with open arms, now has an immigration policy that limits the number of legal immigrants. There are many who believe that the United States should continue to extend an unlimited welcome to anyone yearning to be free.

- **Call on your readers to take action.** If you are writing a persuasive essay, use your conclusion to urge readers to do something or to accept a belief. This approach, called the *direct appeal,* also works for other kinds of compositions, such as this one on athletics and competition.

  > There will always be people who are ready to make an Olympic event out of tying one's shoes. Indeed, it often seems that just about everything in our society is competition based. However, as we've seen, the essence of sport is not competition but cooperation. In business, in our families, and especially in sports, it pays to remember that we humans are all on the same team.

- **Refer to your introduction.** A writer may make a direct reference to something in the introduction. For example, the following conclusion refers to the introduction on page 28.

  > The variety and appeal of these egg dishes prove one thing for sure: Mexicans still value the humble egg.

EXERCISE 5   Writing a Conclusion

Read the introduction and body of the composition on the following page. On your own paper, write a conclusion, using one of the techniques on this page or the previous page. Then get together with a small group of classmates, and discuss your conclusions. Why did you choose one particular technique over another? Which conclusion works best with the composition?

Remember This

You are introduced to a new student in your school. The two of you like each other immediately, so you decide to exchange phone numbers. Just as you are about to recite the familiar numbers, your mind goes blank. You can't remember your own phone number! Your memory has shut down. Luckily, it's only a few seconds before your memory kicks back in. With an embarrassed chuckle, you quickly rattle off your number.

There is no need to be embarrassed. People are always forgetting things. To explain why we sometimes forget even the simplest things, we first have to understand why we remember things. We have to understand how the memory works. Memory is the mind's ability to recall information acquired at an earlier time. There are two main kinds of memory: short-term memory and long-term memory.

Short-term memory is the place where you put information on a temporary basis. For example, when someone gives you directions to the nearest post office, you remember the directions just long enough to find the post office. Only a certain amount of information can be put into short-term memory—directions to the post office, for example. The information in short-term memory is available to you immediately, but once used, it is usually dumped out or transferred to long-term memory.

Long-term memory is where you store all the information you have acquired in your life. It's like a giant attic. Long-term memory helps you recall the events leading up to the Civil War (from last year's social studies class) or what your cabin at summer camp looked like when you were in the first grade. Long-term memory provides you with the ability to learn a skill, such as ice-skating, or to remember when your books are due at the library.

Why, then, do people sometimes forget their telephone numbers? Why do they occasionally forget that their library books are due? Researchers have several explanations for forgetfulness. One is that new memories can interfere with old ones. For example, you have recently memorized your mother's work phone number. This memory may temporarily interfere with the memory of your home phone number. Sometimes we forget things because they get lost in our memory. For instance, suppose that you can't remember where you left your math notebook. You do remember that you had it when you left school yesterday. If you can recall exactly where you went after school yesterday, you can probably find your missing notebook. All you need are the right clues to trigger your memory. We also forget because an experience is unpleasant or painful to remember. Finally, at other times, we forget things because we are ill or under stress.

A PERSONAL IMPRESSION ESSAY

When you write expressively, you share your thoughts and feelings. Some expressive writing you create is just for yourself. Other expressive writing, like this personal expression essay, is meant to be shared.

A *personal impression essay* is a piece of writing that tells how you feel about a person who has been important to you in some way. As you read the essay below, keep in mind the feelings that are expressed.

My Best Friend, Josephine

Josephine is my very best friend. In fact, she is the best and fairest friend anyone ever had.

I met Josephine when I was little. She and I and a bunch of other kids in the neighborhood went out to have a gigantic snowball fight. Most of the other kids ran away when a big St. Bernard dog came trotting up the road, but my mom had bundled me up in so much clothing that I could barely move at all. I tripped, and the huge dog came and sat on me. I was cold and I could hardly breathe. I was terrified. With all the other kids laughing, I also felt humiliated. Josephine was the only one who tried to help me. I could never thank her enough (until the time I saved her life, but that's a different story). Josephine has been my best friend ever since then. Everyone in the neighborhood still makes fun of me every time we see a St. Bernard. It makes me almost cry. But Josephine never laughs. She makes me feel strong and helps me ignore them. She's the kind of friend I want to be.

Another time Josephine helped me was when George Fisher, a huge, mean kid, told me he wanted to be my friend but that I had to do his homework for him. I didn't like George, but I sure didn't want to make him mad at me. I got very depressed. Eventually, I talked it over with Josephine. She suggested that I offer to help him study but not to do his homework for him. I thought this was a good idea. When I told him, he started to look real mad, all red in the face. I felt scared, but I knew I was doing what I had to do. And Josephine was behind me. Well, George finally went away. And later on, he said I was okay, and he asked me to help him study. Josephine said she thought I had done the right thing. She said she was proud of me. I've never felt prouder than when she told me that.

33

Josephine is the best person to do things with and to talk to. She thinks hard about what is fair, and she tries to fix things that aren't fair. I can always count on her. Even if we live far away from each other someday, Josephine and I will always be best friends, because we can rely on each other.

Thinking About the Model

Now that you have read the model personal impression essay, answer the questions on the lines below to help you understand how the writer created it.

1. The purpose of a personal impression essay is to tell how the writer feels about a person. How does the author of the model essay feel about his or her subject?

    _____

    _____

    _____

2. A personal impression essay explains why the writer feels as she or he does about a person. What has Josephine done that makes the author feel this way about her?

    _____

    _____

    _____

3. A personal impression essay tries to use all the senses to describe the thoughts and feelings of the writer. What sensory details does the writer use to give us his or her impression of Josephine?

    _____

    _____

    _____

4. Because a personal impression essay expresses an author's thoughts and feelings, it should have a friendly tone. To achieve this tone, a writer uses informal language, like first-person pronouns (*I, me,* and *our*) and contractions. List some examples of informal language in the essay. (For more information about informal language, see page 87.)

_____

_____

_____

_____

_____

ASSIGNMENT: WRITING A PERSONAL IMPRESSION ESSAY

Write a short personal impression essay describing someone who has been important in your life. In your essay, express your thoughts and feelings about the person. Tell what qualities this person has that you respect or admire. Then relate events in which the person shows these qualities.

Prewriting

Step 1:   First you will want to brainstorm a list of ideas about the subject *Important People.* On your own paper, write this subject at the top of the sheet. Then list every idea that comes to your head. You might list relatives, teachers, or friends. Don't stop to judge any of the ideas. Keep going until you run out of ideas.

Step 2:   From your brainstorming list, choose a person who is important to you to use as the subject for your personal impression essay. This person should be someone you know well and someone about whom you will want to share your thoughts with your readers. Write this person's name on the line below.

_____

Step 3:   Freewrite about this person on your own paper. When you freewrite, you write down whatever comes to mind. Do not stop to judge or edit your thoughts; keep writing until you run out of ideas.

Step 4:   Review your freewriting to choose the most memorable trait about this person. Is he or she loyal? generous? emotionally strong? funny? Select a trait that is important to you and that you are willing to share with your classmates and teacher. State this trait on the line below.

_____

Step 5:   On the lines below, list two experiences you have had with this person that show this person's most memorable trait.

1. _____

2. _____

Step 6: For both of these experiences, tell in chronological order what happened. Tell how the situation began, what the person did, and what happened as a result. On your own paper, answer the following questions:

1. What did the person do?
2. Why did he or she do that?
3. What character trait is this an example of?
4. How did you feel when he or she did that?
5. Why did you feel that way?

 # Writing

Use the following plan to help you write a first draft of your personal impression essay. Write the essay on your own paper. You may want to write on every other line to allow room for your revisions and corrections.

Beginning	<ul><li>Identifies the person and tells your relationship to him or her</li><li>Tells briefly the memorable trait you want to share about this person</li></ul>

Middle	<ul><li>Uses one paragraph to give a detailed description of each experience</li><li>Tells your thoughts and feelings about these experiences</li></ul>

Ending	<ul><li>Restates your choice of the memorable trait</li><li>Gives a final comment, perhaps a look to the future, about this person</li></ul>

Evaluating and Revising

When you evaluate your writing, you judge whether you have accomplished what you set out to do. You may discover ways in which your writing might be improved. When you revise, you make changes to improve what you've written. You can use the following questions to evaluate your personal impression essay before revising it.

Questions for Evaluation

1. Does the beginning identify the person who is the subject of the essay? Does it state the person's most memorable trait? If not, what information should be added?

_____

_____

2. Does the essay describe the writer's thoughts and feelings about this person? If not, what could be added? Where could it be added?

_____

_____

3. Does the essay relate two or three events that show why the writer feels this way? For each event, does it tell what the person did and why he or she did it? If not, what information is missing?

_____

_____

4. Does the essay use details that appeal to all of the five senses? If not, what details can be added?

_____

_____

5. Does the ending tell clearly why the person is important to the writer? Does it give a final comment about the person? If not, what information should be added?

_____

_____

6. Is there information included that is unnecessary and distracting? If so, what information can be cut?

_____

Peer Evaluation

Give your rough draft to a classmate for review. Ask your classmate to follow these steps.

Step 1:   Read the rough draft carefully.

Step 2:   Complete the **Questions for Evaluation** on a separate sheet of paper.

Self-Evaluation

Next, complete your own evaluation of your rough draft. Follow these steps.

Step 1:   Read the peer evaluation written by your classmate. Circle any comments that you plan to use as you revise.

Step 2:   Reread your draft, and write your answers to the **Questions for Evaluation** on your own paper.

Using your answers to the **Questions for Evaluation**, revise your draft. You can use the space in the margins and between the lines of your rough draft for your changes.

Proofreading and Publishing

Use the **Guidelines for Proofreading** on page 10 to find and correct errors in your paper.

Step 1:   a. Check that each word in your paper is spelled and capitalized correctly. If you have any doubt about a word, look it up in a dictionary. Correct any errors you find.

   b. Check for proper punctuation, grammar, and usage. Then correct any errors you find.

Step 2:   Trade papers with a classmate, and proofread each other's paper for spelling, capitalization, punctuation, grammar, and word usage. Mark any errors you find, and return the papers. When you get your own paper back, make any additional corrections that are needed.

Step 3:   Make a clean copy of your revised and proofread paper.

Step 4:   Share your writing in one of the following ways, or think up your own way to reach an audience.

   a.   Work with the class to create a collection of personal impresssions.

   b.   Send or read aloud your personal impression to the person about whom you wrote.

FOR YOUR PORTFOLIO

Write down your answers to these questions, and place them with your essay in your writing portfolio.

1. a.   What have you learned about this person by writing about him or her?

   b.   What do you admire most about this person?

   c.   What can you learn from this person's life that can help you in your own life?

2. What do you think are the strengths of this personal impression essay?

3. What have you learned about expressive writing?

A STORY POEM

What do many poems and song lyrics have in common? Rhythm and rhyme. Poems and song lyrics may also tell stories. A *ballad* is a poem that combines rhythm, rhyme, and a story. The popular music form rap also combines rhythm, rhyme, and story. Here is a poem that follows the rap music style. It is based on "Rip Van Winkle" by Washington Irving.

Rappin' Rip

I'll tell you all a story 'bout a lazy guy,
A good-hearted man with his head in the sky.
Rip Van Winkle was a happy kind of fellow.
He whistled and sang and was always mellow.

There was just one problem with this guy named Rip:
Any hard work he would always skip.
He played and he fished and he visited friends,
But if labor called, his energy would end.

He hiked to the mountains on a bright, sunny day
And met little people along the way.
The little people shared a good-tasting potion
And several sips later, Rip quit all motion.

Some time later Rip awoke sort of groggy,
And the air on the mountain was still and foggy.
Rip seemed confused as he walked to town,
For his beard had grown down to the ground.

Rip traveled through the town at a nervous pace,
For he didn't know a single face.
He sat on a stoop and sighed and sighed.
Folks wondered who he was as they hurried by.

He looked long and hard for his kids and his wife.

He wondered what had happened to his cozy life.

"Hey, I'm Rip Winkle," he shouted, near tears.

"Hey, Rip," someone answered, "you've been gone
twenty years."

Thinking About the Model

Now that you've read the story poem on pages 41–42, think about how the writer created it. Then answer the following questions.

1. People use letters to indicate a pattern of rhyme (called the **rhyme scheme**) in a poem. The first rhyming sound is called *a*; the second rhyming sound is called *b*; and so on. For example:

    The purple *hat a*
    belongs to *Nat. a*

    The green *slacks b*
    belong to *Max. b*

    Please give *Una c*
    the orange *sock. d*

    Please give *Luna c*
    the yellow *smock. d*

Figure out the model poem's rhyme scheme. Write the appropriate letters on the lines below or at the end of each line of the poem.

_____

_____

_____

_____

2. You're probably aware that rap is written in an informal style, using conversational English, slang, and dialect. Sometimes humor is used as well. List some examples of informal words and phrases from the model poem.

_____

_____

3. What is the story that the model poem tells? List the main events below.

   _____

   _____

   _____

   _____

4. The words of story poems and rap songs are not written to be read silently. They are written to be sung or chanted. Read the model poem aloud, snapping your fingers to the beat. How many strong beats does the average line of this poem have?

   _____

ASSIGNMENT: WRITING A STORY POEM

Create your own version of a favorite story, myth, fairy tale, or legend. Keep in mind language, rhythm, and rhyme as you retell a story in this new and interesting way.

 ## Prewriting

Step 1: Think of some possible stories that you might retell as story poems. Write down at least one possibility in each category below: a true story, a myth, a fairy tale, and a legend.

a true story from history (example: the story of the Battle of Gettysburg)

_____

a myth (example: the story of Pegasus, the winged horse)

_____

a fairy tale (example: "Cinderella")

_____

a legend (example: the story of Johnny Appleseed)

_____

Step 2: Now choose the story that you would like to retell as a story poem. Write the title on the line below. Be sure that you are very familiar with your story's content. You may even want to read the story more than once.

_____

Step 3: List the main events from your story on the lines below.

_____

_____

_____

Step 4:   To practice telling part of your story, first choose an event from the list you made in Step 3. List that event on the line below.

_____

Step 5:   Now, on the lines below, write about the event you chose in Step 4. Use the rhyme scheme (*aa*, *bb*, etc.) and the rhythm (four beats per line) of the model poem, or use a rhyme scheme and rhythm of your choice.

_____

_____

_____

_____

_____

_____

_____

 ## Writing

Now combine rhythm, rhyme, and story to begin building your story poem. Use the work you completed in the prewriting section as your guide.

- Know your story well so that you can retell it clearly.

- Focus on the story's key events and the most interesting details.

- Use an informal rap style.

- Keep your rhythm in your head as you write each line.

- Make sure you follow a consistent rhyme scheme.

Evaluating and Revising

You will use these **Questions for Evaluation** when you evaluate your story poem to try to improve it. These questions should help you discover the poem's strengths and weaknesses. You can also use these questions to evaluate a classmate's poem.

Questions for Evaluation

1. Does the poem make sense to readers? Is it clear? If not, what should be added or rearranged?

2. Does the poem use casual, everyday language? If not, where does the language need improvement?

3. Is the rhyme scheme consistent throughout the poem? If not, how can the problem areas be fixed?

4. Do the sentences and the rhymes sound natural? Are there any lines that can be improved? How would you change them?

5. Is the poem lively and full of interesting details? Where might more details be added?

Peer Evaluation

Exchange rough drafts with a classmate. Ask your classmate to follow these steps.

Step 1: Rap is meant to be spoken to a rhythmic accompaniment such as snapping fingers, clapping hands, or a drumbeat. Read the story poem draft aloud, clapping your hands or snapping your fingers as you read it. Think about what parts of the poem might be rewritten to improve the rhythm.

Step 2: Complete the **Questions for Evaluation** above. Try to give specific suggestions for revision.

Self-Evaluation

Next, make your own evaluation of your rough draft. Follow these steps.

Step 1: Read your story poem for rhyme and content, not for grammar and mechanics. Think also about the suggestions you made about your classmate's poem. How might these ideas improve your own work?

Step 2:   Read your poem draft out loud. As you did with your classmate's poem, clap your hands or snap your fingers. Think about how the rhythm works and how it can be improved.

Step 3:   Read your classmate's evaluation. Circle any suggestions you plan to use in your revision.

Step 4:   Reread the **Questions for Evaluation** on page 46. On a separate sheet of paper, jot down notes about specific changes you want to make.

Revise your draft until you can answer yes to each of the **Questions for Evaluation**. If you need to, you might even return to the prewriting stage to generate new ideas.

Proofreading and Publishing

Step 1:   Check your spelling. If you are not absolutely certain that a word is spelled correctly, check a dictionary.

Step 2:   Next, proofread for errors in grammar, usage, capitalization, and punctuation. Use the proofreading checklist on page 10 as a guide.

Step 3:   Make a clean copy of your revised and proofread poem.

Step 4:   Publish your poem by reading it aloud to your classmates or by performing it at a school or a local talent show. If your poem is a version of a children's tale, you may want to take your performance to a local day-care center, a kindergarten class, or to some young relatives.

FOR YOUR PORTFOLIO

If you are keeping a portfolio, you might want to include the answers to the questions below with your poem.

1. What part of creating the story poem did you enjoy most? What did you find most difficult? Write the answers to these questions, and put the answers in your portfolio.

2. The traditional folk ballads of England and Scotland told stories, were written in rhyme, and were passed orally from generation to generation. What similarities and differences are there between rap and this earlier musical form? Write your thoughts in your portfolio.

"I Think that I shall never see, a poem as lovely as a bee, flea, sea, ski, plea, key..."

© 1991; reprinted courtesy of Bunny Hoest and Parade Magazine.

A PRESS RELEASE

Sometimes people or groups want to publicize their plans, events, or successes. They want newspapers, news magazines, or news programs on radio or television to tell the public about an event that the group is planning or a project that the group has completed. One way to get publicity is to send a press release about the event to the editors of news organizations. A press release contains a short news story. News editors sometimes print revised or edited versions of press releases. At other times editors publish press releases, such as the one below, without changing them.

March 14, 1995

Spanish Club
Arcadia High School
Lubbock, Texas
(806) 555-1212

HIGH SCHOOL HOLDS LATIN AMERICAN FESTIVAL

The Spanish Club of Arcadia High School will hold its fourth annual Latin American Festival on Saturday, March 23, from 10:00 A.M. to 2:00 P.M. in the high school auditorium. The public is invited to attend this daylong celebration of Latin American food, dancing, and music.

Las Peruanas, a musical group from Cuzco, Peru, will provide authentic music from Peru, Ecuador, and Bolivia. Home economics students from Arcadia High School will serve a variety of Latin American foods, including empanadas and chiles rellenos.

Ticket prices will be ten dollars in advance and twelve dollars at the door. According to Lupe Martínez, Spanish Club treasurer, proceeds from the festival will finance the Spanish Club's annual field trip to Puerto Rico.

—Chandra Basnayke

Thinking About the Model

When you write a press release, be careful to include all the correct information in an order that makes sense. Read the model press release on the previous page. Then answer the following questions.

1. The information in a press release is usually organized in *order of importance,* from most important to least important. Where does the most important information appear in the model press release?

   _____

2. The first sentence of a press release is called the *lead.* The lead answers several of the *5W-How?* questions: *Who? What? Where? When? Why?* and *How?* Read the lead of the model press release, then answer the following questions.

   What event is being held?

   _____

   Who is holding the event?

   _____

   When is the event being held?

   _____

   Where is the event being held?

   _____

3. What additional information does the press release provide?

   _____

   _____

   _____

   _____

   _____

   _____

   _____

ASSIGNMENT: WRITING A PRESS RELEASE

You are the publicity director for your high school's production of a musical called *Uptown Soundz*. The musical, which combines rap songs and contemporary dance, was written by two students from your school. The directing, acting, lighting, costumes, makeup, and stage design are all being done by students. As publicity director, your job is to announce the play to your community. You have appeared on a local radio program to talk about the musical. Your next goal is to write a press release to send to local newspapers.

 ## Prewriting

Step 1:   Complete the chart below to identify the source of the press release. You will put this information in the upper left-hand corner of your press release.

Organization name (Make up a name for your theater company.)	
School name	
City and State	
Telephone Number	

Step 2:   Write today's date. It will go in the upper right-hand corner of your press release.

_____

Step 3:   Press releases answer the *5W-How?* questions: *Who? What? Where? When? Why?* and *How?* The lead, or first sentence, answers three or four of these questions—the three or four that are most important. Answer the following questions for your press release.

Who is holding the event? _____

What event is being held? _____

Where is it being held?_____

When is it being held? _____

Step 4: Use the information from Step 3 to write a lead for your press release. Remember that the lead should be a single sentence.

_____

_____

Step 5: The **body** of a press release should present additional important information. Gather information for the body of your press release by filling out the following chart. Make up the names, or use the names of your friends or classmates.

Names of musical's writers	
Name of musical's director	
Names of leading actors	
Times of performances	
Price of tickets	
How and Where to buy tickets	

What the musical is about (summary of the story)

_____

_____

_____

_____

_____

Writing

Use the information from your prewriting notes to write a draft of your press release on a separate sheet of paper. Use the press release on page 49 as a model. At the top of your paper, identify the name, address, and telephone number of your organization. Also include today's date. Leave space for the headline.

Next, write the body of your press release. It should be two to four paragraphs long. Each paragraph should be short (two or three sentences). The first paragraph should begin with your lead. Arrange the rest of the information in order of decreasing importance.

Finally, write a **headline**, or title, for your press release. Base the headline on your lead. Your headline should be a short sentence (seven words or less). It should contain a subject and a verb in the present tense. Avoid using the words *a*, *an*, *the*, *is*, and *are* in a headline. [Note: You may want to look at some sample newspaper headlines first.]

Evaluating and Revising

You can use the following questions when you evaluate the strengths and weaknesses of your press release.

Questions for Evaluation

1. Are the date and the source of the press release clear? If not, what should be added?

2. Does the headline have a subject and a verb that is in the present tense? If not, what should be added?

3. Are the words *a*, *an*, *the*, *is*, and *are* left out of the headline? If not, what should be cut?

4. Does the lead answer any of the *5W-How?* questions? If not, how can the lead be fixed?

5. Does the press release use words and sentences that are short and simple? If not, what needs to be cut or replaced?

6. Does the press release contain all the information that readers will need to know? If not, what needs to be added?

7. Is the information arranged in order of decreasing importance? If not, what needs to be rearranged?

Peer Evaluation

Give your rough draft to a classmate to read and evaluate. Then, on his or her own paper, your classmate should answer the **Questions for Evaluation** on the preceding page.

Self-Evaluation

Next, evaluate the draft yourself. Follow these steps.

Step 1: Read the peer evaluation written by your classmate. Circle any comments that you plan to make use of as you revise.

Step 2: Reread your draft, and answer the **Questions for Evaluation.**

Now revise your draft by using your classmate's suggestions and your answers to the **Questions for Evaluation.** You can make corrections directly on your draft; you can rewrite your draft; or you can start all over again with prewriting.

Proofreading and Publishing

Step 1: Proofread the press release for errors in spelling, grammar, usage, and mechanics. Refer to the **Proofreading Checklist** on page 10. Make a clean copy of your revised press release.

Step 2: Publish your press release by creating a collection of class press releases as models for other students to use.

FOR YOUR PORTFOLIO

Write down your answers to these questions to accompany your press release in your portfolio.

1. What was the most important lesson that you learned from writing a press release?

2. Look in a newspaper for stories announcing upcoming events. Cut out one or two that you think are good. Include them with your press release in your portfolio.

A PERSUASIVE LETTER

Is there a change you would like to see in your community? Maybe you'd like the Parks and Recreation Commission to offer more summer art classes, or maybe you'd like a local business to sponsor a basketball tournament. A *persuasive letter* can be an effective means of suggesting a change or arguing in favor of an idea.

16 Cedar Street
Crozet, VA 22932
April 20, 2008

Ms. Laura Rasmussen
Uptown Theater
253 Cross Street
Crozet, VA 22932

Dear Ms. Rasmussen:

After I saw The Joy Luck Club, a film about Chinese American mothers and daughters, I began to think about what it is like for people who come to the United States from another country. I asked my grandmother about people immigrating because she moved here from Poland when she was nineteen years old. She told me stories about her life I'd never heard before. Because this movie is so unforgettable, I am writing to ask you to show The Joy Luck Club once more at your theater.

I think it would be a real service to the community to show it again. The movie was popular and got good reviews. Many people who had read Amy Tan's best-seller, The Joy Luck Club, wanted to see how Hollywood had turned the novel into a movie. When it was shown in our town, there were long lines of people waiting to get in to see it, and many people I know went to see it twice. I also know some people who read the novel after they saw the movie, and now they would like a chance to see the movie again.

Another reason I think it would be good to show the movie is that we have a large population of people in our community who have recently moved to the United States from other countries, such as Russia and Vietnam. I think it would be valuable for everyone to see this film.

The main reason, however, that I would like you to show this film again is that it was the best film I've seen in several years. The story, the subject, and the characters were so interesting that I haven't forgotten them. I am sure I am not the only one in our community who would be glad to have a chance to see it once more.

Thank you for considering my idea.

Sincerely,
Monica Reilly

Thinking About the Model

The writer of the model letter has a strong opinion. Think about how she tries to persuade the movie theater owner to show the film. Answer the following questions on the lines provided.

1. An opinion is a personal belief that one cannot necessarily prove true or false. What opinion is this writer expressing in her letter?

_____

_____

_____

2. An important element of a persuasive letter is a strong opening. You might choose to open with a startling fact or an anecdote. Once you have hooked the reader's attention, you can present your opinion. How does the writer try to catch the reader's attention in the opening paragraph?

_____

_____

_____

3. Once you have presented your opinion, you need to back it up with reasons or evidence. How you organize these reasons is important. You can give the most important reason first, or you may choose to give it last. What reasons does the writer give to support the idea of showing the film again? In what order are these ideas presented?

_____

_____

_____

_____

_____

_____

4. Another way to support your opinion is to show that other people share it. How does the writer of the model letter show that other people liked this movie?

_____

_____

_____

5. Using an example from your personal experience can add an emotional appeal to a persuasive letter. How does the writer use a personal experience to support her viewpoint?

_____

_____

_____

6. The conclusion is important because it is the reader's final impression of your opinion. In it, you can restate your opinion. Or you can end with a *call to action*—what you want the reader to do as a result of being persuaded. You might also want to include a thank-you to the reader for considering your idea or opinion. How does the writer conclude the model letter?

_____

_____

_____

ASSIGNMENT: WRITING A PERSUASIVE LETTER

The owner of a local movie theater has decided not to replay a movie that you would like to see again. Write a letter in which you try to persuade the theater owner to change his or her mind.

 Prewriting

1. Think about the films you've seen that you really enjoyed. They might be recent films, as well as ones you saw when you were younger. Brainstorm a list of titles on your own paper.

2. On your list, circle the name of the film that you would most like to see again. Then, in the space below, list the things you liked about it. Try to list specific details or examples.

    _____

    _____

    _____

    _____

    _____

3. What reasons can you think of to persuade the owner of a theater to show this film again? Can you think of any ways in which you can make an emotional appeal for your viewpoint? List these reasons in the space below.

    _____

    _____

    _____

    _____

    _____

4. Try to add the force of others' opinions to your letter. Did any reviewers give the movie a "thumbs up"? Did it win an Academy Award? List any awards or expert opinions below.

_____

_____

5. Decide how to organize your letter. What will be the strongest support for your opinion? The weakest? On your own paper, list your supporting details and examples. Start with the weakest, and end with the strongest.

 ## Writing

Using your prewriting notes, draft a persuasive letter on your own paper. Here are some suggestions for writing your draft.

Beginning	• Begin with an introduction that will grab the reader's attention. Then state your opinion clearly.

Middle	• Follow your introduction with reasons and evidence to support your opinion. Because you'll get details to support your reasons, you might need a paragraph for each reason.
	• Try to include details that will make an emotional appeal to the reader.
	• Always keep in mind your purpose: You are trying to convince the reader to think or act as you suggest.

Ending	• Create a strong ending. You could summarize your reasons, restate your opinion, or end with a call to action.
	• Add a polite thank-you to the reader for taking the time to read your letter.

Evaluating and Revising

Now that you've written your letter, consider how you can improve it. Use the following **Questions for Evaluation** to evaluate your persuasive letter before revising it.

Questions for Evaluation

1. Does the letter have a strong opening that will catch the reader's attention? If not, what can be added or reworded?

2. Does the letter clearly state an opinion? If not, what can be added or restated?

3. Is the opinion supported with reasons and evidence? Are these reasons well organized? If not, is there a better order in which to present the information?

4. Does the letter make an appeal to the emotions of the reader? If not, can you think of an emotional appeal that could be added?

5. Does the letter include others' opinions to strengthen the argument? If not, what can be added?

6. Does the letter have an effective conclusion that summarizes the reasons, restates the opinion, or calls for action? If not, what could be added to make the ending stronger?

Peer Evaluation

Exchange rough drafts with a classmate. Ask the classmate to follow these steps.

Step 1:   Read the rough draft carefully.

Step 2:   Answer the **Questions for Evaluation** on a separate piece of paper.

Self-Evaluation

Now complete an evaluation of your own rough draft. Follow these steps.

Step 1:   Reread your rough draft carefully.

Step 2:   Think about the suggestions you made for your classmate's rough draft. Do any apply to your own draft?

Step 3: On a separate piece of paper, answer the **Questions for Evaluation** for your rough draft. Be sure to include notes about specific changes you want to make.

Step 4: Study your classmate's suggestions. Circle any suggestions you would like to use in your revision.

Use your answers to the **Questions for Evaluation**, together with your classmate's suggestions, to revise your draft until you are satisfied with it.

Proofreading and Publishing

A polished letter will make a positive impression on the reader. Use these steps to prepare your final version.

Step 1: Begin by checking the spelling of each word. If you are uncertain of the spelling of a word, look it up in a dictionary. Pay special attention to foreign words.

Step 2: Check your letter for correct punctuation, grammar, usage, and capitalization. Make sure that any numbers or statistics you cite are accurate.

Step 3: Make a clean copy of your revised and proofread letter. Use the following format for a business letter.

The Parts of a Letter	
Heading	Begin the heading to the right of the center of the page. Include the following information. • writer's street address • writer's city, state and ZIP Code (A comma follows the name of the city.) • date of letter (A comma separates the day of the month from the year.)
Inside Address	Begin the inside address at the left margin. Include the following information. • the name and, if appropriate, the title of the person you are writing to • the name of the company or organization • street address of company or organization

Salutation	Begin the salutation, or greeting, at the left margin. Begin the first word and all nouns in the salutation with a capital letter. Follow the salutation with a colon.
Body	The body of the letter contains your message. Indent the first line of each paragraph.
Closing and Signature	The closing should be vertically even with the heading. Use *Yours truly,* or *Sincerely,* for the closing. Sign your name in ink in the space just below the closing. Use your legal name.

Step 4:   Use one of the following suggestions to publish your letter.

A. Prepare a bulletin board displaying the letters you and your classmates have written.

B. Post your letter on the refrigerator or in another spot at home so that your family members can read it.

FOR YOUR PORTFOLIO

Look in newspapers or magazines to see if you can find reviews of the movie you wrote about. Study how the reviewer describes the movie. How does the review differ from your letter? Clip the reviews and keep them with a copy of your letter.

B.C. by Johnny Hart. By permission of Johnny Hart and Creators Syndicate.

SENTENCE FRAGMENTS

8a **A *sentence fragment* is a word group that does not have all the basic parts of a complete sentence and does not express a complete thought.**

To find out whether you have written a complete sentence or a sentence fragment, you can use a simple, three-part test.

1. Does the group of words have a subject?
2. Does it have a verb?
3. Does it express a complete thought?

FRAGMENT   Was a great tennis player. [The subject is missing. *Who* was a great tennis player?]

SENTENCE   **Arthur Ashe** was a great tennis player.

FRAGMENT   Arthur Ashe many awards and tennis championships. [The verb is missing. *What* did Arthur Ashe do?]

SENTENCE   Arthur Ashe **won** many awards and tennis championships.

FRAGMENT   Because Ashe wanted to help young tennis players. [This group of words has a subject and a verb, but it doesn't express a complete thought. *What happened* because Ashe wanted to help young tennis players?]

SENTENCE   Because Ashe wanted to help young tennis players, **he wrote many inspiring articles and ran tennis clinics in many cities**.

8b **A *phrase* is a group of words that does not have a subject and a verb. *Verbals* are forms of verbs that are used as other parts of speech. A *verbal phrase* is a phrase that contains a verbal. By itself, a verbal phrase is a fragment because it doesn't express a complete thought.**

FRAGMENT   Watching your game.

SENTENCE   **I enjoyed** watching your game.

FRAGMENT   To become good soccer players.

SENTENCE   **Athletes must practice hard** to become good soccer players.

8c **An *appositive* is a word that identifies or explains the noun or pronoun it follows. An *appositive phrase*, a phrase made up of an appositive and its modifiers, is a fragment. It does not contain the basic parts of a sentence.**

FRAGMENT   A novel about World War I.

SENTENCE   **Ernest Hemingway wrote** *A Farewell to Arms*, a novel about World War I.

> **8d** A *prepositional phrase* is a group of words consisting of a preposition, a noun or pronoun that serves as the object of the preposition, and any modifiers of that object. A prepositional phrase can't stand alone as a sentence because it doesn't express a complete thought.
>
> FRAGMENT   For their sharp wit.
> SENTENCE   **The poems of Dorothy Parker are known** for their sharp wit.

EXERCISE 1   Writing Sentences with Phrasal Fragments

On your own paper, create sentences from the phrases and clauses below. You can either attach the fragment to a complete sentence or develop it into a complete sentence by adding a subject, a verb, or both.

EX.   1. walking on the beach
  1. *Walking on the beach, we found a beautiful shell.*
            or
      Julia and I were walking on the beach.

1. under the table
2. hoping to win first prize
3. to ask a question
4. the captain of the team
5. needing a ride home
6. instead of clouds
7. my cousin in Des Moines
8. to solve this math problem
9. seems to work
10. in the middle of the night
11. watering the yard
12. to look like new
13. with most of the other team members
14. on the roof near the chimney
15. after having a hard rain
16. working after school
17. a new pencil sharpener
18. adding our scores together
19. to believe a story like that
20. our neighbor down the street
21. learn the rules
22. playing chess with us
23. because coming early
24. at the tournament
25. while walking home from school

SUBORDINATE CLAUSE FRAGMENTS

A *clause* is a group of words that has a subject and a verb. An *independent clause* expresses a complete thought and can stand alone as a sentence.

8e A *subordinate clause* does not express a complete thought. It is a fragment and cannot stand by itself as a sentence.

FRAGMENT Because Fred was late for the meeting. [*What happened* because Fred was late for the meeting?]

SENTENCE Because Fred was late for the meeting, **he didn't hear the treasurer's report.**

FRAGMENT Who gave the treasurer's report. [Note that this would be a complete sentence if it ended with a question mark.]

SENTENCE **Fred can easily get the information from Arlene,** who gave the treasurer's report.

 NOTE A series of items is another kind of fragment that's easily mistaken for a sentence.

FRAGMENT A sandwich, an apple, four pieces of celery, and some popcorn.

SENTENCE **I ate several things for lunch:** a sandwich, an apple, four pieces of celery, and some popcorn.

EXERCISE 2   Identifying and Revising Subordinate Clause Fragments

In the following paragraph, underline each fragment. Revise the paragraph on your own paper by joining the subordinate clauses with the independent clauses. [Note: There may be more than one correct way to join the clauses.]

EX. 1   <u>Although the crew members were very busy.</u> They always

2   had a few minutes to spend with the boy.

Although the crew members were very busy, they always had a few minutes to spend with the boy.

1   Roman Inthisith was a six-year-old boy. Who lives in a busy

2   neighborhood in South Philadelphia. Roman moved to the

3   neighborhood recently. Who was born in California. His

4 mother had come to California from Laos. Because

5 Roman was new to the area. He had few playmates. However, all

6 that changed. When a large group of actors, production assistants,

7 camera operators, and carpenters came to South Philadelphia to

8 film a movie. After they chose Roman's block for the filming of

9 many scenes in the movie. Roman met many of the crew

10 members. Suddenly, this curious, friendly boy made several new

11 friends. A photographer loaned Roman a small camera. That was

12 loaded with black-and-white film. One of the carpenters gave

13 Roman a hammer. Who was building sets on the street. Because

14 the crew members liked their young companion so much. They all

15 chipped in and bought him a bicycle.

EXERCISE 3   Using Subordinate Clauses in Sentences

On your own paper, use each of the subordinate clause fragments below as part of a complete sentence. Add whatever words are necessary to make the meaning of the sentence complete. Add capitalization and punctuation as necessary.

EX.   1.   when the telephone rang
      1.   When the telephone rang, it startled me.

1. who called
2. after the meeting ended
3. if you want to see a great movie
4. because I enjoy mystery stories
5. which answered my question
6. since I finished my report
7. that she won the race
8. whom I invited
9. as if they had forgotten
10. where we set up the tent

RUN-ON SENTENCES

8f A *run-on sentence* is two or more complete sentences run together as one.

There are two kinds of run-ons. In a ***fused sentence***, the sentences have no punctuation at all between them.

RUN-ON   Jeremiah moved here from Israel he is my best friend.
CORRECT   Jeremiah moved here from Israel. **He** is my best friend.

The second kind of run-on is called a ***comma splice***. Two sentences are linked together with only a comma to separate them.

RUN-ON   Jeremiah joined the school orchestra, he plays the violin.
CORRECT   Jeremiah joined the school orchestra. **He** plays the violin.

To revise run-on sentences, you can always make two separate sentences. But if the two thoughts are related and are equal to one another in importance, you may want to make a ***compound sentence***.

RUN-ONS   The Delaware River is in eastern Pennsylvania the Ohio River is in western Pennsylvania. [fused]

            The Delaware River is in eastern Pennsylvania, the Ohio River is in western Pennsylvania. [comma splice]

You can revise a run-on sentence by using one of the following techniques.

1. Use a comma and a coordinating conjunction (such as *and, but,* or *or*).

CORRECTED   The Delaware River is in eastern Pennsylvania**, and** the Ohio River is in western Pennsylvania.

2. Use a semicolon.

CORRECTED   The Delaware River is in eastern Pennsylvania**;** the Ohio River is in western Pennsylvania.

3. Use a semicolon and a word such as *therefore, instead, meanwhile, still, also, nevertheless,* or *however*. These words are called *conjunctive adverbs*. Follow a conjunctive adverb with a comma.

CORRECTED   The Delaware River is in eastern Pennsylvania**; however,** the Ohio River is in western Pennsylvania.

EXERCISE 4   Revising Run-on Sentences

On your own paper, revise each of the run-on sentences below. Follow the directions in parentheses. Be sure to use correct end punctuation.

EX.   1. Jamyce has worked hard on her report, it isn't finished yet. (Use a comma and a coordinating conjunction.)

    1. Jamyce has worked hard on her report, but it isn't finished yet.

1. Maria Tallchief was an American Indian she became one of the world's most famous ballerinas. (Split into two sentences.)

2. Reiko Amato designed the cover for our yearbook the design won an award presented by the Houston Art League. (Use a semicolon.)

3. Delaware is one of the smallest states, Rhode Island is even smaller. (Use a semicolon and a conjunctive adverb.)

4. The Andes Mountains are in South America, the Alps are in Europe. (Use a comma and a coordinating conjunction.)

5. We wanted to attend your dress rehearsal, we had to go to a late session of soccer practice. (Use a semicolon and a conjunctive adverb.)

6. The sound of the motorcycle woke me up, I still didn't get out of bed. (Use a coordinating conjunction.)

7. *Fifth Chinese Daughter* by Jade Snow Wong was the book we chose for the book group I am so glad we decided to read it. (Use a comma and a coordinating conjunction.)

8. The storm moved into the area after lunch we had already found shelter. (Use a semicolon and a conjunctive adverb.)

9. Did you attend the concert my mom wouldn't let me go on a school night. (Split into two sentences.)

10. I have always loved animals someday I'd like to be a veterinarian. (Use a comma and a coordinating conjunction.)

11. Chen will march in the New Year's parade his sister will not. (Use a comma and a coordinating conjunction.)

12. Do you enjoy hiking we're planning a trip to New Hampshire next weekend. (Split into two sentences.)

13. We will take nuts, raisins, and a small bottle of water they won't take up much space. (Use a semicolon.)

14. His older brother is coming home for Thanksgiving, his younger brother is, too. (Use a comma and a coordinating conjunction.)

15. Their house has an enormous attic filled with boxes treasures from the past are inside each box. (Split into two sentences.)

REVIEW EXERCISE

A. Identifying Fragments and Run-on Sentences

On the line before each item below, write *frag.* for *fragment, r.o.* for *run-on sentence*, or *C* if the sentence is correct. Then, on your own paper, revise each fragment and run-on to form a clear, complete sentence. [Note: There may be more than one correct way to revise each item.]

EX. _____frag._____ 1. After we saw the movie.

    1. *After we saw the movie, we bought a vegetable pizza.*

_____ 1. Dr. Petrakis is my dentist, she cleaned my teeth.

_____ 2. The character played by Rita Moreno in the movie.

_____ 3. Chili usually contains beans, sometimes it contains no meat.

_____ 4. Spanish settlers brought horses to North and South America.

_____ 5. Photographs taken by my grandfather when my father was a young boy.

_____ 6. Sitting on the back porch, playing a board game.

_____ 7. The Dodgers once played baseball in Brooklyn, New York, today they play in Los Angeles.

_____ 8. The singers went to Russia on a concert tour the Russian teenagers seemed to enjoy their music.

_____ 9. Georgio missed the bus, he was late for school.

_____ 10. Who left this jacket on the playing field after the game.

B. Revising Fragments and Run-on Sentences

In the following paragraph, identify each fragment or run-on sentence. Then, on your own paper, revise each fragment and run-on, changing the punctuation and capitalization as needed to make a clear and complete sentence. [Note: There may be more than one correct way to make each revision.]

EX. 1 Thor Heyerdahl journeyed. To Rapa Nui from Norway.

    1. *Thor Heyerdahl journeyed to Rapa Nui from Norway.*

1   For almost forty years, archaeologists have studied the island

2 of Rapa Nui. Which is part of Polynesia, in the Pacific Ocean. One

3 leading archaeologist who studied Rapa Nui. Thor Heyerdahl.

4   Heyerdahl made many excavations on Rapa Nui in the 1950s,

5   further archaeological studies continue today by archaeologists

6   from Chile and the United States. Uncovered the sites of many

7   early villages and temples. The studies of Rapa Nui by foreign

8   scientists have greatly affected the island's culture, those effects

9   have been both good and bad. Modern people of Rapa Nui great

10   cultural pride from the remains of the beautiful temples. And

11   other hints about the glorious past of Rapa Nui. Books and

12   articles about the archaeological findings on Rapa Nui. Brought

13   many tourists to the island. Helped the island's economy. But

14   there have been bad effects, too, the history of the island has been

15   written largely through the eyes of its visitors. Legends that may

16   not be true appear in many books. As facts. Over the last forty

17   years, the arts and crafts of the island have changed. To match the

18   tastes of the many tourists. Rapa Nui is a beautiful island

19   community with a rich history and culture. Which should be

20   respected, and not changed, by visitors from foreign lands.

C.   Recreating a Message

You are a member of an archaeological team in the year 2500, and you have
been digging at a site outside your school. You have uncovered some torn
pieces of paper. The words on the pieces are shown below. Many contain
sentence fragments. Study these pieces, and use them to reconstruct a
message in complete, clear sentences. Combine fragments to form sentences,
adding whatever words, punctuation marks, and capital letters you need.
Write the message on your own paper.

EX.   stopped running   on the highway   tank was empty
       Our car stopped running on the highway because the gasoline tank was
       empty.

as far as three blocks away   because we were late

missed the big moment   when Darcy kicked the extra point

score 7–0   could hear

jumping up and down   started running

cheering of the fans   greatest games I had ever seen

COMBINING BY INSERTING WORDS

8g You can combine short sentences by inserting a key word from one sentence into another.

You may need to eliminate some of the words in sentences that are combined. You may also need to change the form of the key word.

Using the Same Form	
Original	Ogden Nash wrote many short poems. His poems are funny.
Combined	Ogden Nash wrote many short, **funny** poems.
Changing the Form	
Original	Alexandre Dumas was a famous writer. He was from France.
Combined	Alexandre Dumas was a famous **French** writer.

When you change the form of a word, you often add an ending that makes the word an adjective or an adverb. Usually this ending is *–ed*, *–ing*, or *–ly*.

EXERCISE 5   Combining Sentences by Inserting Words

On your own paper, combine each of the following pairs of sentences by inserting the italicized word from the second sentence into the first sentence. The directions in parentheses will tell you how to change the word form if it is necessary to do so.

EX.   1. My friend Bianca Guerra is a painter. She has *talent*. (Add *–ed* to *talent*.)

   1. My friend Bianca Guerra is a talented painter.

1. Her painting is not finished. It is not *complete*. (Add *–ly* to *complete*.)
2. The painting contains many colors. The colors are *bright*.
3. Bianca has created a painting of a sunset. Her painting is *beautiful*.
4. If you look closely, you can see many details. The details are *hiding*. (Change *hiding* to *hidden*.)

5. Can you see the flock of birds in the sunset? The birds are *flying*.

6. Also, notice the reflection of the sun. The sun is *setting*.

7. In the reflection, a tiny sailboat floats on the water. The boat's floating seems *smooth*. (Add *–ly* to *smooth*.)

8. The sun makes the trees cast long shadows. The sun makes the trees cast *dark* shadows.

9. All of the details make for a beautiful picture. The picture has *drama*. (Change *drama* to *dramatic*.)

10. Bianca used a photograph of a scene as a model for this picture. The scene is in *Spain*, (Change *Spain* to *Spanish*.)

EXERCISE 6   Combining Sentences by Inserting Words

On your own paper, combine each pair of sentences below by inserting words. Add commas and change the forms of words whenever you need to. [Note: There may be more than one correct way to combine each pair.]

EX. 1. The children's museum in our town is on Walnut Street. It is in the second block.

    1. The children's museum in our town is in the second block on Walnut Street.

1. I first went to the museum when I was a child. I was young.

2. In many museums, visitors can't pick up the exhibits. The visitors can't touch the exhibits.

3. At this museum, you can touch all the exhibits. It's a wonderful museum.

4. There are hundreds of exhibits. Each exhibit provides a challenge.

5. Liquid in a tank recreates the movement of ocean waves. The waves roll.

6. On the second floor of the museum, there's an oversized telephone. It is about three feet high.

7. Very young children love this telephone. They can climb all over it.

8. They can call any number on the phone. They can hear the phone ring.

9. A favorite spot of mine is the room called "Grandma's Attic." This room has trunks of old clothes to try on.

10. There is also a box of fancy hats. Some hats are old and some hats are new.

COMBINING BY INSERTING PHRASES

You can also combine closely related sentences by taking a phrase from one sentence and inserting it into another sentence.

8h A *prepositional phrase*, a preposition with its object, can usually be inserted into another sentence with no changes. You may need to leave out some of the words in one of the sentences.

ORIGINAL   The houses along the coast were damaged. They were damaged by the storm.

REVISED   The houses along the coast were damaged **by the storm.**

A ***participial phrase*** acts as an adjective, modifying a noun or pronoun. It contains a verb form that usually ends in *–ing* or *–ed*.

8i   Sometimes you can combine two related sentences by changing the verb from one sentence into a participle and inserting the new participial phrase into the other sentence. When you insert the participial phrase into the sentence, place it close to the noun or pronoun that it modifies. Otherwise, you may confuse your reader.

ORIGINAL   Al saw a herd of wild deer. Al sat on the back porch.

REVISED   **Sitting on the back porch,** Al saw a herd of wild deer.

An ***appositive phrase*** follows a noun or pronoun and helps to explain it.

8j   Sometimes you can combine two related sentences by changing one of the sentences into an appositive phrase.

ORIGINAL   Dr. LaPorte has written a symphony. He is the conductor of the school orchestra.

REVISED   Dr. LaPorte, **the conductor of the school orchestra,** has written a symphony.

EXERCISE 7   Combining Sentences by Inserting Phrases

On your own paper, revise each of the following pairs of sentences to make one sentence. The words you need to insert are italicized, and the directions in parentheses will help you. [Note: There may be more than one correct way to combine the sentences.]

EX.   1. The painting is upside down. The painting *hangs on the living room wall.* (Insert a participial phrase.)

　　　1. The painting hanging on the living room wall is upside down.

1. I had cantaloupe for breakfast. Cantaloupe is *my favorite fruit.* (Insert an appositive phrase.)

2. She wore the suit. The suit had *green and white stripes*. (Insert a prepositional phrase.)

3. The Nile River flows for approximately 4,145 miles. The Nile River is *the longest river in the world*. (Insert an appositive phrase.)

4. The children ran through the sprinkler. The children were *laughing loudly*. (Insert a participial phrase.)

5. Earl won a first-place trophy. Earl *competed in acrobatics*. (Insert a participial phrase.)

6. Judith plays field hockey. Judith is *my oldest sister*. (Insert an appositive phrase.)

7. We moved the desk from my room. We moved the desk *to the garage*. (Insert a prepositional phrase.)

8. Our guide explained Mayan mythology. He used charts of the Milky Way. (Insert a participial phrase.)

9. All afternoon, Lou and I lay on the beach. The beach is *at La Jolla*. (Insert a prepositional phrase.)

10. I like these books. These books were *written by Naguib Mahfouz*. (Insert a participial phrase.)

EXERCISE 8   Combining Sentences by Inserting Phrases

On your own paper, revise each pair of sentences below by inserting a phrase to make one sentence. Use your own judgment as you combine the sentences.

EX. 1. The bones were found in a gravel pit. The pit was in the town of Piltdown.

1. *The bones were found in a gravel pit in the town of Piltdown.*

1. We read about the case of the "Piltdown Man." It was a famous hoax.

2. Parts of a skull and a jawbone were found at Piltdown, England. They were discovered between 1908 and 1912.

3. Scientists examined the bones. Scientists decided that they were very old.

4. Some scientists believed they had found the remains of a human. They believed that the human was from prehistoric times.

5. Other scientists disagreed. Other scientists did not believe the bones were 250,000 years old.

COMPOUND ELEMENTS

8k **You can combine sentences that have either the same subject or the same verb by making a compound subject or a compound verb. Add a coordinating conjunction such as *and, but, or, nor*, or *yet*.**

ORIGINAL Serbia was once part of Yugoslavia. Bosnia was once part of Yugoslavia. [different subjects with same verb]

REVISED **Serbia and Bosnia** were once part of Yugoslavia. [compound subject with same verb]

ORIGINAL The planet Mercury measures 3,100 miles at its equator. The planet Mercury has an average surface temperature of 177° Celsius. [different verbs with same subject]

REVISED The planet Mercury **measures** 3,100 miles at its equator **and has** an average surface temperature of 177° Celsius. [compound verb with same subject]

8l **You can combine two related sentences by making a *compound sentence*. A compound sentence is two or more simple sentences linked by a comma and a coordinating conjunction, a semicolon, or a semicolon and a conjunctive adverb. Before linking two thoughts to make a compound sentence, make sure that the thoughts are related to one another and are equal in importance.**

ORIGINAL Ralph collects old coins. Gina collects postage stamps from South America.

REVISED Ralph collects old coins, **and** Gina collects postage stamps from South America. [comma and coordinating conjunction]
Ralph collects old coins; Gina collects postage stamps from South America. [semicolon]
Ralph collects old coins; **however**, Gina collects postage stamps from South America. [semicolon and conjunctive adverb]

EXERCISE 9 Creating Sentences with Compound Subjects and Compound Verbs

On your own paper, revise each of the following pairs of sentences to make one sentence that contains either a compound subject or a compound verb.

EX. 1. Lemons are citrus fruits. Limes are also citrus fruits.
1. Lemons and limes are citrus fruits.

1. Citrus trees grow wild in parts of Asia. Citrus trees are cultivated on farms in many other places.

2. Citrus trees keep their leaves all year round. They produce fragrant flowers.

3. In the United States, Florida produces a great supply of citrus fruits. Texas produces a great supply as well.

4. Citrus plants thrive in places where there is no frost. They prefer a slightly cool, tropical climate.

5. The kumquat is a citrus fruit with bright orange skin. Similarly, the tangerine is a citrus fruit with bright orange skin.

6. My favorite citrus fruit is grapefruit. My mother's favorite citrus fruit is grapefruit.

7. I usually cut a grapefruit in half. I scoop out the fruit with a spoon.

8. Citrus fruits supply vitamin C. They also contain minerals.

9. The citron tastes sour. The lemon also tastes sour.

10. The rind, or skin, of the citron is often processed. It is used in cakes and candies.

EXERCISE 10   Combining Simple Sentences into Compound Sentences

On your own paper, combine each pair of sentences below to form a compound sentence. [Note: There is more than one correct way to combine each pair.]

EX. 1. My grandfather left France in 1966. My grandmother left Spain at about the same time.

   1. My grandfather left France in 1966, and my grandmother left Spain at about the same time.

1. Granddad worked as a carpenter in New York City. Grandma was a cook in a nearby restaurant.

2. Times were tough back then. Granddad rarely had enough money to eat at the restaurant.

3. But he met my grandmother one day at the vegetable store. They talked and talked.

4. They were married a year later. Granddad's "tough times" suddenly became very full and happy.

5. For years I have heard stories about Grandma and Grandpa. I like to hear these stories.

COMBINING THROUGH SUBORDINATION

A *complex sentence* includes one independent clause—a clause that can stand alone as a sentence. It also has one or more subordinate clauses—clauses that cannot stand alone as sentences.

8m You can combine two sentences by turning one sentence into an *adjective clause*. To do this, insert *who, which,* or *that* in place of the subject. Then use the new subordinate clause to give information about a noun or a pronoun in the other sentence.

ORIGINAL   Lionel Ritchie is a famous singer. He was once a member of a singing group called The Commodores.

REVISED   Lionel Ritchie is a famous singer **who was once a member of a singing group called The Commodores.**

8n You can combine sentences by turning one sentence into an *adverb clause*. Begin the adverb clause with a subordinating conjunction such as *after, although, because, if, when,* or *where*. Choose the subordinating conjunction that shows the relationship between the ideas in the adverb clause and those in the independent clause. Then use the new subordinate clause to give information about a verb, an adjective, or another adverb in the independent clause.

When you use an adverb clause at the beginning of a sentence, use a comma to separate it from the independent clause.

ORIGINAL   The concert was over. I went backstage and met Lionel Ritchie.

REVISED   **When the concert was over,** I went backstage and met Lionel Ritchie. [The subordinating conjunction *when* shows how the ideas are related in time.]

8o You can combine two sentences by turning one sentence into a *noun clause* and inserting it into the other sentence just like an ordinary noun. Begin the noun clause with a word such as *that, how,* or *who*.

When you place the noun clause in the other sentence, you may have to change or remove some words.

ORIGINAL   Lionel Ritchie is friendly to his fans. This fact was made obvious to me by his warm greeting.

REVISED   **That Lionel Ritchie is friendly to his fans** was made obvious to me by his warm greeting. [The word *that* introduces the noun clause, which becomes the subject of the verb *was*.]

EXERCISE 11   Combining Sentences into Complex Sentences

On your own paper, revise each pair of sentences below to make a complex sentence. You may need .to change or take out some words to make smooth combinations. [Note: There may be more than one correct way to combine each pair of sentences.]

EX.   1.   Granville Woods was an African American inventor. He was born in Columbus, Ohio, in 1856.

     1.   *Granville Woods was an African American inventor who was born in Columbus, Ohio, in 1856.*

1. Granville Woods left school at the age of ten. Then he went to work at a machine shop.

2. He worked. At the same time, he went to night school and, later, to college.

3. He was a genius. This fact can be proved by his inventions.

4. He invented a system of electric signals. It helped trains communicate with stations along their routes.

5. The signals told the crews on the moving trains about the locations of other trains. There were far fewer accidents and collisions.

6. Woods sold the device through a company. He established the company himself.

7. He also invented an incubator. It helped poultry farmers.

8. Chickens laid eggs. Then the eggs were put into the warm incubator to hatch.

9. This device led to modern machines. The modern machines can hatch fifty thousand eggs at one time.

10. Granville Woods was a great inventor. He died of a stroke in Harlem Hospital in 1910.

11. Another inventor was Christopher Latham Sholes. He developed his ideas during the late 1800s.

12. With the help of two other men, he invented the first practical typewriter. This typewriter was patented in 1868.

13. Sholes was also a newspaper editor and a state legislator. Sholes held these positions before he invented the typewriter.

14. In 1884, Ottmar Mergenthaler patented the Linotype machine. Mergenthaler was a German living in the United States.

15. The Linotype is a printing machine. This printing machine creates a complete line of type at one time.

IMPROVING SENTENCE STYLE

Combining short sentences to link related ideas can bring variety and interest to your writing. But always avoid *stringy sentences* and *wordy sentences*.

8p A *stringy sentence* **has too many independent clauses strung together. Since all the ideas are treated equally, the reader has trouble understanding how they are related.**

There are two ways you can fix a stringy sentence.

1. Break the sentence into two or more sentences.
2. Turn some of the independent clauses into subordinate clauses or phrases.

STRINGY Marisa and Gina are the leaders of the food festival, so they called a meeting, and the purpose of the meeting was to get volunteers to help, and we were interested in helping, so we went to the meeting.

BETTER Marisa and Gina are the leaders of the food festival, so they called a meeting. The purpose of the meeting was to get volunteers to help. We were interested in helping, so we went to the meeting.

BETTER Marisa and Gina, who are the leaders of the food festival, called a meeting. The purpose of the meeting was to get volunteers to help. Because we were interested in helping, we went to the meeting.

8q A *wordy sentence* **contains too many words or too many fancy words that are difficult to understand.**

Here are three tips for creating sentences that aren't too wordy.

1. Don't use more words than you need to.
2. Don't use fancy words where simple ones will do.
3. Don't repeat yourself unless it's absolutely necessary.

WORDY In the event of a storm involving a downfall of water, we shall forego our plans to participate in the competition of football.

IMPROVED If it rains, we won't play football.

EXERCISE 12   Revising Stringy and Wordy Sentences

The writer of this letter wants to receive information, but the stringy and wordy sentences get in the way. On your own paper, revise the letter. Make it clearer and more effective.

1   Dear Dr. Feliciano:

2   It has come to my attention from the teacher with whom I am
3   studying science at the local junior high school in my community
4   that due to an assignment that I have received and must
5   accomplish after school hours, I have a requirement to receive
6   information and facts and details. Specifically, I have been
7   assigned the task of acquiring knowledge regarding the
8   importance and necessity of such domestic animals as dogs and
9   cats receiving injections and shots to prevent the dangerous and
10   perilous and hazardous disease of rabies. Is it within the realm of
11   possibility for you to transmit to my person a pamphlet or booklet
12   in regards to the dangerous and perilous and hazardous disease
13   of rabies? Looking ahead to the possibility of the receipt of this
14   material from you fills me with gratitude and thanks.

15   Sincerely,

16   Alfred Robinson

Peanuts reprinted by permission of UFS, Inc.

VARYING SENTENCE BEGINNINGS

8r **The basic structure of an English sentence is a subject followed by a verb. But following this pattern all the time makes your writing dull. To make your writing more interesting, use different methods to begin some of your sentences.**

To vary the basic structure of your sentences, you might begin with a single-word modifier, a prepositional or participial phrase, or a subordinate clause.

SINGLE-WORD MODIFIER	**Frightened**, the dog ran under the bed. [adjective]
PHRASE	**Feeling frightened**, the dog ran under the bed. [participial phrase]
SUBORDINATE CLAUSE	**Because it was frightened**, the dog ran under the bed. [adverb clause]

EXERCISE 13   Varying Sentence Beginnings

On the lines provided, revise each of the following sentences by using a variety of sentence beginnings. You may want to add or delete a word to make the sentence sound better. Follow the directions in parentheses.

EX. 1. Dr. Aponte leaped to her feet in surprise. (single-word modifier)
　　 1. Surprised, Dr. Aponte leaped to her feet.

1. Wide-open spaces and rolling meadows are disappearing in many small towns. (phrase) _____

_____

2. We enjoy Cuban music, so we are thrilled with Gloria Estefan's new album. (adverb clause) _____

_____

3. We were confused, so we asked for directions. (single-word modifier) _____

_____

4. They were tired, so they stopped for a rest. (participial phrase) _____

_____

5. There are many beautiful canals in the city of Amsterdam. (phrase)

_____

_____

6. Many people enjoy the essays of Agnes Repplier because she wrote with a sharp sense of humor. (adverb clause) _____

_____

7. The students were excited and rushed onto the court (single-word modifier) _____

_____

8. We saw a mural by Mexican artist Diego Rivera at the National Palace in Mexico City. (phrase) _____

_____

9. Hannah was thoughtful and sent her grandmother a postcard. (single-word modifier) _____

_____

10. I always laugh whenever I read a story by James Thurber. (adverb clause) _____

_____

11. She scored two goals, and she scored them in the first half of the game. (phrase) _____

_____

12. Luis drove down the street, and he waved goodbye. (phrase) _____

_____

13. We visited the Blue Grotto; we visited it before we left Capri. (adverb clause) _____

_____

14. The game was canceled, so we met at Jared's house. (adverb clause)

_____

_____

15. I was startled, so I dropped the platter of food. (single-word modifier)

_____

_____

CHAPTER REVIEW

A. Proofreading a Paragraph for Sentence Fragments and Run-on Sentences

Proofread the paragraph below for sentence fragments and run-on sentences. Then, on your own paper, revise the paragraph. Be sure to change punctuation and capitalization as needed. [Note: There may be more than one correct way to revise each error.]

EX. 1 John Dykstra developed a new camera. For creating special effects in the movies.

   1. John Dykstra developed a new camera for creating special effects in the movies.

1   John Dykstra is a special-effects expert, his work has made
2 such films as *Star Wars* very exciting. Before he entered the movie
3 business, had studied industrial design at Long Beach State
4 College. In California. He began his film career by working with
5 Douglas Trumbull, Trumbull was in charge of all the special effects
6 for *Star Wars*. Dykstra won an Academy Award for the electronic
7 special effects he created. For that film. That achievement made
8 him famous, it also brought him another exciting project. Special-
9 effects creator for a television series called *Battlestar Galactica*. In
10 2002 and 2004, Dykstra was the visual effects designer. To create the
11 visual effects for *Spider-Man* and *Spider-Man 2*.

B. Revising a Paragraph by Combining Sentences

The following paragraph contains many short, dull, choppy sentences. On your own paper, revise the paragraph by combining sentences that contain related ideas. [Note: There may be more than one way to revise the sentences.]

EX. 1. Annuals are delicate flowers. They cannot survive freezing temperatures.

   1. Annuals are delicate flowers that cannot survive freezing temperatures.

1   Most annual flowers have bright colors. Most annual flowers
2 are easy to grow. This makes them popular with gardeners. They
3 are also inexpensive. A garden of annuals is a real bargain. Each
4 seed packet costs about a dollar. Each contains about fifty seeds.
5 A person can grow a plant for about two cents. Marigolds are

6 annual flowers. Petunias are annual flowers, too. A small, sunny
7 spot in a yard is a good place to grow them. You could also grow
8 them in a window box in a sunny space. Follow the directions on
9 the seed packet. Have fun with your bargain garden!

C. Revising a Paragraph

The paragraph below contains many of the problems you have studied in this chapter. Revise the paragraph so that (1) stringy and wordy sentences are corrected, (2) sentences have varied beginnings, and (3) simple sentences are combined into compound and complex sentences. [Note: There are many correct ways to revise and improve this paragraph.]

EX. 1. She was a photographer. She was an artist. Who painted landscapes.

    1. She was a photographer, and she was an artist who painted landscapes.

1   Berthe Morisot was a French painter, and she was part of the
2 movement called Impressionism, and it took place in the
3 nineteenth century. Edgar Degas, Edouard Manet, Claude
4 Monet, and Auguste Renoir were her colleagues in the movement,
5 and they greatly respected her work, in fact she was the only
6 woman invited to join them. In the first impressionist exhibition
7 in 1874. Morisot experimented with color. So did the other
8 impressionist painters. For example, in one painting a woman
9 appears in a white robe. Called *The Bath*. Many other colors
10 appear within the white of the robe, and they include shades of
11 pink, green, beige, and light purple, and they blend, and they
12 make shadows and creases appear in the robe. This arresting,
13 dramatic, incredible, masterful piece of painted art is delightful
14 and marvelous to the eye.

FORMAL ENGLISH

Just as you can change your clothes to suit different occasions, you can also "dress up" or "dress down" your language. Depending on your audience and purpose, your language could be formal, informal, or somewhere in between.

INFORMAL I caught some z's.   I'm hoppin' mad.
FORMAL I napped briefly.   I am extremely angry.

You should use *formal English* when you speak at dignified occasions, such as banquets and dedication ceremonies, or when you write serious papers and reports.

The main differences between formal and informal English are in sentence structure, word choice, and tone. Here are some features of formal English.

SENTENCE STRUCTURE   often long and difficult
WORD CHOICE   precise; often technical or scientific
TONE   serious and dignified

EXERCISE 1   Revising a Paragraph to Replace Inappropriate Language

The following paragraph contains informal language. Above each italicized word or phrase, write language that is more appropriate to a formal report.

EX. [1] The earthquake created a ~~real mess~~. *great deal of damage*

[1] The Incas *sure* knew how to build. [2] They had no modern tools, yet they built these *incredibly neat* foundations. [3] The foundations were made of stones, and some of these were truly *humongous.* [4] *Like,* one was fifteen feet tall, and weighed almost a hundred tons. [5] These *dudes* used stone hammers to shape the stones in the walls. [6] They used no mortar, but it was *no big deal.* [7] The stones fit together so tightly that even *Mother Nature couldn't knock them down with one of her earthquakes.* [8] It took modern

scientists years to *smoke out* their methods. [9] Even so, one step is

still a *big fat question mark.* [10] How the Incas got the stones to the site

is *anybody's guess.*

EXERCISE 2   Identifying Formal English

In each sentence below, underline the word or words in parentheses that are formal English.

EX.   1. That new group plays (groovy tunes, <u>sensational music</u>).

1. I just read (a really rad, an excellent) book on surfing.

2. (Chill out, Relax)! We'll meet our deadline.

3. Alex bought (an attractive, a cool) shirt on sale.

4. That dress is (outta sight, the lastest fashion).

5. Unfortunately, John had a (boring party, bogus bash).

6. The music, flags, and other (attention-getting devices, gimmicks) drew me into the store.

7. Joshua is wearing some (bad threads, fashionable clothes) today.

8. Charlene began to (relax, hang loose) once her homework was completed.

9. We will (skidoo, leave) when the bell rings.

10. (Snap out of it, Stop worrying). This bridge is safe.

INFORMAL ENGLISH

Informal language is the language you hear around you every day. It is probably the language you use when you talk to your friends and family.

Informal English is often used in everyday conversations at home, school, work, and places of recreation. You also find informal English in personal letters, journal entries, and many newspaper and magazine articles.

The main differences between formal and informal English are in sentence structure, word choice, and tone. Here are some features of informal English.

SENTENCE STRUCTURE	short and easy
WORD CHOICE	simple and ordinary; often includes contractions, colloquialisms, and slang
TONE	conversational

Colloquialisms are the informal words and phrases of conversational language. Many colloquialisms are figures of speech that aren't meant to be taken literally.

EXAMPLES   I thought my parents would **have a fit,** but they didn't.
We waited until the rain **let up**, and then we left.
When I wasn't invited to the party, I considered **crashing** it.

Slang is made up of newly coined words or of old words used in unconventional ways. It is usually clever and colorful. It is often created by specific groups of people, such as musicians and computer engineers.

EXAMPLES   The orchestra gave an **awesome** concert last night.
This new MP3 player is **cool.**

 Colloquialisms and slang often fit well in short stories. They can help make your characters believable. However, do not use colloquialisms or slang in test answers, essays, reports, or other types of formal writing.

EXERCISE 3   Replacing Slang and Colloquialisms with Formal English

On your own paper, rewrite each of the sentences below, using formal English. Use a dictionary to find the meaning of any slang or colloquialism that you do not understand.

EX.   1.   That friend of yours certainly is spacey.
      1.   That friend of yours certainly is eccentric.

1.   At the wedding, all they played was this schmaltzy music.
2.   We're going to be late unless you get a move on.
3.   The night before our trip, I was too keyed up to sleep.
4.   I'm psyched that I got an *A* on my term paper.
5.   This is a holiday weekend, so the cops are going to crack down on speeders.
6.   In our building the rule is to keep your junk off the stairs.
7.   The Brazilian soccer team wiped out every other team that year.
8.   Ms. Molina jumped on us for speaking English in Spanish class.
9.   Perhaps Delia needs a vacation; she has a short fuse after a long day at work.
10.   How can I type my paper if you hog the computer?
11.   Give me a ring when you're ready to leave.
12.   Demetri was an old hand at restringing a guitar.
13.   In order to win first place, Stephen must ace the other bowlers.
14.   The lights suddenly going out caused quite a flap in the lab.
15.   Would you slide those noodles this way, please?
16.   That hunk of a meteor created a tremendous crater.
17.   Mother flipped over the flowers that Carlos sent her.
18.   Bonnie shed some light on our math problem.
19.   How could I draw a blank on my own address?
20.   Kaspar is right up there with the best of the hockey goalies.
21.   I'd better hold up here before I forget something.
22.   Tonight's vegetable soup is a hodgepodge from our garden.
23.   My grandfather footed the bill for my parents' wedding.
24.   Our meeting lasted so long, we decided to send out for supper.
25.   Marjorie and Jim were in cahoots on Mom's birthday gift.

DENOTATION AND CONNOTATION

The **denotations** of a word are its dictionary meanings. The **connotations** of a word are the meanings suggested by, or associated with, that word.

Two words can have the same denotation yet have very different connotations. For instance, the words *error* and *blunder* have the same denotation. They both mean "mistake." However, the word *blunder* sounds far more negative. It suggests lack of ability or experience. Words can also be neutral, such as the words *walk* or *car*.

Word choice can have an important effect on readers and listeners. To take advantage of this effect, be aware of the connotations that words have.

EXERCISE 4   Responding to Connotations

For each sentence below, underline the word in parentheses that best fits the sentence. On the line after the sentence, write the reason for your choice.

EX. 1. The evening air felt pleasant, so Miguel (*strolled*, *plodded*) downtown.
Strolled creates a more relaxed image than plodded.

1. My parents (*screamed*, *cheered*) when I crossed the finish line first.

   _____

   _____

2. This antique clock is expensive because it is (*unique*, *strange*).

   _____

   _____

3. No one was surprised when the (*daring*, *reckless*) explorer was injured. _____

   _____

4. Mrs. Cohen is one of my favorite teachers; she's (*stubborn*, *firm*), but she's fair. _____

   _____

EXERCISE 5   Analyzing the Connotations of Words

Decide which of the words below have positive connotations, which have negative ones, and which are neutral. On the line before each word, write *pos.* for *positive*, *neg.* for *negative*, or *neut.* for *neutral*.

EX.   _neg._ 1. dangerous

_____ 1. precious

_____ 2. green

_____ 3. adventuresome

_____ 4. pushy

_____ 5. diagonal

_____ 6. cozy

_____ 7. slimy

_____ 8. gallant

_____ 9. scorch

_____ 10. middle

_____ 11. jealous

_____ 12. magnificent

_____ 13. pastel

_____ 14. sloppy

_____ 15. fascinating

_____ 16. eastward

_____ 17. steal

_____ 18. sixteen

_____ 19. destroy

_____ 20. beautiful

_____ 21. coward

_____ 22. nosy

_____ 23. easy

_____ 24. gossip

_____ 25. brief

_____ 26. dirty

_____ 27. gentle

_____ 28. fake

_____ 29. lying

_____ 30. gleaming

_____ 31. joyful

_____ 32. elementary

_____ 33. conceited

_____ 34. ignore

_____ 35. temporary

_____ 36. cheap

_____ 37. dusty

_____ 38. snuggle

_____ 39. unprepared

_____ 40. neatly

_____ 41. concerned

_____ 42. elegant

_____ 43. last

_____ 44. faithful

_____ 45. twinkle

_____ 46. obvious

_____ 47. thirsty

_____ 48. noisy

_____ 49. distinguished

_____ 50. everlasting

CHAPTER REVIEW

A. Identifying Formal English

In each sentence below, underline the word or words in parentheses that are formal English.

EX. 1. Our last ride at the amusement park was really (*wild*, *exciting*)!

1. The statue is inside a temple, so don't (*act up*, *misbehave*).

2. Those people speak a (*lingo*, *language*) that I don't understand.

3. Our sergeant did not want to hear any (*arguments*, *lip*).

4. I've been feeling (*weak*, *run-down*) since this cough began.

5. One Russian queen had more than fifteen thousand dresses (*hanging*, *squirreled away*) in closets.

6. My (*pal*, *friend*) and I will start with the tabouli.

7. On weekends, I like to (*be*, *hang*) with my friends.

8. The jeans that I want cost thirty-five (*bucks*, *dollars*).

9. Dr. Cabral is the only (*highbrow*, *intellectual*) speaker on the program.

10. This meal is free, so let's (*chow down*, *eat it*) and enjoy it.

B. Revising Informal English

On your own paper, rewrite each of the sentences below using formal English.

EX. 1. That guy doesn't have a clue!
    1. That man does not understand what is happening.

1. When Ali learned he had won, he was on top of the world!

2. Don't bug me about my homework, because it's done.

3. I guess you can kiss that money goodbye.

4. We haven't won a single game, so let's call it quits.

5. Gloria and Margaret raced neck and neck for the finish line.

6. Finally, we were only one light-year away from solving the chemistry equation.

7. Eliot made a mad dash for the door at the same time as Terry.

8. How many teeny-boppers are at the party tonight?

9. For some reason, Terrel is at the tail end of the line every day.

10. The teacher said the scores on our geometry test were bodacious.

C. Analyzing the Connotations of Words

For each sentence below, decide whether the italicized word or phrase has the correct connotation. If it does not, write a better word or phrase choice on the line before the sentence. If it does, write C.

EX. _____mohair_____ 1. One mannequin wore a beautiful, *hairy* sweater.

_____ 1. My father works the night shift, so we all try to *sneak around* the house when he's sleeping.

_____ 2. The entire apartment *reeked* of baking bread.

_____ 3. The new girl that I *confronted* in Spanish class is very pleasant.

_____ 4. Although I did not win first prize, I feel *smug* that I tried.

_____ 5. I love the Canadian flag, with its *garish* maple-leaf design.

_____ 6. Determined women are *wishing for* equal treatment in the job market.

_____ 7. After such a hot day, the *cool* night air felt wonderful.

_____ 8. Each pilgrim enters Mecca wearing a *sanitized* white robe.

_____ 9. Your room is lovely, and it is easy to clean because it's *cramped*.

_____ 10. The politician *nagged* everyone to vote for him.

D. Collaborating on Connotations

Using your own paper, work with two or three partners to list at least ten animals that could have positive and negative connotations when used to describe people. Then choose five animals from your list. On the same page, write five sentences. In each sentence use a different animal to describe a person. Label each sentence as positive, negative, or neutral connotations.

EX. 1. swan
     Consuela is as graceful as a swan. (positive)

NOUNS

The Eight Parts of Speech			
noun	adjective	pronoun	conjunction
verb	adverb	preposition	interjection

10a A *noun* is a word used to name a person, a place, a thing, or an idea.

Persons	sister, Uncle Abdul, weaver, friends
Places	house, Malaysia, Milky Way, Detroit
Things	chopsticks, August, Skylab, table
Ideas	love, hate, cooperation, courage

10b A *proper noun* is a word that names a particular person, place, thing, or idea and is always capitalized. A *common noun* is a word that names any one of a group of persons, places, things, or ideas and is not capitalized.

Common Nouns	Proper Nouns
singer	Leontyne Price, Willie Colon
scientist	Leo Esaki, Marie Curie
country	China, Canada
holiday	New Year's Day, Labor Day
school	Dwight Morrow High School

10c A *concrete noun* names an object that can be perceived by the senses. An *abstract noun* names an idea, a feeling, a quality, or a characteristic.

Concrete Nouns	fog, milk, barrel, key, lightning
Abstract Nouns	enthusiasm, pity, ambition, joy

EXERCISE 1   Identifying Common Nouns and Proper Nouns

Underline all of the nouns in the sentences below. If a noun is a proper noun, underline it twice.

EX.   1. The jogger jumped onto a bus that was going down Broadway.

1. Dan and his wife Lisa have invented a new way of celebrating
     Thanksgiving.

2. The train traveled across Wyoming and into Utah.

3. China was hit by a severe earthquake on Tuesday.

4. A cheetah is known for its speed and beauty.

5. Our new teacher is an expert on jazz.

6. The doctor knew that measles had caused the blindness.

7. In the morning, the mat is rolled up and placed in a small closet.

8. The Great Wall of China is truly an amazing sight!

9. That haiku was written by Matsuo Bashō.

10. The witness rose and placed her right hand on the Bible.

EXERCISE 2   Identifying Abstract Nouns and Concrete Nouns

In the sentences below, underline the abstract nouns once and the concrete nouns twice.

EX.   1. Our first concert was a success.

1. Oneida certainly has the talent to become a great painter.

2. Reverend Ross can discuss all the major religions very well.

3. On Friday the Sargent Memorial Library will be closed.

4. Suddenly the screen was filled with pictures of robots.

5. A variety of dips accompanied the vegetables.

6. For his report, Jonah read a book about the history of airplanes and
     locomotives.

7. People need different kinds of abilities.

8. Uncle Joe wrote a poem about his dreams.

9. After the loss, the players showed their disappointment.

10. Is it true that computers speed up communication?

COMPOUND NOUNS

10d A *compound noun* consists of two or more words used together as a single noun. The parts of a compound noun may be written as one word. They may also be written as two or more words or as a hyphenated word.

One Word	bodyguard, footprint, newspaper
Two or More Words	high school, Kalahari Desert, League of Nations
Hyphenated Word	great-grandmother, left-hander

NOTE If you are not sure how to write a compound noun, look it up in a dictionary. Some dictionaries may give two correct forms for a word. For example, you may find the word *vice-president* written both with and without the hyphen. As a rule, use the form your dictionary lists first.

EXERCISE 3   Identifying Compound Nouns

Underline the compound nouns in the sentences below.

EX.   1.   The Gateway Arch is a beautiful structure.

1.   At last, Cheng Ho reached the Persian Gulf.

2.   Your bill of sale is proof that you paid.

3.   The nation watched in horror as the spacecraft fell.

4.   The experiment will test how long the night light will burn.

5.   The new cast will be listed on the bulletin board in the hallway.

6.   I'm taking this course so that I can be a lifeguard next summer.

7.   We were supposed to find the icecap on the map.

8.   You can take my sleeping bag when you go fly-fishing.

9.   Do you know how many patents Thomas Alva Edison held?

10.   Some arrowheads were made of flint and some of bone.

REVIEW EXERCISE 1

A. Identifying Common, Proper, and Compound Nouns

In the paragraph below, underline the common nouns once and the proper nouns twice. Circle the compound nouns. [Note: Some nouns may fit into more than one category.]

EX.　[1] This (newspaper) stated that Samoyeds are useful animals.

[1] At the beginning of the Space Age, scientists placed a white dog inside *Sputnik II*. [2] The dog, Laika, was a Samoyed, a breed known for its sweet disposition. [3] Samoyeds were originally used by nomadic people in Siberia to herd reindeer and to pull sleds. [4] However, this animal from the former Soviet Union accomplished a new task. [5] Laika became the first living creature to orbit our planet. [6] Laika is also probably the first dog ever to be at an altitude of 1,050 miles above the earth. [7] We do not know exactly why Laika was chosen, but there are three possible reasons. [8] First, its husky build and heavy fur coat allow the Samoyed to stand changes in temperature. [9] Second, the Russians probably wanted a breed of dog from Russia. [10] Third, its strength and intelligence probably helped the Samoyed endure the hardships of the trip.

B. Classifying Abstract and Concrete Nouns

In the sentences below, underline the abstract nouns once and the concrete nouns twice.

EX.　1.　Do I need talent or luck to become an actor?

1.　My sister and I go to the movies on weekends.

2.　She likes films that are full of romance.

3.　I prefer adventures with characters who show courage.

4.　Is this film about people fighting for their freedom?

5.　The Texans, along with many other people, fought with great bravery at the Alamo.

PRONOUNS

10e A *pronoun* is a word used in place of a noun or more than one noun. This noun, called an *antecedent*, gives the pronoun its meaning.

Personal Pronouns	I, me, my, mine, we, us, our, ours, you, your, yours, he, him, his, she, her, hers, it, its, they, them, their, theirs
Reflexive Pronouns	myself, ourselves, yourself, yourselves, himself, herself, itself, themselves
Indefinite Pronouns	all, another, any, anyone, both, each, everybody, one, everything, few, many, most, no one, some, several

EXAMPLES   **Miguel** said that **he** spoke three languages. [*Miguel* is the antecedent of the pronoun *he.*]

Did **Kim** leave **her** wallet on the bus?

Go across the **George Washington Bridge. It** will take you into New York City. [*George Washington Bridge* is the antecedent of the pronoun *It.*]

Notice that a pronoun may appear in the same sentence as its antecedent or in a following sentence.

 NOTE   Some pronouns, such as possessive forms of pronouns (*my, your,* and *her*) and indefinite pronouns (*all, any,* and *some*) may also be classified as adjectives. Follow your teacher's instructions regarding these forms.

Identifying Pronouns

Underline all the pronouns in the following paragraph.

EX.   [1] Kim invited <u>me</u> over to <u>her</u> house.

[1] Kim introduced me to her parents because I had never met them. [2] Kim's father showed me the used envelopes he collects.

[3] Each is special because it has an advertisement printed on it.

[4] Postage meters print the ads while they are printing the postage.

[5] I had never noticed the ads before! [6] On some envelopes you see only words such as "Use Air Mail." [7] However, I particularly liked the ones with pictures on them. [8] Several included animals, appliances, or airplanes. [9] The next time you get commercial mail, look at it carefully. [10] You can look at the postmark to see if an advertisement is printed next to it.

EXERCISE   Identifying Pronouns and Antecedents

Underline all the pronouns in the following paragraph. On the numbered lines after the paragraph, write the pronouns and their antecedents.

EX.   [1] Numerous pirates were men, but not all of them.
    1. them—pirates

[1] Piracy was common in nineteenth-century China, and not only men were practicing it. [2] A woman named Hsi Kai Ching Yih earned herself a place in history as a famous pirate. [3] Her husband, Ching Yih, was a pirate off the coast of China. [4] Ching Yih married Hsi Kai in 1807 and promised her half of his property. [5] At the time, his property included six squadrons of ships. [6] Ching Yih was lost at sea, and his wife took command of the fleet. [7] At one time, she controlled almost two thousand ships! [8] They were crewed by a total of over fifty thousand pirates. [9] Madame Ching later retired from her adventures at sea. [10] The emperor of China wanted peace, so he gave her a position of honor and a palace.

1. _____   6. _____

2. _____   7. _____

3. _____   8. _____

4. _____   9. _____

5. _____   10. _____

ADJECTIVES

10f   An *adjective* is a word used to modify a noun or a pronoun.

To *modify* a word means to describe the word or to make its meaning more definite. An adjective modifies a noun or a pronoun by telling *what kind*, *which one*, or *how many*.

What kind?	**green** leaves, **slow** bus
Which one?	**second** book, **first** one
How many?	**forty** people, **three** tacos

The most frequently used adjectives are *a*, *an*, and *the*. These words are usually called *articles*. *A* and *an* are *indefinite articles*. They indicate that a noun refers to one of a general group. *A* is used before words beginning with a consonant sound. *An* is used before words beginning with a vowel sound.

EXAMPLES   **A** bell rang.   **An** hour had passed.

The is a *definite article*. It indicates that a noun refers to someone or something in particular.

EXAMPLES   **The** bell rang.   **The** hour had passed.

An adjective usually comes before the noun or pronoun it modifies. In some cases, adjectives follow the words they modify. Sometimes, other words separate an adjective from the noun or pronoun that it modifies.

EXAMPLES   The **blue** water attracted us. [adjective comes before noun]
The water, **blue** and **cool**, attracted us. [adjectives follow noun]
The water felt **cool**. [word separates adjective from noun]

EXERCISE 6   Identifying Adjectives

Underline each adjective in the following sentences. Do not include definite or indefinite articles.

EX.   1. A <u>magnificent</u> statue stood in the <u>empty</u> hall.

1. Paul saw many medieval manuscripts in the local museum.

2. One manuscript, old and torn, was about a legendary hero.

3. Rodrigo was young, strong, and handsome.

4. He liked fast horses and vigorous activities, including fencing.

5. He became a fierce warrior and a great leader.

6. He fought many long battles in distant countries.

7. In four battles, he carried a jeweled, gleaming sword.

8. Years later, at a splendid ceremony, he became a knight.

9. Proud Rodrigo welcomed relatives and old friends to the
    ceremony.

10. Knights in colorful clothing and ladies in elegant dresses
    applauded.

EXERCISE 7   Revising Sentences by Supplying Adjectives

Supply adjectives for the sentences below. Write the adjectives on the lines
in the sentences.

EX.   1. Matsu lived in a _____ large _____ apartment building.

1. Down the street was a _____ shopping center.

2. One store had _____ clothes.

3. Another store looked _____ .

4. The _____ bus stopped for me.

5. At dawn the streets were _____ and
    _____ .

6. Our _____ steps are _____ , so be
    careful.

7. _____ people stood impatiently beside the
    _____ sign.

8. Who gave us _____ tickets?

9. You need a _____ jacket and tie for this job.

10. The crowd at the stadium sounded _____ and
    _____ .

PRONOUNS AND NOUNS USED AS ADJECTIVES

10g **Some words may be used as either pronouns or adjectives. When used as pronouns, these words take the place of nouns. When used as adjectives, they modify nouns.**

Pronoun	Adjective
Take **this**.	Use **this** brush.
Neither is home.	**Neither** person is home.

The words *mine, my, your, yours, his, her, hers, its, our, ours, their,* and *theirs* are called pronouns in this book. They are the *possessive* forms of personal pronouns, showing ownership or relationship. Some teachers prefer to call such words adjectives because the words tell *which one* about nouns: *my* radio, *your* ticket. Follow your teacher's instructions in labeling such words.

When a noun is used as an adjective, your teacher may prefer that you call it an adjective. Proper nouns used as adjectives are called *proper adjectives.*

10h **Some words may be used as either nouns or adjectives.**

COMMON NOUNS	autumn	water
ADJECTIVES	autumn leaves	water safety
PROPER NOUNS	**New York**	**Navajo**
ADJECTIVES	**New York** bank	**Navajo** blanket

EXERCISE 8   Identifying Nouns, Pronouns, and Adjectives

Identify each italicized word in the following sentences. Write *n.* for *noun, pron.* for *pronoun,* or *adj.* for *adjective* on the line before each sentence.

EX. _**adj.**_ 1. Mario gave his mother an *electric* wok.

_____ 1. Her birthday is *next* week.

_____ 2. Mrs. Vargas said that woks are very *useful.*

_____ 3. Only *some* are electric.

_____ 4. Most woks need a separate *heat* source.

_____ 5. Now she is cooking summer dishes, such as celery *salad.*

_____ 6. That recipe came from a *Chinese* cookbook.

_____ 7. Soon she will make heartier dishes for *winter*.

_____ 8. *That* is my favorite time of year.

_____ 9. Maybe she will make *that* duck dish we like.

_____ 10. I think it's called *Shanghai* duck.

_____ 11. Did Hideko bring the *cheese* sandwiches or the chips?

_____ 12. Kevin and I need *some* help, Ms. Thompson.

_____ 13. Dr. Kostas is traveling to *Chicago* next Wednesday.

_____ 14. The weather report warned *Texas* residents about a possible hurricane.

_____ 15. Do you like *that*?

_____ 16. *Either* person could work at the concession stand.

_____ 17. The *bitter* cold caused several pipes to freeze.

_____ 18. *Summer* is my favorite time of year.

_____ 19. *Neither* looks good enough to eat.

_____ 20. The *Thanksgiving* choir program was a success.

EXERCISE 9   Revising Sentences by Using Appropriate Adjectives

For each sentence below, add at least one common or proper noun used as an adjective. Write your revised sentences on your own paper.

EX. 1. The cat approached the woman.

    1. *The Siamese cat approached the young woman.*

1. The house was built on a road near me.

2. Trucks rumbled past the store on the corner.

3. A clerk helped me find a sweater.

4. Becky gave a speech in front of the students.

5. On the dresser lay a box.

REVIEW EXERCISE 2

A. Identifying Nouns, Pronouns, and Adjectives

In each of the sentences below, tell how the italicized word is used. Write *comm.* for *common noun,* *prop.* for *proper noun,* *comp.* for *compound noun,* *pron.* for *pronoun,* or *adj.* for *adjective.* [Note: Some nouns may fit into more than one category.]

EX. <u>comm.</u> 1. This *ticket* is yours.

_____ 1. You can almost feel the *excitement*!

_____ 2. *Everyone* is waiting to board the submarine.

_____ 3. Is it a *nuclear* submarine?

_____ 4. This ship can stay underwater for *weeks*!

_____ 5. Didn't *Ferdinand Magellan* travel on this route?

_____ 6. This submarine took *twelve* weeks for its journey.

_____ 7. *This* must be as long as a football field!

_____ 8. The galley, *small* but complete, is below the control room.

_____ 9. This ship even has a *recreation room* on it.

_____ 10. I've never seen *anything* like it.

B. Identifying Abstract and Concrete Nouns

In each of the sentences below, underline the abstract nouns once and the concrete nouns twice.

EX. 1. A <u>day</u> in the <u><u>mountains</u></u> could end your <u>troubles</u>.

1. "Are you ready?" Joe asked Eddie, with excitement in his voice.

2. "Don't we need food and water for the trip?" asked Eddie.

3. Eddie hid his fear when he saw the gigantic mountain.

4. They climbed the mountain with great determination.

5. Because Joe had always wanted to be a mountain climber, his enthusiasm was great .

6. When they reached the top, their spirits soared.

7. As soon as they returned, their mother sighed with relief.

8. "It's an honor to know such brave young men," said their

   neighbor, Sam.

9. Their classmates looked at them with admiration.

10. Joe sat on the front porch and enjoyed his sudden fame.

C. Identifying Nouns, Pronouns, and Adjectives

Underline each noun, pronoun, and adjective in the sentences below. Do not include *a*, *an*, and *the*. In the space above each word, write *n.* for *noun*, *pron.* for *pronoun*, or *adj.* for *adjective*.

EX. 1. This has been a wonderful day.
         pron.   adj.   n.

1. A bad storm is headed this way.

2. Summer storms can be powerful.

3. Are those clouds getting darker?

4. Everything will get wet if I don't cover it.

5. Did you see that rainbow in the sky?

6. Tropical rains can last a long time.

7. They come during the rainy season in certain parts of the world.

8. He told me people run for cover when they see the storms.

9. Can the hard-working men and women rebuild their homes?

10. We have always prepared for big storms.

D. Working Cooperatively to Write an Advertisement

Working with a partner, create an advertisement to describe and sell a new invention that will help students in school.

1. First, think of what the invention would do and what it might look like. Make your advertisement brief, clear, and interesting. Focus on the most important features of your product, and describe what the product does.

2. Write your advertisement on your own paper. Use at least three nouns and three adjectives in your advertisement. Then underline and label them.

EX.   adj.   n.   adj.   n.
    End bookshelf clutter forever! The amazing Presso Paperweight
              adj.   n.   n.   n.
    will compress huge piles of paper. Buy Presso Paperweight!

VERBS

10i   A *verb* is a word used to express an action or a state of being.

Words such as *do, come, go,* and *write* are ***action verbs.*** Sometimes action verbs express actions that cannot be seen: *believe, understand, love.*

A ***transitive verb*** is an action verb that expresses an action directed toward a person or thing named in the sentence.

EXAMPLES   Lorie **welcomed** the visitors to the game. [The action of the verb *welcomed* is directed toward *visitors.*]
Juan **served** the bread and the herb butter. [The action of the verb *served* is directed toward *bread* and *butter.*]

The action expressed by a transitive verb passes from the doer—the subject—to the receiver of the action. Words that receive the action of a transitive verb are called ***objects.***

An ***intransitive verb*** expresses action (or tells something about the subject) without passing the action from a subject to an object.

EXAMPLES   A cold wind **blew** over the tundra.
We **rode** in silence.

A verb may be transitive in one sentence and intransitive in another.

EXAMPLES   Liang **left** his book. [transitive]
Liang **left** early. [intransitive]

EXERCISE 10   Identifying Action Verbs

In each of the following sentences, underline the action verb once. If the verb is transitive, underline its object twice.

EX.   1. Tom <u>conducted</u> an <u>experiment</u> in his kitchen.

1. In science class, Mrs. Velade discussed chemical reactions.

2. She provided glasses and various liquids.

3. Tom filled a glass with water.

4. He stirred soda into the water.

5. Another student found a bottle of vinegar nearby.

6. Rosa poured some vinegar into a second glass.

7. No one noticed anything special about the mixtures.

8. Then Tom poured the vinegar into the soda solution.

9. Many small bubbles suddenly rose to the surface.

10. The reaction between the two different liquids created a gas.

EXERCISE 11   Identifying Transitive and Intransitive Verbs

Underline the verb in each sentence below. On the line before the sentence, write *trans.* if the verb is transitive or *intr.* if it is intransitive.

EX.   _____ 1. My train tickets arrived today.

_____ 1. Many families waited at the station.

_____ 2. Two men boarded the train ahead of me.

_____ 3. Haruo read my travel plans very carefully.

_____ 4. The train moved quickly along the smooth track.

_____ 5. A woman sold food to the hungry passengers.

_____ 6. After lunch, I slept for about an hour.

_____ 7. The train reached the station at exactly three o'clock.

_____ 8. We studied the subway maps on the wall.

_____ 9. Our visit to Boston ended too soon.

_____ 10. We took the same train home on Sunday afternoon.

EXERCISE 12   Using Transitive and Intransitive Verbs

Choose five verbs from the list below. On your own paper, use each verb in two sentences. The verb should be transitive in one sentence and intransitive in the other. After each sentence, label the verb *intr.* for *intransitive* or *trans.* for *transitive*.

ate	answered	flew
read	remember	cheered
study	watched	struck

EX.   1. I ate after she did. (intr.)

Danielle ate her salad. (trans.)

LINKING VERBS

10j A *linking verb* serves as a link between two words. The most commonly used linking verbs are forms of the verb *be*.

Forms of *Be*			
am	can be	will be	may have been
are	could be	would be	might have been
is	may be	have been	shall have been
was	might be	has been	should have been
were	shall be	had been	will have been
being	should be	could have been	would have been

Here are some other frequently used linking verbs.

Other Linking Verbs			
appear	grow	seem	stay
become	look	smell	taste
feel	remain	sound	turn

The noun, pronoun, or adjective that follows a linking verb completes the meaning of the verb and refers to the noun or pronoun that comes before the verb.

EXAMPLES The writer **is** Sandra Cisneros. [writer = Sandra Cisneros]
The writer **is** talented. [talented writer]

Many linking verbs can be used as action (nonlinking) verbs as well.

EXAMPLES Roger **felt** happy this morning. [linking verb—happy Roger]
Roger **felt** the rough fabric. [action verb—object *fabric*]

Even *be* is not always a linking verb. It is sometimes followed by only an adverb.

EXAMPLES They are **inside**.

To be a linking verb, the verb must be followed by a noun or a pronoun that names the subject, or by an adjective that describes the subject.

EXERCISE 13   Identifying Linking Verbs and the Words They Link

In each of the sentences below, underline the linking verb once. Draw two lines under the words that are linked by the verb.

EX.   1.   Sue Ann seems interested in horses. .

1.   This ranch in Wyoming is a camp for riders.

2.   The riders appeared calm during the show.

3.   The campers felt tired after a long day on the trail.

4.   The horses are probably hungry and thirsty by now.

5.   When the sky grew dark, the campers went into their tents.

6.   The pack horses should be ready by now.

7.   Food from an open fire tastes wonderful!

8.   Even after a day of riding, everyone remained cheerful.

9.   I felt sore only on the first day, Friday.

10.   Soon the boys and girls were comfortable outdoors.

EXERCISE 14   Writing Appropriate Linking Verbs

On the line in each sentence below, write a linking verb. Use a different verb for each sentence. You may use the verbs from the charts on page 107.

EX.   1.   The sky _____ looked _____ threatening.

1.   The storm _____ scary.

2.   That thunder _____ so loud!

3.   Nadim _____ nervous as the storm approached.

4.   The air _____ moist and heavy.

5.   That lightning _____ very close now.

6.   You and I _____ safe inside the house.

7.   The electricity _____ off for only a few minutes.

8.   Severe storms _____ dangerous.

9.   The air _____ cool after the rain.

10.   The grass _____ wet for a long time.

VERB PHRASES.

> **10k** A *verb phrase* consists of a main verb preceded by at least one *helping verb* (also called an *auxiliary verb*). Besides all forms of the verb *be,* helping verbs include
>
> | | | | | |
> |---|---|---|---|---|
> | can | do | has | might | should |
> | could | does | have | must | will |
> | did | had | may | shall | would |
>
> Notice how helping verbs work together with main verbs to make a verb phrase.
>
> EXAMPLES   **is** leaving   **may** become   **might have** been
>   **had** seemed   **should** move   **must have** thought
>   **shall be** going   **could** jump   **does** sing
>
> Sometimes the parts of a verb phrase are interrupted by other parts of speech.
>
> EXAMPLES   **Did** you **finish** your history paper?
>   You **could** always **stay** at my house.
>
> NOTE   The word *not* is always an adverb. It is never part of a verb phrase, even when it is joined to a verb as the contraction *–n't.*
>
> EXAMPLES   We **would** not **have left** by that time.
>   We **would**n't **have left** by that time.

EXERCISE 15   Identifying Verbs and Verb Phrases

Underline the verbs and verb phrases in the following sentences. [Hint: The parts of a verb phrase may be separated by other words.]

EX.   1.   Our plane <u>should arrive</u> around 2:00 P.M.

1. We will not be staying in Richmond Friday.

2. People in Indiana are always talking about basketball!

3. Well, you should see the trophies at Indiana University.

4. The state has long been known for its basketball teams.

5. My sister's team could be playing in the semifinals this year.

6. Did you watch the game last night on Channel 5?

7. The game must not have started on time.

8. Well, the team might not have arrived on schedule.

9. Has everyone visited the Basketball Hall of Fame?

10. That building should have been built in Indiana instead of Massachusetts.

11. Do basketball players from Indiana ever become members of professional teams?

12. I haven't been practicing my jump shot.

13. My uncle has never enjoyed contact sports.

14. An interview with a professional team might be exciting.

15. A lot of people from Indiana must really like basketball.

16. The game of basketball was invented in 1891.

17. Wasn't the game developed by a physical education instructor?

18. The new game was played with a soccer ball and two peach baskets.

19. Didn't the first basketball team have nine players?

20. Originally, only one or two players on the team could shoot the ball.

EXERCISE 16   Writing Verb Phrases

Complete each sentence below by creating a verb phrase that uses the verb in parentheses. Write the verb phrases on your own paper.

EX.   1. I (*shop*) for a birthday present for my brother.
     1. have been shopping

1. My brother (*take*) an English course.

2. Betty (*finish*) a book in an evening.

3. For her birthday, I (*give*) Sally a special photograph.

4. I (*look*) for a good science fiction story.

5. He (*enjoy*) one of those!

6. The teacher (*talk*) to the parent committee.

7. We (*watch*) a film of last week's game.

8. Who (*won*) the Pulitzer Prize this year?

9. The Pyrenees Mountains (*locate*) between Spain and France.

10. Toshi never (*see*) this movie.

ADVERBS

10l An *adverb* is a word used to modify a verb, an adjective, or another adverb.

An adverb answers the questions *where, when, how,* or *to what extent* (*how long* or *how much*).

Where?	Let's go **inside**. Will you stand **there**?
When?	We can leave **now**! The rain will stop **soon**.
How?	The alarm rang **wildly**. Speak **slowly**.
To what extent?	She **hardly** noticed. The path is **quite** steep.

Adverbs may come before or after the verbs they modify. Sometimes adverbs interrupt parts of a verb phrase. Adverbs may also introduce questions:

EXAMPLES **Recently** we learned about a new law. [The adverb *recently* modifies the verb *learned,* telling *when* we learned.]
How can we **quickly** climb the rope? [The adverb *how* introduces the question and modifies the verb phrase *can climb.* The adverb *quickly* interrupts the verb phrase and tells *how* we climbed.]

If you aren't sure whether a word is an adjective or an adverb, ask yourself what it modifies. If a word modifies a noun or a pronoun, it is an adjective. If it modifies a verb, an adjective, or an adverb, it is an adverb.

EXAMPLES Jogging is part of my **daily** routine. [*Daily* modifies the noun *routine,* telling *which* one. In this sentence, *daily* is used as an adjective.]
I run **daily**. [*Daily* modifies the verb *run,* telling *when.* In this sentence, *daily* is used as an adverb.]

EXERCISE 17   Identifying Adverbs

Underline the adverbs in the sentences below. Then draw an arrow to the word or words that each adverb modifies.

EX.   1. Recently, little rain has fallen.

1. Newscasters are now warning us about forest fires.

2. Forest fires can spread rapidly.

3. Our scout leader often discusses fire safety.

4. Scouts in this area listen carefully.

5. We never burn fires in windy weather.

6. A gust of wind can quickly spread a small fire.

7. Soon we will find a safe location.

8. Mr. Stamos always pours water over his fires.

9. He stirs the coals thoroughly as he pours.

10. Then he shovels dirt over the wet ashes.

EXERCISE 18   Revising with Adverb Modifiers

Revise the sentences below by adding one adverb modifier for each italicized word or phrase. Use a different adverb in each item. Write your answers on your own paper.

EX.   1. *Water* the plants.
      1. Water the plants weekly.

1. We *ran* to school.

2. She *wore* a beautiful coat.

3. Three guitars *were playing* all at once.

4. Leticia *dances*.

5. Severe thunderstorms *are expected*.

6. The rain *fell*.

7. We *ate* the tasty apples.

8. Lamont *quotes* his grandfather.

9. I *studied* for my math test.

10. The baby *is crying*.

OTHER USES OF ADVERBS

10m **Adverbs that modify adjectives often come before the adjectives.**

EXAMPLES   This painting is **almost** complete. [The adverb *almost* modifies the adjective *complete*, telling *how complete.*]

This watch is **exceedingly** accurate. [The adverb *exceedingly* modifies the adjective *accurate*, telling *how accurate.*]

The most frequently used adverbs are *too, so,* and *very*. In fact, these words are often overused. Here are some other choices.

Adverbs That Frequently Modify Adjectives		
completely	especially	quite
dangerously	extremely	rather
definitely	largely	surprisingly
dreadfully	mainly	terribly
entirely	mostly	unusually

EXERCISE 19   Identifying Adverbs That Modify Adjectives

Underline the adverb that modifies an adjective in each sentence below. Draw an arrow to the adjective that the adverb modifies.

EX.   1.   The Owens family was rather poor.

1. J. C. Owens was quite unhealthy as a child.

2. His parents were really happy about his running.

3. Running was amazingly good for the boy's health.

4. The Owens' Cleveland home was entirely different from their first home.

5. The boy was too shy to explain that his name was J. C. and not Jesse.

6. In high school, one coach was especially kind to Jesse.

7. Coach Riley noticed that the young man was surprisingly fast.

8. The 1936 Summer Olympics were terribly exciting.

9. Winning four track-and-field gold medals was extremely unusual, so Jesse became a star.

10. Definitely talented, in 1976, Jesse Owens won one of America's highest civilian awards—the Medal of Freedom.

10n   Adverbs can modify other adverbs.

EXAMPLES   Don't eat **too** quickly. [The adverb *too* modifies the adverb *quickly*, telling *to what extent*.]
The water covered the town **almost** completely. [The adverb *almost* modifies the adverb *completely*, telling *to what extent*.]

NOTE   Although many adverbs end in *–ly*, the *–ly* ending does not automatically mean that a word is an adverb. Many adjectives also end in *–ly*: a *daily* prayer, a *silly* cartoon, a *lovely* day. Even though some words do not end in *–ly*, they are often used as adverbs. These words include *now, then, far,* and *already.* To identify a word as an adverb, ask yourself two questions.

- Does this word modify a verb, an adjective, or another adverb?
- Does it tell *when, where, how,* or *to what extent*?

EXERCISE 20   Identifying Adverbs That Modify Other Adverbs

Underline the adverb that modifies other adverbs in each sentence below. Draw an arrow to the other adverbs being modified.

EX.   1.   Cheetahs can move very quickly.

1.   A sloth almost never travels on the ground.

2.   Those armadillos sleep much more than most animals!

3.   A sifaka, a type of lemur, lives almost totally in trees.

4.   You will be able to read this book on animals quite quickly.

5.   Can red kangaroos jump exceedingly high?

6.   Wild turkeys, you know, can run surprisingly fast.

7.   Gray parrots talk much better than other birds.

8.   A few birds fly so slowly that you might expect them to fall from the sky.

9.   One bullfrog jumped quite far during our contest.

10.   The tiny bristlemouth fish lives almost everywhere!

PREPOSITIONS

> **10o** A *preposition* is a word used to show the relationship of a noun or a pronoun to some other word in the sentence.
>
> EXAMPLES We hung the picture **beside** the sofa.
> We hung the picture **above** the sofa.
> We hung the picture **near** the sofa.

Commonly Used Prepositions				
aboard	because of	by	like	past
above	before	concerning	near	since
according to	below	during	next to	through
across	beneath	except	of	to
against	beside	for	off	toward
along	between	from	on	underneath
around	beyond	in addition to	out	until
as of	but (meaning	inside	over	upon
at	*except*)	into	owing to	with

NOTE Many words in the list above can also be adverbs. To be sure that a word is a preposition, ask whether the word relates a noun or a pronoun following it to a word that comes before it.

EXAMPLES One person lagged **behind**. [adverb]
One person lagged **behind** the others. [preposition]

EXERCISE 21 Distinguishing Prepositions from Adverbs

On the line before each of the following sentences, write *prep.* if the word in italics is a preposition or *adv.* if the word is an adverb.

EX. <u>prep.</u> 1. This exhibit has many pictures *of* children.

_____ 1. The name *on* many pictures is Mary Cassatt's.

_____ 2. The sketch for this scene is *beside* the painting.

_____ 3. One woman is sipping tea from a tray that is sitting *near* the chair.

_____ 4. The other woman is sitting just *beyond* her.

_____ 5. Look at the big picture as you go *out*.

_____ 6. Mary Cassatt lived in Paris *for* many years.

_____ 7. Once, she painted a scene of Paris *from* her balcony.

_____ 8. She included her dog, which she loved to have *around*.

_____ 9. The dog has the rails of the balcony to lean *against*.

_____ 10. *According to* a biographer, it was one of the few times she painted a picture of the city.

EXERCISE 22   Revising Sentences by Using Appropriate Prepositions

Revise the following paragraph by writing an appropriate preposition or compound preposition on the line in each sentence.

EX.   [1] The shield had a picture of a turtle _____*on*_____ it.

[1] Each summer, Native American people _____ many places gather for powwows. [2] In fact, I went to one _____ Saturday. [3] I stood _____ a Chippewa dancer. [4] He wore a colorful costume and had beaded, leather moccasins _____ his feet. [5] He danced beautifully_____ the regular beat of the drums. [6] My sister learned some traditional dances _____ a powwow.   [7] Many Native American people in the Northwest live and work _____ cities. [8] Those who want to keep their traditions alive are sometimes caught _____ two cultures. [9] At the powwows, people dance _____ prizes. [10] Native American culture is remembered and preserved _____ powwows.

CONJUNCTIONS AND INTERJECTIONS

10p A *conjunction* is a word used to join words or groups of words.

Coordinating conjunctions always connect items of the same kind. They may join single words or groups of words. Coordinating conjunctions include *and, but, for, nor, or, so,* and *yet.*

EXAMPLES   songs **and** lyrics [two nouns.]
in sickness **or** in health [two prepositional phrases]
First it rained, **but** the rain stopped quickly. [two complete ideas]

Correlative conjunctions also connect items of the same kind. However, unlike coordinating conjunctions, correlatives are always used in pairs. Correlative conjunctions include *both...and, either...or, neither...nor, not only...but also,* and *whether...or.*

EXAMPLES   **Both** dogs **and** cats make good pets. [two nouns]
You should set flowers **not only** on the table **but also** in the basket. [two prepositional phrases]
Either borrow a book **or** buy a magazine. [two complete ideas]

A third kind of conjunction—the *subordinating conjunction*—is discussed on page 165.

EXERCISE 23   Identifying and Classifying Conjunctions

In the following sentences, underline the coordinating conjunctions once and the correlative conjunctions twice. Some sentences contain more than one conjunction.

EX.   1. I like most fruits, <u>but</u> I don't like <u><u>either</u></u> currants <u><u>or</u></u> blueberries.

1. Most fruits and vegetables are good sources of nutrients.

2. Milk is high in calcium, but it also can be high in fat.

3. Both cereals and pasta are rich in B vitamins yet low in fat.

4. Vitamin C is found not only in oranges, but also in strawberries, green peppers, and tomatoes.

5. I don't know whether to cook this in oil or bake it in the oven.

6. Sara wants neither lettuce nor sprouts on her sandwich.

7. Baked, steamed, or boiled potatoes are low in calories, so don't add butter or sour cream.

8. To make the sauce, use either a blender or an electric mixer.

9. Joel is concerned about additives, so he has started reading food labels.

10. May I have both juice and water with my meal?

10q An *interjection* **is a word used to express emotion. It has no grammatical relation to the rest of the sentence.**

Since an interjection is unrelated to other words in the sentence, it is set off from the rest of the sentence by an exclamation point or a comma.

EXAMPLES   **Hooray!** We won the game!
Oh, I guess it's okay.
Dinner was good, but, **ugh,** that dessert was awful.
No! Our television picture just disappeared.

EXERCISE 24   Writing Sentences with Interjections

On your own paper, use each of the interjections below to create a sentence.

EX.   1. ouch
1. Ouch! That branch scratched me!

1. goodbye	6. ha
2. well	7. yippee
3. yipes	8. shh
4. goodness	9. oh dear
5. wow	10. phew

CHAPTER REVIEW

A. Identifying the Parts of Speech

On the line before each sentence, identify the part of speech of the italicized word. Write *n.* for *noun*, *v.* for *verb*, *adv.* for *adverb*, *adj.* for *adjective*, *pron.* for *pronoun*, *conj.* for *conjunction*, *prep.* for *preposition*, or *intj.* for *interjection*.

EX. __adj.__ 1. Joseph Haydn composed *many* symphonies.

_____ 1. The composer and musician created 104 symphonies, 84 string quartets, *and* many other works.

_____ 2. Did you know that he was *once* expelled from his school?

_____ 3. At the time, Haydn was attending a *choir school* in Vienna.

_____ 4. The choir *sang* in St. Stephen's Cathedral.

_____ 5. In school, a boy with a pigtail stood *in front of* Hyden.

_____ 6. One day, Haydn cut *it* off.

_____ 7. Haydn was seventeen years *old* at the time.

_____ 8. *Well*, the adults at the school were displeased by this.

_____ 9. Haydn was *no* longer a student at that school.

_____ 10. This event did not *seem* to affect his later life, though.

B. Writing Sentences Using the Same Words as Different Parts of Speech

On your own paper, write two sentences for each of the words below, showing how the word can be used as two different parts of speech. Then label how you used each word.

EX. 1. down
1. Jonathan looked down. (adv.)
He tossed the ball down the hill. (prep.)

1. race	6. milk	11. for
2. over	7. dark	12. jump
3. building	8. some	13. both
4. game	9. well	14. kick
5. purple	10. beyond	15. knot

C. Working Cooperatively to Determine Parts of Speech in a Message

You have discovered a letter and a treasure map that have been hidden in an attic for many years. Unfortunately, parts of the letter have crumbled away, leaving numerous holes. Work with a partner to supply a word that makes sense for each hole. Write its part of speech in the space above the line. You may use the following abbreviations: *n.* for *noun, v.* for *verb, pron.* for *pronoun, adj.* for *adjective, adv.* for *adverb, prep.* for *preposition, conj.* for *conjunction,* and *intj.* for *interjection.* [Note: Each part of speech is used at least once. You may wish to read the entire letter before you try to fill in the blanks.]

EX.   Look for a ___<u>flat</u>____{adj.}___ stone.

My dear [1] _____ ,

     I buried [2] _____ bars of gold and a hundred pieces

of silver. If something happens to me, I want [3] _____

to have them. Be sure to follow my [4] _____

exactly, and use the map as a reference. On the map, you will see a

[5] _____ hut. In this hut is a closet. The closet is

[6] _____ feet to the right of the [7] _____ .

The floor [8] _____ the closet [9] _____

false. It will lift [10] _____ . Dig [11] _____

about three feet and look for a metal ring. Pull it [12] _____

as hard as [13] _____ can. [14] _____ !

You have discovered the [15] _____ box. The box is

[16] _____ of gold [17] _____ silver. If

you are reading [18] _____ , I might be dead. Good luck!

One of [19] _____ , at least, will get rich.

                                        Your [20] _____ ,

                                        Lemuel

THE SENTENCE

11a A *sentence* is a group of words that contains a subject and a verb and expresses a complete thought.

If a group of words does not express a complete thought, it is a *fragment*, or incomplete part, of a sentence.

FRAGMENT	the man in the white coat
SENTENCE	The man in the white coat is my uncle.
FRAGMENT	standing in line
SENTENCE	We were standing in line.
FRAGMENT	before you go to the meeting
SENTENCE	Do you want some lunch before you go to the meeting?

Notice that a sentence always begins with a capital letter and ends with a period, a question mark, or an exclamation point.

EXERCISE 1   Identifying Complete Sentences and Sentence Fragments

On the line before each word group below, write *sent.* if it is a sentence or *frag.* if it is not a sentence. Add correct capitalization and end punctuation to the sentences.

EX. _sent._ 1. W̶would you like a bowl of soup

_____ 1. waiting for your phone call

_____ 2. help me carry this huge package

_____ 3. after the basketball game was over

_____ 4. three of my favorite animals

_____ 5. did you finish your science project

_____ 6. it doesn't bother me

_____ 7. someday if we are fortunate

_____ 8. the fastest runner on the whole team

_____ 9. there is very little money in the treasury

_____ 10. hoping to win a scholarship to college

EXERCISE 2   Revising Fragments to Create Complete Sentences

On your own paper, revise each word group below so that it is a complete sentence. Add modifiers and any other words to make the meaning of your completed sentence clear.

EX.   1. in the center of the room
   1. In the center of the room stood a large statue.

1. standing in the lobby
2. nevertheless, I
3. after the concert
4. out in the driveway
5. the men were
6. climbing to the top of the mountain
7. it often
8. this exciting movie
9. late last night while walking home
10. four students on the bus
11. boardsailing in the California surf
12. in ink on a postcard
13. want to try the shrimp
14. now Heidi
15. feeds her chickens
16. in almost every letter
17. were finding shells on the beach
18. from the two new students
19. must reach the Evlers
20. is one of the most dedicated people
21. to apply for this job
22. adjusting the throttle
23. working on a computer
24. changes in fashions
25. should write or read
26. a serious discussion
27. floating in the pool
28. therefore, we
29. just around the corner
30. wanted the answer

SUBJECT AND PREDICATE

11b   A sentence consists of two parts: the subject and the predicate. The *subject* is the part that names the person or thing spoken about in the rest of the sentence. The *predicate* is the part that says something about the subject.

The subject may be one word or a group of words. The ***complete subject*** contains all the words that name the person or thing spoken about in the rest of the sentence. The complete subject may appear at the beginning, in the middle, or at the end of a sentence.

EXAMPLES

               cmpl. s.
The woman in the red car just got a speeding ticket.
          cmpl. s.
Did **Phoebe's brother** win the poetry contest?
              cmpl. s.
Into the water dove **a brown pelican**.

Like the subject, the predicate may be one word or a group of words. The ***complete predicate*** contains all the words that say something about the subject. Like the complete subject, the complete predicate can appear in many different places in a sentence.

EXAMPLES

                      cmpl. pred.
The woman in the red car **just got a speeding ticket**.
                 cmpl. pred.
Did Phoebe's brother **win the poetry contest**?
      cmpl. pred.
Into the water dove a brown pelican.

EXERCISE 3   Identifying the Complete Subject

Underline the complete subject in each of the following sentences.

EX.   1. <u>What</u> is the source of your information?

1. Martin Miller is a geologist and a photographer.

2. In the September 1993 issue of *Earth* magazine, readers can see examples of his photographs.

3. Did you see his pictures of desert landscapes?

4. In the desert, strong winds can carve deep ridges in the rocks.

5. Similarly, those fierce winds blast clouds of flying sand against the rocks.

6. Sand and dust in the wind leave behind a hard surface of bare rocks.

7. The sand is eventually redeposited elsewhere in the desert, often as sand dunes.

8. Standing in a dramatic row in one of Miller's desert photographs are huge sand dunes.

9. The dunes are constantly shifting and changing shape because of strong winds.

10. The powdery dunes may be compressed into hard layers of sandstone after many thousands of years.

EXERCISE 4   Writing Complete Predicates

On your own paper, write ten complete sentences by adding a complete predicate to each of the subjects below. Be sure to use correct capitalization and end punctuation in your sentences.

EX.   1. the clerk in that store
   1. The clerk in that store is extremely helpful.

1. one of the buildings on our street
2. my favorite poem
3. a popular tourist attraction in our area
4. dinosaurs
5. several people
6. the most interesting books
7. political leaders
8. a good way to get exercise
9. the escalator at the north end of the mall
10. the artist
11. llamas and alpacas
12. a sifaka, a kind of lemur,
13. your best friend
14. a group of sixth-graders
15. my favorite holiday

THE SIMPLE SUBJECT AND SIMPLE PREDICATE

11c The *simple subject* is the main word or group of words within the complete subject.

EXAMPLE	**The letter from Sharon** is on your desk.
COMPLETE SUBJECT	The letter from Sharon
SIMPLE SUBJECT	letter
EXAMPLE	Did **that mysterious Colonel Potter** return my call?
COMPLETE SUBJECT	that mysterious Colonel Potter
SIMPLE SUBJECT	Colonel Potter

NOTE   In this book, the term *subject* refers to the simple subject unless otherwise indicated.

EXERCISE 5   Identifying Complete Subjects and Simple Subjects

In each sentence below, underline the complete subject once, and draw a second line under the simple subject.

EX.   1. The talented Ansel Adams was a photographer, a
conservationist, and a writer.

1. Ansel Adams' photographs of Yosemite Valley are very dramatic.

2. Time after time, Adams filmed the stark beauty of the canyons.

3. His experiments with light and shutter speed made him unique.

4. Many talented photographers have tried to duplicate Adams' work, without success.

5. The photographer wrote in his many books about his photographic techniques.

6. He often photographed mountains, forests, and rivers.

7. Adams' style of photography is called *straight photography*.

8. *Straight photography* shows the subjects of the pictures simply and directly.

9. Adams established photography departments in several schools.

10. One of these departments is at the San Francisco Art Institute.

11d The *simple predicate*, or *verb*, is the main word or group of words within the complete predicate.

EXAMPLE	He **wasn't going to the movie.**
COMPLETE PREDICATE	wasn't going to the movie
SIMPLE PREDICATE	was going
EXAMPLE	**In a little while**, the fireworks **should begin.**
COMPLETE PREDICATE	should begin in a little while
SIMPLE PREDICATE	should begin

The simple predicate may be a single verb or a verb phrase. A **verb phrase** is a main verb and its helping verbs.

EXAMPLES   is walking   has been called   will have seen

When you look for the simple predicate in a sentence, be sure to include all parts of the verb phrase. Keep in mind the various helping verbs, such as *am, is, were, do, have, can, will,* and *could.*

 In this book, the word *verb* refers to the simple predicate unless otherwise indicated.

EXERCISE 6 Identifying Complete Predicates and Simple Predicates

In each sentence below, underline the complete predicate once, and draw a second line under the simple predicate. Be sure to include all parts of a verb phrase.

EX.   1. Ravi <u>was leading the band at practice yesterday.</u>

1. The high school band has finally gotten new uniforms after many years.

2. They are black with orange stripes down the pant legs and the sleeves.

3. A committee raised the money for the uniforms.

4. They earned almost three thousand dollars through car washes, bake sales, and a flea market.

5. Everyone in the band helped with these activities.

6. The band members will appear in their new uniforms tonight.

7. Dr. Beach has arranged for the appearance of four other high school bands from various parts of the city.

8. All the band members will march into the stadium in uniform.

9. Then they will play the "Star-Spangled Banner" together.

10. Are you going to the concert?

FINDING THE SUBJECT

The best way to find the subject of a sentence is to find the verb first. Then ask "Who?" or "What?" in front of it.

EXAMPLES   Next week at the library, you can meet the author of *The Pelican Brief*. [The verb is *can meet*. *Who* can meet? *You* can meet. *You* is the subject.]
The fuel for the lantern is in the shed. [The verb is *is*. *What* is in the shed? *Fuel* is in the shed. *Fuel* is the subject.]

11e   The subject of a verb is never in a prepositional phrase.

EXAMPLES   The secretary to the principal is Ms. Gómez. [*Secretary* is the subject. The prepositional phrase *to the principal* modifies the subject.]
The car with the flat tire limped into the service station. [*Car* is the subject. The prepositional phrase *with the flat tire* modifies the subject.]

11f   You can find the subject in a question by turning the question into a statement. Find the verb in the statement and ask "Who?" or "What?" in front of it.

Questions often begin with a verb, a helping verb, or a word such as *what, where, when, how,* or *why.* The subject usually follows the verb or helping verb.

EXAMPLE   Has the plane left? **becomes** The plane has left. [*What* left? The *plane* left.]

11g   Do not mistake the word *there* for the subject of a sentence. To find the subject in this type of sentence, omit *there* and ask "Who?" or "What?" before the verb.

There is often used to get a sentence started when the subject comes after the verb.

EXAMPLE   There are many worms in the compost pile. [*What* are in the compost pile? The *worms* are. *Worms* is the subject.]

NOTE   Like *there*, the adverb *here* is often used to get a sentence started. To find the subject in such a sentence, omit *here* and ask "Who?" or "What?" before the verb.

EXAMPLE   Here is your ticket. [*What* is? *Ticket* is. *Ticket* is the subject.]

11h   In a request or a command, the subject of a sentence is usually not stated. In such sentences, *you* is the *understood subject*.

REQUEST   Please feed the cat. [*Who* should feed the cat? *You* should feed the cat. *You* is the understood subject.]

COMMAND   Don't talk during his speech. [*Who* shouldn't talk? *You* shouldn't talk. *You* is the understood subject.]

Sometimes a request or command will include a name. Names used in commands or requests are called *nouns of direct address*. They identify the person spoken to or addressed, but they are not subjects. *You* is still the understood subject.

EXAMPLE   Marie, (you) please deliver this note for me.

EXERCISE 7   Identifying Subjects and Verbs

In the sentences below, underline each subject once. Underline the verb twice. If the understood subject is *you*, write *you* on the line before the sentence.

EX.   _____   1.   There are almost forty new houses on this road.

_____   1.   Rodney, return your books to the library.

_____   2.   When will the candidate make a speech here?

_____   3.   Here are the directions to my house.

_____   4.   Take the dog for a walk around the block.

_____   5.   Did your mother enjoy the concert?

_____   6.   There is a new movie at the Fox Theater tonight.

_____   7.   Will you need a ticket to the lecture?

_____   8.   Is Harrisburg the capital of Pennsylvania?

_____   9.   Priscilla, watch the children in the pool.

_____   10.   Be quiet!

_____   11.   Can you play badminton?

_____   12.   The quarterback, along with the coach, left early.

_____   13.   Learn the rules by Wednesday.

_____   14.   Dorothea Dix, with Elizabeth Blackwell, helped the sick.

_____   15.   There was a nail in my shoe.

COMPOUND SUBJECTS AND COMPOUND VERBS

11i **A *compound subject* consists of two or more subjects that are joined by a conjunction and have the same verb.**

The conjunctions most commonly used to connect the words of a compound subject are *and* and *or*.

EXAMPLE **Lucia** and **Donald** brought refreshments for the team. [*Who brought refreshments? Lucia* brought them. *Donald* brought them. *Lucia* and *Donald* form the compound subject.]

When more than two words are included in the compound subject, the conjunction is generally used only between the last two words. Also, the words are separated by commas.

EXAMPLE Lucia**,** Donald**, and** Sophia brought refreshments for the team. [Compound subject: *Lucia, Donald, Sophia*]

Correlative conjunctions may be used with compound subjects.

EXAMPLE **Either** Lucia **or** Donald will bring refreshments for the team. [Compound subject: *Lucia, Donald*]

11j **A *compound verb* consists of two or more verbs that are joined by a conjunction and have the same subject.**

EXAMPLES The photographer **ran** up the aisle and **snapped** the president's picture.
I **listened** to the game on the radio but **missed** the fourth inning.
Our team **won** four games, **lost** two, and **tied** three.
Congress **will** either **approve** the bill or **suggest** some changes.

Notice that in the last sentence, the helping verb *will* is not repeated before the second verb, *suggest*. In compound verbs, the helping verb may or may not be repeated before the second verb if the helper is the same for both verbs.

EXERCISE 8   Identifying Compound Subjects and Their Verbs

In each of the following sentences, underline the compound subject once and the verb twice.

EX.   1. Birds and lizards might be modern relatives of dinosaurs.

1. Either Tanya or Mae Ellen will win the election.

129

2. There are your shoes and socks, under your bed.

3. Are Helena and Miguel staying for dinner?

4. In the cold waters of this stream, many trout, bass, and pickerel live.

5. At the bottom of the drawer were needles, thread, and even extra buttons.

6. Bottles of juice and cartons of milk were standing in the cooler.

7. Neither my brother nor my sister can come to the concert on Friday.

8. Only Jeremy and I know the location of the buried treasure.

9. Here are Jim and Sandy at the bus stop, right on time.

10. In April, my sisters and I are visiting colleges in Maine and Utah.

EXERCISE 9 Identifying Subjects and Compound Verbs

In each sentence below, underline the subject once and the compound verb twice. Be sure to include any helping verbs.

EX. 1. They visited Canada but did not go to Banff.

1. The fielder shielded her eyes, saw the ball, and moved quickly to her left.

2. I opened the door but saw no one on the porch.

3. Tomorrow morning we will either go to the beach or walk into town for breakfast at the diner.

4. Odessa will direct the play and perform the role of Lady Macbeth.

5. Ray Charles wrote the music and lyrics for his songs and played the piano extremely well.

6. You can come to Puerto Rico, relax on the beach, and visit our great shops and restaurants.

7. At night you can eat dinner and look out at the Caribbean Sea.

8. The new computers at the library have flat-screen monitors and are available for everyone's use.

9. My cousin joined the Houston Museum of Natural Science last year and has gone to many interesting programs there.

10. Could you meet me right after school today or come to my house after soccer practice?

COMPLEMENTS

11k **A *complement* is a word or group of words that completes the meaning of a predicate.**

Notice how the following sentences need the complements to complete the meaning of the predicates. The complement may be a noun, a pronoun, or an adjective, and may be compound. The best way to find the complement in a sentence is to ask who or what receives the action of the verb.

EXAMPLES

          s   v   c
Denzel Washington is a great **actor.** [noun]

         s   v   c
The coach advised **us.** [pronoun]

  s v   c   c
She is always **friendly** and **polite.** [compound adjective]

         s   v   c   c
Dr. Ramírez helped **Velma** and **me.** [noun and pronoun]

NOTE   The complement of a sentence is never part of a prepositional phrase.

EXAMPLES   She fed the **dog.** [*Dog* is the complement.]
She called to the **dog.** [*Dog* is part of the prepositional phrase *to the dog.*]

EXERCISE 10   Identifying Subjects, Verbs, and Complements

In each of the following sentences, underline the simple subject once and the verb twice. Then put brackets around the complement. [Hint: Some sentences may have a compound complement.]

EX.   1. Marie rented an old [movie] last night.

1. Her great-grandfather had recommended the movie to her.

2. Marie enjoys mysteries and courtroom dramas.

3. The name of the movie was *Witness for the Prosecution.*

4. Three very famous actors from Great-Grandpa's era had the leading roles.

5. Charles Laughton, famous as the hunchback in *The Hunchback of Notre Dame*, played the defense attorney in *Witness for the Prosecution.*

6. A very famous actor, Tyrone Power, played the defendant.

7. Marlene Dietrich was one of the most beautiful and most talented women in film history.

8. She played the defendant's wife and the chief witness for the prosecution.

9. Throughout the movie, twists and turns in the plot keep viewers on the edges of their seats.

10. Do not reveal the surprise ending to anyone!

11. We often rent old movies at our house, too.

12. My favorite old movie is *It Happened One Night.*

13. This movie stars Clark Gable and Claudette Colbert.

14. It received the Academy Award for best picture in 1934.

15. The same year, Gable and Colbert each received an Academy Award for best actor and best actress, respectively.

EXERCISE 11   Writing Sentence Complements

Complete the sentences below by adding a complement to each group of words. Add any other words necessary to make your sentences clear.

EX.   1. Tomorrow Penny will give ___a speech___ .

1. Gina sometimes seems _____ .

2. Do you need _____ or _____ ?

3. Last Thursday, I finished _____ and _____ .

4. Barbara won _____ .

5. This bread tastes _____ .

6. That painting is really _____ .

7. Could I borrow your _____ ?

8. My favorite musician today is _____ .

9. Is Donald Duck a _____ ?

10. The best book I ever read was _____ .

11. Tonight's practice session became _____ but _____ .

12. Our neighbor brought home _____ .

13. With paper clips, you can make _____ .

14. Next Monday I begin my new _____ .

15. How soon will you finish _____ ?

THE SUBJECT COMPLEMENT

11l A *subject complement* is a noun, pronoun, or adjective that follows a linking verb. It describes or explains the simple subject.

☞ **REFERENCE NOTE:** For more information on linking verbs, see page 107.

There are two kinds of subject complements—the *predicate nominative* and the *predicate adjective*.

(1) A *predicate nominative* is a noun or pronoun in the predicate that explains or identifies the subject of the sentence.

EXAMPLES   Termites are dangerous **pests**.
The new attorney general is **she**.
Mario is a very talented **musician**.

(2) A *predicate adjective* is an adjective in the predicate that modifies the subject of the sentence.

EXAMPLES   The wind feels **cold**. [cold wind]
The ground is **wet**. [wet ground]

Subject complements may be compound.

EXAMPLES   Two great songwriters were **Richard Rodgers** and **Oscar Hammerstein II**. [compound predicate nominatives]
The pizza is **hot** and **spicy**. [compound predicate adjectives]

To find the subject complement in an interrogative sentence, rearrange the sentence to make a statement.

EXAMPLE   Was Barbra Streisand the director?
Barbra Streisand was the **director**. [predicate nominative]

To find the subject complement in an imperative sentence, insert the understood subject *you*.

EXAMPLE   Be proud of your achievements!
(You) Be **proud** of your achievements! [predicate adjective]

EXERCISE 12   Identifying Subject Complements

In each of the following sentences, underline the subject complement. On the line before the sentence, write *p.n.* for *predicate nominative* or *p.a.* for *predicate adjective*. [Hint: Some sentences may contain compound subject complements.]

133

EX.   _p.a._   1. The woods were full of wildflowers and animals.

_____ 1. Marah is a canoeing counselor at a camp in Maine.

_____ 2. Most of the campers are boys and girls from big cities.

_____ 3. At first, some of the new arrivals seem a little scared and shy of the woods of Maine.

_____ 4. To most of them, canoes seem dangerous.

_____ 5. Marah is patient with these new wilderness campers.

_____ 6. She becomes their guide to new experiences.

_____ 7. Many rivers and river valleys in northern Maine are home to bears, moose, and other wild creatures.

_____ 8. With Marah's help, children from the city become skilled and knowledgeable about the treasures of the wilderness.

_____ 9. I was one of Marah's first campers, twelve years ago.

_____ 10. Thanks to Marah, I am now a seasoned wilderness traveler and the author of two books about the rivers of Maine.

EXERCISE 13   Writing Subject Complements

Complete each sentence below by adding a subject complement. Add any other words that you feel are necessary to make your sentences clear. On the line before each word group, identify the complement in your completed sentence. Write _p.n._ for _predicate nominative_ or _p.a._ for _predicate adjective._ [Hint: Some sentences need a compound complement.]

EX.   _p.a._   1. The river was _wide_ and _deep_ .

_____ 1. Suddenly, the sky became _____ .

_____ 2. My favorite food is _____ .

_____ 3. Is that man _____ or _____ ?

_____ 4. Nancy looked_____ but _____ .

_____ 5. The winner of the race was _____ .

_____ 6. Two inventions that changed the world are_____

and _____ .

_____ 7. Remain_____to your friends.

_____ 8. The mountains appear_____ yet _____ .

_____ 9. Today the weather seems_____ .

_____ 10. Is Ms. Ramillo a _____ ?

OBJECTS

Objects are complements that do not refer to the subject.

11m A *direct object* is a noun or pronoun that receives the action of the verb or shows the result of the action. It answers the question "Whom?" or "What?" after an action verb.

EXAMPLES   Gina called **me**. [Gina called *whom*? *Me* is the direct object.]
Hot soup may burn your **throat**. [Hot soup may burn *what*? *Throat* is the direct object.]

Direct objects are never found in prepositional phrases.

EXAMPLES   Yosef rode the **horse**. [*Horse* is the direct object.]
Yosef rode on the **horse**. [*Horse* is part of the prepositional phrase *on the horse*.]

11n An indirect object is a noun or pronoun that precedes the direct object and usually tells *to whom* or *for whom* (or *to what* or *for what*) the action of the verb is done.

EXAMPLES   The coach gave **Josh** and **him** awards. [*Josh* and *him* are the compound indirect object of the verb *gave*, telling *to whom the coach gave the awards.* The noun *awards* is the direct object.]
Juan built his **sister** a shelf for her books. [The noun *sister* is the indirect object of the verb *built*, telling *for whom Juan built a shelf.* The noun *shelf* is the direct object.]

If the word *to* or *for* is used, the noun or pronoun following it is part of a prepositional phrase and cannot be an indirect object.

PREPOSITIONAL PHRASE   I made a card **for you**.
INDIRECT OBJECT   I made **you** a card.
PREPOSITIONAL PHRASE   He gave the extra ticket **to Tom**.
INDIRECT OBJECT   He gave **Tom** the extra ticket.

☞ **REFERENCE NOTE**: For more information on action verbs, see page 105.

EXERCISE 14   Identifying Direct Objects

Underline the direct object in each of the following sentences.

EX.   1. George's father and mother, Mr. and Mrs. Ristevski, own the <u>Liberty Deli</u>.

1. Students from the university and staff from the hospital often buy lunch there.

2. Early each morning, Mrs. Ristevski bakes the bread for the deli sandwiches.

3. Twice a month, Mr. Ristevski makes his own sausage.

4. During the cold winter months, the neighbors especially like the convenient location of the delicatessen.

5. For twenty-five years the Ristevski family has owned and managed the delicatessen.

EXERCISE 15   Identifying Direct Objects and Indirect Objects

In each sentence below, underline the direct object once and the indirect object twice. Some sentences may not contain an indirect object. [Hint: Both direct objects and indirect objects may be compound.]

EX.   1. Ms. Sanchez gave Trudy and us directions to her office.

1. Can you loan Marley and Pat enough money for their tickets?

2. He left your jacket in the hall closet.

3. Dr. Fuller gave the children some good advice about poison ivy.

4. Please read me the opening paragraph of your composition.

5. Before the hike, Pierre gave each girl and boy trail maps.

6. At the wildlife park, we took photographs of zebras and monkeys.

7. Could you please show me the fastest route to Monterey?

8. Take Marshall Boulevard to the top of the hill and turn right.

9. I'll give you this book about interesting sights in Monterey.

10. Thank you very much, sir.

11. Amy Tan published her first novel in 1989.

12. Did you study the life of Sauk chief Black Hawk?

13. He teaches his students the concepts of t'ai chi ch'uan, a system of self-defense and meditation.

14. My grandfather visited three cities in the Southwest.

15. The archaeologist Howard Carter found Tutankhamen's tomb.

CLASSIFYING SENTENCES BY PURPOSE

11o Sentences may be classified as *declarative*, *imperative*, *interrogative*, or *exclamatory*.

(1) A *declarative* sentence makes a statement. All declarative sentences are followed by periods.

EXAMPLE   The famous painter Arshile Gorky was born in Armenia in 1904.

(2) An imperative sentence gives a command or makes a request. Imperative sentences are usually followed by periods. Very strong commands, however, may be followed by exclamation points.

EXAMPLES   Please shut the window.
Don't swim alone.
Watch out for the sharks!

Notice that a command or request has the understood subject *you.*

(3) An *interrogative* sentence asks a question. Interrogative sentences are followed by question marks.

EXAMPLE   What is your favorite poem?

(4) An *exclamatory* sentence expresses strong feeling. Exclamatory sentences are always followed by exclamation points.

EXAMPLES   That car is rolling down the hill!
What an incredible race that was!
I can't believe I won a trip to Paris!

EXERCISE 16   Identifying the Four Kinds of Sentences

Add the correct punctuation mark to the end of each of the following sentences. On the line before the sentence, indicate which type of sentence it is. Write *dec.* for *declarative, inter.* for *interrogative, imp.* for *imperative,* or *excl.* for *exclamatory.* [Hint: Some imperative sentences may end in exclamation points.]

EX.   _____imp._____   1. Stop fighting at once !

_____   1.   Have you seen all of the Indiana Jones movies

_____   2.   The first one, *Raiders of the Lost Ark,* came out in 1981

_____   3.   What a fantastic movie it was

_____ 4. Although audiences had seen Harrison Ford as Han Solo in *Star Wars*, he became a star when he took on the role of Indiana Jones

_____ 5. Call the video store, and ask if they have *Raiders of the Lost Ark* in stock

_____ 6. Wow, there must have been at least a billion snakes in that scene

_____ 7. Are you afraid of snakes

_____ 8. Watch out for the falling rocks, Indy

_____ 9. Critics did not give the second Indiana Jones movie, *Indiana Jones and the Temple of Doom*, the great reviews that they gave the first one

_____ 10. Did you think that Karen Allen was a better heroine than Kate Capshaw

EXERCISE 17   Writing the Four Kinds of Sentences

You are sitting in a restaurant. Suddenly you notice that the diner at the next table is a large penguin. On your own paper, write a dialogue that might take place between you and the penguin. Add stage directions if you wish. Write ten sentences, and use at least two examples of each of the four kinds of sentences. Label each of your sentences to identify its classification.

EX.   1. Me: (with a puzzled expression) *We don't usually see penguins in this neighborhood.* (dec.)

"What was it like back in the days when people talked and wrote in complete sentences?"

CHAPTER REVIEW

A. Identifying the Parts of a Sentence

In the paragraph below, classify each underlined word according to its function in the sentence. Write *s.* for *subject*, *p.n.* for *predicate nominative*, *d.o.* for *direct object*, *v.* for *verb*, *p.a.* for *predicate adjective*, and *i.o.* for *indirect object*.

EX.   Romesh Gunesekera has published a [1] <u>book</u> *d.o.* of short stories.

Romesh Gunesekera is a [1] <u>native</u> of Sri Lanka. [2] <u>Sri Lanka</u> is an island nation located in the Indian Ocean. Gunesekera now [3] <u>lives</u> in London, where he has published [4] <u>*Monkfish Moon.*</u> His book is quite [5] <u>good</u> in its blending of appearance and reality. Its nine short [6] <u>stories</u> give [7] <u>readers</u> several interesting [8] <u>views</u> of life in Sri Lanka. [9] <u>Some</u> of the stories are [10] <u>frightening.</u> They [11] <u>tell</u> of events related to Sri Lanka's long and cruel civil war. Only the [12] <u>setting</u>, however, will seem [13] <u>unfamiliar</u> to readers outside of Sri Lanka. All of the stories contain complex [14] <u>characters</u> and vivid details. Because Gunesekera [15] <u>has based</u> this excellent [16] <u>collection</u> of stories on his native land, he has given the [17] <u>East</u> and the West a new and powerful [18] <u>link</u>. His book [19] <u>is</u> both a masterpiece of literature and a [20] <u>tribute</u> to a beautiful and complex country.

B. Identifying and Punctuating the Four Kinds of Sentences

Add the correct punctuation mark to the end of each of the following sentences. On the line before the sentence, classify the sentence. Write *dec.* for *declarative*, *imp.* for *imperative*, *inter.* for *interrogative*, and *excl.* for *exclamatory*.

EX.   __imp.__ 1. Please pass the salt

_____ 1. In 1991, Paul Sereno discovered a dinosaur fossil in Argentina

_____ 2. What a fierce animal that dinosaur must have been

_____ 3. Read the article about it in the September 1993 issue of *Earth* magazine

_____ 4. That dinosaur has been given the name *Eoraptor*

_____ 5. Did it live about 228 million years ago

_____ 6. Another dinosaur lived at about the same time

_____ 7. What was its name

_____ 8. It was called *Herrerasaurus,* and Sereno found its fossil in the same rock formation, along with *Eoraptor*

_____ 9. Do you believe that dinosaurs once roamed these woods

_____ 10. Wow, they must have been terrifying

C. Writing Sentences

On your own paper, write fifteen sentences according to the guidelines below. Underline the part or parts called for in the guidelines.

EX. 1. a declarative sentence with a compound verb
1. Barbra Streisand produced and directed the movie *The Prince of Tides*.

1. a declarative sentence with a predicate adjective

2. an interrogative sentence with a direct object

3. an interrogative sentence with a compound subject

4. an imperative sentence with an indirect object and a direct object

5. an imperative sentence that ends with a period

6. an imperative sentence that ends with an exclamation point

7. a declarative sentence with a compound indirect object and a direct object

8. an exclamatory sentence with a predicate adjective

9. a sentence that begins with *there* and contains a compound subject

10. a sentence with the understood subject *you*

11. a declarative sentence with a predicate nominative

12. an exclamatory sentence with a compound verb

13. a declarative sentence with a compound predicate nominative

14. an interrogative sentence with a compound verb

15. a sentence with the understood subject *you* and a compound verb

PREPOSITIONAL PHRASES

12a A *phrase* is a group of related words that is used as a single part of speech and does not contain both a predicate and its subject.

EXAMPLES   should have listened [verb phrase; no subject]
between Marika and Martin [prepositional phrase; no subject or verb]

12b A *prepositional phrase* is a group of words consisting of a preposition, a noun or pronoun that serves as the object of the preposition, and any modifiers of that object.

Some prepositions are made up of more than one word, like *in front of* or *prior to.* Also, an article or some other modifier often appears in a prepositional phrase.

EXAMPLES   Zahara built a model airplane **for her brother.** [The object of the preposition *for* is *brother.* The possessive pronoun *her* modifies *brother.*]
When will she give the birthday present **to him**? [The object of the preposition *to* is *him.*]
Our new bus stop is **in front of the supermarket.** [The object of the preposition *in front of* is *supermarket.* The adjective *the* modifies *supermarket.*]

Objects of prepositions may be compound.

EXAMPLES   Heavy snow fell **throughout the day and night.** [Both *day* and *night* are objects of the preposition *throughout.*]
In addition to you and me, six other people are coming. [The preposition *in addition to* has a compound object, *you* and *me.*]
Our new bus stop is **in front of the supermarket and the laundromat.** [The objects of the preposition *in front of* are *supermarket* and *laundromat.* The adjective *the* modifies *supermarket* and *laundromat.*]

 REFERENCE NOTE: For a list of commonly used prepositions, see page 115.

EXERCISE 1   Identifying Prepositions and Their Objects

In each of the following sentences, underline the preposition, and draw an arrow from the preposition to its object.

EX.   1. Our voices echoed loudly inside the empty house.

1. Two of Mr. Johnson's children play the violin.

141

2. Today, you can buy almost anything from a catalog.

3. That girl with the catcher's mitt plays baseball well.

4. Imagine what the world would be like without television.

5. We spotted a doe and two fawns running across the grassy meadow.

6. The Forty-first and Forty-second Congresses had among their members the first African American representatives and the first African American senator.

7. The coach will award the medals at tonight's sports banquet.

8. Rain has been falling since dawn.

9. According to this article, nearly ten thousand Chinese immigrants helped construct the Central Pacific Railroad.

10. The baseball sailed over the fence, the street, and the parking garage.

EXERCISE 2   Writing Notes for TV

You are a writer for the show *Wildlife Facts*. Your next program is on snakes. Use the following notes to write ten sentences that might be used for the voice-over for this program. Include at least five prepositional phrases in your sentences. Underline the phrases and draw an arrow from the prepositions to their objects. Write these sentences on your own paper.

EX.   1.   True vipers are found in Africa and Eurasia.

NOTES

1. world's largest poisonous snake—king cobra

2. cobras—Malaysia, China, India, the Philippines

3. true vipers—Africa, Eurasia, and the East Indies

4. pit vipers—facial pits

5. rattlesnake—eats small animals, lifts tail to make sounds

6. African saw-scaled viper—rubs side scales together to produce rasping sound

7. North American sidewinder—moves sideways

8. water moccasin—southern swamps and bayous in North America

9. Indian cobra—hooded, lift up for battle

10. asp—also called Egyptian cobra

ADJECTIVE PHRASES AND ADVERB PHRASES

12c **A prepositional phrase that modifies a noun or pronoun is called an *adjective phrase*.**

Adjective phrases answer the same questions that adjectives answer: *What kind? Which one? How many?* or *How much?* An adjective phrase usually follows the noun or pronoun that it modifies. More than one phrase may modify the same word. An adjective phrase may also modify the object of another prepositional phrase.

EXAMPLES The names **of the contest winners** will be announced tomorrow. [The phrase *of the contest winners* modifies the noun *names*, telling *which* names.]
Please bring me that big ball **of string in the garage.** [Both phrases modify the noun *ball. Of string* tells *what kind; in the garage* tells *which one.*]
The painting **of the girl with the dog** won first prize. [The phrase *of the girl* modifies the noun *painting*, telling *which painting.* The phrase *with the dog* modifies the object *girl*, telling *which girl.*]

EXERCISE 3 Identifying Adjective Phrases

Underline each adjective phrase in the sentences below. Draw an arrow to the word it modifies. [Note: Some sentences have more than one adjective phrase.]

EX. 1. My grandparents tape-recorded stories of our family's history.

1. The walls around us were a brilliant yellow.
2. The flowers along the path are geraniums and petunias.
3. Leon took a picture of a blue heron next to a snowy egret.
4. The heavy winds of the storm spun the weather vane on the roof.
5. The cat ate all of the sardines in the tin.
6. *Hunger of Memory* is an autobiographical story by Richard Rodriguez.
7. The plays in the game were very exciting.
8. Mom opened the can of beans carefully.
9. Which of these books do you want?
10. The castle beside the ocean belonged to Prince Edward.

> **12d** An *adverb phrase* is a prepositional phrase that modifies a verb, an adjective, or an adverb.
>
> Adverb phrases answer the same questions that adverbs answer: *When? Where? How? To what extent?* (*How long? How many? How far?*)
>
> EXAMPLES **Within a few minutes**, the concert will begin. [The phrase *Within a few minutes* modifies the verb phrase *will begin*, telling *when* the concert will begin.]
> The water is deeper **on the far end**. [The phrase *on the far end* modifies the adjective *deeper*, telling *where* the water is deeper.]
>
> Like adjective phrases, more than one adverb phrase may modify the same word.
>
> EXAMPLE **With a final sprint**, Takara won the marathon **by three seconds**. [Both phrases modify the verb *won*. *With a final sprint* tells *how*; *by three seconds* tells *to what extent*.]

EXERCISE 4   Identifying Adverb Phrases and the Words They Modify

Underline the adverb phrases in the sentences below. Draw an arrow from each phrase to the word or words it modifies. [Note: Some sentences have more than one adverb phrase.]

EX.   1. After our classes, Germaine and I played basketball in the schoolyard.

1. Germaine pointed to the dark clouds that were gathering in the sky.

2. In a few minutes, thunder cracked loudly above our heads.

3. From the house, we watched the storm.

4. Lightning flashes appeared repeatedly for an hour.

5. Soon the lightning seemed closer to the house.

6. The whirligig was spinning out of control.

7. I thought the beets and carrots would be ripped out of the ground by the wind.

8. The rain grew from a drizzle to a downpour.

9. Germaine's dog Rosamunda hid under the bed.

10. His sister Elena ran through the house, pretending she was a rescue worker.

VERBALS AND VERB PHRASES

Verbals are formed from verbs. Like verbs, they may be modified by adverbs and may have complements. However, verbals are used as other parts of speech. There are three kinds of verbals: *participles, gerunds,* and *infinitives.*

12e   A *participle* is a verb form that can be used as an adjective.

EXAMPLE   The divers discovered **sunken** treasure off the coast of Key Largo. [The participle *sunken*, formed from the verb *sink*, modifies the noun *treasure*.]

(1) *Present participles* end in *–ing*.

EXAMPLE   The photographer took a picture of the **laughing** baby. [*Laughing* is a present participle modifying the noun *baby*.]

(2) *Past participles* usually end in *–d* or *–ed*. Other past participles are irregularly formed.

EXAMPLES   Please pass your **completed** test to the front of the room. [The past participle *completed* modifies the noun *test*.]
Her only son, **grown** and **gone** from home, visits her often. [The irregular past participles *grown* and *gone* modify the noun *son*.] ·

 NOTE   Although participles are forms of verbs, they do not stand alone as verbs. However, a participle may be used with a helping verb to form a verb phrase. When a participle is used in this way, it is part of the verb and is therefore not an adjective.

EXAMPLES   Matthew **has been studying** Spanish.
Her son **is grown** and **has been gone** from home for years.

EXERCISE 5   Identifying Participles and the Words They Modify

Underline the participles used as adjectives in the following sentences. Then draw an arrow from each participle to the noun or pronoun that it modifies.

EX.   1. Splashing paint on the canvas, the artist created a masterpiece.

1. The museum, known for its collection of modern art, has a new exhibit.

2. Most of the pieces seen in this show are from private collections.

3. A crowd gathered around a sculpture of a group of people sitting on a bus.

4. The figures, assembled from plaster casts, seemed real.

5. Expressing his opinion loudly, one man obviously did not like the artist's work.

6. Framed and hung on the wall, an enormous picture of a mother and child captured the attention of many people.

7. For a long time, Marissa stood in front of the picture, staring and thinking.

8. Lecturing on the artists of the mid-1900s, the museum guide talked about the work of the sculptor Alexander Calder.

9. Some people believe that Calder's sculptures have a charming quality.

10. Connected with rods and wires and suspended in the air, Calder's mobiles are probably his most popular pieces.

EXERCISE 6   Choosing Appropriate Participles

On the line in each of the sentences below, write a participle that fits the meaning of the sentence.

EX.   1. The _____rising_____ tide washed over the beach.

1. The _____ sun cast a purple haze across the evening sky.

2. _____ her head, the baby fell asleep.

3. The whale, _____ suddenly out of the water, startled the people on the boat.

4. _____ in the sand, the clam was not visible to the hungry sea gulls.

5. We spent the day with our friends at the teen center, _____ .

PARTICIPIAL PHRASES

12f A *participial phrase* is a phrase containing a participle and any complements or modifiers it may have.

A participial phrase should be placed as close as possible to the word it modifies. Otherwise the sentence may not make sense.

EXAMPLES **Hiking in the Sierra Nevada**, Paulo encountered a mountain lion. [The participle is modified by the prepositional phrase *in the Sierra Nevada.*]

Did you see that lioness **carrying her cubs**? [The participle has an object, *cubs.* The possesive pronoun *her* modifies *cubs.*]

The hiker, **acting quickly**, snapped a picture of the lion. [The participle is modified by the adverb *quickly.*]

 REFERENCE NOTE: The punctuation of participial phrases is discussed on pages 265 and 267. The participle as a dangling modifier is discussed on page 227. Combining sentences by using participles is discussed on page 73.

EXERCISE 7   Identifying Participial Phrases

Underline the participial phrase in each of the following sentences. Draw an arrow from the participial phrase to the word or words the phrase modifies.

EX.   1. Listening to the story of the princess and the frog, the children are enchanted.

1. Every Saturday morning, Shanti spends time at the library, telling stories to children.

2. Leaving their children at story hour, the parents run their errands.

3. Shanti reads with the children gathered in a circle around her.

4. The stories, chosen from among Shanti's own childhood favorites, are usually fairy tales and folk tales.

5. Enhanced by Shanti's unique style, each story delights the children.

6. Once, as I passed by the story-hour room, I overheard Shanti speaking gruffly.

7. Speaking in the voices of different characters, she was telling the story of the three little pigs.

8. The children held their breath when the wolf, huffing and puffing with all its might, tried to blow down the house of the third little pig.

9. The house built of bricks did not fall down, of course, and the pig survived.

10. Clapping and cheering at the end, the children showed how much they loved that folk tale.

EXERCISE 8   Identifying Participles and Participial Phrases

Underline each participle or participial phrase in the paragraph below. Draw an arrow from the participial phrase to the word or words that it modifies.

EX.   [1] Using an old tale, a poet provides a different view of a familiar character.

[1] Thinking about tomorrow's assignment, I decided to talk about a poem. [2] Skimming through my literature book, I came across an interesting poem titled "The Builders." [3] The poem, written by Sara Henderson Hay, does not actually identify its topic—"The Three Little Pigs." [4] The speaker of the poem is the pig who built his house of bricks, protecting himself from the starving wolf. [5] The pig, recalling recent events, tells the story in a scolding tone. [6] He points out that he told his brothers to build with bricks, but, being stubborn, they wouldn't listen to him. [7] The pig seems to be sorry that his brothers are gone, having been eaten by the wolf. [8] Having heard "The Three Little Pigs" so many times as a child, I found much to say about Hay's poem. [9] Looking for something to use as my first prop, I found a shoebox in my closet. [10] The shoebox, painted with a pattern of small bricks, would represent the pig's house.

GERUNDS

12g **A *gerund* is a verb form ending in *–ing* that is used as a noun.**

SUBJECT	**Walking** is good exercise.
PREDICATE NOMINATIVE	My favorite activity at the beach is **snorkeling**.
DIRECT OBJECT	Mom enjoys **golfing**.
OBJECT OF A PREPOSITION	A sturdy, thick-soled shoe is recommended for **hiking**.

Like nouns, gerunds may be modified by adjectives and adjective phrases.

DIRECT OBJECT	I watched **the incredible** diving **of the Olympic gold-medal winner**. [The article *the*, the adjective *incredible*, and the adjective phrase *of the Olympic gold-medal winner* modify the gerund *diving*.]
SUBJECT	**The sloppy** writing **of the note** made it impossible to understand. [The article *The*, the adjective *sloppy*, and the adjective phrase *of the note* modify the gerund *writing*.]

Like verbs, gerunds may also be modified by adverbs and adverb phrases.

SUBJECT	Cheering **loudly at the game** gave Geraldo a sore throat. [The gerund *Cheering* is modified by both the adverb *loudly* (telling *how*) and the adverb phrase *at the game* (telling *where*).]
DIRECT OBJECT	I would enjoy sitting **quietly for a while**. [The gerund *sitting* is modified by both the adverb *quietly* (telling *how*) and the adverb phrase *for a while* (telling *for how long*).]

Gerunds, like present participles, end in *–ing*. To be a gerund, a verbal must be used as a noun. In the following sentence, three words end in *–ing*, but only one of them is a gerund.

EXAMPLE	**Thinking** about the trip, Earline was **packing** suitable clothes for **sightseeing**. [*Thinking* is a present participle modifying *Earline*. *Packing* is part of the verb phrase *was packing*. Only *sightseeing*, used as the object of the preposition *for*, is a gerund.]

EXERCISE 9   Identifying and Classifying Gerunds

Underline the gerunds in the following sentences. On the line before each sentence, identify how each is used. Write *s.* for *subject*, *p.n.* for *predicate nominative*, *d.o.* for *direct object*, or *o.p.* for *object of a preposition*.

EX. __s__   1. Fishing relaxes my dad.

_____   1. Tomás enjoys gardening.

_____   2. Bicycling is a sport that can be enjoyed at any age.

_____   3. After the accident, she was bothered by a painful throbbing in her knee.

_____   4. My favorite part of graduation was the singing, but Dad liked the speeches better.

_____   5. Running in a marathon is Aretha's goal.

_____   6. Acting in such plays as *Othello* and *The Emperor Jones* earned national attention for the renowned African American actor Paul Robeson.

_____   7. On a hot day like today, the only work I want to do is writing.

_____   8. The new puppies enjoy chasing each other playfully around the house.

_____   9. When we went to Mexico, we took along a Spanish-English dictionary for translating.

_____   10. Nestled in our sleeping bags, we heard the howling of a coyote, which sounded lonely to me.

EXERCISE 10   Writing About Hobbies

On the lines below, write five sentences about hobbies or activities that you enjoy. In each sentence, use a gerund, and underline it. In the space above the gerund, label its use in the sentence. Write *s.* for *subject*, *p.n.* for *predicate nominative*, *d.o.* for *direct object*, or *o.p.* for *object of a preposition*.

                     s.
EX.   1. Playing the Japanese game Go is fun.

1. _____

_____

2. _____

_____

3. _____

_____

4. _____

_____

5. _____

_____

GERUND PHRASES

12h A *gerund phrase* contains a gerund and any modifiers or complements it may have.

SUBJECT	**The loud roaring of the wind** could be heard inside the cabin. [The gerund *roaring* is modified by the article *The*, the adjective *loud*, and the prepositional phrase *of the wind*.]
DIRECT OBJECT	Thelma enjoyed **racing swiftly on her bike**. [The gerund *racing* is modified by the adverb *swiftly* and by the prepositional phrase *on her bike*.]
PREDICATE NOMINATIVE	His hobby is **sending friends old postcards**. [The gerund *sending* has a direct object, *postcards*, and an indirect object, *friends*.]
OBJECT OF A PREPOSITION	She improved her composition by **rewriting the last paragraph**. [The gerund *rewriting* has a direct object, *paragraph*.]

NOTE Whenever a noun or a pronoun comes before a gerund, the possessive form should be used.

EXAMPLES The **parrot's** endless squawking made us laugh.
Her cooking has really improved.

EXERCISE 11   Identifying and Classifying Gerund Phrases

Underline the gerund phrases in the following sentences. On the line before each sentence, identify how each phrase is used. Write *s.* for *subject*, *p.n.* for *predicate nominative*, *d.o.* for *direct object*, or *o.p.* for *object of a preposition*.

EX. _____s._____ 1. Traveling to exotic places would be fun.

_____ 1. The people on the Samoan island of Upolu in the South Pacific showed their hospitality to the magazine photographer by welcoming her warmly.

_____ 2. The photographer's job was taking pictures of the island's scenery for a travel article.

_____ 3. She liked talking to the people about their remote South Pacific island.

_____ 4. Swimming in the warm waters of Upolu is possible all year.

_____   5. A popular entertainment on the island is torch dancing.

_____   6. Tourists enjoy diving from the reef.

_____   7. Almost one hundred years ago, writer Robert Louis Stevenson found paradise by sailing to the island of Upolu.

_____   8. Finding an island paradise is the dream of many writers.

_____   9. After chartering a yacht, Robert Louis Stevenson set sail in search of his dream island.

_____ 10. Flying to Apia, the capital of Western Samoa, is the fastest and simplest way to reach this dream island today.

_____ 11. Driving over Cross Island Road takes you from one coast to the other.

_____ 12. Moving from Los Angeles to Polynesia must be a big change.

_____ 13. Losing your job might cause you to make such a move.

_____ 14   A way to honor the local leaders is by taking a Samoan name.

_____ 15. I don't know if I'd like moving to Samoa, but I'd vacation there if I could afford it.

EXERCISE 12   Working Cooperatively to Write Sentences with Gerund Phrases

Working with a partner, create ten sentences that use the gerund phrases below. Write on your own paper. Underline each gerund phrase, and write above the phrase *s.* for *subject,* *p.n.* for *predicate nominative,* *d.o.* for *direct object,* or *o.p.* for *object of a preposition.*

EX.   1. throwing the javelin

                s.
   1. <u>Throwing the javelin</u> was the second field event on the schedule.

  1. putting on my running shoes
  2. pole-vaulting at the track meet
  3. pushing off from the starting block
  4. firing the starting gun
  5. passing the baton
  6. running a marathon
  7. crossing the finish line
  8. lying on the grass to rest
  9. landing in the sandpit
 10. cheering for the athletes

INFINITIVES AND INFINITIVE PHRASES

> **12i** An *infinitive* is a verb form, usually preceded by *to*, that can be used as a noun, an adjective, or an adverb.
>
> NOUNS **To sing** with a rock band is Jon's dream. [*To sing* is the subject of the sentence.]
>
> I had hoped **to finish** my story, but Joey's plan was **to leave** early. [*To finish* is the direct object of the verb phrase *had hoped*. *To leave* is the predicate nominative.]
>
> ADJECTIVE The person **to ask** is the information director. [*To ask* modifies the noun *person*.]
>
> ADVERB Eager **to rest**, we sat down on the grass. [*To rest* modifies the adjective *eager*.]
>
> **12j** An *infinitive phrase* consists of an infinitive together with its modifiers and complements.
>
> NOUN **To find a job quickly** is Rita's goal. [The phrase is the subject of the sentence. The infinitive has a direct object, *job*, and is modified by the adverb *quickly*.]
>
> ADJECTIVE Roses are the flowers **to give for a special occasion**. [The phrase modifies the predicate nominative *flowers*. The infinitive is modified by the adverb phrase *for a special occasion*.]
>
> ADVERB He seemed afraid **to say a word**. [The phrase modifies the predicate adjective *afraid* and has a direct object, *word*.]
>
> An infinitive may have a subject. The infinitive, together with its subject, complements, and modifiers, is sometimes called an *infinitive clause*.
>
> EXAMPLE Mom asked **me to buy milk on my way home.** [*Me* is the subject of the infinitive *to buy*.]
>
> Sometimes the *to* of the infinitive is omitted in a sentence.
>
> EXAMPLE Will you help me **find** my missing watch?

EXERCISE 13 Identifying and Classifying Infinitives

Underline the infinitives in the sentences below. On the line before each sentence, identify how each infinitive is used. Write *n.* for *noun*, *adj.* for *adjective*, or *adv.* for *adverb*.

EX. __n.__ 1. To be a member of the hockey team was important to Chris.

_____ 1. Slow to start, the car was old and unreliable.

_____ 2. Does anyone wish to respond to the mayor's comments?

_____ 3. Dan is the person to follow, because he always knows exactly where he's going.

_____ 4. Mr. Petrakis ran to catch his train so that it would not leave without him.

_____ 5. We left our seats to get some popcorn.

EXERCISE 14   Identifying and Classifying Infinitive Phrases

Underline the infinitive phrases in the sentences below. On the line before each sentence, identify how the infinitive phrase is used. Write *n.* for *noun*, *adj.* for *adjective*, or *adv.* for *adverb*.

EX. __n.__ 1. To make pizza requires some planning ahead.

_____ 1. Earlier, Luisa and Josh went to get the ingredients at the market.

_____ 2. To prepare the most delicious pizza ever was their objective.

_____ 3. They had already decided to heap lots of fresh vegetables on the pizza.

_____ 4. They needed advice from Luisa's mother on the best way to make the tomato sauce.

_____ 5. She was happy to share her old family recipe with them.

_____ 6. To stretch the dough properly was another technique that she demonstrated for them.

_____ 7. Once the dough was stretched and the sauce was cooked, Luisa and Josh were ready to assemble their pizza.

_____ 8. Josh asked Luisa to ladle the sauce on the dough.

_____ 9. After mushrooms, peppers, artichokes, onions, and cheese were piled on the dough, it was time to bake the pizza in a very hot oven.

_____ 10. Then they invited some friends for dinner, because, Josh said, "Pizza is a food to eat with friends!"

REVIEW EXERCISE

A. Identifying and Classifying Prepositional Phrases

Underline all the prepositional phrases in the paragraph below. In the space above each phrase, identify how the phrase is used. Write *adj.* for *adjective* and *adv.* for *adverb.*

EX. [1] I. M. Pei is just one <u>of the many architects</u> whose work enhances city landscapes worldwide.
[adj. above "of the many architects"]

[1] I. M. Pei, born in Canton, China, in 1917, was the son of a successful Chinese banker. [2] Pei came to the United States to study architectural engineering when he was eighteen years old. [3] Because of a war between China and Japan, Pei could not go home after his college graduation. [4] He obtained a master of architecture degree from Harvard University and, in 1948, joined the staff of an important architectural firm. [5] Before this time, Pei had never designed any actual buildings, but the head of the firm was impressed by Pei's architectural drawings. [6] He wanted Pei on his staff. [7] With this important job, Pei had his chance to alter modern urban environments. [8] Many cities are more beautiful because of Pei's decision to join that firm. [9] Among the buildings he has designed are the Mile High Center in Denver, Colorado, the East Building of the National Gallery of Art, and the Dallas City Hall. [10] If you are looking at Boston's Government Center or Montreal's Place Ville Marie, you are looking at Pei's designs.

B.   Identifying and Classifying Verbals and Verbal Phrases

Underline the verbal or verbal phrase in each of the following sentences. On the line before each sentence, identify the verbal or verbal phrase. Write *ger.* for *gerund*, *ger. phr.* for *gerund phrase*, *inf.* for *infinitive*, *inf. phr.* for *infinitive phrase*, *part.* for *participle*, or *part. phr.* for *participial phrase.*

EX.   _____ger. phr._____   1.   Imagining a world without computers is impossible for me.

_____   1.   The photo in the book showed bats hanging upside down.

_____   2.   Although I've tried, I can't seem to take a really good photograph of a sunset.

_____   3.   Theo's one passion is acting.

_____   4.   Lost, the young boy worried that he might never find his way home.

_____   5.   She had a question she wanted to ask.

_____   6.   We came to a tidal pool where we saw crabs, shrimp, and other ocean creatures swimming around.

_____   7.   The fire was about to spread to other buildings when the fire trucks arrived.

_____   8.   Walking beneath the bridge, we could hear the rumble of the train on the tracks above.

_____   9.   It seems obvious, but the only way you'll ever become a better dancer is by dancing more.

_____   10.   The growling lion frightened away the birds.

C.   Writing a Compugram with Verbals and Verbal Phrases

You are on a space team that is exploring Saturn. Once a month, you are allowed to send home an interplanetary compugram (a telegram sent and received by computers) ten sentences long. On your own paper, write a compugram to your friend. Explain what you've been doing. Describe your most exciting discoveries. You may also want to tell your friend what you do for relaxation and entertainment on your days off. Include at least one of each type of verbal and verbal phrase. Underline each verbal or verbal phrase in your sentences. Identify each verbal or verbal phrase by writing *ger.* for *gerund*, *ger. phr.* for *gerund phrase*, *inf.* for *infinitive*, *inf. phr.* for *infinitive phrase*, *part.* for *participle*, or *part. phr.* for *participial phrase.*

EX.   *part. phr.*
Being involved in interplanetary exploration, I have a new appreciation of our entire universe.

APPOSITIVES AND APPOSITIVE PHRASES

12k **An** *appositive* **is a noun or a pronoun given beside another noun or pronoun to identify or explain it.**

EXAMPLES My friend **Janet** invited me to her family's cabin. [The noun *Janet* identifies the noun *friend*.]
Linda Ronstadt, a popular **singer**, has recorded an album of Mexican songs. [The noun *singer* explains the noun *Linda Ronstadt*.]

12l **An** *appositive phrase* **is made up of the appositive and its modifiers.**

EXAMPLES Joseph, **star pitcher of our baseball team**, sprained his wrist.
The movie *La Bamba* was based on the life of Ritchie Valens, **one of the great rock musicians of the 1950s.**

NOTE An appositive phrase usually follows the noun or pronoun it refers to. Sometimes, however, the appositive precedes the noun or pronoun explained.

EXAMPLE **A volunteer worker at the library**, Pamela knows exactly where to look for a book.

Appositives and appositive phrases are usually set off by commas unless the appositive is a single word closely related to the preceding noun or pronoun. Commas are always used with appositives that refer to proper nouns.

ESSENTIAL Our cat **Snowball** likes to sleep under the couch. [The writer has more than one cat. The appositive is necessary to tell which cat is referred to.]

NONESSENTIAL Our cat, **Snowball**, likes to sleep under the couch. [The writer has only one cat. The appositive is not necessary to identify the cat.]

EXERCISE 15   Identifying Appositives and Appositive Phrases

In the following sentences, underline all appositive phrases once. Underline twice the word or words an appositive phrase identifies or explains.

EX. 1. Summer, my favorite time of year, is a great time for hiking.

1. The magazine *Music* is a guide to the enjoyment of classical music.

2. One dessert on the menu, the fresh fruit, is not available today.

3. This article discusses the life and works of Langston Hughes, a poet, novelist, and short-story writer.

4. Tanya wants to become an occupational therapist, a person who treats people with sports injuries and other kinds of injuries.

5. Marjorie, the director of the senior community center, is looking for volunteers to work at the center two days a week.

6. A nuisance to everyone, the mosquitoes seem to be bigger and hungrier this summer.

7. Have you ever played charades, a game in which you have to act out titles for your teammates to guess?

8. My sister Kimiko just got her driver's license.

9. Ina returned the blouse to the store for a refund, twenty-two dollars.

10. What did you think of the movie *Harry Potter and the Goblet of Fire*?

EXERCISE 16　Adding Appositives

On the line in each of the sentences below, write an appositive or appositive phrase that fits the meaning of the sentence.

EX. 1. Fluffy, _____*my house cat*_____, lapped some milk and curled up again on my lap.

1. My friend _____ and I are going to the library.

2. Our library, _____, is open on Saturdays.

3. We are giving a presentation, _____, in class.

4. My parents, _____, say television is harmful.

5. We would like to see some research, _____, to decide for ourselves.

6. The jury, _____, reached a verdict.

7. My sister _____ sang in the choir.

8. Is your favorite dish, _____, being served?

9. James asked everyone where his dog _____ had gone.

10. Two students, _____ and _____, won the contest.

CHAPTER REVIEW

A. Identifying and Classifying Prepositional Phrases

Underline each prepositional phrase in the paragraph below. Then draw an arrow from the phrase to the word or words it modifies. In the space above the phrase, write *adj.* for *adjective phrase* or *adv.* for *adverb phrase*. A sentence may have more than one phrase.

EX. [1] The concerts always start with "The Star-Spangled Banner."

[1] Every Friday evening during the summer, something very special happens in our seaside town. [2] That's when Mr. Turner, who is eighty-four years old, takes his place in front of the Pleasantville Town Band. [3] For forty-six years Mr. Turner has been leading the band in rousing songs that celebrate and reflect the American spirit. [4] Each Friday night, thousands gather at the Vernon Turner Bandstand and watch Mr. Turner conduct. [5] Mr. Turner has loved music throughout his life. [6] As a college student he studied music, and he eventually became a music teacher in the Pleasantville area. [7] Although Mr. Turner has considered retirement several times, the adoration he receives from band and community members keeps him working.

B. Identifying Verbals and Appositives

On the line before each of the following sentences, identify the italicized word or word group. Write *prep.* for *preposition*, *part.* for *participle*, *ger.* for *gerund*, *inf.* for *infinitive*, or *app.* for *appositive*.

EX. __inf.__ 1. Molly wants *to keep* a journal during the summer.

_____ 1. The *stolen* notebook was never recovered, and so the results of his experiments remain a mystery.

_____ 2. Were you planning *to attend* the junior class play?

_____ 3. Hector described his trip, the *one* that he took to Mexico.

159

_____ 4. *Instead of* taking the bus, let's walk to school today.

_____ 5. Many people associate *knitting* with grandmothers, but my uncle Tim knits sweaters that are works of art.

C.   Writing Sentences with Phrases

On your own paper, write ten sentences, following the directions given below. Underline your phrase in each sentence. If your phrase is a modifier, draw two lines under the word or words it modifies.

EX.   1. Use an adjective phrase to modify the subject of a sentence.
     1. The <u>tree</u> <u>in front of our house</u> is a weeping cherry tree.

1. Use an adjective phrase to modify the object of a preposition.
2. Use an adverb phrase to modify an adjective.
3. Use an adverb phrase to modify a verb.
4. Use a participial phrase to modify a subject.
5. Use a participial phrase to modify a direct object.
6. Use a gerund phrase as the object of a preposition.
7. Use a gerund phrase as a predicate nominative.
8. Use an infinitive phrase as a noun.
9. Use an infinitive phrase as an adjective.
10. Use an appositive phrase beside a direct object.

D.   Working Cooperatively to Create a Cluster

Work with a partner to think of situations that are associated with smiles and frowns. On your own paper, fill in a prewriting cluster for smiles and frowns. Use gerund and prepositional phrases, and include at least one infinitive or infinitive phrase in your cluster.

EX.

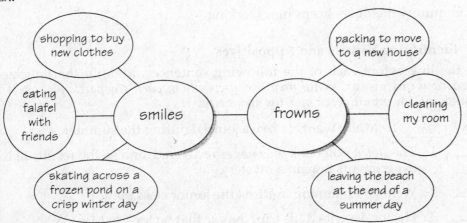

KINDS OF CLAUSES

13a A *clause* is a group of words that contains a verb and its subject and is used as part of a sentence.

13b An *independent* (or *main*) *clause* expresses a complete thought and can stand by itself as a sentence.

EXAMPLES   Elena is studying astronomy.
            She wants to be an astronaut.

Each independent clause has its own subject and verb and expresses a complete thought. These clauses can be joined by a comma and a coordinating conjunction such as *and, but, or, for, so,* or *yet.* They could also be written with a semicolon between them or with a semicolon followed by a conjunctive adverb and a comma.

EXAMPLES   Elena is studying astronomy, and she wants to be an
            astronaut.
            Elena is studying astronomy; she wants to be an astronaut.
            Elena is studying astronomy; indeed, she wants to be an
            astronaut.

13c A *subordinate* (or *dependent*) *clause* does not express a complete thought and cannot stand alone.

A subordinate clause must be joined to at least one independent clause to express a complete thought. Words such as *whom, because, what, if,* and *when* signal the beginning of a subordinate clause.

SUBORDINATE CLAUSES   if the fog lifts
                       when the show begins
                       whom we have met before

SENTENCES   **If the fog lifts**, we can go sailing.
             Did you ask **when the show begins**?
             Sumio, **whom we have met before**, will take us to
             the site.

EXERCISE 1   Identifying Independent and Subordinate Clauses

In the following paragraph, identify each italicized clause. On the line before each sentence, write *indep.* for *independent* or *sub.* for *subordinate.*

EX.   [1] __indep.__ Before 2000 B.C. *there were no post offices for the general public.*

[1] _____ Egypt is most likely *where the first postal system was*

developed. [2] _____ *Postal systems were developed* because ancient

governments needed to relay messages. [3] _____ The central

government could control provincial administration only *if there*

was a system of communication linking the capital and the provinces.

[4] _____ Later postal systems employed relay stations, *which*

would provide fresh horses and riders. [5] _____ *Since this*

idea is so practical, it was probably thought of quite soon.

[6] _____ Evidence *that postal relay stations were used,* however,

is no older than 500 B.C. [7] _____ *The Roman Empire*

needed a postal system because it was so enormous in every regard.

[8] _____ The Roman Empire's postal system was important

enough *that it was preserved by the succeeding Islamic Empire.*

[9] _____ In the Middle Ages, *additional postal routes were set up*

privately so traders could conduct business. [10] _____ *It was*

not until the middle of the sixteenth century A.D. that private persons and

businesses were allowed to use the government's postal system.

[11] _____ *United Parcel Service and Federal Express are*

contemporary versions of these privately run postal systems.

[12] _____ Private citizens' using the postal system was begun

in Europe by the prince Thurn und Taxis, *who ran the Imperial postal*

system of his country. [13] _____ *This practice began the era of the*

postage stamp, which was invented as a way to charge private persons

who sent mail. [14] _____ *Before the stamp was invented,* people

had to pay to receive mail sent to them. [15] _____ Some

people today want to revert to this practice *because they think it would*

cut down on junk mail.

THE ADJECTIVE CLAUSE

13d An *adjective clause* is a subordinate clause that modifies a noun or a pronoun.

An adjective clause follows the word it modifies. If a clause is essential to the meaning of the sentence, it is not set off with commas. If a clause only gives additional information and is nonessential to the meaning of a sentence, it is set off by commas.

EXAMPLES   The pond, **which is a landing place for migrating birds**, lies in a protected area. [The clause *which is a landing place for migrating birds* is not necessary to identify *pond* and is set off by commas.]
Baseball is the sport **that I like best.** [The clause *that I like best* is essential to the meaning of the sentence and, therefore, is not set off by commas.]

Adjective clauses are usually introduced by *relative pronouns*. These words relate an adjective clause to the word that the clause modifies.

Relative Pronouns				
that	which	who	whom	whose

EXAMPLES   Sarah, **who had lived in the Philippines**, still had many friends there. [The relative pronoun *who* relates the adjective clause to *Sarah*. *Who* is the subject of the adjective clause.]
Stephen Hawking is a scientist **whom I greatly admire.** [The relative pronoun *whom* relates the adjective clause to the subject. *Whom* is the direct object of the verb *admire* in the adjective clause.]
The author, **whose new book was published this week,** spoke to our class. [The relative pronoun *whose* relates the adjective clause to *author*. *Whose* is used as a possessive pronoun in the adjective clause.]

In many cases, the relative pronoun in the clause may be omitted.

EXAMPLE   Here is the video **you wanted.** [The relative pronoun *that* is understood. *That* relates the adjective clause to *video* and is the direct object in the adjective clause.]

EXERCISE 2   Identifying Adjective Clauses

Underline the ten adjective clauses in the paragraph below.

EX.   [1] Cesar Chavez, who was born in 1927, helped migrant workers
          improve their lives.

[1] Cesar Chavez, who spent much of his life trying to improve the
lives of migrant farm workers, believed in the power of nonviolent
protests. [2] His parents owned a store, which they lost in the Great
Depression of the 1930s. [3] The Chavez family moved to California
and joined the migrant workers who moved throughout the state,
harvesting crops. [4] Chavez learned firsthand about the miserable
conditions which these people had to endure. [5] He searched for
ideas and methods that would improve the lives of farm laborers.
[6] He organized a boycott of California grapes that spread
throughout the United States. [7] The boycott helped workers win a
contract, which was the first in the history of farm laborers. [8] In
1968, Chavez began a fast that lasted twenty-five days. [9] It was the
first of three times he fasted to protest the low pay and poor working
conditions of the farm laborer. [10] Chavez, who died in 1993, saw
several improvements in farm labor practices in his lifetime.

EXERCISE 3   Revising Sentences by Supplying Adjective Clauses

Revise the following pairs of sentences by substituting an adjective clause
for one of the sentences. Write the revisions on your own paper.

EX.   1. We were lucky to see a minke whale. This whale rarely swims
          into this area.

      1. We were lucky to see a minke whale, which rarely swims into this area.

1. Lian planned the menu for the fund-raiser. The fund-raiser was
    successful.
2. Two reporters moderated the debate. The reporters are well known.
3. Amy and Cheng questioned the results of the experiment. This
    experiment was the first.
4. The hikers agreed to try a less difficult route. The hikers were tired.
5. The audience became restless during the presentation. The
    presentation was long.

THE ADVERB CLAUSE

13e An *adverb clause* is a subordinate clause that modifies a verb, an adjective, or an adverb.

An adverb clause tells *how, when, where, why, how much, to what extent* or *under what condition* the action of the main verb takes place. Adverb clauses are introduced by *subordinating conjunctions*.

Common Subordinating Conjunctions			
after	because	since	when
although	before	so that	whenever
as	even though	than	where
as if	if	though	wherever
as long as	in order that	unless	whether
as soon as	once	until	while

EXAMPLES **After the judge announced her decision,** the attorneys held a press conference. [The adverb clause *after the judge announced her decision* tells *when* the attorneys held a press conference.]
We will go on to the summit **if the good weather holds.** [*If the good weather holds* tells *under what condition* we will go to the summit.]
Because traffic was so heavy, the Parks decided to take a different route. [*Because traffic was so heavy* tells *why* the Parks decided to take a different route.]

NOTE   Introductory adverb clauses are usually set off by commas.

EXAMPLE   If you want to come, call me.

EXERCISE 4   Identifying and Classifying Adverb Clauses

Underline the adverb clause in each of the following sentences. Above each adverb clause, write whether the clause tells *how, when, where, why, how much, to what extent*, or *under what condition*.

EX.   1. We go camping every year before school starts.
when

1. While we were camping in August, we saw a meteor shower.

2. Meteor showers occur when rock or iron particles called meteoroids enter earth's atmosphere from space.

165

3. As these particles enter the earth's atmosphere, they heat up and glow brightly.

4. We call the burning particles "shooting stars" even though they are not really stars.

5. Meteor showers are spectacular because you can see many shooting stars in one night.

6. November is a good month to watch for meteors because the Leonid meteor shower occurs every November.

7. Where space debris is abundant, the showers are more brilliant.

8. Unless you can get away from cities, light pollution makes it hard to see meteors.

9. Once we had driven far enough from the city, we started looking for a campsite.

10. After we viewed the sunset, we watched the sky and saw a fine show.

EXERCISE 5   Building Sentences That Have Adverb Clauses

On your own paper, write ten sentences, using a clause from the list below in each sentence. Do not use the same subordinate clause twice. In each sentence you create, underline the adverb clause once and the word or words it modifies twice. You may combine two of the clauses below or add words of your own.

EX.   some people are always hungry   the lunch bags appear right away

   1. Because some people are always hungry, the lunch bags appear right away.

after we get to the Museum of Science

where our class goes on an outing

before we will allow radios with speakers

as Mr. Henshaw gets off the bus

once Mr. Favaloro starts talking

while someone makes a joke

as if we agree

if Mr. Henshaw acts like a tour guide

unless we ban radios with speakers

in order that we eat lunch

wherever no one can hear

because we left the parking lot

since some people are always hungry

until we can agree on music

as long as we meet at the cafeteria

whenever we see a video of an animal

so that the bus can leave at nine o'clock

as soon as we eat lunch

although Mr. Favaloro laughs hardest

when we scatter through the museum

THE NOUN CLAUSE

13f A *noun clause* is a subordinate clause used as a noun.

A noun clause may be used as a subject, a complement (predicate nominative, direct object, indirect object), or the object of a preposition.

SUBJECT	**What I liked best about my trip to Mexico** was seeing the Aztec ruins.
PREDICATE NOMINATIVE	The loser is **whoever has the final piece to the puzzle.**
DIRECT OBJECT	We thought we knew **what Kwam's gift would be.**
INDIRECT OBJECT	The chef will tell **whoever asks** the recipe for her specialty.
OBJECT OF A PREPOSITION	She carefully checked the applications of **whoever applied for the job.**

Noun clauses are usually introduced by *that, what, whatever, who, whoever, whom,* and *whomeve*r. Sometimes, however, noun clauses do not have an introductory word.

EXAMPLE   Joey wished he could join the group. [The introductory word *that* is understood.]

EXERCISE 6 Identifying and Classifying Noun Clauses

Underline each noun clause in the following paragraph. Above it, identify how it is used. Write *s.* for *subject*, *p.n.* for *predicate nominative*, *d.o.* for *direct object*, *i.o.* for *indirect object*, or *o.p.* for *object of a preposition*.

EX.   [1] My sister always said <u>that she did not like animals</u>.
                                                     d. o.

[1] What changed her mind was her discovering a baby opossum in our backyard. [2] She realized that it was too tiny to survive on its own. [3] She didn't know what to do with it or who could help her. [4] That our town had a wildlife rescue center proved to be the answer to her problem. [5] My sister carefully wrapped the baby opossum in whatever soft rags were at hand and took it to the center.

167

[6] The director told her the center would care for the opossum until it was old enough to return to the wild. [7] My sister asked whoever was free many questions. [8] Now she is a volunteer at the center, helping in whatever way she can. [9] A veterinarian is what she wants to be. [10] Whatever animals she treats will be in good hands.

EXERCISE 7   Writing Sentences by Inserting Noun Clauses

On your own paper, add noun clauses to the sentences below. Then label the function of the noun clause in each sentence.

EX.   1.   Eliza told me   <u>that Ramón is going to the carnival tonight. (d.o.)</u>
(Use *that*)

1. _____
   _____ is a sad fact. (Use *that*.)

2. _____
   _____ had better tell me. (Use *whoever*.)

3. _____
   _____ is a good vacation. (Use *what*.)

4. Did you know _____
   _____? (Use *that*.)

5. Mom always gives _____
   _____a reward. (Use *whoever*.)

6. The teacher limited test items to _____
   _____ . (Use *whatever*.)

7. _____
   _____will probably always be a mystery to me. (Use *where*.)

8. The best answer is _____
   _____ . (Use *whatever*.)

9. Was your question _____
   _____? (Use *how*.)

10. We all wanted to know _____
    _____ . (Use *who*.)

SENTENCE STRUCTURE

13g **According to their structure, sentences are classified as** *simple,* *compound, complex,* **and** *compound-complex.*

(1) A *simple sentence* **has one independent clause and no subordinate clauses. It may have a compound subject, a compound verb, and any number of phrases.**

EXAMPLE   After studying Russia and listening to their grandmother's stories, Tanya and Alexis decided to prepare a Russian meal for their friends.

(2) A *compound sentence* **has two or more independent clauses but no subordinate clauses.**

In effect, a compound sentence consists of two or more simple sentences joined by a comma and a coordinating conjunction, by a semicolon, or by a semicolon followed by a conjunctive adverb and a comma.

EXAMPLES   They had eaten many of their grandmother's Russian specialties**, but** they had never prepared them.
They had eaten many of their grandmother's Russian specialties**, but** they had never prepared them.
Tanya's favorite was piroshki**;** Alexis liked dumplings, latkes, and blini.
They had watched their grandmother prepare these dishes**; consequently,** they knew it was a lot of work.

(3) A *complex sentence* **has one independent clause and at least one subordinate clause.**

EXAMPLES   Tanya suggested that they also serve a soup, a salad, and Russian tea.
When they told their grandmother about their plans, she offered to help.

(4) A *compound-complex sentence* **contains two or more independent clauses and at least one subordinate clause.**

EXAMPLES   Tanya and Alexis wanted to invite everyone who was interested in their plans, and so they had a long guest list.
Before the party began, the two had spent many hours cooking, and so had their grandmother, who said the feast was first-rate.

EXERCISE 8   Classifying Sentences According to Structure

Classify each sentence in the paragraph below. On the line before each sentence, write *simp.* for *simple,* *comp.* for *compound,* *cx.* for *complex,* and *cd.-cx.* for *compound-complex.*

EX. _____cx._____ [1] Machu Picchu, which is located on a mountaintop in Peru, was the capital city for the Incas a thousand years ago.

_____ [1] Built on a peak in the Andes and overlooking a deep canyon, the ancient city contains the ruins of four hundred houses, as well as temples, plazas, and palaces. _____ [2] It was constructed of granite blocks; how the Incas, who had only simple tools, transported this stone up the steep mountain remains a puzzle. _____ [3] A Peruvian legend says that the ancient Incas were helped by angel architects who made the granite fall off cliffs and fly to the building site. _____ [4] Some modern engineers believe this explanation as much as any other! _____ [5] Incas lived in Machu Picchu until the population outgrew the food supply; then they moved the capital to Cuzco, which is on the western slope of the Andes. _____ [6] Machu Picchu was no longer inhabited, but perhaps it was not entirely forgotten. _____ [7] The Spaniards came to Peru hundreds of years after Machu Picchu was abandoned. _____ [8] The Spaniards, who were searching for gold, attempted to seize a convent where Inca women devoted their lives to the service of the Sun God.

_____ [9] They found the convent empty; the women had vanished.

_____ [10] Many Incas believed that the Sun God lifted the women into the sky; but after explorers discovered Machu Picchu in 1911, some people came to believe that the women took refuge there.

CHAPTER REVIEW

A. Classifying Subordinate Clauses

Classify each italicized clause in the paragraph below. Write *adj.* for *adjective*, *adv.* for *adverb*, or *n.* for *noun* above the clause.

EX. [1] *Although rock climbing looks difficult*, it is a sport [2] *that nearly everyone can try*.

                   adv.   adj.

The variety of the sport is [1] *what makes it open to anyone* [2] *who is interested*. Rock climbing can be climbing [3] *in which the climber stays close to the ground without a rope or special gear*, or it can be big wall-climbing, a feat [4] *that requires much more training*. [5] *Although physical strength and coordination are useful*, expert climbers say [6] *that these are not all there is to climbing*. Determination and courage are also qualities [7] *that a climber must have*. [8] *What you need first of all* is an experienced teacher [9] *with whom you can climb*. [10] *After you have followed an expert up enough rocks*, you may be ready to lead a climb yourself.

B. Identifying and Classifying Clauses

In the following sentences, underline the subordinate clauses. On the line before each sentence, identify the way each clause is used. Write *s.* for *subject*, *d.o.* for *direct object*, *i.o.* for *indirect object*, *p.n.* for *predicate nominative*, *o.p.* for *object of a preposition*, *adj.* for *adjective*, or *adv.* for *adverb*. [Note: Some sentences have more than one clause.]

EX. <u>adv.</u> 1. <u>When Maryssa gave a report on frogs</u>, the class was fascinated.

_____ 1. I had always thought that frogs were boring.

_____ 2. What Maryssa described showed that she had done a lot of research.

_____ 3. She said that West Africa is home to the world's largest frog, which can grow to a length of three feet.

_____ 4. The smallest known frog is found in Cuba and is only one-half inch long when it is fully grown.

_____ 5. If a person could jump proportionately as far as one small North American frog, the world's long-jump record would be 215 feet.

_____ 6. Because eggs are easy prey, some frogs have developed interesting strategies for protecting their eggs.

_____ 7. It is the male parent of the Darwin's frog in South Africa who guards the eggs.

_____ 8. When the eggs show signs of life, the male frog swallows five to fifteen of them and holds them in his croaking sac until they hatch.

_____ 9. Maryssa also described a male frog who guards newly laid eggs by carrying them wound around his leg.

_____ 10. My favorite story was about the helmet frog, who uses its bony head as a door for its home inside a tree.

C.   Rewriting a Paragraph to Include a Variety of Sentence Structures

After researching a topic for an essay, you have jotted down the draft of the paragraph below. On your own paper, rewrite the paragraph to improve its style. You will need to vary the sentence structure, and you may want to delete, reword, or add details. Write at least one sentence with each kind of structure: simple, compound, complex, and compound-complex. Be ready to identify the structure of each sentence you write.

1   Dr. Maria Montessori was a pioneer in the field of education.
2   She was also the first woman in Italy to attend medical school. She
3   was born in Italy in 1870. That year Italy became a nation. As a
4   teenager she was interested in mathematics. Her parents suggested
5   she become a teacher. This was practically the only career open to
6   women at that time. She decided that she wanted to attend medical
7   school. She was told this was impossible. She persisted and won
8   entrance to medical school. She even won scholarships. As the only
9   female student, she endured great hardships in medical school. She
10 graduated in 1896. After graduation, she worked at a psychiatric
11 clinic. She became interested in children with learning problems.
12 She came to believe that with the proper education, their lives
13 could improve. She became director of a school for children who
14 were considered hopeless. The progress of the children in her
15 school surprised everyone. She went on to develop theories of
16 education for all children. The equipment she designed for
17 teaching and her ideas about how young children learn are used
18 now in Montessori schools all over the world.

SUBJECT-VERB AGREEMENT

> *Number* is the form of a word that indicates whether the word is singular or plural.
>
> **14a** **When a word refers to one person or thing, it is *singular* in number. When a word refers to more than one, it is *plural* in number.**
>
> | SINGULAR | plumber | mouse | I | chopstick |
> |---|---|---|---|---|
> | PLURAL | plumbers | mice | we | chopsticks |

Classifying Nouns and Pronouns by Number

In the sentences below, identify each italicized word by writing *sing.* for *singular* or *pl.* for *plural* above the word.

EX. 1. The tiny *peaches* were carved from a *piece* of green jade.

1. Cleon said that Irene and *he* can rehearse their *scenes* later.

2. When the ball came flying toward the plate, *Vincente* swung the bat with all *his* strength.

3. The political *cartoons* are usually on the editorial *page*.

4. Florence Griffith Joyner has certainly won a lot of *medals* and *awards* in track-and-field events!

5. An auto *mechanic* can adjust your *brakes* easily.

6. The new stained-glass *windows* replaced the *ones* that had been damaged during the hailstorm.

7. Each person in the *class* created colorful *drawings* of people or animals.

8. An antique silk *kimono* was displayed in a glass *case*.

9. The driver asked *us* if *we* wanted to stop at Monticello.

10. Corey is teaching his twin *sisters* how to ride *their* bikes.

14b A verb should always agree with its subject in number.

(1) Singular subjects take singular verbs.

EXAMPLE   **Julie kicks** the ball to me. [The singular verb *kicks* agrees with the singular subject *Julie*.]

(2) Plural subjects take plural verbs.

EXAMPLE   The **players run** toward the goal. [The plural verb *run* agrees with the plural subject *players*.]

Like single-word verbs, verb phrases also agree with their subjects. However, in a verb phrase, only the first helping (auxiliary) verb changes its form to agree with the subject.

EXAMPLES   **Maribeth has** been working on my campaign.
             Maribeth and **Eula have** been working on my campaign.

EXERCISE 2   Identifying Verbs That Agree in Number with Their Subjects

For each sentence below, underline the verb in parentheses that agrees with the subject.

EX.   1. First, the pilot (*checks*, *check*) the controls.

1. (*Has, Have*) you ever seen Alvin Ailey's ballet?

2. The Pachecos all (*laughs, laugh*) at the same jokes.

3. These folk tales (*is, are*) about how the world began.

4. First, the students (*picks, pick*) up their pencils.

5. Mama (*has, have*) made sopapillas for dessert.

6. Several trains (*runs, run*) on that track.

7. My youngest cousin (*spins, spin*) the dreidel first.

8. The Indian monetary system (*is, are*) based on the rupee, not the dollar.

9. The two boys (*collects, collect*) baseball cards.

10. Since July, Lorenz (*has, have*) painted four pictures.

11. Bradley (*earns, earn*) his blue belt in tae kwon do this year.

12. Dexter and Paul (*enjoys, enjoy*) our school carnivals.

13. The band from Mexico City (*plays, play*) for us frequently.

14. The Herb Show (*has, have*) many interesting booths.

15. Next week, business leaders (*is, are*) hosting a job fair.

INTERVENING PHRASES

14c The number of the subject is not changed by a phrase following the subject.

Remember that a verb agrees in number with its subject. The subject is never part of a prepositional phrase.

EXAMPLES That **curtain** behind the actors **is** new. [The verb *is* agrees with the subject *curtain*.]
The **books** on that shelf **are** dictionaries. [The verb *are* agrees with the subject *books*.]

Compound prepositions such as *together with, in addition to, as well as,* and *along with* following the subject do not affect the number of the subject.

EXAMPLES **Leona**, as well as her parents, **is** visiting us.
The **lettuce**, in addition to the tomatoes, **has** been washed.

EXERCISE 3 Identifying Subjects and Verbs That Agree in Number

In each of the following sentences, underline the verb form that agrees with the subject. Then underline the subject twice.

EX. 1. Several cars in the parking lot (*needs*, *need*) washing.

1. A pattern of changing colors (*appears*, *appear*) on the screen when the computer is not in use.

2. The people from our town (*is*, *are*) celebrating Nisei Week.

3. The actor, in addition to the producers, (*calls*, *call*) the daily meetings.

4. The pedestrians in this city (*hears*, *hear*) the muezzin every day.

5. Two students, together with their teacher, (*is*, *are*) collecting blankets for flood victims.

6. The signature below the printed name (*was*, *were*) difficult to read.

7. Ben, as well as Aunt Elaine, (*makes*, *make*) good couscous.

8. The keys on this keyboard (*feels*, *feel*) sticky.

9. A huge bouquet of flowers (*was*, *were*) delivered to my mother.

10. The twins, together with Duane, (*is*, *are*) taking the bus.

11. Roberto Garcia, Jr., a bronze sculptor who lives south of Kingsville, Texas, (*has, have*) an unusual job.

12. All the work on a bronze sculpture (*is, are*) done by Garcia, himself.

13. Bronze, wax, and clay, along with steel, (*is, are*) materials he works with every day.

14. Two clay statues outside his garage (*guards, guard*) his workshop.

15. Sketches, as well as small models, (*makes, make*) up the first step of a new bronze sculpture.

16. A full-size structure of steel and clay (*goes, go*) together next.

17. Mr. Garcia's kiln, at temperatures of about fifteen hundred degrees Farenheit, (*melts, melt*) the wax in a mold.

18. The wax between the mold's layers (*drains, drain*) out.

19. Bronze for the statue (*is, are*) poured into the gap left by the drained wax.

20. Welding, along with sandblasting and grinding, almost (*finishes, finish*) the process.

EXERCISE 4   Proofreading a Paragraph for Subject-Verb Agreement

In the paragraph below, draw a line through each verb that does not agree with its subject. Write the correct verb form in the space above the incorrect word.

EX.   [1] A student in my biology class ~~have~~ an interesting terrarium.
(above "have": has)

[1] A fish tank, a gift from Pedro's parents, are the container.

[2] The plants in it is mostly nonflowering. [3] The moss, as well as the lichens, have spores, not flowers. [4] The mosses near the front comes from the woods near the school. [5] The lichens on the rock is about five years old, according to my biology teacher. [6] The bright red tips on the lichen is partly fungus. [7] One name for the lichens are "British soldiers." [8] In addition to mosses and lichens, a fern thrive in the terrarium. [9] Our teacher, along with us students, want to start a class terrarium. [10] Some students in the class knows where to get a fish tank and some plants.

AGREEMENT WITH INDEFINITE PRONOUNS

Indefinite pronouns are pronouns that do not refer to a specific person or thing.

14d The following pronouns are singular: *each, either, neither, one, everyone, everybody, no one, nobody, anyone, anybody, someone, somebody.*

EXAMPLES   **Neither** of the books **is** difficult. [Neither one is difficult.]
Someone does have the key.

14e The following pronouns are plural: *several, few, both, many.*

EXAMPLES   **Several** of the books **are** easy.   **Both have** keys to the house.

14f The pronouns *some, all, most, any,* **and** *none* **may be either singular or plural.**

These pronouns are singular when they refer to a singular word and plural when they refer to a plural word.

SINGULAR   **All** of the report **is** factual.
Most of the lawn **has** been raked.
PLURAL   **All** of the facts **are** true.
Most of the leaves **have** been raked.

The words *any* and *none* may be singular even when they refer to a plural word if the speaker is thinking of each item individually. *Any* and *none* are plural only if the speaker is thinking of several items as a group.

EXAMPLES   **None** of the windows **was** broken. [*Not one window* **was** broken.]
None of the windows **were** large. [*No windows* **were** large.]
Is any of the windows open? [*Is any one window* open?]
Any of the windows **are** good places for a plant. [*All the windows* are good places for a plant.]

EXERCISE 5   Using Indefinite Pronouns Correctly

On your own paper, use each of the following word groups as a subject in a sentence. Underline the subjects once and the verbs twice in your sentences.

EX.   1. Most of my homework
    1. <u>Most</u> of my homework <u>is finished</u>.

1. Several of my friends   3. Everybody in the room

2. Both Nikki and Emilio   4. Someone from school

5. Neither of the movies	13. Some of Mr. Dodd's pecans
6. Somebody upstairs	14. Most of the movies
7. All of the guitars	15. Any of the ribbons
8. Everyone at the meeting	16. No one from our office
9. Many of the puppets	17. None of the bread
10. Each fish in the tank	18. Most of her progress
11. None of the streams	19. Nobody within the class
12. Few among the volunteers	20. Any of the softball games

EXERCISE 6   Proofreading a Paragraph for Subject-Verb Agreement

Draw a line through each verb that does not agree with its subject. Write the correct verb form in the space above the incorrect word. Some sentences may contain no agreement errors.

EX. [1] One of my term papers ~~are~~ ^{is} on Hausa proverbs from the people of northern Nigeria and the Sudan.

[1] All of the proverbs I found makes me really think. [2] Neither of these two proverbs are easy to understand: "It is not the eye which understands, but the mind" and "Lack of knowledge is darker than the night." [3] Both proverbs gives insight into how people think. [4] Some proverbs reflects the Hausa way of life. [5] "A chief is like a trash heap where everyone brings his or her rubbish" seems to show us that the Hausa bring their problems to their leader. [6] Someone like that chief have to be very patient, I think. [7] Several proverbs contains words I had to look up in a dictionary. [8] Most of the unfamiliar words are natural objects, such as cowries and groundnuts. [9] No one I know have clearly explained the proverb "It is by traveling softly, softly that you will sleep in a distant place." [10] One of my teachers have suggested that I also read the proverbs of the Ashanti, one of the native peoples of West Africa.

THE COMPOUND SUBJECT

A *compound subject* has two or more nouns or pronouns that are the subject of the same verb.

14g Subjects joined by *and* usually take a plural verb.

EXAMPLES **Cao** and **I are** building the model together. [Two people are building the model.]

Light, warmth, and **water act** together. [Three things act together.]

14h Compound subjects that name only one person or thing take a singular verb.

EXAMPLE **Red beans** and **rice is** inexpensive and healthful. [*Red beans* and *rice* is one dish.]

14i Singular subjects joined by *or* or *nor* take a singular verb.

EXAMPLES **Either Grandfather** or **Julie has** the scissors. [Only one person has the scissors, not both.]

Neither fog nor **rain stops** this train! [Neither one stops the train.]

14j When a singular subject and a plural subject are joined by *or* or *nor*, the verb agrees with the subject nearer the verb.

ACCEPTABLE Either the peaches or the **watermelon is** fine for dessert.
Either the watermelon or the **peaches are** fine for dessert.

BETTER The **peaches are** fine for dessert, and so **is** the **watermelon.**
The **watermelon is** fine for dessert, and the **peaches are**, too.

You can usually avoid such awkward constructions by rewording the sentence so that each subject has its own verb.

EXAMPLE Either **Darren is** bringing the children to the ceremony, or his mother and **father are.**

EXERCISE 7   Choosing Verbs That Agree in Number with Their Subjects

In each of the following sentences, underline the correct form of the verb in parentheses.

EX.   1. Charles and Pang (*is, are*) on the team.

1. Either the tuba or the saxophones (*plays, play*) first.

2. Neither my mother nor my father (*is, are*) eager to go.

3. Either Yori or Sheila (*has, have*) extra flyers.

4. Macaroni and cheese (*is, are*) our favorite food.

5. The audience and the actors (*likes, like*) that play.

6. David Ben-Gurion and Golda Meir (*was, were*) prime ministers of Israel.

7. Either Jun or Asa (*has, have*) time to saw the boards.

8. Blocks and a drum (*is, are*) all a two-year-old child needs for entertainment.

9. Neither pencil and paper nor a calculator (*was, were*) available.

10. Rock-and-roll always (*catches, catch*) my sister's attention.

11. Jordan's sketch and Meg's painting (*was, were*) finished.

12. My brother and sister never (*enjoys, enjoy*) arguing.

13. Tents, backpacks, and food (*has, have*) been packed.

14. Neither the pharmacy nor the front desk (*is, are*) answering.

15. (*Was, Were*) chicken and dumplings on the menu today?

16. Both salsa and gazpacho (*requires, require*) tomatoes as ingredients.

17. Patricia, Susan, and Guy (*works, work*) well together.

18. Scissors and paper (*does, do*) need to be on the list.

19. Paula, her brothers, and her sister (*wishes, wish*) to help Mrs. Landowski.

20. Either Mrs. Columbo or Mr. Andrews (*is, are*) able to help them, too.

21. Pencil or pens (*writes, write*) equally well on this type of paper.

22. Bonnie and Rolando (*has, have*) agreed to run for office.

23. How soon (*is, are*) Etta and Albert leaving on vacation?

24. Mark and Coretta (*watches, watch*) the runners carefully.

25. (*Does, Do*) Erica or Han-Ling cast the last vote?

DOESN'T / DON'T *AND COLLECTIVE NOUNS*

14k *Don't* and *doesn't* **must agree with their subjects.**

Contractions are two words combined into one, with one or more letters omitted. *Don't* is the contraction for *do not*. *Doesn't* is the contraction for *does not*.

With the subjects *I* and *you* and with plural subjects, use *don't* (*do not*).

EXAMPLES   I **don't** see anything.   They **don't** care.
You **don't** need one.   Sales **don't** last long.

With other singular subjects, use the singular *doesn't* (*does not*).

EXAMPLES   He **doesn't** work here.   The sweater **doesn't** fit.
This **doesn't** look hard.   Lily **doesn't** feel sick.

14l **Collective nouns may be either singular or plural.**

Collective nouns are singular in form, but they name a *group* of persons or things.

Collective Nouns		
army	committee	herd
assembly	family	jury
audience	fleet	public
class	flock	swarm
club	group	team

Use a plural verb with a collective noun when you refer to the individual parts or members of the group acting separately. Use a singular verb when you refer to the group acting together as a unit.

EXAMPLES   The **jury have** not been home yet. [*Jury* is thought of as individuals.]
The **jury has** finally reached a verdict. [*Jury* is thought of as a unit.]

EXERCISE 8   Using *Doesn't* and *Don't* Correctly

Use *doesn't* or *don't* correctly to complete each sentence below.

EX.   1. I ___don't___ need help with this.

1. We _____ serve any Moroccan food here.

2. _____ you serve couscous?

3. Well, our dish _____ contain meat.

4. You _____ need to use lamb, but it adds good flavor.

5. These recipes _____ require a special steamer.

6. The supermarket _____ sell lamb broth.

7. _____ Jolon need more chickpeas?

8. The vegetables _____ need a separate bowl.

9. It _____ look hard to make.

10. _____ this taste delicious!

11. Some newspapers _____ have many recipes like this.

12. _____ you grow some of these vegetables?

13. Herbs _____ seem to be difficult to grow.

14. Preparing the garden _____ take long.

15. _____ overwater the herbs and vegetables.

EXERCISE 9   Writing Sentences with Collective Nouns

Select five collective nouns from the chart on the preceding page. On your own paper, write a pair of sentences using each noun. Each pair of sentences should show how the collective noun may be either singular or plural.

EX.   1. The swarm is huge!
      1. The swarm are flying in different directions.

OTHER PROBLEMS IN AGREEMENT

14m **A verb agrees with its subject, not with its predicate nominative.**

              S   V   P.N.

EXAMPLES   The **prize is** two concert tickets.

                            S   V   P.N.

                Two concert **tickets are** the prize.

14n **When the subject follows the verb, find the subject and make sure that the verb agrees with it.**

The most common cases in which the subject follows the verb are in questions and in sentences beginning with *here* or *there*.

EXAMPLES   Here **is** a **menorah**.
                Here **are** some **candles**.

                There **is** a new **student** in class.
                There **are** new **students** in class.

                Does the **map** show this road?
                Do these **roads** appear on the map?

14o **Words stating an amount are usually singular.**

EXAMPLES   **Six dollars is** a lot for that.
                Your **five minutes is** up.

Sometimes, however, the amount is thought of as individual pieces or parts. If so, a plural verb is used.

EXAMPLES   **Two** of the dollars **are** silver dollars.
                Three fourths of the pencils **are** sharpened.

14p *Every* or *many a* before a subject calls for a singular verb.

EXAMPLES   **Every** shelf **has** a kachina doll on it.
                Many a doll **was** made of cottonwood root.

14q **A few nouns, although plural in form, take singular verbs.**

EXAMPLES   The **news is** grim this week.
                Unfortunately, **measles is** showing up in young adults.

NOTE   Some nouns that end in –*s* take a plural verb even though they refer to a single item.

        EXAMPLES   The **scissors are** on the table.
                    Your **pants are** clean.

EXERCISE 10   Identifying Subjects and Verbs That Agree in Number

In each sentence below, underline the verb form that agrees with the subject. Then underline the subject twice.

EX.   1. A relay team (*is*, *are*) three people.

1. Eight miles (*is*, *are*) a long race.
2. Two different prizes (*was*, *were*) given at the party.
3. Many a trophy (*has*, *have*) been won by that team!
4. Politics (*determines*, *determine*) the choice of team captain.
5. (*Does*, *Do*) Ulani have the same coach?
6. The winner (*is*, *are*) the first-year runners.
7. There (*is*, *are*) professional recruiters in the bleachers today.
8. Every race (*has*, *have*) a clear favorite.
9. Here (*is*, *are*) the name of the best runner.
10. Many unknown runners (*has*, *have*) won the steeplechase.
11. (*Does*, *Do*) Gisela have a good chance of winning in the next race?
12. Where (*is*, *are*) your friend Rudy now?
13. That relay team always (*goes*, *go*) on to the regional meet.
14. Every heat (*has*, *have*) six runners in it.
15. The shorts with green and while stripes (*is*, *are*) Emilio's.
16. Why (*does*, *do*) Caron and Aponte always get here early?
17. Twenty minutes (*has*, *have*) passed since the starting gun went off.
18. Five kilometers (*is*, *are*) the distance of the cross-country race.
19. Three of those kilometers (*leads*, *lead*) up steep hills.
20. Tonight the news (*covers*, *cover*) some of the races.
21. Here (*is*, *are*) the books you were looking for.
22. Few varieties of oak tree (*grows*, *grow*) in our state.
23. (*Hasn't*, *Haven't*) Andrés passed his driving test?
24. Gayle's trousers (*is*, *are*) a dark shade of green.
25. There (*is*, *are*) a new family on our block.

REVIEW EXERCISE

A. Choosing Verbs That Agree in Number with Their Subjects

In each of the sentences below, underline the correct form of the verb in parentheses.

EX. 1. The men in the picture (*is, are*) artists.

1. Each (*has, have*) a brush, some black ink, and a sheet of paper.

2. (*Does, Do*) your sister use a camel's hair brush?

3. The audience (*likes, like*) the bamboo with the drooping leaves.

4. Many in the room (*enjoys, enjoy*) painting.

5. (*Does, Do*) the artists often make their own inks?

6. The ink, the brush, and the silk (*affects, affect*) the finish of a painting done on silk.

7. Either Mr. Tsai or his teacher (*is, are*) demonstrating different kinds of brush strokes.

8. Where (*is, are*) the scrolls that contain all the writing?

9. Neither the words nor the drawing (*is, are*) red.

10. Forty dollars (*seems, seem*) reasonable to me.

11. You (*wasn't, weren't*) home when we telephoned.

12. One of the articles (*is, are*) about N. Scott Momaday.

13. We (*was, were*) talking about these machines in French class.

14. Nobody in these stores (*sells, sell*) my kind of shoe.

15. (*Does, Do*) apples and oranges come in the next shipment?

16. Each of the contestants (*seems, seem*) pleased with the judges' final decision.

17. Theo, Jerry, and Ed (*wants, want*) to work for you.

18. Jeanine and her parents (*gets, get*) all of the mail.

19. Either Gloria or Sandra (*has, have*) a watch with a second hand.

20. The effects of the long dry spell (*was, were*) deadly for crops and cattle.

B. Proofreading a Paragraph for Subject-Verb Agreement

In the sentences below, draw a line through each verb that does not agree with its subject. Write the correct verb form in the space above the incorrect word. Some sentences have no errors in subject-verb agreement.

EX. [1] One of my cousins ~~are~~ *is* a great collector.

[1] The news are full of stories about lucky breaks. [2] You might read about how somebody find a rare book in an attic. [3] Few of these stories is completely true. [4] Still, my cousin and I like to hear them. [5] We has spent many weekends going to yard sales. [6] There is often collections of baseball cards for sale. [7] These sales offers a great opportunity for collectors. [8] People often don't know which cards are special. [9] Several of the older cards has greater value today than ever before. [10] The cards in my collection was made before 1960.

C. Writing Trivia Questions

Your job as a copywriter is to write questions for a television trivia game show. Your category for the next program is the Olympics. Use reference books, magazines, or encyclopedias to learn some details about the Olympics. Then, on your own paper, create fifteen questions from your notes. Underline the subjects once and the verbs twice in your questions, and make sure they agree.

EX.   Notes: games held in Olympia, Greece, every four years between 776 B.C. and A.D. 393

Question: Where were the first games held?

PRONOUN-ANTECEDENT AGREEMENT

A pronoun usually refers to a noun or another pronoun that comes before it. The word that a pronoun refers to is called its *antecedent.*

14r   A pronoun should agree with its antecedent in number and gender.

Some singular personal pronouns have forms that indicate the gender of the antecedent. Masculine pronouns (*he, him, his*) refer to males. Feminine pronouns (*she, her, hers*) refer to females. Neuter pronouns (*it, its*) refer to things that are neither male nor female, and often to animals.

EXAMPLES   **Sean** took **his** calculator with **him.**
Mrs. Torres said that **she** would share **her** lunch.
The **trunk** is missing **its** key.

The gender of other pronouns is determined by the phrase that follows the pronoun.

EXAMPLES   **Neither** of the **women** forgot **her** lines.[*Women*, in the phrase that follows *Neither*, determines the pronoun's gender.]
One **person** left **her** or **his** scarf. [*Person* could be either masculine or feminine.]

(1) Use a singular pronoun to refer to *each, either, neither, one, everyone, everybody, no one, nobody, anyone, anybody, someone,* **or** *somebody.*

EXAMPLES   **Each** cast **his** or **her** vote.
One of the striped socks lost **its** mate.

(2) Use a singluar pronoun to refer to two or more singular antecedents joined by *or* **or** *nor.*

EXAMPLES   Either **Lucia** or **Marna** will explain **her** experiment.
Neither my **father** nor **Rudy** brought **his** camera.

(3) Two or more antecedents joined by *and* **should be referred to by a plural pronoun.**

EXAMPLES   **Lionel** and **Laura** were proud of **their** son.
Mr. Tower, **Todd**, and **I** will do **our** best.

EXERCISE 11   Identifying Antecedents and Writing Pronouns

On the line in each sentence below, write a pronoun that agrees with its antecedent. Underline the antecedent.

EX.   1. Mr. Sharp offered ___his___ opinion.

1. No one in the party had forgotten _____ ticket.

2. For many people, this trip to the jungle was _____ first.

3. Flora always carried _____ camera.

4. The train stopped four times on _____ way to the plantation.

5. Neither my sister nor Hazel needed _____ snacks.

6. At the many stops, local people sold _____ goods.

7. One person left _____ hat on the seat.

8. Toshiro and Greg struggled to get _____ seats by the window.

9. The banana plantation ships much of _____ fruit to other countries.

10. One of the men brought _____ puppy on the train.

11. Tara took _____ lamb to the county fair.

12. Our town had _____ centennial celebration last week.

13. Renaldo and Kazuo always go to _____ gymnastic classes.

14. Either Nora or Rosa will invite _____ mother to the open house.

15. Both of the boys went to _____ extra practices to prepare for the Olympic trials.

16. The new motor scooter received _____ first dent.

17. Nobody in our family forgets to wear _____ seat belt when riding in the car.

18. The truck and bicycle had mud all over _____ wheels.

19. Wendy decided that _____ could meet us after all.

20. Did Dr. Bryan agree that she should make _____ speech for our health class?

CHAPTER REVIEW

A. Proofreading Sentences for Subject-Verb and Pronoun-Antecedent Agreement

For each error in agreement in the following sentences, draw a line through the incorrect word, and write the correct form above it. If the sentence is correct, write C.

EX. _____ 1. Politics ~~are~~ *is* not as interesting as science.

_____ 1. Where are your report on meteorites?

_____ 2. The students in the front row hears Ms. Swift better than I do.

_____ 3. Somebody in my class forgot to write their name on a paper.

_____ 4. The chart is actually several different photographs put together.

_____ 5. Neither Nancy nor Yolanda want to give their report.

_____ 6. Every comet were seen as an omen of things to come.

_____ 7. Few of my classmates has ever seen an aerial photograph of our city.

_____ 8. Fifteen minutes are a long time to talk!

_____ 9. Do each of the boys want some of this salad?

_____ 10. Each of the women presented their findings separately.

_____ 11. Lori and Yoko, besides arriving early, has brought our dessert.

_____ 12. Many of us agree that Robert Frost is one of America's greatest poets.

_____ 13. Several of my classmates is going to the amusement park today.

_____ 14. Have any of the group members brought the paper and paint for the banners?

_____ 15. Some of the father's answers to his son's questions is funny.

_____ 16. Room and board is included in the summer camp fee.

_____ 17. The garden don't take as much work as I thought it would.

_____ 18. Which questions on the test is hardest for you?

_____ 19. At noon, the posse are leaving to begin the search.

_____ 20. There is twenty students in my Chemistry I class.

B. Proofreading a Paragraph for Subject-Verb and Pronoun-Antecedent Agreement

In the paragraph below, draw a line through each incorrect verb or pronoun. Write the correct form in the space above the incorrect word. Some sentences have no errors in agreement.

EX. [1] There *is* many people in my family.
        are

    [1] My entire family visit Nara every summer. [2] Everybody look forward to this trip. [3] My father and grandfather always plays *Go* for one evening. [4] Neither my mother nor my grandmother enjoy the game. [5] She both prefer to walk though the streets of Nara. [6] During the day we all likes to wander in the park. [7] Each of us has their favorite part of the park. [8] Grandfather and Grandmother always spends an hour or two at the statue of Buddha. [9] The most interesting part for me are all the people from many nations. [10] Everyone in the family tries to guess a person's home country.

C. Writing a Letter to a Pen Pal

After waiting many months, you have finally learned the name and address of your new pen pal. On your own paper, make notes about things you might want this person to know about you. You might tell about your family, your birthday, your age, and what grade you are in. Your new friend might like to know your favorite food, movie, sport, color, or holiday. Use your notes to write ten sentences in a letter to introduce yourself to your pen pal. Be sure to put your address in your letter so your new friend will know where to mail his or her answer. In your sentences, check that your verbs agree with their subjects and that your pronouns agree with their antecedents.

EX.

                                    Mara Aboud
                                    157 Middle St.
                                    Grants Pass, OR 97526

    Dear Lani,
    My name is Mara, and I'd like to be your new pen pal. I'll tell you about myself.

REGULAR VERBS

15a The four principal parts of a verb are the *base form*, the *present participle*, the *past*, and the *past participle*.

EXAMPLES   We **walk** to school. [base form of *walk*]
We are **walking** home. [present participle of *walk*]
We **walked** to the store. [past of *walk*]
We have **walked** for hours. [past participle of *walk*]

Notice that the tenses made from the present participle and past participle use helping verbs, such as *am, is, are, has,* and *have*.

15b A *regular verb* is a verb that forms its past and past participle by adding *–d* or *–ed* to the base form.

Base Form	Present Participle	Past	Past Participle
happen	(is) happening	happened	(have) happened
create	(is) creating	created	(have) created
carry	(is) carrying	carried	(have) carried

The present participle of most regular verbs ending in *–e* drops the *–e* before adding *–ing*.

 NOTE   A few regular verbs have an alternate past form ending in *–t*. For example, the past form of *burn* is *burned* or *burnt*.

EXERCISE 1   Writing the Correct Forms of Regular Verbs

For each of the following sentences, decide what the correct form of the italicized verb should be. Write the correct verb form on the line in the sentence.

EX.   1. Last night's train (*arrive*) _____arrived_____ on time.

1. Ashur has (*admit*) _____ that he forgot the flowers.

2. Before she left, Lien (*pledge*) _____ to return.

3. Yes, we have (*create*) _____ a new gumbo.

4. My sister, who loves gardening, is (*plant*) _____ both fruits and vegetables.

5. Although we (*hurry*) _____ , we missed the bus.

6. During World War II, hundreds of Navajos in the U.S. Marines (*work*) _____ as Code Talkers.

7. The club members are (*urge*)_____ us to join.

8. What has (*happen*) _____ to that building?

9. The method that Thelma is (*use*) _____ was developed in India.

10. Yesterday morning the class (*watch*) _____ a film about pollution.

11. The rest of the workers have (*decide*) _____ to follow my suggestion.

12. Every morning last month we (*listen*) _____ to a weather report.

13. Ms. Perkins has (*correct*) _____ the errors.

14. I think that dog is (*follow*) _____ us!

15. The radio station (*play*) _____ my two favorite songs last night.

16. Our neighbor down the street is (*move*) _____ to another town.

17. I (*promise*)_____ that I would feed the cat every morning.

18. Sheila (*search*) _____ for hours, but she could not find her keys.

19. Our art class is (*visit*) _____ the museum today.

20. Because the fans have (*wait*) _____ for a long time, they are getting restless.

SALLY FORTH   **BY GREG HOWARD**

Sally Forth reprinted with special permission of North America Syndicate, Inc.

IRREGULAR VERBS

15c An *irregular verb* is a verb that forms its past and past participle in some other way than by adding *-d* or *-ed* to the base form.

Irregular verbs form their past and past participle by changing vowels, changing consonants, adding *-en*, or making no change at all.

Base Form	Past	Past participle
begin	began	(have) begun
go	went	(have) gone
take	took	(have) taken
set	set	(have) set

Since most English verbs are regular, people sometimes try to make irregular verbs follow the same pattern. However, words such as *knowed* and *thinked* are considered nonstandard. If you are not sure about the parts of a verb, look in a dictionary which lists the principal parts of irregular verbs.

When the present participle and past participle forms are used as main verbs (simple predicates) in sentences, they always require helping verbs.

Present Participle	+	Helping Verb	=	Verb Phrase
running		⎡ forms ⎤		am running
driving	+	⎢ of ⎢	=	was driving
seeing		⎣ *be* ⎦		were seeing

Past Participle	+	Helping Verb	=	Verb Phrase
run		⎡ forms ⎤		have run
driven	+	⎢ of ⎢	=	has driven
seen		⎣ *have* ⎦		had seen

 REFERENCE NOTE: Sometimes a past participle is used with a form of *be*: *was found, is heard, are located*. This use of the verb is called the *passive voice*. See page 199.

IRREGULAR VERBS FREQUENTLY MISUSED

Base Form	Present Participle	Past	Past Participle
begin	(is) beginning	began	(have) begun
blow	(is) blowing	blew	(have) blown
break	(is) breaking	broke	(have) broken
bring	(is) bringing	brought	(have) brought
burst	(is) bursting	burst	(have) burst
choose	(is) choosing	chose	(have) chosen
come	(is) coming	came	(have) come
dive	(is) diving	dove (or dived)	(have) dived
do	(is) doing	did	(have) done
drink	(is) drinking	drank	(have) drunk
drive	(is) driving	drove	(have) driven
eat	(is) eating	ate	(have) eaten
fall	(is) falling	fell	(have) fallen
freeze	(is) freezing	froze	(have) frozen
give	(is) giving	gave	(have) given
go	(is) going	went	(have) gone
grow	(is) growing	grew	(have) grown
know	(is) knowing	knew	(have) known
make	(is) making	made	(have) made
put	(is) putting	put	(have) put
ride	(is) riding	rode	(have) ridden
ring	(is) ringing	rang	(have) rung
run	(is) running	ran	(have) run
see	(is) seeing	saw	(have) seen
shake	(is) shaking	shook	(have) shaken
shrink	(is) shrinking	shrank (or shrunk)	(have) shrunk
sink	(is) sinking	sank	(have) sunk
speak	(is) speaking	spoke	(have) spoken
steal	(is) stealing	stole	(have) stolen
sting	(is) stinging	stung	(have) stung

IRREGULAR VERBS FREQUENTLY MISUSED			
Base Form	**Present Participle**	**Past**	**Past Participle**
strike	(is) striking	struck	(have) struck
swear	(is) swearing	swore	(have) sworn
swim	(is) swimming	swam	(have) swum
take	(is) taking	took	(have) taken
tear	(is) tearing	tore	(have) torn
throw	(is) throwing	threw	(have) thrown
wear	(is) wearing	wore	(have) worn
write	(is) writing	wrote	(have) written

EXERCISE 2   Writing Forms of Irregular Verbs

Change each of the verb forms below. If the base form is given, change it to the present participle. If the present participle is given, change it to the past form. If the past form is given, change it to the past participle. Use *have* before the past participle form and *is* before the present participle form.

EX.   1. is diving ___*dove*___   2. ran   ___*have run*___

1. see   _____
2. spoke   _____
3. is freezing   _____
4. threw   _____
5. is breaking   _____
6. brought   _____
7. grow   _____
8. drove   _____
9. is swimming   _____
10. began   _____

11. speak   _____
12. is choosing   _____
13. wear   _____
14. knew   _____
15. ride   _____
16. shook   _____
17. is eating   _____
18. went   _____
19. take   _____
20. drank   _____

EXERCISE 3   Identifying Correct Forms of Irregular Verbs

For each of the following sentences, underline the correct form of the verb in parentheses.

EX.   1. Those plants have (*grew, grown*) taller.

1. The class (*chose, chosen*) new officers last week.
2. Did you know your rear axle has (*broke, broken*)?

3. An earthquake (*struck, strike*) Antigua earlier today.

4. I'm afraid your sweater (*shrank, shrunk*) in the wash.

5. About four inches of rain has (*fell, fallen*) since yesterday.

6. Anica angrily (*tore, torn*) the letter into bits.

7. My grandfather has (*wrote, written*) several articles for *National Geographic*.

8. You can try after Rudy has (*dove, dived*) off the board.

9. The concert has (*began, begun*), but you have not missed much.

10. Mr. Katz (*shaken, shook*) his head in reply.

EXERCISE 4   Proofreading a Paragraph for Correct Verb Forms

Proofread the paragraph below. If a sentence contains an incorrect verb form, draw a line through the wrong form and write the correct form above it. Some sentences may have no errors in verb forms.

EX.   1. Last year we ~~seen~~ some of the studios in Bombay.
                    saw

[1] The film industry in India has grew tremendously. [2] Today India's film industry was the largest in the world. [3] Since 1979, India has made more than seven hundred films each year! [4] Only lately have I began to notice the number of Indian films. [5] I had went to an Indian film festival to see a film by Satyajit Ray. [6] I seen several others while I was there. [7] When one film began, I recognized the lead actor. [8] I could have swore that he was in two other films at the same festival. [9] Later, I done a little research on him. [10] He had maked more than a dozen films that year.

EXERCISE 5   Using Irregular Verbs

On your own paper, write fifteen sentences using verbs from the charts on pages 194-195. Use the participle forms of the verbs in five of your sentences. Underline the verbs you use.

EX.   1. Frederick has <u>brought</u> us a bushel of potatoes.

15d   The time expressed by a verb is called the *tense* of the verb.

Every verb in English has six tenses.

Tense	Examples
Present	I throw, you throw, he throws, we throw
Past	I threw, you threw, she threw, they threw
Future	I will (shall) throw, you will throw, they will throw
Present Perfect	I have thrown, you have thrown, he has thrown
Past Perfect	I had thrown, you had thrown, she had thrown
Future Perfect	I will (shall) have thrown, you will have thrown, we will have thrown

Each of the six tenses has an additional form, called the *progressive form,* which expresses a continuing action. It consists of a form of the verb *be* plus the present participle of a verb. The progressive is not a separate tense but an additional form of each of the six tenses.

Form	Examples
Present Progressive	am/are/is throwing
Past Progressive	was/were throwing
Future Progressive	will (shall) be throwing
Present Perfect Progressive	has/have been throwing
Past Perfect Progressive	had been throwing
Future Perfect Progressive	will (shall) have been throwing

15e   Do not change needlessly from one tense to another.

NONSTANDARD   Elia drove to the store and buys lunch. [*Drove* is past tense; *buys* is present tense.]

STANDARD   Elia **drove** to the store and **bought** lunch. [*Drove* and *bought* are both past tense.]

EXERCISE 6   Identifying Verb Tenses

For each sentence below, identify the tense of the verb. Write your answers on your own paper.

EX.   1. Kam had seen the movie.
      1. *past perfect*

1. The team traveled by bus.
2. Leila has taken her medicine.
3. The conference will begin on Monday.
4. We swim on Friday evenings.
5. Phillip had already seen the movie.

EXERCISE 7   Proofreading a Paragraph for Consistent Verb Tenses

Decide whether the paragraph below should be written in the present or past tense. Then draw a line through each incorrect verb form, and write the correct form above it.

EX.   [1] I ~~eat~~ too quickly, so I got these hiccups.
    ate

[1] Most times, hiccups are not dangerous, but they are a nuisance. [2] Also, most people found them funny. [3] Yesterday, my hiccups continue for a while, so my friends gave me advice. [4] Maripat tells me to hold my breath and count to ten. [5] Shing says that I should quickly drink a tall glass of water. [6] Other people suggest ideas that sound really strange. [7] My mother says that I should put a pail or a wastebasket over my head and have someone beat on it. [8] My sister gave me the best idea of all. [9] She went into the kitchen and comes back with a paper bag. [10] I place it over my head, and my hiccups vanished.

EXERCISE 8   Using Verb Tenses and Forms Correctly

On your own paper, write five sentences showing the correct use of the verb *bring*. Use as many different verb tenses and forms as you can. Underline each verb, and label its tense or form.

EX.   1. Dad <u>is bringing</u> my sister Leta to watch my game. (present progressive)

ACTIVE AND PASSIVE VOICE

15f **A verb in the *active voice* expresses an action done *by* its subject.**
A verb in the *passive voice* expresses an action done *to* its subject.

ACTIVE VOICE   Mr. Noor **helped** Sarah. [The subject, *Mr. Noor,* performed the action.]

PASSIVE VOICE   Sarah **was helped** by Mr. Noor. [The subject, *Sarah,* received the action.]

NOTE   In a passive sentence, the verb phrase always includes a form of *be* and the past participle of the main verb. Other helping verbs may also be included.

The passive voice emphasizes the person or thing receiving the action. It may be used when the speaker does not know or does not wish to say who performed the action.

                         SUBJECT

PASSIVE VOICE   A window **was broken** by someone last night.

                    SUBJECT   OBJECT

ACTIVE VOICE   Someone **broke** a window last night.

In general, you should avoid using the passive voice because it makes your writing sound weak and awkward. Using the active voice helps make your writing direct and forceful.

EXERCISE 9   Classifying Sentences by Voice

Identify each of the following sentences as active or passive. On the line before each sentence, write *act.* for *active* or *pass.* for *passive.*

EX.   *act.* 1. Pat Cummings illustrates books.

_____ 1. She has been inspired by Tom Feelings.

_____ 2. Her work is created in Brooklyn.

_____ 3. Cummings uses a variety of materials in her work.

_____ 4. *Jimmy Lee Did It* was illustrated by Cummings.

_____ 5. Our school library owns several of her books.

_____ 6. My sister can be counted among her first big fans.

_____ 7. Sarita was surprised by the invitation.

_____ 8. Was Pat Cummings asked by the art teacher to visit our school?

_____ 9. Did she ever really come?

_____10. The program was enjoyed by all of us.

_____11. I hope we get more programs.

_____12. How many books were suggested?

_____13. Wynona reads several books each month.

_____14. Our teacher wants us to form a book club.

_____15. Did she give you any ideas for a club name?

EXERCISE 10   Using Verbs in the Active Voice and the Passive Voice

In the cartoon below, Blondie, Dagwood, Daisy, and Mr. Dithers are the subjects and objects of many actions that are occurring. On your own paper, write ten sentences to describe the cartoon. Use the active voice in six sentences and the passive voice in four sentences. After each sentence, write *act.* for *active* or *pass.* for *passive* to identify the voice you used.

EX.   1. *Blondie's dog watches the action.* (act.)

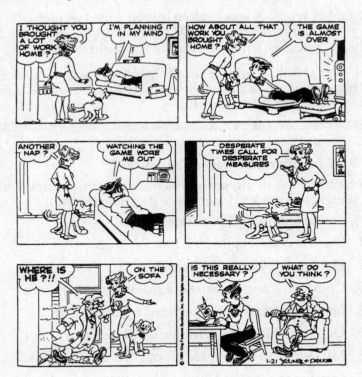

Blondie reprinted with special permission of King Features Syndicate, Inc.

LIE AND LAY

15g The verb *lie* means "to rest," "to recline," or "to remain in a lying position." *Lie* rarely takes an object. The verb *lay* means "to put" or "to place" (something). *Lay* usually takes an object.

EXAMPLES The dog **is lying** in the doorway.
Sarah **lay** the mat in front of the door.

PRINCIPAL PARTS OF *LIE* AND *LAY*			
Base Form	**Present Participle**	**Past**	**Past Participle**
lie (to recline)	(is) lying	lay	(have) lain
lay (to put)	(is) laying	laid	(have) laid

NOTE The verb *lie* may be used to describe the lying position of inanimate objects as well as of people and animals. Even though someone puts an object down, it *lies* (not *lays*) there.

EXAMPLE Your book **is lying** on the table.

When deciding whether to use *lie* or *lay*, ask yourself two questions.

QUESTION 1: What do I want to say? Is the meaning "to be in a lying position," or is it "to put something down"?

QUESTION 2: What time does the verb express, and which principal part is used to show this time?

The following examples show how you can apply these questions to determine which verb—*lie* or *lay*—should be used.

EXAMPLE That blanket has always (*lain, laid*) on the back of the couch.

QUESTION 1: Meaning? The meaning is "to be in a lying position." Therefore, the verb should be *lie*.

QUESTION 2: Principal part? The verb expresses the past, and the sentence requires the past participle with *has*. The past participle of *lie* is *lain*.

ANSWER: That blanket **has** always **lain** on the back of the couch.

EXERCISE 11   Choosing the Correct Forms of *Lie* and *Lay*

For each of the following sentences, underline the correct form of *lie* or *lay*.

EX.   1.   The mummy had (*laid*, *lain*) in the ground for centuries.

1.   Early Egyptians sometimes (*laid*, *lay*) bodies in dry sand.

2.   Other mummies have been (*lying*, *laying*) in frozen earth for hundreds of years.

3.   About 2,100 years ago, someone in Hunan, China, had (*lain*, *laid*) the body of a woman in a burial mound.

4.   The mummy (*laid*, *lay*) there until the Chinese government decided to build a hospital on that site.

5.   Native Americans sometimes (*laid*, *lay*) bodies inside dry caves.

6.   One such mummy had (*lain*, *laid*) in a Kentucky cave for two thousand years.

7.   Egyptian embalmers (*lain*, *laid*) strips of linen over their dead.

8.   Often, a person's organs (*lay*, *laid*) inside a separate jar.

9.   The friends of John Paul Jones (*lain*, *laid*) his body in a lead casket that was full of alcohol.

10.   His mummy had (*lain*, *laid*) there for over one hundred years.

11.   Instead of (*lying*, *laying*) down, some mummies are put in a seated position.

12.   Did you know that Egyptian mummies at one point in the process (*lay*, *laid*) in sodium carbonate?

13.   Before being (*laid*, *lain*) in a tomb, mummies were given a treatment lasting seventy days.

14.   The body of King Mer-en-re was found (*lying*, *laying*) in a tomb in 1880.

15.   Besides the mummy, articles from a person's life were (*laid*, *lain*) in the tomb.

EXERCISE 12   Using *Lie* and *Lay* Correctly

On your own paper, write five sentences using the different forms of *lie* correctly. Then write five sentences using the different forms of *lay* correctly. Use all of the principal parts at least once in your sentences. Underline and label all the forms of *lie* and *lay* in your sentences.

EX.   1.   Chandra laid her pen beside her book. (past)

SIT *AND* SET *AND* RISE *AND* RAISE

SIT *AND* SET

15h The verb *sit* means "to rest in an upright, seated position." *Sit* almost never takes an object. The verb *set* means "to put" or "to place" (something). *Set* usually takes an object. Notice that *set* does not change form in the past or past participle.

PRINCIPAL PARTS OF *SIT* AND *SET*			
Base Form	**Present Participle**	**Past**	**Past Participle**
sit (to rest)	(is) sitting	sat	(have) sat
set (to put)	(is) setting	set	(have) set

EXAMPLES   **Sit** here.   **Set** your end down first.
The box **sat** on the table.   The driver **set** it there.

EXERCISE 13   Using the Forms of *Sit* and *Set*

In each of the following sentences, write the correct form of *sit* or *set* on the line provided.

EX.   1. Thi and I will both _____*sit*_____ in the back seat.

1. Thi has _____ a pad of paper between us.

2. When I _____ down, I felt a pencil on the seat.

3. We _____ on the floor playing word games and talking about school.

4. Don't _____ your lunch box on the window ledge, or your food will spoil.

5. When the car stopped, I _____ our picnic basket on the table.

6. Thi was reading about Lewis Carroll, but she _____ the book down.

7. We have _____ here for an hour playing *Mischmasch*, one of Carroll's games.

8. I wrote the letters "HTH" on the page and then _____ the pencil beside me.

9. Thi _____ for a long time, trying to think of a word containing that letter combination.

10. When we _____ at lunch the next day, I whispered, "Lighthouse."

RISE AND *RAISE*

15i **The verb *rise* means "to go in an upward direction." *Rise* rarely takes an object. The verb *raise* means "to move something in an upward direction." *Raise* usually takes an object.**

PRINCIPAL PARTS OF *RISE* AND *RAISE*			
Base Form	**Present Participle**	**Past**	**Past Participle**
rise (to go up)	(is) rising	rose	(have) risen
raise (to move something up)	(is) raising	raised	(have) raised

EXAMPLES   My parents **rise** at about 6:30 most mornings.
I'm glad you **raised** that issue!
The price of oranges will **rise** again.
The store **raised** the price of its fruit.

EXERCISE 14   Using the Forms of *Rise* and *Raise*

Write the correct form of *rise* or *raise* on the line in each sentence below.

EX.   1. If you add yeast, the dough will _____*rise*_____.

1. Matzo contains no yeast, so the dough does not _____.

2. My aunt _____ at dawn to start her bread.

3. She has _____ earlier than usual.

4. At dinner, my uncle _____ the napkin and peeked underneath.

5. Before a particularly good dessert, everyone's excitement will

_____.

CHAPTER REVIEW

A. Writing Sentences Using the Correct Forms of Verbs

On your own paper, write twenty sentences using the following verbs.

EX. 1. sunk
   1. The raft had sunk last summer.

1. laid
2. (have) walked
3. seen
4. swam
5. (had) set
6. lying
7. rose
8. thrown
9. drove
10. (had) used

11. froze
12. (have) shaken
13. (is) bringing
14. stole
15. stung
16. (have) chosen
17. raise
18. began
19. (have) given
20. (is) doing

B. Proofreading a Paragraph for Correct Verb Forms

In the following paragraph, if a sentence contains an incorrect verb form, cross out the incorrect verb. Then write the correct form above the verb. Some sentences will be correct. Others may have more than one incorrect verb form.

EX. [1] Cochise and Thomas Jeffords ~~beginned~~ began a long friendship.

[1] In the late 1800s, the Apache leader Cochise was arrest on a false charge. [2] He escaped and later striked back at the settlers. [3] At one point, his people had killed more than a dozen mail carriers. [4] Thomas Jeffords, the man in charge of the mail, decides to visit Cochise. [5] When they met, he sets his own weapons aside. [6] Then the two men set and talked for days. [7] After this meeting, the men had became good friends, and Jeffords was chose to be the agent for the Apache reservation. [8] The men's friendship lasted

until the chief's death in 1874. [9] Shortly thereafter, Jeffords was

replace by a different agent, and a new leader raised to power among

the Apaches. [10] His name, Geronimo, was soon knew throughout

the United States.

C. Writing a Weather Report

You are a weather forecaster on a local television station. For tonight's show, you will be using the weather map that is shown below. When you display the map, you will describe the weather situation to your audience.

1. First, use the weather symbols to determine what the weather is in different parts of the country.

2. Next, make notes on your own paper. Write five sentences about the weather. Use each of the following verbs at least once: *sit*, *lie*, and *rise*.

EX.   1.   A stationary front is sitting over northern Florida.

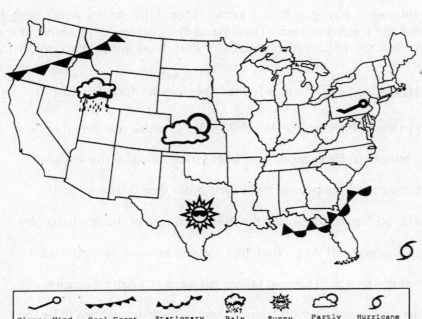

CASE OF PRONOUNS

Case is the form of a noun or pronoun that shows its use in a sentence. In English, there are three cases: *nominative, objective,* and *possessive.*

The form of a noun is the same for the nominative and objective cases.

NOMINATIVE CASE   The **judge** has issued a ruling. [noun used as subject]

OBJECTIVE CASE   I respect the **judge**. [noun used as direct object]

A noun changes its form only in the possessive case, usually by adding an apostrophe and an *s*.

POSSESSIVE CASE   The **judge's** ruling was fair.

 REFERENCE NOTE: For more about forming possessives with apostrophes, see page 285.

Unlike nouns, most personal pronouns have different forms for the nominative, objective, and possessive cases.

PERSONAL PRONOUNS			
	Nominative Case	**Objective Case**	**Possessive Case**
Singular	I you he, she, it	me you him, her, it	my, mine your, yours his, her, hers, its
Plural	we you they	us you them	our, ours your, yours their, theirs

 NOTE   Some teachers prefer to call possessive forms of pronouns (such as *hers, your,* and *their*) adjectives. Follow your teacher's instructions regarding possessive forms.

EXERCISE 1   Identifying Personal Pronouns and Their Cases

Identify the case of the italicized pronoun in each sentence below. On the line before each sentence, write *nom.* for *nominative*, *obj.* for *objective*, or *poss.* for *possessive*.

EX. __poss.__ 1. Benito Pablo Juárez earned *his* place in history as one of the greatest leaders of Mexico.

_____ 1. *His* birthplace was Oaxaca, Mexico.

_____ 2. In 1847, *he* was elected governor of the Mexican state of Oaxaca.

_____ 3. At that time, the people of Mexico had few freedoms; Santa Anna ruled *them* with an iron hand.

_____ 4. Juárez and other local leaders opposed *him*.

_____ 5. *Their* dreams for greater freedom stalled when Santa Anna sent Juárez out of Mexico.

_____ 6. When Juárez returned to Mexico in 1855, *he* became minister of justice.

_____ 7. *Our* textbook states that one of Juárez's greatest deeds was putting through the Juárez Law.

_____ 8. *It* took away some powers from the army and the clergy and gave more rights to the citizens of Mexico.

_____ 9. Juárez was rewarded in 1861 when the people elected *him* president of Mexico.

_____ 10. Today, *we* credit Juárez for bringing religious freedom and civil rights to the people of Mexico.

EXERCISE 2   Writing a Poem with Personal Pronouns

On your own paper, write a poem of at least ten lines about how friendship can exist between people who are very different. In your poem, describe the differences between two friends. Use at least two examples of each of the three cases of pronouns. Underline each pronoun that you use.

EX. I am wildfire.

You are rain.

And yet we are friends.

NOMINATIVE CASE PRONOUNS

16a   The *subject of a verb* is always in the nominative case.

EXAMPLES   Do **they** enjoy country music? [*They* is the subject of *Do enjoy*.]
He and **I** watched the show. [*He* and *I* are the two parts of the compound subject of *watched*.]

To choose the correct pronoun for use in a compound subject, try each form of the pronoun separately.

EXAMPLE   Oskar and (*me, I*) play in a band.
Me play in a band. [incorrect use of objective case]
I play in a band. [correct use of nominative case]

ANSWER   Oskar and I play in a band.

16b   A *predicate nominative* is always in the nominative case.

A ***predicate nominative*** is a noun or pronoun that follows a linking verb and explains or identifies the subject of the sentence. A pronoun used as a predicate nominative always follows a form of the verb *be* or a verb phrase ending in *be* or *been*.

EXAMPLES   The captain of the team is **I**. [*I* follows the linking verb *is* and identifies the subject, *captain*.]
The owners of the store are Marsha and **he**. [*He* follows the verb *are* and identifies, along with *Marsha*, the subject, *owners*.]

EXERCISE 3   Identifying Nominative Case Pronouns

Complete each of the following sentences by underlining the correct pronoun or pronoun pair in parentheses.

EX.   1.   Elsie and (*he*, *him*) are planning an Earth Day project.

1. The contestants on the quiz show were (*him and me*, *he and I*).

2. The person who called may have been (*she*, *her*).

3. Naturally, (*she and I*, *her and me*) will help at the carwash.

4. The most comfortable shoes are (*they*, *them*).

5. Dr. Ramírez and (*us*, *we*) are meeting to plan the tournament.

6. Amanda and (*I*, *me*) are working together on our research reports.

7. The judges for the creative writing contest might be Ms. Robinson and (*them, they*).

8. It was (*we, us*) who donated the set of encyclopedias for the library book sale.

9. Have (*they, them*) visited South America before?

10. Could it have been (*him, he*)?

11. The big winners would be (*she, her*) and Ramona.

12. Did (*I, me*) ever seem this happy before?

13. (*They, Them*) always work together on their boat.

14. (*We, Us*) sat down to think it over.

15. Karen and (*I, me*) joined the soccer team on the same day.

EXERCISE 4   Proofreading Sentences for Correct Use of Nominative Case Pronouns

If a sentence below contains the wrong form of a pronoun, draw a line through the pronoun, and write the correct form above it. Some sentences are correct.

EX.   1. Juan Carlos the First and ~~her~~ *she* were the rulers of Spain.

1. Our foreign exchange students this year are Kamaria and him.

2. The team member who scored the most points was he.

3. Him and I were both born in Laos.

4. Two successful Cuban American singers are Gloria Estefan and her.

5. Will he and me perform after Juanita?

6. The winners of the award should have been her and I.

7. Was it he who said, "Don't give up yet"?

8. Perhaps you and me should volunteer for cleanup duty.

9. That night, they announced that the winners were us!

10. The drama coach said that he and me could apply for the two jobs as understudies.

PRONOUNS AS DIRECT OBJECTS

16c   The *direct object* **of a verb is always in the objective case.**

A *direct object* is a noun or pronoun that receives the action of a verb or that shows the result of the action.

EXAMPLES   The officer directed **me** to the right address. [*Me* tells *whom* the officer directed.]
Teresa gave **them** to her sister. [*Them* tells *what* Teresa gave.]

To choose the correct pronoun for use as a compound direct object, try each form of the pronoun separately.

EXAMPLE   The audience applauded Geraldo and (*I, me*).
The audience applauded *I*. [incorrect use of nominative case]
The audience applauded *me*. [correct use of objective case]

ANSWER   The audience applauded Geraldo and **me**.

EXERCISE 5   Choosing Correct Pronoun Forms

Complete each sentence below by writing an appropriate pronoun on the line or lines provided. Use a variety of pronouns, but do not use *you* or *it*. Make sure that each pronoun you choose makes sense in the sentence.

EX.   1. Fran took her brother and _____me_____ to a concert.

1. Someone called _____ extremely late last night.

2. Please help _____ with the assignment.

3. Did you see _____ at the library?

4. The child answered _____ politely.

5. Professional scouts contacted _____ and _____ after the game.

6. Simon and Rebecca told _____ about their visit to Israel.

7. Tomorrow night my brother will drive _____ to the mall.

8. Dr. Maldonado treated _____ and the other hikers for frostbite.

9. The orchestra leader thanked _____ and _____ for attending the concert.

10. Aunt Maribeth surprised _____ by coming to rehearsal.

EXERCISE 6   Proofreading for Correct Pronoun Case

Draw a line through each pronoun that is used incorrectly in the paragraph below. Write the correct pronoun in the space above the word. Some sentences are correct.

EX.   [1] They sent Zahara and ~~I~~ *me* to the regional meeting.

[1] The members of our International Club surprised and pleased Zahara and I at the last meeting. [2] They chose she and me as representatives for the regional meeting. [3] They told me it was because Zahara is from East Africa and I am from Santiago, Chile. [4] Our international experiences have introduced we to many different cultures and beliefs. [5] Many students in our school, and particularly members of the International Club, have helped her and I in our new surroundings in the United States. [6] Now they are helping she and I in a whole new way. [7] They are sending us to the meeting to talk about how the city government might help students from foreign countries. [8] Zahara and I will tell you and they all about the meeting as soon as we return. [9] Or can you join she and I at the next meeting of the International Club? [10] Our meetings are on the first Tuesday of the month; I'm sure you'll enjoy they. [11] Zahara showed I some African artwork from her country. [12] I showed she a painting my father had done. [13] Zahara enjoys museums and often goes to visit they. [14] I enjoy them, too, but I like soccer games more. [15] All in all, everyone has treated we very well.

INDIRECT OBJECTS AND OBJECTS OF PREPOSITIONS

16d The *indirect object* of a verb is always in the objective case.

An *indirect object* is a noun or pronoun that tells *to whom* or *for whom* something is done.

EXAMPLES   Hadiya sent **him** a birthday card. [*Him* tells *to whom* Hadiya sent a birthday card.]

Could you make **me** a sandwich? [*Me* tells *for whom* you could make a sandwich.]

To choose the correct pronoun for use in a compound indirect object, try each form of the pronoun separately in the sentence.

EXAMPLE   Emilio Estevez sent Melba and (*she, her*) an autographed photo.
Emilio Estevez sent *she* an autographed photo. [incorrect use of nominative case]
Emilio Estevez sent *her* an autographed photo. [correct use of objective case]

ANSWER   Emilio Estevez sent Melba and **her** an autographed photo.

EXERCISE 7   Using Pronouns as Indirect Objects

Complete each of the following sentences by writing an appropriate pronoun on the line or lines provided. Use a variety of pronouns, but do not use *you* or *it*.

EX.   1.   Did Lorenzo loan his sister and _____*him*_____ money for the tickets?

1.   We gave _____ an award for being such a great coach.

2.   Will you loan _____ your copy of the script?

3.   When she returned to Somalia, Tabia sent _____ a note.

4.   The counselor gave Kareem and _____ some very good advice about scholarships.

5.   At lunch, Dolores told _____ and _____ a joke.

6.   When I did the job well, the boss offered _____ a better one.

7.   She mailed _____ all of our camping equipment.

8. Mattie cooked _____ his favorite meal after the show.

9. Ginette blushed when Alfredo handed _____ the flowers.

10. It took six months for my cousin to write _____ a letter.

16e   The *object of a preposition* is always in the objective case.

A *prepositional phrase* is a group of words consisting of a preposition, a noun or pronoun that serves as the object of the preposition, and any modifiers of that object.

EXAMPLES   for **me**   after Meredith and **him**   in front of **us**

☞   **REFERENCE NOTE:** For a list of prepositions, see page 115.

EXERCISE 8   Choosing Correct Pronouns as Objects of Prepositions

Complete each sentence below by underlining the correct pronoun or pair of pronouns in parentheses.

EX.   1. The musical was directed by (*he and she, him and her*).

1. To my classmates and (*I, me*), Anzu and Ima Asato are very talented twin sisters.

2. They wrote our class musical for (*we, us*).

3. Thanks to (*them, they*), our musical won second place in the city music festival.

4. Perhaps you read the article in the *Kansas City Star* about their family and (*they, them*).

5. Because their father, a member of the Kansas City Symphony, helped them, we should send a thank-you note to (*he, him*).

6. Between (*you and I, you and me*), the music was beautiful.

7. Listen to (*I, me*) while I play the main theme on the piano.

8. Jim and I were lucky that Ima was standing right in front of (*we, us*) in the chorus during the performance.

9. We could listen to (*she, her*) as she sang, and we followed along.

10. The entire cast got tapes of the music from (*they, them*) as gifts on opening night.

REVIEW EXERCISE

A. Identifying Correct Pronoun Form

Complete each sentence below by underlining the correct pronoun in parentheses. On the line before the sentence, identify the pronoun's use in the sentence. Write *s.* for *subject*, *p.n.* for *predicate nominative*, *d.o.* for *direct object*, *i.o.* for *indirect object*, or *o.p.* for *object of a preposition*.

EX. _p.n._ 1. That must be (*her*, *she*) at the door.

_____ 1. Please save two seats for Maisie and (*I, me*).

_____ 2. Our coach offered the younger students and (*they, them*) some pointers.

_____ 3. Many people thanked Ms. Tan and (*we, us*) for our posters in the cafeteria.

_____ 4. You never guessed that the person in the gorilla costume was (*I, me*)!

_____ 5. Whenever it rains hard, my sisters and (*I, me*) have to put towels around the door.

_____ 6. The Korean family that just moved into the neighborhood thanked (*we, us*) for the welcome basket.

_____ 7. Maria shared her grandmother's recipe for salsa with Jamyce and (*he, him*).

_____ 8. Somewhere along the way, Shani and (*she, her*) misplaced their house keys.

_____ 9. Show Ada May and (*I, me*) your drawing when you are finished.

_____ 10. It may have been (*they, them*) who sent these flowers.

_____ 11. Was it (*we, us*) who had the winning ticket?

_____ 12. Ontario is a place that (*he, him*) has always wanted to visit.

_____ 13. Thanks to (*they, them*), there are no more mosquitoes in the backyard.

_____ 14. If you hurry, (*I, me*) will be able to meet you at the restaurant.

_____ 15. The drama club honored Rita by giving (*she, her*) the prize for best play.

B.   Proofreading for Correct Pronoun Forms

Draw a line through each pronoun that is used incorrectly in the paragraph below. Write the correct pronoun in the space above the word. Some sentences are correct.

EX.   [1] To Mavis and ~~I~~, Ronnie Milsap is the greatest country singer of
      me
      all time.

[1] Country singer Ronnie Milsap, who is blind, has given we

many memorable songs. [2] When Ronnie was six, his parents sent he

to the Governor Morehead School for the Blind in Raleigh, North

Carolina. [3] There, his classmates and him received excellent

training in music. [4] Ronnie and them learned to play musical

instruments, and he became especially interested in the piano and the

violin. [5] After he left Morehead, he went to college in Georgia.

[6] He entered the music business, and it is him that one can hear

playing the piano on several of Elvis Presley's early hits. [7] By 1973,

many people had heard about he because of his work on Presley's hit

"Kentucky Rain" and many others. [8] In 1973, RCA offered him a

contract to record his own songs. [9] My sister Mavis and me have

collected all twenty-three of the albums he recorded with RCA.

[10] The hit singles "Smoky Mountain Rain" and "Stranger in My

House" are the favorites of both Mavis and I.

C.   Writing a Friendly Note

On your own paper, write a note to a friend, telling about a movie you recently saw and enjoyed. Describe the major characters and the main events. In your letter, use five nominative and five objective case pronouns correctly. When you have finished writing, underline all of the pronouns. Above each pronoun, identify its use. Write *s.* for *subject*, *p.n.* for *predicate nominative*, *d.o.* for *direct object*, *i.o.* for *indirect object*, or *o.p.* for *object of a preposition*.

EX.   Dear Marvin,
            s.   s.   o.p.
      I just saw a great movie today. You will enjoy all the action in it.

WHO *AND* WHOM

16f Use *who* and *whoever* in the nominative case. Use *whom* and *whomever* in the objective case.

In spoken English, the use of *whom* is becoming less common. In fact, when speaking, you may correctly begin any question with *who*, regardless of the grammar of the sentence.

16g The use of *who* or *whom* in a subordinate clause depends on how the pronoun functions in the clause.

When choosing whether to use *who* or *whom* in a subordinate clause, follow these steps.

Step 1: Find the subordinate clause in the sentence.
Step 2: Decide how the pronoun is used in the clause—as subject, predicate nominative, object of the verb, or object of a preposition.
Step 3: Determine the case of the pronoun according to the rules of standard English.
Step 4: Select the correct form of the pronoun.

EXAMPLE   I know (*who, whom*) wrote the note.

Step 1: The clause is (*who, whom*) *wrote the note.*
Step 2: In this clause, the pronoun is used as the subject of the verb *wrote.*
Step 3: A pronoun used as a subject should be in the nominative case.
Step 4: The nominative form is *who.*

ANSWER   I know **who** wrote the note.

No words outside the clause affect the case of the pronoun. In the example above, the entire clause is used as a direct object of the verb *know*, but the pronoun *who* is used as a subject (nominative case) within the clause.

Frequently, *whom* in subordinate clauses is omitted (understood).

EXAMPLE   The man (whom) I voted for is Julian Washington.

EXERCISE 9   Classifying Pronouns Used in Subordinate Clauses and Identifying Correct Forms

Complete each sentence below by underlining the correct pronoun form in parentheses. On the line before the sentence, identify the pronoun's use in the clause. Write *s.* for *subject*, *p.n.* for *predicate nominative*, *d.o.* for *direct object*, or *o.p.* for *object of a preposition*.

EX. __p.n.__ 1. Do you know (<u>*who*</u>, *whom*) they are?

_____ 1. The student for (*who*, *whom*) I'm saving this seat should arrive shortly.

_____ 2. (*Whoever*, *Whomever*) you invite to the concert will be happy to go with you.

_____ 3. Did you talk to (*whoever*, *whomever*) you gave the plates for the party?

_____ 4. Mr. Ignacio is the Navajo artist (*who*, *whom*) we saw on television last night.

_____ 5. I haven't decided for (*who*, *whom*) I made this necklace.

_____ 6. Can you predict (*who*, *whom*) will win the class election?

_____ 7. Please tell me (*who*, *whom*) the owner of the store is.

_____ 8. The South American ruler (*who*, *whom*) we are now studying is Juan Perón.

_____ 9. (*Whoever*, *Whomever*) enters the contest must write a poem.

_____ 10. Tell us (*who*, *whom*) you saw at the bowling alley last night.

_____ 11. The sentry hailed (*whoever*, *whomever*) came up the path.

_____ 12. The judges will vote for (*whoever*, *whomever*) seems to be most worthy.

_____ 13. Can't you see (*who*, *whom*) really wants it more?

_____ 14. They named (*who*, *whom*) the winner is.

_____ 15. It's easy to see that (*whoever*, *whomever*) runs the fastest will arrive the soonest.

_____ 16. We thanked Deniz because he was (*who*, *whom*) brought the latkes.

_____ 17. Isabel gave the costumes to the actors to (*who*, *whom*) they were assigned.

_____ 18. Do you know Maribeth, (*who*, *whom*) I met yesterday?

_____ 19. How did Justin learn (*who*, *whom*) our new neighbor is?

_____ 20. Ken sent oranges to (*whoever*, *whomever*) he heard from first.

APPOSITIVES AND INCOMPLETE CONSTRUCTIONS

16h **Pronouns used with *appositives* are in the same case as the words to which they refer.**

An *appositive* is a noun or pronoun that follows another noun or pronoun to identify or explain it.

EXAMPLES   The judge announced the winners, Bart and **me**.[Since *winners* is the direct object of the verb *announced*, the pronoun *me*, in apposition with *winners*, must be in the objective case.]
We runners must train hard.[As subject of the sentence, *We* is in the nominative case. The noun *runners*, which identifies *We*, is the appositive.]

To choose the correct pronoun for use with an appositive or as an appositive, try the sentence with only the pronoun.

EXAMPLE   Two actors, Gina and (*me, I*), won awards on opening night.
Gina and *me* won awards on opening night.[incorrect use of objective case]
Gina and *I* won awards on opening night.[correct use of nominative case]

ANSWER   Two actors, Gina and I, won awards on opening night.

EXERCISE 10   Identifying Correct Pronouns as Appositives

Complete each of the following sentences by underlining the correct pronoun form in parentheses.

EX.   1. My cousins, Rachel and (<u>he</u>, *him*), are visiting from San Juan.

1. The coach gave the fullbacks, Paulo and (*he, him*), a pep talk.

2. The doctors thanked the nurses, Jobelle and (*I, me*).

3. At the end of the concert, the musicians, (*we, us*), played four encores.

4. Please offer more food to your guests, Charles and (*she, her*).

5. The best athletes in the class, you and (*he, him*), might be called to the stage.

6. Several people, the board and (*they, them*), elected a new president last year.

7. The head cheerleaders, she and (*I, me*), ran the practice.

8. The school newspaper paid a lot of attention to the basketball players, the forwards and (*we, us*).

9. The last campers in the water, Manuel and (*I, me*), still reached the raft on time.

10. The task of going for help was given to the best sailors on the lake, (*she, her*) and (*he, him*).

16i   When *than* or *as* introduces an incomplete construction, use the form of the pronoun that would be correct if the construction were completed.

Notice how pronouns change the meaning of sentences with incomplete constructions.

EXAMPLES   I like Cleon better than **she**.
I like Cleon better than **her**.

In the first example, the nominative case pronoun *she* is the subject of an understood verb; *I like Cleon better than she [likes Cleon].* In the second example, the objective case pronoun *her* is the object of an understood verb; *I like Cleon better than [I like] her.*

EXERCISE 11   Completing Incomplete Constructions and Classifying Pronoun Forms

Beginning with *than* or *as*, write the understood clause for each of the following sentences, on the line after it. Use the correct form of the pronoun. Then identify the pronoun in the completed clause by writing s. for *subject* or *obj.* for *object*. Some items may have more than one correct answer.

EX.   1. Leroy is taller than (*I, me*). ___than I am (s.)___

1. Can you swim to the end of the pool as fast as (*she, her*)?

   _____

2. You have called Mateo more often than (*I, me*).

   _____

3. I am just as good a writer as (*he, him*).

   _____

4. We have known Phoebe longer than (*they, them*).

   _____

5. Many people pay higher monthly rents than (*we, us*).

   _____

CHAPTER REVIEW

A. Correcting Pronoun Forms

Draw a line through each incorrect pronoun in the sentences below. On the line before each sentence, write the correct pronoun form.

EX. _____I_____ 1. Both of the applicants, Johan and me, took part-time jobs.

_____ 1. Katya speaks Spanish far better than her.

_____ 2. Mrs. Macavoy rented a canoe and prepared a picnic for Percy and I.

_____ 3. After the ballgame, the coach and me talked about my pitching.

_____ 4. Us residents of Benton Avenue have begun a neighborhood recycling campaign.

_____ 5. I can't believe that it was him who sent me this beautiful poem!

_____ 6. Do you know yet who you are inviting to the class dance?

_____ 7. The letter may have been written by one of my brothers, Juan or he.

_____ 8. I will give a reward to whomever finds my lost cat.

_____ 9. Have you decided to work for they?

_____ 10. The store owner gave both clerks, Mona and I, generous raises.

_____ 11. Someone should ask we students our opinion.

_____ 12. Wouldn't you like to go with she and me to the party?

_____ 13. To who do you think the principal was speaking?

_____ 14. We invited Helen and Frank to stay, but them wanted to get an early start.

_____ 15. Well, they did a good job, whomever it was.

_____ 16. Her and I have been friends since the first day of school.

_____ 17. Our history teacher told we honor students that we could do extra work.

_____ 18. Sometimes in the evenings my sister and him would sing folk songs together.

_____ 19. Mother wondered whom would speak first.

_____ 20. Us scuba divers like to explore coral reefs.

B.   Proofreading a Paragraph for Correct Pronoun Forms

Draw a line through each pronoun that is used incorrectly in the paragraph below. Write the correct pronoun in the space above the word. Some sentences are correct.

EX.   [1] The people ~~whom~~ who see the baskets say that they are beautiful.

[1] When my family and me were in South Carolina last summer, we bought a beautiful sweet-grass basket. [2] The women whom make the baskets are African American. [3] Them and their relatives have woven and sewn these beautiful crafts for many years. [4] The people to who credit is given for bringing this art form to the United States were brought here as slaves from West Africa about three hundred years ago. [5] We had never seen sweet-grass baskets before, so we asked the women all about them. [6] Mrs. Washington told my sister and I that the other basket makers and her go to marshy fields to collect the sweet grass that grows wild there. [7] Then they bind together the coarse grass and stitch it into place. [8] The lady to who we spoke said that she takes at least ten hours to sew a basket. [9] Then she told my father and I about new problems that are facing the basket makers. [10] The fields of sweet grass are disappearing, and the art and the tradition of the basket makers might very well disappear with them.

C.   Writing Interview Questions and Answers

As a feature writer for a sports magazine, you are to interview a celebrity sports figure. He or she might be a star in hockey, auto racing, basketball, or any other sport that you choose. On your own paper, write at least ten questions that you would ask about this person's background, accomplishments, and future goals. From magazines, newspapers, and biographies, gather information and details about this person. Use your research to write the answers that the person might give. Be sure to use the correct forms of personal pronouns in your questions and answers.

EX.   *Gordie Howe*
  1. *Among all the positions, why did you choose to be a goalie?*

COMPARISON OF MODIFIERS

Positive, *comparative*, and *superlative* are the three degrees of comparison for adjectives and adverbs.

POSITIVE	Robert told a **funny** joke.
COMPARATIVE	Kim told a joke that was **funnier** than Robert's was.
SUPERLATIVE	Of all of them, Charlie told the **funniest** joke.

17a **A one-syllable modifier regularly forms its comparative and superlative degrees by adding** *–er* **and** *–est.*

POSITIVE	My cat is **wet** from the rain.
COMPARATIVE	My dog is **wetter** than my cat is.
SUPERLATIVE	My horse is the **wettest** of my three pets.

17b **Some two-syllable modifiers form their comparative and superlative degrees by adding** *–er* **and** *–est.* **Others form these degrees by using** *more* **and** *most* **or** *less* **and** *least.*

Positive	Comparative	Superlative
windy	windier	windiest
careful	more careful	most careful
anxious	less anxious	least anxious

NOTE Some two-syllable modifiers, such as *common*, may use either *–er* and *–est* or *more/less* and *most/least.*

17c **Modifiers that have more than two syllables form their comparative and superlative degrees with** *more/less* **and** *most/least.*

Positive	Comparative	Superlative
original	more original	most original
beautiful	less beautiful	least beautiful

17d **Some modifiers use irregular methods of forming their comparative and superlative degrees.**

Do not add *–er* and *–est* or *more/less* and *most/least* to irregularly formed comparisons.

Positive	Comparative	Superlative
good	better	best
bad	worse	worst
many/much	more	most

EXERCISE 1   Forming Degrees of Comparison with Modifiers

On the lines below, write the comparative and superlative degrees of each of the following modifiers. Use a dictionary as necessary.

EX. 1. large   _____larger_____   _____largest_____

1. exciting   _____   _____

2. happy   _____   _____

3. delightful   _____   _____

4. little   _____   _____

5. quickly   _____   _____

6. blue   _____   _____

7. afraid   _____   _____

8. suspicious   _____   _____

9. round   _____   _____

10. far   _____   _____

EXERCISE 2   Proofreading for Correct Comparative and Superlative Forms

Underline the comparative or superlative form of the modifier in each sentence below. If the form is incorrect, write the correct form above it.

EX. 1. Avis will be <u>carefuller</u> than your last mechanic.   *more careful*

1. Pelé was certainly one of the successfullest soccer players in the world.

2. The judges thought that Alice's poem was originaller than mine.

3. This hurricane was the destructivest that we've had in years!

4. That man looks like the most happy worker in the city.

5. Of all the foods here, sushi is the least likely to contain fat.

6. Which do you like better, traveling by train or by airplane?

7. I'm not sure which of those two is the more safe way to travel.

8. Of all the cities we visited in Japan, Kyoto is the beautifullest.

9. I saw several silk kimonos on sale, but I decided to buy the

   least expensive one.

10. This trip was even gooder than the one we took last year.

USES OF COMPARATIVE AND SUPERLATIVE FORMS

17e Use the comparative degree when comparing two things. Use the superlative degree when comparing more than two.

COMPARATIVE   The little red pepper is **spicier** than the green one.
SUPERLATIVE   This little red pepper is the **spiciest** one of all.

NOTE   In everyday conversation, people sometimes use the superlative degree when comparing two things: *I pitch best with my right hand.*

17f Include the word *other* or *else* when comparing one thing with others that belong in the same group.

NONSTANDARD   Anaba writes better than any student in her class.
STANDARD   Anaba writes better than any **other** student in her class.

NONSTANDARD   Uncle Luis is funnier than anyone in my family.
STANDARD   Uncle Luis is funnier than anyone **else** in my family.

17g Avoid double comparisons.

A *double comparison* is incorrect because it contains both *–er* and *more/less* or *–est* and *most/least.*

NONSTANDARD   I think Tom Landry is more older than your father.
STANDARD   I think Tom Landry is **older** than your father.

17h Be sure your comparisons are clear.

UNCLEAR   The restaurants in Rockport are cheaper than New York City.
CLEAR   The restaurants in Rockport are cheaper than the restaurants in New York City.

EXERCISE 3 Identifying and Correcting Modifiers

For each of the following sentences, underline the error in the use of modifiers. Rewrite each sentence correctly on the line provided.

EX.   1. This film is <u>better than any</u> I've seen.

_____

1. Indian films are often more longer than American films.

_____

2. Bombay must contain the greater number of film posters in the world.

_____

3. Tien liked this film more than anyone who saw it.

_____

4. This comedy is the least funniest in this film festival.

_____

5. The films of Mr. Satyajit Ray are more seriouser than those of Mr. B. Kapoor.

_____

6. Of my two sisters, Nora knows most about film directors.

_____

7. This theater is much less comfortable than yesterday.

_____

8. The movies made by students are not as polished as experienced directors.

_____

9. It is certainly more hotter outside than it is in the theater.

_____

10. Directors in India make more films than directors in any country in the world.

_____

11. In India, the price of a movie ticket is cheapest than in the United States.

_____

12. The length of the movie is least important than the entertainment it provides.

_____

13. Kapoor wants to get the most best stars and the most best music for his movies.

_____

14. Will Kapoor continue to be India's bigger filmmaker?

_____

15. One of his movies was the larger production ever made in India.

_____

DANGLING MODIFIERS

17i   A modifying phrase or clause that does not clearly and sensibly modify a word or group of words in a sentence is called a *dangling modifier*.

When a modifying phrase containing a verbal comes at the beginning of a sentence, the phrase is followed by a comma. Immediately after that comma should come the word that the phrase modifies.

UNCLEAR   Visiting Philadelphia, several museums interested me.
  CLEAR   Visiting Philadelphia, I was interested in several museums.

UNCLEAR   To see Henry Ossawa Tanner's work, a visit to the Philadelphia Museum of Art is necessary.
  CLEAR   To see Henry Ossawa Tanner's work, you must visit the Philadelphia Museum of Art.

To correct a dangling modifier, rearrange the words in the sentence, and add or change words to make the meaning logical and clear.

 DANGLING   Arriving on a holiday, the museum was closed.
CORRECTED   Arriving on a holiday, we found the museum closed.

 NOTE   A sentence may appear to have a dangling modifier when *you* is the understood subject. In such cases, the modifier is not dangling; it is modifying the understood subject.

EXAMPLE   To paint well, (you) spend a lot of time drawing.

EXERCISE 4   Revising Sentences by Eliminating Dangling Modifiers

On the line after each of the following sentences, indicate how you would revise the sentence to eliminate the dangling modifier. As shown by the example, you need not write the whole sentence.

EX.   1.   Looking at one drawing, the signature surprised me.
       drawing, I was surprised by the signature.

1.   Displayed in one gallery, we enjoyed the Japanese woodcuts. _____

_____

2.   To see everything on this floor, a plan is necessary. _____

_____

3. Looking at the watercolors, some looked like oil paintings. _____

_____

4. Hung on several walls, Sharon read placards telling about the artist's life.

_____

5. To prevent damage, many pieces were covered with plastic shields by the officials.

_____

6. There will be a special show next month of local photography.

_____

7. Some winter scenes gave us chills painted in grays and whites.

_____

8. My favorite colors were used in several paintings, which are mainly reds and yellows.

_____

9. Along the New England coast, one group of photographs showed storm scenes.

_____

10. Expecting a large crowd, arrangements were made by the museum to change the viewing hours.

_____

EXERCISE 5   Writing Sentences with Introductory Modifiers

Write ten complete sentences using the introductory modifiers below. Be sure the word that the phrase modifies immediately follows the comma. Write your sentences on your own paper.

EX.   1. Wearing bug repellent,
           Wearing bug repellent, we ventured into the woods.

1. Waving a camera,
2. To create memorable pictures,
3. Working quickly,
4. Covered with mosquito bites,
5. To photograph hummingbirds,
6. After listening to the report,
7. Walking to school,
8. Made from leather,
9. Creeping around the door,
10. To talk on this pay telephone,

MISPLACED MODIFIERS

17j   A *misplaced modifier* is a phrase or clause that sounds awkward because it modifies the wrong word or group of words.

Modifying phrases should be placed as near as possible to the word or words they modify.

MISPLACED   The picture was taken at the August Moon Festival of the little girl in a yellow costume.

CORRECTED   The picture **of the little girl in a yellow costume** was taken at the August Moon Festival.

Adjective clauses and adverb clauses should be placed so that they are clearly linked to the words they modify.

MISPLACED   Before you leave, get the atlas from the table that you need.

CORRECTED   Before you leave, get the atlas **that you need** from the table.

EXERCISE 6   Revising Sentences by Correcting Misplaced Modifiers

Underline the misplaced modifier in each of the following sentences. Indicate where the modifier should appear in the sentence by inserting a caret (∧).

EX.   1.   The detective ∧ questioned Ms. O'Rourke <u>with the dark beard</u>.

1.   Written by Henry David Thoreau, I admire the simple country life portrayed in *Walden*.

2.   We could hear the tornado approaching from our basement shelter.

3.   Leonora went to her room after her brother had left for the video arcade to do some homework.

4.   The car will win an award that is the most fuel-efficient.

5.   We read about the candidates who are running for mayor in the Sunday paper.

6.   In the sky last night, our astronomy class enjoyed watching a meteor shower.

7.   Their dog was waiting at the door looking very excited and wagging its tail.

8. We drove Mr. Mason from his house to the mall, who needed to run an errand.

9. Always a very caring person, Rebecca decided to become a nurse at the age of twelve.

10. The neighbor's dogs frightened the Yamaguchis' new baby barking at night.

11. The salad is in the refrigerator for your lunch.

12. I willingly admit that I might have given up and gone home in her situation.

13. Mrs. Worthington gave some of her prize-winning roses to her neighbor arranged in a white basket.

14. The rusty, green van belongs to our next-door neighbor that is parked in the driveway.

15. Nikki drove the family car wearing sunglasses and a leather cap.

16. The Allentown Community Choir rehearsed a new song paying careful attention to the rhythm.

17. Cheering the loudest, the prize was awarded to the team.

18. During the fire drill, the students were asked to leave the room quietly by the teacher.

19. The puppy sat in the doorway scratching its head.

20. Phoebe got all the supplies from the store that she needed.

21. Granny told me a story about getting caught in a storm sitting in her chair near the window.

22. They fixed the bike's flat quickly working together.

23. I work for my money hard.

24. You can find the photographs that Dad took of your great-grandparents in one of these old photo albums.

25. The old family home sat on a hill needing repair.

CHAPTER REVIEW

A. Revising Sentences by Correcting Modifiers

In the sentences below, correct all errors in the use of modifiers. Rewrite each sentence on your own paper.

EX. 1. Yo-Yo Ma must be one of the famousest cellists in the world.
  1. *Yo-Yo Ma must be one of the most famous cellists in the world.*

1. These seats are more better than the ones we had last month.
2. In his seat I told my young cousin to sit quietly.
3. That pianist is better than any musician I've heard.
4. Sitting in the center of the hall, the music surrounded us.
5. The trio is playing the piece that you liked onstage now.
6. There are many families in the audience with children.
7. Later, a chorus will sing the familiarest songs from *The Wizard of Oz*.
8. Having seen the movie, the songs were enjoyed by the children.
9. Which song is your more favorite?
10. Moving her arms gracefully, we watched the conductor.

B. Using Modifiers Correctly in a Paragraph

In the following paragraph, underline any misplaced or incorrect modifiers. For misplaced modifiers, indicate where the modifier should appear in the sentence by inserting a caret (∧). For all other errors, write the corrections above the sentence.

EX. [1] Many people ∧ visit Nashville <u>who like music</u>.

[1] Of all the U. S. cities, Nashville is probably the one that is more famous for country music. [2] However, people can enjoy a great variety of music who go there. [3] In 1980, my parents enjoyed a performance of the Royal Laotian Classical Dance Troupe, whose vacation included a visit to Nashville. [4] Before performing, fancy costumes and masks were put on. [5] Then the dancers told traditional stories using their costumes and their bodies. [6] The stories about ancient Laos that they told were more than six hundred years old. [7] The music is played on stringed and percussion

231

instruments that accompanies the dances. [8] Originally performed

only for the king of Laos and his court, the Nashville audience

seemed to appreciate the royal dances. [9] These dances for centuries

have been passed from one generation to the next. [10] Taking over

Laos in 1975, the royal dancers' safety was threatened by the

Communists.

C.   Using Modifiers in an Adventure Story

As an author of adventure stories, you have jotted down the following list of
phrases and clauses as prewriting for a new tale. On your own paper, use
ten of the following phrases and clauses correctly to write your opening
paragraph. To make sure that your paragraph does not have any dangling
or misplaced modifiers, underline the modifiers you use, and draw arrows
to the words they modify.

speeding down the mountainside	rubbing my bruised leg
while enjoying a brief rest	which I discovered by accident
to avoid falling in the canyon	from my experience as a rider
chased by a wild beast	to avoid being seen
that seemed safer	hearing a moaning sound
diving into the water	that caused my hair to curl
jumping off the speeding freight train	to escape the extreme engine heat
that was hidden inside a cave	creeping silently along
to save myself from certain disaster	hoping for some daylight
which later saved my life	that was under a rotted log

EX.   that seemed safer
       My eyes darted around frantically as I searched for a path that seemed safer.

This chapter presents an alphabetical list of common problems in English usage. Throughout the chapter, examples are labeled *standard* or *nonstandard*. **Standard English** is the most widely accepted form of English. **Nonstandard English** is language that does not follow the rules and guidelines of standard English.

a, an   These *indefinite articles* refer to one of a general group.

EXAMPLES   Jaime ate **a** banana and **an** orange.
             Crystal bought **an** umbrella and **a** uniform for work.

Use *a* before words beginning with a consonant sound; use *an* before words beginning with a vowel sound. In the example above, *a* is used before *uniform* because the *u* in *uniform* has a consonant sound.

affect, effect   *Affect* is a verb meaning "to influence." *Effect* used as a verb means "to accomplish." Used as a noun, *effect* means "the result of some action."

EXAMPLES   Did the happy story **affect** your mood?
             The coach gave a speech to **effect** a change in the team's
                 morale.
             The sad story had a negative **effect** on me.

all the farther, all the faster   These phrases are used in some parts of the United States to mean "as far as" or "as fast as."

NONSTANDARD   One mile is all the farther he can run.
   STANDARD   One mile is **as far as** he can run.

among   See **between, among**.

and etc.   *Etc.* is an abbreviation of the Latin phrase *et cetera*, meaning "and other things." Thus, *and etc.* means "and and other things." Do not use *and* with *etc.*

EXAMPLE   During baseball practice, Philip worked on batting, fielding,
               throwing, *etc.* [not *and etc.*]

anywheres, everywheres, nowheres, somewheres   Use these words without the final *s*.

EXAMPLE   I looked **everywhere** for that recipe. [not *everywheres*]

as   See **like, as**.

at   Do not use *at* after *where*.

NONSTANDARD   I don't know where she's at.
    STANDARD   I don't know **where** she is.

beside, besides   *Beside* is a preposition that means "by the side of" someone or something. *Besides* as a preposition means "in addition to." As an adverb, *besides* means "moreover."

EXAMPLES   Lily sat **beside** Natalya on the bus. [preposition]
    Besides cleaning his room, he has to wash the dishes. [preposition]
    I don't have enough money for the movie. **Besides**, I haven't finished my homework. [adverb]

EXERCISE 1   Solving Common Usage Problems

For each sentence below, underline the correct word or expression in parentheses.

EX.   1.   I like to use (*a*, *an*) straw.

1.   "This is (*all the farther*, *as far as*) I can swim," he panted as he climbed into the boat.

2.   (*Beside*, *Besides*) Shanaz, no one did well on the test.

3.   The pollution from that factory (*affects*, *effects*) the air quality of the entire region.

4.   Shiloh's puppy follows him (*everywheres*, *everywhere*).

5.   Sometimes I don't know where your head (*is*, *is at*)!

EXERCISE 2   Proofreading Sentences for Correct Usage

In each sentence below, draw a line through the error in usage, and write the correct form above it.

EX.   1.   The trunk with Grandma's heirlooms is ~~somewheres~~ somewhere in the attic.

1.   I hope Nicholas sits besides me at the play.

2.   The missing key was nowheres to be found.

3.   Does Rodrigo really practice the trombone for a hour each morning?

4.   No one seems to know where our next basketball game is at.

5.   Max has to dust the living room, set the table, arrange the flowers, and etc., before the guests arrive.

BETWEEN, AMONG / FEWER, LESS

between, among   Use *between* when you are referring to two things at a time, even though they may be part of a group consisting of more than two. Use *among* when you are thinking of a group rather than of separate things.

EXAMPLES   Place that plant **between** the piano and the chair.
Greetings were exchanged **between** the six guests. [Although there were more than two guests, the guests greeted one another in pairs, or two at a time.]
There was excitement **among** the fans when Irisa scored a goal. [The fans are thought of as a group in this situation.]

could of   Do not write *of* with the helping verb *could*. Write *could have*. Also avoid *ought to of, had of, should of, would of, might of*, and *must of*.

EXAMPLES   Jamila **could have** helped you. [not *could of*]
I **ought to have** made souvlakia for dinner. [not *ought to of*]

discover, invent   *Discover* means "to be the first to find, see, or learn about something that already exists." *Invent* means "to be the first to do or make something."

EXAMPLES   Edmond Halley **discovered** the comet that bears his name.
The piano was **invented** by Bartolomeo Cristofori in 1709.

effect, affect   See **affect, effect.**

everywheres   See **anywheres,** etc.

fewer, less   *Fewer* is used with plural words. *Less* is used with singular words. *Fewer* tells "how many"; *less* tells "how much."

EXAMPLES   **Fewer** people attended the festival this year.
The festival took up **less** space this year.

EXERCISE 3   Identifying Correct Usage

For each of the following sentences, underline the correct word or expression in parentheses.

EX.   1.   My ancestors lived (*somewheres, somewhere*) in El Salvador.

1.   We (*should have, should of*) left earlier.

2.   Thomas Edison (*discovered, invented*) the electric light.

3. Did that hurricane (*affect, effect*) your town?

4. I (*might have, might of*) taken that phone message.

5. Mika sat on the lawn (*among, between*) the dandelions.

6. The heat had a negative (*affect, effect*) on my energy level.

7. When we checked the returns, we were surprised that (*fewer, less*) people donated money this month than last month.

8. Lan (*must have, must of*) rehearsed for hours.

9. I searched (*everywhere, everywheres*) for books about Indira Gandhi, a former prime minister of India.

10. Jonas Salk (*discovered, invented*) a cure for polio.

11. There was (*fewer, less*) room in the car than we had expected.

12. Samuel and Liona (*ought to have, ought to of*) studied harder for their grammar quiz.

13. My grandfather lives in Laos, a country (*among, between*) Vietnam and Thailand.

14. Marco needs to (*affect, effect*) a detailed plan for our project.

15. I had (*less, fewer*) homework assignments than usual, so I (*could have, could of*) helped you.

16. I (*could have, could of*) won the race if only I hadn't gotten a cramp.

17. The television program showed that the four thieves split the stolen money (*among, between*) themselves.

18. Nathaniel has been having (*fewer, less*) headaches since he improved his diet.

19. Working in their father's shop, the boys (*discovered, invented*) a burglar alarm.

20. Thaddeus (*ought to have, ought to of*) signed up for that class when there was an opening.

HAD OF / OUGHT TO OF

had of   See **could of**.

had ought, hadn't ought   Unlike other verbs, *ought* is not used with *had*.

NONSTANDARD   Jake had ought to budget his money; he hadn't ought to
spend so much that he can't save any money.

STANDARD   Jake **ought** to budget his money; he **ought not** to
spend so much that he can't save any money.

invent, discover   See **discover, invent**.

kind, sort, type   The words *this, that, these,* and *those* should always
agree in number with the words *kind, sort,* and *type*.

EXAMPLE   Is **this type** of music more relaxing than **those** other **types**?

learn, teach   *Learn* means "to acquire knowledge." *Teach* means "to
instruct" or "to show how."

EXAMPLE   I want to **learn** to speak Italian; do you think you can **teach** me?

leave, let   *Leave* means "to go away" or "to depart from." *Let* means "to
allow" or "to permit."

NONSTANDARD   Leave Jamal go home.
STANDARD   **Let** Jamal go home.

less   See **fewer, less**.

like, as   In informal English, the preposition *like* is often used as a
conjunction meaning "as." In formal English, use *like* to introduce a
prepositional phrase, and use *as* to introduce a subordinate clause.

EXAMPLES   That building looks **like** a castle.
Please do the project **as** our teacher described.

might of, must of   See **could of**.

nowheres   See **anywheres,** etc.

of   Do not use *of* with prepositions such as *inside, off,* or *outside*.

EXAMPLES   I went **inside** the pantry. [not *inside of*]
I took some crackers **off** the top shelf. [not *off of*]
I walked **outside** the building. [not *outside of*]

ought to of   See **could of**.

EXERCISE 4   Identifying Correct Usage

In each sentence below, underline the correct word or expression in parentheses.

EX.   1. Leon (*had ought, ought*) to attend the spring festival.

1. Ms. Gabriel will (learn, teach) the class about Martin Luther King, Jr.

2. Please (let, leave) my puppy play in the yard.

3. Did you find evidence that this (type, types) of moccasin was worn by many Native Americans?

4. Wyatt looks (as, like) his older sister.

5. We walked around (inside, inside of) the White House when we were in Washington, D.C.

EXERCISE 5   Correcting Errors in Usage

In the sentences below, draw a line through each error, and write the correct form above it. Some sentences contain more than one error.

EX.   1. Martina climbed ~~off of~~ her bicycle.
                       off

1. I would like to play my cello like Anthony does.

2. These kind of books learned us all about several kinds of inventions in ancient China.

3. That cave looked as a good camping spot, so we walked inside of it and looked around.

4. This kinds of enchilada is spicier than those kind.

5. We hadn't ought to swim without a lifeguard, even though the camp counselors learned us how to swim.

6. Please leave me go with you to the Cinco de Mayo parade.

7. The sea lion has whiskers like a cat does.

8. Those type of rugs are made in Afghanistan.

9. The ball flew over the outfield wall and landed outside of the park.

10. We had ought to wear our rain gear for the hike to the summit.

SHOULD OF / WOULD OF

should of See **could of.**

some, somewhat In writing, do not use *some* for *somewhat* as an adverb.

NONSTANDARD I enjoyed hiking in the woods some.
    STANDARD I enjoyed hiking in the woods **somewhat.**

somewheres See **anywheres.**

sort See **kind**, etc.

teach See **learn, teach.**

than, then *Than* is a conjunction; *then* is an adverb.

EXAMPLES That lamp is brighter **than** this one.
    I will stop at the market; **then** I will visit you.

them *Them* should not be used as an adjective. Use *those* or *these*.

EXAMPLE Milagro enjoyed **those** long walks on the beach. [not *them*]

this here, that there The words *here* and *there* are unnecessary after *this* and *that*.

EXAMPLE I like **this** wallpaper. [not *this here*]
    Ida likes **that** style. [not *that there*]

type See **kind,** etc.

when, where Do not use *when* or *where* incorrectly in writing a definition. Do not use *where* for *that*.

NONSTANDARD A bialy is when you make a flat breakfast roll.
    STANDARD A bialy is a flat breakfast roll.
    STANDARD I heard in class **that** school is being canceled. [not *where*]

which, that, who The relative pronoun *who* refers to people only; *which* refers to things only; *that* refers to either people or things.

EXAMPLES Annmarie is the one **who** ordered that sandwich. [person]
    That afghan, **which** is in the closet, was a birthday gift. [thing]
    Eli was the person **that** I wanted to meet. [person]
    The salsa **that** I made is in the refrigerator. [thing]

would of See **could of.**

EXERCISE 6 Correcting Errors in Usage

For each sentence below, underline the correct word or expression in parentheses.

EX. 1. (*Them*, *Those*) books are about tropical rain forests.

1. Shina is (*some*, *somewhat*) interested in (*this*, *this here*) topic.

2. Rain forests, (*which*, *who*) have rain almost every day, have no frost.

3. Hundreds of kinds of trees grow in (*these*, *them*) forests.

4. Shina told me (*where*, *that*) the canopy is the tops of the trees, and animals living there climb a long (*way*, *ways*) in search of food.

5. Southeast Asia's rain forest is taller (*than*, *then*) most.

EXERCISE 7 Correcting Errors in Usage

In the sentences below, draw a line through each error, and write the correct form above it. Some sentences contain more than one error.

EX. 1. I am ~~some~~ familiar with the Red Cross.
       somewhat

1. A short ways down the street, people were donating blood.

2. This here blood drive was being run by the Red Cross.

3. Them Red Cross volunteers help people all over the world.

4. Volunteers are when people give their time and services without having to and often without being paid.

5. Red Cross volunteers, which can be found in many countries, are paid with grateful smiles from them people they help.

6. The Red Crescent, who operates in Muslim countries, is part of the same group.

7. When there's a natural disaster, they might have to carry blood and medical supplies a long ways.

8. Often, their work is some dangerous.

9. Red Cross and Red Crescent volunteers often can help better then governments can.

10. My friend Mr. Azakian learned me about these volunteers.

DOUBLE NEGATIVES

In a *double negative*, two negative words are used when one is sufficient. Avoid double negatives in both writing and speaking.

hardly, scarcely   The words *hardly* and *scarcely* both convey a negative meaning. Never use one of these words with another negative word.

EXAMPLES   **I can hardly** believe that my sister is graduating. [not *can't*]
The park **has scarcely** enough swings. [not *hasn't*]

no, nothing, none   Do not use one of these words with another negative word.

NONSTANDARD	We don't have no library books.
STANDARD	We **don't have any** library books.
STANDARD	We **have no** library books.
NONSTANDARD	I don't want nothing to do with the problem.
STANDARD	I **don't want anything** to do with the problem.
STANDARD	I **want nothing** to do with the problem.
NONSTANDARD	Kareena wanted tickets, but there weren't none left.
STANDARD	Kareena wanted tickets, but there **weren't any** left.
STANDARD	Kareena wanted tickets, but there **were none** left.

EXERCISE 8   Correcting Errors in Usage

Each of the sentences below contains at least one error in usage. Draw a line through each error, and write the correct form above it.

EX.   1.   Hector ~~can't hardly~~ *can hardly* believe he made the team.

1.   I didn't have no plans last night, so I went for a long walk.

2.   Kali's family owns a wonderful restaurant that hasn't scarcely ever had a slow moment.

3.   Ricardo didn't buy nothing at the fruit and vegetable market.

4.   Asa and I don't have no time to practice today, and we didn't hardly have any time yesterday.

5.   We wanted to build a real wigwam, but there weren't no poles for the frame.

EXERCISE 9   Proofreading Paragraphs for Double Negatives

In the paragraph below, draw a line through the errors in usage. Write the correct form above the underlined error. Some sentences contain no errors.

EX.   [1] I ~~can't hardly~~ believe that I have never heard of this poet.
can't (or can hardly)

[1] Born in 1917 in Topeka, Kansas, Gwendolyn Brooks didn't hardly live there for long. [2] She wasn't no adult, but just a teenager, when her poetry was first published in the *Chicago Defender* and *American Childhood*. [3] At college, and later at the South Side Community Art Center, Gwendolyn didn't miss no chance to improve her writing. [4] As a result, she didn't hardly surprise people by winning several local poetry contests. [5] Her poetry hadn't scarcely appeared in *Poetry* magazine before she published her first book of poems, *A Street in Bronzeville*, in 1945. [6] The critics didn't have nothing but praise for her work, and she received two awards in a row. [7] Winning the awards meant that she wouldn't have to do nothing but write poetry for a while.

[8] In 1949, Ms. Brooks published *Annie Allen*, which didn't include none of her previous work. [9] For these new poems, she won nothing no less important than the 1950 Pulitzer Prize in poetry. [10] No other black woman had never won this before. [11] Ms. Brooks's style became more casual through the 1950s and 1960s, but the change did not take away nothing from her humor and skill. [12] In the 1970s, the themes of her writing were not different from the social issues of the times. [13] Her children's stories and novels of the 1970s and 1980s didn't reflect these themes no less than her poetry had. [14] At various times over the years, she went back to college— not as a student, but as a teacher of poetry. [15] Perhaps nothing couldn't match the honor given to Ms. Brooks in 1968 when she became the poet laureate of Illinois.

CHAPTER REVIEW

A. Identifying Errors in Usage

For each sentence below, underline the correct word or expression in parentheses.

EX. 1. The discussion (*between*, <u>*among*</u>) my classmates was about trains.

1. Did you read (*where*, *that*) railroads have been used since the 1500s?

2. These early (*types*, *type*) of rails were made of wood.

3. Trains were wagons that had to be pulled (*everywheres*, *everywhere*) by horses.

4. Steam railroads were (*discovered*, *invented*) in the 1800s.

5. Steam engines looked much (*like*, *as*) the diesel engines of today.

6. George Stephenson had a big (*effect*, *affect*) on this (*kinds*, *kind*) of transportation.

7. (*This here*, *This*) man built trains so that people could ride (*inside*, *inside of*) the cars.

8. Our teacher (*learned*, *taught*) us about the transcontinental railroad.

9. This (*must have*, *must of*) been one of the most important projects in U.S. history.

10. The construction of a nationwide railroad system immensely (*effected*, *affected*) the country's growth.

11. One thing that (*hadn't ought*, *ought not*) to be ignored is that immigrants (*which*, *who*) were mostly from China built this railroad.

12. Before the transcontinental railroad, there were (*fewer*, *less*) people in the West.

13. After the railroad was built, the United States went a long (*way*, *ways*) in growing as a nation.

14. The transcontinental railroad, (*beside*, *besides*) transporting people, enabled industries to expand to new areas.

15. For my project on the railroad, I am building (*a*, *an*) steam engine out of folded paper.

B.   Using Words Correctly in Sentences

Because your friends respect your opinion, they often ask your advice on how to handle their problems. On your own paper, use fifteen of the words or expressions in this chapter to write sentences suggesting solutions to a few of your friends' problems. Underline the words or expressions you use.

EX.   1. <u>Learn</u> the rules for using diving equipment before you try diving.

Peanuts reprinted by permission of UFS, Inc.

C.   Writing a Letter

You are a diver on an expedition. Exploring the sea one morning, you come across a large sunken ship. You and your partner decide to enter it and look around. Later, when you are back on your ship, you decide to sit down and write a letter to a friend, describing your day and all that you saw in the sunken ship. In your letter, use five of the words or expressions covered in this chapter. Underline the words and the expressions that you use.

EX.   Dear Lucia,
          You <u>would have</u> been interested in our discovery today.

SENTENCES, PRONOUN I, AND INTERJECTION O

19a   Capitalize the first word in every sentence.

EXAMPLES   **The** bus is late.
We may be late for the game.

Traditionally, the first word of a line of poetry is capitalized.

EXAMPLE   **We** wandered freely in the park
Until the summer sky grew dark.

NOTE   Some writers do not always follow these capitalization rules. If you are quoting, use letters exactly as the author uses them in the source of the quotation.

☞ **REFERENCE NOTE:** For more information about using capital letters in quotations, see page 281.

19b   Capitalize the pronoun *I* and the interjection *O*.

Although it is rarely used, *O* is always capitalized. Generally, it is reserved for invocations and is followed by the name of the person or thing being addressed. You will more often use the interjection *oh*, which is not capitalized unless it is the first word of the sentence.

EXAMPLES   When **I** wake up my brother, **I** sometimes say, "**O** Sleepyhead, you will miss your bus."
We paddled safely through, but **oh**, what a struggle we had!

EXERCISE 1   Capitalizing Sentences in a Paragraph

In the following paragraph, circle the words that should begin with a capital letter.

EX.   (my) favorite section of the orchestra is the percussion section

1   drums, castanets, and xylophones are all percussion

2   instruments. the player strikes these instruments in some way to

3   make a sound. for striking, the player may use sticks, mallets, or

4   sometimes brushes. pitch, though, is not adjustable on some

5   percussion instruments. for a xylophone, the length of the bars

6 determines the pitch when you play it, but many drums are tuned

7 by a player. have you ever watched the timpanist tune a

8 kettledrum? the player adjusts the skin of the drum to make the

9 pitch higher or lower. in order to do this, the player uses a special

10 key to loosen or tighten the tuning pegs. i love to hear the

11 timpani in *Thus Spoke Zarathustra*. next year I hope to learn to

12 play the timpani in our school orchestra.

EXERCISE 2 Correcting Capitalization Errors in Sentences

In the sentences below, underline the words that have errors in capitalization.

EX. 1. If i could have three wishes, one would be "Give me three more wishes, o genie!"

1. Do some holy books often address their readers, "o faithful believers"?

2. the first snowfall is beautiful, but Oh, how i wish it were spring!

3. We laughed when he said the punch line, "So i bit him."

4. have you ever heard anyone say, "Woe is me!"?

5. The team chanted, "o you Tigers! go! go! go!"

6. are you buying cookies this year from the Girl Scouts?

7. we studied the works of the Danish poet Johannes Ewald.

8. Adolfo López Mateos was, i believe, president of Mexico from 1958–64.

9. the Chinese poet Li Po lived from A.D. 701–762.

10. have you ever heard of the first-century Greek critic Longinus?

PROPER NOUNS AND ADJECTIVES

19c   **Capitalize proper nouns and proper adjectives.**

A *common noun* names one of a group of people, places, or things. A *proper noun* names a particular person, place, or thing. *Proper adjectives* are formed from proper nouns.

   REFERENCE NOTE: For more about proper nouns, see page 93. For more about proper adjectives, see page 101.

Common nouns are not capitalized unless they begin a sentence or a direct quotation, or are included in a title. Proper nouns are always capitalized.

Common Nouns	Proper Nouns	Proper Adjectives
a country	Mexico	Mexican artist
a ruler	Napoleon	Napoleonic period
a city	Paris	Parisian styles
a poet	Dante	Dantean verses

Some proper nouns consist of more than one word. In these names, short prepositions (generally fewer than five letters) and articles are not capitalized.

EXAMPLES   Statue of Liberty   Alexander the Great

   Proper nouns and adjectives sometimes lose their capitals through frequent usage.

EXAMPLES   china   pasteurize   sandwich

EXERCISE 3   Identifying Correct Capitalization

For each of the following pairs of phrases, write the letter of the correct phrase on the line provided.

EX. _____ 1. a. visit a University
                  b. visit Stanford University

_____ 1. a. last tuesday
              b. last Tuesday

_____ 2. a. the Brooklyn Bridge
              b. a Bridge in New York City

_____ 3. a. Kanes county
              b. Kanes County

_____ 4. a. Mississippi River
              b. Mississippi river

_____ 5. a. a european tour
        b. a trip through Europe

_____ 6. a. a famous film actor
        b. actor danny glover

_____ 7. a. a man named Eric the Red
        b. a man named Eric The Red

_____ 8. a. nation's laws
        b. mexican laws

_____ 9. a. Cajun dishes
        b. cajun dishes

_____ 10. a. World Trade Center
         b. World Trade center

EXERCISE 4   Correcting Errors in Capitalization

In the sentences below, underline each error in capitalization. Write your correction in the space above the error.

EX.   1. Last ~~october~~, my brother Earl and I went to ~~new york city~~.
            October   *New York City*

1. We took a bus from newark, new jersey, after lunch.

2. When we arrived at the greyhound station, we took another bus.

3. The bus went to Central park.

4. Sharika led the group of canadian tourists through the egyptian exhibit at the museum.

5. Many people were dressed in the latest italian styles.

6. We got off the bus and walked to lexington avenue.

7. On the way, we stopped to talk with a man called binti, an African Artist.

8. He had recently arrived from zanzibar, an island off the coast of africa.

9. He was selling persian rugs and tapestries.

10. The rugs had pictures of the united nations seal.

11. Every ten years, the bureau of the census counts the U.S. population.

12. Tagalog is the language used by the austronesian people of the same name.

13. The ukrainian Sculptor archipenko was born in 1887.

14. The Lammermuir hills are in the borders and lothian regions of Scotland.

15. Laos, formerly a state of french indochina, is in southeast Asia.

PEOPLE AND PLACES

19d Capitalize the names of people.

EXAMPLES   Maya Angelou, Herman Melville, Joyce Chen, Eva Perón

19e Capitalize geographical names.

Type of Name	Examples
continents	South America, Australia
countries	Sri Lanka, Israel, Albania
cities, towns	Oklahoma City, Acton
counties, townships	Essex County, Niles Township
states	Arizona, North Carolina
islands	Staten Island, Key West
bodies of water	Bay of Fundy, Pacific Ocean
streets, highways	South Marshall Street, Ford Boulevard
parks and forests	Natchez National Park, Sherwood Forest
mountains	Andes Mountains, Mount Everest
regions	the South, the Northwest

NOTE   Words such as *east, west, north,* and *south* are not capitalized when they indicate directions.

EXAMPLES   Drive **south** two miles and take a left. [direction]
Citrus fruits grow throughout the **South**. [region]

However, these words are capitalized when they name a particular place.

EXAMPLES   in the No**r**thwest   by the South

NOTE   In a hyphenated street number, the second part of the number is not capitalized.

EXAMPLE   West Ninety-third Street

EXERCISE 5   Correcting Errors in Capitalization

In the sentences below, underline each error in capitalization. Write your correction in the space above the error.

EX.   1.   The <u>appalachian mountains</u> stretch from <u>georgia</u> to <u>maine</u>.
> Appalachian Mountains   Georgia   Maine

1. The country of argentina is in the southern part of south america.

2. Just South of the city of new orleans, the mississippi river empties into the Gulf of Mexico.

3. The novelist jorge amado was born in brazil in 1912.

4. We traveled to the southwest to study the varieties of cactus that grow there.

5. When the bus reaches herald square, how much farther will I ride to Thirty-Fifth Street?

6. As you know, cochise was a famous American indian.

7. The hetch hetchy valley is located in yosemite national park.

8. Mountains known as the alps tower over much of europe.

9. The states of new jersey and pennsylvania are separated by the delaware river.

10. We visited my friend Ramón in jefferson city, the capital of missouri.

11. Why did we count fifteen streets between Eleventh Street and Twenty-First Street?

12. Penzance is a port in cornwall in the southwest part of England.

13. The urubamba river, flowing through peru, joins a second river to become the Ucayali River.

14. Have you ever visited the Dinaric alps Northeast of Italy?

15. The Little Karroo mountains are part of the Drakensburg mountains in south africa.

GROUPS, EVENTS, AND NATIONALITIES

19f **Capitalize the names of organizations, teams, businesses, institutions, and government bodies.**

Type of Name	Examples
organizations	American Legion
teams	Houston Oilers
businesses	Ford Motor Company
government bodies	Department of Agriculture
institutions	University of Rochester

NOTE Do not capitalize words such as *hotel, theater, college, high school, post office,* and *courthouse* unless they are part of a proper name.

EXAMPLES   Gloucester High School
my high school

19g **Capitalize the names of historical events and periods, special events, and calendar items.**

Type of Name	Examples
historical events, periods	World War I, Middle Ages
special events	Olympic Games, Summerfest
calendar items	Monday, May, Arbor Day

NOTE Do not capitalize the name of a season unless it is personified or used in the name of a special event.

EXAMPLES   We felt Winter's rule.
the annual Dartmouth Winter Carnival

19h **Capitalize the names of nationalities, races, and peoples.**

EXAMPLES   Spanish, Caucasian, Asian, Cherokee, Zulu

NOTE The words *black* and *white* may or may not be capitalized when they refer to races.

EXAMPLE   Both Blacks and Whites [*or* blacks and whites] have
worked to protect our civil rights.

EXERCISE 6   Proofreading Sentences for Correct Capitalization

In the sentences below, underline each error in capitalization. Write your correction in the space above the error.

EX.   1.   My neighbor, Mr. <u>johnson</u>, works for <u>bell</u> telephone. *(Johnson / Bell Telephone)*

1.   Our local bank, first federal savings, is closed on thanksgiving day.

2.   Many doctors belong to the American medical association.

3.   One well-known egyptian leader was anwar sadat.

4.   People celebrated the end of world war I on armistice day.

5.   After he graduated from the university of maryland, John Lucas played basketball for the houston rockets.

6.   The Veterans of Foreign Wars helps soldiers from world wars I and II.

7.   In Canada, Christmas day is the day before Boxing day.

8.   Among Spanish leaders of the Middle ages, el cid was quite famous.

9.   We gladly said farewell to summer and her long, hot days.

10.   Fans throughout the stadium cheered the team from the university of arizona.

EXERCISE 7   Identifying Correct Capitalization

For each of the pairs of phrases below, write the letter of the correct phrase on the line provided.

EX.   __a.__   1.   a.   the Chicago Bulls
                     b.   the New York mets

_____   1.   a.   a pleasant stay at the Bellevue hotel
              b.   a pleasant stay at the Bellevue Hotel

_____   2.   a.   a Service Bureau
              b.   the Internal Revenue Service

_____   3.   a.   an Italian opera
              b.   a french artist

_____   4.   a.   raced in the New York City Marathon
              b.   raced in the Marathon

_____   5.   a.   Stone age humans
              b.   Iron Age humans

OBJECT, STRUCTURES, AND SCHOOL SUBJECTS

19i **Capitalize brand names and trade names.**

EXAMPLES   Chicken of the Sea, Apple, Xerox

NOTE   Do not capitalize a common noun that follows a brand name: Chicken of the Sea tuna, Apple computer.

19j **Capitalize the names of ships, monuments, awards, planets, and other particular places or things.**

Type of Name	Examples
ships, trains	the *Mayflower*, the *Orient Express*
aircraft, spacecraft, missiles	*Hindenburg*, *Apollo I*, *Patriot*
monuments, memorials	Bunker Hill Monument, Martin Luther King, Jr., Memorial Center
buildings	Town Hall, Lincoln Center
awards	Nobel Prize
planets, stars	Mercury, the North Star

19k **Do not capitalize names of school subjects, except for languages or course names followed by a number.**

EXAMPLE   Besides math and art, I'm taking Italian and History 102.

EXERCISE 8   Proofreading Sentences for Correct Capitalization

In the following sentences, underline each error in capitalization. Write your correction in the space above the error.

EX.   1. Our school recently bought a <u>macintosh</u> computer.
　　　　　　　　　　　　　　　　　　　　Macintosh

1. The *Spirit of st. louis* was Charles Lindbergh's Airplane.

2. The Passenger Ship named *titanic* struck an iceberg.

3. Did *Gone with the Wind,* the famous movie that was set during the american civil war, win an academy award?

4. I am giving my sister a timex watch for Graduation.

5. The First Star you see at night is often the planet venus.

6. Roberto has to choose between Algebra II and American History.

7. Did the spacecraft called *skylab* travel to any Planets?

8. When you're in washington, d.c., be sure to visit the white house and the vietnam veterans war memorial.

9. The french novelist Jules Verne wrote about a fictitious submarine called *nautilus*, piloted by Captain nemo.

10. The Poet Richard Wilbur won the pulitzer prize in 1957 and in 1989.

11. Have you checked the records on file at city hall?

12. Scientists wonder what the environments of saturn and pluto might be like.

13. Did Rayjean tell you the old joke about who is buried in grant's tomb?

14. The Bay area rapid transit system helps workers get to their jobs.

15. Chuck won the most valuable player award again this year.

EXERCISE 9   Writing Sentences Using Correct Capitalization

You are a reporter covering the International Trade Fair in Tokyo, Japan. You are writing down notes that you can later use in an article. On your own paper, write ten sentences. In your sentences, include at least two of the rules for capitalization covered in this lesson. You might include types of products, companies represented, and awards won.

EX. 1. The U.S. Waterbed Co. won the Most Unusual New Product Award for its collapsible waterbed.

TITLES

19l   Capitalize titles.

(1) Capitalize the title of a person when it comes before a name.

EXAMPLES   **Dr.** Schweitzer, **Senator** Boxer, **Ms.** Katz

Do not capitalize a title that is used alone or that follows a person's name. Often, these titles are preceded by *a* or *the*.

EXAMPLES   A **president** whom I admire was Abraham Lincoln.
My friend Samantha is **vice-president** of the Stamp Club.

When a title is used alone in a direct address, it is usually capitalized.

EXAMPLES   I would like to interview you, **Senator.** Thanks, **Doctor.**

EXCEPTIONS Yes, **Sir** [or sir]. I will, **Ma'am** [or ma'am].

(2) Capitalize words showing family relationship when used with a person's name, but *not* when preceded by a possessive.

EXAMPLES   **Grandmother** Smith · **Aunt** Tanya   my grandfather   your father

(3) Capitalize the first and last words and all important words in titles of books, periodicals, poems, stories, historical documents, movies, television programs, works of art, and short musical compositions.

Unimportant words in titles include articles (*a, an, the*), coordinating conjunctions (*and, but, for, nor, or, so, yet*), and prepositions of fewer than five letters (*by, for, on, with*).

Type of Name	Examples
books	*A Tale of Two Cities*
periodicals	the *Chicago Tribune*
poems	"The Hollow Men"
stories	"The Open Window"
historical documents	**Bill of Rights**
movies	*In the Line of Fire*
television programs	*Sixty Minutes*
works of art	*View of Toledo*
short musical works	"A Minor Variation"

EXERCISE 10   Proofreading Sentences for Correct Capitalization

In the sentences below, underline each error in capitalization. Write your correction in the space above the error.

EX.   1.   Annie Lennox was interviewed in that issue of *rolling stone.* [Rolling Stone]

1.   In 2004, senator John Kerry lost the election to president George Bush.

2.   Uncle dan gave me a copy of Dorothy Parker's story, "a telephone call."

3.   I read a review of Tom Clancy's book, *the teeth of the tiger,* in the Sunday paper.

4.   My Cousin Adrienne and I have learned to play Willie Nelson's song "stranger" on the piano.

5.   I got interested in poetry only after I read "break, break, break" by Tennyson.

6.   "I gave it to your Father," said professor Jones.

7.   Let's get the march issue of *harper's.*

8.   I don't remember who wrote the declaration of independence, but I know that john hancock signed it.

9.   constable's painting *wivenhoe park, essex* is of the actual Wivenhoe Park.

10.   My Mother hopes to write a book called *cooking for others,* about her days at *La Cantina.*

11.   Have they read any of the books by doctor Joyce Brothers?

12.   Please ask Gerry to find out how many Presidents have been elected since 1900.

13.   King john of england did not want to sign the magna carta.

14.   Grandma moses painted *Out for Christmas trees* in 1987.

15.   The musical *Sunday In The Park With George* is based on the life of the French painter Georges Seurat.

CHAPTER REVIEW

A. Correcting Errors in Capitalization

In the sentences below, underline each error in capitalization. Write your correction in the space above the error.

EX. 1. When <u>i</u> finish <u>High School</u>, I want to go to <u>allegheny college</u>.
             I   high school   Allegheny College

1. Yes, doctor, i did read the article about you in *the denver post*.

2. The japanese city of hiroshima is located on a large Bay.

3. In philadelphia, the franklin institute is on benjamin franklin parkway.

4. Ana's Uncle Georgio wrote an article about the Spacecraft *challenger*.

5. When you're in the northwest, be sure to visit the city of seattle.

6. candace bergen, a television star, spoke at the spring women's conference at the University where my aunt Flo teaches.

7. We received a letter from governor rick perry of texas.

8. I bought this perdue chicken at hal's market on Fifty-Third Street.

9. Was this house really the inspiration for Nathaniel Hawthorne's book *the house of the seven gables?*

10. My Grandmother always says, "Waste not, want not."

11. Shall I take Biology I, English I, or Algebra?

12. West Indian music combines African, spanish, and other styles.

13. The National science fair is scheduled for early in the winter.

14. Marlene's new poem begins, "Say, Let me tell you a story."

15. Is Thanksgiving day always celebrated on a thursday ?

B. Proofreading a Paragraph for Correct Capitalization

In the paragraph below, all capital letters have been omitted. Underline each word that should be capitalized. Write your correction in the space above the word.

EX. [1] <u>next tuesday</u> the students at <u>west chester junior high</u>
        Next Tuesday   West Chester Junior High

will celebrate <u>earth day</u>.
               Earth Day

[1] my friend bobby ray robinson and i are making an exhibit called "steel from trash." [2] last week, we drove east on route 30 to interview doctor ramón martínez of the lukens steel company in the city of coatesville. [3] he assured us that his company is very interested in purchasing clean, used steel cans from the residents of west chester. [4] when bobby ray heard that, he said, "Let's get this recycling project off the ground!" [5] we are thinking about writing a letter to the *west chester gazette*.

C. Working with a Partner to Report on a Space Journey

The year is 2110, and you and your partner are newspaper reporters. Your editor has asked you to accompany an astronaut as she journeys into space. The purpose of your trip is to interview the astronaut, gathering details about her childhood and education, her training as an astronaut, the goals of her mission, and her hopes for the future.

1. Working together, use reference books and science magazines to make notes about current space missions. Add science fiction details to put your journey clearly into future times. Create character details for the astronaut. What might she have studied in school? How might she have trained for this mission?

2. On your own paper, write a news story based on your notes. Identify the name of the spacecraft, the name of the astronaut's school and hometown, the astronaut's cultural background, and the planets or stars the astronaut plans to visit. Be sure to capitalize correctly.

3. Be sure to include the name of your newspaper and your editor.

EX.   *Astronaut June Villarmo is proof of how important Science 102 can be!*

END MARKS AND ABBREVIATIONS

End marks are used to show the purpose of a sentence.

20a   A period follows a statement (or declarative sentence).

EXAMPLE   My father speaks Yiddish fluently**.**

20b   A question mark follows a question (or interrogative sentence).

EXAMPLE   Can you open this jar**?**

20c   An exclamation point follows an exclamation.

EXAMPLE   What a terrible storm that was**!**

20d   Either a period or an exclamation point may follow an imperative sentence.

EXAMPLES   Please wait here**.** [a request]
Don't touch that**!** [a command]

20e   A period usually follows an abbreviation.

Abbreviations with Periods	
Personal Names	I. M. Pei, H. H. Munroe
Titles Used with Names	Mrs., Ms., Mr., Dr., Jr., Sr.
States	Calif., N.H., Wash.
Organizations and Companies	Co., Inc., Assn.
Addresses	St., Rd., Ave., P.O. Box
Times	A.M., P.M., B.C., A.D.
Abbreviations Without Periods	
Government Agencies	HUD, IRS, FBI, WHO
States followed by ZIP Codes	Encinitas, CA 92024
Units of Measure	mg, cm, g, pt, gal, lb
Other Organizations	NASA, YMCA, NAACP

EXERCISE 1   Adding End Marks to Sentences

Write the end mark that should appear at the end of each sentence below.

EX.   1. On what day does the Vietnamese holiday Tet begin**?**

1. We will be fine if the rain doesn't start
2. How wonderful it is to meet you at last
3. Where do you leave newspapers for recycling
4. Tamara will proofread my book report
5. Were those pots made by a Maricopa potter
6. Please hold the door for me
7. How can we fix this bicycle
8. Stop that noise immediately
9. What a great interview Laurence Yep gave
10. This dog doesn't seem to have a license or rabies tag
11. Which museum will we visit on this field trip
12. Return these books to the library, please
13. A seismograph records earthquake data
14. Don't jump off a seesaw too quickly
15. Why can't we go to lunch together

EXERCISE 2   Proofreading for the Correct Use of Abbreviations

Add or delete periods where needed in the items below. On the line before each name or phrase, write *C* if the name or phrase is correct.

EX.   _____ 1. Mrs**.** Violette A**.** Johnson

_____ 1. is 12 cm. long
_____ 2. at 311 Catalpa Dr
_____ 3. U S Senator Joseph Montoya
_____ 4. Ed Begley, Jr
_____ 5. West Warwick, RI 02893
_____ 6. inside FBI headquarters
_____ 7. weighs 6 g
_____ 8. at 2:30 AM
_____ 9. E L Baines Enterprises, Inc
_____ 10. the room is 6 ft 6 in long

_____ 11. Dr Laura Stans
_____ 12. in the third century BC
_____ 13. Juan Sánchez, Sr.
_____ 14. by 3:00 P.M.
_____ 15. Ms. J R Peale
_____ 16. with the I.R.S.
_____ 17. San Diego, Calif
_____ 18. San Diego, CA 92119
_____ 19. 18 mg.
_____ 20. PO Box 87

COMMAS IN A SERIES

20f   Use commas to separate items in a series.

EXAMPLES   I will have hummus, tahini, and pita bread. [words]
They found locusts in their car, on their porch, and even in their kitchen. [phrases]
The drawings that Tena had dreamed about, that she had struggled to create, and that she had carefully matted were sold in a week. [clauses]

(1) If all items in a series are joined by *and* or *or*, do not use commas to separate them.

EXAMPLE   The bronco kicked and bucked and reared.

(2) Semicolons usually separate independent clauses in a series. Commas may separate short independent clauses, however.

EXAMPLES   We arrived well before dawn; we scrubbed the walls and ceilings; and we painted the rooms a pale blue.
We arrived, we cleaned, and we painted.

20g   Use commas to separate two or more adjectives preceding a noun.

EXAMPLE   This sari is a fine, beautiful silk.

When the last adjective in a series is thought of as part of the noun, the comma before the adjective is omitted. Compound nouns like *orange juice* and *lunch box* are considered single units.

EXAMPLE   My father grabbed his steel lunch box.

 Try inserting *and* between the adjectives in a series. If *and* fits sensibly, use a comma. For example, *fine and beautiful* sounds sensible, so a comma is used. *And* cannot be logically inserted in *steel lunch box*, however.

 REFERENCE NOTE: For more about compound nouns, see page 95.

EXERCISE 3   Proofreading Sentences for the Correct Use of Commas

Add commas where needed in the following sentences. On the line before each sentence, write *C* if the sentence is correct.

EX.   _____ 1. We rode through forests, up mountains, and across a desert.

_____ 1. French, Spanish and German will be offered next year.

_____ 2. Look for shrubs that are short rounded and dense.

_____ 3. Duane stared across the vast cornfields.

_____ 4. Invite Tyree to sing to dance or to tell jokes.

_____ 5. Jennifer sputtered coughed and finally took a deep breath.

_____ 6. Heat drought and poor soil were our biggest obstacles.

_____ 7. Someone drove up saw your sign and left a dollar.

_____ 8. We invited all of our aunts uncles and cousins.

_____ 9. Aretha was so determined to find her ring that she searched in the house in the yard and even out in the orchard.

_____ 10. Our bus soon began to produce clouds of black greasy smoke.

_____ 11. The poets that we studied included Robert Frost and Zora Neale Hurston.

_____ 12. The salsa that my mother makes is thick red and spicy.

_____ 13. You would have time to visit São Paulo stop in Rio de Janeiro and still meet your cousin in Recife.

_____ 14. All you have to do is nod and smile and keep quiet.

_____ 15. People write from right to left in Egypt Iran and Israel.

_____ 16. We sat on the metal fire escape to enjoy the cool air.

_____ 17. That character has appeared in books plays poems and films.

_____ 18. This is a person who is honest fearless and admired.

_____ 19. Shanghai seemed stylish successful and busy when we visited last year.

_____ 20. Postcards books and magazines are for sale in this store.

Peanuts reprinted by permission of UFS, Inc.

COMMAS WITH COMPOUND SENTENCES

20h Use commas before *and, but, for, or, nor, so,* and *yet* when they join independent clauses.

EXAMPLE   Chico dove for the ball**, but** Shing reached it first.

 NOTE   A comma is always used before *for, so,* and *yet* when they join two independent clauses. The comma may be omitted, however, when the independent clauses are very short; before *and, but, or* or *nor;* and when there is no possibility of misunderstanding.

EXAMPLE   Dad washed and I dried.

Do not be misled by compound verbs, which often make a sentence look as if it contains two independent clauses.

SIMPLE SENTENCE   Lian **sharpened** her pencil and **sat** down to write. [one subject with a compound verb]

COMPOUND SENTENCE   First Lian sharpened her pencil**, and** then she began to write. [two independent clauses]

EXERCISE 4   Correcting Compound Sentences by Adding Commas

For each of the following sentences, add commas where needed. On the line before the sentence, write *C* if the sentence is correct.

EX.   _*C*_   1. Amy climbed on her horse, but then she had to wait for us.

_____   1. The falafel contained no meat yet it was very filling.

_____   2. A dark cloud approached from the east and gradually filled up the sky.

_____   3. The river was crowded for today was market day.

_____   4. The first pictures of Venus came in and they were startling.

_____   5. You can read for an hour or you can make the salad.

_____   6. Amy could not even see her hand nor could she find the light switch.

_____   7. Before the show started, Chad climbed on stage and tested the microphones.

_____   8. I wasn't wearing repellent yet the mosquitoes didn't bite me.

_____ 9. Neither my cousin in Ohio nor my cousin in Texas drives yet.

_____ 10. The calendar is very old and it is made of stone.

_____ 11. How far did you have to go for the milk and eggs?

_____ 12. We haven't started school yet but we will begin on Monday.

_____ 13. Charlotte laughed but I didn't.

_____ 14. Douglas lost his dollar so he had to go home.

_____ 15. The sign said we had to pay ten dollars but the woman at the gate let us in for free.

EXERCISE 5   Combining Sentences

On your own paper, rewrite each pair of sentences as a single compound sentence. Use a comma and *and, but, for, nor, or, so,* or *yet.*

EX. 1. We could go to a movie. We could rent one.
   1. *We could go to a movie, or we could rent one.*

1. We can go to the station now. The bus doesn't leave for two hours.
2. I swam for hours. I wasn't tired.
3. The fiesta began on Thursday. It continued for three days.
4. I studied hard for this quiz. I am as ready as I can be.
5. Most dogs aren't allowed in here. Guide dogs are always welcome.
6. I fed that plant and watered it. It still won't grow.
7. Long ago, that woman died of smallpox. She wasn't allowed to be buried with the other townspeople.
8. Some beads were made of shell. These are made of bone.
9. Put the spoiled food in the compost heap. Grind it up in the disposal.
10. This letter is very fragile. It was written almost two hundred years ago.
11. We left the party early. We were not having fun.
12. Put covers on your textbooks. They will stay clean.
13. Volunteers stacked sandbags along the riverbank. The river flowed over the sandbags.
14. Maxine was our best hockey player. She wanted to try out for the track team.
15. Roland likes apples. Abby prefers peaches.

COMMAS WITH NONESSENTIAL WORDS

> **20i** **Use commas to set off nonessential clauses and nonessential participial phrases**.
>
> A *nonessential* (or *nonrestrictive*) clause or participial phrase adds information that is not necessary to the main idea in the sentence.
>
> NONESSENTIAL PHRASE   The cook, **smiling broadly,** bowed at us.
> NONESSENTIAL CLAUSE   This fabric, **which is tie-dyed,** came from
> East Africa.
>
> When a clause or phrase is necessary to the meaning of a sentence—that is, when it tells *which one*—the clause or phrase is *essential* (or *restrictive*), and commas are not used.
>
> ESSENTIAL PHRASE   The car **sitting on the trailer** is a dragster. [*Which* car?]
> ESSENTIAL CLAUSE   The book **that I reserved** is for a report. [*Which* book?]
>
> NOTE   An adjective clause beginning with *that* is usually essential.

EXERCISE 6   Using Commas Correctly

On the line before each sentence, identify each italicized phrase or clause by writing *e.* for *essential* or *n.e.* for *nonessential*. Insert commas where necessary.

EX.   *n.e.*   1.   The speech was by Chief Joseph, a Nez Perce chief.

_____   1.   This manuscript *which is very old* belongs in a museum.

_____   2.   The kimchi *that Bob makes* is spicier than mine.

_____   3.   Don't you wonder why that diamond *lost for centuries* should suddenly turn up here?

_____   4.   The mural *that you liked* was painted by Diego Rivera.

_____   5.   Lobster Newburg *which was named for a man named Wenberg* is made with a delicious sauce.

_____   6.   This little menorah is the one *that we light during Hanukkah.*

_____   7.   Ricardo owns a brown-and-white horse *which looks like an appaloosa to me.*

_____   8.   Circle any words *that you don't understand.*

_____ 9. Geothermal energy *already popular in Denmark* is gradually finding supporters in the United States.

_____ 10. The woman *on the camel* is a Mongolian sheepherder.

_____ 11. Juan de la Cierva is one of the two men *who perfected the helicopter.*

_____ 12. The novel <u>The Age of Innocence</u> *which was written by Edith Wharton* has been made into a movie.

_____ 13. A band of dust *which some scientists blame on the eruption of Mt. Pinatubo* is now circling the globe.

_____ 14. The large dog *on the right* is a Great Dane.

_____ 15. Labor Day *which the Mexicans celebrate on May 1* is a festive holiday.

_____ 16. The Braille alphabet *which consists of patterns of raised dots* was named for its inventor.

_____ 17. The statue shows Thomas Gallaudet *for whom Gallaudet College is named.*

_____ 18. Millions of people perished as a result of the Black Death *which was a form of bubonic plague.*

_____ 19. Early hockey teams *playing on frozen lakes* sometimes had thirty players on a team.

_____ 20. The lucky astronauts were the ones *who rode in Apollo 11.*

_____ 21. Nancy lives next door to the new recreation center *which is made of red brick.*

_____ 22. Turn the handle *attached to the left side* to operate the jack-in-the-box.

_____ 23. A jaguar is a fierce forest cat *resembling a leopard.*

_____ 24. Professor Dunlap *who teaches driver safety* is originally from New Hampshire.

_____ 25. Quicksand will quickly swallow any heavy object *falling into it.*

COMMAS WITH INTRODUCTORY WORDS

20j **Use a comma after words such as *well, yes, no,* and *why* when they begin a sentence.**

EXAMPLES **No,** we won't be late.
Well, it's finally finished.

20k **Use a comma after an introductory participial phrase.**

EXAMPLE **Jumping up,** Carlotta grabbed the ball.

20l **Use a comma after a series of introductory prepositional phrases.**

A short introductory prepositional phrase does not require a comma unless the comma is necessary to make the meaning clear.

EXAMPLES **In the front of the store,** two clerks were ringing up purchases.
After dinner we talked for hours.
After dinner, time seemed to stand still.[The comma is needed to avoid reading "*dinner time*"]

20m **Use a comma after an introductory adverb clause.**

EXAMPLES **When you're finished,** please help me here.

20n **Use commas to separate items in dates and addresses.**

EXAMPLES On **September 5, 1968,** a star was born!
I will be at **54 Howard Lane, Bartow, FL 33830.**

20o **Use a comma after the salutation of a friendly letter and after the closing of any letter.**

EXAMPLES Dear Ms. Hoy,   Sincerely yours,

20p **Use a comma after a name followed by an abbreviation such as Jr., Sr., and M.D.**

EXAMPLES Martin Luther King, Jr.   Ben Casey, M.D.

EXERCISE 7   Adding Commas with Introductory Elements

In each of the following sentences, add commas where needed. On the line before the sentence, write *C* if the sentence is correct.

EX. _____ 1. Washing my clothes in the river, I saw an alligator.

_____ 1. In the back of the closet Jared noticed a small door.

_____ 2. Yes the writer Miguel Angel Asturias did win a Nobel Prize.

_____ 3. Singing at the top of her lungs Heather attracted quite a bit of attention.

_____ 4. Before you leave, look at this picture of Lou Gehrig.

_____ 5. As you read the chapter ask yourself questions about it.

_____ 6. Next to the kayak a much larger boat was being built.

_____ 7. At noon everyone took a short break for lunch.

_____ 8. Climbing over the fence Guido noticed a nest of rabbits.

_____ 9. Before you lock up check the alarm system.

_____ 10. Why one of my friends made it for me.

_____ 11. Say do you know Frieda?

_____ 12. Because Mother worked all day, she is tired tonight.

_____ 13. However we know that you did the best job that you could.

_____ 14. At the sound of the bell everyone should leave the building.

_____ 15. Why do onions make a person's eyes water?

EXERCISE 8   Using Commas Correctly

On your own paper, rewrite the sentences below, inserting commas where needed.

EX.   1. March 9 1943 was a truly memorable day.
      1. March 9, 1943, was a truly memorable day.

1. On September 9 1957 Congress established the Commission on Civil Rights.
2. A terrible blizzard struck New York City on March 11 1888.
3. In a letter to the editor of our school paper Duncan wrote about our lunchroom schedule.
4. You can write to the American Hockey League at 425 Union Street West Springfield MA 01089.
5. After we moved into our new house we met our neighbor Harriet Barlow Ph.D.
6. This note arrived yesterday: "Dear Aunt Jo Thanks. Kisses Kim."
7. I need the address of Fran Ahola M.D. of Dayton Ohio.
8. On April 7 1992 Debra began her job as office assistant.
9. Wow what an exciting concert that was last night!
10. Why was the letter dated May 28 1900 so late in being delivered?

COMMAS WITH SENTENCE INTERRUPTERS

20q   Use commas to set off elements that interrupt the sentence.

Two commas are used around an interrupting element—one before the "interrupter" and one after. If the interrupter comes at the beginning or the end of the sentence, only one comma is needed.

EXAMPLES   Roberto Clemente, **the ball player,** once lived there.
Furthermore, the whales are protected.
I need some help, **Kai.**

(1) Appositives and appositive phrases are usually set off by commas.

EXAMPLES   Inez, **my pen pal,** is an artist.
The documentary told about spelunkers, **people who explore caves for a hobby**.

If an appositive is closely related to the word preceding it, it should not be set off by commas.

EXAMPLE   I am looking for my friend **Greg**.

(2) Words used in direct address are set off by commas.

EXAMPLES   **Mrs. Ignacio,** your cab is here.
I know, **Mai,** that you will do your best.
We want to thank you, **Jolon**.

(3) Parenthetical expressions are set off by commas.

Parenthetical expressions are side remarks that add information or relate ideas.

EXAMPLES   The bronze lion, **in fact,** is quite common.
For instance, look at this butterfly.

EXERCISE 9   Proofreading Sentences for the Correct Use of Commas

For each of the following sentences, underline the appositive word or phrase. Add commas where needed.

EX.   1. The animal, a guanaco is related to the camel.

1. My sister Kate knows all about camels and guanacos.

2. East of the Andes a mountain range in South America live the guanacos.

3. Another relative of the camel the alpaca is also used for wool.

4. Alpacas descendants of the guanaco are bred for their wool.

5. The bigger animals the llamas are becoming popular pets.

6. Llama wool a very coarse fiber is used for making rope.

7. Llamas sturdy animals are also used as pack animals.

8. The country that I visited Peru still uses llamas.

9. Another pack animal the dromedary lives in Asia and Africa.

10. Dromedaries the camels with one hump can carry heavy loads.

EXERCISE 10   Punctuating Sentence Interrupters

In the sentences below, add commas where needed.

EX.   1. Mah-jong, I believe, is an ancient game.

1. To be honest I never understood the appeal.

2. Please tell me what you think Ms. Karas.

3. My grandmother for example loved her sports car.

4. Uncle Marco do you remember the 1960s?

5. The beauty of the orchid I suppose isn't in its scent.

6. By the way did everyone in the 1920s love jazz?

7. I understand Keiko that you want a new kimono.

8. Nevertheless I refuse to use pesticide.

9. *Alice in Wonderland* was written in English; it has however been translated into many other languages.

10. Like all fads of course pet rocks lost popularity.

11. Toni Morrison my favorite author won the Nobel Prize in literature in 1993.

12. At any rate a majority of the senators will vote to pass the legislation.

13. One of these days Marcia we must find your jacket.

14. What happened at the end of the movie Dennis?

15. My aunt Mae an avid gardener loves her roses.

REVIEW EXERCISE

A. Proofreading Sentences for Correct Use of Commas

In the sentences below, insert commas where needed.

EX. 1. Caves, after all, can be rich sources of history.

1. I have visited caves in Virginia Pennsylvania and Kentucky.

2. In some caves scientists have found traces of ancient tools.

3. Thousands of years before Columbus arrived people were living in North American caves.

4. Scientists have found these caves and sometimes people discover tools inside them.

5. Some caves had walls some had roofs and some had separate rooms.

6. The tools which were made of stone were buried in the dirt.

7. They were preserved naturally by the hot dry air.

8. In limestone caves in the Southwest archaeologists even found mummies.

9. In one cave pet dogs were found buried next to bones.

10. Indeed these early people had baskets blankets and pets.

B. Proofreading a Paragraph for Correct Use of Commas

In the following paragraph, insert commas where needed.

EX. [1] This park, I think, was designed by Olmsted.

[1] Frederick Law Olmsted was born on April 26 1882. [2] He began life in Hartford Connecticut. [3] He went to college at Yale University and he studied agriculture and engineering. [4] After he graduated he traveled through Europe to study gardens. [5] When he returned he became both the architect and the superintendent of Central Park in New York City. [6] He went on to design parks in Boston Chicago Detroit and Montreal. [7] Why did you know that the University of California in Berkeley California had Olmsted design

its campus? [8] It is certainly a beautiful place. [9] Olmsted's son

another Frederick also designed parks. [10] In fact he designed a

whole system of parks for Boston Massachusetts.

C. Writing Brief Descriptions

You are writing to someone your age who is moving to your area. This
person will be attending your school. You have included a list of some of the
activities and clubs available at school that you think this person would like
to know about. Write brief descriptions of four of these activities or clubs.

1. First, choose four school activities or clubs.

2. Choose three details about each of them. Write at least two
    sentences about each activity or club, and use at least one comma
    in each sentence.

EX.   1.   *One club you might like, the Chess Club, meets twice a month.*

1. _____

_____

_____

_____

2. _____

_____

_____

_____

3. _____

_____

_____

_____

4. _____

_____

_____

_____

SEMICOLONS

20r **Use a semicolon between independent clauses if they are not joined by *and, but, or, nor, for, so,* or *yet.***

EXAMPLES   Selma pressed the button and waited**;** nothing happened.
Our bathroom leads a double life**;** it's also a darkroom.

20s **Use a semicolon between independent clauses joined by conjunctive adverbs or transitional expressions.**

Commonly Used Conjunctive Adverbs			
accordingly	furthermore	meanwhile	otherwise
also	however	moreover	still
besides	indeed	nevertheless	then
consequently	instead	next	therefore
Commonly Used Transitional Expressions			
as a result	for instance	in fact	on the other hand
for example	in addition	in other words	that is

EXAMPLES   I have a cat**; therefore,** I have cat hair on my clothes much of the time.
Stacking wood is no fun**; on the other hand,** it is good exercise.

20t **A semicolon (rather than a comma) may be needed to separate independent clauses joined by a coordinating conjunction when there are commas within the clauses.**

CONFUSING   You must bring boots, socks, and a backpack, but fruit, nuts, and a cup would be nice.
CLEAR   You must bring boots, socks, and a backpack**;** but fruit, nuts, and a cup would be nice.

20u **Use a semicolon between items in a series if the items contain commas.**

EXAMPLE   I have lived in Beaufort, North Carolina**;** New Orleans, Louisiana**;** Evanston, Illinois**;** and Gloucester, Massachusetts.

EXERCISE 11 Using Semicolons Correctly

In each sentence below, add the missing semicolon.

EX. 1. The flag of the United States has fifty stars; each star stands for a state.

1. Almost everyone recognizes our country's flag however, few recognize our state's flag.

2. All states have flags some are quite beautiful.

3. Some have pictures on them the flag of California, for example, shows a bear.

4. Arkansas was our twenty-fifth state as a result, its flag has twenty-five white stars on it to show the states.

5. The Arkansas flag is red, white, and blue and it has three blue stars beneath the name *Arkansas* representing Spain, France, and the United States.

6. Texas has had many flags flown over it at one point France, Spain, and Mexico all claimed it.

7. Ohio's flag is different from other flags it is swallow-tailed instead of rectangular.

8. The Ohio flag's stripes represent roads and waterways its stars represent the original states and its circle represents the Northwest Territory.

9. The flag of West Virginia shows a wreath of rhododendron, the state flower a cap of liberty and a ribbon with the state name.

10. The American Legion in Alaska sponsored a flag-design contest Benny Benson, from the Jesse Lee Mission Home, was the winner.

11. This thirteen-year-old boy designed Alaska's flag the flag shows the constellation known as the Big Dipper.

12. Alaska became the forty-ninth state on January 3 the year was 1959.

13. Michigan and Arkansas became states at the same time on the Arkansas flag, a pair of stars on the blue band represents this relationship.

14. Some flags use stars to show that they were once territories others use circles.

15. The state of Washington was named for George Washington he was our first president.

COLONS

20v **Use a colon to mean "note what follows."**

(1) Use a colon before a list of items, especially after expressions like *the following* and *as follows*.

EXAMPLES   Your test will contain the following items: definitions, multiple-choice questions, and two essay questions.
Please bring these when you come: two sharp pencils, a calculator, and one sheet of scratch paper.

NOTE   Do not use a colon before a list that follows a verb or a preposition.

INCORRECT   Pay special attention to: the size, the shape of the tail, and the shape of the bill.

CORRECT   Pay special attention to these features: the size, the shape of the tail, and the shape of the bill.

(2) Use a colon before a long, formal statement or a long quotation.

EXAMPLE   This is how I feel about friends: "By helping you today, I give you the chance to help me tomorrow."

20w **Use a colon in certain conventional situations.**

(1) Use a colon between the hour and the minute.

EXAMPLES   The film starts at 7:00 P.M.   Try to call before 10:00 A.M.

(2) Use a colon between chapter and verse in referring to passages from the Bible.

EXAMPLES   Genesis 43:29–34   James 3:7–11

(3) Use a colon after the salutation of a business letter.

EXAMPLES   Dear Mr. Blanco: Dear Personnel Manager:

EXERCISE 12   Adding Colons to Sentences

In each of the following sentences, add the missing colon.

EX.   1.   Make sure that the names of the following cities are on your tickets : Portland, Seattle, and Vancouver.

1.   Many couples include Ruth 1 16 in their wedding ceremonies.

2. These are my favorite breakfast foods waffles, fresh fruit, and orange juice.

3. Every morning, Dad rides the 7 45 commuter train into town.

4. You will need these items before beginning bobsled training a helmet, gloves, and kneepads.

5. We will dismiss classes at 2 30 P.M. on school days before holidays.

6. We should ask these people to help with the science project David, Susan, Anna, and Tony.

7. Please write "Dear Sir or Madam" for your business letter salutation.

8. This year's transportation show includes a variety of vehicles cars, trucks, vans, and motorcycles.

9. Do you have these things on the grocery list onions, apples, paper towels, soap?

10. Mathew has appeared in two plays *The Diary of Anne Frank* and *High Noon*.

EXERCISE 13   Using Colons Correctly

Proofread the following business letter. Add, delete, or replace punctuation as necessary.

1   Dear Ms. Reynolds,

2   I am writing to confirm your speaking engagement at our church

3   on Sunday, April 10. Pastor Reeves will open the proceedings at

4   3;00 P.M. with a reading of Isaiah 40.28–31.

5   We have the following audiovisual equipment available for your

6   use, a slide projector, a VCR, and an audiocassette player. Please let

7   me know if you require any other equipment or supplies.

8   Sincerely:

9   Maureen A. Brown

CHAPTER REVIEW

A. Proofreading Sentences for Correct Use of Commas

For each of the sentences below, add commas where needed.

EX. 1. Mary Cassatt ,I heard ,was an interesting woman.

1. Well she was born just before midnight on May 22 1844.

2. Shortly after that her family moved to Allegheny City Pennsylvania.

3. At the age of seven she moved to France with her family.

4. The three other children in the family were Lydia Alexander and Robert.

5. When Mary was a young woman she returned to Paris to study art.

6. She drew she painted and she met other artists.

7. Many of her early works in fact were destroyed in a fire that hit Chicago on October 8 1871.

8. One of her most famous paintings *The Bath* shows a mother bathing a child.

9. Besides working at her art Cassatt strongly supported women's rights.

10. In her later years however her eyesight failed and this failure forced her to stop painting.

B. Using End Marks, Commas, Semicolons, and Colons Correctly in a Paragraph

Add the missing punctuation to the following paragraph.

1   July 15 1993 was a red-letter day we started driving across the

2   United States For the past two years my family has talked about

3   making this trip and we finally did it On our first day we drove by

4   these cities Providence Rhode Island Hartford Connecticut Albany

5   New York and Cleveland Ohio Why did we drive so far Well we

6   had seen all these places before When we crossed the Mississippi

7   River we slowed down and started sightseeing We reached Arizona

8   my favorite state during the last week in July We all loved the state

9   indeed we stayed there two weeks Arizona has a lot to see Navajo

10   and Hopi communities Grand Canyon National Park and several

11   national monuments

C.   Proofreading a Letter

Add the missing punctuation to the business letter below.

1   590 Washington Street

2   Waverly PA 18471

3   October 10 1994

4   Dr Tonya Powell

5   426 Lane Drive

6   Bangor PA 18013

7   Dear Dr Powell

8   I understand that you are seeking volunteers for the

9   Community Supper which you hold every Wednesday evening

10   between 6 30 and 8 00 P M Our class advisor Ms Rice explained

11   your program and asked for volunteers.

12   Many students were interested consequently we can fully staff

13   the supper during the months of November December and

14   January Will you need additional volunteers after that date If you

15   will, just let us know Your volunteers for November will include

16   the following four students Margaret Lee Flavio Torres Rebecca

17   Solomon and me

18   We have all been told what to expect Dr. Powell According to

19   Ms Rice you need people to cook to serve and to clean up

20   afterward Everyone who volunteered is willing to do any of those

21   tasks, I believe We are delighted to be able to help and we look

22   forward to meeting you As you requested we will arrive at 6 15

23   the first night for an orientation tour

24   Sincerely

25   Farah Davis

                                                        Farah Davis

UNDERLINING (ITALICS)

21a Use underlining (italics) for titles of books, plays, periodicals, films, television programs, works of art, long musical compositions, ships, aircraft, and spacecraft.

Type of Name	Examples
Books	*Annie John, A Separate Peace*
Plays	*Raisin in the Sun, Macbeth*
Periodicals	*International Herald Tribune, Smithsonian*
Films	*Casablanca, Glory*
Television Programs	*Nightline, Entertainment Tonight*
Works of Art	*The Footballer, Urban Freeways*
Long Musical Compositions	*Treemonisha, Messiah*
Ships	*Titanic, Columbia*
Aircraft	*Spirit of Columbus, Air Force One*
Spacecraft	*Apollo 12, Sputnik II*

NOTE The article *the* is often written before a title but is not capitalized unless it is part of the official title. The official title of a book is found on the title page. The official title of a newspaper or periodical is found on the masthead, which usually appears on the editorial page.

EXAMPLE   I read the editorial in **the** *Houston Post.*

21b Use underlining (italics) for words, letters, and figures referred to as such and for foreign words.

EXAMPLES   The words *bite* and *bight* are homophones.

There are two digits in *10*.

The word does not have an *e* at the end.

Do you like to eat *akara?*

EXERCISE 1   Using Underlining (Italics) Correctly

For each sentence below, underline the word or item that should be italicized.

EX.   1.   Which actor played the policeman in the film <u>Casablanca</u>?

1. The song is about a train called <u>The City of New Orleans</u>.

2. Many artists and photographers have done funny versions of the painting <u>American Gothic</u>.

3. Tonight Channel 5 is showing two different episodes of <u>Star Trek</u>.

4. Electricity had just arrived in this town the year that <u>Sputnik I</u> was launched.

5. I don't think you spell the name with a <u>k</u> at the end.

6. My parents took these pictures on board the <u>Queen Elizabeth 2</u>.

7. Did you read the interesting editorial in <u>The Des Moines Register</u> last Wednesday?

8. After we read the play <u>Hamlet</u>, we'll see the movie, which is on video.

9. I enjoyed the book <u>Nisei</u>, which is by Bill Hosokawa.

10. The word <u>kvetch</u>, which means to complain, actually comes from Yiddish.

EXERCISE 2   Proofreading Sentences for the Correct Use of Underlining (Italics)

In the sentences below, underline each word or item that should be italicized.

EX.   1.   Mom looked in <u>Newsweek</u> to see what's available in entertainment.

1. <u>Friday Night Lights</u>, based on the movie, got good reviews.

2. The book <u>Harry Potter and the Goblet of Fire</u> is as popular as the movie <u>Harry Potter and the Goblet of Fire</u>.

3. A new production of the old opera <u>Xerxes</u> is opening in Santa Fe.

4. The classic book, <u>Jane Eyre</u>, has been made into a movie several times.

5. Mom said that if we don't want to go out, we can stay home and watch re-runs of <u>I Love Lucy</u>.

QUOTATION MARKS

21c Use quotation marks to enclose a direct quotation—a person's exact words.

EXAMPLE   "Wait here," said the officer, "until the woman with the flag waves you on."

21d A direct quotation begins with a capital letter.

EXAMPLE   Shane said, "The earlier arrowheads were larger than the later ones."

21e When the expression identifying the speaker interrupts a quoted sentence, the second part of the quotation begins with a small letter.

EXAMPLE   "The clay," said Kelly, "comes from an area near the bottom of the cliffs."

When the second part of a divided quotation is a sentence, it begins with a capital letter.

EXAMPLE   "Look at this," said Mr. Park. "It is a piece of amber."

21f A direct quotation is set off from the rest of the sentence by a comma, a question mark, or an exclamation point, but not by a period.

EXAMPLES   "They will ask for time out," whispered Palani.
"What good will that do?" asked Jason.
"We won!" shouted Teresa.

21g A period or a comma should always be placed inside the closing quotation marks.

EXAMPLES   Kwam said, "That's a beautiful serape."
"My grandmother gave it to me," said Flora.

21h A question mark or an exclamation point should be placed inside the closing quotation marks when the quotation itself is a question or an exclamation. Otherwise, it should be placed outside.

EXAMPLES   "Who has an extra pencil?" I asked.   [The quotation is a question.]
Why did you say, "Space aliens did it"?   [The sentence, not the quotation, is a question.]

When both the sentence and a quotation at the end of the sentence are questions (or exclamations), only one question mark (or exclamation point) is used. It is placed inside the closing quotation marks.

EXAMPLE   Did Arthur ask, "Who's in charge here?"

EXERCISE 3   Punctuating Quotations

For each sentence below, insert quotation marks and other marks of punctuation where needed.

EX.   1.   "Who was Daniel Hale Williams?" asked Marty.

1. Dr. Williams was the doctor said Virgil who founded the first interracial hospital in this country

2. He did more than that explained Lori He also started the first training school for African American nurses

3. What did people do before that asked one student Were they treated at home

4. They were either treated at home said Brian or they were put into dirty wards

5. This doctor even performed heart surgery exclaimed Lina That was unheard of in 1893

EXERCISE 4   Proofreading Sentences for the Use of Quotation Marks

In the sentences below, correctly punctuate and capitalize all direct quotations. If a sentence is correct, write *C* on the line before the sentence.

EX.   _____   1.   "Look out for the cars!" yelled Karas

_____   1. We came Ming said to celebrate Kosciuszko Day

_____   2. Hey, Mark Angelo whispered did you finish your homework

_____   3. Will you help me asked Lani

_____   4. What a great way to decorate the invitations exclaimed Gan

_____   5. You were right she said the store opens at eight o'clock

Using Quotation Marks

On your own paper, create five sentences that each illustrate a rule from this lesson. Then label the sentences with the correct rule number.

EX.   1.   "Did you know," asked Marta, "that I was chosen?" (21c)

21i When a quotation consists of several sentences, put quotation marks only at the beginning and the end of the whole quotation.

EXAMPLE   "Now, you're galloping toward the first barrel. You know you're going to turn and go around it, but the horse doesn't know. So you squeeze with your right knee, " said Ron.

21j When you write dialogue (conversation), begin a new paragraph every time the speaker changes.

EXAMPLE   Chad looked nervous as he said, "You guys are not going to believe what I saw last night. Coming home from practice, I saw this thing glowing in the sky, just above the horizon."
"Did you think it was a UFO?" asked Jodie.
"I don't know what it was, but it sure was strange."
"Look," said Umeko, "let's call the state police. They'll know if anyone else reported it."

21k Use quotation marks to enclose the titles of short works such as short stories, poems, articles, songs, episodes of television programs, and chapters and other parts of books.

EXAMPLE   Did she sing "Love is the Thing" at the concert?

21l Use single quotation marks to enclose a quotation within a quotation and to punctuate the title of a short work used within a quotation.

EXAMPLES   Luana said, "I spoke to the principal, and she said, 'Remember that everyone has the right of free speech.' "
"Have you ever read the poem 'Refugee in America'?" asked Juan.

EXERCISE 6   Punctuating Quotations

In each of the following sentences, insert quotation marks where needed.

EX. 1. " That poem, called' Preciosa and the Wind', is by Federico García Lorca," said Ms. Lee.

1. Who said He who hesitates is lost? asked Ali.

2. When she walks in said Belinda, we'll sing Happy Birthday.

3. Before you leave, read the article called The New Youth Brigades.

4. The first day is the hardest, said Byron. After that you get used to eating less salt.

5. Did your mother say Patti is always welcome? asked Patti.

6. Kathy handed me the book and said, The funniest chapter is the one called The Solar Democrat.

7. Is the title of that poem The Silent Crowd?

8. The reviewer said, This book would have been better if it had been shorter. In fact, it might have been wonderful.

9. Did Nikki Giovanni write the poem Knoxville, Tennessee, or did someone else?

10. And then, said Julia, someone started singing The Bear Went Over the Mountain. It was wild!

11. Nathan, Billy asked did you know that there really are dragons in the world?

12. No there aren't countered Nathan.

13. Yes, I read about the Komodo dragon, the forest dragon, and the bearded dragon in the article Amazing Real-life Dragons, answered Nathan.

14. Kiu asked, did Ms. Jeffery say Include material about the Haitian artist Roosevelt in your report?

15. Jerome wants a copy of the brochure Careers in Computers and Electronic Engineering.

EXERCISE 7   Punctuating Paragraphs

On your own paper, rewrite the passage below, adding paragraph breaks and quotation marks where needed.

EX.   [1]   Now listen up! said Ms. Vacca.

   1.   "Now listen up!" said Ms. Vacca.

[1] Today you will learn something new, said Ms. Vacca. [2] You will learn how to check your spelling with your computer. [3] That's what I need, said Amir. [4] I'm not a really good speller. [5] Ms. Vacca said, This program can help you. [6] However, it won't find certain kinds of mistakes. [7] What kinds won't it find? asked Sopa. [8] Sometimes, said Ms. Vacca, you can misspell one word by writing another word correctly. [9] You mean, like writing "t-h-e-i-r" instead of "t-h-e-r-e"? asked Amir. [10] That's exactly what I mean, said Ms. Vacca, and most computers won't catch that kind of mistake.

APOSTROPHES

The *possessive case* of a noun or a pronoun shows ownership or relationship.

Ownership	Relationship
Toby's poncho **my** homework **everyone's** award	a **night's** sleep **dogs'** leashes **anyone's** guess

21m **To form the possessive case of a singular noun, add an apostrophe and an *s*.**

EXAMPLES   the teacher**'s** desk   Jess**'s** grades   this morning**'s** paper

 NOTE   A proper noun ending in *s* may take only an apostrophe to form the possessive case if the addition of *'s* would make the name awkward to say.

EXAMPLES   Miss Rawlings**'** book   Jesus**'** teachings   Diaz**'** home

21n **To form the possessive case of a plural noun ending in s, add only the apostrophe.**

EXAMPLES   students**'** names   two-days**'** growth   the Stones**'** home

21o **To form the possessive case of a plural noun that does not end in s, add an apostrophe and an *s*.**

EXAMPLES   sheep**'s** coats   men**'s** barracks   teeth**'s** hardness

 NOTE   Do not use an apostrophe to form the plural of a noun. Remember that the apostrophe shows ownership or relationship.

INCORRECT   Two players' have red jerseys.
CORRECT   Two **players** have red jerseys
CORRECT   The two **players'** jerseys are red.

21p **Do not use an apostrophe with possessive personal pronouns.**

EXAMPLES   Is this book **yours**?   Is the marker **hers**?

285

EXERCISE 8   Proofreading for the Use of Apostrophes for Singular Possessives

In the paragraph below, underline each word that needs an apostrophe, and insert the apostrophe. Some sentences have no errors in the use of apostrophes.

EX.   [1] These <u>families'</u> homes were in West Virginia.

[1] The coal miners lives were different from mine. [2] About half of the workers houses had once belonged to the company. [3] Now local families own them. [4] In this community, the mens jobs were basically farming and mining. [5] The womens tasks included factory work, farming, and child care. [6] I visited one mine and was allowed to go down into the mines tunnels. [7] The ones that I visited were about four hundred feet underground. [8] All the miners talk was cheerful until an alarm rang. [9] Everyones face then became serious as we rode to the surface. [10] Although the days work was cut short, no one was hurt.

EXERCISE 9   Writing Possessives

On your own paper, rewrite each of the expressions below by adding an apostrophe to create the correct possessive form.

EX.   1.   the shoes of the dancer
       1.   the dancer's shoes

1. the desk of the boss
2. the games of the children
3. the beds of the soldiers
4. the color of the tooth
5. the kimono that belongs to somebody

6. the popcorn of Ms. Thomas
7. the food of the geese
8. the chairs of the speakers
9. the streets of the city
10. the tortillas of the customer

OTHER USES OF THE APOSTROPHE

A *contraction* is a shortened form of a word, a number, or a group of words.

21q **Use an apostrophe to show where letters, numbers, or words have been omitted (left out) in a contraction.**

Common Contractions	
you are ....you're	they have.................they've
1995 ....'95	she had..........................she'd
she will...............she'll	where is ....where's
of the clock......o'clock	who will.....................who'll
I will........................I'll	I would............................I'd

The word *not* can be shortened to *n't* and added to a verb, usually without any change in the spelling of the verb.

EXAMPLES   are not..........aren't   could not.........couldn't
                 has not ....hasn't   should not ....shouldn't
EXCEPTIONS will not ....won't   cannot....................can't

Be careful not to confuse contractions with possessive pronouns.

Contractions	Possessive Pronouns
It's late. **[It is]**	**Its** voice was loud.
You're here! **[You are]**	**Your** chili was spicy!
Who's there? **[Who is]**	**Whose** jacket is this?
There's the car. **[There is]**	The red ones are **theirs**.

21r **Use an apostrophe and an *s* to form the plurals of letters, of numerals, and of words referred to as words.**

EXAMPLES   Dot your *i*'s and cross your *t*'s.
               No, there are two *1*'s and two *2*'s.
               Try not to begin all sentences with *then*'s.

EXERCISE 10   Using Apostrophes Correctly

In the sentences below, underline each word that needs an apostrophe, and insert the apostrophe. On the line before the sentence, write C if the sentence is correct.

EX. _____ 1. The boat you're looking at is handmade.

_____ 1. Stay for a while, and well look through the whole museum.

_____ 2. Youll notice that most of the boats are made from animal skins.

_____ 3. Theyre stretched over frames that are made from wood or bone.

_____ 4. The kayak that youre looking at holds just one person.

_____ 5. The bigger boat on your left isnt a kayak, though.

_____ 6. You can tell that boat is an umiak because its hull is much larger.

_____ 7. Some linguists spell *kayak* with *q*s instead of *k*s.

_____ 8. These boats havent been used in many years.

_____ 9. Which of these kayaks was theirs?

_____ 10. Whos talking to your friend about the Inuit hunters?

EXERCISE 11   Writing Contractions

On the line before each sentence below, write a contraction for the italicized word or word pair.

EX. ___Who's___ 1. *Who is* that woman?

_____ 1. I *do not* remember her first name, but her last name was Taylor.

_____ 2. I think *it is* a picture of Anna Edson Taylor.

_____ 3. I *cannot* guess why she went over Niagara Falls in a barrel.

_____ 4. *I am* sure she just wanted to prove that it could be done.

_____ 5. I *will not* say if she was brave or if she was foolish.

CHAPTER REVIEW

A. Proofreading for the Correct Use of Apostrophes, Quotation Marks, and Underlining (Italics)

Rewrite each of the following sentences, using apostrophes, quotation marks, and underlining correctly. [Note: A sentence may contain more than one error.]

EX. 1. The English words their and theyre sound the same, said Inez.

"The English words their and they're sound the same," said Inez.

1. For homework, we are supposed to read the chapter called Cells in the book called Real Life. _____

_____

2. Whos going to play lead guitar? asked Irina. May I? _____

_____

3. Have you ever, asked Jamal, heard the song called Texas Flood? _____

_____

4. This letter was probably written during the 1800s, said Mr. Koski. It uses words like verily and beshrew. No one writes like that today. _____

_____

_____

5. I love this new jacket! shouted Ms. MacPherson. Lets buy one! _____

_____

6. Was Harry kidding me? asked Selma. Did anyone really write a book called A Wrinkle in Time? _____

_____

_____

7. Some people make their capital qs look like large 2s. _____

_____

8. Brads parents are going to be pleased because he got an A and two Bs. _____

_____

9. Theres a picture of the new ocean liner Queen Mary in this volume of the New Encyclopaedia Britannica. _____

_____

10. Sofie asked, Why would anyone even try to say The sixth sheiks sheep is sick? _____

_____

11. The three broadcasters reports did not agree about the game. _____

_____

12. What do you want to do with yesterdays menus? _____

_____

13. Two managers employee rules were being discussed. _____

_____

14. Walt, have you read that article about Miriam Makeba, titled Mama Africa? asked Abby. Its about her U.S. tours. _____

_____

15. Yes, answered Walt. I heard her perform with Paul Simon in 1987. _____

_____

B. Writing a Dialogue

On your own paper, create a dialogue based on the following old joke. Write the dialogue in sentence form with direct quotations, and be sure to use quotation marks and other marks of punctuation correctly. In addition to punctuation marks, you will need to add dialogue tags to identify who is speaking (*shouted Al; said Earline*).

> Three people were riding on a loud subway. They couldn't hear each other very well. When Al said it was *windy*, Tranh thought that Al had said *Wednesday*. Tranh then remarked that today was Thursday, not Wednesday. Then Earline spoke up. She thought that Tranh had said *thirsty*, and she admitted that she was thirsty, too.

EX. "Tranh, it is windy today," shouted Al.

THE DICTIONARY

A dictionary entry is divided into several parts. Study the parts of the sample dictionary entry below.

> **hap•py** (hap′ē), *adj.*, –**pi•er**, –**pi•est** [Old English *haep*, convenient, suitable] **1.** having a feeling of pleasure [a *happy* person] **2.** giving a feeling of pleasure [a *happy* birthday] **3.** lucky; suitable and fitting [a *happy* chance] **4.** INFORMAL silly or too quick to act [see *slap-happy*] –**hap′pi•ly**, *adv.* –**hap′pi•ness**, *n.*
>
> *SYN.* ***Happy*** suggests "a feeling of pleasure." ***Glad*** suggests "a reaction of pleasure." ***Cheerful*** means "showing bright spirits." ***Joyful*** and ***joyous*** mean "feeling very happy." *ANT.* sad, melancholy.

1. **Entry word.** The entry word shows the correct spelling of a word. An alternate spelling may also be shown. The entry word shows how the word should be divided into syllables and may also show if the word should be capitalized.
2. **Pronunciation.** The pronunciation is shown using accent marks, phonetic symbols, or diacritical marks. Each *phonetic symbol* represents a specific sound. *Diacritical marks* are special symbols placed above letters to show how those letters sound.
3. **Part-of-speech labels.** These labels are usually abbreviated and show how the entry word should be used in a sentence. Some words may be used as more than one part of speech. In such a case, a part-of-speech label is also given either before or after the set of definitions that matches each label.
4. **Other forms.** Sometimes a dictionary shows spellings of plural forms of nouns, tenses of verbs, or the comparative forms of adjectives and adverbs.

5. **Etymology.** The·*etymology* tells how a word (or its parts) entered the English language. The etymology also shows how the word has changed over time.
6. **Definitions.** If there is more than one meaning, definitions are numbered or lettered.
7. **Sample of usage.** Some dictionaries include sample phrases to illustrate particular meanings of words.
8. **Special usage labels.** These labels identify how a word is used (*Slang*), how common a word is (*Rare*), or how a word is used in a special field, such as botany (*Bot.*).
9. **Related word forms.** These are forms of the entry word created by adding suffixes or prefixes. Sometimes dictionaries also list common phrases in which the word and its related forms appear.
10. **Synonyms and antonyms.** Words similar in meaning are *synonyms*. Words opposite in meaning are *antonyms*. Many dictionaries list synonyms and antonyms at the ends of some word entries.

EXERCISE 1   Using a Dictionary

Use a dictionary to answer the questions below.

EX.   1. How many syllables are in the word *retaliation*?___five____

1. How is the word *delirious* divided into syllables? _____

2. What is the spelling for the plural form of *flamingo*? _____

3. Give three different meanings for the word *mean*. _____

_____

4. What is the past tense of *arise*? _____

5. What is the etymology of the word *maverick*? _____

_____

EXERCISE 2   Writing Words with Alternate Spellings

For each of the words below, write the alternate spelling on the line after the word.

EX.   1. archaeology _archeology_____

1. catalog _____   4. ameba _____

2. theater _____   5. enroll _____

3. yogurt _____

SPELLING RULES

ie and *ei*

22a Write *ie* when the sound is long *e*, except after *c*.

EXAMPLES chief, believe, piece, relief, receive, deceit
EXCEPTIONS either, neither, leisure, seize, weird

22b Write *ei* when the sound is not long *e*, especially when the sound is long *a*.

EXAMPLES weight, height, veil, neighbor, eight, reign
EXCEPTIONS lie, pie, tie, friend, mischief

EXERCISE 3 Writing Words with *ie* and *ei*

On the line in each word below, write the letters *ie* or *ei* to spell each word correctly. Use a dictionary as needed.

EX. 1. for _ei_ gn

1. n _____ ce
2. th _____ r
3. f _____ ld
4. fr _____ ght
5. h _____ r

6. gr _____ f
7. br _____ f
8. sh _____ ld
9. de _____ ve
10. ach _____ ve

11. b _____ ge
12. c _____ ling
13. misch _____ f
14. y _____ ld
15. conc _____ t

–cede, –ceed, and *–sede*

22c In English, the only word ending in *–sede* is *supersede*. The only words ending in *–ceed* are *exceed, proceed,* and *succeed*. All other words with this sound end in *–cede*.

EXAMPLES concede, recede, precede, secede, intercede

EXERCISE 4 Proofreading a Paragraph to Correct Spelling Errors

The following paragraph contains ten spelling errors. Underline the misspelled words. Write the correct spelling above each misspelled word.

EX. [1] In the <u>preceeding</u> week, Alexis and I visited the Carnegie Science Center.

preceding

293

[1] The staff of the Carnegie Science Center has succeded in creating a museum that is truly an "amusement park for the mind." [2] The museum has recieved rave reviews from the residents of Pittsburgh. [3] It has also gained worldwide publicity because of its many foriegn visitors. [4] Visitors to the Science Center can liesurely examine more than two hundred and fifty hands-on exhibits. [5] They can then procede to either the planetarium or the aquarium. [6] Believe me, niether Alexis nor I had ever been to such an exciting aquarium. [7] The giant tank rises to a great hieght. [8] Swimming together in the tank are thousands of fish and many wierd creatures from the deep. [9] The fish seem very freindly and calm, although we did see a brief battle between two barracudas. [10] We also saw a giant tortoise that must have wieghed two hundred pounds.

BORN LOSER® by Art Sansom

Born Loser reprinted by permission of NEA, Inc.

PREFIXES AND SUFFIXES

A *prefix* is a letter or a group of letters added to the beginning of a word to change the word's meaning. A *suffix* is a letter or a group of letters added to the end of a word to change its meaning.

22d   When adding a prefix to a word, do not change the spelling of the word itself.

EXAMPLES   mis + spell = **mis**spell   im + possible = **im**possible
over + ripe = **over**ripe   un + rehearsed = **un**rehearsed

22e   When adding the suffix –*ness* or –*ly* to a word, do not change the spelling of the word itself.

EXAMPLES   fair + ness = fair**ness**   open + ness = open**ness**
soft + ly = soft**ly**   real + ly = real**ly**

EXCEPTION   For most words that end in *y*, change the *y* to *i* before –*ly* or –*ness*.

EXAMPLES   happy + ness = happ**iness**   busy + ly = bus**ily**

22f   Drop the final silent *e* before a suffix beginning with a vowel.

Vowels are the letters *a, e, i, o, u,* and sometimes *y*. All other letters of the alphabet are *consonants*.

EXAMPLES   gentle + est = gentl**est**   skate + ing = skat**ing**
note + able = not**able**   race + er = rac**er**

EXCEPTION   In words ending in *ce* and *ge*, keep the silent *e* before a suffix beginning with *a* or *o*.

EXAMPLES   notice + able = notic**eable**
courage + ous = courag**eous**

22g   Keep the final *e* before a suffix beginning with a consonant.

EXAMPLES   hope + less = hope**less**   late + ness = late**ness**
grace + ful = grace**ful**   sure + ly = sure**ly**

EXCEPTIONS   argue + ment = arg**ument**   true + ly = tru**ly**

EXERCISE 5   Spelling Words with Prefixes and Suffixes

On the line after each partial word equation below, write the word, including the prefix or suffix that is given.

EX.   1. final + ly   _finally_

1. thick + ness   _____   11. il + legal   _____

2. a + rise   _____   12. up + set   _____

3. un + noticed   _____   13. dis + satisfy   _____

4. cheerful + ly   _____   14. im + mortal   _____

5. ir + responsible _____   15. easy + ly   _____

6. return + able   _____   16. anti + toxin   _____

7. baby + ish   _____   17. waste + ful   _____

8. joy + ous   _____   18. haste + y   _____

9. state + ing   _____   19. en + counter   _____

10. outrage + ous   _____   20. rake + ed   _____

EXERCISE 6   Spelling Words with Suffixes

On the line after each partial word equation below, write the word, including the suffix that is given.

EX.   1. ride + ing   _riding_

1. admire + able _____   11. brown + ness _____

2. quick + ly   _____   12. bake + er   _____

3. large + est   _____   13. joke + ing   _____

4. primary + ly   _____   14. argue + ment   _____

5. aviate + or   _____   15. nine + ty   _____

6. bossy + ness   _____   16. range + ing   _____

7. rise + ing   _____   17. mighty + ly   _____

8. peace + able   _____   18. change + able _____

9. skate + er   _____   19. lazy + ly   _____

10. usual + ly   _____   20. mis + state   _____

SUFFIXES

22h For words ending in *y* preceded by a consonant, change the *y* to *i* before any suffix that does not begin with *i*; keep the *y* before a suffix that does begin with *i*.

EXAMPLES   mystery + ous = myster**ious**   easy + ly = eas**ily**

                dry + ing + dr**ying**   hurry + ing = hurr**ying**

EXCEPTIONS   dry + ness = dr**yness**   sly + ly = sl**yly**

22i Words ending in *y* preceded by a vowel do not change their spelling before a suffix.

EXAMPLES   boy + hood = bo**yhood**   pray + ed = pray**ed**

EXCEPTIONS   say + ed = sa**id**   day + ly = dail**y**

22j Double the final consonant before adding *–ing*, *–ed*, *–er*, or *–est* to a one-syllable word that ends in a single consonant preceded by a single vowel.

EXAMPLES   step + ing = ste**pping**   hit + er = hi**tter**

                ship + ed = shi**pped**   sad + est = sa**ddest**

With a one-syllable word ending in a single consonant that is not preceded by a single vowel, do not double the consonant before adding *–ing*, *–ed*, *–er*, or *–est*.

EXAMPLES   wail + ing = wailing   near + er = nearer

                seem + ed = see**m**ed   cool + est = coolest

EXERCISE 7   Spelling Words with Suffixes

On your own paper, write each of the following words, including the suffix that is given.

EX.   1. dim + er

     1. dimmer

1. crazy + ness	6. stray + ed	11. pay + ing	16. big + est
2. spin + ing	7. drop + ing	12. vary + ous	17. fool + ing
3. wait + ed	8. clear + est	13. play + ed	18. warm + er
4. hot + er	9. worry + ed	14. swim + er	19. try + ing
5. crusty + est	10. hazy + er	15. snap + ed	20. glory + ous

REVIEW EXERCISE

Proofreading to Correct Spelling in a Paragraph

In the paragraph below, underline the twenty spelling errors. Write the correct spelling above each incorrect word.

EX.   [1] Sparky Rucker is *making* history interesting.

[1] Rucker, an African American storyteller from Tennessee, has been delighting audeinces for many years. [2] In his new show, which is called *Concieved in Liberty*, he discusses fameous historycal figures and tells stories about the culture and music of West Africans who were brought to the United States as slaves. [3] His shows usualy contain many songs; this show includes "Amazeing Grace" and "Hambone." [4] Through his work, Rucker has succeded in teaching many people about their African American heritage. [5] In the process, he has truely been makeing history more real. [6] In many of his shows, he explains the meannings of such slave songs as "Follow the Drinking Gourd." [7] Rucker has sayed that this song was realy a map of the Underground Railroad. [8] Its first line is "Follow the drinking gourd, for the old man is waitting to carry you to Canaan." [9] The drinking gourd is the Big Dipper, and Canaan is Canada, the land where the couragous slaves hopeed to gain their freedom. [10] Storytelling was not unatural in Rucker's family. [11] He remembers his aunts and uncles telling some of the same stories in varyous ways. [12] He often includes hand-clapping rhythms as well. [13] His beleif that no one can easly separate politics and culture shows in his storytelling.

PLURALS OF NOUNS

22k Form the plurals of most nouns by adding −*s*.

SINGULAR	shoe	date	desk	donkey	radio	hymn
PLURAL	shoe**s**	date**s**	desk**s**	donkey**s**	radio**s**	hymn**s**

22l Form the plurals of nouns ending in *s, x, z, ch,* or *sh* by adding −*es*.

SINGULAR	glass	tax	waltz	lunch	dish
PLURAL	glass**es**	tax**es**	waltz**es**	lunch**es**	dish**es**

NOTE Proper nouns usually follow these rules, too.

EXAMPLES   the Espinoza**s**   the Bendex**es**
the Jenkins**es**   the Moskowitz**es**

EXERCISE 8 Spelling the Plurals of Nouns

On the line after each noun, write the correct plural form.

EX.   1. ax   _axes_

1. bench _____   14. rodeo _____

2. stereo _____   15. area _____

3. box _____   16. tray _____

4. Cortez _____   17. Vélez _____

5. wish _____   18. switch _____

6. class _____   19. pencil _____

7. kiss _____   20. mask _____

8. rash _____   21. moth _____

9. grass _____   22. donkey _____

10. nickel _____   23. fizz _____

11. piano _____   24. guess _____

12. Katz _____   25. Kirkpatrick _____

13. Delgado _____

22m Form the plurals of nouns ending in *y* preceded by a consonant by changing the *y* to *i* and adding *–es*.

SINGULAR   story   berry   army   sky   jury
  PLURAL   stor**ies**   berr**ies**   arm**ies**   sk**ies**   jur**ies**

EXCEPTION   With proper nouns, simply add *–s*.

  EXAMPLES   the Reillys, the Brodskys

22n Form the plurals of nouns ending in *y* preceded by a vowel by adding *–s*.

SINGULAR   tray   key   Sunday   boy   play
  PLURAL   tray**s**   key**s**   Sunday**s**   boy**s**   play**s**

22o Form the plurals of most nouns ending in *f* by adding *–s*. The plurals of some nouns ending in *f* or *fe* are formed by changing the *f* to *v* and adding either *–s* or *–es*.

SINGULAR   roof   belief   reef   knife   wife   leaf
  PLURAL   roof**s**   belief**s**   reef**s**   kni**ves**   wi**ves**   lea**ves**

 NOTE   When you are not sure how to spell the plural of a noun ending in *f* or *fe*, look in a dictionary.

EXERCISE 9   Spelling the Plurals of Nouns

On the line after each noun, write the correct plural form.

EX.   1. baby   _babies_

1. theory   _____

2. calf   _____

3. bay   _____

4. cherry   _____

5. life   _____

6. valley   _____

7. Tuesday   _____

8. shelf   _____

9. injury   _____

10. toy   _____

11. gulf   _____

12. Sablosky   _____

13. honey   _____

14. reply   _____

15. filly   _____

16. thief   _____

17. day   _____

18. raspberry   _____

19. Daly   _____

20. scarf   _____

22p **Form the plurals of nouns ending in *o* preceded by a vowel by adding –*s*. The plurals of many nouns ending in *o* preceded by a consonant are formed by adding –*es*.**

SINGULAR	stereo	zoo	hero	tomato
PLURAL	stereos	zoos	heroes	tomatoes

EXCEPTIONS	tuxedo	tuxedos	hello	hellos

Form the plurals of most musical terms ending in *o* by adding –*s*.

SINGULAR	solo	cello	soprano	contralto
PLURAL	solos	cellos	sopranos	contraltos

> **NOTE** To form the plurals of some nouns ending in *o* preceded by a consonant, you may add either –*s* or –*es*.
>
> | SINGULAR | flamingo | grotto | volcano |
> |---|---|---|---|
> | PLURAL | flamingos | grottos | volcanos |
> | | *or* | *or* | *or* |
> | | flamingoes | grottoes | volcanoes |

22q **The plurals of a few nouns are formed in irregular ways.**

SINGULAR	child	man	tooth	goose	mouse
PLURAL	children	men	teeth	geese	mice

22r **Form the plural of a compound noun consisting of a noun plus a modifier by making the modified noun plural.**

SINGULAR	sister-in-law	man-of-war	stock market
PLURAL	sisters-in-law	men-of-war	stock markets

EXERCISE 10   Spelling the Plurals of Nouns

On the line after each noun, write the correct plural form.

EX. 1. radio ___radios___

1. veto _____
2. gaucho _____
3. woman _____
4. studio _____
5. father-in-law _____

6. blue jay _____
7. foot _____
8. baby sitter _____
9. potato _____
10. video _____

EXERCISE 11   Proofreading to Correct Spelling in a Paragraph

In the paragraph below, underline the fifteen errors in spelling. Write the correct spelling above each misspelled word.

EX.   [1] All of the ~~childs~~ *children* in the international chorus visited our school.

[1] Because they have naturally high voices, most of the singers are sopranoes, and only a few are altoes. [2] During the concert, echos of soaring voices, almost like those of Baltimore oriolees or other singing birds, filled the hall. [3] The singers were accompanied by two womans who played grand pianoes and two mans who played piccoloes. [4] Afterwards, the singers met with members of our school chorus to tour our practice studioes. [5] Then we all had lunch on the patioes, which were only a few foots away from the music wing and the art department. [6] Two mans from a television station interviewed the singers and taped videoes for tonight's news broadcast. [7] Two radio stations are planning to play excerptes from the concert on separate broadcasts next week. [8] Tonight, several members of the chorus will sing soloes during the City Symphony's performance.

EXERCISE 12   Using Plurals Correctly

On your own paper, write a sentence, using the plural form of each word below.

EX.   1. foot
      1. Please wear shoes to protect your feet.

1. hobo   3. great-uncle   5. cargo   7. rodeo   9. mosquito
2. ox   4. banjo   6. maid of honor 8. lingo   10. Congo snake

CHAPTER REVIEW

A. Correcting Spelling Errors in Sentences

Underline all misspelled words in each sentence below. Then write each misspelled word correctly in the space above the word.

EX. 1. Tamara and Louis had a ~~breif~~ *brief* meeting to discuss the film.

1. My nieghbor, Takara Asano, is a foriegn exchange student from Japan.

2. Two soloes by a famous opera singer will preceed tonight's concert.

3. I know she will easily succede as leader of the altoes.

4. I was disatisfied with the overipe fruit.

5. Suddenly the two children burst into an outragous arguement.

6. We bought plentyful supplyes before the storm.

7. Dentists usualy offer new teethbrush to their patients after yearly checkups.

8. The Sanchezs will spend a liesure weekend in Galveston.

9. The factories are shiping the stereoes in heavy boxes to avoid damage.

10. Our ponys wear colorful harnesses when pulling the slieghs.

11. The receeding floodwaters had ruined the crops in the feilds.

12. I admire my freind's openess.

13. Were you planing to make such a gracful entrance?

14. The spot on the carpet is realy noticable!

15. The store recieved ninty hatboxes today.

16. How many flys ball did you catch in the outfeild today?

17. After traceing the vase's outline, Melba easly added the color.

18. The men carriing the bags were my shipsmate.

19. The students wanted to meet all of thier facultys sponsor.

20. The flock of wild geeses flying above us was a beautyful sight.

B. Proofreading a Paragraph to Correct Spelling Errors

The paragraph below contains twenty spelling errors. Underline each misspelled word, and write the correct spelling above it.

EX.   [1] Diver Michael Grofik found a treasure in the <u>reeves</u> off the
       Florida coast.

[1] Grofik is one of the memberes of a team sent to the Florida

waters by a company nameed Historical Research & Development,

Inc. [2] He and his freinds and partners were diveing about one

hundred yards off the coast of Sebastian, Florida, in eight foots of

water. [3] When the other mans and womans on the team took their

dayly break to eat their lunchs, Grofik did not. [4] He decided that

continueing his searchs for treasure might be more rewarding than

stoping for lunch. [5] That decision luckyly payed off; in fact, it

exceded even Grofik's bigest dreams and expectationes. [6] He

found many peices of gold jewelry, which historyans beleive came

from a Spanish ship that sank off the Florida coast in 1715!

C. Identifying Correctly Spelled Words

For each of the following items, underline the correctly spelled word in parentheses.

EX.   1. a (<u>brief</u>, breif) vacation

1. a (belief, beleif) in children

2. the (weight, wieght) of the package

3. a painted (ceiling, cieling)

4. a (mispelled, misspelled) word

5. many (skaters, skatters)

6. a silly (argument, arguement)

7. an (immpossible, impossible) dream

8. (*skateing, skating*) on the pond

9. a (*changeable, changable*) nature

10. (*drying, driing*) the towels

11. an (*unatural, unnatural*) appearance

12. two new (*radioes, radios*)

13. serving mashed (*potatos, potatoes*)

14. living near the (*Kirkes, Kirks*)

15. washing the (*knives, knifes*)

16. (*trays, trayes*) for the salad

17. three (*sopranoes, sopranos*)

18. eight (*geese, gooses*)

19. several (*man-of-war, men-of-war*)

20. (*their, thier*) new home

D. Writing a Language Workshop Lesson

You are a student intern who has been asked by the United Nations to travel to another country. Your assignment is to run a spelling workshop for students who are learning English as a second language. Select five spelling rules from this chapter to present in your first class. On the lines on the following page, write each rule. Then provide examples. Finally, for each rule, create five exercise items to give to the students to check their understanding of the rule. For each exercise, create a list of answers on a separate piece of paper.

EX. 1.   RULE: To form plurals of nouns ending in s, x, z, ch, or sh, you must add −es.
EXAMPLES: glass, glasses; box, boxes; waltz, waltzes; beach, beaches; wish, wishes
EXERCISE ITEM: 1. fox   1.   foxes

COMMONLY MISSPELLED WORDS

The following list contains seventy-five words that are often misspelled. To find out which words give you difficulty, ask someone to read you the list in groups of twenty-five. Write down each word; then check your spelling. Make a list in your spelling notebook of any word you misspelled. Keep reviewing your list until you have mastered the correct spelling.

75 Commonly Misspelled Words

ache	forty	speak
across	friend	speech
again	grammar	straight
all right	guess	sugar
almost	half	surely
always	having	tear
answer	heard	though
belief	hour	through
built	instead	tired
business	knew	together
busy	know	tomorrow
buy	laid	tonight
can't	likely	tough
color	making	trouble
coming	meant	truly
cough	minute	Tuesday
could	often	until
country	once	wear
doctor	ready	Wednesday
doesn't	really	where
don't	safety	which
eager	said	whole
easy	says	women
every	shoes	won't
February	since	write

SPELLING WORDS

Learn to spell the following words if you don't already know how. They're grouped so that you can study them ten at a time.

300 Spelling Words	
absence	authority
absolutely	available
acceptance	basically
accidentally	beginning
accommodate	believe
accompany	benefit
accomplish	benefited
accurate	boundary
accustomed	calendar
achievement	campaign
acquaintance	capital
actually	category
administration	certificate
affectionate	characteristic
agriculture	chief
amateur	circuit
ambassador	circumstance
analysis	civilization
analyze	column
announcement	commissioner
anticipate	committee
apology	comparison
apparent	competent
appearance	competition
approach	conceivable
approval	conception
arguing	confidential
argument	conscience
assurance	conscious
attendance	consistency

300 Spelling Words (continued)

constitution	embarrass
continuous	emergency
control	employee
cooperate	encouraging
corporation	environment
correspondence	equipped
criticism	essential
criticize	evidently
cylinder	exaggerate
debtor	exceedingly
decision	excellent
definite	excessive
definition	excitable
deny	exercise
description	existence
despise	expense
diameter	extraordinary
disappearance	fascinating
disappointment	fatal
discipline	favorably
disgusted	fictitious
distinction	financier
distinguished	flourish
dominant	fraternity
duplicate	frequent
economic	further
efficiency	glimpse
eighth	glorious
elaborate	grabbed
eligible	gracious

300 Spelling Words (continued)	
graduating	knowledge
grammar	leisure
gross	lengthen
gymnasium	lieutenant
happiness	likelihood
hasten	liveliness
heavily	loneliness
hindrance	magazine
humorous	maneuver
hungrily	marriage
hypocrisy	marvelous
hypocrite	mechanical
icy	medieval
ignorance	merchandise
imagination	minimum
immediately	mortgage
immense	multitude
incidentally	muscle
indicate	mutual
indispensable	narrative
inevitable	naturally
innocence	necessary
inquiry	negligible
insurance	niece
intelligence	noticeable
interfere	obligation
interpretation	obstacle
interrupt	occasionally
investigation	occurrence
judgment	offense

300 Spelling Words (continued)

official	practically
omit	precede
operation	precisely
opportunity	preferred
oppose	prejudice
optimism	preparation
orchestra	pressure
organization	primitive
originally	privilege
paid	probably
paradise	procedure
parallel	proceed
particularly	professor
peasant	proportion
peculiar	psychology
percentage	publicity
performance	pursuit
personal	qualities
personality	quantities
perspiration	readily
persuade	reasonably
petition	receipt
philosopher	recognize
picnic	recommendation
planning	referring
pleasant	regretting
policies	reign
politician	relieve
possess	remembrance
possibility	removal

300 Spelling Words (continued)

renewal	sponsor
repetition	straighten
representative	substantial
requirement	substitute
residence	subtle
resistance	succeed
responsibility	successful
restaurant	sufficient
rhythm	summary
ridiculous	superior
sacrifice	suppress
satire	surprise
satisfied	survey
scarcely	suspense
scheme	suspicion
scholarship	temperament
scissors	tendency
senate	thorough
sensibility	transferring
separate	tremendous
sergeant	truly
several	unanimous
shepherd	unfortunately
sheriff	unnecessary
similar	urgent
skis	useful
solemn	using
sophomore	vacancies
source	vacuum
specific	varies

A

a, an, 233
abbreviations
    with periods, 259
    without periods, 259
abstract noun, defined, 93
action verb, defined, 105
active voice, 199
adding, 9
addresses and dates, commas
    used to separate items in,
    267
adjective
    commas used to separate,
      261
    defined, 99
    following a linking verb,
      107
    predicate, 133
    proper, 101, 247
    used to modify gerunds,
      149
adjective clause
    commas used with, 163
    defined, 163
    using to combine
      sentences, 77
adjective phrase
    defined, 143
    used to modify gerunds,
      149
adverb
    conjunctive, 67, 273
    defined, 111
    list of, 113
    used to modify adjectives,
      113
    used to modify gerunds,
      149
    used to modify other
      adverbs, 114
adverb clause
    comma used after
      introductory, 267
    defined, 165
    introduced by
      subordinating
      conjunctions, 165
    using to combine
      sentences, 77
adverb phrase
    defined, 144
    used to modify gerunds,
      149
affect, effect, 233

agreement
    with *any* and *none*, 177
    with compound subjects,
      179
    of *don't* and *doesn't*, 181
    with *every* and *many a*, 183
    with indefinite pronouns,
      177
    with intervening phrases,
      175
    of pronoun and
      antecedent, 187
    of subject and verb, 173–74,
      183
    with words stating an
      amount, 183
all the farther, all the faster, 233
among, between, 235
an, a, 233
and etc., 233
anecdote, defined, 27
antecedent
    defined, 97, 187
    gender of, 187
    and pronoun agreement,
      187
antonyms, in a dictionary
    entry, 292
anywheres, everywheres,
    nowheres, somewheres, 233
apostrophe
    in contractions, 287
    to form the plurals of
      letters, of numerals, and
      of words referred to as
      words, 287
    to form the possessive case
      of a plural noun, 285
    to form the possessive case
      of a singular noun, 285
appositive
    commas used to set off, 269
    defined, 63, 157, 219
    pronoun used as, 219
appositive phrase
    commas used to set off, 269
    defined, 63, 157
    using to combine
      sentences, 73
arranging ideas, 5
article, 99
as, like, 237
as or *than*, used to introduce
    an incomplete
    construction, 220

asking questions, 3
at, 234
auxiliary (*or* helping) verb
    in a compound verb, 129
    list of, 109
    in a verb phrase, 109, 145
awards, capitalization of, 253

B

ballad, defined, 41
base form
    of an irregular verb, 193
    of a regular verb, 191
be, forms of, 107
beside, besides, 234
between, among, 235
body
    of a composition, 27
    of a press release, 52
    of a letter, 62
brainstorming, 2
brand names, capitalization
    of, 253
businesses, capitalization of,
    251

C

calendar items, capitalization
    of, 251
capitalization, 245-55
    of brand names and trade
      names, 253
    of common nouns, 247
    of a direct quotation, 281
    of first word, 245
    of geographical names, 249
    of the interjection *O*, 245
    of names of historical
      events and periods,
      special events, and
      calendar items, 251
    of names of nationalities,
      races, and peoples, 251
    of names of organizations,
      teams, businesses,
      institutions, and
      government bodies, 251
    of names of people, 249
    of names of school subjects,
      253
    of names of ships,
      monuments, awards,
      planets, and other
      particular places of
      things, 253

number of, 175
plural, 174, 179
simple, 125
singular, 174, 179
understood, 128, 133
subject complement
compound, 133
defined, 133
in an imperative sentence,
133
in an interrogative
sentence, 133
predicate adjective as, 133
predicate nominative as,
133
subject-verb agreement,
173–174, 183
subordinate (*or* dependent)
clause
defined, 65, 161
in a complex sentence, 77,
169
in a compound-complex
sentence, 169
used as a noun, 167
using to vary sentence
beginnings, 81
using *who* and *whom* in,
217
subordinating conjunction
in an adverb clause, 77,
165
list of common, 165
suffix
defined, 295
spelling of a word when
adding, 295, 297
superlative degree
forming, 223
using, 225
synonyms, in a dictionary
entry, 292

T

teach, learn, 237
teams, capitalization of, 251
telling a story, 21
tense, verb, 197
than or *as,* used to introduce
an incomplete
construction, 220
than, then, 239
that, who, which, 239
that there, this here, 239
them, 239
there, mistaken for the
subject of a sentence, 127
thesis statement, defined, 27

this here, that there, 239
titles, capitalization of, 255
tone, defined, 27
topic outline, 25-26
topic sentence
defined, 13
and main idea, 13
trade names, capitalization
of, 253
transitional expression
list of, 273
used to join independent
clauses, 273
transitional words and
phrases
defined, 18
to show connections
between ideas, 18
transitive verb, defined, 105
type, sort, kind, 237

U

underlining (italics), 279
understood subject, 128, 133
unity, 15
usage, glossary of, 233-41

V

varying sentence
beginnings, 81
verb (*or* simple predicate)
action, 105
agreement with subject,
174, 179
compound, 75, 129
defined, 105, 126
helping (*or* auxiliary), 109,
129
intransitive, 105
irregular, 193-95
linking, 107
phrase, 109, 126, 145, 193
plural, 174, 179
principal parts of, 191
regular, 191
singular, 174, 179
tense, 197
transitive, 105
verbal
defined, 63, 145
gerund as, 145, 149
infinitive as, 145, 153
participle as, 145
phrase, 63
voice, 199
vowel
defined, 295

spelling rules, 295, 297,
300–301

W

"What if?" questions, 3
when, where, 239
which, that, who, 239
who and *whom,* 217
who, which, that, 239
whoever and *whomever,* 217
word lists, spelling, 307-312
wordy sentence, 79
would of. See could of, 235
writer's journal, 1
writing
conclusions, 30-31
a first draft, 6
introductions, 27-28
a personal impression
essay, 37
a persuasive letter, 59
a press release, 53
a story poem, 45

Y

you, as the understood
subject of a sentence, 128,
133

Making Learning Happen

A Guide for Post-Compulsory Education

Phil Race

Los Angeles | London | New Delhi
Singapore | Washington DC

Third
Edition

Los Angeles | London | New Delhi
Singapore | Washington DC

SAGE Publications Ltd
1 Oliver's Yard
55 City Road
London EC1Y 1SP

SAGE Publications Inc.
2455 Teller Road
Thousand Oaks, California 91320

SAGE Publications India Pvt Ltd
B 1/I 1 Mohan Cooperative Industrial Area
Mathura Road
New Delhi 110 044

SAGE Publications Asia-Pacific Pte Ltd
3 Church Street
#10-04 Samsung Hub
Singapore 049483

Editor: Marianne Lagrange
Editorial assistant: Rachael Plant
Production editor: Nicola Marshall
Copyeditor: Gemma Marren
Proofreader: Emily Ayers
Indexer: Author
Marketing manager: Catherine Slinn
Cover design: Naomi Robinson
Typeset by: C&M Digitals (P) Ltd, Chennai, India
Printed and bound by CPI Group (UK) Ltd,
Croydon, CR0 4YY

MIX
Paper from
responsible sources
FSC
www.fsc.org   FSC™ C013985

First edition published 2005, reprinted 2007, 2008, 2009
(twice). Second edition published 2010, reprinted 2010

Library of Congress Control Number: 2013951867

British Library Cataloguing in Publication data

A catalogue record for this book is available from
the British Library

ISBN 978-1-4462-8595-4
ISBN 978-1-4462-8596-1 (pbk)

Praise for the previous edition

'This is a very practical resource for teachers who are developing their skills as educators in the post-compulsory education sector, for practising teachers and for use by those engaged in staff development in the area. Race provides a range of tools and checklists which can be used to promote reflection on practice, and to support improvement if necessary. Throughout the book, the reader is exposed to practical resources, while being introduced to theories and concepts about learning at this level in accessible and concise language.'
  Ms Angela Higgins, School of Education Studies, Dublin City University

'Excellent resource, especially for those making the transition from practice roles to academia. Phil Race explains his ideas in a way that is simple yet very effective. This book has helped me prepare for my role as a nurse lecturer and helped to reduce many of the stressors I expected to find in entering the classroom environment. The chapter on "What can I do when ...?" is invaluable and has already helped me resolve several teaching dilemmas. Highly recommended.'
  Paul Smith, Lecturer in Nursing, School of Nursing and Midwifery, Dundee University

'Simply the clearest, most concise text for an aspiring lecturer I have read.'
  Cameron Rough, School of Nursing and Midwifery, Dundee University

'Should be mandatory reading for anyone in the HE/FE sector. Cannot say more than that; buy it, read it, apply what you have learned.'
  Mr Andrew Holmes, Centre for Life-Long Learning, Hull University

'Another wonderful book offering a multitude of ideas and common sense from an excellent educator who has the learners firmly at the heart of learning. Absolutely recommended for all those involved in learning.'
  Mrs Helen Handyside, Teacher Education, CB Learning and Assessment Ltd

'This is a bible for all fledgeling teachers.'
  Ms Tina Duffy, Health and Social Care, NWRC

CONTENTS

ACKNOWLEDGEMENTS

I am grateful to countless workshop participants for their permission to share the products of our combined thinking and discussion. I remain indebted to my wife, Sally Brown, for innumerable relevant day-to-day discussions about formative feedback, assessment design and fit-for-purpose approaches to teaching and learning in universities, and for encouraging feedback about some of the new additions present in this edition, particularly the sets of tips I have added to this edition, and some of the new diagrams. I am grateful to the eight people who gave detailed feedback on the second edition when approached by Sage about this third one, for their really valuable and penetrating analysis of the strengths and weaknesses of the former version, and I have built on their wisdom and advice substantially in this new edition. I dedicate this book to all the students who have helped me to learn about learning, and continue to inspire me to work towards making learning happen successfully.

Phil Race

ABOUT THE AUTHOR

Professor Phil Race is passionate about helping people to learn successfully. Now retired from full-time employment, he runs workshops and gives keynotes throughout the UK and abroad, working with university and college staff on teaching, assessment and feedback methods. He is known for his highly participative style and humour, and getting participants working with Post-its!

He lives in Newcastle-upon-Tyne. His wife is Professor Sally Brown, known internationally for her work on fit-for-purpose assessment. Originally a scientist, Phil quickly became interested in teaching and assessment. He has worked at several universities, and is now Visiting Professor at Plymouth University and University Campus Suffolk. He was awarded a National Teaching Fellowship in 2007, and in 2012 became a Principal Fellow of the Higher Education Academy. He publishes widely, but regards *Making Learning Happen* as the favourite of his many books.

He can be contacted through his website: http://phil-race.co.uk

PREFACE TO THE THIRD EDITION

WHAT'S NEW?

Who could have imagined how much, and how rapidly, post-compulsory education has been changing in various parts of the world in the years since I completed earlier editions of this book! Now we live in a world where the internet is
an accessible everyday source of a vast amount of information, easily downloaded to our laptops, tablets and smartphones. Now we can send information
and correspondence in seconds around the world, and communicate with each
other using social media as well as email. Now, massive open online courses
(MOOCs) dominate many discussions about the future of educational institutions.
Since I completed the last edition, I have continued to give keynotes and to run
hundreds of workshops on assessment, learning and teaching around the UK and
in various other parts of the world, talking to thousands more teachers and learners, continuing to reflect on what makes learning happen. This third edition is, in
my view, not only expanded, but substantially improved, for example:

- I have completely reworked Chapter 1, to include discussion of MOOCs, communication using social media, and I have introduced four 'literacies', which learners now need when participating in post-compulsory education. I've also ended
  with some informal tips for would-be university entrants entitled 'How to do uni'.

- I have improved Chapter 2, by making the unfolding of the seven factors less
  'jerky', and removing the diagrams until all factors have been introduced.

- In Chapter 3, I've added some tips for students on how best they can make
  use of intended learning outcomes.

- I have extended Chapter 4 on 'Assessment Driving Learning' by including
  what is now required of institutions in the UK by the Quality Assurance

Agency as an example of how we can approach improving assessment, and by adding a large table helping readers to compare the pros and cons of a wide range of assessment processes and instruments, as well as some tips for students themselves.

- I've added some tips for students on using feedback to Chapter 5.

- I have reworked much of Chapter 6, now calling it 'Making Lectures Inspiring', as large-group learning has evolved very significantly in the age of ready access to online resources and courses, and as the use of handouts has all but ceased in lectures. I've also added some tips for students on getting the most from lectures.

- In Chapter 7 on 'Making Learning Happen in Small Groups', I've now brought in discussion of links to developing employability and enterprise skills, and added a section on personal tutoring – and some tips for students themselves.

- To Chapter 8 on 'Learning through Observing and Reflecting' I've added some tips on peer-observation, to help colleagues get the most from both observing and being observed.

- By popular request, and using many ideas from readers, I have expanded the range of problems addressed by Chapter 9, 'What Can I Do When …?', which provides some creative tactics for addressing some of the common problems colleagues experience in teaching in post-compulsory education.

To make room for these additions to the book, some things had to go! I have discarded the short chapter on 'Employability' from the previous edition, and worked suggestions on helping learners become employment-ready in several of the mainstream chapters of the book. I have also mainstreamed discussion about helping students with special needs into the main content of the book.

PUTTING THE BOOK IN CONTEXT

People have been trying to make learning happen throughout the recorded development of the human species – and no doubt for some time before any-one tried to describe it in words. There is now a vast literature, online and in print, about learning and teaching. Some of it is scholarly. There is also an abundant 'how to do it' literature, spanning learning, teaching and assessment. It sometimes feels as though there is a gulf between the two kinds of literature, with some academics climbing ever higher up their ivory towers, and some practice-based writers ignoring the wisdom that emanates from those towers. Both kinds of literature constitute a huge database of evidence about teaching and learning, and in the best traditions of evidence-based practice, this book is my attempt to bridge the gap. In some chapters I have referred to some of what I believe to be the most important scholarship underpinning best practice.

However, this book does not set out to be a scholarly text, but rather is an attempt to integrate how best we can make learning happen in post-compulsory education by focusing on learners themselves, and on key factors underpinning successful learning.

Essentially, this book is rooted in my own experience during the last four decades, where I have been working on four fronts of the interface between teaching, learning and assessment.

- Working with learners, both in subject-related contexts and learning strategy development, has helped me to get closer to how best we can talk with learners about their learning, and help them to prepare for our ways of trying to measure their progress.

- Working with lecturers and tutors in universities and colleges has helped me to work out how to help them to make learning happen with their students, and how to go about the difficult tasks of measuring learners' achievement, and getting feedback to them to aid their learning.

- Working with learning resource designers has helped me to see the necessary processes which learning resources need to have in place to play their part in making learning happen.

- Continuing to work with experienced and skilled trainers on training design has helped me to 'keep my feet on the ground' and pick out the useful processes from the spurious theories or artefacts.

During this time I have come to believe that the best way forward on all of these fronts is to address, quite deliberately and consciously, seven factors which underpin effective learning:

- *wanting* to learn – often referred to as 'intrinsic motivation' by others

- taking ownership of the *need* to learn – perhaps what others call 'extrinsic motivation'

- *learning by doing* – practice, repetition, trial and error, learning through experience

- learning through *feedback* – from fellow learners, from tutors, from learning resources, from results

- *making sense* of what has been learned – getting one's head around ideas, concepts and theories. This is something we can't do for our learners, our job as teachers is to increase the probability that *they* do it successfully

- *verbalizing or speaking* – putting what has been learned into spoken words – explaining, coaching or teaching: purposefully using these processes to help people (and indeed ourselves) to deepen learning, in other words to intensify the *making sense* part of it

- *making informed judgements – assessing*: this is to enable learners to fully deepen their learning and *making sense* process, and also allows a great deal more 'learning through feedback' to occur, especially in the context of student self-assessment and peer assessment.

These factors may look obvious – indeed simple. Yet Einstein suggested that 'everything should be made as simple as possible – but not simpler'. *How* these seven factors interact with each other is indeed complex, as is how best we can set out consciously to address these factors in our bid to make learning happen for our students. My aim in this book is to tackle some of these complexities, based on the experience of many thousands of learners, teachers and trainers, as well as on my own experience.

I was first alerted to these factors through my work with students on study-skills development. Since then, and in the last 20 years in particular, I have continued to develop the links between these factors and just about everything we try to achieve in post-compulsory education, and this book summarizes this work. I have become ever more convinced that addressing these factors works in day-to-day practice. I have to date got several thousands of people arguing, debating and extrapolating from the factors at staff development workshops in several countries and cultures, and this book owes much to the wisdom which has been shared and the insights which have developed through these discussions.

SUMMARY OF THE CONTENT

In Chapter 1, 'Setting the Scene', I start by asking 'What are universities and colleges for?' in the age of online learning and MOOCs. Then four 'literacies' which are needed by learners are introduced. The chapter concludes by addressing the question: 'Integration or fragmentation?' in the world of social media and MOOCs.

Chapter 2, 'Factors Underpinning Successful Learning', unpacks seven factors, and the way they continuously affect each other (like 'ripples on a pond') rather than functioning consecutively in a cycle. Chapter 2 is the heart of this edition, and many of the later chapters link to how these factors can be addressed purposefully in various teaching/learning contexts in our bid to make learning happen effectively, efficiently and enjoyably for our students (and indeed for ourselves).

Chapter 3, 'Designing the Curriculum for Learning', starts with a discussion of the design of learning outcomes and their place in learning. Next follows a case study, illustrating the kinds of activities which can help colleagues to align the curriculum constructively, so that learning outcomes and assessment criteria align fluently with evidence of achievement produced by students, and with assessment and feedback processes. The chapter concludes with some thinking about 'learning incomes' and 'learning outgoings', and '*emergent* learning outcomes' as worthy of consideration in the overall process of curriculum design and development.

Chapter 4, 'Assessment Driving Learning', is the biggest chapter in the book. I now start by asserting that assessment is presently 'broken' in post-compulsory education, in the context that for most learners, learning is largely driven by assessment ('When's the deadline?', 'What's the pass mark?', 'What standard is expected?' and so on) and that we over-assess greatly. I continue by discussing the need to make assessment valid, reliable, transparent and authentic, and then look at some of the things that are presently wrong with assessment in general in post-compulsory education. In the next section, 'A critical look at exams and essays!', two commonly used assessment formats are analysed in some detail against the factors underpinning successful learning. The chapter goes on to present a table showing a critical comparison of eleven assessment types. Finally, 'Towards assessment *as* learning' provides a tool to enable you to interrogate your assessment design against a range of factors linked to learning as well as in terms of reliability, validity, and so on.

In Chapter 5, 'Learning through Feedback', I go into more detail about the various ways that learners can be given formative feedback on their own work by lecturers, tutors, teachers and, most importantly, by each other, and how this feedback links to the other factors underpinning successful learning.

In Chapter 6, 'Making Lectures Inspiring', I relate the seven factors to large-group teaching, exploring what we can get our learners to do to maximize their learning pay-off in such contexts, but also analysing what lecturers and teachers can do to *cause* learners to increase their learning pay-off, ending with tips respectively for lecturers and for students. Similarly, in Chapter 7, 'Making Learning Happen in Small Groups', I aim to get you thinking about your tutorial or seminar groups, and on what we can cause learners to do while working together to increase their learning pay-off. The links between small-group learning and developing employability and enterprise are explored. A new section on personal tutoring addresses the one-to-one aspects of learning. The chapter ends with tips for lecturers and for students.

Chapter 8, 'Learning through Observing and Reflecting', is partly about reflection in broad terms, but mostly about using peer observation to enhance your own teaching. This chapter contains a range of suggestions for designing peer observation schemes to get the most out of the processes involved, and a checklist you can adapt to help you to reflect on your own teaching.

Chapter 9, 'What Can I Do When …?', brings together ideas from throughout the book, addressing an extended range of frequently occurring problems experienced by teachers in post-compulsory education, and offering short, sharp suggestions for tactics to try out when facing such problems.

CHAPTER 1

SETTING THE SCENE

O═══ **Key topics in this chapter**

- Language of learning
- Massive open online courses
- Social media
- Assessment literacy
- Information literacy
- Social literacy
- Academic literacy
- Integration or fragmentation?

WHY THIS BOOK?

There is a massive literature about teaching, learning and assessment, in print and online, referring to all levels of education and training. Some of this literature is about scholarship and research into how human beings learn, and how best to cause them to learn more effectively. Some scholarship is more practical in nature, advocating ways to go about designing our teaching and monitoring how learning is happening. There is a great deal of evidence available to us, on which to build our practices. So what is intended to be different in *this* book?

One principal difference is that this book aims to get back to straightforward language about teaching and learning, and avoid some of the jargon which so often gets in the way of helping teachers in post-compulsory education reflect on their work. Perhaps the main difference is that this book also goes deep into assessment and feedback, which can be regarded as the main drivers for most learning, and which take even more time for most practitioners than simply preparing and doing teaching. In addition, this third edition takes the discussion forward into our present age of online information, digital communication, social media and the emergence of massive open online courses (MOOCs) from some of the leading institutions around the world.

The approach I am using in this book is to leave aside the questionable thinking about learning styles and theories of learning, and probe much deeper into the factors underpinning *all* learning. It can be argued that these factors are actually quite easy to identify. Moreover, once identified, they are relatively straightforward to address in the design of all manner of teaching–learning contexts and environments.

STARTING WITH EINSTEIN

Einstein is reported to have said: 'Everything should be made as simple as possible, but not *too* simple'. It can be argued that much of what has been written about learning in the last half-century or more has not been as simple as possible in the words and language used, but at the same time has been *too* simple in terms of many of the models proposed.

Another Einstein maxim is 'Knowledge is experience – everything else is just information'. We are now in an age where information is more abundant than could ever have been imagined. It is also easily obtained – in other words, it is plentiful and cheap – more often than not, entirely free. When I myself was a student, most students left most lectures with about as much *information* as they could write in an hour or so, a few hundred words or equivalent, from what the lecturer said, did and showed. Nowadays, students are likely to emerge from an hour's learning with links to many thousands of words or equivalent in downloadable files from an intranet or the web, and sometimes handout materials, but it is all still just *information* until they have done things with it to turn it into the start of their own *knowledge* about the subject concerned, and link it up to other things they already know about that subject and about the rest of the universe.

Now that we are in the age of MOOCs (massive open online courses), much of the best *information* in the world is free for all to consume, and in conventional lecture rooms and classrooms the age of the 'lecture' is gone in the traditional sense ('stand and deliver' is no longer the game) – but that does not mean we can't achieve very useful learning by having large groups of learners breathing the same air for an hour or so.

Yet perhaps the most relevant thought from Einstein is 'it is simply madness to keep doing the same thing, and expect different results'. Our educational practices are too slow to adapt to the rapidly changing context around us. We know, for example, from feedback since 2005 from UK students in the National Student Survey, that assessment and feedback are weak links in our attempts to make learning happen for them. Therefore, in many parts of this book I pose the question, 'What *else* may work better?' We continue to use outdated ways of giving feedback to learners, for example, and traditional approaches to assessing what has been learned. This book aims to help us to keep up with our learners. Regarding subject content, it could be argued that 'it is simply madness to keep doing lectures in colleges in the same old ways, when thousands of the best lectures in the world are now available to anyone, free, online'. Our learners know this too.

So perhaps at one level the quest to make learning happen in post-compulsory education boils down to the question: how best can we help our learners to turn information into their own knowledge, using all the resources now available to them? I argue in this book that we can go a long way towards achieving this mission by carefully and systematically addressing the factors underpinning successful learning identified in Chapter 2. But first, I would like you to address the question: why come to an educational institution at all nowadays, when so much is available free online?

WHAT ARE UNIVERSITIES AND COLLEGES FOR?

Institutions of higher education have existed for centuries, with the University of Bologna (founded in 1088) being among the first to function continuously across the ages, with Oxford and Cambridge claiming origins as far back as 1167 and 1209 respectively. So universities existed long before 'compulsory education' existed widely. Nowadays, post-compulsory education comprises universities and a wide range of colleges of further and higher education, most of which afford pathways for learners to gain degrees. In much of the history of universities, the reasons for going there included that these were the places where the scholars lived and worked, and where the books resided. Since 1440 when Johannes Gutenberg invented the printing press, books became much more widely available, and the places where learning could happen widened. In 1991 the World Wide Web designed by Tim Berners-Lee was released by CERN, the European Organisation for Nuclear Research, and the internet spread rapidly.

Recently, Betsy Sparrow et al. at Columbia University described the internet as:

> an external memory source that we can access at any time. ... Just as we learn through transactive memory who knows what in our families and offices, we are learning what the computer 'knows' and when we should attend to where we have stored information in our computer-based memories. We are becoming symbiotic with our computer tools ... growing into interconnected systems that remember less by knowing information than by knowing where the information can be found. This gives us the advantage of access to a vast range of information – although the disadvantages of being constantly 'wired' are still being debated. (Sparrow et al., 2011)

The development and impact of the printing press occurred over a considerable time span, yet the speed of the development of the internet in recent years seems to have been a revolution of comparable proportions. The internet naturally makes a huge impact on what happens at universities and colleges, but also on how readily anyone can get information wherever they are able to connect. With rapidly increasing usage of smartphones, tablets and laptops, the internet has indeed become 'an external memory source' that is readily available to a rapidly increasing proportion of the world's population.

The tendency is for information online to become free. Publishers naturally want to sell e-books and e-journals, but educational institutions often want their brand to be promoted, and offer all sorts of tasters and samples for free online. This has resulted in MOOCs, with Harvard, MIT and the UK's Open University taking pioneering roles since around 2008, and now a plethora of free online courses exists. The quality of some of these freely available educational opportunities is extremely good in terms of the presentation and the authoritativeness of the information.

A useful summary about MOOCs, with links to providers, is 'What campus leaders need to know about MOOCs' published online by Educause (2012), with links to main providers, and is accessible free from www.educause.edu/library/resources/what-campus-leaders-need-know-about-moocs. A later version of this resource summarizes the educational access position as follows:

> Massive open online courses – MOOCs – are online courses that are free and open to anyone, with essentially unlimited enrollment.
>
> How MOOCs Work: MOOCs are online courses where lectures are typically 'canned', quizzes and testing are automated, and student participation is voluntary. They attain large scale by reducing instructor contact with individual students; students often rely on self-organized study and discussion groups. An alternative model allows students to vote on which questions should rise to the professor's attention (e.g., Coursera). edX encourages students to rely on each other, awarding 'Karma points' to students who correctly answer other students' questions. As points accrue, students' roles can expand, e.g., to a teaching assistant. (Educause, 2012)

(Note, however, online briefings such as this change day by day, and it would be worth going to the Educause website to find how this may have changed by the time this book is printed.)

The big players – Harvard and MIT – have invested large sums of money in setting up MOOCs. Tim Goral wrote:

> Perhaps the biggest issues, however, are revenue and sustainability. MIT and Harvard each pumped $30 million into launching edX. Coursera began with $16 million in venture capital. But, with courses and materials typically provided free to students, the question of how these programs will sustain themselves is a big one. (Goral, 2013)

Goral continues by discussing the concept of SPOCs (Short Private Online Courses), an offshoot of the MOOC model that may have revenue potential. Anant Agarwal, president of edX, says of SPOCs: 'It's a business-to-business concept that Armando Fox at University of California, Berkeley has dubbed SPOC, for small, private online courses. You create a course and license it to a university or an organization or corporation'. (Goral, 2013)

The term SPOCs has already entered the debate, and the Financial Times Lexicon defines it as follows, commenting on how SPOCs might prove more realistic than MOOCs to educational intuitions:

> Small private online courses (Spocs) are a competing model to the Mooc (massive open online course). Despite much excitement about how Moocs might transform the education system, they have so far not been able to show how they will fund themselves. In addition, the 'open' nature of the Mooc courses encourages large numbers of participants with very varied abilities because anyone with an internet connection can participate. This raises problems with assessment and therefore how much a Mooc can be worth on someone's curriculum vitae as they go on to jobs or further study. Spocs offer some solution in that students are selected, which limits numbers of participants, and ensures they satisfy some entry requirements for the course. Spocs allow educational establishments to use them in a 'blended learning' approach that combines classroom teaching with online learning. (Financial Times Lexicon, 2013)

However, when there is information on just about everything imaginable available online, why should one go to a university or college ever again? Back to Einstein – for the experience, not for the information. Essentially, the learning experience that we can offer in our institutions is more about people than about information, and the feedback and support than human tutors offer learners. But the main things which institutions offer, that MOOCs don't yet, are assessment and accreditation.

Things have changed, however. Martin Hall, Vice-Chancellor of Salford University, recently blogged about MOOCs (after studying himself online on one):

> They could finish off the lecture as a form of conveying information, and the teacher becomes an expert guide in a world of abundance rather than a lecturer passing down wisdom from the podium. (Hall, 2013)

However, higher education never has been just about gaining knowledge, it is also about becoming qualified. This means learning being supported by feedback, and having evidence of achievement measured and assessed and accredited. Martin Hall continues:

> Validation: the only validation on this MOOC was online acceptance of an honor [sic] code. If MOOCs are to provide credit with any currency, then this will have to change. (Hall, 2013)

So what is an 'honour code'? What do MOOC users commit to? An example is that used by one of the prevalent providers of MOOCs, Coursera, and typically users click their acceptance of statements such as the following:

1. I will register for only one account.

2. My answers to homework, quizzes and exams will be my own work (except for assignments that explicitly permit collaboration).

3. I will not make solutions to homework, quizzes or exams available to anyone else. This includes both solutions written by me, as well as any official solutions provided by the course staff.

4. I will not engage in any other activities that will dishonestly improve my results, or dishonestly improve/hurt the results of others. (Coursera, 2013)

I showed this example of an 'honour code' to an audience containing lawyers. They just smiled! We are already well aware of the dangers of copying and plagiarism in normal college courses, where we have many ways of triangulating our focus on evidence of achievement (traditional exams, face-to-face questioning on written work, and so on), and there is simply no way of guaranteeing in a MOOC that conditions such as those listed in this example of an 'honour code' have been met. Nevertheless, some MOOCs attract many thousands of students, most of whom seem to have degrees already, and many of whom have high-status management roles in educational institutions. Retention rates for MOOCs are typically low, from 1–10 per cent, but with high numbers enrolled, even low completion rates can mean a significant number of successful learners, who are typically rather proud of their 'certificates of completion' or 'badges'. There is already evidence that, despite the non-completion, a great many MOOC users get involved simply to find out more about something in particular that relates to their work, and after they've got what they wanted, they discontinue. The extent to which MOOCs transcend national and international boundaries can be seen from the following example of data:

During its first 13 months in operation, ending March 2013, Coursera registered about 2.8 million learners with:

27.7% from the United States

8.8% from India

5.1% from Brazil

4.4% from the United Kingdom

4.0% from Spain

3.6% from Canada

2.3% from Australia

2.2% from Russia

41.9% from the rest of the world. (Waldrop, 2013)

At the time of writing this new edition, discussion of MOOCs has 'gone viral' in the press and online, with discussion of this new phenomenon addressing it as a 'disruptive technology': something described as an innovation providing a product or service which is so compelling that everyone rapidly abandons their current ways of doing things and flocks to what is new. If you Google 'MOOCs', you now get through to a rich array of examples and information about this online revolution, and despite the reservations many academics express about Wikipedia, the links from there are far more wide-ranging and up to date than from any scholarly published papers on the topic that have yet come my way. It seems, however, unlikely that lecture theatres and classrooms will vanish from educational institutions in the near future, but it is quite possible that what goes on in institutions will need to accommodate what is becoming available to anyone from the world outside. It could be said that 'learning can happen' (and does happen) by many people using MOOCs, but that the role of an educational institution is to 'make learning happen' – ensuring that learning outcomes are achieved, evidenced and accredited.

I will return to the implications of the technological revolution lying behind MOOCs towards the end of this chapter, but first I would like you to think about three dimensions intimately involved in making learning happen: language, literacies and the 'speed' of learning.

MINDING OUR LANGUAGE

Learning? Knowing? Understanding?

In a book with the words 'making learning happen' in the title it is useful to stop and reflect upon what we really *mean* by 'learning' and, since the words 'knowing' and 'understanding' (among others) naturally creep into any such reflections, to try to work out what we're really about when we attempt to 'make learning happen'.

For a start it is, of course, *learners* who learn; we can't do it to them, we can't do it for them. One way or another, they have to do it themselves. The mission of teaching is about actions increasing the probability that learning will happen. 'Teaching' at any level can surely be summarized as a purposeful attempt to cause learning to happen by those being taught. We can, however, structure the environment so that learning becomes easier, more productive, more efficient, more likely, and so on. I am now tired of the term 'learning environment' – and worse, 'virtual learning environment'. All environments can be learning ones, and learners themselves make no distinction between 'virtual' and everyday. The internet, smartphones and laptops are so readily available to most of today's learners (and teachers) that it seems unwise now to refer to parts of what's around us all as 'virtual'.

Understanding – and evidence-based practice

The word 'understanding' has long caused problems in designing learning. 'Understanding' is a journey, and we can never measure the extent to which anyone has progressed in the journey, other than through what 'comes out' from them at various stages of the journey. Knight and Yorke (2003) acknowledged that there is a problem with 'understanding', and also pointed out that the kinds of assessments learners meet in post-compulsory education have a significant effect upon the extent to which learners develop understanding.

> There is uncertainty about what counts as understanding. Side-stepping some important philosophical issues, we suggest that a student who understands something is able to apply it appropriately to a fresh situation (demonstration by far transfer) or to evaluate it (demonstration by analysis). Understanding cannot be judged, then, by evaluating the learner's retention of data or information; rather, assessment tasks would need to have the student *apply* data or information appropriately. This might not be popular in departments that provide students with a lot of scaffolding because their summative assessment tasks only involve near transfer, not far transfer. Where far transfer and evaluation are the hallmarks of understanding, assessment tasks will not be low-inference, right or wrong tasks, but high-inference ones, judged by more than one person with a good working knowledge of agreed grade indicators. (Knight and Yorke, 2003: 48, emphasis in original)

Perhaps we have a problem in the English language in that words such as learning, knowing and understanding overlap so much in their everyday usage. If we intend learners to become able to soft-boil an egg, it is normally enough that they become able to soft-boil an egg, and do so successfully most times they attempt the task. We could say then that they have learned to soft-boil an egg, and equally we could say that they then 'know how to soft-boil an egg'. But we wouldn't (I trust) say that they 'understand' about soft-boiling eggs until a lot more had happened in their brains, not least all of the chemistry of the colloidal processes varying with temperature within the egg, the physics of the differences in boiling temperature of water at different heights above sea level, the meteorology of the effects of the variation in air pressure under different climatic or weather conditions, not to mention the zoological considerations of the differences between different kinds of egg, and so on. But such knowledge is not necessary to boil an egg (fortunately), though for some people such knowledge may indeed enrich the thinking which might just accompany the routine process of making a soft-boiled egg.

One of the problems of formulating a curriculum is that in the English language people tend to use the word 'understand' much too loosely. Intended learning outcomes are too often badly phrased along the lines 'by the end of this course students will understand x, y and z'. Nor is it much use to soften the outcomes along the lines 'this course will help students to deepen their understanding of x, y and z'. Yes, the course may indeed help students to *deepen* their understanding, but do they know how much they are deepening it, and can we measure how much they have deepened it? In short, we can't measure what students *understand*. We can only measure the evidence that students produce to *demonstrate* their understanding. That evidence is all too easily limited by techniques of demonstrating understanding – their written communication skills perhaps, or whether they are note-perfect in music. We can measure such things, and give students feedback about them, but we can't ever be sure that we're measuring what is present in learners' minds. In some religions, blessings are phrased along the lines 'the peace of mind which passes all understanding'. Perhaps in education we need to be aware of 'the piece of understanding which passes all attempts to measure it'! Or, when it comes to understanding, 'if we *can* measure it, it almost certainly isn't *it*'.

Similar problems surround the words 'know', 'knowing' and 'knowledge'. I've already quoted Einstein's 'Knowledge is experience – everything else is just information'. Think of a person you know. What do you *mean* by know? There are all sorts of levels of knowing someone. Even at the closest levels, people often find out (usually too late) that they never *really* knew whoever-it-was.

Carole Dweck (well known for her writing on 'fixed' and 'malleable' approaches to thinking about intelligence), in an interview which can be accessed online, said of knowing:

> The things you know today are not enough. Facts change, new challenges arise, and so you can never think, '*I know this*' and call it done. To do so would assume that the question stays static or that the knowledge set necessary for solving a problem is permanently the same. To say 'I know' is to assume that your ideas are non-revisable, and that the question or problems haven't shifted. (Dweck, 2013)

So where does this leave us with 'making learning happen'? Setting out on the journey towards developing learners' understanding may well be a useful direction to go in, but we need to be really careful to spell out exactly *how far* learners are intended to develop their understanding, and what *evidence* they need to be aiming to produce to prove that they have developed their understanding, and what *standards* this evidence must measure up to, to indicate that they have successfully developed their understanding sufficiently.

We are now in an age where evidence-based practice is to the fore. The fields of health, medicine and agriculture have successfully embraced evidence-based practice, and Geoff Petty (2009) points to the need for a similar revolution in education. He starts his book by linking four principles of evidence-based practice to teaching as follows:

> You need all the evidence to make sound decisions.
>
> It is not enough to know what works, you need to know why.
>
> You need to find the critical success factors that are failing in your teaching context, and fix these.
>
> You need to review your teaching constantly in the light of the evidence above. (Petty, 2009: 4)

We need to think hard about which *processes* are best to help learners to develop their understanding, and to recognize that different processes and environments suit different learners best. We can use similar arguments about knowing and knowledge. We only measure what learners *know* as far as we can assess the evidence which learners produce. In other words, we can only measure what learners *show* of what they know. And what they show depends so much on what we *require* them to show in our various assessment contexts.

Slow learning, repetition and building on what learners already know

Perhaps when, in two or three decades, we look back at the development of post-compulsory education, in the UK in particular but often enough elsewhere as well, we may be surprised at the speed with which we rushed into modular provision in the 1990s. In many higher education institutions, this was coupled with semesterization, splitting the academic year into two main sections (rather than three terms), with what has often turned out to be an awkward and uncomfortable inter-semester break, towards the end of January (in the Northern hemisphere). Many institutions are now moving back in some subject disciplines to the design of 'long thin modules' which last a full year. Yet outside our institutions, the plethora of present-day massive open online courses is perhaps the biggest collection of 'modules' ever to be available, but largely asynchronously rather than to any academic timetable. So what about the 'speed' of learning?

Claxton (1998) referred to the idea of 'slow learning', suggesting that some learning takes weeks, months or even years to construct. This resonates well with work by Meyer and Land (2003) on 'threshold concepts' or 'troublesome knowledge'.

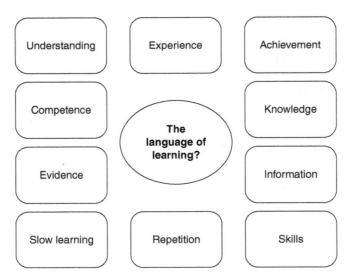

Figure 1.1 Some words from the 'language of learning'?

Knight and Yorke argue that 'complex learning is almost invariably slow learning, taking longer to grow than most modules last' (2003: 53). They also suggest that 'an advantage of monodisciplinary programmes is that, almost without the need for curriculum planning, some of the learning can take place over the full span of the programme' (2003: 140).

Another problem which can be exacerbated by too wide-ranging a mixture of available modules is that learners begin any element of study with widely differing amounts of existing knowledge. Ausubel stated: 'If I had to reduce all of educational psychology to just one principle, I would say this: The most important single factor influencing learning is what the learner already knows. Ascertain this, and teach (him) accordingly' (1968: 235). Now with all sorts of free learning opportunities available online, for example cherry-picked sections of massive open online courses, the availability of learning opportunities has never been wider – and more confusing. This leads me in Chapter 3 on curriculum design to suggest the importance of balancing 'learning incomes' alongside intended learning outcomes.

Knight and Yorke (2003) go further into the assessment implications of some learning being 'slow', and the problems this causes when the curriculum is too fragmented. Practising teachers in post-compulsory education can often cite aspects of their own subject which seem to be necessarily learned slowly. In my own former discipline, the Second Law of Thermodynamics is one such topic. It has to be 'lived with' for quite a while before it begins to make sense. It is an example of what many refer to as 'troublesome knowledge', or a 'threshold concept' (see Meyer and Land, 2003) which has to be passed. It is often quite some time after being able to *use* it successfully, and solve problems with it, that the meaning of it gradually dawns. This is not just because historically it tends to have been expressed in rather forbidding terminology, perhaps following on from the precedent of Newton's *Principia* (containing his Laws of Motion) in the 1690s, of making concepts intentionally difficult to understand, leading to his masterpiece being described as 'one of the most inaccessible books ever written'. Notwithstanding, Dennis Overbye (1991) (adapted by Bill Bryson, in *A Short History of Nearly Everything*, 2004: 107) is not far from simplifying the truth when he sums up the three main laws of thermodynamics as: (1) you can't win (that is, can't create energy from nothing), (2) you can't break even (that is, there is always some energy wasted) and (3) you can't get out of the game (that is, can't reduce the temperature to absolute zero).

For many years, when teaching thermodynamics to chemical engineers on Friday afternoons, I found that by saying 'You don't have to *understand* the Second Law; all you've got to become able to do is solve problems with it' the relief on their faces was very evident. When later the students came up to me after practising solving problems sufficiently, and proudly said 'I've got it now', I would congratulate them and reply, 'Great. I'm really glad. But of course I can't measure what's in your head, I can only measure how you apply it'.

In our present systems of post-compulsory education driven by targets and league tables, there seems little room for *not-yet-successful* learning. Yet the more elusive ideas and concepts, which can only be learned relatively slowly, often need to be re-learned several times during that pathway where slow learning leads to successful achievement. It is in fact useful to encourage learners to celebrate *forgetting* things as part of the natural process of becoming less likely to forget them next time round. The most complex ideas probably need to be grasped then lost several times before they are gradually retained more permanently and safely. Learners, however, often feel frustrated and disappointed when they have mastered something one moment, and then find that it has slipped shortly afterwards. For example, the light may dawn during a lecture or online presentation, then be found to have 'gone out again' when learners try to do the same things on their own as they seemed to be doing perfectly successfully a short while before.

One way of helping learners take ownership of the benefits of slow learning, when appropriate, is to point out to them that repetition not only pays dividends in the permanence of learning, but can be a very efficient way of using time and energy as part of an intentional learning strategy. For example, if a particular concept takes one hour to get one's head around first time, but then slips away, it may only take 10 minutes to regain the ground a few days later. If it slips away again, it may only take five minutes to get it back a few more days later, and so on. By the twentieth time round it may only take a minute or less of re-learning and it will be safely recaptured. Encouraging learners that 'it's not how long you spend learning it, it's how *often* you've learned it and lost it and regained it that counts' is a way of allowing them to feel ownership of a successful strategy for approaching those things which are best learned slowly. It is also worth encouraging them *not* to spend too long on trying to learn anything the first time round, but to come back to it frequently until it begins to make sense. Meanwhile, rather than struggling to force the brain to make sense of a difficult concept, they can spend the time more productively between attempts, refreshing their learning on things already learned successfully and ensuring that these don't just slip away. Let's next go much further into some essential skills and competences learners need to make learning happen.

DEVELOPING SKILLS FOR LEARNING: FOUR LITERACIES?

Making learning happen is not just about becoming better at given subjects, but is equally about developing as an effective, rounded, balanced, skilled human being. For those who move successfully into post-compulsory education straight from school, and then need to progress towards maximizing their potential towards evidencing their achievement fully, such learners need to acquire or develop at least four kinds of 'literacy' to bring to bear upon making learning happen successfully. Those entering as mature learners may have already developed one or more of these literacies, or indeed may be lagging some way behind their younger counterparts in some of them. The four literacies I propose here overlap, but can be summarized as follows. Learners need:

- *Assessment literacy*: needed to maximize their opportunities to provide excellent evidence of achievement 'when it really counts', in assessment whether written, oral, practical or collaborative;

- *Academic literacy*: tuning in to exactly how the world of post-compulsory education works, and where to focus their energies in the quest to succeed;

- *Information literacy*: becoming ever more able to interact with the information and communication technologies around them, particularly to locate subject material electronically, then select what they need from a wide range, and finally make good use of what they have chosen;

- *Social literacy*: further developing the skills to work effectively with each other, and interact fluently with all the other people they meet on the way through higher education towards gaining suitable career opportunities.

Many learners enter post-compulsory education already having developed these four kinds of skills to a significant extent, but are often quite different in their profile regarding these on entry, and we need to alert them how best to apply the strengths they may already have, and help them to focus productively on other areas which will help them to achieve success. More discussion of each of these literacies follows.

ASSESSMENT LITERACY

Many learners already have achieved at least a good start on assessment literacy. Those coming straight from school are already likely to be well versed in, for example, preparing for and taking exams, and to some extent will also have developed their writing skills for assessment. However, assessment in post-compulsory education is often quite different from that already known by school-leavers. For example, with written coursework or essays, it is no longer common practice in post-compulsory education to give learners feedback on drafts (as might have happened at school) so that by the time their work is assessed it needs to be as successful as they can make it. It is more common for essays and assignments to be assessed 'as they stand' at the point of assessment, and to give learners feedback and feed-forward to help with the next similar kind of assessment.

Some of the aspects of assessment literacy most needed by many entrants to post-compulsory education include:

- The ability to successfully undertake a wider variety of assessment methods than hitherto experienced, including assessed presentations, posters, portfolios, reflective accounts, practical work, online participation as well as the more familiar essays, assignments and exams.

- Being wisely strategic in the amount of time and energy they devote to competing demands, and focusing on those aspects of assessment which count most.

- Being willing and able to identify and clarify exactly what is required of them in each of the different assessment contexts they encounter, and knowing how best to interpret relevant wording in published assessment criteria, learning outcomes and evidence-of-achievement specifications in course documentation.

- Becoming familiar with how assessment works, including regulations, procedures about any re-sits or resubmission of work, how pass-marks operate, what is meant by standards such as '1st class', '2.1', '2.2', '3rd' and so on in degree classifications as used in the UK, for example, and 'Distinction', 'Merit', 'Pass' in vocational qualifications, or the A+, A, A–, B+, etc. grades common in the US, and now being linked in the UK to a proposed numerical scale from zero to 4.25 to augment the interpretation of degree classifications.

- How to handle e-assessment. This links to online submission of assessed work, computer-based exams, and the preparation of evidence of achievement electronically, such as e-portfolios.

There is naturally a rapid growth of the use of e-assessment, accompanying the increased tendency for learning to happen using online and digital resources. For this, learners need to develop appropriate aspects of 'digital' literacy as part of their overall assessment literacy. One of the problems that can occur when universities and colleges use institution-specific platforms is that students may lose access to their own work when they graduate and can no longer use the institutional virtual learning environment. Commercial platforms similarly have risks, since educators have no control over when or how sites are removed from public availability. However, there are risks to this, for example if students are unaware of what they are doing when they accept terms and conditions on some of these sites, whereby they are actually signing away ownership of their own ideas, which in some areas such as design can have very serious implications. A far better strategy for e-portfolios is to choose and use platform-independent systems, where students' ownership of their evidence is asserted. There can also be issues about equality of opportunity if students with plenty of money can buy commercial systems, which are showier and easier to use than open-access systems, for example to showcase their portfolios.

We need to include within the curriculum robust advice for students not just on how to assess the look and the usability of sites and platforms, but also on building the confidence with which students can use them. Rather than mandating the use of particular sites or tools, we need to support the development of students' own judgement capabilities, so they are capable of making sophisticated and thoughtful choices rather than just going for the first options they find.

Academic literacy

Academic literacy overlaps with assessment literacy, but also extends wider. Learners attending a college or university need to acquire and develop a further range of abilities, including:

- Knowing about protocols of conduct in educational institutions, and knowledge of how to benefit from large-group settings such as lectures, small-group settings such as tutorials and seminars, and a further range of learning contexts such as individual work, private study, online study, and use of laboratories, studios, workshops and placements.

- How to choose and use reading approaches which are fit for purpose in each study context. Reading for learning can be quite different from reading for pleasure, and needs pen in hand or Post-its, to sift and sort important information while reading. Also learners need to go beyond the 'click-and-go' approach when web browsing, which gets little into the reader's head. It rarely works to read through something for quite a long time, then conscientiously go back and make notes about the important things – the latter stage normally just doesn't happen!

- The ability to recognize what plagiarism is, how seriously it is regarded in assessed contexts, and how to avoid doing it or being accused of doing it.

- Knowledge about how they are expected to write, such as when to use formal ways of writing (third person passive voice: 'It was found that ...'), as opposed to less-formal first person active voice: ('What I found was ...'), for example in reflective accounts.

- The level to pitch the vocabulary of writing, expectations regarding sentence length, choice of wording, the avoidance of repetition, and so on.

- How to meet expectations regarding accurate spelling, context-appropriate grammar, punctuation conventions – things they may be expected to be able to do well already, even when they can't! (Sadly, there are those who think 'literacy' is entirely about this tiny sub-set of the literacies being discussed here.)

- Requirements and expectations not just to make arguments and proposals, but to back these up with authoritative quotes from the relevant literature.

- Appreciation that it may no longer work just to 'hand it in for assessment as soon as it is finished', but that a few more drafts may be needed before it is really ready for assessment – the skills to edit and improve are essential in post-compulsory education.

There are now excellent supporting materials to help students develop key aspects of academic literacy, not least Bryan Greetham's *How to Write Better Essays* (Greetham, 2013), and Jeanne Godfrey's *The Student Phrase Book* (2013b), a source which not just students, but just about everyone could usefully spend time using, and *How to Use Your Reading in Your Essays* (Godfrey, 2013a).

Information literacy

Information literacy is partly about being able to make good and quick use of the technologies now available to find information, and to manipulate it and store it. It overlaps with what I have already referred to as 'digital' literacy – competence at navigating these technologies quickly and efficiently. This side of literacy is of course very relevant to the ability to make good use of all the information already available free in massive open online courses, as well as the rest of the plethora of online information readily accessible from any laptop, tablet or smartphone. Many staff in universities and colleges are amazed at the information literacy skills some students already have developed when they arrive, especially regarding using technology. However, information literacy is perhaps more importantly about the need to *search* for information skilfully and wisely, and *handle* it well once found. It has never been easier to *find* information, but perhaps it gets harder and harder to *distinguish* what is really good information from all the dross, and then *use* selected information in a purposeful way. So it's not just about digital literacy. Learners nowadays need to be able to:

- Search for relevant information quickly and efficiently, combining all the online tools now available, but also making good use of print-based resources in libraries. (A recent newspaper article gained a lot of publicity by including a finding that learners who never visited their institution's library were seven times more likely to drop out without achieving anything. 'Not visiting the library' is perhaps part of the bigger picture of visits to public libraries in general having fallen by as much as a third in recent years.)

- Be really selective during information searching, and avoid downloading or photocopying vast amounts of 'possibly useful' material.

- File useful information in findable ways. (How often have you wished you could remember what you called something important you downloaded? Or searched through everything on your machine using the approximate date you downloaded it?)

- Avoid simply collecting loads and loads of information, however relevant (precious little learning happens in this process), without processing it and distilling just a few of the most vital parts into manageable proportions (much more learning happening).

- Cite and reference journal articles, books and web sources appropriately and accurately in accepted formats in their own writing – particularly in coursework which is going to be assessed.

- Question the veracity of information, and triangulate where necessary to check how trustworthy particular elements of information are likely to be.

- Know when to stop reading, when to stop collecting and when to start turning the most relevant findings into real learning and evidence of achievement.

Social literacy

Social literacy links to digital literacy, but goes much further. With various social media now widely used, by no means exclusively by the younger generation, we might wonder if learners in post-compulsory education need even the slightest amounts of development in this aspect of literacy. However, social literacy is by no means just about competences in using social media. 'Emotional intelligence' is increasingly seen as a very necessary part of human development, and it could be argued that some of the uses of social media may be very effective regarding communication, yet can be far from developing emotional intelligence. It is worth reminding ourselves that newcomers to post-compulsory education may be subjected to one or more of the situations below:

- Some may have been widely connected before they came to college, with a circle of friends which may quickly become out-of-date as they settle into a new environment.

- Some of their new lecturers and tutors may be enthusiastic about using social media for communication, while others are antagonistic or hostile to such media: they therefore need to respond appropriately to these different attitudes as they meet them.

- The informality of the tone and style of social media communications may be seen as quite inappropriate by at least some of their new tutors.

- The expectation that a response to a text message or email will be quick may lead to disappointment when a tutor with a pile of work to mark fails to respond so quickly – or at all.

- Thoughts, opinions and views can 'go viral' on social media; this can cause problems when, for example, a criticism of a poor lecturer turns into a media storm.

It can be argued that higher education is for maturing and transforming, and part of this is developing social and emotional intelligences, which include improving skills such as:

- relating to other people, not least fellow students

- practising using empathy to achieve targets

- interacting successfully with a wider range of people of various nationalities, cultures and views

- noticing the non-verbal cues from other people, and regulating one's own non-verbal behaviour to minimize problems or offence

- communicating appropriately face-to-face in widely differing contexts, and adjusting ways of communicating according to the climate as picked up by careful and rapid observation of how others are behaving

- communicating appropriately online with people known and unknown

- balancing written communication to oral communication, in all the different contexts where both may be involved.

Social literacy may make all the difference to the experience of being a learner in post-compulsory education, helping learners to learn about them themselves and each other more effectively. All of these skills relate strongly to employment-readiness and successful career development. These 'people skills' can be essential in the processes of moving on into employment and embracing the challenges (and joys) of working with colleagues, bosses and clients.

STUDENTS AT THE CENTRE OF LEARNING

The present book focuses largely on what can be done by practitioners in universities and colleges to make learning happen by students. However, learners themselves can do a great deal to make their learning effective, efficient and successful. Getting a degree or any other qualification depends enormously on the successful development of well-honed study skills. I would argue that just about all educational qualifications boil down to a measure of how well learners have demonstrated their study skills. The approach and wisdom of Stella Cottrell, in an extensive range of materials now available for students, perhaps most of all her *Study Skills Handbook* (Cottrell, 2013), is now widely recognized as one of the most powerful aids to students on their journey towards making their learning happen successfully in post-compulsory education, and her work provides vital reading for lecturers and tutors to help them gain insight into the learning side of the teaching–learning equation.

Trying to sort out the picture

I quoted Einstein earlier as advocating 'Everything should be made as simple as possible, but not *too* simple'. I argue that the plethora of terms and processes that have arisen in the models of learning widely available in the literature of pedagogy are not at all simple enough to describe adequately something as fundamental as how our species learns – but perversely that the 'going around in a circle' idea in a particular direction, as in a learning cycle, is much *too* simple. In other words, although all of the processes may have a part to play in successful learning, they are unlikely to follow on from each other in a neat cycle. In fact, they are much more likely to interact with each other, and affect each other and to occur concurrently rather than consecutively. How then can we simplify the picture, but at the same time enrich it? My belief is that the way ahead is to find out what factors are involved in all the main processes involved in learning – what is the underlying picture?

One of the most detailed critical reviews of models of learning in general, and learning styles approaches in particular, is the work of Coffield et al. (2004). They were robustly critical of learning cycles and learning styles, as the following quote illustrates:

> Kolb clearly believes that learning takes place in a cycle and that learners should use all four phases of that cycle to become effective ... But if

Wierstra and de Jong's (2002) analysis, which reduces Kolb's model to a one-dimensional bipolar structure of reflection versus doing, proves to be accurate, then the notion of a learning cycle may be seriously flawed. (Coffield et al., 2004: 153)

And concerning the origins of the learning cycle:

Finally, it may be asked if too much is being expected of a relatively simple test which consists of nine (1976) or 12 (1985 and 1999) sets of four words to choose from. What is indisputable is that such simplicity has generated complexity, controversy and an enduring and frustrating lack of clarity. (Coffield et al., 2004: 154)

For some time in my own workshops and keynotes, I have been critical of the learning cycle approach to thinking about learning, and have posed questions about 'What's missing?', and discussed some of the factors illustrated in Figure 1.2 below.

In Chapter 2, and then throughout the rest of this book, I have addressed how all of these 'missed dimensions' are vitally important to us in our bid to make learning happen. Not least, for example, we can only measure what students communicate, and not what's in their heads.

Coffield et al. are also dismissive about learning styles, and refer us to the work of Reynolds among others (concerning matching learning styles in teaching):

Figure 1.2 Dimensions missed by learning cycles?

The most telling argument, however, against any large-scale adoption of matching is that it is simply 'unrealistic, given the demands for flexibility it would make on teachers and trainers' (Reynolds 1997, 121). It is hard to imagine teachers routinely changing their teaching style to accommodate up to 30 different learning styles in each class, or even to accommodate four ... Should research into learning styles be discontinued, as Reynolds has argued?

We ourselves have been reminded yet again how complex and varied that simple-sounding task is and we have learned that we are still some considerable way from an overarching and agreed theory of pedagogy. In the meantime, we agree with Curry's summation (1990, 54) of the state of play of research into learning styles: 'researchers and users alike will continue groping like the five blind men in the fable about the elephant, each with a part of the whole but none with full understanding'. (Coffield et al., 2004: 157)

Coffield et al. conclude their large-scale report as follows, in words which repay revisiting in the present-day world where online learning can happen anywhere, and where students do not need to go to educational institutions to gather information:

Finally, we want to ask: why should politicians, policy-makers, senior managers and practitioners in post-16 learning concern themselves with learning styles, when the really big issues concern the large percentages of students within the sector who either drop out or end up without any qualifications? Should not the focus of our collective attention be on asking and answering the following questions?

- Are the institutions in further, adult and community education in reality centres of learning for *all* their staff and students?

- Do some institutions constitute in themselves barriers to learning for certain groups of staff and students? (Coffield et al., 2004: 157)

It is with these conclusions and questions resounding in my own mind that I set about the task of preparing this book about making learning happen in post-compulsory education. But before we get down to the task of looking at the factors which underpin successful learning, let's dig deeper into the state of the world now surrounding our colleges and universities.

MOOCS AND SOCIAL MEDIA: INTEGRATION OR FRAGMENTATION?

In this age of Facebook, Twitter, LinkedIn (to name but a few of the recent ways people now use technology to communicate) we are gaining unimagined speed and sophistication in how we can send and receive information (textual, visual, audio-visual) to and from fellow human beings anywhere on our planet. On our laptops, PCs, tablets and smartphones we can link to the largest collection of digitized resources there has ever been, via the internet. Communication and information have 'gone viral' – surely an irreversible change?

Yet what is happening to our brains? We all now learn with a plethora of stimuli, but without dataports in our heads, the same old brains have to learn to deal with extracting what's needed (or wanted) from all the information and images that pass our eyes and ears every day. The internet has become an external memory source that we can access at almost any time or place; we don't need to store things in our heads like once was the case. As long as we know how to find it, or (better) where we put it last time we found it, there's little point remembering most things.

Integrating the technologies, but fragmenting the stimuli?

Claims can be made that a lot of integration has taken place between technologies of communication and information retrieval. More often than not, systems can talk to each other. So we are now bombarded with stimuli from a range of 'platforms' such as Facebook, Twitter and so on, and our lives are changed by the constant pressure to respond to these stimuli quickly and suitably. Speed has become of the essence. If a text message or email remains unanswered, or a voicemail un-responded to, have we failed? If we tweet, and no one re-tweets us, is this worse than a lousy record in citation reviews? Our busy lives are carried out amid a plethora of communications stimuli – whether they are social, work-related, or quite irrelevant to us (do we not delete more of the messages we receive than those we read?). In the midst of this fragmentation of data, communication and stimulation, we go about the normal processes of living and working. Indeed, much of the fragmented communication makes our working and living more efficient and more enjoyable. But what about longer-term thinking and learning? Have we sufficient uninterrupted time left to think? Have we time to reflect, before the next tweet, email or text message pings? Is the 'big picture' in our heads enhanced or damaged overall?

Versatility with communications and information technologies is (naturally) expected by modern employers. But they still expect graduates who can write in joined-up language and fine-tune proposals and reports to maximize impact. And they expect graduates who can 'concentrate' – just the sort of skill our modern environment tends to destroy. The new media help enormously when it comes to 'being well informed', but are we sacrificing thinking skills?

Some cultures value meditation highly. Meditation is usually thought of in terms of lack of interruptions to thinking. This can allow the brain to make connections between ideas, and to generate new ideas and hypotheses, which could not have happened in other circumstances. Meditation affords, among other things, the luxury to ponder the answer to a question – quite different from having to respond immediately or instinctively on demand. Even in the calm of an exam room, there is at least some possibility of pondering the answer to a question before (and while) putting pen to paper or fingers to keyboard. But the expectation remains in exams to answer questions in a limited time – meditation is a luxury, and there's little pay-off for any thinking that is above and beyond the required answers to the exam questions.

Open learning has come of age

The learning environment is already digital. Online communication is normal for most of us. Young people don't need to read manuals to find out how to work things – they just get on with trial and (very little) error until things work. That sort of learning still works. When 'open learning' started to develop in the last century, who could have imagined the online possibilities which would emerge with MOOCs? The founding ideals of open learning – own pace, own place, own choice of time – are all now endemic in modern learning environments. The learner is now in control of so many of the variables, and can navigate (or fail to navigate) the subject matter at will. And perhaps more important, learners can communicate with each other so easily and effectively, synchronously and asynchronously, and with tutors, mentors and anyone else who has a bearing on their learning – a dimension of 'openness' unimaginable in the early days of paper-based open learning. Open learning is finally realized in all its glory. But how good are we at assessing the evidence of achievement arising from open learning?

Measuring learning

At the centre of any learning, whether in traditional contexts or on a MOOC, is the human brain. Learning happens in brains one at a time, though (as ever) other brains can be learning resources. We can't transfer knowledge from one brain to another – never could – each brain has to do some learning. 'Knowledge transfer' was the silliest of phrases. Perhaps the internet is – and has been since its inception – a rapidly expanding massive open online course? The difference is in the last word: 'course'. There's the rub. That's about organization of content and processes – but, more importantly, implies some way of measuring the degree of success with which individual brains have assimilated and mastered sufficient knowledge from the mass of information to be worthy of that knowledge being somehow measured and accredited. Will MOOCs be able to measure how much we've learned, and how well we can demonstrate our learning? Probably – this is already happening to some extent in fact. We've long been able to use multiple-choice online testing to calibrate many dimensions of what people's brains can do with what they've learned. This depends of course on the quality of the assessment questions, which in turn depends on how well they've been trialled before being used for real. With the sophistication of technologies now available to us, the basic multiple-choice question seems strangely old-hat. We can now, if we choose, follow up a 'correct' choice with a series of options regarding why exactly the best choice is better than the distractors, and 'which of the following reasons is why Distractor C was wrong? ...' – multi-layered multiple-choice questions, reducing the 'guess factor' from 25 per cent in an old four-option question down to single figures. This means that the reliability of the assessment is improved, and it can be argued that the validity is also enhanced.

Assessment remains at the heart of learning. We only know that learning has happened if we can measure the results. In conventional learning environments such as schools, colleges and universities, assessment drives learning. Institutions compete on the basis of success at assessment. Educational institutions have responsibility for the quality of assessment: validity, reliability and authenticity, as well as inclusiveness, transparency and manageability. Where assessment is done online in a MOOC, how do we know that it is the brain of the candidate that we're assessing? Ingenious solutions include characterizing each user's keyboarding skills, and requiring them to demonstrate that it is indeed their fingers at work on the keyboard by typing out given samples of text, and verifying their keyboarding profile. But when they are being assessed, how different may the environment be from a traditional examination?

Traditional assessment processes attempt to measure what's in a head in terms of what comes out of a pen in a silent room, at the very end of a period of learning. The extent to which what's in a head can be measured by what comes out of a pen has been disputed ever since the first written exam in Europe in Cambridge in 1791, prior to which candidates were grilled orally. Oral assessment allows for probing questions to ascertain that the candidate actually knows what she or he is saying, in a way that written assessment fails to do. But of course, a MOOC could well use oral online assessment, with video helping to establish authenticity. But that would cost a lot – MOOCs are usually free, so who would bear the cost?

Back to the learner

What about the personal dimension? In the original incarnation of open learning, thought was given to learners having choice regarding what was being learned, as well as when, where, why and how they studied. In universities and colleges, today's students are increasingly critical about feedback from tutors supporting their learning. Students want the feedback to be intimate and personal, about their particular triumphs and disasters, and about things to bear in mind next hurdle on. Surely with all the possibilities offered in a MOOC context, not least learners giving and receiving feedback on each other's efforts, the personal dimension is better met. Learners will still want 'authoritative' feedback, however – that from an expert. Perhaps that is where *we* come in?

The possibilities of integration are most encouraging. Technology can help combine the benefits of rapid access to information, communication with fellow learners and supporters or assessors, and allow own place, own time, own pace and own choice of content to happen. But assessment remains what it's all about, and the design of assessment has to live up to the quality of the learning resources which abound. But there's still to be considered the interface between MOOCs and their associated assessment, with the world of benchmarks and standards and specified intended learning outcomes and standardized expectations regarding evidence of achievement that has grown around the arena of formal human learning. How else can we have the (dubious) satisfaction of making league tables comparing providers of learning opportunity? How else can funding be allocated to the right people, according to the displayed merits of the products of their systems? Is it the case that in this exciting new age of possibilities, we still hanker after the comfort of the constraints which open learning long ago started to erode? Are we grown-up enough to enter the age of MOOCs properly yet? Time will tell. As always, the proof of the pudding will be in the assessing. This is why Chapter 4 on assessment is the biggest in this book.

CONCLUSIONS

We have got to be really careful about the language we use to *describe* learning, and we must accept that we can never really measure *learning*, but only evidence of achievement as a result of learning. Evidence of achievement is our best proxy in attempts to quantify learning, understanding, knowing, and so on, so we need to become ever more skilled at describing intended evidence of achievement in terms which will provide learners with targets to aim towards (and aim to exceed). To succeed, our learners need the literacies outlined in this chapter, if they are to thrive in the world of abundance of information and ease of digital communication.

Most importantly, we need to think about the *processes* of learning, and avoid the danger of oversimplifying them. *How* does learning happen best? This leads nicely towards the purpose of Chapter 2 – to think about learning in straightforward language which we can share with our learners, so that all of us can cooperate and play our respective parts in making learning happen, but to avoid oversimplifying the processes an instrument as complex as the human brain uses when learning.

To end this chapter, however, I'd like to share some informal advice I sometimes give to students who are thinking of taking the plunge and going to university ('uni' as they tend to call it in the UK). You might wish to adapt or improve this for your own students.

 Tips for students: how to do uni

This short guide aims to help you make it at uni. But I can't do it for you – here's how you can make it.

1 *It's not like school*. For example, you don't get to do an essay and get feedback on your drafts so you can make it better. When you hand an essay (or report, or whatever) in at uni to be assessed, that's it. You're marked on what you hand in.
2 *It's a lot bigger than school was*. At school, you may have been one of the brightest of the bunch, and you knew everybody. At uni, you're one of a much bigger,

brighter bunch, and most folk don't know you. You've got to sink or swim – and it's much more fun swimming.

3 *Your success depends most on what comes out of your pen.* It's not really about how well you get your head around your subjects at uni, as only you know how well you do that. You're assessed on what comes out – mainly through your pen in exams, and your keyboard in coursework.

4 *Your lecturers won't know you like teachers used to know you.* There may be hundreds in your class, especially in the first year. If you're slipping behind, lecturers may not notice. It's up to you at uni – less chance of help unless you ask for it.

5 *How much work you do is up to you.* No one will tell you that you should be doing more. Many of your fellow students won't seem to be doing much work (even those who are doing a lot behind the scenes). Only you can make sure you're doing enough.

6 *Yes, do enough, but don't burn yourself out.* Doing too much studying is as dangerous as doing too little. What you really need to do is to make your studying efficient, so you don't waste time and energy. You'll need a fresh set of study skills at uni. What worked fine at school is no longer up to the mark at uni.

7 *You can't do it all at the end.* At school, you could mug up for exams and get away with it. At uni, there's so much more to get to grips with, and it's harder, and you've really got to keep at it all the way through so that when exams come up you're right there, ready and waiting.

8 *There will be loads of distractions.* That doesn't mean don't ever get distracted from studying, but it does mean you've got to manage your distractions. Those who don't, don't succeed. What a waste of time and money that is. Life is too short not to make a good go of Uni.

9 *Sounds like all hard work?* No, for most successful students, uni is one of the best times of their lives. Successful students, however, tune in fast to what's wanted in essays, reports and exams, and draft and re-draft their coursework to score most marks. Successful students listen for all the cues, clues and hints that lecturers give about what counts. Teachers used to tell you what counts, lecturers don't – but they do give you clues, cues and hints.

10 *Your fellow students are a great resource for you.* Talk to them. Listen to them. Explain things to them. Get them explaining things to you. The more you talk and listen, the more you learn – even more than just reading or writing. You need to do the learning before you can write well, so talk and listen to make the most of the folk around you.

If you succeed, you'll be really glad you went to uni. But I said 'if'. Whether you succeed at uni is, as you can see above, up to you. I hope you do. *You can.*

CHAPTER 2

FACTORS UNDERPINNING SUCCESSFUL LEARNING

O— **Key topics in this chapter**

- Wanting to learn
- Needing to learn
- Learning by doing
- Making sense
- Learning through feedback
- Verbalizing orally
- Assessing: making judgements

BACKGROUND

In this chapter, I introduce you to investigations I have been doing for the last three decades, asking by now well over 160,000 people about how they learned (and what went wrong in their learning). The responses continue to prove to be very convergent. From marked trends in their responses we can identify that there are distinct factors which underpin successful learning. Moreover, it is really important to consider how these factors overlap with and interact with each other. The way of thinking about learning presented in this chapter has been developed from asking all these people six two-part questions about how they learned and further deepened their learning. The factors identified in this chapter form the basis of much of the rest of this book, as we link them in turn to assessment, feedback, large-group teaching, small-group learning, reflection and various other aspects of higher education.

Who are all these people?

The respondents to my questions come from the following main groups:

- students I work with on developing their study skills approaches to further and higher education
- lecturers and teachers in higher and further education, during courses and workshops on the design of teaching, learning and assessment
- large groups of people from higher education, and various other professions, at conference interactive keynote sessions I run in the UK and beyond
- trainers I work with on the design of training processes and resources.

I've often developed the discussion of these factors at conferences, as well as in training workshops and staff development programmes. I've also asked similar questions to groups of school pupils, and have found that their thinking about learning is very close to that of adults (further increasing my reservations about 'andragogy' having a special nature, or whether 'heutagogy' ('self-determined learning') is confined to adult learning!). The ages of respondents spans 8 to 80 years, and I've worked with people from the UK and Ireland, but also in Australia, New Zealand, Holland, Denmark and, occasionally, in Singapore, Canada, Sweden and Switzerland. I therefore feel able to argue that the common ground which emerges is about fundamental processes underpinning successful learning by adults from several cultures, rather than pertaining only to a relatively focused cross-section of learners.

The main stage of this investigation involves me asking people the first four questions, each in two parts, and getting them to jot down their responses to the second part of each question, in no more than about half-a-dozen words for each response – in other words, headline responses. The first part of each question asks them to identify an element related to one instance of their own learning, whether formal or informal. I then ask them to jot down their answers to the second part of each question, and sample the responses if working with a large group, or take everyone's response when working with 20 or fewer people. Then I ask two further questions, this time asking people to indicate by show of hands the extent to which they believe that their own learning was deepened by two more processes.

To enter into the spirit of this book, however, I prefer not to say too much more about the factors which emerge from people's answers to these questions, until you have had a go at answering them yourselves. You may of course already know at least something about the factors from the Preface of this book or from previous editions, or from having been present when I've used the questions. Whatever the case, you might like to jot down your own responses to the questions in the following box.

Questions about your own learning

Please use this table to focus on your own learning – past or present. Part (a) of each of the first four questions which follow is to get you thinking about particular instances in your own learning. Part (b) then asks you to put pen to paper (or fingers to keyboard) to capture some of the processes which led to the success – or otherwise – of the respective instances of your learning.

1 (a) Think of something you are good at – something which you know you do well. (This may be an academic subject, but equally could be a hobby or skill – in short, anything at all that you're good at.)

  (b) Now jot down a few words about *how* you became good at this.

2 (a) Think of something about yourself which you *feel* good about – something which you like about yourself. This could be anything about yourself which gives you a sense of pride.

  (b) Now jot down a few words about how you know that you can be proud of this – in other words, upon what evidence is this positive feeling based?

3 (a) Think of something which you don't do well! This could be the result of an unsuccessful learning experience, maybe long ago or maybe recently. If you've nothing in this category, you can miss out question 3. (I usually add that no one has admitted, so far, to have nothing in this category!)

  (b) Now jot down a few words about each of the following: what went wrong, do you think, in your learning relating to this thing you do not do well? And who, if anyone, might have been to blame for this?

4 (a) Think of something you can indeed do well, but that you didn't *want* to learn at the time you learned it. This could be something like 'driving', 'swimming', 'cooking' or, equally, it could relate to a particular area of academic study – perhaps 'statistics' or 'economics' and so on. Whatever it is, you're probably pleased *now* that you succeeded with it – it's likely to be useful to you now, or to have served its purpose some time ago.

  (b) Jot down a few words about what kept you going, so that you did indeed succeed in this particular episode of learning.

5 (a) Think of something which you've helped other people to learn. This could include teaching people, coaching them, training them and so on. Think back particularly to the first time you explained it to other people, particularly by putting it into spoken words.

  (b) To what extent did you find that you 'had your own head around it' much better after putting it into spoken words that first time? Choose one of the following options:

- Very much better
- Somewhat better
- No better

6 (a) Still thinking of the first time you helped other people get a grip on that particular topic, think back to the first time you attempted to see how well they'd 'got it'.

  (b) To what extent did you find that after that first occasion of measuring or assessing their learning, you yourself had made sense of the topic even more deeply? Choose one of the three options which follow:

- Very much better
- Somewhat better
- No better

IDENTIFYING THE FACTORS UNDERPINNING SUCCESSFUL LEARNING

In the next section, I summarize the responses I have had to the questions in the box above, and draw from the strongest trends in these responses the factors which underpin successful learning.

1 How most people become good at things

What people think of as something they do well ranges enormously – everything imaginable has been covered in the responses of those who have shared with me their replies to the first part of question 1. Most people's answers to the second part of question 1 are much more convergent, along the following lines:

- practice (far and away the most common response)
- learning from mistakes, through getting it wrong at first
- experimenting
- trial and error
- repetition
- experience
- having a go

And so on. All of the above answers have one thing in common – they're about 'doing' of one kind or another.

There's nothing new about this of course. The ancient Greeks and Chinese knew a lot about the importance of learning by doing. Sophocles is reported to have said words to the effect that 'Though one thinks one can do something, one has no certainty until one tries to do it'. Indeed, many of the Ancients could have said this.

Ancient wisdom about learning is worth revisiting. *How* we learn has not changed much over the millennia. Even though there have been vast changes in *what* we learn, and indeed in the resources and tools we *use* to aid our learning, those essential processes of 'learning by doing' remain. Or, in other words, there may have been huge changes in our learning environments over the years, but the human brain evolves very slowly, and the processes underpinning successful learning are slow to evolve.

Included in learning by doing is trial and error – learning through mistakes. Niels Bohr, the Danish nuclear physicist, is reported to have defined 'an expert' as follows: 'Someone who has made all of the mistakes which it is possible to make – in a very narrow field!' Sadly, at present we often seem to undervalue the potential of learning through mistakes. There's a tendency to take note of people's mistakes and use these against them in evidence. I now regularly encourage lecturers and trainers to help their students to *celebrate* learning by trial and error as a productive and efficient way of learning many things – so long as the environment in which the mistakes are made is productive, unthreatening, safe and without the risk of humiliation or embarrassment.

Although most replies about how people became good at things relate to *doing* of various kinds, at least some relate to ways in which they were affected by other people. In particular, there are usually some responses about how other people caused or enabled practice or repetition, and even 'training' comes up occasionally – but quite rarely 'being taught'. 'Being inspired' comes up rather more often, along with 'being enthused'. Later in this book we'll explore how we can aim to be inspiring.

2 How people come to feel good about things

Question 2 yields very convergent replies to 'how you *know* that you can be proud of this – in other words, upon what evidence is this positive feeling based?' Typical answers include:

- feedback
- other people's reactions
- praise
- compliments
- people come to me for help
- seeing the effect on other people
- seeing the results.

All these can be summed up as 'feedback' of one kind or another. Feedback clearly plays a vital part in helping people to develop positive feelings about things they do, and things they are. The majority of such feedback arises from other people, including fellow learners, tutors, teachers, trainers, mentors, friends, just about everyone or anyone. Some feedback is also linked to self-assessment or self-evaluation, for example the 'seeing the results' replies often refer to looking at the *evidence* arising from the learning – the visible side of the achievement (including drawings, paintings, musical compositions, sculptures, and many other artefacts which are products of the learning concerned).

While most people readily accept that feedback plays a vital role in helping them to learn, there are two key problems which can get in the way of feedback reaching its optimum value:

- the feedback needs to be provided very soon after the actions on which it is based
- feedback needs to be actively taken on board and reflected upon and acted on, and not rejected or dismissed.

A further response often arises from question 2: this is 'my confidence increased'. This too, on probing, often links back to feedback from others, or confidence gained by seeing the results of the learning concerned.

In Chapter 5, I go into much more detail about how adjusting the timing of feedback can make a lot of difference to its value to learners, and about how a wide range of feedback processes can be analysed in terms of which are the most effective for learners in various contexts, and which are most efficient for teachers.

3 Learning going wrong!

Question 3 yields a rich harvest of causes of learning going wrong. People's replies to the questions 'what went wrong, do you think, in your learning relating to this thing you don't do well? And who, if anyone, might have been to blame for this?' show that a wide range of things can be the causes of unsuccessful learning – 'things people aren't good at' – and that although many people accept the 'blame' for this, even more blame other people. In fact, the blame is often directed at particular teachers and lecturers at virtually any stage of learning.

Many replies link back to the overlap between question 3 and the previous two questions. For example:

- didn't get enough practice
- I didn't work hard enough at it
- I got poor feedback
- poor communication between myself and teachers (or trainers, tutors, fellow learners)
- I was made to feel small about it
- no one explained to me how to become better at it.

And so on. But even more replies bring in some important further factors:

- I didn't want to learn it in the first place
- I couldn't see the point of it
- I couldn't see what I was supposed to be aiming to do with it
- I couldn't get my head around it
- I just didn't understand it
- the light wouldn't dawn
- I couldn't make sense of it.

A further, even more common factor is:

- poor teaching!

When running this exercise with learners themselves, they often write down the *names* of teachers here (more often than not maths teachers, but teachers of French for some reason often share the blame attributed!).

A further dimension underpinning successful learning is clearly to do with getting one's head around it, or *making sense* of it. This is all about developing deeper understanding of what is being learned, but bearing in mind my reservations about the word *understanding*, as expressed in Chapter 1, I prefer to use 'making sense' as there is less risk of thinking that the process is necessarily 'complete' or 'final'. In addition, replies to question 3 often bring in aspects of motivation. In particular, when learners don't really *want* to learn something, we should not be surprised that they may be unsuccessful at learning it well. Conversely, when learners *really* want to learn something, little will stop them from succeeding. There are countless tales of learners who had a very strong *want* to succeed in learning difficult and complex things, who succeeded even when people around them did not think they would make it.

It can be useful to think of the *making sense* process as mentally *digesting* the experience of learning, and *digesting* the feedback being received. The everyday use of the word 'digesting' is about extracting what we need from what we eat and drink – taking what will sustain us for the next few hours or days. But just as important in normal 'digesting' is discarding what we don't need – 90-odd per cent of the total amount eaten and drunk no less.

We can think of *digesting* as being a parallel process where the human brain sorts out the floods of information sent to it by the various senses, and keeps just a little of this information in one form or another, discarding perhaps 99.9 per cent of it quite rapidly. We can therefore regard the process of *digesting* to be turning information into knowledge. The metaphor linking *making sense* to digesting food and drink can, of course, be extended much further. We can think of mental *indigestion* arising from various conditions and environments. We can think of some *ailments* which can be caused by exposure to adverse kinds of information or inappropriate amounts of information, or failure to *digest* caused by poor reception of feedback or even total lack of feedback. Too much of one kind of information may be bad for us. Low-quality information can't be good for us. Incomplete processing of important information decreases the amount of *making sense* we achieve. Extending the metaphor even further, different parts of the digestive system have distinct parts to play in extracting particular minerals and elements from our food, so perhaps different learning contexts and environments are needed by our brains to maximize our acquisition of particular kinds of knowledge?

4 What keeps learners going when the going is tough?

Just about everyone to whom I have posed question 4 has no difficulty in thinking of something they did learn successfully, but didn't actually *want* to learn at the time. Often they are now glad that they did succeed – whatever it was has proved worthwhile in the long run. The things people have learned in this way include just about everything imaginable, for example:

- swimming
- driving
- cooking
- ironing
- keyboard skills.

Moreover, all sorts of academic learning come into this category for many learners, not least:

- statistics (e.g. SPSS: the Statistical Package for the Social Sciences, first developed in 1968)
- calculus
- thermodynamics
- critical theory
- counterpoint.

And so on.

So what then keeps learners going, when they don't really *want* to learn something? People's answers to the second part of the question reveal at least three factors.

- Some learners are kept going by strong support and encouragement. Such support often comes from teachers or tutors, but also from mentors, friends, family and just about anyone. In a large group, however, it is usually only about one in 10 people who attribute their 'being kept going' to strong support and encouragement. For these people, that support is indeed critical, and without such support they probably would not have succeeded – or would have taken much longer to succeed. This has implications for the feedback we give learners on their work. It is all too easy for carelessly phrased feedback to stop such learners in their tracks. Also, those learners who *need* strong support and encouragement could wilt without it.

- Rather more learners are kept going by something which at first sight seems rather negative – not wanting to be found lacking, or not wanting to be humiliated, or wanting to prove to other people that they can indeed do it – sometimes to people who may have implied that they did not expect them to succeed. Some learners need to prove to *themselves* that they can succeed – they take ownership of the challenge and put everything into meeting the challenge head on. They have determination. The implications of feedback are more profound when learners don't want to be seen to fail, however. Any critical feedback can all too easily stop them in their tracks, and we need to be particularly careful with the wording of feedback when they have not yet accomplished something. In practice, this range of 'negative' drivers of learning is surprisingly common – about one in three learners seem to be kept going by not wanting to be seen to fail.

- The majority of learners (typically six out of 10), however, give different accounts of what kept them going when they didn't actually *want* to learn something, the common factor being 'need' or 'necessity'. People say 'I kept going because I needed to become able to do it' or 'It was a necessary step in the pathway I was heading along' or 'I needed this to open the door to what I really *wanted* to do', and so on. But it's not just about there being a need, it's usually about people accepting *ownership* of the need. This is all perfectly *rational* of course. Learners who take ownership of a particular *need* to learn are quite robust – they are not easily stopped, even by critical feedback when they get things wrong. They too are determined.

5 Learning through verbalizing orally – teaching, explaining, coaching

When asked about how my respondents helped other people to learn face-to-face, the vast majority say they got their own heads around some learning 'very much better' by putting it into spoken words to other people, by 'verbalizing' or 'vocalizing' it. We've all heard of 'walking the talk' as being desirable, but 'talking the walk' is perhaps even more essential. People remember surprisingly well the very first time they attempted to teach something, or to explain it to others, or to coach others in it. They often remember that they didn't at that stage do it particularly well, but more importantly, they remember that they made sense of the topic a great deal more than they had done hitherto. They were learning fast as they tried to teach it or explain it or provide coaching in it. And they were learning 'deep'. We can therefore think of verbalizing or speaking as a further process which causes the factors we've looked at already (wanting, needing, making sense, feedback) to intensify. We could argue that learning hasn't happened fully without this additional step of putting things into words to people face-to-face.

We can interpret this as evidence for the processes of putting things into spoken words yielding a high learning pay-off for teachers. Good news for teachers, explainers, coaches! But we can of course turn this round, and get our students putting things into words. Often, learning is indeed judged on the basis of how well people can explain things orally. Putting things into written words may help, but spoken words also involve hearing one's own words as we speak, giving a further opportunity to adjust our words as we speak. Many people who learn *coach* other people in the subject they're learning. This is, in a way, different from teaching, and deeper than just explaining. Coaching can be regarded in many ways as the highest form of teaching, as it is such an interactive and intimate process, and the feedback between both parties has to be extremely good for it to work at its best.

So why exactly is putting things into spoken words so good at helping 'the explainers' to deepen their own learning? Think now of what happens to us when we teach.

- We gain vast amounts of *feedback* as we teach. All the eyes in a classroom or lecture theatre are feedback to us. All the things our learners do give us feedback – the work they do successfully as a result of our teaching and their learning is feedback to us. Even more so, all the mistakes they make are further feedback to us. It is not surprising that all this feedback helps us to deepen our own learning while we teach.

- We're *making sense of the topic* ourselves all the time that we teach. How often have you found yourself, while in the middle of explaining something to learners, *getting your head around it properly* for the very first time as you explain it? It is often halfway through the process of explaining things to other people that the real meaning dawns in the mind of the explainer.

- We're also *doing* when we teach. We're not only learning by doing things ourselves, but we're learning by getting other people doing things too. So teaching is full of experiential learning for us, as well as for our learners.

- We're addressing the *need* as we teach. We are trying to help learners to see the point of what they're learning. We're trying to help them to see what it's for, what it will do for them and where it fits in to the bigger picture. We're trying to convince them that the intended learning outcomes are for them, not just for us.

- And we're confronting the *want* all the time we teach. More acutely, often we're confronting the *lack of want* as we teach, and using all our skills to try to 'warm up' learners and arouse their curiosity, so that they take ownership of the need to learn *and* want to learn as well.

It therefore should not surprise us how much we learn as we teach. And particularly that *first* time we try to teach something, we're plotting our own course in uncharted territory regarding *how* we explain things to learners, *what* we get them to do, *how* we help them to get feedback, and so on.

If teaching is so good in terms of the learning pay-off for us, the obvious question is 'should we be getting our learners themselves to maximize their learning pay-off through teaching?' My answer is 'Definitely!' Imagine, for example, a maths lesson, where the teacher has explained a proof or derivation to the extent that a third of the learners in the room have seen the light. That is the time, I argue, for the teacher to stop, and get the learners into threes, each containing one who has seen the light and can now *do* it, and two who haven't yet seen the light and can't yet do it. Then get the one who can do it to talk the other two through until they too can do it. When one does this, the *explainers* remember it forever! It's one of the deepest learning experiences there is, to see the light about something, then within minutes, talk a couple of fellow human beings through it until they too can do it. The explainers are benefiting from the high learning pay-off associated with teaching.

The 'explainees' are having a good deal too. They are *now* having it explained to them by someone who remembers how the light dawned. For us as teachers, all too often we've known things for so long that we've forgotten how the light dawned that vital first time round. Perhaps the moral is that we are better able to teach things that we can clearly remember *not* understanding? If it seems that we've always understood something, we probably are not the best person to try to teach it to others.

6 Learning through assessing – making informed judgements

The final question in the box above is about the learning gain which happens when we try to measure other people's learning – assessing. Just about all of my respondents to question 6 recall that they got their heads around a topic much better when they made judgements about other people's learning of the topic. For example, as we mark students' work, right from the very first time:

- we find out all the mistakes that we never imagined anyone would make

- we discover the different ways in which individual learners have made their own sense of whatever it was

- we gain a great deal of feedback about how to go about teaching the same thing next time round, to minimize the mistakes learners will make and maximize their learning pay-off.

We can think of the act of *assessing* as causing all the processes in our own learning we've already looked at to intensify and deepen. While we make assessment judgements:

- we're getting a great deal of feedback on how our learners' learning has gone

- we're finding out a lot about how our teaching has gone, and what to do to make it better next time

- we're continuing to make sense both of the topic and of other people's disasters and triumphs as they learn the topic

- we're learning by doing yet again – this time particularly by applying criteria and designing feedback for learners about their achievements and their problems

- we're continuing to learn by explaining and coaching, as we formulate feedback for learners and help them to improve their learning

- we're defining – and redefining – the standards of learners' evidence of achievements of the intended learning outcomes, clarifying in our own minds priorities and balances

- we're gaining yet more information about learners' *need* to learn and their *want* to learn.

In short, the process of assessing deepens our own learning every time we make informed judgements on learners' work, but particularly those first few times we engage in the process, where we find out a great deal very rapidly. In other words, learning through assessing has a very high learning pay-off indeed *for us*.

Once more, we can ask: 'If the process of *assessing* yields such a high learning pay-off, should we be causing *learners* to assess rather than just assessing their work for them?' I believe that we should indeed do so. Causing learners to self-assess their own work leads to deepening their learning in ways which just don't happen if we do it all for them.

As long ago as 1989, the Australian guru on feedback and assessment, Royce Sadler, wrote:

> The indispensable conditions for improvement are that the student comes to hold a concept of quality roughly similar to that held by the teacher, is able to monitor continuously the quality of what is being improved *during the act of production* itself, and has a repertoire of alternative moves or strategies from which to draw at any given point. In other words, students have to be able to judge the quality of what they are producing and be able to regulate what they are doing *during the doing of it*. (Sadler, 1989: 121, emphasis added)

In 2010, Sadler went on to suggest:

> Students need to be exposed to, and gain experience in making judgements about, *a variety of works of different quality* ... They need planned rather than random exposure to exemplars, and experience in *making judgements about quality*. They need to create *verbalised* rationales and accounts of how various works could have been done better. Finally, they need to engage in *evaluative conversations* with teachers and other students. Together, these three provide the means by which students can develop a concept of quality that is similar in essence to that which the teacher possesses, and in particular to understand what makes for high quality. Although providing these experiences for students may appear to add more layers to the task of teaching, it is possible to organise this approach to peer assessment so that it becomes a powerful strategy for higher education teaching. (Sadler, 2010: 544, emphasis added)

Causing learners to peer-assess each other's work achieves a great deal:

- they may get a great deal more feedback from each other than we ourselves would have been able to give them

- they may find it easier to take feedback from a fellow learner than from figures of authority such as teachers or tutors

- they deepen their own learning by making informed judgements of fellow learners' work

- they find out about things that other learners did better than they did themselves, and can emulate these things in their future work

- they see mistakes that they themselves avoided making, and increase their awareness of what to avoid doing in future.

Once learners are convinced of the value of self-assessment and peer assessment, it can become one of our strongest teaching tactics to set this up and facilitate it. However, there are always some learners who will argue that 'This is *your* job, not mine' or 'You're paid to do this, not me!' We therefore have to work hard sometimes to convince learners that the act of assessing is one of the best ways to deepen their own learning, and a useful pathway towards their own success and achievement.

You may notice that I've expanded quite a lot on the responses I get to questions 5 and 6 in the box above. This is not least because I would now go so far as to argue that learning is only 'complete' when it has been deepened both by some form of teaching/explaining/coaching and assessing. In earlier versions of my 'ripples on a pond' model of learning I focused on the central five factors, but now believe that the outer two are indispensable. It could be argued that these two are not as 'distinguishable' as the central five factors, but serve to make those five resonate so that learning is deepened.

Summary of the factors underpinning successful learning

From people's answers to these six questions, the following factors can be seen to be involved in successful learning.

1 *Wanting* to learn. We could call this 'intrinsic motivation' but hardly anyone uses these words in answer to any of my questions. Such language may *mean* the same as 'wanting to learn', but remains cold, remote and academic-sounding. Everyone knows what a 'want' is, and that if the want to learn is powerful enough, success is likely to follow.

2 *Needing* to learn – or, to put it more precisely, *taking ownership* of the need to learn. This could be called 'extrinsic motivation' but again learners (or their teachers and trainers) rarely use this sort of language when describing what kept them going when the going was difficult.

3 *Learning by doing* – practice, experience, having a go, repetition, trial and error. This fits well with all that has been said about 'experiential learning'.

4 *Learning through feedback* – other people's reactions, confirmation, praise, compliments and simply seeing the results. Constructive critical feedback helps too, particularly in the context of learning by trial and error. Feedback, of course, is directly connected to everything under the 'learning by doing' banner. The quicker the feedback, the better it helps learning.

5 *Making sense of things* – getting one's head around it or 'digesting'. This process is perhaps the most important in most learning situations. This is about 'the light dawning' or 'gaining understanding', and so on. But this is very firmly linked to each and all of the other factors in the list above. For example, *feed-back* plays a vital part in helping most people make sense of the results of their *learning by doing*. If there was already a strong *want* to learn, it is not surprising that the *making sense* is catalysed dramatically. Even if there is only a distinct *need* to learn, *making sense* is aided. This factor is different from the first four, however, in that we can't *make sense* of things for our learners – only *they* can do it. So our job becomes to provide them with the best possible environment in which they can achieve the *making sense* parts of their learning.

6 *Verbalizing orally* – this helps us to make sense of it even better than we had done hitherto. It's not just about 'putting it into words' as that could be done in writing. It's about speaking it, face-to-face with other people, with all the feedback entailed in that context. It's about hearing our own voices as we try to explain something, and adjusting and readjusting our words as we speak until our mission is achieved.

7 *Assessing – making informed judgements*. This process too intensifies many of those listed already, and it can be argued that learning is not at all complete until we've attempted to assess other people's learning, which helps us to self-assess our own learning, thereby developing our own learning very sharply.

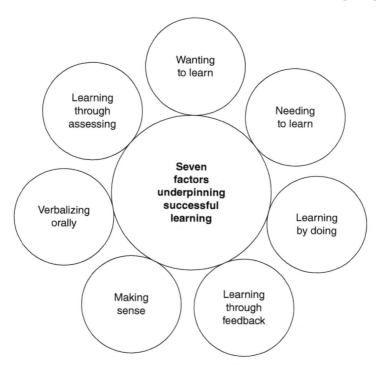

Figure 2.1   Seven factors underpinning successful learning

Figure 2.1 summarizes the seven factors we've explored so far in this chapter, but how do they interact with each other? As I suggested in Chapter 1 – definitely not in a cycle!

RIPPLES ON A POND

We've seen the factors which can be identified from asking a vast number of human beings to reflect on their own learning experiences. Next to the vital matter of how these factors interact with each other. They don't just follow on from each other in a particular order, nor are they necessarily *different* stages of an ongoing process. My argument is that they all affect each other, and all may occur more or less simultaneously and concurrently. One way of thinking about this is to imagine them as ripples on a pond, bouncing backwards and forwards and interacting with each other in the same way as ripples do when a pebble falls into a pond.

Imagine that initially the water on the surface of the pond is mirror-smooth. Then a pebble falling into the pond starts the water rippling. The energy to start learning happening can arise from *wanting* to learn. It can also arise from *needing* to learn. Better still, both may be involved. When learners really want to – and need to – learn, it is very likely that some learning will take place. But how often

Figure 2.2 Factors affecting each other like ripples on a pond

do we know that we *want* to do something – or indeed *need* to do something – but we don't actually get round to it? All too easily, if we do nothing more, the *want* or *need* just fades away. We could think of this as the pond smoothing itself out again as if nothing had happened.

However strong the *want* or *need* to learn may be, nothing tangible happens unless some *learning by doing* happens next. This can take many forms – practice, trying something out, experimenting, trial and error, repetition, application, and so on. However, just *doing* something is no guarantee that learning is happening. For example, I often talk to learners coming out of other people's classes, and ask them about what they feel has happened during the last hour or so. They often say that they have *enjoyed* the last hour, and feel inspired and empowered to go on learning whatever it was. But all too often when I ask them to tell me a little about what they learned during the session, their replies are along the following lines: 'Sorry, I haven't actually *read* it yet, I've just seen details of the weblinks to follow up later', and so on. In other words, they've got the *information* but they haven't yet really started to convert it into their own knowledge.

Put bluntly, they've been wasting their time during the session. They may have been *taking* notes, but often without even thinking about what they were writing down. They've sometimes been copying things down from the screen or board, and copying things down verbatim that the teacher or lecturer said, but without thinking about the meaning. There has been precious little *making sense* going on. Sometimes they have been far too busy trying to capture all the information and they have not even had time to try to make sense of what they have been writing. Or they may have been skim-reading loads of information on screens. Now if they had been *making* notes rather than *taking* notes, things might have been much better and they would then be able to tell me a lot about what had been going on in their minds during the session.

So for effective learning to be taking place, *doing* needs to be linked to *making sense* or *getting one's head around it*. Learners need to be *processing* information and turning it into their own knowledge, not just capturing information.

So how can learners know that they've *made sense* of the subject matter they have met? It's one thing to *feel* that they've made sense of it, but another thing to *know* that they've made sense of it. That's where *feedback* comes in. If they have been getting a lot of feedback on their thinking during a teaching session or while working through learning resource materials, they are in a much better position to know whether they've got their heads around the subject matter that has been the content of the session. Feedback from whom? The lecturer or teacher of course, but also from each other, and from comparing their own thinking with what is contained in the resources materials associated with the session.

The feedback helps them to *make sense* of their own *learning by doing*. The feedback helps them to digest the information they have been processing, and turn it into a start towards building their own knowledge from it. The feedback also clarifies the *purpose* of the information – for example, by linking it to the frame of reference provided by the intended learning outcomes for the session. Feedback allows learners to see *why* an element of learning will be useful to them or relevant to them. It helps them to gain a sense of ownership of what they *need* to learn. If they already *wanted* to learn it, feedback may confirm that they have succeeded or help them find out what they still need to do to achieve the intended outcome.

Thinking of ripples on a pond as a metaphor, we can imagine the feedback ripples bouncing back towards the middle of the learning ripple, strengthening the *making sense* process, causing more *doing* to occur, clarifying the *need* and, when constructive and helpful, enhancing the *want* to continue learning. Without feedback, much less *making sense* is likely to occur – perhaps none at all.

Yet learning is still not complete until we have gone through the processes of putting things into words to other people, face-to-face, orally. And our learning still isn't complete until we have also intensified our own thinking by assessing other people's learning.

It is useful to think of these factors as continuously affecting each other, not just in a particular sequence, but simultaneously and concurrently, just as ripples bounce backwards and forwards on a pond. More importantly, all these processes are tangible and easily understood by teachers and learners alike. However, perhaps the real breakthrough is that these factors can be addressed and harnessed both by teachers and by learners themselves. As teachers, we can set out to:

- enhance or initiate the *want* to learn

- clarify the *need* to learn, and help learners to take ownership of this need

- cause learners to *learn by doing* – practice, trial and error, repetition, and so on

- help learners to *make sense* of what they are learning, rather than just store information for later processing that may never happen

- cause learners to receive *feedback* on what they do, and on what they think about what they have done, and so on

- get our learners themselves to *vocalize orally* the material they're learning, and talk each other (or indeed anyone else) through the material

- cause our learners to *assess,* for example using peer assessment, or self-assessment, or simply getting them to apply criteria to evidence we give them to assess.

Several parts of this book refer in much more detail to what we can do to make learning happen in learners' minds.

The time factor

We've been thinking about these seven factors, and the way they all affect each other, and 'bounce backwards and forwards' to impact on each other. One thing, however, that I'm keen to remind you is that this does not mean they always happen in a linear fashion when it comes to timing. In particular, the *making sense* part of the process happens a bit at a time in several iterations. For example, we can start to make sense of something in the act of *learning by doing*, but this is unlikely to be 'complete' making sense if the topic is complex. We proceed to make more sense of it when we gather and analyse feedback on our learning by doing. But even then, we may not have made complete sense of it. We continue to increase the extent to which we've made sense of it by explaining it to others, or coaching other people in it, or teaching it. Even then, as many teachers agree, we may still not have made complete sense of it in our own minds. We can, however, go even further towards making sense of it by making informed judgements, for example in assessing students' work relating to the topic, or facilitating their self-assessment or peer assessment of it. So the *making sense* stage is part of the picture which is accomplished little by little, in a series of iterations backwards and forwards across the various factors underpinning successful learning.

Moreover, we've probably *never* made complete sense of it! More than once, a very skilled and experienced teacher has asked me 'What can I do when I realize that the thing I'm about to teach yet again is something I now know I don't completely understand?' This can be regarded as yet another positive stage in learning it. We're more knowledgeable about it when we realize we don't fully understand it than when we thought we did! This is another way of arguing that the idea of *understanding* something is fragile, and that it is better to think of learning as gradually making more and more sense of something but without imagining that there is an end to this journey. Even very accomplished teachers admit that their *making sense* journey continues for the foreseeable future. Admitting this to learners is very reassuring to them. 'Don't worry too much about trying to understand it', a good teacher might say, 'You'll gradually make more and more sense of it the more often you revisit it, especially if you try explaining it to others, and extend this to trying to make informed judgements about your own learning of it, and about other people's learning of it'. So in a way, we could argue that it's the number of times the seven processes have resonated backwards and forwards that governs the extent of that vital process – *making sense* of what is being learned. It's not just about the time taken!

But what can we do if there isn't a want and if learners are not even conscious of a need?

Sadly, many groups of learners nowadays contain at least some learners who don't really *want* to learn anything at a given moment in time, and who may also be quite oblivious of any real *need* to put in the effort to learn something. We can try to initiate a *want* but that can be an uphill struggle. We may, however, be able to convince at least some of the 'unwilling' learners that they have a *need*. One of the most useful ways of approaching this task is to remind ourselves that we may need to convince learners of the benefits which will accrue when they have put in some effort to achieve some learning.

When faced with an array of disinterested, bored-looking faces in a class, it can be worth asking ourselves 'What station am I broadcasting on just now?' I sometimes suggest to staff that the most appropriate one is 'WIIFM' – 'what's in it for me?' In other words, we need to try to help our students to take ownership of the *need* to learn, and spelling out the benefits they will derive from having learned something successfully can sometimes win them round. We can point ahead to:

- what they will be able to do when they have learned something successfully
- what doors this may open for them in their future lives and careers
- how learning this bit will make the next bit achievable.

And so on. But even these tactics leave some learners unmotivated, especially if they are there against their will in the first place. So what else can we try? Experience suggests that the best approach is to get them *doing* something. Choose something that:

- does not take long
- is interesting in its own right
- can be linked back at least in some way to a relevant intended learning outcome
- will stretch them a bit, but not intimidate them
- may win them over to the idea of doing something more very soon.

Then, as soon as possible, get them *making sense* of what they have been doing by getting them to compare with each other, argue, discuss, debate – in other words, deepen their learning through feedback and vocalizing orally. If they enjoyed the episode of learning by doing, found that making sense of it was interesting too and liked gaining and giving feedback about it, the ripple can 'bounce back' right to the centre and alert them to the *need* they have now addressed. In other words, we can help them to realize that the small increment of learning they have just done links to something worthwhile and relevant to them. The more they enjoyed it, the more likely they are to be willing to engage in the next element of learning by doing – in other words, they now have at least some degree of *wanting* to continue learning.

In at the deep end: teaching and assessing?

We explored earlier how *doing* can start off the whole process, when there isn't a *want* or a *need*. What about *teaching* and *assessing*? Every teacher has tales to tell of how quickly they learned things they had previously never encountered when they were plunged in at the deep end and given a new topic to teach at short notice. This can be very frightening, but it often works surprisingly well. We can easily examine the situation and draw out that there is indeed a great deal of *learning by doing* and *trial and error* in teaching a new subject, and a great deal of *feedback* gathered in action. This in turn causes a lot of *making sense* and so on.

Similar arguments can be applied to *assessing*. Suppose you were appointed as an examiner for a major examining body and your first big pile of exam scripts included one or two topics that were quite new to you – a scary prospect. However, many examiners report that this has happened to them quite often, though they would have been wary of admitting this to a Chief Examiner at the time! Nevertheless, the act of applying assessment criteria to other people's evidence of *doing* (even when that 'doing' is just writing things down in exam halls) causes accelerated *making sense* to occur. Those unfamiliar elements of the syllabus may take considerably more time and energy to mark, but where is all that extra energy going? – into *making sense* of the new topic.

This flexibility is perhaps the most significant aspect of a way of thinking about learning which allows the process to begin at quite different starting points. That said, I would hesitate to suggest that as teachers or trainers our main approach to making learning happen should be intentionally to drop learners into the deep end of the pond! However, we would do no harm in alerting them to the fact that they can indeed survive and prosper when they unexpectedly find themselves in these deeper waters.

So where may 'understanding' come in?

In Chapter 1 I suggested that the word 'understand' is not a useful one for various reasons – especially that it's unsuitable as a key word when we express intended learning outcomes, and (more importantly) we can never really *measure* understanding, only echoes of it as manifested by various kinds of evidence of achievement. Perhaps understanding lies outside and beyond the last ripple in Figure 2.2. It can be argued that one never really *understands* something until one has learned it, then taught it, then assessed it. In other words, *understanding* something can perhaps be regarded as the cumulative effect of:

- taking ownership of the need to learn, and clarifying the evidence of achievement which will match successful attainment of the intended learning outcome

- wanting to achieve the learning outcome and to continuously make informed judgements on the learning as it is happening

- purposefully learning by doing – not just during practice, trial and error, repetition, but also in teaching, explaining, coaching and making informed judgements during self-assessing and peer-assessing

- building on feedback gained about evidence of achievement, and feedback arising from making informed judgements on other learners' evidence

- maximizing the learning pay-off arising from all the *making sense* which accompanies learning in the first place, and continues in the acts of explaining, teaching, coaching and assessing.

Noel Entwistle (2009) provides perhaps the most in-depth account of understanding in the context of university education to emerge in recent years, distinguishing between the idea of 'personal understanding', as developed by students, and 'target understanding', as perceived by their tutors. Entwistle comments that:

> Relying too much on the teacher's understanding may leave the student without a fully functional personal understanding, being able to pass exams by mimicking the lecturer's understanding, but not able to use it in other situations. (Entwistle, 2009: 50)

Also discussed is difference between 'fixed understanding' and 'flexible understanding' – a continuous restructuring and reframing of facts and knowledge. Fascinating as this discussion is, my concern remains with what we actually measure with our various assessment processes and instruments, and I remain unconvinced that we measure anything more than echoes of understanding in most contexts.

The value of 'time out'

However, *understanding* does not usually just 'stop'. As we continue to teach something over the years, continue to assess learners' work on it and continue to refine our teaching through all the feedback we get in these processes, it is not surprising that our own understanding continues to deepen. Yet even this is not as straightforward as it seems. For example, if we just continue teaching and assessing, we get to a certain level in our own understanding. But if we move on to different things for a year or two and *then* revisit the original topic in our teaching and assessing, we are often surprised at how much *more* we feel that we now understand it. We could think of this as 'different' ripples in our own learning adding to 'previous' ones – or the whole pond becoming more agitated. Many an experienced teacher has admitted to me how scary it was when teaching something again after many times doing so, they suddenly realized 'I don't quite understand this now!' This goes to show that the understanding stage has perhaps endless depths, and at any one moment we've only reached a particular level of this – greater understanding may follow. It is not surprising that industrious teachers sometimes feel that they are learning so much that it's almost like becoming seasick – a good excuse to laze on a beach somewhere to recharge our batteries now and then!

'Look – no teacher!'

Learners, too, can be involved in taking charge of how these seven factors work for them. In my work with learners developing study skills, I encourage them to:

- explore their own motivation, seeking good reasons which will fuel their *want* to learn – in other words, building their own rationale for *why* they are learning and what they want to *become* as a result of their learning

- clarify exactly what they *need* to learn – in other words, identify exactly what they need to become able to do as a result of their learning, taking ownership of the real purpose of the intended learning outcomes involved

- recognize that *learning by doing* is how it all happens in practice, encouraging them to put their energy into practice, repetition, trial and error, and so on

- accept that *making sense* of what is being learned is important, and is something that only *they* can do, and that we can't do it for them. Encourage them to try hard to *digest* information, selecting from it the really useful parts, rather than just collecting and attempting to store as much information as possible

- make the most of *feedback* on their learning from all possible sources – from each other, from teachers or trainers, from books and articles, and from anyone else who can give them feedback on their actions, their evidence, their *making sense*, and so on

- take every opportunity to verbalize things face-to-face with other people, explaining things, teaching others, coaching fellow students, to maximize the learning pay-off which accompanies putting ideas into words orally, showing others how to do things, and so on

- create opportunities to make informed judgements about their own learning, to self-assess their evidence of achievement of the learning outcomes, and even better to peer-assess others' evidence, to gain the vast amount of making sense which accompanies the act of assessing, and work towards being able to continuously monitor their own learning as suggested by Sadler (1989).

Learners find it perfectly acceptable that the actions listed above all affect and enhance each other, and that any combination, or indeed all, of the actions can be happening at any instant during their learning.

Since learners themselves can take control of all these factors and address them for themselves, it is not surprising just how much learning takes place without any teaching, training, instructing or tutoring processes. The phrase 'self-taught' has always been in widespread use, often in contexts where particular people have reached outstanding levels of achievement without teaching interventions. It could often be said that the people concerned have simply found their own ways of mastering how they learn, and have developed their own ways to address the factors described above.

Imagine you yourself needed to learn something new, and there was no one to help you to learn it. Imagine you found yourself in a library, surrounded by books, articles, videos, web access, and so on – in other words, adrift in a sea of information about the topic. This taxes our imagination rather weakly because most people have been exactly there! The modern equivalent is perhaps to have just started out on a MOOC. What do we do about it? What works is to start *processing* all that information – finding out what the important parts really are, finding out what they mean and rearranging the information in ways where we can handle it. We learn by doing – practice, repetition, trial and error. We reduce the vast sea of information down to manageable proportions – summarizing it. We try to get feedback on how our learning is going. We gradually digest and make sense of the information. We test our learning by communicating it – explaining things to others, having a go at teaching it.

And of course, we're looking ahead towards our own evidence of achievement being assessed. We look for detail about the sorts of judgements which will be made on our learning. We look for past assessment criteria and apply them to our own learning. Even better, we try to get others to make some judgements on our learning, or have a go at getting into the assessor's mind by making judgements on other people's learning.

Perhaps, therefore, in our bid to make learning happen in post-compulsory education, we need to be spending much more time helping learners to see how learning really happens. I firmly believe, of course, that we should be starting to help people to be in control of their own learning long before they reach post-compulsory education. Developing learners' control of their learning is already happening under a variety of labels – key skills, transferable skills, and so on – but, possibly because we so often use the word 'skills' for such things, people don't yet quite realize that these are exactly the 'skills' which underpin even the most sophisticated levels of knowledge or understanding. And perhaps the most important outcome of any element of learning is that of becoming a better *learner* bit by bit. This chapter ends with some suggestions for learners themselves regarding how they can address the factors we've been exploring.

CONCLUSIONS

The main factors underpinning successful learning, as developed in this chapter, form an agenda for much of the rest of this book. They are just as useful for learners as for tutors. Their strength lies in their simplicity – at least in terms of the language we can use to describe them – and is easily shared by teachers and learners alike. But the strength of this way of thinking about learning also lies in its complexity – the way the factors all interact with each other and don't need to occur in a set order or pattern. And perhaps the most significant factor is that any or all of these processes can be going on at any instant in our learning – and we can choose to address any or all of them quite intentionally at any moment in our teaching.

 Tips for you, and your students: helping learners to make learning happen

There are numerous sources of study skills advice for learners, many suggesting tried-and-tested approaches to learning. One of my own contributions to the genre (Race, 2007) is built around helping learners to get their heads inside the processes of assessment so that they optimize their performance when their achievement is being measured formally. I have chosen to end this chapter on learning with a set of 25 key suggestions written directly to learners, which you may find useful to copy for your learners or, better still, adapt for them, tuning the suggestions into the particular contexts of their own studies in your own discipline.

1   *Want to succeed.* Don't just *hope* to be successful. Be determined to get your result and to do everything you need to do to make it happen. Think positive. Keep reminding yourself of 'What's in it for me?' Think ahead to how much better your life will be *having* succeeded: more choices available in your career; a better developed brain.

2   *Make good use of the intended learning outcomes.* These tell you a lot about what you need to become able to do to actually get to your target. These help you to sort out what to learn from what not to learn. These help you to find out about what is fair game as an exam question and what is not. These help you to work out what your assessors are looking for in assignments. (There are some more detailed suggestions about how to make good use of intended learning outcomes in Chapter 3.)

3   *Don't bury your head in the sand.* Getting your learning to work for you is a big job, but like any big job, is done a little bit at a time. Keep doing little sections of the job all the time rather than hiding from the enormity of the whole task. You get your result for doing all the *little* jobs, not just for tackling the whole task.

4   *Confront your work avoidance tactics.* It's all too easy to put off the evil moment of starting a task. Meanwhile, you could have got the task well under way. Don't waste time feeling miserable about the backlog of work you've got – just do one thing from the backlog and you'll immediately feel better. Then do another thing, and you'll feel ahead of the game.

5   *Don't mix up 'important' with 'urgent'.* The danger is that if you're too busy doing things that seem urgent, you'll miss out on things that are really important. Do one short important thing *before* you do the urgent thing you've got to do that day. That's one less thing that will become urgent. Revising last week's lecture for 10 minutes is often more important than the first 10 minutes you will spend writing up this week's assignment.

6   *Don't confuse being busy with working effectively.* It's all too easy to be busy working at something which will only contribute a mark or two towards your overall result, when you could have spent the same time on something that would count for a lot more. Being busy can actually become an advanced work-avoidance tactic. Keep your eye on the big picture, not the small detail.

7   *Don't spend too long on any one thing.* Don't get so involved in writing a particular essay or report that you miss out on spending time getting your head around the important concepts and ideas from the last couple of weeks' lectures. An extra two hours might just get you one more mark on that essay. Two hours spent consolidating the last two weeks' learning might pave the way to earning you 20 marks in a forthcoming exam.

8   *Take charge of your workload.* Don't just respond to the pressures around you. Be your own manager. Do what's expected of you, and what's required of you, but also do things that no one has told you to do – for example, going back over things you've already learned, making sure they're not just slipping away again.

9   *Think questions.* Any important fact or concept is just the answer to a question or two. If you know all the questions, you're well on your way to being able to

(Continued)

(Continued)

answer any question that will come your way. Write your own questions down all the time – in lectures, when you're reading, when you're thinking, when you wake up, any time.

10   *Find out the answers to important questions.* Look them up. Ask fellow students. Ask lecturers when necessary. Don't just guess the answers – check whether your guess is good enough. Life is too short to learn 'wrong' stuff.

11   *Learning happens by doing.* Don't just read things or listen to lectures or browse websites or books, handouts and articles. *Do* things all the time. Make your own headline notes. Practise solving problems. Practise answering questions. Do it again – repetition deepens learning. Find out about those things you need to do *six* times before you get your head around them – these will usually be more important than something you only have to do once.

12   *Make notes – don't just take notes.* When reading, or sitting in a class, or working online, you're only really *doing* something useful if you've got a pen in hand or fingers to keyboard, and you're *not just copying things down*. Capture your own thoughts, questions, ideas and so on, and link them to what you're seeing and hearing.

13   *Find out how you're doing – all the time.* Get as much feedback as you can – from lecturers, from fellow students and by comparing your own work with what's in books, articles, websites, everything. Don't just wait for feedback to come to you – go looking for it. Don't be defensive when the feedback is critical – learn from it. Don't be glib when the feedback is complimentary, build on it consciously.

14   *Keep records of all the feedback you get.* Written feedback from tutors is easy to return to, and re-learn from, but make sure you also keep short notes of advice received in face-to-face feedback too – it's easy to forget important points otherwise.

15   *Use your friends.* Show your draft assignments to anyone who will read them – fellow students, friends, family members, anyone who can read. Even people who don't know anything about your subject can give you some useful feedback – even if only on spelling or punctuation.

16   *Don't think that studying is something you have to do alone.* It's much more sociable studying with like-minded fellow learners. The only time it's really important to do things on your own is writing up the final versions of assessed coursework – you don't want to risk being accused of copying then.

17   *Practise communicating what you've learned.* In due course, it's what you communicate that gets you your qualification, not just what's inside your head. Use every opportunity to explain things to other people. Do this with fellow learners, family, friends, everyone. Even explaining things to a dog helps you become better at making sense of what you've learned (and dogs love being talked to about anything!).

18   *Self-assess all the time.* Don't just wait for someone to assess your work. Apply the assessment criteria to your own work before you hand it in for tutor assessment. Cross-reference your work to the intended learning outcomes, and work out which of these you've achieved and which you have not yet achieved. The more you know about the standard of your own work, the better you'll fare when others judge your work.

19   *Make the most of peer assessment too.* Get fellow students to give you feedback about your work. Take every opportunity to apply assessment criteria to their

work. Making informed judgements about their work helps you to become better at continuously monitoring your own work as you do it, and thereby to produce work of better quality, gaining higher marks.

20   *Practice makes perfect.* Exams measure how good you are at answering exam questions under exam conditions. Practise answering questions as your main revision strategy. The more *often* you've jotted down the answer to a tricky question, the *faster* you can do it correctly one more time in the exam itself. Don't just hope it will be all right on the day in the exam – *make* it all right by practising all the way up to the day itself.

21   *Have a life.* Getting your result isn't *all* hard slog. You need time out for your brain to be refreshed. But build this time out *into* your overall strategy, rather than feeling guilty about it. There's no better way to enjoy some time out than to take it at the point of just having achieved a useful chunk of learning. So earn your time out, then enjoy it.

22   *Be cue-conscious.* All the time, your lecturers are giving you cues about what's really important and what's less important. The intended learning outcomes give you cues too. You'll get lots of cues from past exam questions. You'll get even more cues by talking to fellow students and finding out what they think is important. But don't let all these cues evaporate away – jot them down, preferably in the form of questions you need to become able to answer or things you need to become able to do. When you know where you're heading, you're much more likely to become able to get there.

23   *Take setbacks in your stride.* A low mark for an assignment is a useful learning experience – find out what to avoid doing again so that you don't lose the same sorts of marks next time. Don't just grumble that you deserved better marks. Learn what you can from each setback, then let it go and don't brood over it.

24   *Take pride in your achievements.* Don't just worry about all the things you haven't yet done – learn from things you've done well and build on that learning. There's no way you can ever feel that you're doing everything possible towards getting where you're heading, so be reasonable with yourself.

25   *Keep becoming better at studying.* At the end of the day, your learning is a measure of how well you've developed your study techniques, not just how much information you've crammed into your brain. Become ever more conscious about how you learn best. Explore all the possibilities. Find out the techniques which really work for you, and develop them.

CHAPTER 3

DESIGNING THE CURRICULUM FOR LEARNING

O🔑 Key topics in this chapter

- Evidence of achievement
- Assessment briefings
- Rationale for assessments
- Draft learning outcomes
- Marking criteria
- Feedback to students
- Post-pilot adjustments

EVIDENCE-BASED PRACTICE

Many fields of human endeavour now focus on evidence-based practice, including what has been seen as a revolution in health care. A well-designed set of intended learning outcomes is evidence of good curriculum design, but more importantly should link really strongly to the evidence of achievement which will be developed by successful learners. After all, it is such evidence of achievement which is drawn from learners in assessment contexts, and such achievement can be regarded as the whole point of education and training. The word 'attainment' is sometimes used by policy-makers, but I don't think this adds much to our thinking about curriculum design, as attainment is only 'real' to the extent that we are able to quantify and accredit achievement.

You may well have come across the use of taxonomies as a way of formulating the wording which ends up in statements of intended learning outcome, notably (historically) that of Bloom et al. (1956) and a much later one involving one of Bloom's original collaborators (Krathwohl, 2002). While I support taking all reasonable care in formulating the wording of learning outcomes, I am convinced that lists of words as comprised in taxonomies are a poor substitute for looking carefully in each context at the evidence of achievement which is intended to be demonstrated by learners. The same words can have very different manifestations in different disciplines, different levels and different learning contexts. Also, some of the words listed in taxonomies can have quite different meanings in different languages, not least different varieties of even the English language as used in different parts of the world. I am unconvinced by one of the results of employing taxonomies: where particular words are associated with different 'levels' of achievement, such as where certain learning outcomes are designated 'final year' as opposed to 'first year', and so on. In my experience, a seven year old can often provide evidence of achievement of just about all of the so-called 'higher' levels of achievement. In the discussion in this chapter, I urge readers to leave behind any preconceptions resulting from the use of taxonomies, and proceed to use language to arrive at fit-for-purpose learning outcomes linking directly to intended evidence of achievement.

TOWARDS LEARNING OUTCOMES THAT WORK FOR LEARNERS

Whenever the topic of 'curriculum design' comes up, we tend to think of learning outcomes – whether we like them or not. In this chapter, I'd like to help you to work towards formulating learning outcomes that will be really useful for your learners. After all, learning outcomes are for students. It's their learning we're talking about. They need to know what they're supposed to become able to do, so they can set their sights on some definite targets and work purposefully towards being able to show that they've achieved these. That said, wisely chosen and well-developed learning outcomes are extremely useful to us as teachers. They help us to map the curriculum, so that we can plan the routes we use to navigate our learners through their learning.

'Constructive alignment' – a 'slice' of the pond?

The term 'constructive alignment', following from the work of Biggs and Tang (2011), is widely used to indicate a desirable way of designing curriculum. Constructive alignment, to me, boils down to 'joined-up thinking' linking sensibly learners' evidence of achievement to each of the following:

- the assessment criteria used to measure the standard of the evidence of achievement

- the learning outcomes specifying the anticipated nature of the achievement

- the learning-by-doing processes through which the achievement will be developed

- the ongoing feedback which helps learners gauge their achievement, and work towards evidencing it more successfully.

In the previous chapter we looked at the seven factors underpinning successful learning, including in particular how teaching and assessing can increase learning pay-off. But what about the documentation – the paperwork associated with some of these processes? Important parts of this documentation are of course the learning outcomes, and the assessment criteria we apply to learners' evidence of achievement of the outcomes. All this can be thought of as a 'slice' of the central parts of the pond discussed in Chapter 2, as shown in Figure 3.1.

We can think of intended learning outcomes as right at the centre of the picture. These should define the *need* to learn. Better still, if the outcomes can be designed in such a way that learners find them attractive, we may even manage to link them more strongly to their *want* to learn, especially if we can build the 'What's in it for me?' dimension into the outcomes.

Learning by doing: this leads directly to *evidence*. This evidence of achievement can take many forms:

- written assignments done by learners – essays, reports, problem sheets, and so on

- practical work – laboratories, studios, fieldwork, work-based learning, and so on

- written test and exam answers

- performances, interviews, presentations, discussions, debates, and so on.

Regarding the *making sense* part of learning, this evidence of achievement needs to link to our assessment criteria, defining the expected *standards* of

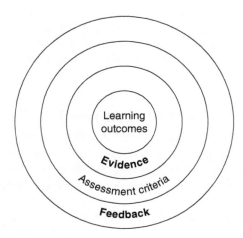

Figure 3.1 A cross-section of the pond?

achievement of the intended learning outcomes we are aiming our learners towards.

Feedback: this should enable us to help learners to see to what extent their *evidence* in all its different forms has demonstrated their achievement of the *intended learning outcomes* to the standards specified by the *assessment criteria*. Linking strongly learning outcomes to evidence of achievement and assessment criteria can be regarded as one way of thinking about what Biggs and Tang mean by 'constructive alignment' of the curriculum.

DESIGNING CURRICULUM TO ACHIEVE CONSTRUCTIVE ALIGNMENT

I believe that it's best *not* to start drafting learning outcomes as the first step in designing an element of curriculum. Starting with learning outcomes has too often ended up as a triumph of hope over experience! It is much more productive to start our thinking in terms of *evidence* of achievement. It's really helpful for students to know what success *looks* like. Indeed as Royce Sadler (2010) reminds us, it is even better for students to see a range of examples of evidence of achievement, so they can work out for themselves how good the evidence needs to be to indicate real success.

Having worked out the desired evidence of achievement, we can then work backwards towards the intended outcomes for which this evidence is valid, and choose how best to measure reliably students' achievement, and work out the criteria which will set the standards for this achievement. Then go backwards and forwards until the whole lot are in harmony. It's an iterative business. We should not just start with some outcomes, then work out some criteria whereby we measure whether students have achieved them or not. The evidence of achievement is what it's all about – the learning outcomes are merely a means of setting the scene for the arena in which students will head towards furnishing this evidence.

In most of this chapter, we will explore how to link learning outcomes to the seven factors we've explored in Chapter 2, and how to work backwards from evidence of achievement so that we end up with learning outcomes which align really well to assessment and everything else!

Then we can give students feedback about the extent to which their evidence shows that they have achieved the learning outcomes to the level of the assessment criteria. That's what 'constructive alignment' means to me. But keep in mind that all of these iterate – they all affect each other, as do the processes underpinning successful learning outlined in Chapter 2. Feedback helps tease out the evidence of achievement, and helps us to fine-tune the learning outcomes and the assessment criteria until they all resonate. 'Ripples on a pond' continues to be the analogy which I suggest.

Learning outcomes should be heard as well as seen!

You can't *hear* a module handbook page, or even a web screen (well, you can in fact be enabled, using appropriate technology, to hear the latter, but not with

the various subtleties which teachers can add to the words in person, as below).
Learners need the additional communication of what the learning outcomes actually mean, as given through:

- tone of voice

- emphasis on particular words

- the power of a pause in a sentence or phrase

- speed of speech

- repetition, when something is important enough to hear again and again.

And when possible:

- eye contact

- facial expression

- body language

- gesture.

All of these dimensions of communication add enormously to the power of
printed or on-screen words, helping learners to work out exactly what the
intended learning outcomes mean for them. All these additional dimensions can
be achieved in our use of learning outcomes – if we provide them – in each lecture, tutorial or practical briefing we give.

Stepping back from this, it's very useful for *us* to hear our learning outcomes
read out to us, as we go through the process of putting a curriculum element
together. If we get someone else to read out one of our draft learning outcomes
to us, we can almost always improve them, for example as follows:

- If the reader has difficulty reading out the outcome, it is probably too long or
  too clumsy; if breath has to be taken in mid-sentence, the 'thought' is probably
  too long as expressed in the present draft to be comfortable to a learner meeting the idea for the first time.

- While listening to someone else reading our words, we often think to ourselves, 'Ah, that's not quite what I meant here' and have the chance to change
  key words to make the real meaning clearer.

- If it *sounds* boring, it will no doubt be read as boring by learners!

Linking learning outcomes to the seven factors underpinning successful learning

In Chapter 2, we explored how successful learning is underpinned by seven factors, which all affect each other and interact with each other rather like 'ripples

on a pond'. So how exactly should a set of intended learning outcomes address these seven factors?

1   *Wanting* to learn: the learning outcomes need to arouse curiosity, and be attractive and interesting. At best, the learning outcomes should trigger the 'wow' factor. At worst, they should at least manage to address the 'So what?' as well as the 'Why should I bother to learn this?', and 'What's the point of me paying attention to these learning outcomes?'

2   Regarding ownership of the *need* to learn: the learning outcomes should *define* the need, helping students to see exactly what they need to work towards becoming able to achieve. Learners may simply wish to know 'What exactly do I need to do?' Some will go much further, and look carefully at the learning outcomes to find out 'What do I need to do to get a really good qualification?' Others will take a more strategic view, asking of the outcomes 'What's the minimum I must do just to pass?'

3   *Doing*: this relates most directly to the production of evidence of achievement. 'What exactly should I be expecting to be required to do as I learn this topic?' This also needs to include clear answers to the questions: 'When and where will I need to do these things on my way to achieving the learning outcomes, and provide evidence of my achievement for the various assessment contexts I will meet?' Learners may also be asking 'What's the difference in "doing" between a first-class degree and a pass?' Learning outcomes need to be designed to help students to see exactly what they should be practising, what they should be learning from trial and error and from experimenting, and should indicate where repetition is going to be useful.

4   *Feedback*: learners are likely to look at a set of learning outcomes with the following questions in their minds: 'How will I know I'm on the right track while learning this material? How will I know that my evidence of achievement is pitched at the right level? What can I do to get back on track if I've slipped?' Learners need feedback on their achievement of the learning outcomes – not just at the end, but all the way along the route. Learners don't just need feedback on what they've done, but also feedback on where they are in their journey towards evidencing their achievement of the learning outcomes.

5   *Making sense*: 'How will I know that I've really achieved the outcomes? How will I know that I've reached the standard that's being looked for? How will I know my evidence isn't just a fluke and that I've really got there?' Learning outcomes need to help students to see what's supposed to be going on in their heads at the end of the journey, and at points along the route. Of all the seven factors discussed in Chapter 2, 'making sense' is the process we can't do for our learners. We can, however, illustrate what it looks like to have 'made sense' of something, and we can show evidence specifications so that learners can test out for themselves the extent to which they have made sense of things along the learning journey.

6 *Verbalizing, vocalizing*: actions such as teaching, explaining and coaching all relate to communicating the achievement resulting from successful learning, but more importantly cause that learning to be deepened and strengthened. Learning outcomes need to clarify as well as possible what we want learners to become able to show for their learning, and very often that boils down to becoming able to explain things fluently. Many an exam question includes 'explain' as a key word. We want learners to make sense of what they're learning so well that learners can coach fellow learners, or teach someone starting to learn the topic concerned. It is useful if learners can see from the way we design the curriculum for them that we intend them not just to sit in solemn silence filling their heads with information to communicate back to us, but to practise communicating their knowledge to fellow human beings on the journey towards demonstrating their evidence of achievement to us in formal settings such as exams or assignments.

7 *Assessing – making informed judgements*: we need to encourage learners, through every available means, to optimize the deepening of their learning by applying assessment criteria to the evidence they produce of achievement of their learning. We can partly achieve this by making sure that learning outcomes show that we're not merely requiring learners to reproduce information for us as evidence of their learning. Where possible, we need to illustrate by the wording of learning outcomes that we're looking for high-level critical analysis as evidence of achievement, encouraging learners to practise producing this kind of evidence using self-assessment and peer assessment to raise the standard of that evidence. We need to point towards the value of the self-interrogation which can accompany real reflection as learners analyse from themselves how well they are approaching mastery of clearly expressed intended learning outcomes.

It is no mean feat to produce a set of learning outcomes which links well, as proposed above, to these seven factors underpinning successful learning. As I suggested at the beginning of this chapter, the best way of arriving at this destination is *not* to start with the learning outcomes, but to work backwards from evidence of achievement, and iterate the process until everything fits fluently in the big picture. In the next section, we'll look in more detail at how we can go about this design process.

CURRICULUM DESIGN FROM SCRATCH

In the following discussion, I would like to share how I work with staff who are planning a new curriculum element. In practice, of course, it's quite rare that we have the luxury of starting from scratch. We've usually got some existing learning outcomes to start with – and they're not always good ones! We've often got pre-specified evidence of achievement to think about, and existing ways of assessing learners' achievement. Nevertheless, the ideas in this section can be used even when we're not starting from scratch, so long as we are willing to make adjustments to what we're already starting with. What follows is a description of a set of processes that I use with participants at curriculum design workshops, and I invite you to adapt the various stages to meet your own needs.

1 Start with evidence of achievement

As mentioned above, I suggest that we start by working out *evidence of achievement* first, even before thinking of draft learning outcomes. By half-way through a day's workshop on curriculum design, I have participants in groups, each group with a flipchart marked out as shown in Figure 3.2.

Intended learning outcome	Assignment task briefing	Marking scheme	Notes
Evidence of achievement of the learning outcome …	Rationale for choosing the particular assessment process to link the evidence to the intended outcome …		
1			

Figure 3.2   Start by thinking about evidence of achievement

 Photocopiable *Making Learning Happen* © Phil Race, 2014 (SAGE)

The aim is to populate the various boxes on the chart. However, rather than write on the charts, I get participants to stick Post-its on to them, as the Post-its can be edited, improved or replaced as discussion goes on during the workshop, starting with the box numbered '1' in Figure 3.2. In practice, participants end up with layers of Post-its in each box, showing the successive improvements and adjustments made to each area of the chart as the links are strengthened between the various elements. The first step is then to think ahead to different aspects of evidence of achievement (e.g. some written evidence, some practical evidence, some oral evidence, some collaborative evidence, and so on) and jot the details down on various Post-its, numbered E1, E2, E3, and so on, to remind us that these are evidence descriptors.

2 From evidence of achievement to assignment briefing

Next, I ask groups of participants to work out how they are going to 'get at' the evidence of achievement, so that it can be measured and duly accredited. I ask them to come up with (on Post-its) draft examples of any or all of the following:

- test or exam questions
- draft briefs for written assignments
- practical exercises
- briefings for reports

and so on, each measuring in its own way a facet of the evidence of achievement identified in box 1, and to stick their Post-its on the box labelled '2' in Figure 3.3. Box 2 is about assessment, and the Post-its can be numbered A1, A2, A3, and so on.

Intended learning outcome	Assignment task briefing	Marking scheme	Notes
	2		
Evidence of achievement of the learning outcome ...	Rationale for choosing the particular assessment process to link the evidence to the intended outcome ...		
1			

Figure 3.3 Now design assessment to link to evidence of achievement

I ask groups to fine-tune boxes 1 and 2 so that the assignment briefings and evidence of achievement match each other more and more closely. For example, assessment A1 should be a good way of getting at evidence E1, and A2 for E2, and so on. If something does not lend itself to some kind of measurement, it may need to disappear from box 1, or better, ways need to be thought of to set some kind of task which does measure it. Equally, if something important which was not already in box 1 is being measured in box 2, it may need to be duly added to the evidence in box 1.

3 Rationale – learning by explaining

It's now time to tackle the rationale for choosing particular assessment processes to link evidence of achievement, in due course, to the intended learning outcome. See Figure 3.4.

Intended learning outcome	Assignment task briefing	Marking scheme	Notes
	2		
Evidence of achievement of the learning outcome ...	Rationale for choosing the particular assessment process to link the evidence to the intended outcome ...		
1	3		

Figure 3.4 Work out rationale linking assessment to evidence of achievement

Box 3 is for *rationale*. I ask groups to sketch out on Post-its justifications for why particular assessments or assignments in box 2 are indeed fit for purpose to get at the 'evidence of achievement' specifications in box 1. So rationale R1 should be a good reason for choosing assessment type A1 to get at evidence of achieve-ment E1, and so on.

Then I ask groups to exchange membership, so that each group retains one or two of its original members, but has one or more members from *other* groups present. I then ask the 'resident' members of each group to explain the rationale in box 3 to the newcomers. This leads to quite a lot of opportunity to further improve the links between boxes 1 and 2, and the Post-its in all three boxes can be amended as necessary to make these links ever more transparent and direct.

I then ask the groups to return to their original formation and bring what has been learned from the explaining (and listening to others' explanations) to bear on further improving the contents of boxes 1 to 3. Invariably, groups significantly improve the contents of all three boxes by the end of these processes, learning a great deal from each other's attempts to put the rationale into words.

4 First-draft intended learning outcomes

Now it's time for each group to think of how the *evidence of achievement* is going to be expressed to learners in the form of learning outcomes, ensuring that these too will link to the rationale already established for the assessment processes. See Figure 3.5.

Intended learning outcome	Assignment task briefing	Marking scheme	Notes
4	2		
Evidence of achievement of the learning outcome …	Rationale for choosing the particular assessment process to link the evidence to the intended outcome …		
1	3		

Figure 3.5 Next make first draft of intended learning outcome

Box 4 is for draft learning outcomes. Groups now draft (on Post-its) intended learning outcomes and stick them in box 4. Learning outcome O1 should point seamlessly towards evidence E1, which can be measured by assessment A1 for the reason specified in R1, and so on. As groups start to populate the outcomes box, it is useful to have pause for thought about the actual wording of the outcomes in general.

I have found that the best way forward is to ask each group to work up some learning outcomes as well as they can, copy them on further Post-its, and then, returning to plenary formation, I ask participants to swap Post-its so no-one knows who has their Post-it. I then ask participants individually to read out the draft learning outcomes as written on these Post-its, usually reading them out more than once, while we all join together in any suggestions for clarifying, editing or refining the wording of the outcomes. When participants return to their groups, they usually have a range of ideas to bring to improving the learning outcome drafts in box 4 on their charts.

5 Sharpening the alignment by thinking about marking

By this stage, each group has drafted parts of the curriculum, aligning learning outcomes to assessment, informed by the rationale for choosing particular assessment formats to measure appropriate facets of the desired evidence of achievement. As you will know from your own assessment work, nothing sharpens up assessment better than actually getting down to marking students' work. Therefore, the next stage is to ask each group to draft out marking schemes (including draft assessment criteria) for each of the assessment elements they have devised in box 2, and attach details (as Post-its or, more usually, as small Post-its linking to separate numbered sheets) in box 5. See Figure 3.6.

Intended learning outcome	Assignment task briefing	Marking scheme	Notes
4	2	5	
Evidence of achievement of the learning outcome …	Rationale for choosing the particular assessment process to link the evidence to the intended outcome …		
1	3		

Figure 3.6   Design marking scheme

Designing a marking scheme almost always leads to adjustments in assignment or assessment briefings, and groups are encouraged to make these and amend the Post-its in box 2 as necessary. This in turn impacts on exactly what parts of the evidence specifications in box 1 are in fact addressed by the assessment elements, and to the rationale in box 3. Naturally, to maintain the alignment between assessment and evidence of achievement, it is now necessary to make further adjustments to the intended learning outcomes in box 4. See Figure 3.7.

Intended learning outcome	Assignment task briefing	Marking scheme	Notes
4a	2a	5	
Evidence of achievement of the learning outcome …	Rationale for choosing the particular assessment process to link the evidence to the intended outcome …		
1a	3a		

Figure 3.7   Make adjustments to all previous drafts

6 Designing how exactly students will get feedback

The next consideration is feedback. This of course depends a lot on which of the assessment elements in box 2 are formative and which are summative (and not so suitable for feedback). I suggest to groups that in box 6 they draft out the feedback processes (e.g. written, face-to-face, and so on) which best lend themselves to giving students feedback on their achievement as measured by successive assessment tasks, choosing which process is likely to be most effective depending on the nature of the evidence of achievement being measured, and the extent to which feed-forward can usefully be provided to help learners to optimize their performance of oncoming tasks. It is clearly important that students get formative feedback on their evidence of achievement of the learning outcomes to as great an extent as can reasonably be achieved without increasing the burden of assessment unduly. So it is now time to have another iteration right round the boxes in the chart, as assessment elements, marking schemes (including assessment criteria) and the intended learning outcomes themselves are fine-tuned to take into account the matter of optimizing feedback to students on the evidence of achievement which they produce. This is demonstrated in Figure 3.8, where I have indicated the further adjustments as '5b', and so on.

Intended learning outcome	Assignment task briefing	Marking scheme	Notes
4b	2b	5b	
Evidence of achievement of the learning outcome …	Rationale for choosing the particular assessment process to link the evidence to the intended outcome …	How learners will get feedback on their achievement	
1b	3b	6	

Figure 3.8 Think about feedback, and make further adjustment to all previous drafts

7 Improving curriculum design after teaching it and assessing it for the first time

We all know that after teaching a new chunk of curriculum for the very first time, we gain all sorts of ideas on how to do it better next time. And we normally go on to do just that! Moreover, after we've run the various assessment elements for the first time, done the marking and given feedback to students, *and* found out how best that feedback can be further adjusted on a future occasion to help students even more, we have a great deal of information about how best to express the curriculum concerned. The sad thing is that too often the curriculum documentation does not get upgraded, and languishes in its initial state in filing cabinets and module handbooks alike. I suggest next the best way to capitalize on the experience gained through teaching a curriculum element.

At the curriculum review stage, preferably very closely after completing the first run of teaching and assessing, it is useful to get staff back together to adjust all of the elements in the chart we've been thinking about, on the basis of replies to various questions, including the ones I've now added to the right-hand column of the chart (see Figure 3.9). Successive versions of learning outcomes, assessment elements, etc., are now labelled '4c', '2c', and so on.

The list of questions I've put into the right-hand column is only meant to be a start here. Further questions could include:

Intended learning outcome	Assignment task briefing	Marking scheme	Adjustments after teaching it the first time ...
4c	2c	5c	How well did the assessment elements, A1, A2, A3, and so on actually work?
Evidence of achievement of the learning outcome ...	Rationale for choosing the particular assessment process to link the evidence to the intended outcome ...	How learners will get feedback on their achievement	How well did the marking schemes work? What adjustments were made to the assignments then?
1c	3c	6c	What parts of evidence E1, E2, E3, and so on were actually measured? What changes were made to the outcomes O1, O2, O3, and so on at each stage? ...

Figure 3.9   Make further adjustments after the first teaching run

- What worked best about this curriculum element, and why was this?
- What didn't work so well, and how could this be adjusted?
- Was there any unwanted duplication, for example elements of evidence which were measured more than necessary?
- What *else* might it have been useful to include in evidence of achievement?
- How *else* might that evidence of achievement have been assessed?
- How *else* might feedback have been given to learners?

A consequence of this kind of developmental review of curriculum is that the specification should never be more than a year old! This is, of course, contrary to existing practice, where all too often curriculum design can be set in stone for five years or more, or until some sort of external review (or change of staffing) causes us to revisit the design of teaching, learning and assessment.

How well do learners know how to use the intended learning outcomes?

I've included a self-assessment checklist (Table 3.1) which you can give to learners (or better still, fine-tune and adapt for your own learners) to help them get a sense of how well they're using your intended learning outcomes. In practice, the reflection that such a checklist can start off may alert learners to the fact that they *can* actually make good use of the outcomes. Moreover, reflecting on learners' completions of this checklist (provided of course they're willing to let you see them) can tell you a lot about how well your learning outcomes are working

Table 3.1   Putting learning outcomes to work

	Please tick one or more of the columns for each row, as appropriate	This is what I do	I would like to do this, but do not manage to	I don't think this is necessary	This just is not possible for me	I'll try to do this in future
1	I locate the intended learning outcomes in my course documentation					
2	I already use the intended learning outcomes as a frame of reference for my studying					
3	I find it easy to work out exactly what the intended learning outcomes mean in practice					
4	I carefully work out exactly what I'm supposed to become able to *do* to show my achievement of each learning outcome					
5	I keep the intended learning outcomes to hand, so I can see how each study element relates to them					
6	I know how to link learning outcomes to assessment, and to what I need to be able to do in assignments and exam questions to show I've achieved them					
7	I find it useful when tutors give me feedback about the extent to which I've demonstrated my achievement of each learning outcome involved in an assignment					
8	I ask for clarification when I'm not sure about the standards I need to meet in the context of an intended learning outcome					
9	I discuss the meaning of intended outcomes with fellow students, helping me to get a better idea about which are the really important outcomes					
10	I've made sure that the intended learning outcomes for each taught session are included in or with my notes					
11	I've checked how well I reckon I've already achieved each of the intended learning outcomes, and have marked these decisions against the outcomes for future reference					
12	When I can't find out exactly what the intended learning outcomes are, I design some myself and check with tutors and fellow students whether I've made a good attempt at this					

for your learners, and how you may be able to improve the links between outcomes and evidence of achievement, and between your choices of assessment and your rationale for using each kind of assessment.

Good and bad learning outcomes?

Let's take this particular chapter as a case study, and attempt to think about it in terms of intended learning outcomes. An unsuccessful attempt to do so might look like:

> To understand the use of learning outcomes in curriculum design.

This is poor because the word 'understand' is (as always) elusive and unmeasurable, but also because there is no indication of what the intended evidence of achievement might look like, nor any sense of the intended journey towards such evidence. A better attempt might be as follows:

> After working through this chapter, you should be better able to design some curriculum by systematically linking the following:
>
> - evidence of achievement
> - assessment elements: showing how the above evidence will be sought and measured
> - rationale for linking particular kinds of evidence to specific assessment processes
> - intended learning outcomes which link naturally to evidence of achievement and assessment processes.

BEYOND LEARNING OUTCOMES

In this chapter on curriculum development, we've explored how intended learning outcomes need to be developed and adjusted iteratively, so that they fit naturally into the bigger picture of syllabus content, assessment, feedback and teaching. But intended learning outcomes can be thought of as part of an even bigger picture, which also includes *learning incomes, emergent learning outcomes* and *intended learning outgoings*. Having sprung on you three things you won't find mentioned yet in the literature about curriculum design, let me explain and illustrate what I mean by these terms, and how we might usefully address them in curriculum design.

Learning incomes

These may be different for each different learner. By learning *incomes*, I mean all the things learners are bringing to the learning situation. These include:

- what they already know about the subject
- what they can already do, related to the subject
- hang-ups or preconceptions about the subject which may need to be addressed
- other things in their experience which they can link to the new subject.

As long ago as 1968, Ausubel wrote:

> If I had to reduce all of educational psychology to just one principle, I would say this: the most important single factor influencing learning is what the learner already knows. Ascertain this, and teach him accordingly. (Ausubel, 1968, 235)

So how can we find out, before we start teaching them, what our learners already know? Ask them!

Finding and using learning incomes

When about to start a new topic 'x' with a large group of learners, it can be useful to give each of them two Post-its of different colours (e.g. pink and blue).

- On the blue Post-it, ask everyone to jot down their response to, 'The most important thing I already know about "x" is ...'. Learners are always quite pleased to do this, and it always amazes me how much is already collectively known by a large group about most topics.
- On the pink Post-it ask everyone to jot down their response to, 'One question I really want to know the answer to about "x" is ...'. Learners are very relaxed about doing this, as 'not knowing' is being legitimized.
- Next get learners to show their Post-its to each other and discuss, gradually passing the Post-its towards the ends of rows. Learners are usually quite heartened to find out that several others questions on the pink Post-its are similar to their own.
- Next, arrange that they stick all the Post-its up on charts or walls. The most important step is then for us to collect all these Post-its, and sift through what they already know and what they want to find out.
- It is then possible to return to the group next time having analysed the Post-its, and put up a slide with one of the frequently occurring questions on it, saying, for example, 'Over 50 of you had a question similar to this one ...'. You can then ask, 'How many of you had a question similar to this one?' and many hands will be raised. You can then sometimes say, '14 of you know the answer to this question, as it was what was written on your blue Post-it last time. Please raise your hands and keep them raised until you've got at least three of your colleagues who had asked the question sitting close to you. Then please explain to each other'.

This is a quick way of finding out more about what the learners in the group *want* to know, and building discussion around things that some of them already do know.

Finding out about learning incomes helps you to avoid spending too much time telling the class all sorts of things they already know. We still may need to cover some of these things for the sake of the learners who don't yet know them, but we can minimize the tedium for those who already do know them, by:

- giving learners the chance to explain things they already know to each other – the explainers learn a great deal and we avoid boring them with our own explanations

- spotting misconceptions that some of our learners may have about things we're going to build on – we can then put them right on these as we introduce topics

- building on what members of the class *want* to find out: this helps learners to feel an increased degree of ownership of what we tell them – in effect, we're structuring the curriculum around *their* questions.

Emergent learning outcomes

Let's think about the *emergent* learning outcomes, which learners achieve at the same time as they achieve the *intended* ones. In just about everything we do as human beings, there are emergent outcomes as well as intended ones. We often talk about 'unforeseen consequences' or even 'unintended consequences' accompanying every human endeavour. Sometimes the emergent learning outcomes turn out to be even more important than the intended ones. As teachers, every time we explain things to learners, and assess their learning, as discussed in Chapter 2, *we* gain a lot in terms of our own learning. We can think of this as our own emergent learning outcomes. But think again about *students'* learning. When they work through an element of curriculum, much more happens to them than merely achieving our intended learning outcomes. What *else* might they have learned? They learn all sorts of additional things, which might include:

- things they learned about the subject concerned above and beyond what we intended them to learn

- things they learned about the links between *our* subject and other subjects they are learning

- things they learned by getting things wrong on their journey towards achieving the intended learning outcomes

- things they learned *about themselves* as learners – for example, techniques they developed while learning this particular bit of curriculum which will be useful to continue to apply to other learning contexts

- things they learned from each other, and skills they gained in working with each other.

We can find out from students a lot about emergent learning outcomes. I have often issued Post-its to a large class and asked everyone to jot down responses to the question, 'What *else* did you learn?' I've then asked students to stick these on a chart on their way out of the teaching session. More often than not there are many *emergent* learning outcomes which prove to be just as relevant and important as any of the *intended* outcomes, and are well worth adding into the intended outcomes next time round.

So what about *assessment* of the emergent learning outcomes? We can't really do this! This would be unfair. After all these were not part of the published, overt targets – even when they are important and desirable. And besides, the emergent learning outcomes are going to be different for different learners. But we can still give learners *feedback* on their *evidence* of achievement of their own emergent learning outcomes, alongside giving them feedback on the extent to which their evidence demonstrates their achievement of the *intended* learning outcomes. It would be tragic to refrain from congratulating learners on particular aspects of their achievement just because these aspects weren't part of the picture as defined by our curriculum.

Intended learning outgoings

How often have you told learners, 'This will be really useful to you later in your career', and so on? In vocational teaching, we're often preparing learners for the world of work, and aiming to equip them with skills and knowledge which they will need in years to come. Very often, these things are above and beyond what we're actually going to be able to get learners to *show* for their learning while they're with us. In other words, some of these things can't be included in the evidence of achievement upon which we base our assessment, and therefore can't be included formally in the intended learning outcomes as discussed in this chapter. But we can refer to them as intended learning *outgoings*, to help learners to see where they fit in to the bigger picture of the curriculum, and indeed to link the intended learning outcomes to the wider world of future learning and employment.

One way of achieving this is to present the intended learning outgoings alongside the intended learning incomes so that learners can see what is on the immediate agenda, compared to the bigger picture of their ongoing learning and development. This can help them to gain increased ownership of the curriculum, addressing their 'What's in it for me?' question more fully.

CONCLUSIONS

This chapter on 'Curriculum design for learning' has focused strongly on making the curriculum flexible and learner-centred, and avoiding the curriculum becoming dominated merely by the detail of the subject content itself. We've looked at the importance of thinking about *evidence of achievement* as the first stage in working towards our documentation describing the curriculum. We've explored how to arrive at specifications of intended learning outcomes as a result of considering assessment and feedback before, rather than after, reaching the wording of the outcomes. By adding in thinking about learning *incomes* and researching with learners their *emergent* learning outcomes in practice, and by including in the picture the intended learning *outgoings* which learners will need later in their lives and careers, I believe we can make curriculum design address the full picture of student learning, assessment and feedback, working towards making it fit for purpose as part of our bid to encourage lifelong learning, rather than just the short-term achievement of particular targets.

 Tips for students: using learning outcomes

The following suggestions for students may help them make better use of intended learning outcomes, as part of structuring their learning.

1 *Find the learning outcomes*. They are usually there somewhere. They should give you a reasonable indication of the shape of the curriculum, and of what is included (and not included).

2 *Think 'evidence'*. Look for information about how you will, in due course, be expected to show what you've learned, especially when it comes to formal assessments, not least written assessments such as exams, essays and reports.

3 *Find out as much as you can about past and present assessments*. See what kinds of things are being measured. See what eludes measurement. Your success depends on being able to provide those parts of evidence of achievement which are actually (likely to be) measured.

4 *Look for information about standards*. Think about what might be regarded as 'excellent' evidence of achievement of the outcomes, as opposed to 'passable' evidence, and so on.

5 *Prioritize*. Some learning outcomes are likely to be significantly more important than others; see if you can strike a sensible balance about how much time and effort to devote to particular learning outcomes.

6 *Seek clarification*. When in doubt, seek to find out 'what it really means', especially when the evidence of achievement is not sufficiently clear. Ask tutors, but also ask fellow students what they make of the descriptions of particularly elusive parts of evidence of achievement.

7 *Think timescales*. Seek to find out where and when you will need to be able to show that you've achieved learning outcomes by providing related evidence of achievement of them.

8 *Keep track of your own progress*. Tick off learning outcomes that you are happy to describe as 'fully mastered', and those 'needing more attention'.

9 *Don't get disheartened*. Some learning outcomes take time to achieve, and these can sometimes be the really important ones. Keeping in sight what you're aiming for is a good tactic to getting there sooner or later.

10 *Balance your act*. Only some of the evidence of achievement you're trying to master will in fact be measured, and some of your best achievements may never be measured. Simply aim to maximize the likelihood that your achievement will be seen to be successful.

 Some of the resources in this chapter are available to print for your own use on the companion website. To access these, along with some video clips of the author, please visit: **www.sagepub.co.uk/makinglearninghappen**

CHAPTER 4

ASSESSMENT DRIVING LEARNING

O━━ Key topics in this chapter

- What students think
- Validity
- Fairness
- Whodunit?
- Assessment as learning
- Is assessment broken?

This chapter is one of the most important in the book, and it has grown even more in this edition. To make it easier to navigate, it is now divided into four parts:

Assessment is broken in higher education! The first section ranges widely, exploring what's wrong with assessment, examining some links between assessment and learning, and discussing validity, reliability, transparency and authenticity, as well as pointing forwards to how we can work our way out of the problems which are endemic today.

A critical look at exams and essays! This section focuses first on time-constrained, unseen written exams, links between these and the factors underpinning successful learning, with short notes about some of the better alternatives that exist. Next follows a similar discussion of that other most-common assessment format – the essay. It is worth noting straightaway that most people who graduate from higher education don't sit an exam or write an essay ever again.

A critical comparison of eleven assessment types. This table, new to this edition, supplements the discussion in the previous section, by providing a comparative table widening the discussion further, and helping you to compare and contrast the advantages and disadvantages of various assessment approaches.

Towards assessment *as* learning. This final section consists of a tool to enable you to interrogate any assessment instrument or process of your choice (written, online, oral) against factors such as validity, reliability, and so on, and also against the factors underpinning successful learning developed in Chapter 2. This section ends with some overall recommendations for improving assessment in post-compulsory education, and some tips you could give your students (or better, adapt for them) to help them give assessment in general their best shot.

ASSESSMENT IS BROKEN IN HIGHER EDUCATION!

Several indicators tell us this, including:

- Students' perceptions (for example, as gathered from final-year students annually in the National Student Survey in the UK since 2005) tell us that assessment and feedback continue to be the least satisfactory elements of the higher education experience, that the assessment criteria are not clear, and that students do not believe that marking and grading are fair.

- Academic staff responding to the starter 'Teaching would be much better for me if only I ...' mention 'had more time' more frequently than any other factor, and when further questioned usually cite the time it takes to mark students' work as the main oppressing factor. Indeed, staff often grumble that they have to spend more than twice as much time marking students' work as they actually spend with their students.

How has assessment become broken in higher education?

What are the factors which make it harder and harder to make assessment work well for students, and make the processes of marking and giving feedback to students unmanageable for staff? The factors which have caused our present problems include:

- Student numbers have grown: we can't use the same processes and instruments for a system where nearly 50 per cent of the 18–30 year-old population study at university level, compared to 5 per cent a couple of decades ago.

- The world has opened up, so that our assessment processes and practices need to be more compatible with those in markedly different cultures and traditions.

- It is widely accepted now that assessment is the major driver for student learning, and if assessment is not working as a *good* driver for learning, learning is not happening well and the effectiveness of our entire higher education provision is jeopardized.

- We now know much more about the standards we should strive towards in assessing students' work, in particular the need to improve assessment to make it more valid, more fair, more transparent to students, better linked to the world outside higher education, and more inclusive so that assessment does not disadvantage students with identified special needs, and enables them to demonstrate their learning in ways where they can show their optimum achievement.

- Rapidly increasing usage of online assessment, including online submission of coursework assignments, and the increasing awareness of the difficulty in establishing veracity in many contexts – in other words, who exactly did the coursework?

- We need to continue to diversify the assessment processes and instruments we use, so that no students are repeatedly disadvantaged by the predominance of particular assessment formats.

In short, we need a richer mix of high-quality assessment formats, and we also need to *reduce* the overall burden of assessment for ourselves and for our students. We need to measure less, but measure it better. We need to measure a wider spectrum of students' evidence of achievement, with a broader, more versatile set of tools. Presently, we spend far too much of our (and students') time on things they write, at the expense of other ways they can show evidence of how they have achieved the learning outcomes. But to repeat myself, we still need to *reduce* the burden of assessment: more assessments, but much shorter ones.

Fortunately, help is at hand. There now exists a rich literature about assessment, containing a great deal of authoritative wisdom to bring to bear on assessment design, helping us to address the factors listed above, and work towards making student perceptions of assessment more satisfactory, while at the same time allowing us to make it a more reasonable and realistic proportion of our jobs as academics in post-compulsory education.

What students think

In the National Student Survey, administered to all final-year students every year in the UK since 2005, in the section on 'assessment and feedback', statements 5 and 6 link directly to students' experience of assessment. The design of this particular survey is far from ideal, but its use right across the higher education sector in the UK makes it an important indicator of at least some of students' feelings about their higher education experience. Students are asked to make judgements as follows:

- definitely agree
- mostly agree
- neither agree nor disagree
- mostly disagree
- definitely disagree
- not applicable

on the following two statements (numbers 5 and 6 out of the 22 in the survey):

5 The criteria used in marking have been clear in advance.

6 Assessment arrangements and marking have been fair.

Widely across the sector, institutions have been dismayed at students' negative responses to these statements, compared to most of the rest of the survey, and this trend has continued throughout the use of the survey as implemented so far. Many factors can account for student dissatisfaction with assessment, including:

- For students, assessment is of course the sharp end of their overall experience in higher education – it's what determines their qualifications.

- When students are paying for their higher education, they are quick to pin-point assessment as one of the most important things they are buying, and naturally start looking hard at what they are getting for their money.

- Even when the assessment criteria have been clearly formulated in module hand-books or on course websites, students may not have *heard* the criteria sufficiently in face-to-face contexts, allowing them to know better exactly what they mean in terms of evidence of achievement of the intended learning outcomes.

- Even when assessment and marking *are* fair, students often do not know the lengths institutions go to in order to achieve this. Students may know little of the detail of assessment questions being moderated and improved by external examiners, for example.

- Overall, students do not have sufficient opportunity to get their heads inside the assessment culture of higher education – it is sometimes a 'black box' to them, where they do their best and hope it will all work out well in the end.

- Students do not have sufficient opportunity to really get their heads around the assessment criteria applied to their work, for example by *making informed judgements* themselves on their own and each other's work.

Sometimes, of course, students are right, and assessment is far from being perfect! Assessment criteria are not always made clear to them in advance, and sometimes assessment and marking are far from fair!

However, going back to the design of the survey, both of the statements involved in this section are in fact 'bipolar'. In other words, is it the wording 'clear' or 'in advance' (or both) which triggers the student's choice of options for statement 5, and is it 'assessment arrangements' or 'marking' (or both) being 'fair' which triggers students' choices for statement 6? I regard it as unfortunate that such a widely used instrument incorporates (and repeats annually!) such clumsiness. Nevertheless, the discussion in this chapter aims to address all of the reasons why students are dissatisfied with the assessment culture they meet in higher education.

Similar problems with assessment are shared in many parts of the world. Flint and Johnson (2011) in Australia have built their excellent book, *Towards Fairer University Assessment*, around the concerns of students themselves, which are very close to the reservations expressed above. They report that:

Student evaluations frequently reveal poor assessment practices that:

- lack authenticity and relevance to real world tasks;
- make unreasonable demands on students;
- are narrow in scope;
- have little long-term benefit;
- fail to reward genuine effort;
- have unclear expectations and assessment criteria;
- fail to provide adequate feedback to students;
- rely heavily on factual recall rather than on higher-order thinking and problem-solving skills. (Flint and Johnson, 2011: 2)

I have now showed this list to several thousand staff at workshops and keynotes, each time inviting them to 'raise a hand if not guilty on any of these eight counts' and to date have only had one hand raised (by someone who had just been appointed the day before).

Why assessment counts

This book is about making *intentional* learning – or *purposeful* learning – happen. Perhaps the most significant difference is that learning in post-compulsory education ends up being *assessed* in various ways. Some of this assessment usually relates to *completion* of stages of learning. Not all learners in post-compulsory education complete their learning programmes. Yorke (2002) has analysed 'leaving early' in higher education (i.e. non-completion) and finds that:

> Roughly two-thirds of premature departures take place in, or at the end of, the first year of full-time study in the UK. Anecdotal evidence from a number of institutions indicates that early poor performance can be a powerful disincentive to continuation, with students feeling that perhaps they were not cut out for higher education after all – although the main problems are acculturation and acclimatisation to studying. Having recognised that deleterious consequences of early summative assessment and that the first year of full-time study is typically only a kind of qualifying year for an honours degree, some institutions are removing from their assessment regulations the requirement that students pass summative assessments at the end of the first semester. This should allow students more of an opportunity to build confidence and to come to terms with academic study, and ought to allow more of the vital formative assessment to take place. (Yorke, 2002: 37)

People lose interest in learning for a range of reasons and become at risk of dropping out. How and when assessment takes place is one of the more important critical factors which can influence people's decisions to drop out. As we will see in the next chapter, the timeliness, quality and nature of formative feedback is perhaps the most critical of the factors under our control in post-compulsory education, especially when such feedback 'goes wrong' for various reasons. And students need early feedback, so that they can adjust the time and energy they put into their learning, and therefore some early assessment can be valuable.

Getting assessment right should be seen as an opportunity, not a threat. Sally Brown (2009), in the closing keynote at a conference on the first-year experience, used the following words:

> Concentrating on giving students detailed and developmental formative feedback is the single most useful thing we can do for our students, particularly those who have had a struggle to achieve entry to higher education. Assessment and feedback are two of the best tools available to us, to support student achievement, progression and retention. Getting assessment and feedback right from the beginning of the first year makes a real difference. (Brown, 2009)

There are also economics to consider. Making learning happen in post-compulsory education costs money – a great deal of money. So it is natural that accountability is necessary, not least in times of recession, such as at the time of preparing the present edition of this book. It is now more important than ever that we are efficient and effective in post-compulsory education. We can only measure what students produce as evidence of their learning. That's where assessment – and, indeed, completion – come in. 'Making learning happen' is not just about causing learning to happen; it's about 'making learning *being seen* to have happened'. It's about results. These affect funding. We're not paid just to make learning happen; we're paid on the basis that we can *show* that learning has happened and that we've played a part in making it happen. We've got to take care with making sure that what we measure is indeed learners' *achievement* of these outcomes, as directly as possible, and not, for example, just a measure of how well learners can communicate with a pen in exam rooms, how well they may have achieved those parts of the outcomes which are amenable to showing on written scripts. That would be only an echo of the achievement we are seeking to measure – perhaps only a ghost of the learning. We need to be very careful that our attempts to measure the achievement of intended learning outcomes are not skewed or muffled by filters such as exam technique, which may have little to do with the intended outcomes, or (more serious perhaps) speed and legibility of handwriting.

Gibbs and Simpson (2002) share concerns about assessment practices and policies driving learning in the opposite direction from improving learning, as follows:

> When teaching in higher education hits the headlines it is nearly always about assessment: about examples of supposedly falling standards, about plagiarism, about unreliable marking or rogue external examiners, about errors in exam papers, and so on. ... Where institutional learning and teaching strategies focus on assessment they are nearly always about aligning learning outcomes with assessment and about specifying assessment criteria. All of this focus, of the media, of quality assurance and of institutions, is on assessment as measurement. ... The most reliable, rigorous and cheat-proof assessment systems are often accompanied by dull and lifeless learning that has short lasting outcomes – indeed they often directly lead to such learning. ... Standards will be raised by improving student learning rather than by better measurement of limited learning. (Gibbs and Simpson, 2002)

This is the main reason that assessment is the principal driving force for learning for so many learners in post-compulsory education. Their exam grades, certificates, degrees and even higher degrees depend on them being able to prove that they have met standards, demonstrated achievement and communicated their learning. Learners are rewarded for what they *show*, not just for what they know. Indeed, we can even argue that *showing* is actually *more* important than knowing. In some assessment contexts learners can gain credit by becoming competent at writing *as if* they had mastered something, even when they have not!

Assessment and deep, surface and strategic learners

Deep learning

Deep learning gets a good press in the scholarly literature. Deep learning is, we might argue, closer to developing real *understanding*. But we've already seen that this is difficult or even impossible to measure. So deep learning may be the wrong approach to wean our learners towards, when our assessment may only be measuring something rather less than deep learning. Deep learning may, of course, be much more appropriate for those learners going on to higher levels, and is doubtless the kind of learning which leads to the most productive and inspired research. Perhaps that is why deep learning is regarded so favourably by educational researchers on the whole. However, 'Save your deep learning for your postgraduate years. For now, your priority is to make sure that you get to *having* some postgraduate years' could be wise advice to give undergraduates!

Surface learning

Surface learning gets a bad press in the literature. However, much of the learning done by most people in post-compulsory education is actually only surface learning. Learners learn things 'sufficient to the day' – the exam day or the assessment week, for example. When it has been learned successfully enough to serve its purpose – pass the module, gain the certificate – it's ditched. It's not entirely wasted, however. Something that's been surface learned is a better starting point for re-learning, or for learning more deeply, than something which has not been learned at all. But learners can all tell us tales of the countless things they have learned only well enough to give back when required to demonstrate their achievements, which have been quite deliberately 'eased out' of their minds as they moved on to the next stage of their learning journey. 'You are what you learn' may be a noble sentiment, but it can be argued that our assessment processes and instruments cause learners to learn far too many things which aren't important, diluting the quality of learning that is afforded to those things that *are* important.

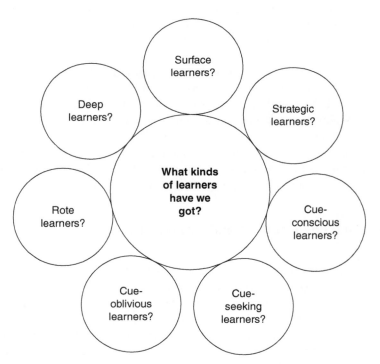

Figure 4.1 Different kinds of learner, or different approaches from any learner?

Despite the criticisms of surface learning approaches, sometimes it is a fit-for-purpose choice. Where a limited amount of factual information needs to be available at will in a particular scenario, but will not be needed after that scenario is completed, surface learning can be a wise enough choice. There are things that just are not important enough to warrant a lot of time and energy being invested in learning them deeply. An example could be the statistics relating to stopping distances in wet and dry conditions, which need to be learned to pass parts of the driving test in the UK. Few experienced drivers can quote these facts and figures correctly a few years after passing their driving tests, but probably are perfectly capable of judging stopping distances well enough simply based on experience. This aspect of the learning for the test seems to be almost entirely a surface learning business.

What's wrong with strategic learning?

Strategic learning has perhaps had the worst press of all. It's not just *accidental* surface learning. It is perhaps sometimes *deliberate* surface learning, consciously engaged in at the expense of deeper learning. Strategic learning is regarded as 'learning for the exam'. It's associated with 'seeking out the marks or credit' quite consciously in essays, reports, dissertations and theses, and extends readily to preparing strategically for job interviews, promotion boards, and so on. Moreover, it can be argued that strategic learners may make informed judgements about *what* to learn deeply and what to learn *just* at a surface level.

Strategic learners tend to be successful, or at least moderately successful. Deep learners may well *deserve* success, but quite often shoot themselves in one foot or the other by mastering *some* parts of the curriculum very very well while leaving other parts of the curriculum underdeveloped, and not getting the overall credit that they might have achieved had they spread their efforts more evenly across the curriculum. Surface learners can also fare well enough if and when all that is really being measured in our assessment systems is surface learning. Strategic learning is often thought of in terms of doing the *minimum* to get by. But there are various 'minima'. In the present degree classification system in the UK, perhaps there's the minimum to get by and get a degree at all, the (different) minimum to get by and get a 2.1, the (different again) minimum to get by and get a first-class degree, and perhaps the minimum to get by and get a first-class degree with a margin for safety?

So what *is* strategic learning? We could regard it as making informed choices about when to be a deep learner and when to be a surface learner. It could be viewed as investing more in what is important to learn and less in what is less important to learn. It could be regarded as setting out towards a chosen level of achievement and working systematically to become able to demonstrate that level of achievement in each contributing assessment element.

There is growing recognition that the curriculum in post-compulsory education is content-bound. There is just so much subject matter around in every discipline. Any award-bearing programme of study necessarily involves making informed decisions about what to include in the curriculum and what to leave out. But is not this the very same thing that strategic learners do? Isn't being an *effective* strategic learner to do with making wise and informed choices about where to invest time and energy, and where not? It can be argued that strategic learning, when done well, is a demonstration of a useful kind of *intelligence* – that of handling quite vast amounts of information, narrowing the information down to a smaller proportion and then processing only that smaller proportion into knowledge. It can also be argued that those learners who go far are the strategic ones, rather than the deep ones. It can be argued that they know *when* to adopt a deep approach and when it is sufficient to adopt a surface approach.

In the UK, for example, every year there is an annual clamour about the A level results. The clamour echoes the usual protests that standards have not fallen, that there has been no 'dumbing down'. Could it not be that A level candidates are becoming better prepared to achieve at A level? Could it not be that they know more about what is being looked for in good exam answers? Could it not be that they are more aware about what is required for good grades in associated course-work? Could it not, indeed, be that they are now better versed in the virtues of strategic learning? And is this really a 'bad thing'?

'I'm sorry, but I haven't got a cue!'

As long ago as 1974, Miller and Parlett discussed what can now be thought of as one way of thinking about strategic learning: 'cue-consciousness'. They proposed three approaches which learners can use in the ways that they structure their learn-ing in systems where assessment is a significant driving force – an assessment regime which then in the UK was mainly comprised of written exams. They wrote of:

- cue-seeking learners: more likely to get first-class degrees

- cue-conscious learners: more likely to get upper second-class degrees

- cue-deaf learners: less likely to succeed.

Gibbs and Simpson (2002) expand on, and quote from, Miller and Parlett's work as follows:

> Miller and Parlett focussed on the extent to which students were oriented to cues about what was rewarded in the assessment system. They described dif-ferent kinds of students: the cue seekers, who went out of their way to get out of the lecturer what was going to come up in the exam and what their personal preferences were; the cue conscious, who heard and paid attention to tips given out by their lecturers about what was important, and the 'cue deaf', for whom any such guidance passed straight over their heads. This 'cue seeking' student describes exam question-spotting: *'I am positive there is an examina-tion game. You don't learn certain facts, for instance, you don't take the whole course, you go and look at the examination papers and you say "looks as though there have been four questions on a certain theme this year, last year the professor said that the examination would be much the same as before", so you excise a good bit of the course immediately …'*. (Miller and Parlett, 1974: 60)

In contrast these students were described as 'cue-deaf': '*I don't choose ques-tions for revision – I don't feel confident if I only restrict myself to certain topics.' 'I will try to revise everything ...'.* (Miller and Parlett, 1974: 63)

Miller and Parlett were able to predict with great accuracy which students would get good degree results. '*... people who were cue conscious tended to get upper seconds and those who were cue deaf got lower seconds*'. (Miller and Parlett, 1974: 55)

Things have not really changed much in four decades. I am, however, readily persuaded by Sally Brown's suggestion that the phrase 'cue-deaf' is unfortunate, and indeed unacceptable. 'Cue-blind' is equally problematic. 'Cue-oblivious' is a better way of thinking about those learners who just don't take any notice of cues about how assessment is going to work, or about how useful the intended learn-ing outcomes may be as a framework upon which they can prepare for assess-ment, or about how valuable formative feedback on assessed coursework can be to help them improve their techniques for future assessments.

Knight and Yorke (2003) put the matter of cue-consciousness in perspective as follows:

Learned dependence is present when the student relies on the teacher to say what has to be done and does not seek to go beyond the boundaries that they believe to be circumscribing the task. The construction of curricula around explicit learning outcomes risks the inadvertent building-in of cir-cumscriptions or, for the 'strategic' student seeking to balance study and part-time employment, a welcome 'limitation' to what they have to do. For-mal and informal feedback can be interrogated for what it can tell about what is expected, and can become part of a vicious spiralling-in towards 'playing it safe', basing action on perceptions of the implicit – as well as the explicit – expectations. It is a paradox that active 'cue-seekers' (Miller and Parlett, 1974) can exhibit a form of learned dependence, through 'playing it clever' (at least, superficially) by hunting for hints that will help them to maximise the grade received for their investment of effort. Over-reliance on the teacher can thus give achievements a meretricious ring: these may look worthier than they actually are. (Knight and Yorke, 2003: 134)

It is interesting to think a little more about cue-seekers, cue-conscious learners and cue-oblivious learners, and to analyse how the factors underpinning suc-cessful learning may be at work in their respective cases as they tune in to their differing ways of looking forward to assessment in their choices of learning approaches.

Cue-seeking learners These could be regarded as strategic learners, who are setting out to find out how assessment works so that they can produce their optimum performances in each assessed situation. They are likely to be much more receptive to *feedback*, using critical constructive feedback to fine-tune their learning, and to work out what gets them good marks and what doesn't. They are likely to probe quite deeply into feedback – both positive and critical – to find out as clearly as they can where they are meeting assessment expectations and where their shortfalls presently lie. They are likely to be particularly skilled regarding taking ownership of the *needing to learn* dimension, paying close attention to the cues they can draw from published intended learning outcomes, evidence descriptors and assessment criteria. Likewise, they may consciously seek explanation and interpretation of the real meaning of criteria and standards, so that they know more about just how to optimize evidence of their own achievement.

The *wanting to learn* dimension may still be strong, but is steered in the direction of investing time and energy in what they *need* to learn, as above. The *learning by doing* dimension is likely to be governed by their thinking about what is really *worth* doing and what is not. They may indeed invest in practice and trial and error where they see that there are likely to be dividends at the end of the road for them, and may deliberately *not* do things which they see as not paying such dividends in due course.

The *making sense* dimension is perhaps the most profoundly affected, with cue-seekers making strategic decisions about what they *try* to make sense of, and about what they will be perfectly content to use surface approaches to learn. Cue-seeking learners are likely to make the most of opportunities to find out how assessment works by making informed judgements on their own work, and each other's work. They are also amenable to encouragement that explaining things to each other is a good rehearsal for formal assessment.

Cue-seeking can therefore be thought of as a rich approach to learning, linking directly to each of the seven factors underpinning successful learning explored in this book. It is therefore not surprising that cue-seekers are usually identified as the learners most likely to succeed.

Cue-conscious learners   This group of learners may include at least some deep learners, but who are balancing their intrinsic *want* to learn with more strategic approaches to ensure that they do indeed achieve what they believe they *need to learn* as well. They are likely to be almost as receptive to *learning through feedback* as their cue-seeking counterparts, but are not likely to go the extra mile to *seek* additional feedback or to ask for clarification of aspects of feedback they are not sure about. They may remain conscious of cues in structuring their *learning by doing*, but may be less likely to be as analytical as their cue-seeking counterparts in deciding how much time and energy to invest in each element of their studying.

Cue-conscious learners are likely to use cues to help them to *make sense* of what they are learning, but perhaps gain more from the cues they derive from teaching sessions and learning materials, and are likely to be less aware of cues in assessment contexts than their cue-seeking counterparts. That said, cue-conscious learners may benefit considerably from the process of *making informed judgements* in self-assessment and peer assessment opportunities, bringing home to them some of the more important cues which will help them in formal assessment contexts. They are perhaps less likely to regard time and energy spent in verbalizing their learning orally in *explaining, coaching* or *teaching* as really relevant to developing their own learning more deeply.

Cue-conscious approaches can therefore be seen as relating directly to at least some of the processes underpinning successful learning. There are some parallels with strategic learning approaches, but the strategy can be regarded as underdeveloped. However, the difference between cue-seeking and cue-consciousness may too often end up as a difference in achievement between the most successful and the adequately successful learners.

Cue-oblivious learners   Whatever else, these are probably *not* to be regarded as strategic learners. Sometimes, they can be more like deep learners or, alternatively, surface learners.

Some of these may be learners whose *want* to learn is very high but who perhaps do not make sufficient use of establishing a real sense of ownership of the *need* to learn. They are less likely to draw on published intended learning outcomes, evidence specifications or assessment criteria to structure their learning. Their motivation may, however, be so strong that they learn some parts of the curriculum really deeply, but thereby increase the risk that they fail to achieve on those parts of the curriculum which interest them less strongly. They may derive much less value from *feedback* than their cue-seeking or cue-conscious counterparts and, indeed, may become demotivated by critical feedback, which otherwise they could have used to their advantage.

Their *learning by doing* may be more haphazard, following their interests rather than attending to the parts of the curriculum in which they may need to invest some practice. They may *make sense* very well of those parts of the curriculum which interest them, and do so much less well where they lack such interest.

Cue-oblivious learners are less likely to internalize the benefits of learning by *making informed judgements* in self-assessment or peer assessment processes, and while they may still engage in explaining things to each other, this can happen at a somewhat superficial level, without them really optimizing the *making sense* which accompanies such actions for cue-seekers or cue-conscious learners.

Among the constituency of cue-oblivious learners, however, may be those learners who have not got much *want* to learn at all, and who are likely to end up as the casualties of assessment in due course. They, too, are unlikely to take ownership of the *need* to learn, as might have been indicated had they been aware of the cues connected with learning outcomes and assessment criteria.

All in all, it is not surprising that cue-oblivious learners are not nearly so successful as their cue-seeking or cue-conscious counterparts, as they miss out on the contribution which making use of cues can make to all seven of the factors underpinning successful learning.

How then can we assess what students have learned? Figure 4.2 shows some possibilities.

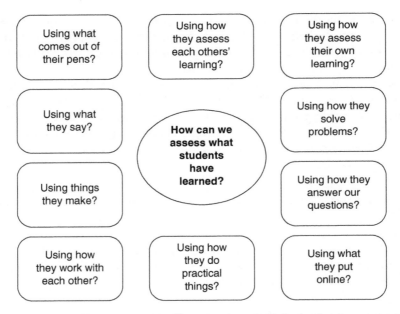

Figure 4.2   Just some ways of assessing what students have learned – there are many more!

Validity, fairness, 'whodunit?', transparency and real-world dimensions

We've already seen that it is widely accepted that for most learners assessment drives learning to a quite profound extent. This is particularly the case for cue-seeking learners and strategic learners, and unsurprisingly they fare best in most common assessment processes and procedures. But is this state of things satisfactory? Institutional policies on teaching, learning and assessment make much of the design of assessment processes and instruments being adjusted to address the following qualities:

- validity – how well are we actually measuring what we're supposed to be measuring – evidence of achievement of intended learning outcomes?

- fairness – how reliable is the assessment – e.g. will different markers award identical marks for the same piece of work or exam script? Fairness can also be thought of as 'justice'.

- 'whodunit?' – was the assessed work done by the candidate, or by other people? Another word for this could be 'veracity' (but I quite like 'whodunit?' as it reminds us of the central question involved).

- transparency – how well do learners know how the system works?

- real-world dimensions – how closely does the assessment link to things learners may need to do in employment? This issue is also often referred to as authenticity.

So assessment should be valid, fair, transparent and linked to the real world, and we need to be certain regarding who did the assessed work. Anyone who cares about the quality of the assessment they design for learners will say how they strive to make it so. We are also *required* in the UK, for example, to make assessment valid, fair and transparent in higher education by the Quality Assurance Agency. As an example of what we need to do to 'mend' assessment, it is worth listing in full in this chapter the 18 indicators of sound practice listed in the QAA's *UK Quality Code for Higher Education* (2013) in the section on the 'Assessment of students and the recognition of prior learning', subsection 'Indicators of sound practice' as follows in Table 4.1.

Table 4.1 Indicators for sound assessment practice from the Quality Assurance Agency's *UK Quality Code for Higher Education* (2013)

The basis for effective assessment

1 Higher education providers operate effective policies, regulations and processes which ensure that the academic standard for each award of credit or a qualification is rigorously set and maintained at the appropriate level, and that student performance is equitably judged against this standard.
2 Assessment policies, regulations and processes, including those for the recognition of prior learning, are explicit, transparent and accessible to all intended audiences.
3 Those who might be eligible for the recognition of prior learning are made aware of the opportunities available, and are supported throughout the process of application and assessment for recognition.
4 Higher education providers assure themselves that everyone involved in the assessment of student work, including prior learning, and associated assessment processes is competent to undertake their roles and responsibilities.
5 Assessment and feedback practices are informed by reflection, consideration of professional practice, and subject-specific and educational scholarship.
6 Staff and students engage in dialogue to promote a shared understanding of the basis on which academic judgements are made.
7 Students are provided with opportunities to develop an understanding of, and the necessary skills to demonstrate, good academic practice.
8 The volume, timing and nature of assessment enable students to demonstrate the extent to which they have achieved the intended learning outcomes.
9 Feedback on assessment is timely, constructive and appropriately developmental.
10 Through inclusive design wherever possible, and through individual reasonable adjustments wherever required, assessment tasks provide every student with an equal opportunity to demonstrate their achievement.
11 Assessment is carried out securely.
12 Degree awarding bodies assure themselves that the standards of their awards are not compromised as a result of conducting assessment in a language other than English.
13 Processes for marking assessments and for moderating marks are clearly articulated and consistently operated by those involved in the assessment process.
14 Higher education providers operate processes for preventing, identifying, investigating and responding to unacceptable academic practice.
15 Degree awarding bodies specify clearly the membership, procedures, powers and accountability of examination boards and assessment panels, including those dealing with the recognition of prior learning; this information is available to all members of such boards.
16 Boards of examiners/assessment panels apply fairly and consistently regulations for progression within, and transfer between, programmes and for the award of credits and qualifications.
17 The decisions of examination boards and assessment panels are recorded accurately, and communicated to students promptly and in accordance with stated timescales.
18 Degree awarding bodies systematically evaluate and enhance their assessment policies, regulations and processes.

Institutional teaching and learning strategies in the UK are now required to embrace these qualities in the design of assessment. But hang on – why have we all got 'teaching and learning' strategies in our institutions? Why have most institutions got 'teaching and learning' committees? (Or, indeed, 'learning and teaching' committees – small difference?) Why haven't we got 'teaching, learning and assessment' strategies – or, indeed, 'assessment, learning and teaching' committees, which would be the way round I would name them? Because assessment is the weakest link, I suggest. It's much easier (and safer) to fiddle around with the quality of teaching or learning than to tackle the big one: assessment. It's actually quite hard to *prove* that some teaching has been unsatisfactory, but only too easy to demonstrate when something has gone wrong with assessment. But, as shown below, there are significant shortfalls in the extent to which many of the most common assessment practices measure up to bringing these qualities to bear on assessment, particularly, as we shall see, exams and essays.

Validity?

Valid assessment is about measuring that which we should be trying to measure. But still too often, we don't succeed in this intention. We measure what we can. We measure echoes of the manifestation of the achievement of learning outcomes by learners. Whenever we measure what they *write* about what they *remember* about what they once *thought* (or what we once *said* to them in our classes), we're measuring ghosts. Now, if we were measuring what they could now *do* with what they'd *processed* from what they thought, it would be better.

'But we *do* measure this!' assessors justify themselves. But ask learners, they know better than anyone else in the picture exactly what we end up measuring. For a start, let's remind ourselves that we're still very hung up on measuring what learners *write*. We don't say in our learning outcomes, 'When you've studied this module you'll be able to write neatly, quickly and eloquently about it so as to demonstrate to us your understanding of it'. And what do we actually measure? We measure, to at least some extent, the neatness, speed and eloquence of learners' writing. What about those who aren't good at writing? Or to be more critical, what about those learners who have at least some measure of *disability* when it comes to writing? And in exams, the 'writing' tends to be *handwriting*. Where else, one may ask, in this age of keyboards, computers, tablets and smartphones are significant tracts of wording composed with a pen in hand? How divorced has our assessment become from everyday life?

In the UK, the writing is on the wall for us regarding any tendency for our assessment instruments and processes to discriminate against learners with disabilities. Since 2002, the Special Educational Needs and Disabilities Act (SENDA) and subsequent amendments to disability legislation have caused us to make far-reaching changes to our assessment just to keep it within the law. We are required to make 'reasonable adjustments' so that no learner should be unfairly discriminated against by our education provision, not least the assessment-related aspects of this provision. Legislation also requires these reasonable adjustments to be made in an *anticipatory* manner. In other words, they should not just deal with instances of discrimination when they are found to have happened. This is a tricky situation, as in one sense the purpose of assessment *is* to *discriminate* between learners, and to find which learners have mastered the syllabus best, and least, and so on. If we're honestly discriminating in terms of ability, that might be lawful. But if we're discriminating in terms of disability, it won't be lawful. But aren't they the same thing? Where does ability stop and disability begin?

For a long time, there have been those of us strongly arguing the case for diversifying assessment, so that the same learners aren't discriminated against *repeatedly* because they don't happen to be skilled at those forms of assessment that we over-use (such as, in some disciplines, tutor-marked, time-constrained, unseen, written examinations, tutor-marked coursework essays and tutor-marked practical reports).

We're entering an era where *inclusive* assessment will be much more firmly on the agenda than it has ever been to date. We now know much more about the manifestations of dyslexia in assessment, and are beginning to work out the effects of dyscalcula, dysgraphia, dyspraxia, and so on. Many of us are beginning to realize for the first time that, even in that packed lecture theatre, we do have learners with disabilities, not just the occasional learner visibly in a wheelchair, but perhaps a quarter or a third of our learners who are affected at some time in their learning by factors which we don't know about and which many of them don't even know about themselves. So is it ever going to be possible for us, in our assessment practices, to be satisfied with the levels of validity or fairness to which we aspire?

So we're not really in a position to be self-satisfied regarding the appropriateness of even our most used, and most practised, assessment instruments and processes. But the situation isn't new – we've used these devices for ever it seems. That doesn't make them more valid, but we are experienced in using them. Admittedly, that makes us better able to make the best of a bad job with them. But should we not be making a better job with something else?

Fairness?

For many, this word is synonymous with 'reliability' and 'consistency' and indeed 'justice'. Fairness is easier than validity to put to the test. If several assessors mark the same piece of work and all agree (within reasonable error limits) about the grade or mark, we can claim we're being reliable. This is not just moderation, of course. Fairness can only be tested by blind multiple marking. Double marking is about as far as we usually manage to get. And, of course, we agree often enough, don't we? No we don't, in many disciplines.

There are some honourable exceptions. 'Hard' subjects, such as areas of maths and science, lend themselves better to measures of agreement regarding fairness than 'softer' subjects, such as literature, history, philosophy, psychology, you name it. By 'hard' and 'soft' I don't mean 'difficult' and 'easy' – far from it. Not surprisingly, staff are resistant to the suggestion that they may need to undertake yet more marking. 'But multiple marking just causes regression to the mean' can be the reply. 'And after all, the purpose of assessment is to sort learners out – to discriminate between them – so it's no use everyone just ending up with a middle mark'. 'And besides, we spend quite long enough at the assessment grindstone; we just haven't room in our lives for more marking'.

Sadler (2009a) suggests four propositions which have a bearing on the difficulties we face in ensuring that assessment is fair and reliable. He proposes:

(1) Students deserve to have their work graded strictly according to its quality, without their responses to the same or similar tasks being compared with those of other students in their group, and without regard to the students' individual histories of previous achievement.

(2) Students deserve to know the basis on which judgements are made about the quality of their work. There should be few if any surprises.

(3) Students deserve their grades to have comparable value across courses in the academic program in which they enrol, and across the institution. Courses should not exhibit characteristically tough or lenient grading.

(4) Students deserve grades that are broadly comparable across institutions and maintain value over time, so that the standing of their educational qualifications is protected not only by the college or university in which they study, but also in higher education as a social institution. (Sadler, 2009a: 809)

Sadler's propositions here show that there is much more to be achieved, in the context of fairness, than simply reliability within the marking of a set of assignments.

So why else is fairness so important? Not least, because assessing learners' work is the single most important thing we ever do for them. Many staff in education regard themselves as teachers, with assessment as an additional chore (not to mention those who regard themselves as *researchers*, with teaching and assessing as additional chores). Perhaps if we were all to be called *assessors* rather than teachers it would help. And perhaps better still, if we all regarded ourselves as researchers into assessment, alongside anything else we were researching into, it would help more. 'Students can escape bad teaching, but they can't escape bad assessment' after David Boud (1995: 35).

In countries with a degree classification system, our assessments can end up with learners getting first-class degrees or thirds. This affects the rest of their lives. Now if our assessment were really fair, we could sleep easily about who got firsts or thirds. The learners who worked hardest would get better degrees and the learners who lazed around wouldn't. This indeed is often the case, but most of us can think of exceptions, where learners got good degrees but didn't really deserve them, or where learners who seemed worthy of good degrees didn't come up with the goods in the assessed components of their courses, so we couldn't award these to them. So perhaps it's not just that our assessment isn't fair, it's our discrimination that's sometimes faulty too.

Whodunit?

This one seems straightforward. It's about knowing that we're assessing the work of the candidate, not other people's work. It's about the safety of assessment. We could call it 'veracity'. In traditional, time-constrained, unseen written exams, we can be fairly sure that we are indeed assessing the work of each candidate, provided we ensure that unfair practices, such as cheating or copying, are prevented. But what about coursework? In the age of the internet, word processing and electronic communication, learners can purchase and download ready-made essays and incorporate elements from these into their own work. Some such practices can be detected electronically, but the most skilful plagiarists can remain one step ahead of us and make sufficient adjustments to the work they have found or bought to prevent us from seeing that it is not their own work.

Plagiarism is becoming one of the most significant problems which coursework assessors find themselves facing. Indeed, the difficulties associated with plagiarism are so severe that there is considerable pressure to retreat into the relative safety of traditional, unseen written exams once again, and we are coming round full circle to resorting to assessment processes and instruments which can guarantee safety regarding 'whodunit?' but at the expense of validity.

However, probably too much of the energy which is being put into tackling plagiarism is devoted to *detecting* the symptoms and punishing those found guilty of unfairly passing off other people's work as their own. After all, where are the moral and ethical borderlines? In many parts of the world, to quote back a teacher's words in an exam answer or coursework assignment is culturally accepted as 'honouring the teacher'. When learners from these cultures, who happen to be continuing their studies in the UK, find themselves accused of plagiarism, they are surprised at our attitude. Prevention is better than the cure. We need to be much more careful to explain exactly what is acceptable and what is not. While some learners may deliberately engage in plagiarism, many others find themselves in trouble because they were not fully aware of how they are expected to treat other people's work. Sometimes they simply do not fully understand how they are expected to cite others' work in their own discussions, or how to follow the appropriate referencing conventions.

It is also worth facing up to the difficulty of the question, 'Where are the borderlines between originality and plagiarism?' In a sense, true originality is extremely rare. In most disciplines, it is seldom possible to write anything without having already been influenced by what has been done before, what has been read, what has been heard, and so on.

Transparency?

One way of describing 'transparency' is the extent to which learners know where the goalposts are. The goalposts, we may argue, are laid down by the intended learning outcomes, matched nicely to the assessment criteria that specify the standards to which these intended outcomes are to be demonstrated through evidence produced by learners, and also specify the forms in which learners will present that evidence of their achievement. There's a nice sense of closure matching up assessment criteria to intended learning outcomes. But how well do learners themselves appreciate these links? How well, indeed, do assessors themselves consciously exercise their assessment-decision judgements to consolidate these links? Learners often admit that one of their main problems is that they still don't really know where the goalposts lie, even despite our best efforts to spell out syllabus content in terms of intended learning outcomes in course handbooks and to illustrate to learners during our teaching the exact nature of the associated assessment criteria – and sometimes even our attempts to clarify the evidence indicators associated with achievement of the learning outcomes are not clear enough to learners. In other words, learners often find it hard to get their heads inside our assessment culture – the very culture which will determine the level of their awards.

The learners who have least problems with this are often the ones who do well in assessment. Or is it that they do well in assessment *because* they have got their minds into our assessment culture? Is it that we're discriminating positively in the case of those learners who manage this? Is this the ultimate assessment criterion? In systems with degree classification, is it *this* difference which is the basis of deciding between a first and a third? And is this the *real* learning outcome, the achievement of which we're measuring? If so, is this stated transparently in the course handbook?

Therefore, we're not too hot on achieving transparency either. In fact, the arguments above can be taken as indicating that we often fail ourselves on all three qualities – validity, fairness and transparency – when considered separately. What, then, is our probability of getting all three right at the same time? Indeed, is it even *possible* to get all three right at the same time?

The real world

Under the heading 'whodunit?' we've so far taken up the matter of *ownership* of assessed work. There is, however, another thing to consider – the extent to which the work being assessed relates to the real world beyond post-compulsory education. We need to be thinking more about making assessed tasks as close as possible to the performances that learners will need to develop in their lives and careers in the real world. Doctors, lawyers, accountants and managers don't, in their day-to-day work, sit *writing* about medicine, law, accountancy and management – they *do* these things. There is often a considerable gap between what we get learners to do in our assessment, and what they will need to be good at throughout their careers. The more we can bridge that gap by making assessment feel relevant to learners, the more we can expect them to take ownership of the need to become able to evidence their achievement in assessed contexts.

Why is now the time to move towards mending assessment?

By now, you may be convinced that assessment is broken in higher education. OK, there's a problem, but we just haven't got enough time to fix it. *Why* haven't we got time to fix it? Because we're so busy doing, to the best of our ability and with integrity and professionalism, the work which spins off from our existing patterns of assessment, so busy indeed that we haven't left ourselves time to face up to the weaknesses of what we're doing. Or maybe we simply *dare not* face up to the possibility that we may be making a mess of such an important area of our work? It can help to pause and reflect on just how we got into this mess in the first place.

Three decades ago, the proportion of the 18–30-year-old population of the UK participating in higher education was in single figures; now it's well on the way to 50 per cent. When it was only 5 per cent, it could be argued that the average ability of those learners who participated in higher education was higher, and they were better able to fend for themselves in the various assessment formats they experienced. Indeed, they usually got into higher education in the first place because they'd already shown to some extent that they'd got at least a vestigial mastery of the assessment culture (from the tips of their pens at least). Now, there are far more learners who haven't yet made it in getting their heads around our assessment culture, let alone gearing themselves up to demonstrate their achievement within it.

At the same time, when we were busy assessing just a few per cent of the population, we had time to try to do it slowly and carefully, using the time-honoured traditional assessment devices at our disposal. Trying to do the same for five or ten times as many learners is just not possible. We can't do it. We can't do it well enough. We're assessing far too much to do it fairly and reliably, for a start.

And what about the learners? Their lives are dominated by assessment. The intelligent response to this (thank goodness our learners remain intelligent) is to become strategic. In other words, if there aren't any marks associated with some learning, strategic learners will skip that bit of learning. If it counts, they'll do it. It's easy to go with the flow, and make everything important 'count' so that learners will try to do all of it. But in the end this just leads to surface learning, quickly forgotten as the next instalment of assessment looms up. We're in danger of using assessment to *stop* learning instead of to start learning. It's no use us bemoaning the increased extent to which learners have become strategic when our assessment is the cause of this.

Who *owns* the problem of mending assessment?

We can only ever really *solve* problems which we own. But the assessment problem is so widely owned. It's dangerously easy to feel there's nothing that any one constituency among 'the owners of the problem' can do about it. It's easy enough to identify scapegoats, including:

- professional bodies, in whose name we feel we need to stick to the status quo

- pre-university education systems, which cast the die and train pupils into particular expectations of learning and assessment

- institutional, faculty and departmental assessment regulations, which limit our room for manoeuvre

- teaching and learning strategies, which are so detailed and all-encompassing that we can't suspend belief and start afresh

- heads of department or school, who are often seen (sometimes wrongly) to be content with the status quo

- external examiners, who would have to be convinced when radical changes may need to be made (despite the fact that the best of these would welcome us making these changes)

- learners themselves who could or would complain about rapid changes to the level of the playing field or the position of the goalposts (even if the whole field is enveloped in thick fog at present)

- the world outside academe, where there's a view about what a graduate should be, and so on (sometimes held deeply by those who prospered under the older order of things)

- journalists, broadcasters and editors, who would give us a hard time if anything were to be found wrong in the way we did the job we are paid to do

- politicians and policy-makers, who got to where they are by succeeding in the system of assessment we already have, and dare not admit that it might have been flawed

- the people who foot the bill for education: parents, employers, taxpayers and students themselves.

However, if we're perfectly frank about it, each assessment judgement is almost always initially made in the mind of one assessor in the first instance. True, it may well then be tempered by comparisons with judgements made in other people's minds, but to a large extent assessment remains dominated by single acts of decision-making in single minds, just as the evidence which is assessed is usually that arising from the product of a single learner's mind at a given time within a given brief. Living on a crowded planet may be a collaborative game, but we tend to play the assessment game in predominantly singular circumstances, and competitive ones at that.

The fact of the matter is that to fix assessment in post-compulsory education will require individuals to change what they do, but that won't be enough to change the culture. Teams of individuals with a shared realization of the problem will need to be the first step.

Assessment Agency: who does the assessment?

It can be worth thinking carefully about the advantages and drawbacks of assessment being undertaken by tutors, group members, student self-assessment and external examiners. Table 4.2 shows a number of factors to consider.

Table 4.2 Assessment Agency: some factors to consider

External assessment	Tutor	Inter-peer group	Intra-peer group	Self-assessment
External examiners assess students' work	e.g. lecturer assesses work	Groups assess other groups' work	Group members assess work of other members	Students assess their own work
Can encourage tutors and students to feel 'on the same side', working together to achieve shared goal of success.	Relatively easy process to be managed.	Relatively neutral, as students can judge other groups' work using criteria and evidence.	Requires effective engagement of students, to evaluate peer contributions to their own group.	Can foster useful approaches to study in general.
Can cause 'teaching to the (expected) test', and miss out on other useful learning.	Students often say they prefer this.	High learning pay-off, as plenty of discussion can be involved.	Students can back away from confronting others' non-contribution to the group's work.	Can promote student independence and autonomy.
Eliminates possible bias or prejudices on the part of assessors.	Low student engagement.	Good student engagement.	Responsibility for assessment judgement shared.	Can cause students to reflect usefully on their work, in ways which would not have happened if they just passed it on for tutors to judge.
Assessors only see the evidence being assessed, and may know little about the journeys through which that evidence was created.	Neutral for the student.	Responsibility for judgements shared.	Can be complex to manage.	Responsibility lies with individual students to apply criteria to their own evidence of achievement.
Tutors' responsibility is mainly getting students ready for assessment, and not that of judging students' evidence of achievement.	Assessor prejudices may go unnoticed.	Students can get a lot of feedback from each other while assessing, and may also get feedback from the other students who are assessing them.	Can be unpopular with students who may not want to make judgements on those they are working with.	Students who don't engage well can get little out of the process, and may be unaware of their work's shortcomings.
	Feedback may be good and quick or may be poor and slow.	Students assessing other groups' work can also be thinking about the quality of their own work, and learning from peers' attempts.	Can be high learning pay-off.	Can be hard to manage.
	Discourages student collaboration, even when this may have been useful.	Can be complex to manage.	Good training regarding managing group behaviours and avoiding passengers.	
	Can encourage students to plagiarise or copy, and skilfully disguise that they have done this.	Can be unpopular with students.		
	Students may just take notice of marks or grades, and not make good use of feedback.			

Student engagement in assessment and feedback processes

Low ← —————————————————————————————————— → High

How can we mend assessment?

We need to work out a strategy. But any strategy has to be made up of a suitably chosen array of tactics. Sometimes it's easier to start thinking of the tactics first. What could be a shopping list of tactics to play with for starters in the mission to get assessment right in post-compulsory education? They include:

- getting learners into our assessment culture, by using peer assessment and self-assessment more, so that learners are better tuned into our assessment culture when *we* assess them

- reducing the quantity of assessment (say by a factor of three) so that *we* have time to do it well, and learners have time for their learning not to be completely driven by assessment

- increasing the quality of assessment, so that it is fit for purpose and more valid, fairer, more transparent, better linked to the real world, and with less possibility for doubt about who actually did the work being assessed

- increasing the diversity of assessment instruments and processes, so that learner casualties (where particular learners are discriminated against repeatedly by the same old assessment formats) are not so frequent

- training (yes, training, not just educating) our learners to be better able to play the game of working out where the goalposts are, and practising how to demonstrate their achievement of our intended learning outcomes

- training (not leaving it to the chance of them becoming educated) our assessors to tackle head-on the problems we know about, and make assessment fit for purpose.

To sum up the problems with assessment, therefore, there are three principal weaknesses in assessment in post-compulsory education at present:

- assessment often drives learning away from what we might agree would be *good* learning

- there's far too much assessment going on, leaving us little time to work out how to do it better

- despite the importance of assessment, we're not very good at getting it right!

So what can *you* do to mend assessment?

Turning tactics into a strategy is a big job, and beyond the scope of a single chapter in a book such as this. I have, however, added an interrogation tool – 'Towards assessment *as* learning' – to this chapter to help you to analyse particular examples of assessment, as a start towards making them better. Meanwhile, that big job won't even get started unless people are convinced that it needs to be done, and that has been the purpose of this chapter so far. My intention in this chapter has been to employ challenging language to convince you that you've got a problem regarding changing assessment so that it makes learning happen in post-compulsory education.

What are *you* going to do about it? I suggest that we can improve things by interrogating our various assessment processes and practices, putting them under the spotlight and looking hard at what exactly they measure. But, perhaps more importantly, we can analyse how they relate to how learners learn in post-compulsory education. This is the way forward to adjusting our assessment to contribute positively to making learning happen, rather than to continue to allow surface or reproductive learning to be the outcome of post-compulsory education. With this in mind, I would like you to consider how the assessment processes and instruments which you use contribute to making learning happen for your learners.

A CRITICAL LOOK AT EXAMS AND ESSAYS!

In the analysis which follows, I am selecting two of the most common assessment processes, traditional exams and essays, and suggesting how they may impact on the factors underpinning successful learning. Although I am only interrogating two of the available assessment processes and instruments, they presently represent a large proportion of the assessment in post-compulsory

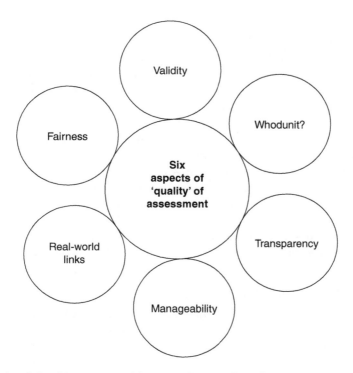

Figure 4.3 Six of the things to consider regarding quality of assessment

education in the UK, for example, and I hope that this may help you to look in a similar way at other assessment processes you employ, and think through the implications in parallel to my analysis below. The analysis which follows is based not just on my work helping teaching staff in post-compulsory education to develop assessment processes and instruments, but even more on my parallel work over three decades in helping learners to develop the skills they need to demonstrate their optimum performance in a range of different assessment conditions and environments.

After this analysis, I would like to widen the field, and get you thinking about the pros and cons of a wider range of assessment possibilities, continuing to hold in mind the detail of the two particular kinds of assessment interrogated below against the factors underpinning learning.

Traditional exams

In particular, let's take the example of time-constrained, unseen written examinations. In other words, candidates don't know the questions until they see them in the exam room. They work against the clock, on their own, with pen and paper. Assessment systems in the UK are quite dominated by this kind of assessment, usually at the end point of increments of learning. The assessment can therefore be described as summative.

As an assessment process, exams can be *reliable or fair* – if there is a well-constructed marking scheme, each candidate can be reasonably confident that the marking will be fair and consistent.

The main problem with many traditional exams is that they don't rate highly on *validity*. In other words, too often they measure what the candidate can *write* about what they have learned, in the relatively artificial conditions of solemn silence, against the clock. Where, however, exams are based on problem-solving, case study analysis, and so on, validity can be much higher.

Exams can be improved in terms of *transparency* where candidates have been involved in applying assessment criteria to their own or other people's exam answers, and have found out all they need to know about how the examiner's mind works.

One of the major advantages of exams is that we are reasonably certain (with due precautions) that the work of the learner is being marked – in other words, that side of *whodunit?* is assured. The extent to which the assessed performance relates to the normal conditions in which the learning is intended to be applied is less assured, and in some traditional exams the conditions under which achievements are measured are quite alien.

1 Traditional exams and wanting to learn

For many exam candidates, the 'want' to learn is damaged by the mere thought of looming exams. Many learners, if given the choice, go for learning modules that are continuously assessed rather than assessed by examination because of their fear – and even dread – of exams. Few assessment processes induce such high emotions. This is not the case for everyone, however. Some candidates love exams – and are very good at preparing for them and doing them. Not surprisingly, the cue-seekers mentioned earlier in this chapter are among those who are good at traditional exams. Their cue-seeking approach is thus rewarded by this pervasive assessment format.

2 Traditional exams and needing to learn

This is where the intended learning outcomes should come into their own. Ideally, if learners have systematically prepared to demonstrate their achievement of these outcomes, and practised doing so sufficiently, they should automatically remain able to demonstrate the same achievements under time-constrained, written exam conditions. However, there is often a gulf between the intended learning outcomes as published and what is *actually* measured by traditional exams. Due attention to achieving constructive alignment can overcome this problem. But there is another side to needing to learn. Candidates who prepare successfully for exams by mastering the intended learning outcomes so that they can demonstrate their achievement in answering likely exam questions often concentrate very firmly on what they perceive they need to learn, and don't invest time or energy in things they decide can't (or won't) come up in the exams. We are therefore favouring strategic learners by the use of exams (and, of course, cue-seeking strategic learners do best).

3 Traditional exams and learning by doing

There is plenty of learning by doing *before* traditional exams. But not much further learning by doing happens *during* traditional exams. It can, however, be claimed that a looming exam is as good a way as any of causing learners to get their heads down and do some learning. We could argue, however, that preparing for an oral exam (viva) would have just as much effect on learning by doing.

4 Traditional exams and learning through feedback

This is where traditional exams do really badly. As far as feedback is concerned, they are mostly lost opportunities. By the time the scripts are marked, learners have often moved on to the next part of their learning and are no longer really interested in which questions they answered well and why, or (more importantly) in where they lost marks. Many learners were very interested in these matters immediately after the exam, and spend hours in post-mortem mode trying to work out how their answers measured up to what was being looked for by their examiners. All the feedback that most learners receive – after some time – is their score, or their grade, or simply whether they passed or failed. It is feedback of a sort, but hardly formative feedback. We can, of course, argue that exams are intended to be summative measures, but they still seem to represent lost feedback opportunities. Where feedback *is* provided very quickly after an exam (for example, in computer-marked multiple-choice exams, where a feedback printout can be handed to each candidate on leaving the exam room), feedback can, indeed, play a much more powerful role even in summative testing.

5 Traditional exams and making sense of what is being learned

This, too, links badly to traditional exams. As with learning by doing, a great deal of making sense of the subject matter occurs *before* an exam and, indeed, could be argued to be happening *because of* the exam. But few exam candidates report later that the moment when the light dawned was *during* the exam. More often, they report that they only found out that the light had *not* dawned during the exam. And then we need to ask whether traditional exams are measuring the extent to which learners have made sense of what they learned. Too often, exams seem to measure what learners can *reproduce* rather than what they can *do*. Many learners can tell us about the frequent occasions where surface learning was all that they needed to engage in to address the task of answering a particular exam question.

6 Traditional exams and learning through verbalizing

In Chapter 2, we explored the significant benefits to learners resulting from them verbalizing orally, explaining things to each other, coaching each other, and so on. Sadly, traditional exams only really get at verbalizing in writing – and usually with a pen at that. One of my worries about traditional exams is that learners tend not to discuss things with each other, but to go into competitive mode, and hide their learning achievements from each other rather than celebrating such achievements. We can, of course, try to counter this tendency, and encourage learners to work together in their preparation for exams, quizzing each other, explaining things to each other, and so on, providing good rehearsal for doing similar things in writing on their own in the exam room.

7 Traditional exams and learning through assessing – making informed judgements

We could argue that in the context of traditional exams, most of this kind of learning occurs in the minds of examiners, not learners! Too often, *exactly how* the informed judgements are made by examiners is hidden from learners; examiners seem to fear the consequences of sharing with learners details of how marking schemes work in practice, possibly dreading future appeals by learners against 'academic judgement'. We can indeed encourage learners to self-assess practice exam performance, and to peer-assess each other's practice as they head towards exams, but the competitive ethos of exams militates against them doing either of these wholeheartedly. Moreover, there is fear involved – fear of finding out that the performance is not going to be up to the standards desired – and this can lead to self-fulfilling prophecy and lower attainment in exams.

Perhaps the main problem regarding learning through making informed judgements in the context of traditional exams is that such assessments are often the 'mystery black box' in nature, where learners do the best they can, hoping it will be found to be satisfactory or better. Other assessment formats tend to be more open to learners regarding exactly how they work (though this is not always the case).

Traditional exams: summary

The picture painted above of the links between traditional exams and the factors underpinning successful learning is very bleak. It does not *have* to be so bleak, however. With care, exams can be designed which are much better at measuring 'making sense' than suggested above. Problem-solving exams and case study exams are much better at *not* rewarding reproductive learning. But the concerns remain about the damage that can be inflicted on many candidates' *want* to learn, the artificial way that exams can skew the *need* to learn and the fact that so much work may be done by examiners making sure that the exams have been fair and reliable, yet very little feedback usually reaches learners. In some ways, it seems that traditional exams are diametrically opposed to all of the central factors underpinning successful learning! Couple this with the problems of achieving validity, fairness and transparency, and it is surprising that in some assessment cultures (including much post-compulsory education provision in the UK) traditional exams continue to hold sway to the extent that they do.

Other kinds of exams

The discussion above focused on the most common kind of exams – against-the-clock, written exams, and with candidates not seeing the questions until they sit at their exam desks. There are, however, many other kinds of exam, which overcome some of the problems about fairness, validity, transparency and links to the real world in suitable contexts and discipline areas. These alternatives can also be thought of in terms of the factors underpinning successful learning, and some 'food for thought' implications are summarized below for just two of the alternatives.

Computer-marked multiple-choice exams

If candidates are aware that it is their decision-making that will be measured rather than their ability to put their knowledge into words in writing, then *wanting* to learn will not be threatened as much as it is by traditional exams. Ownership of the relevant *need* to learn can also be improved, so long as learners become practised and rehearsed regarding *which aspects* of their achievement of the intended learning outcomes can indeed be measured by this sort of exam. *Learning by doing* in such exams is primarily of the decision-making variety, but with skilful attention to the design of questions and option choices, decision-making can cumulatively be used to yield a good measure of the extent to which learners have *made sense* of what they have learned. At least we can be assured that the *learning by doing* that is measured by computer-assisted assessment is not skewed by such mundane factors as the speed of handwriting or its legibility. Perhaps the most significant link between computer-assisted assessment and making learning happen is *feedback*. There are many possibilities. Learners can be provided with on-screen feedback as they go through a computer-based exam, allowing them to avoid the possibility of carrying forward errors of thinking into their answers to the next questions they meet. Or they can be given feedback on-screen or in print-outs at the end of each exam, when at least the feedback is quick enough for them to still remember what their thinking – and their decisions – were as they answered the questions. The availability of speedy and specific feedback can help learners to *make sense* of the subject matter they have been working with, admittedly too late for the computer-based exam they have just undertaken, but better late than not at all. Learning by *making informed judgements* is of course involved in multiple-choice exams, especially when there is plenty of this kind of practice in advance of the actual test. Learning by *explaining* can be involved if much of this practice is done in small groups of students, discussing the reasoning for choosing particular options.

I include more discussion about multiple-choice exams in the third section of this chapter, 'A critical comparison of eleven assessment types', where you may find it easier to compare its pros and cons with those of several other assessment approaches.

OSCEs

Objective structured clinical examinations (OSCEs) are widely used in medical education and health care studies, and lend themselves to many other disciplines where practical *doing* is important in the intended learning outcomes. Essentially, OSCEs are exams where each candidate *does* something at each of a number of assessment stations located around the exam room. In medicine, for example, candidates may visit successive stations and perform a series of assessed tasks, such as:

- interpreting some X-rays
- looking through a set of notes on a patient and approaching a diagnosis
- prescribing medication for a given condition in a given context
- briefing a ward sister about the pre-operative preparation of a patient
- talking to a patient to diagnose a condition (though in practice the 'patient' is an actor, as it is hard to get real patients to tell the same story to successive doctors).

The key claim made for OSCEs is that the assessment is valid, in that candidates are assessed on exactly the sorts of things they have been intended to become able to *do* in practice and not just on what they may have written in traditional exams about hypothetical cases.

Clearly, OSCEs link closely to learning by doing – practice, repetition and trial and error. Furthermore, the more feedback candidates get on their practice before such an exam, the more they can improve their performance. OSCEs also link strongly to well-defined *needing to learn* agendas, and as practitioners can see the relevance of developing their skills and knowledge to cope with such situations, the *want* to learn is enhanced. The variety of tasks which can be built into an OSCE add to the depth of *making sense* of what is being learned and assessed, as triangulation is possible, approaching key tasks from different angles. While it can take a considerable amount of time to design a good OSCE, when candidate numbers are large, this is time well spent, and the time spent *marking* an OSCE can be much less than a corresponding written exam, not least because most of the assessment decisions can be made at the assessment stations while the exam is in progress. In practice, it is wise to get groups of learners to design OSCE scenarios – they will often design better ones than we can! This also maximizes the learning pay-off they gain from discussing and arguing with each other, and making informed judgements about the material involved and the assessment criteria being addressed.

Essays: a critical examination

In some subject areas (notable exceptions include maths, science and technology-based disciplines), essays are key elements of both coursework and exams. We can again pose questions about how successfully essays relate to validity, fairness, transparency and the world outside education. Essays do not do very well as an assessment method on such interrogation. But perhaps worst of all, essays (except handwritten ones in exams) fall short regarding *whodunit?*, as it becomes easier to download information and paste it into word-processed essays. At least in exam-based essays we can be reasonably certain whose work is being marked, but in coursework essays we can't. However, in time-constrained essay-type exams we are perhaps penalizing the slower learners – perhaps by measuring speed of writing rather than quality of thought.

There are also particular problems with *fairness* where subjectivity in marking is all too easily present and inter-marker reliability is a problem (different markers giving the same essay different marks), as is also intra-marker reliability (the same marker giving the same essay different marks on different occasions – for example, among the first half-dozen marked or the last half-dozen marked).

Validity is perhaps the weakest link for essays as an assessment device. If we look hard at 'what are we *really* measuring?', it is often essay-writing skills rather than mastery of the subject matter concerned. Academics often defend the importance of essay-writing skills, but in practice for most learners, these tend to be skills that they are unlikely to need when they leave post-compulsory education, unless they too are heading towards becoming academics! Moreover, writing scholarly contributions to the literature involves much more than essay-writing skills – not least addressing fully the intended target audience of the writing and critically reviewing the existing literature in the field. Writing essays for an examiner is just a limited special case of this wider picture.

Transparency can be improved by involving learners in self-assessing and peer assessing essays so that they become much more aware of how marks are earned and lost, and how the assessment criteria work in practice – and, indeed, how the assessment links to the associated intended learning outcomes.

The connection between essays and the real world is problematic. The link between essays and the context in which learning may be intended to be applied is often tenuous. There are many learners in post-compulsory education who will never again put pen to paper (or fingers to keyboard) to compose an essay after leaving education.

Meanwhile, let's continue with our analysis of how essays may relate to the factors underpinning successful learning. I should point out at once that there are *very* significant differences here between coursework essays (with feedback in due course) and exam-based essays. As many factors relating to the latter overlap with what I've already said about traditional exams, the discussion which follows is mostly about the coursework essays.

1 Essays and wanting to learn

The effects here are widely variable. Some learners really enjoy 'sorting out their minds' by putting pen to paper to construct essays, particularly when they then get detailed and helpful feedback on their learning. Such feedback is unlikely to be forthcoming for exam-based essays. For other learners, actually getting round to putting pen to paper (or fingers to keyboard) is a major challenge. Ask a group of learners 'What was your best work-avoidance tactic that you used to delay starting to put together that essay?' and you will soon see how, for many learners, the task of getting started was the daunting part.

2 Essays and needing to learn

On one level, essays help learners to take ownership of the need to learn, by giving them something to do to cause them to get their heads into the books and resources relating to the task. However, the agenda of taking ownership of the intended learning outcomes is less successfully addressed, as all too often the links between these outcomes and a particular essay-writing task are not spelled out clearly enough in the briefings learners receive.

3 Essays and learning by doing

Essays certainly involve learning by doing. There are several kinds of *doing* in play, including information retrieval and sorting, planning, communicating in writing, comparing and contrasting ideas, making decisions and judgements, and summarizing. So this aspect of learning can be regarded as being satisfactorily addressed by the use of essays. Similarly, during the processes of drafting and redrafting an essay, a great deal of reflection and deepening of ideas can take place, and the act of writing the essay becomes much more than simply learning by doing.

However, it is worth asking how many of the same aspects of learning by doing are involved in constructing *essay plans* rather than writing fully-fledged essays. Such plans may miss out on some of the finer points of communicating in writing and on the reflective dimension, but making essay plans can involve many of the other important aspects of learning by doing. And if, let us suppose, 10 essay plans can be produced in the same time as it takes to write one fully-fledged essay, the learning pay-off associated with writing essay plans becomes all the more attractive.

Where, however, essays are primarily being used to train learners in the arts of marshalling their ideas, presenting them coherently and logically, and coming to a well-thought out conclusion or summary, and these are the primary intended learning outcomes, writing full essays will meet these aims to a much greater extent than simply preparing essay plans.

4 Essays and learning through feedback

Coursework essays can be very valuable in the context of making feedback available to learners. Feedback in general is discussed in more detail in the next chapter of this book. Meanwhile, it is worth bearing in mind that the timing and nature of the feedback on formative essays need to be managed well for optimum learning through feedback. It can be well worth considering ensuring that at least some of the feedback can be intentionally developmental. For example, if an essay is 'marked' three times, once where feedback is given on an essay plan, again when a rough draft is submitted and, finally, when the last version of the essay is completed, feedback on the first two stages can lead to much higher quality in the final products. This clearly takes extra assessor time, but the two earlier feedback stages do not need to be quantitatively 'marked', and can be required simply as conditions to be satisfied before the final essay version is submitted. However, most higher education institutions don't offer feedback on draft work, as learners who've been used to formative feedback at school find to their dismay – the handed-in version is the one that determines their mark.

5 Essays and making sense of what is being learned

Coursework essays coupled with formative feedback can be very valuable in helping learners to get their heads around ideas and concepts, and also in helping them make sense of other people's ideas from the literature. It is often the act of trying to communicate an idea which causes the human brain to clarify it and put it into perspective. This is equally true of oral responses, but writing out ideas and progressively making them more coherent is probably one of the best ways of causing reflection and deepening learning. 'I don't know what I think until I've written about it' is said by many authors, who recognize the value of putting ideas down on paper as a way of helping the brain to make sense of them. Coursework essays can also cause learners to find and retrieve information from the literature and from other sources, and then to sift it and analyse it, and distil from the source materials their own conclusions or thinking about a topic, issue or question.

6 Essays and learning by verbalizing – explaining orally

Though coursework essays do indeed involve the development of skills of *written* explaining, essay-writing tends to be a somewhat solitary activity, and learners are rather unlikely to spontaneously involve themselves in orally explaining things to each other or coaching each other, especially if the competitive nature of assessment-by-essays is in the forefront of their consciousness. We can, of course, encourage learners to think that their final essays are likely to be much better if they have spent a fair amount of time and energy working together at least before nearing their final drafts, but both learners and assessors have justified worries that at least some plagiarism may then happen.

7 Essays and learning through assessing – making informed judgements

More often than not, it's the assessors who gain all of this learning – not the learners. This can be counteracted by well-planned use of peer assessment, allowing learners to benefit from seeing work that is better than their own and worse than their own. Furthermore, learners can be encouraged to undertake self-assessment of their coursework essays, using the same criteria as will be used by their assessors. This practice can also help them to become more self-assessing when they come to write essays in exams.

Essays: summary

As can be seen from the above analysis, essays used formatively in a coursework context (rather than summatively in exam contexts) can involve many of the seven factors underpinning successful learning. Perhaps partly because they are time-consuming to plan, draft and polish, they are perhaps better than many assessment-related artefacts in enabling reflection and consolidation (important aspects of 'making sense'). They are, however, often solitary learning journeys, at least until the points where feedback is received. Peer review, peer assessment and peer editing processes can be used profitably to enable learners to benefit from feedback along the way.

Beyond exams and essays

What other assessment choices can we think about? Brown and Knight (1994) identified over 80 alternatives to exams and essays. I will only list a few alternatives here, with just the briefest of indications about how these may link more successfully to some or all of the factors underpinning successful learning. There is some further discussion in Table 4.3 which follows this section.

Question banks

Question banks are where learners compile a list of a specified number (for example, 300) of short, sharp questions about a topic or subject, and make a parallel list of answers to the questions or clues leading towards the answers. My own experience shows that this increases learners' *want* to learn, as it helps them break down the daunting task of getting to grips with a topic area into the more manageable steps of working out what questions they need to become able to answer, and linking the questions to the answers. Those learners who do not revel in trying to write in sophisticated language like the fact that the questions are intended to be short and direct, and the quality of a question bank depends on the relevance of the questions rather than the use of language.

Question banks also give learners a strong sense of ownership of the *need* to learn, as they translate the meaning of the intended learning outcomes into a practical tool which they can use to develop their ability to achieve the outcomes. *Learning by doing* is involved in making a question bank in the first place. Then it lends itself to practice, repetition and trial and error as learners put it to use. What is more, they have control and ownership of all stages of the learning by doing. Learners get immediate feedback as they use their question banks, especially when fellow learners quiz them with the questions and check whether their answers are satisfactory. All this practice and repetition does a great deal to help learners to *make sense* of the subject matter covered by the questions and answers, at least to the extent of equipping them to be better able to answer questions in traditional exam contexts.

Using a question bank instead of a conventional coursework assignment can get learners to build themselves useful learning tools, where high learning pay-off results both from making the tools in the first place and then practising with them from there onwards.

Annotated bibliographies

Learners can be asked, for example, to select what they consider to be the best 20 sources on a topic, and write just a few lines relating to what they think is most useful (or most important) in each source. This then equips them with a useful learning tool and gives them valuable practice at referencing sources accurately. The task of making an annotated bibliography involves a lot of learning by doing – for example, finding the sources, making decisions about which are the most appropriate sources, then working out what is special to each source.

This in turn causes learners to *make sense of* the subject matter, as they compare and contrast the different viewpoints or emphases of the various sources. As with question banks, there can be much more thinking per hundred words in making an annotated bibliography than just writing an essay or an exam answer. In other words, the learning pay-off can be much higher. Annotated bibliographies can be an excellent way of breaking down a lot of information into useful summaries, and can serve as useful learning tools, aiding revision and preparation for traditional exams.

I discuss annotated bibliographies in greater detail in Table 4.3.

Presentations

These are often part of an assessment mix. Learners can be asked to prepare a presentation with supporting materials (handouts, slides, posters) and then give the presentation to an audience of their peers (including tutors). Usually presentations are followed by a question-and-answer session with the audience. When the presentations are peer-assessed, and especially when the learners themselves have been involved in designing the assessment criteria and establishing their respective weighting, they learn not only from preparing and giving their own presentations, but also from applying the criteria to each other's presentations.

Learners often take presentations very seriously, and to some extent preparing and giving their first presentation might damage their *want* to learn, at least temporarily. When learners have ownership of the criteria, however, they feel more positive about the *need* to try to achieve them. There are several aspects of *learning by doing* involved, not least researching the content, preparing the support materials, rehearsing the presentation itself and preparing to be able to answer questions after giving the presentation.

Perhaps the most significant link between presentations and learning is the *making sense*, which occurs as a result of their preparation and delivery. Learners are usually able to answer questions on the topic involved long after the event, and their learning about the subject matter can be said to be much deeper than if they had just written an essay or assignment on the topic.

Learners can also gain a great deal of *feedback* during the various processes, not least from fellow learners during rehearsal and during the presentation itself. Further feedback can be provided by tutors or other assessors. The skills which learners develop as a result of preparing and giving presentations, and answering questions about the topic concerned, link strongly to employability. In particular, oral communication skills can be developed and practised alongside the subject-matter learning process. I've expanded on the above in Table 4.3 which follows.

A CRITICAL COMPARISON OF ELEVEN ASSESSMENT TYPES

In the discussion in the previous section, two of the most commonly used kinds of assessment (traditional exams and essays) fared rather poorly in one way or another, when we looked at how they linked to making learning happen. In the next section, we will compare several assessment types (including these traditional ones) in terms of advantages and disadvantages, but this time also discussing validity, fairness, whodunit?, links to the real world, and the extent to which feedback to learners can be provided and made useful.

Table 4.3 illustrates the pros and cons of several kinds of assessment. In each case, in the 'status' column I have included judgements regarding how well (or how poorly) each assessment type listed measures up to validity, fairness, whodunit? (whether there could be serious doubts or not regarding whose work is being assessed), links to the real world, and the extent to which feedback to learners may be available, or useful.

Comparing computer-based assessment with hand-marking

There are now a number of assessment platforms which can be used for computer-based marking of students' electronically submitted assignments and tests. Typically, these platforms are licensed for use in a particular educational institution, with costs varying according to the number of students who will use them.

Table 4.3 Comparison of advantages and drawbacks of various forms of assessment

Type of assessment	Status	Advantages	Disadvantages
1 Traditional exams Exams are often referred to as the 'gold standard' because of their widespread use in secondary and higher education. Still the most common kinds of exam are handwritten, invigilated, against-the-clock, with questions not being known by candidates beforehand. Exams remain prevalent on many post-compulsory education courses, sometimes where questions are set by external examiners, and sometimes by the staff who teach the learners. Timescales vary, but two hours and three hours are relatively common in universities, though much shorter exams are perfectly possible (and perhaps desirable). Many traditional exams offer candidates a choice of questions (e.g. attempt any five out of eight questions, each carrying equal marks), but increasingly there may be a compulsory section, then a section providing choices.	**Validity**: poor, limited to what comes out of pens. **Fairness**: can be good, but poor when answers are essay-type, and different markers would award very different marks for the same essay. **Whodunit?**: relatively safe (though stories of ingenious cheating are legion!). **Real world**: written exams are not at all close to the workings of the real world; most people never do a written exam again after leaving university. **Feedback to learners**: very limited indeed, usually just a score/grade or pass/fail, which can leave candidates having very little idea about what they did well or badly.	Can avoid plagiarism and cheating. Give data which can be ranked and handled quantitatively. Exams are relatively familiar to learners entering higher education, as they've already experienced them at school. Exams are already 'hard-wired' into many university systems, so a case doesn't have to be made for continuing to use them. Written exams are much better for some subjects than others: for example, they can work well for mathematical and quantitative subject matter, and tend to work really badly for 'wordy' or descriptive matter.	As has been argued already in this book, exams tend only to measure what comes out of pens, a poor proxy for what might be in heads. Many otherwise capable learners never show their best efforts under exam conditions. It can take a long time to mark a set of exam scripts (properly). (There are economies of scale for large numbers of candidates as examiners become familiar with the marking scheme being used.) Problems with speed of writing and legibility, and difficulties candidates face when using a pen. 'Sudden death': a bad day can mar a lifetime. A snapshot of achievement, rather than a real measure of it. One of the main skills measured tends to be time-management – dividing the available time sensibly between the questions being attempted. Promotes surface-learning: filling heads with information to use 'on the day' and forget as quickly as possible thereafter. Question-spotting by candidates can pay off substantially, meaning that at least some candidates pass without having learned the whole syllabus reasonably well. Where candidates have a choice of questions, it is really hard to get all of the questions to be of equal difficulty – leading to at least some candidates ending up with an easier exam than others overall. Long-answer written exams contribute to the continuing trend for post-compulsory education to remain 'elitist' – i.e. to favour those who are good at such exams.

(Continued)

Table 4.3 (Continued)

Type of assessment	Status	Advantages	Disadvantages
2 Short-answer exams Short written responses to a large number of questions. Usually the whole exam is compulsory, reducing the tendency for candidates to use question-spotting as a means of deliberately only learning some of the syllabus.	**Validity**: often a lot better than long-answer exams, as evidence of achievement of learning outcomes can be covered much more fully, rather than the 'write down everything you happen to know' tendency which long-answer questions can engender. **Fairness**: can be good. **Whodunit?**: safe under exam conditions. **Real world**: closer than traditional exams, as success may involve knowing the overall subject really well. **Feedback to learners**: poor, usually just a score or grade.	Can cover a wide range of topics in a limited time. Not so much affected by speed of writing or legibility. Can be somewhat faster to mark than long-answer exams (but not always). Can measure breadth of knowledge. Is fairer than exams where there are choices of question, as all candidates are effectively taking exactly the same exam.	Can miss out on depth of knowledge. Can deprive high-fliers of the opportunity to excel. It can take much longer to design a short-answer exam paper than a traditional long-answer one. It can be quite difficult to apportion marks across the various elements in a short-answer exam paper.
3 Multiple-choice exams Paper-based or computer-based: e.g. select the 'best' option from four or five alternatives for each of a fairly long list of questions. Such exams are usually time-constrained, but often most candidates complete the exam with plenty of time to spare.	**Validity**: can be good if questions are well-designed. A wide range of syllabus knowledge can be addressed in quite a short time. **Fairness**: can be really good, if questions are well designed and trialled. **Whodunit?**: safe under exam conditions; not safe if asynchronous, for example in distance learning contexts.	Gets away from 'what comes out of pens' limitations of other kinds of exams. When questions are well-designed, can quickly test quite a wide range of subject knowledge. Can be useful in areas where rapid decision-making is a useful skill for learners. Possible to provide feedback on-screen after each decision in computer-based uses, or a	It is much harder than people think to design really good multiple-choice questions. The 'key' is the best option, and is the one intended to be chosen by candidates who know the topic properly. However, it is sometimes hard to design a 'key' which is *always* right – high-fliers can often spot when even this choice is not correct. It can be difficult to design good 'distractors'. Options such as 'all of the above' or 'none of the above' are still too often included (usually through laziness regarding thinking of more distractors), and which are very rarely the 'best' option in any case.

Type of assessment	Status	Advantages	Disadvantages
Note that these can be extended to be **multiple-response exams**, where each question is along the lines of 'Which (one or more) of the following options is true?'. This can cause candidates to think harder about *all* of the options, rather than just picking the 'best' then moving on.	**Real world**: can be better than other kinds of exams, as multiple-choice exams tend to measure what goes on in heads, and aren't limited by what comes out of pens – they can measure decision-making well. **Feedback to learners**: possible to be excellent in speed and quality (but not often achieved). Excellent feedback can address, for each option: 'was I right?' and (particularly) 'if not, *why* not?'	complete feedback printout (feedback on the distractors as well as the correct choices) on leaving the exam. (Such printouts can make really useful revision tools for future candidates.) Can be useful for candidates who have difficulty stringing together fluent prose in written answers, but who can still think clearly through options.	Questions need to be well piloted and tested before being used in exams. Still an element of 'luck' picking the best option. (In a test using four-option questions, the average monkey should score 25 per cent). Quite a lot of emphasis now goes onto *reading* the questions and options well; learners with limited skills or speed in reading can be disadvantaged.
4 Essays Essays are highly regarded as an assessment type, despite the many disadvantages listed in this table! At university level, a coursework essay is often an extended account (such as 3000 words), usually submitted in word-processed form, and often passed through plagiarism-detection software.	**Validity**: rarely good. (Prose which comes out of a pen in an exam, or through a keyboard in coursework, is rarely the best way of measuring evidence of achievement of intended outcomes). **Fairness**: poor. (A great deal of research evidence is available showing that different markers award very different marks).	Allow learners to demonstrate ability to construct written arguments and to write fluently. Can give candidates who show 'depth' fair reward.	Essays take forever to mark, and marking is unreliable (unfair) anyway, as proved by a great deal of research! Tends to advantage learners who are good at written 'waffling'! Unless there are tight word-limits, a longer essay will usually score higher than a shorter one. Where there is an element of choice (e.g. coursework essays) some choices may prove harder to bring off in practice than others, disadvantaging some learners. In coursework essays, there can be a tendency to copy in (suitably rephrased) sentences from literature sources, without really thinking about the meaning of the elements copied in.

(Continued)

Table 4.3 (Continued)

Type of assessment	Status	Advantages	Disadvantages
However, handwritten essays (shorter) in exams are still widely used. In the case of coursework essays, learners may be given an essay title or theme, or may be allowed to choose from a list of topics, or may have leeway to choose an appropriate topic of their own, or negotiate a topic with a tutor.	**Whodunit?**: very unsafe, except for essays under exam conditions. Essays can be commissioned and purchased online from well-practised, skilled writers! However, concerns about whodunit? are minimal with small groups of learners, where tutors regularly talk to learners and would usually quickly know if submitted work was not their own. **Real world**: not close to the sorts of writing relevant to most careers. **Feedback to learners**: can be useful, but usually too late, not least because of the length of time it takes to mark a set of essays. There is usually no feedback at all on essays handwritten in exams.	Can give an indication of the quality, depth and breadth of reading that has been done by candidates.	Spelling, punctuation and grammar may disproportionately affect marking. 'Coherence', flow, ease of reading essays disproportionately influences most markers. A 'smooth' essay is usually awarded higher marks than a 'jerky' one, even if the content of the latter is much better. Where essays are handwritten in exams, it is not at all easy to edit and adjust along the way, e.g. to go back and rephrase the start of the essay appropriately after the main thrust has been addressed. Handwritten essays in exams are subject to concerns about measuring 'what comes out of a pen' rather than 'what's in a head', and are subject to the effects of speed of writing, legibility, and so on. Handwriting an essay in an exam is quite a different game from composing a word-processed coursework essay, so coursework is poor preparation for the exam experience, and feedback on coursework essays may not help exam candidates.
5 Annotated bibliographies This kind of assessment works best when various elements of the task are specified, including one or more of: • overall word count, preferably with quite tight limits • number of sources to include – preferably an exact number in practice	**Validity**: can link well to learning outcomes about breadth of reading, and prioritizing quality of sources. **Fairness**: can be much better than essays or reports, as high-flying candidates quickly distinguish themselves by the quality of their comments on sources, and their rationale for the sources they choose.	A really useful way to cause learners to read around a topic, rather than just dip into random sources during their studies. 'Wikipedia' (for example) could be allowed to be linked to only one of several required sources.	The easiest sources to find tend to be via Google (especially the first page in a search) and Wikipedia, and it may be necessary to prevent learners from making more than limited use of these sources. Annotated bibliographies essentially require learners to demonstrate their academic literacies, but any lack of relevant information literacies may get in the way of this.

Type of assessment	Status	Advantages	Disadvantages
<ul><li>any expected balance between kinds of sources, e.g. journal articles, reviews, book chapters, web sources</li><li>whether to include (say) four 'given' sources, and four more that individual learners have found</li><li>whether to prioritise the sources in order of any particular aspect, e.g. usefulness, authority, relevance to topic, and so on</li><li>whether the list should be a comparative one, e.g. with pros and cons of each source in the context of the bibliography</li><li>whether there is free choice regarding the 'age' of the sources, e.g. in some contexts it can be useful to ask students to limit contents to sources published within the last three years</li><li>the extent to which the comments on each item should include the learner's own view.</li></ul>	**Whodunit?**: good, as any unwanted collaboration or copying would be fairly obvious (e.g. same sources selected, in same order, and with identical mistakes in the referencing!). **Real world**: high relevance to many careers, where learners will need to be able to review a range of sources and select and justify those most relevant to a given context. **Feedback to learners**: this can be harder to achieve than with some other assessment types, but can be really valuable when done well (e.g. it would have been good for you to have included source 'x' because ...; source 'y' was not a good one to include, because ..., and so on).	Learners can be given the opportunity to demonstrate the breadth of their learning (range of sources) as well as depth (their judgemental comments about respective sources). It can be useful if one of the assessment criteria relates directly to the correct 'citing' of each source (e.g. Harvard system), so that learners gain practice in getting references exactly right, which may be important for future research-related writing. A set of annotated bibliographies can be retained as an online resource, to show future cohorts of learners how to do this task, and for these learners to practise making judgements to establish criteria for their own work. A '300-word annotated bibliography prioritising five sources' can be far faster to mark than an essay where similar literature reviewing was intended – and can be marked much more reliably (fairly) than such an essay.	There is the danger that the extent of sources chosen by learners may mask the depth of thinking about individual sources, therefore it is important to not simply get learners listing a lot of sources. Learners may need some rehearsal before undertaking this sort of task for assessment. For example, a whole-class session could be taken up with learners assessing some past examples of annotated bibliographies, so that they find out how the assessment works in practice before making their own contributions to the genre.

(Continued)

Table 4.3 (Continued)

Type of assessment	Status	Advantages	Disadvantages
6 Reports For example, write-ups of practical work, field work, investigations, and so on. Usually word-processed these days.	**Validity:** can be reasonably high. **Fairness:** not great, but much better than essays. Can allow room for good candidates to shine. **Whodunit?:** can be unsafe, unless other ways of checking are used, e.g. face-to-face quizzing. **Real world:** can be good, report writing is relevant to many careers. **Feedback to learners:** can be useful, but usually comes too late.	Avoids 'sudden death' aspects of assessment, as reports are usually built up over a period of time. Assessment can be broken down usefully, such as agreed proportions of marks for 'Abstract', 'Method', 'Interpretation of Data', 'Conclusions', 'Plans for further work' and so on. Can be on work done collaboratively, but with individual write-up. Learners who write up quickly (before they have forgotten what they actually did) can be advantaged, therefore encouraging good study habits of 'keeping up' and 'avoiding backlogs'.	Word limit may need to be controlled strictly, as long reports would otherwise almost always score more marks than short ones, whereas in the real world a really good short report may be much more useful in practice. There is the danger that learners can spend more time on writing reports than is reflected by the marks they carry overall in the bigger picture of assessment. Those learners who end up with a backlog of reports may spend far too much time catching up on this backlog at the expense of preparing for summative exams, which may carry much more weight in the overall assessment.
7 Portfolios of evidence For example, built up over a period of time on a course or module, often with intermediate feedback opportunities for learners.	**Validity:** can be good, as different elements of a portfolio can relate to each different aspect of evidence of achievement of a range of learning outcomes. **Fairness:** can be good, but different assessors may be looking for different things in a portfolio, in which case fairness can be poorer.	Allows for a wide range of kinds of evidence of achievement, for example drawings, photos, videos, recordings, reviews, reflective commentaries. Can extend well beyond the 'read-write' domain. Can build in opportunities for learners to reflect on their learning, and provide evidence of such reflection.	It can take a very long time to mark a set of portfolios, and they can be very bulky to carry around from one marking place to another (work to home, and so on). Can be difficult to balance marks for portfolios evidencing different strengths.

Type of assessment	Status	Advantages	Disadvantages
In the present climate of 'evidence-based practice', assessment by portfolios is naturally gaining momentum. As can be seen in this table, the 'status' aspects (validity, etc.) are favourable, and there are many advantages, but the crunch comes in the disadvantages column – portfolios take a great deal of time to mark, and there are distinct problems regarding fairness of assessment.	**Whodunit?:** can be questionable, but improved where face-to-face probing is also used. **Real world:** can be better than many other kinds of assessment, depending on what's included in the portfolio specification. **Feedback to learners:** can be good, especially if their progress is reviewed at various times during construction of a portfolio.	Can be interdisciplinary, helping learners to link together aspects of different subjects and topics. Allows candidates to demonstrate originality and creativity. Portfolios can be useful evidence to show prospective employers. Portfolios can be maintained and updated beyond the assessment period.	A big portfolio will normally attract higher marks than a small one, so there is a tendency to reward 'cramming in as much as possible' rather than quality of evidence. One of the most significant dangers with such a 'big' assessment element is non-completion. When portfolio assessment is used, the portfolio may often make up a substantial part of the overall assessment, which can mean for those candidates who are not at their best in this element, assessment is unduly prejudiced against them.
8 Oral exams These are essentially about interrogating individual learners face-to-face, often with two or three assessors present. Sometimes the questions may be about the course or module in general, and/or about a particular submitted element of coursework (for example, a portfolio or dissertation). An oral exam does not necessarily have to be lengthy. Even a five-minute oral exam can be useful to gain assurance about the 'whodunit?' aspect of a portfolio or dissertation. (Note that in many parts of the world there is much more oral assessment than written assessment, as was the case in the UK before written exams started in 1791 towards becoming endemic!)	**Validity:** can be high, but still can favour candidates who can 'talk well' over those who know it just as well but are not so good at 'talking it'. **Fairness:** can be good when successive candidates are asked exactly the same questions (but 'security' of questions needs to be safeguarded, so they don't 'leak' to later candidates). **Whodunit?:** one of the safest kinds of assessment. **Real world:** strong links to the sorts of questioning learners will need to be able to handle in most careers. **Feedback to learners:** can be quick and useful, but also can be stressful and rather transient (e.g. quickly forgotten).	Allows for probing questions, to test real mastery rather than surface learning. Gets over reservations about 'Whodunit?'! Learning pay-off during preparation for an oral exam can be wider, deeper and better than, for example, just writing an essay or report, as anything may be asked. When learners are encouraged to engage in practice and rehearsal, they can learn a great deal from each other, as well as improving their skills relating to oral performance.	Some candidates can be let down by nerves. With a large class of learners, a round of 'orals' can take a lot of time, and 'the word inevitably gets around' about the sort of experience it is going to be. Evidence of achievement as demonstrated orally is somewhat ephemeral, and it can be difficult to think back over several candidates' performance and remember accurately who did better or worse. It can be difficult to guarantee fairness, when different degrees of probing may have been used with different candidates.

(Continued)

Table 4.3 (Continued)

Type of assessment	Status	Advantages	Disadvantages
9 Individual presentations Typically, assessed presentations are given before a relatively small group rather than a large class, in the presence of a tutor (who assesses), but often some peer assessment is built in as well. Sometimes presentations are made by groups, but then it is much harder to allocate credit appropriately to individuals, so for assessed presentations, individual performance is preferable. It is useful if the briefing is really clear to learners in advance, including: • the duration • a range of topics to choose from – or the chance to choose something original • any guidance about supporting materials (e.g. slides, handouts, exhibits) • the assessment criteria • the extent of any 'question and answer' episode after each presentation.	**Validity**: can be good when learning outcomes include oral communication skills. **Fairness**: it can be difficult to maintain fairness during a set of presentations, as there is a tendency for later candidates to learn from earlier ones, and do better. **Whodunit?**: one of the safest forms of assessment. **Real world**: high relevance; in many careers candidates will need the skills involved in giving presentations. **Feedback to learners**: possible to give quick and useful feedback, but this may be somewhat ephemeral and quickly forgotten. Peer feedback during rehearsal can, however, be really valuable.	Allows oral communication skills to be demonstrated alongside mastery of subject matter. Can allow candidates as much time as they need for preparation and rehearsal. Depth of learning tends to be high; learners tend to remember very well things they researched and practised as preparation for a presentation. Can be used in a peer assessment context, where learners can gain a lot from making informed judgements on each other's presentations. Can allow individual learners to demonstrate particular strengths. Can include the opportunity for 'probing' to test depth of knowledge, where questions are posed for a few minutes after each presentation.	It can take a very long time to assess a large number of presentations. Choice of topic can affect marks significantly. What seemed like an interesting and stimulating topic can end up being harder than imagined, and so on. There can be some drift in standards, where 'later' candidates are judged more rigorously than 'earlier' ones, or conversely benefit themselves from seeing earlier presentations. Some candidates can be unduly disadvantaged by nerves. Impression marks associated with the quality of slides or handout materials used during the presentations may overshadow the quality of the actual mastery of the topic concerned. It is sometimes difficult to collect evidence to put forward for moderation (for example, external examiner scrutiny), though recordings can be made for this purpose.

Type of assessment	Status	Advantages	Disadvantages
10 Posters For example, preparation of a visual display in a specified format – e.g. on an A1 sheet – using photos, drawings and text to address a particular brief.	**Validity**: can often be high, allowing good links between evidence of achievement and intended learning outcomes. **Fairness**: likely to be at least some subjectivity when it comes to judgements, but this can be offset by having multiple judgements (possibly peer assessment, and assessment by externals). **Whodunit?**: questionable, as learners may use varying amounts of external help in producing posters, and may collaborate with each other. The whodunit? aspect can be made much better when the assessment also includes learners talking about their poster or being questioned about their poster. **Real world**: visual displays are used in many professions, for example to back up a proposal, or present findings to colleagues. **Feedback to learners**: can be very effective, especially when tutor and peer feedback is offered on drafts in class (i.e. nothing 'secret') before the preparation of the final submission.	Can allow learners flexibility in choice, where they have significant control of the topic and the way they present their findings. Gives room for learners to organise their thinking visually rather than in words alone. Exhibitions of posters can be kept online, and used for future learners as indications of the kinds of evidence they may aim to emulate, and (better) for getting future learners to learn by assessing, before they set out to make their own posters.	It can be really hard to make relative assessment judgements about different topics handled in different ways to different depths. Wealth may come into the picture; learners who can afford good colour printing and photos may be advantaged over those whose resources are more limited. The visual aspects of the poster can dominate too much when being assessed. Judgements on visual evidence such as in posters is always to some extent subjective, with different assessors looking for different things in a 'good' poster. (This problem can be offset by having several assessors, or including one or more externals in the assessment.)

(Continued)

Table 4.3 (Continued)

Type of assessment	Status	Advantages	Disadvantages
11 Artefacts These can include paintings, designs, models, sculptures, items of metalwork, engineering outputs, teaching materials, plans, accounts, prototypes, furniture, display items and so on.	**Validity:** this can be high, where the intended outcome of a particular curriculum element includes the production of specific items. **Fairness:** this can be harder to achieve in assessment of artefacts, as originality and creativity are likely to be among the assessment criteria, and therefore there is bound to be at least some subjectivity in the assessment. **Whodunit?:** on this dimension, artefacts are relatively safe, although there remain possibilities for others to have helped in their production. **Real world:** artefacts often link strongly to the sorts of skills which learners need for particular vocations or careers. **Feedback to learners:** this can be done well, for example, 'things I like best about this example' and 'one suggestion which could have improved this example would have been ....'.	When a course or module involves learners in practical work in workshops or studios, it makes a big difference if the quality of their work there counts towards their overall assessment. The competitiveness which is encouraged by some sort of measure of the quality of the things learners make encourages them to put more effort into their practical work. Artefacts can be retained by learners after assessment, and can be useful evidence of their achievement to show prospective employers. A photographic record of assessed artefacts (or the artefacts themselves if not needed by their creators) can provide the next cohort of learners with valuable targets to aim towards – and exceed.	Where some learners may have benefited from external help in the production of artefacts, the fairness of assessment can be compromised. When individuals are to be assessed on the basis of artefacts they produce, collaboration between learners is discouraged, and may deprive them of things they could have learned from and with each other. It can sometimes be difficult to work out how much the assessment of artefacts should contribute to the overall assessment of a particular curriculum element. Where some learners have special needs which limit how well they can produce particular kinds of artefact, it can be difficult to make 'reasonable adjustments' to allow them alternative assessment possibilities.

These platforms can do a lot of the routine management of assessment submission, which can be particularly advantageous with large cohorts of students. Receipts dating submission times can be automatically sent to students. Some of these platforms allow for students to review each other's assignments and give feedback to each other. Some allow for feedback from tutors to be made online. Figure 4.4 shows a series of 'tradeoffs' – in other words differences between web-based assessment and traditional tutor marking, to be considered when deciding the advantages and drawbacks of either kind of assessment.

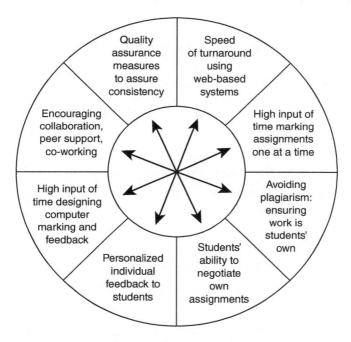

Figure 4.4 Tradeoffs: computer-designed assessment versus hand-marked assessment

TOWARDS ASSESSMENT *AS* LEARNING

It is widely accepted that in higher education internationally, assessment drives students' learning. As a consequence, students become ever more strategic, and only put energy into things that count towards their overall assessment. The section which follows offers you a practical way of setting about reflecting on the assessment processes and instruments *you* use. Many institutions have now adopted 'assessment for learning' approaches, to make better links between assessment and learning. I argue here that we can go even further and work towards 'assessment *as* learning', where all of our elements of assessment are designed with learning at the centre of our thinking.

This section provides you with a scoring grid, which you can use to interrogate your own assessment elements and determine how well they measure up to a combination of 'assessment for learning' and 'assessment as learning'.

Assessment design: seven key terms to address

In this chapter we've already explored five key variables: *validity, fairness, who-dunit?, transparency* and *real-world links.* Now I'd like you to extend this thinking by adding two more factors (which have, of course, already entered into the discussion of assessment presented in this chapter):

- *manageability* – both for us as assessors and for learners themselves

- *inclusiveness* – ensuring that no particular categories of learners are disadvantaged significantly by each particular assessment format being used.

Too often, terms such as these seven are explained in language which does not make addressing them any easier. Also, addressing them all at once is rarely possible, and is at the very least a highly complex balancing act. Later in this section, I will provide straightforward briefings to help you to interrogate your own assessment elements in terms of how well each of these variables is successfully addressed.

Linking assessment to the processes underpinning successful learning

We need to set out to address, in our assessment design, the seven factors underpinning successful learning:

1 *Wanting* to learn.

2 Taking ownership of the *need* to learn.

3 *Learning by doing*: practice, trial and error, experimenting, experience, repetition when appropriate.

4 Learning from *feedback*: praise, criticism, seeing the results of learning.

5 *Making sense* of what is being learned: 'getting one's head around it', 'light dawning'.

6 *Verbalizing orally – explaining* to others, *coaching* others and *teaching* what has been learned.

7 *Making informed judgements* on one's own work, other people's work, self-assessment and peer assessment.

Within the grid which follows (see Figure 4.5), there are 20 decisions to be made for each assessment element of a course or module. The grid contains space to interrogate four separate assessment elements, but it is suggested that you start with a single element (Element A), and work through the discussion which follows first, using this element (as rehearsal) before returning to further elements of assessment. In this discussion 'element of assessment' simply means any assessed task or activity which counts towards the overall award being studied for, and has marks or grades associated with the level of performance students show in it. Typical examples include those shown below, but any other assessment elements can be considered.

Written exam	Drawing	Oral exam
Presentation	Sculpture	Interview
MCQ exam	Dance	Short-answer exam
Essay	OSCE	Written reflection
Practical test	In-tray exam	Report

For each of the 20 lines of the grid, a decision is to be made on a 1–5 scale: 5 is where the design of the assessment element fits very well indeed with 'assessment as learning' as a goal, or is of very high quality in the context of the variables of 'validity', 'fairness', and so on. In each case, the discussion which follows provides guidance on how decisions may be made on this 1–5 scale.

Why 1–5 rather than 0–5?

The scale begins at 1 so that an assessment element which is very poor at addressing the assessment variables, and has very little to do with 'assessment as learning', can still have a score. The minimum total score is 20, which can be said to describe an assessment element which has little to do with anything other than assessment *of* learning, and was also poor regarding validity, fairness, and so on.

Why are all the 20 lines interrogated on the same scale of 1–5?

The scale is used as a first approximation towards balancing the 20 factors considered towards an overall judgement of how well the assessment element approaches the goal of 'assessment as learning'. It is likely that adjustments to this 'equal rating' position will be desirable in future. This grid is simply meant as a starting point towards interrogating assessment on a complex and interrelated set of variables, in a relatively straightforward manner.

Why not just fill in the grid straightaway, without reading further to find out how?

You may, in fact, wish to do this for a chosen element of assessment, and then revisit each item in turn on the basis of the discussion which follows for each line of the grid, to self-assess how well your instinct about your assessment element lines up with the thinking behind the scoring suggestions made in the discussion which follows. However, the meanings of terms such as 'validity', 'fairness', and so on may need to be further clarified in the context of this exercise to allow you to make informed judgements as you interrogate your own assessment elements, and for your scores to be compared to others' scores for their assessment elements, and so on. Furthermore, you would be wise to consult your students to help you make a scoring decision for several of the items in the grid.

Another reason not to fill the grid in straightaway is that relatively familiar variables, such as validity and fairness, are interspersed with factors relating to the quality of learning associated with the assessment, and the final three lines of the grid refer to the place of this particular assessment element in the overall assessment pattern for the course or module. So the discussion which follows takes you through the agenda in a manner that is intentionally non-linear.

Guidance on making your 1–5 scoring decisions for each item

1 Students love it (wanting to learn)

If the assessment element is one that students dread (possibly a traditional exam) this might warrant a score of 1 – the minimum. If it's the sort of assessment which students really look forward to, and enjoy doing while they are performing it, that would be nearer a 5. Of course, different students will have different views about how much they enjoy any particular form of assessment, so you may like to ask 20 or more students and average their views to help you make your 1–5 decision here.

2 Students learn by doing while preparing for it

This line is about the kind of learning students perform leading up to the assessment (and to some extent also any learning they achieve while actually doing the assessment). The minimum score of 1 would be warranted by any assessment where students merely 'filled their heads up with information' ready to regurgitate it during the assessment itself. This might apply to some traditional written exams in some disciplines, and equally to some kinds of essay or report where the learning by doing is quickly forgotten after the task is completed. Higher scores may be associated with useful practice, problem-solving, explaining things to each other (or to anyone else who would listen), learning by getting things wrong and finding out exactly why, and so on. Decide as honestly as you can the extent to which students' learning is active while preparing for this particular assessment element on the usual scale: 1–5. If you can, ask students themselves.

3 Students make sense of their learning while preparing for it

This is linked to but is sufficiently different from item 2 above to warrant a separate line on the grid. This is more about *how permanently* students get their heads around things in the way that this assessment causes them to prepare for it. A low score might be warranted if students simply prepare themselves in a way where they are 'OK on the day' and then let their learning slip, perhaps quite intentionally, as they prepare for the next assessment on their schedule. A high score for this item would be where you know that most students prepare for this assessment in a way which really consolidates their learning (and not merely that you *intend* them to prepare in such a way!). You may indeed wish to check this out with a sample of students.

Assessment element	A	B	C	D
Your name:				
Course or module:				
Assessment element A:				
Assessment element B:				
Assessment element C:				
Assessment element D:				
Assessment element	**A**	**B**	**C**	**D**
Factors relating to the particular assessment element in isolation				
1 Students love it (wanting to learn)				
2 Students learn by doing while preparing for it				
3 Students make sense of their learning while preparing for it				
4 Students verbalize orally when preparing for it				
5 Students practise making informed judgements				
6 Students design the criteria				
7 Students own the weighting of the criteria				
8 Validity				
9 Fairness				
10 Transparency				
11 Whodunit?				
12 Real-world relevance				
13 Manageability – efficiency for students				
14 Manageability – efficiency for you				
15 Inclusiveness				
16 Students get *and use* feedback as a result of it				
17 Alignment: how well it links visibly to learning outcomes				
Factors relating to the particular assessment element in the overall context				
18 Students use several ways of communicating and explaining				
19 Diversity: overall range of assessment types				
20 The 'wow' factor, as gained from student feedback				
Total/100				

Figure 4.5   Towards assessment as learning: the 'interrogation' grid

4 Students verbalise orally when preparing for it

This time, the student activity represented by this item is quite explicit. If students are involved in coaching or teaching each other as they work towards this assessment, the score could be as high as 5. If they prepare entirely on their own, in solemn isolation, it could be 1. If they're involved in discussing, explaining to each other, and so on, the score could be nearer 5. Remember, it's what students actually do that governs the score for this, and not necessarily what you *hope* they do. Ask them.

5 Students practise making informed judgements

If students' preparation for this assessment centres mainly around self-assessing their own learning and peer-assessing the products of fellow students' learning, this would score a 5. If this assessment does not involve students making informed judgements in such ways, it's more likely to be a 1. If students do at least some self-assessment or peer assessment, the score might be somewhere between 1 and 5. Making informed judgements on material from the literature is, of course, still useful (perhaps warranting a score of 2 or 3), but almost certainly less intense an experience than self-assessing their own work, or peer-assessing each other's work, where their judgements need to be able to be supported by feedback to each other.

6 Students design the criteria

This relates particularly to the extent to which students 'take ownership of the need to learn'. When they have worked together to establish the criteria, the assessment is much more 'owned' by them. When they are using self-assessment and peer assessment, using criteria whose design they have shaped, the ownership is at its best, and a 5 might be warranted for this item. If students have merely been given the 'official criteria', the score might only be 2 or so, and if students have no idea of the exact nature of the criteria, the minimum of 1 might be appropriate here.

7 Students own the weighting of the criteria

While this might at first sight seem to overlap with item 6 above, the process of students sorting out what is important and what isn't, in their design of the criteria, has so much to do with their 'making sense' of the topic that this criterion deserves a line of its own. If students have collectively worked out the marking scheme, a 5 may be warranted for this line, especially if this was done in the context of something they self-assessed or peer-assessed.

8 Validity

The crux here is the answer to the question 'Is this assessment really measuring what it is intended to measure?' rather than 'Is it simply measuring what happens to be easily measurable?'. For example, a traditional unseen written exam might score a 1 here, if it is just measuring what students can do on their own, in a quiet room, with what comes out of their heads and gets through in handwriting on to their answer scripts legibly enough to score them marks. That said, a written maths exam measures quite well whether students can do maths, and a problem-solving kind of exam does measure whether students can solve some kinds of problems, and the scores could be higher for this item.

However, higher scores may be more readily warranted on the grounds of validity for assessments such as an OSCE (objective structured clinical exam), as used by medical students, where what is measured is essentially what practitioners are intended to be able to do, such as interpreting a set of X-rays, scanning a patient's case notes to arrive at a prescription, talking to a patient (an actor in practice) to work out what is wrong, and so on. Similarly, a presentation may have high validity as an assessment format, if students not only need to master some learning but also to present it authoritatively and clearly to others. An oral exam (viva) may also score highly on validity, if it is felt that this is the most effective way of determining the extent of students' learning. Furthermore, an exam of the 'in-tray' variety may also score highly, as this depends on students making a series of informed decisions based on information supplied to them over the time of the exam.

9 Fairness

This would attract the minimum score of 1 for an assessment element where there are known to be problems regarding two or more people agreeing on the mark or grade for students' work (not least, essays!), but also in forms of assessment which may be more valid than essays, notably portfolios, but where different assessors can often come to quite different judgements. Even dissertations fare quite badly regarding fairness, as different assessors often look for different things while assessing them, and their overall marks can be influenced disproportionately by the presence or lack of particular things. A high score for this item might be associated with, for example, a multiple-choice test or exam, where the scoring is no longer likely to be influenced by human frailty (though the question design may still be!).

10 Transparency

This is about the extent to which students know how the assessment works, and how exactly it is marked, and how scores or grades are reached. If, as far as the students are concerned, it is a 'black box' assessment – they do their best, then find out if that was good enough – the assessment element probably merits the minimum score of 1 here. If it's something where students have had practice at marking examples you've given them, or better still their own or each other's work, the score may be a 5, if they feel they know exactly how the assessment works. It is important to distinguish between 'transparency' and 'familiarity'. For example, students can be quite familiar with traditional exams, while still not knowing exactly how they are marked. The same often goes for essays, dissertations and reports. 'Transparency' here is about how well students have a grasp of what will be going on in the minds of their assessors as they come to assessment judgements about their work.

11 Whodunit?

This is in part about how well the assessment avoids plagiarism. Here, a traditional exam might score a 5, if precautions are sufficient to ensure that no one can substitute for candidates. Similarly, a solo presentation or an oral exam (viva) may score 5 as an assessment element. Assessment formats where plagiarism is possible score much lower on this item, including essays, reports, dissertations and other written work, where it is possible for students to copy other people's work, buy or download work from the internet, and so on. In rating your assessment element on 'whodunit?', it is perhaps wisest to step back from any feelings of 'I'm sure none of my students would do this', or 'The anti-plagiarism software makes this highly unlikely', as the most skilled plagiarists are never caught! For this item, it is best to consider the *possibility* rather than the *probability* of plagiarism occurring when deciding your 1–5 score.

12 Real-world relevance

This is about how well the assessment element links to the real-world professions students may be qualifying to enter. For example, doctors, lawyers, accountants and managers hardly spend their working lives *writing* about medicine, law, accountancy or management – they *do* it, rather than write about it. So essays are likely to score a 1 in disciplines such as these, and in several others.

At the other end of the scale, OSCEs (objective structured clinical exams) in medical education are likely to deserve a 5 here, if they are designed to be what doctors need to be able to show that they can do, not just write about. The practical part of a driving test would be high on real-world authenticity, whereas the theory part which accompanies such a test in some countries is more of a memory test and less well-linked to authenticity. (Do you still remember the stopping distance at 50 miles per hour on a wet road?)

13 Manageability – efficiency for students

This is essentially about the value of the time spent by students preparing for the assessment. You may need to ask a sample of your students about your particular assessment element to help you towards your 1–5 rating for this item. How much time do they know they *waste* in their preparations for this assessment? How do they see their time-efficiency relating to this item of assessment in the overall context of the bigger picture of their total assessment menu? Both of their answers to these questions need to be informed by how much this assessment element *counts* overall. The score for this item could be as low as 1 if students feel it takes them forever to prepare for this assessment element, compared to other elements contributing to their overall assessment.

14 Manageability – efficiency for you

Whereas in many of the other items on the grid you may need to consult students to help you decide how assessment links to their experience of learning, this time you will know only too well how much time and energy the assessment element takes from you. Perhaps one factor to help you decide your 1–5 score for this item is how well you think the time you spend marking this element is spent, considering the contribution of the element to students' overall award. For example, if the element involves you in marking a large pile of essays or reports, but only contributes 5 per cent or less to the overall award for students, the score will probably need to be a 1! If it's a computer-based multiple-choice exam for a large cohort of students, even if the design time was very significant, but the marking is automated, the score may be nearer a 5.

15 Inclusiveness

This is a very complex issue. Its significance may depend a great deal on the composition of the student group, and to some extent on the size. Factors which may need to be considered here include:

- how well the assessment provides a level playing field for students learning in a second language

- the extent to which the assessment may disadvantage students with particular needs, such as dyslexia, visual impairments, hearing impairments, and so on

- whether some particular students, for whatever reason, are less successful than their optimum in this particular kind of assessment.

For this item, therefore, you will need to bear all manner of factors in mind when deciding your rating for 'inclusiveness' on the 1–5 scale. Sometimes you will have a very clear idea of how well the assessment concerned provides a level playing field for the particular student cohort, and at other times you may need to make judgements as best you can on the basis of what you know about the students.

16 Students get and use feedback as a result of it

The key words here are 'and use'; we all know how common it is for students to get feedback and fail to use it. For summative assessment elements, students often get little feedback (perhaps just a pass/fail award, or a score or a grade), and for this item the score may only be 1. Then there are the cases where students get quite a lot of feedback, but the feedback comes too late for them to put it to any real use – that too may warrant a 1 score. Or there may be cases where students don't seem to take any notice of the feedback, or don't even pick up their marked work containing feedback – that too could warrant a score of 1. Some forms of assessment are much richer in feedback than others (including student peer assessment and student presentations to an audience), and you will need to take this into account when working out the score for this item.

Of course all students are different, and some may be making good use of the feedback they get, while others make much less use of it, so for the assessment element concerned you may need to consider an averaged score for this item.

17 Alignment: how well it links visibly to learning outcomes

This links both to the perceived quality of the design of the assessment and also to how well students have information about the targets they are meant to attain, as can be expressed through well-used, intended learning outcomes. In particular, this boils down to how aware students are of the kinds of evidence of achievement which will be measured by the assessment. When curriculum is validated or reviewed, either internally or externally (for example, by professional bodies), the alignment to learning outcomes is often required to be made more explicit. This also links to the extent to which students have developed ownership of the need to learn.

If students are not aware of the intended learning outcomes, or don't realize that such outcomes reflect their attainment targets, the score for this item is likely to be 1. If students are fully aware of the links, the score could be closer to 5. The score you decide could be regarded as a measure of the 'constructive alignment' of the assessment element in the context of students' learning, and the design of the curriculum as a whole.

18 Students use several ways of communicating and explaining

This item (along with 19 and 20 below) refers to the overall picture of assessment elements A to D (or more), so when you make your decision for assessment element A, you need to think about the nature of B, C and D as well. A single assessment may well focus on just one method of students communicating their learning, for example in writing or orally or in group contexts or online, and so on. And even 'in writing' can take many forms, for example unseen written exams, coursework essays and reports, written reviews, written reflections, and so on. If all of the assessment elements use very similar ways of students communicating their learning, the score for this item might be as low as 1 for each of the elements involved. If overall there is a rich mix in how students communicate their learning, the score could be 5.

19 Diversity: overall range of assessment types

This item also refers to the overall picture of the complete set of assessment elements for the course or module. Every assessment format disadvantages some students. Therefore, the more variety of forms of assessment making up the overall picture, the less likely that the same students will be repeatedly disadvantaged by any one format. The score for this item needs also to be considered in terms of the extent to which any particular assessment format dominates the overall picture. For example, if a written exam counts for 80 per cent or more of the overall award, the score for diversity should be as low as 1. If there is a mix of four quite different forms of assessment, each counting for 25 per cent overall, a score of 5 may be justified. Note that there is a danger in attempts to achieve diversity of assessment of ending up with *too much* assessment (affecting the two 'manageability' items addressed earlier). It is best to work towards diversity by appropriately reducing the size of assessment elements as the range is broadened.

20 The 'wow' factor, as gained from student feedback

This too refers to the overall picture of the assessment of the course or module, but this time in terms of students' *feelings* about the assessment element concerned. Of all the measures in this grid, this is necessarily the most subjective one! However, it is linked to the value of the assessment as a positive driving force for students' learning, and links in its own way to the enhancement of their 'want' to learn the subject matter linked to the assessment element, but even more to the actual learning pay-off they derive while preparing for, and then undertaking, the assessment element. It is likely that only the occasional assessment element will, in practice, attract a 'wow' factor score from students, but when it does, it is important to recognize it.

Interpretation of scores for this exercise

Linking assessment firmly to learning can be regarded as one of the most complex of our tasks in higher education. In many of my workshops since 2009, I have talked participants through each item of the grid in turn (and in different orders), and then invited them to add up their scores for the assessment element they chose to interrogate. Quite often, traditional forms of assessment have scored considerably lower (for example, scores in the 30s) than more innovative forms, which have sometimes scored as high as the mid-80s. Putting the grid to work with staff in higher education is showing that this attempt to interrogate assessment design can be a valuable prelude to working systematically towards 'assessment *as* learning', as it causes staff to reflect very deeply on the design of their assessment elements. I hope that this exercise helps you to think critically and developmentally in ways which will assist your own assessment design, not only to make learning happen better for your students, but also develop your assessments to rate highly in such dimensions as validity, fairness, and so on.

It is hoped that this step-by-step process of trying to analyse 20 separate aspects of assessment design may contribute towards making assessment a more efficient and effective driver leading to better student learning.

Towards assessment becoming a *better* driver for learning

Let me end this chapter by returning to some tactics which can play their part in helping to bring assessment closer to our intention to make learning happen. First, ten suggestions for tutors (and then at the very end, ten tips for students themselves).

1 *Diversify assessment more and move away from overuse of just two or three assessment formats.* In particular, we need to ensure that our assessment systems do not end up just measuring how skilled (or unskilled) our learners are in a limited range of assessment contexts, such as *just* a mixture of time-constrained, unseen written exams, tutor-marked essays and reports.

2 *Make assessment fit for purpose so that we measure what we really should be measuring – not just ghosts of learners' learning.* We need to revisit the validity of each and every form of assessment we employ, and choose those which are good at measuring suitable evidence showing what students have really learned.

3 *Make assessment a high-learning pay-off experience for learners by making the most of feedback to students.* We need to think ahead to how we will give feedback to students after each element of assessment, and to how useful that feedback can be, even when the main purposes of assessment are summative rather than formative.

4 *Reduce the burden of assessment for learners and for ourselves.* We have got our education systems into a state where assessment all too often militates against deep learning and takes much of the enjoyment out of learning. Reducing the amount quite dramatically – by a factor of three or four perhaps – can be part of the pathway towards increasing the quality of assessment and the usefulness of associated feedback to learners.

5 *Assess evidence of what learners have learned, not just what we have tried to teach them.* It may be instinctive to try to find out what students have learned as a direct result of what we have tried to teach, but there should be more to assessment than this. We need to be able to credit learners for their achievements in learning which they have done for themselves and with each other.

6 *Assess students' evidence of their learning more fairly.* Most assessors are aware that assessment is rarely an exact science, yet with so much depending on the marks and grades we award learners, we need to be constantly striving to make each assessment element as fair as we can, so we can make learners feel more assured that they are being assessed justly – and so that employers and others can have more trust in the results of our assessments.

7 *Focus learning outcomes on 'need-to-know' rather than 'nice-to-know' material – and stop measuring things which are 'nuts to know'!* Too often, it is possible to look at what is really being measured by an exam question or assignment and find ourselves asking 'Why on earth are we causing learners to learn this bit?' Sometimes, our reply to ourselves – if we're honest – is as banal as 'Well, at least this lends itself to being measured!' Not a good enough reason. What is measured by assessment should be easily recognized as being important, not just interesting.

8 *Measure 'know-how' and 'know-why' much more, and 'know-what' much less.* In other words, move learning away from information recall and regurgitation,

and strive to use assessment to encourage learners to make sense of what they have learned, and towards being able to explain it and apply it rather than merely describe it.

9 *Involve learners in assessing their own and each other's work to deepen their learning, and help them to get their heads around how we conduct assessment.* The more learners know about how assessment really works, the better they can do themselves justice in preparing for it and demonstrating their learning back to us. There is no better way than helping them to develop self-assessment and peer assessment skills, to deepen their learning and acclimatize them to the assessment culture they are part of.

10 *Get our wording right in our outcomes, briefings, tasks and criteria – write them all in English, not in 'academese'.* Too often, whether in exams or other assessment contexts, learners who are skilled at working out exactly what our assessment tasks actually *mean* achieve better results than equally deserving learners who are not so skilled. Teaching is about effective communication, not playing word games.

 Tips for students: assessments

These tips may help your students do better in assessment, and may make your work as an assessor rather happier. Better still, fine-tune and add to these tips before giving them to your students.

1 *You're assessed on what you show, not on what you know.* (Of course, if you don't know it, you've got very little chance of showing it anyway, but the problem is knowing it and not managing to show it; just knowing it is far too risky). Whatever form of assessment you're preparing for, practise giving evidence of what you know – writing it, talking it, repeating it, and gaining speed and confidence in showing it when it matters (such as in exams).

2 *With any kind of assessment, read the briefing properly.* You're measured on how well you do exactly what is being asked. You're not measured on all the things you might do that aren't asked for. Even in an exam, keep looking back at the question, and make sure you're still answering it and not going off on a flight of fancy.

3 *Keep your eyes and ears open for clues and cues.* You can work out a lot about what is going to be assessed from things said by tutors, and from syllabus documentation (look at the intended learning outcomes, for example), and from all the information you can dig up about past assessments or exams. When possible, also talk to some students who've already succeeded on the course or module.

4 *Build your own question bank.* Collect and compose lots and lots of short, sharp questions to practise answering. The more often you've answered a question (in writing, in speaking, any way you wish) the faster and better you get at answering it. Exams, for example, really just measure how practised you have become at answering exam questions, rather than how much you know.

(Continued)

(Continued)

5 *With coursework, be your own editor.* The mark you get for coursework depends on the edition you hand in. You can do a lot of improving by editing several times before you hand it in, each version getting just a bit better. Editing on a computer is so easy, but save it as something different every time – don't risk losing something you may want to go back to. Besides, if you've edited your material well all the way along, there won't be any obvious errors left (spelling, grammar, and so on). Such errors would have given the impression it's a hasty last-minute attempt – not likely to put any assessor into a generous mood!

6 *Get ahead of schedule.* Fend off dangers of crises, illness or anything unexpected getting in the way of your progress. With coursework, it can be really good to draft it really early, put it away for a week or two, then edit it all the better by being able to have a fresh look at what you actually wrote, and seeing how much you can improve it to turn it into what you meant to write. This is much happier than wasting a lot of time putting off the evil moment of getting stuck into it.

7 *Talk a lot to fellow learners.* Talk about the work you're doing. Listen to them – you'll get ideas which will make your own work better. Explain things to them – every time you explain something you become better at explaining it, and can do so better when you come to do your own assessed work. But beware – make sure that (if it's coursework) when you come to do it in earnest, it's *your* work. The earlier talking is to help you get your head around it – but your assessed work needs to be about how well your head has now got round it.

8 *Use all the feedback you can get.* Take particular note of previous feedback from tutors. Things they liked may well increase your marks in future work. Things they didn't like may well be worth avoiding in future. Feedback needs to be used – otherwise it's wasted. Past critical feedback is really, really useful.

9 *Before you hand in coursework, have yet another good look at the instructions.* Check that you've followed these really closely. Check any briefings on word count, layout and, particularly, what exactly is asked for. It can even be worth doing a quick spell-check on someone else's machine, in case (like me) you've accidentally taught your own machine some incorrect spellings!

10 *Before you hand in coursework – do one more thing.* Mark it yourself! Apply the assessment criteria yourself. You will often find out, in time, about marks you would have lost if you hadn't done this bit of self-assessment. If you haven't got the criteria, make some up on the basis of experience. Then make final improvements to your work so that it scores marks against all the likely criteria.

Some of the resources in this chapter are available to print for your own use on the companion website. To access these, along with some video clips of the author, please visit: **www.sagepub.co.uk/makinglearninghappen**

CHAPTER 5

LEARNING THROUGH FEEDBACK

🔑 Key topics in this chapter

- Feed-forward
- National Student Survey
- Written, printed, on-screen
- Face-to-face oral
- Efficiency
- Timing: 24 hours!
- Language of feedback

Already in this book, feedback has been identified as one of the seven principal factors underpinning successful learning. Feedback should interact with the other factors continuously, as follows:

- Feedback should help learners to *make sense* of what they have done.

- Feedback should help learners to clarify and take ownership of the *need* to learn as defined by the evidence of achievement of the intended learning outcomes defining their studies.

- Feedback ideally should enhance learners' *want* to learn by increasing their self-esteem and confidence whenever possible, and by helping them to believe that they can indeed achieve the intended learning outcomes *and* demonstrate this in ways where they will be duly credited for this achievement.

- Feedback should motivate learners to move forward into their next episodes of *learning by doing* and focus their efforts more sharply towards bringing the experience from their past work to bear on making their next work better.

- Feedback gained while *explaining, coaching* and even *teaching* fellow learners can add enormously to learners' mastery of what they have learned, and increase their confidence as they work towards communicating their knowledge in formal assessments.

- Involving learners in *assessing – making informed judgements* can open up to them a great deal of further feedback on how their learning is progressing, and how well they are becoming able to provide evidence of their achievement in each of the forms which will make up their overall assessment.

FEEDBACK OR FEED-FORWARD?

Some writers already use the term 'feed-forward' to describe those aspects of feedback which particularly point towards what to do next, rather than merely looking backwards at what has (or has not) already been achieved by learners. Hounsell (2008) described feed-forward as follows:

> Feedforward is a strategy that aims to 'increase the value of feedback to the students by focusing comments not only on the past and present ... but also on the future – what the student might aim to do, or do differently in the next assignment or assessment if they are to continue to do well or to do better'. (Hounsell, 2008: 5)

Feed-forward can offer help along the following lines:

- Details of what would have been necessary to achieve better marks or grades, expressed in ways where learners can seek to improve their future assignments or answers.

- Praise relating to things which learners have done really well, so that they don't simply shrug off their success, but take on board what to *continue* to do well in future assignments and assessment contexts.

- Direct suggestions for learners to try out in their next piece of work to overcome problems or weaknesses arising in their last assignment.

- Suggestions about sources to explore, illustrating chosen aspects of what they themselves are being encouraged to do in their own future work.

Feed-forward can be regarded as *formative* – in other words, pointing towards improving and developing future work. This contrasts with *summative* feedback, referring back principally to what was – and what was not – achieved in past work. Ideally, feedback needs to achieve both purposes, but the danger is that it sometimes is not sufficiently formative and is too dominated by summative comments.

IS FEEDBACK BROKEN TOO?

In Chapter 4, it was argued that assessment is broken in higher education. The same arguments extend to feedback, as very often it is linked to assessment. For example, in the National Student Survey, administered to all final-year students every year in the UK since 2005, in the section on 'assessment and feedback', statements 7, 8 and 9 link directly to students' experience of feedback. Students are asked to make judgements as follows: 'definitely agree', 'mostly agree', 'neither agree nor disagree', 'mostly disagree', 'definitely disagree', or 'not applicable' on each of the following three statements:

7 Feedback on my work has been prompt.

8 I have received detailed comments on my work.

9 Feedback on my work has helped me clarify things I did not understand.

As with the survey results on assessment, students' responses about feedback have continued to show that this is one of the least satisfactory areas in their overall experience of higher education. Many institutions in the UK have taken action to try to improve students' perceptions of the value of feedback, but the problem still continues to perplex staff. It could be argued that:

- Students are right about statement 7, feedback is often *not* prompt. Even with turnaround times for assessed work being prescribed by institutions, it is often weeks before students get their marked work back. Later in this chapter, I suggest ways of speeding up substantially at least some of the feedback we give to students.

- Staff often defend themselves by saying 'But students didn't take any notice of the detailed comments I put on their work', or 'Some of them didn't even bother to collect their marked work'. This is at least partly due to the mark being more important in students' minds than the feedback. Later in this chapter I suggest ways round this problem.

- One of the roles of formative feedback is indeed to help students to clarify things that they did not understand. However, written comments on students' work play only a limited role in this mission. Face-to-face feedback plays a more important role, and in the context of the survey, students may be forgiven for thinking the 'feedback' refers only to the written comments rather than the rest of the feedback they get from tutors. Moreover, in the context of the factors underpinning successful learning, feedback is only part of the toolkit available to us for helping students to clarify things they didn't understand. We need to be adopting all of the tactics available to us for helping them to make sense of what they're learning, not least getting *them* to make informed judgements on their work, and not just leave that to us.

Now that students in England, for example, are presently paying around £9,000 per academic year for tuition fees in universities, unsurprisingly they regard formative feedback as a very important aspect of tuition, and the pressure on tutors to provide timely and useful feedback is increased even further.

FEEDBACK, ACHIEVEMENT AND FAILURE

There is now a substantial and rich literature on the potential role of feedback in formative assessment contexts. This section of the chapter focuses on just a few important sources of wisdom and expertise on using feedback to make learning happen in post-compulsory education. Positive feedback brings few problems to learners or to staff giving it. However, it is the feedback on unsuccessful work which causes most heartache to staff and learners alike. Peelo (2002) writes tellingly on the difficult subject of failure, as follows:

> However correctly dealt with by the system, a student who is failing in a system which is built on academic success may well experience a sense of isolation and strangeness. Similarly, few students suddenly and unexpectedly fail academically – there is usually prior warning. For many, *failing is not an event but a series of hesitations*, a combination of moments of failure. For others, *experiencing failure is not about external criteria, but about falling below their own, personal standards*. Externally, everything may be fine and they may well be passing their courses successfully. But internally, the pressure and striving can be enormous. If something else goes wrong in life then the fragile structures which support such students through university assignments can begin to crumble. (Peelo, 2002: 2, emphasis in original)

The key to all this is of course timely, helpful and supportive feedback. Bowl (2003: 93) illustrates poignantly, through student quotes, the need they have for such feedback. For example, one of the case studies around which her book is written includes the following scenario:

> Planning assignments is my worst, it's my weakness definitely. I can say what I want to put in it, but it's how do I do it? What comes top, second, third? I know I can write. It's just that initial help to say that should go first, second or whatever. Once I've got that, I can do an assignment ... Some give you guidelines, and some don't. It's like, how do you want us to write this? How do you want us to do it? I would go out and know how to work practically. But writing, it's like – what do you want? ... It's getting it structured the way that it suits them and suits their needs. (Sandra, first-year student)

But what makes feedback work to make learning happen? Knight and Yorke (2003) explain it thus:

> Formative assessment can clearly be said to have 'worked' if the student demonstrates having learned as a result of the feedback provided. This requires that the student has a concept of learning that allows them to take in what the assessor has sought to convey and they then act on the basis of this developed understanding. (Knight and Yorke, 2003: 135)

It is also argued that it is the lower fliers who are most in need of feedback, for example Bandura (1997: 217) argues: 'The less individuals believe in themselves, the more they need explicit, proximal, and frequent feedback of progress that provides repeated affirmations of their growing capabilities'.

Knight and Yorke (2003) have a wealth of useful food for thought concerning the role of feedback in formative assessment. They describe the purposes of formative assessment in general as follows:

1 To give credit for what has been done, with reference to the expected standard.

2 To correct what is wrong, thereby helping the student to avoid repeating the error (hence merely saying that something is wrong is insufficient).

3 To encourage emancipation by alerting the student to possibilities which they may not have hitherto discerned. (Knight and Yorke, 2003: 35)

It can be argued that giving learners feedback is just about the most important dimension of the work of teachers in post-compulsory education, second only perhaps to that of making assessment judgements which can affect the future careers and lives of our learners. But perhaps all told, formative feedback is *the* vital dimension as, given at the right time and in the best possible way, it can lead learners steadily towards successful achievement in summative assessment contexts.

Among Sadler's many valuable contributions to the literature on feedback is the following extract:

> Giving students detailed feedback about the strengths and weaknesses of their work, with suggestions for improvement, is becoming common practice in higher education. However, *for many students, feedback seems to have little or no impact*, despite the considerable time and effort put into its production. With a view to increasing its effectiveness, extensive theoretical and empirical research has been carried out into its structure, timing and other parameters. For students to be able to apply feedback, they need to understand the meaning of the feedback statements. They also need to *identify, with near certainty, the particular aspects of their work that need attention*. For these to occur, students must possess critical background knowledge. This article sets out the nature of that knowledge and

how students can acquire it. They must appropriate for themselves three fundamental concepts – task compliance, quality and criteria – and also develop a cache of relevant tacit knowledge. (Sadler, 2010: 535, emphasis added)

Nicol and MacFarlane-Dick (2006) propose seven principles for good feedback practice as follows:

Good feedback practice:

1. Helps clarify what good performance is (goals, criteria, expected standards);
2. Facilitates the development of self-assessment (reflection) in learning;
3. Delivers high quality information to students about their learning;
4. Encourages teacher and peer dialogue around learning;
5. Encourages positive motivational beliefs and self-esteem;
6. Provides opportunities to close the gap between current and desired performance;
7. Provides information to teachers that can be used to help shape the teaching. (Nicol and MacFarlane-Dick, 2006: 205)

The research literature on feedback confirms the importance of formative feedback as a vital step in successful learning, with Sadler recommending 'conversations' and Nicol and MacFarlane-Dick advocating dialogue, but it remains well known that presently the most commonly used methods of getting feedback to students in higher education simply don't work at all well – particularly written comments on their work. At my own workshops I frequently suggest that feedback on paper is probably the most time-wasting, least effective and most dangerous way to give students feedback.

VARIETIES OF FORMATIVE FEEDBACK

What sorts of feedback can help to make learning happen more successfully? There are many ways in which feedback can reach learners, each with advantages and disadvantages. Perhaps the more *different* ways we use to get feedback to learners, the more likely we are to ensure that they receive at least some feedback in ways which suit their own personal approaches to learning.

Written, printed and on-screen feedback

All this can be regarded as feedback in the 'read-write' domain of Neil Fleming's VARK® inventory (2001–13). Such feedback can take many forms, including:

- handwritten comments directly entered on to learners' work

- summary overall comments on learners' assignments – handwritten, word-processed or emailed directly to learners

- model answers or specimen solutions, giving feedback to learners on what may have been looked for in their own work

- generic feedback on a batch of learner work, in print, emailed to all learners, or put up on an electronic discussion list, virtual learning environment or computer conference

- sheets listing 'frequently occurring problems' or 'frequently needed explanations' specific to a particular assignment, allowing learners to see feedback on some of the problems they may themselves have encountered, but also alerting them to other potential problems they may not have been aware of themselves, but which may be useful to avoid in their next work.

Feedback on other learners' work

I've already suggested that written comments on learners' work are not usually a successful feedback tactic, despite how endemic this process is at present. However, learners can benefit a great deal from feedback on each other's work. For example, when Sue reads the feedback on her own work, high emotions can come into play if there is some criticism, and she may well shrug off encouraging comments as she looks for the next critical bit. But if Sue is reading the feedback on Janet's work, when there is some encouragement Sue may well say to herself, 'Ah, that's the thing to do, I can do this next time', and when Sue reads some criticism on Janet's work Sue may think, 'Mmm, that's what not to do, I'll make sure I avoid this myself in future', and so on. My own view is that learners can get a great deal more from reading the feedback on each other's work than that on their own work. We have to be careful how we set this up, however, and it's best if the choices of who reads each other's feedback are left to learners themselves to arrange informally. It can be counter-productive if learners feel they have been 'set up' to read particular elements of feedback.

Audio feedback on mp3 files

Many tutors nowadays are experimenting with sending students (for example by email attachment) audio files of spoken feedback on their work. Findings of a JISC-funded project at Leeds Metropolitan University can be found at https://sites. google.com/site/soundsgooduk/ (Soundsgood, 2010). The feedback can be spoken into a small digital audio recorder (or a suitable mobile phone), then uploaded on to a computer and sent directly to the individual student. Students quite like having their tutor's voice talking them through their work, and are often reported as listening to the recordings several times. The voice can be much more encouraging than mere printed or written words. Sometimes, the mark for the work can be included only in the audio feedback, which means students need to listen to find out their marks.

Face-to-face feedback

This extends feedback into the auditory, visual and kinesthetic areas of Neil Fleming's VARK® inventory (2001–13), and brings into play the enhanced communication power of tone-of-voice, facial expression, body language, gesture, and so on. Face-to-face feedback can take several forms, including:

- feedback to whole lecture groups on work that has already been marked and is now being returned to them

- feedback to similar groups, but at the time they have just handed in their work, while it is still fresh in their minds. This feedback of course addresses *anticipated* problems or mistakes, but can be really valuable to learners, still remembering the fine detail of their own attempts at the work

- feedback to small groups of learners, for example, in tutorials, allowing more interaction – learners can probe deeper into what exactly the feedback means

- face-to-face, one-to-one feedback, by appointment, or in other learning contexts such as practical classes or studio work, where tutors can often chat to individual learners in a context less formal than individual appointments.

Feedback on learners' own self-assessments

Where learners are briefed to carry out a self-assessment of their assignments at the point of handing them in for marking, tutors can then not only give learners feedback on the assignments themselves, but also on the self-assessment reflections. In practice, this can help tutors to give learners feedback which is much more focused on learners' real needs rather than giving feedback without knowing what learners themselves already thought about their own strengths and weaknesses relating to the assessed work.

Feedback associated with peer assessment

Where groups of learners are assessing each other's work (whether written assignments, essays, reports, presentations, artefacts, exhibitions or posters), learners can get a great deal of feedback from their peer assessors. They also get what is perhaps even more useful feedback individually, directly from the processes of applying assessment criteria to other examples of work – some better than their own, and some not as good. All this helps them to place their own work in context and to work out what they may need to do next time to improve or develop their own future work.

FEEDBACK, EFFICIENCY AND LEARNING PAY-OFF

Most tutors and lecturers already know how important feedback is to their learners. Few, however, feel that they have got themselves into a position where the feedback is really working. Ideally, we need to make informed decisions about how best to maximize the learning pay-off associated with our feedback, but at the same time to improve our own efficiency in composing and delivering the feedback. In many workshops, I have asked groups of participants to write down on separate Post-its the different ways they use to give their learners feedback (adding also *other* ways learners get feedback – for example, from each other, from web sources, from books and handouts, and so on). I then ask them to place the Post-its on to the chart shown in Figure 5.1.

The feedback processes which people consider to have the highest learning pay-off are positioned well up the vertical axis. Those which are most efficient for us are placed towards the left of the chart. Those which are most efficient *and* have the highest learning pay-off go towards the top left-hand corner of the chart.

Scales 1 to 5 can then be drawn on each axis, and the product of 'efficiency' × 'learning pay-off' can be worked out for the position of each of the Post-its on the chart (Figure 5.2). The highest scoring feedback methods are frequently those involving peer assessment or peer marking, and 'live' feedback in class including peer discussion. Self-assessment also attracts some high scores. This is not least because the 'efficiency for us' tends to be high, especially when large groups of learners are involved. Further high scoring elements emerge, such as 'feedback from clients', 'feedback from externals', 'feedback from employers', and so on. The lecturers concerned rightly justify these scores along the lines, 'Students take far more notice of this feedback than they do of that we give them', and 'It is very efficient for us as it's not us spending the time doing it!'

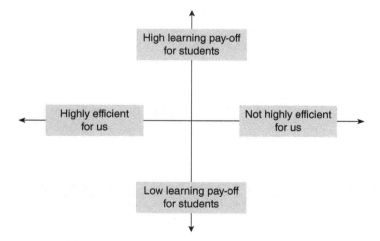

Figure 5.1 Mapping the student learning pay-off resulting from feedback, to the efficiency for staff providing it

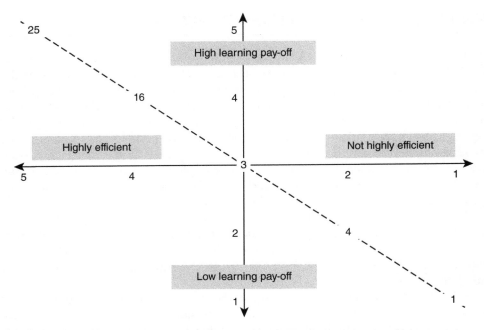

Figure 5.2 A semi-quantitative approach to learning pay-off and staff efficiency

Written comments on students' work – despite being widely employed – usually scores only around 4! One-to-one feedback often attracts low scores, not least because it is inefficient for us, even when the learning pay-off is felt to be high. However, the lowest scoring feedback processes frequently include 'just a mark' or 'grades'. In other words, most tutors know only too well that learners don't learn much from just being given a number or grade for their work. In this exercise, 'no feedback at all' is sometimes an entry, and attracts a score of 5, as it takes no time at all, and is therefore very efficient (in terms of time only, of course), and the learning pay-off is minimal. It can be argued that all feedback methods which score *less* than 5 in this exercise are *worse than useless*!

Working through this kind of discussion about learning pay-off versus efficiency often encourages tutors to make more and better use of peer assessment, self-assessment and clients or externals as tactics in a strategy to provide learners with more and better feedback using existing resources. It also helps tutors to appreciate the limitations of just giving scores or grades.

JUST A MARK IS THE LEAST USEFUL FORM OF FEEDBACK!

In the 'effectiveness versus efficiency' explorations summarized above, 'just a mark' often scores 1. In other words, it is very ineffective as feedback for learners, but takes us a lot of time to do! There are problems here.

- Learners *expect* marks – and may complain if we don't give them marks.

- When learners get marks, that is the first thing they look at, and they get blinded by the mark.

- Feedback is often then ignored – or (worse) interpreted in an emotive way, depending on the mark.

- If the mark is high, learners are likely to ignore the feedback, and 'smile and file'. They may well be missing out on finding out *why* the mark was high, and thereby becoming better able to continue in future work to do the things that got them the high mark.

- If the mark is low, learners often bin the assignment concerned, and miss out on all the feedback which might have helped them to work out how to get better marks for similar work next time.

What can we do about these problems? I suggest the following process:

1 At a whole-class session, give students back their marked work, but with feedback comments only and no marks (keeping your own record of their scores).

2 Remind them of the assessment criteria and tell them to use the next week to work out their marks from the feedback, and return next week with their scores for the work.

3 Tell the class that their marks count! Suggest that if their scores are within 5 per cent (or one grade) of the scores you've given them, the *higher* score will go forward into their assessment records, but that if they are outside 5 per cent, you will talk individually to them and sort out the score face to face.

4 Suggest that they don't just look at the feedback on their own work, but also the feedback on a few fellow learners' work. Explain that every time they look at some work which is better than theirs, they will learn something useful, and will be better able to get higher marks next time they do something similar. Also explain that every time they see someone else's work which has attracted critical feedback that their own work missed, they will learn something useful and will be able to *avoid* similar mistakes in future work. In other words, the time spent comparing their work with that of others will always be productive in terms of *making sense* of the subject matter, and (even more importantly) they will be *learning by making informed judgements* about their own and each other's work (the 'informing' being done through the feedback they see).

5 Next week, pass a board around the group asking everyone to enter their mark against their name. This can be achieved in just a few minutes of a whole-class session, even with hundreds of students there.

6 Two important things have happened over the week, and with no extra cost of time to you: just about all of your learners have read your feedback and

many of them have learned from the feedback that some of their classmates have received too.

7   In practice, nine out of ten learners are likely to arrive at scores within 5 per cent of your own scores, and the higher numbers can go forward. This means that nine out of ten of your learners are very satisfied with the marking and feedback, as follows:

o   they have been awarded the mark they awarded themselves, or

o   they have got a small number of extra marks, where either you gave them a slightly higher mark than they gave themselves, or they got away with a slightly higher mark than you gave them!

8   Make time to talk individually to the remaining one in ten of the learners, now of course using the full human communication range including facial expression, eye contact, tone of voice, and so on.

9   Where they underestimated their scores, point out to them where they deserved more marks than they had awarded themselves. Show them where they had in fact achieved the outcomes which they didn't think they had achieved. These learners go away with a spring in their step, even happier than the nine out of ten referred to earlier. After all, they've just found that they're doing better than they thought they were.

10 Where they overestimated their scores, go through their work with them until you find out where the main difference arose. It's usually because of a blind spot – something they thought they'd cracked but which they haven't yet mastered in fact. Talk them through this blind spot until they can see exactly why they lost the marks concerned, and get them to talk you through it so you can check that they have really seen the light about why they lost those marks, and what they can do to avoid losing similar marks in the future. (Don't just say, 'Do you understand now?' Make sure they do by getting them to show you.) These learners go away happiest of all – and they are *very* unlikely ever to lose those particular marks again.

Figure 5.3 summarizes the processes described above.

Let's just summarize what has been achieved by getting learners to work out their own marks:

•   Learners have taken much more notice of the feedback than if you'd given them marks.

•   100 per cent of them are very happy with the process and end result.

•   You've spent relatively little additional time achieving all this.

•   You've spent that additional time giving really useful face-to-face feedback to the one in ten who really needed face-to-face feedback, and you've avoided wasting time with all the learners who don't really need such face-to-face feedback.

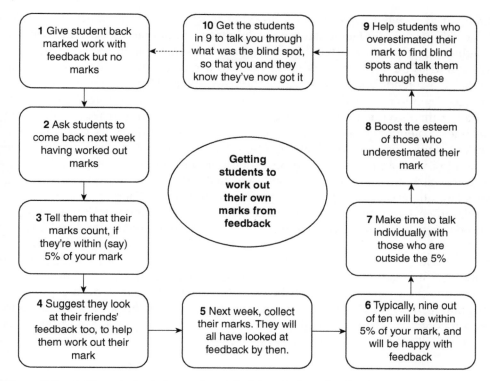

Figure 5.3   Getting students to work out their marks from feedback

- You've optimized the learning of your students by getting them to *make informed judgements*.

- You've got something really interesting to add to your teaching portfolio, or to please your external examiner.

In the light of all the benefits of getting students to work out their own marks, the original problem of 'students expect marks' fades somewhat into insignificance. You may, however, come up against the occasional learner who says, 'It's your job to assess my work. I'm paying for this course'. My own reply tends to be along the lines, 'Fine, I'll give you your mark. But I'm not very good at marking. And you'll miss out on a lot of learning. And you may miss out on some marks you might otherwise have got. But it's up to you'.

THE LANGUAGE OF FEEDBACK

A lot has been written about the wording we use in feedback to learners. There are problems with what some call 'final language', including such words and phrases as 'excellent', 'good', 'satisfactory', 'adequate', 'poor'. Such feedback may give an indication of the quality of a piece of work, but does not provide any direction as to what to do about it, in other words, no feed-forward. Words like those above are judgemental and somewhat authoritarian. Would you be delighted to receive some feedback along the lines that something you had done was found to be 'adequate'? We also need to avoid the danger of concentrating much of our feedback effort towards the lower-fliers. High-fliers can feel short-changed by minimal feedback even when marks or grades indicate their success.

Rather than saying 'excellent' or 'good', it can be better to offer feedback along the lines 'splendid – keep doing this', or 'this will continue to get you good marks – don't stop', because learners often don't notice praise when they've done something well, and may never repeat their demonstration of strength otherwise. Feed-forward along the lines of 'You could make this even better by ...' can also help. High-fliers quite like to have targets to aim towards. When work is much less good, rather than point out all the inadequacies it can be more fruitful to suggest 'Three things you can do to make this kind of work much better are as follows ...'.

Most learners like the personal touch in feedback. Phrases such as 'I really like the way you ...' can warm their feelings about the feedback as a whole. Talking to learners themselves, the thing that makes a massive difference is when a tutor notes how well they've taken on board a feedback suggestion from a previous assignment. This does of course mean from the tutor's point of view we need to keep records of what has been said to whom – and the whole thing becomes impossible if marking is anonymized.

FEEDBACK WITHIN 24 HOURS!

At workshops and conferences, I often alarm participants by stating 'Feedback is of little use unless students get it within 24 hours!' Delegates shake their heads sadly. I remind them of the real-life experiences of a day where things go badly – one may remain upset for the rest of that day, but on waking the following morning, it's rarely quite as bad as it seemed to be. And a few days later, it's faded from the mind quite a lot. It's rather similar with feedback – we need it while our thinking is still fresh in our minds. After a few days, feedback is much less readily received – the work has receded into the past. But there are ways of achieving 24-hour feedback, as discussed in this section and previously developed in Race and Pickford (2007).

There's nothing new about the idea that feedback has to be quick to be effective. It is widely accepted that feedback on students' work is most effective when it is received quickly, while they still remember clearly what they were trying to do in their efforts. The work in Australia of Sadler (1989, 1998, 2003, 2009a, 2009b, 2010) has consistently emphasized the role of formative feedback in leading students towards successful learning. Gibbs and Simpson (2002) look critically at a decline in the quantity and quality of formative feedback which students receive as class sizes grow in a climate of policies about widening participation in higher education. Bowl (2003) provides a wealth of detail about how students react to feedback (or the lack of it) in her book based on interviews with non-traditional entrants to higher education. Yorke (2002) writes convincingly of the role (and speed) of formative feedback in addressing student non-completion, and Knight and Yorke (2003) continue the argument that there are major problems in higher education with assessment and formative feedback, an argument developed further in this book.

Some feedback can be nearly instantaneous, for example when using computer-based or online multiple-choice exercises, where the feedback to choosing distractors (or correct options) can appear on-screen as soon as students select an option. Feedback on practical work can be relatively instantaneous too. However, it is often the case that students get feedback on essays, reports, problems sheets, and so on much too late – it can take weeks to mark their work, particularly if the class size is large. By the time students receive their feedback, they may well have moved on, and then they take very little notice of the feedback. Colleagues in many institutions complain that too many students don't even bother to pick up their marked work. Even when much care and effort and time have been put into writing the feedback, it often ends up entirely wasted! Life is too short to waste time on composing feedback that won't be read or used.

In this section, I suggest processes that enable feedback (on paper and face-to-face with whole groups) to be given to large (or indeed small) groups of students within 24 hours of them engaging with the work they hand in for assessment.

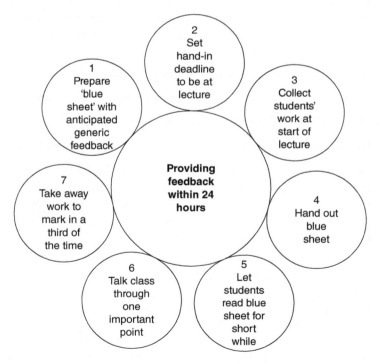

Figure 5.4 A way of getting feedback to a large group of students within 24 hours of them doing the work

No 'yes, buts …' please, at least not yet. Before you read this discussion, please prepare to abandon any reservations to the ideas you are about to see – at least for the next two pages or so. Then we'll address some of the 'yes, buts …'.

1 You've issued the class with an assignment, including all the usual detail about assessment criteria, links to intended learning outcomes, suggested sources, and so on. In the meantime, you prepared a feedback sheet on the assignment concerned.

2 Ask your class to bring the completed assignment (essay, report, whatever) to a particular whole-class session, for example a lecture – say the 10.00–11.00 lecture next Tuesday morning.

   Explain that the *absolute* deadline for receipt of their work is 10.03 on Tuesday morning, and the (only) place they can hand in that assignment is at this particular lecture during the first few minutes.

3 On the day, ask all students to place their work in a pile on a table at the front of the lecture room, in the first three minutes of the lecture period. By 10.03 or so, you have all their work (and a good attendance).

4 As soon as you've got all of their work, distribute to everyone in the group copies of a pre-prepared feedback sheet on the assignment concerned – on a coloured sheet of paper (different colours for successive assignments, so you can say 'the blue sheet', 'the pink sheet', and so on to refer to particular examples of these feedback sheets). On the sheet, use numbered points, so you can say 'point 3 on the blue sheet' to refer to a particular explanation, for example. This feedback sheet can contain:

   o explanations to anticipated, frequently occurring problems

   o illustrations of components of a good answer to the assignment question

   o examples of useful source materials and references

   o model solutions of quantitative parts of the assignment (if applicable).

5 Allow your class three minutes to scan through the feedback sheet (10.03–10.06). It goes very quiet! Suddenly, lots of students are finding out things about what they missed out of their attempts at the assignment, things they got wrong, but also things that were good about their attempts, and so on. Your class is getting quite intense read–write feedback in these three minutes or so.

6 Next, for just three minutes (10.06–10.09) talk the whole group through only one or two of the most significant of the feedback areas on the sheet, adding tone of voice, body language, eye contact to help the meaning of your feedback to be really clear to the students, augmenting one or two of the paragraphs on your feedback sheet. Don't try to cover the whole sheet – that would be too boring for the class and would take too long. *Which* points should you cover? Watch carefully students near to you between 10.03 and 10.06. See where they look serious as their eyes rest on particular parts of the

sheet. These give you clues about which points will be most valuable to expand on between 10.06 and 10.09.

7   Everyone in the class has now had three minutes benefiting from your feedback sheet, and a further three minutes getting some richer feedback on particularly important points about the assignment. Then proceed with the lecture as normal, and at the end take away the work to mark in a third of the time.

The point of all this?

Most of the students will still have been finishing off the assignment – or at least giving it a final check – *within the last 24 hours*. Moreover, more students than you might imagine will in fact have only *started* on the assignment during the last 24 hours – it's worth asking them! These are likely to be the ones who need the feedback the most, and they are very receptive to it at this time. This means they are now getting feedback:

*   while they still have a very clear view on what they were trying to do in the assignment

*   while they remember what their difficulties may have been

*   while they still remember very clearly what they were pleased with about their work on the assignment

*   while they really *want* to know how their work will fare in assessment

*   while they are thirsty for feedback!

Now you can mark that assignment in much less time!

When you actually go away to mark your students' work, you can save up to two-thirds of the time you would normally have spent marking it. You save time and energy as follows:

*   You don't have to write the same things on many different students' assignments – the common mistakes and difficulties have already been covered by your feedback sheet, and you can simply write, 'Please see point 5 on the blue sheet', and so on. (Most tutors admit that in 'normal' marking, they get fed up of writing the same explanations time after time on different students' work, and that they get less and less patient doing so!) It is, however, important to take the few seconds needed to write that 'Please see ...' briefing on the student's work, and not to assume that because the explanation the student needs has already been given out that the student will see the link to his or her own work.

*   You can now concentrate in the time you devote to marking the assignment to giving students feedback on particular things they need as individuals – in other words focusing your expertise where it is most helpful to your students.

- If, as you are marking the work of a large class, additional frequently needed explanations arise (over and above the ones you had on the blue sheet, for example), you can compose a new supplement to the blue sheet (probably just half a page or so in practice), covering perhaps points 8 to 10 to supplement the 7 points already on the blue sheet. You can then, where necessary, abbreviate many of your feedback remarks on students' work to 'Please see point 9 on the blue sheet supplement attached', continuing to save you time and spare you the tedium of repetition.

- Because you've debriefed your students *orally* in the whole group about the most important points in your pre-prepared feedback, there's little need to mention these points in any additional feedback you write on to their assignments, other than to sometimes remind them of your oral debriefing.

- Since you're now marking the pile of assignments in a third of the time it would otherwise have taken, it's likely you'll be able to get the marked work back to the class much more quickly than hitherto, which means that students are getting the rest of the feedback while the assignment has not completely faded from their minds.

- Your growing collection of feedback sheets continues to be available as evidence of your good teaching practice, and can be included in submissions to external examiners, professional bodies and in your appraisal or review documentation.

Now for those 'yes, buts ...'!

'But what about students who don't hand it in on time?'

There are no extensions! The real world works on deadlines – for funding bids, conference contributions, job interviews, and so on. It's good to train students to meet deadlines. Deadlines are deadlines are deadlines. A number of universities I know have now abandoned 'mitigating circumstances', 'extensions', and so on. It's worth reminding students that there are quite clear links between punctuality and excellence! Long ago, when marking laboratory scripts, I used to say to my students: 'The marks for the scripts will be more or less in the order you hand them in. First in gets the highest mark, and so on'. In fact, it surprised me how frequently the first scripts to be handed in were the best ones.

You can, however, explain to your students in advance that anyone who misses the deadline is not completely stuffed. They have the opportunity to do alternative assignment B instead, which more or less addresses the same learning outcomes as the original but where the coloured feedback sheet for the original assignment A will be of no help. They then hand the alternative assignment in at another deadline. (You may find ways of giving subtle hints making alternative assignment B somehow less attractive than the original assignment!) Assignments A and B can be issued at the same time, so that students who know they're going to have a real problem with deadline A (family crisis, illness, whatever) can set their sights on deadline B.

With a large group, don't be surprised if three students approach you and say, 'Is it OK for me to have a go at both assignment A *and* assignment B please?' I always used to reply, 'Of course'. And to the one student who will turn back to you after the other two have gone and say, 'And can I be credited to whichever assignment I get the best mark for?' I naturally used to reply, 'Of course'!! These students are often the higher-fliers in any case.

Putting late submissions and extensions into perspective, think of it this way. Imagine you had 100 students, and 95 of them handed the work in at the deadline of 10.03 on Tuesday, but five of them were not there. If you delayed the issue of the 'blue sheet' till next week while you waited for the five missing assignments, you would be depriving 95 students of the very strong benefits of feedback within 24 hours. This is educationally irresponsible, to say the least.

'If the feedback on the coloured sheet is so valuable, why can't we give out this guidance in advance of students doing the assignment?'

We can indeed give out the guidance in advance – but it doesn't work! Even when students have detailed guidance, many of them read it but soon become so busy doing the assignment that they ignore or forget most of the guidance and still get into the (anticipated) difficulties that the coloured feedback sheet addresses. If in doubt about this, give out the blue sheet three weeks before setting the assignment, simply saying, 'Keep this safe, it will be useful to you'. Then at 10.03 on the hand-in date, issue the same blue sheet again, and listen to the chorus of surprised, plaintive comments, 'I never noticed *that* on the blue sheet!' Feedback only really seems to work *after* students have done something.

FEEDBACK FOR HIGH-FLIERS AND FOR LOW-FLIERS

Some feedback processes are much more suitable for successful learners than struggling learners. For example, just a mark or a grade may be all that is needed by high-fliers, while a combination of written and oral feedback may be much more suitable for learners who need significant help. At the same time, learners without any problems may find it irritating to be given detailed feedback on things they have already mastered. However, learners without problems may equally feel short-changed if their less able course mates are seen to be getting more time and attention from tutors. An appropriate balance needs to be struck, where high-fliers get useful feedback too – perhaps a combination of positive comments about their work *and* some constructive suggestions about how they can make their next piece of work even better. It is well known how desolate a learner can feel when, having consistently achieved A grades, an out-of-the-blue B grade hits them. This can all too often be tracked down to a lack of tutors explaining to them *why* they had been achieving A grades to date. 'If you don't know how you did it, you're less likely to be able to do it again'.

FORMATIVE AND SUMMATIVE FEEDBACK

So far in this chapter, most of the discussion has been about feedback in formative assessment contexts. Another dimension which is useful to explore when reviewing the range of feedback approaches available to us is the question of which processes best lend themselves to providing formative feedback and which are more suitable for summative feedback? In some cases, the conclusions are obvious. For example, 'just a mark or grade' serves summative purposes and 'suggestions for your next assignment' serves formative purposes. However, some are much more complex, and the feedback associated with peer assessment, for example, can play a significant formative role even when it is received in contexts where the overt intention is closer to being summative. This is partly because, in some contexts, learners may actually take on board more deeply things they learn from each other, where there is no 'authoritarian' agenda present, than from when they receive feedback directly from their tutors.

Formative and summative assessment processes can be regarded as two ends of a continuum. All too often, for example, what sets out to be formative feedback ends up as summative feedback. For example, when learners don't get the feedback until they have already moved on to another topic or another module, they are very unlikely to take any notice of formative feedback given on work from weeks (sometimes months) ago, and the feedback ends up as no more than summative. In other words, learners may notice the mark or grade, but not bother to read the hard-wrought comments their assessors may have added to their work. It can be argued that there is very little point providing detailed formative feedback if no notice will be taken of it, and that it would, in such circumstances, be just as well to limit things to marks or grades and spend the time saved on providing *real* formative feedback on ongoing work, where learners have the opportunity to make good use of the feedback in improving and developing their work accordingly.

Yorke (2002) argues that we need to spend time helping learners to make better use of formative feedback. He suggests:

> There is a case to be made for spending considerable time and resources on students undertaking their first programmes of study to help them understand the purposes of formative feedback and how their own self-beliefs can impact on the ways they receive it. Inevitably this would eat into available time for content delivery, which academic staff no doubt would be unwilling to see slimmed down, but if an institution is serious about retaining students as a key means of survival in an increasingly competitive world, then tough decisions might have to be made. (Yorke, 2002: 39)

One way of helping learners to put feedback to better use is to cause them to reflect on feedback, and evidence their reflections as part of an ongoing process of becoming increasingly conscious of how they learn – and in this case increasing their awareness of how much they can in fact gain from feedback on their assessed work. The following reflective checklists can be used as a starting point to design your own reflection devices to allow learners to develop their

	Please tick one or more columns for each of the options below	This is what I did	I would have liked to do this, but didn't manage it	I didn't think this necessary	This just was not possible for me	I'll do this next time
1	I started thinking about this essay in plenty of time					
2	I started to collect my reading materials well in advance					
3	I discussed the ideas associated with this essay with someone, virtually or live, prior to starting writing					
4	I had a timetable in mind for pre-reading, planning, drafting, writing, checking, doing the references					
5	I planned out the structure of the essay logically, so my train of thought was continuous					
6	I made reasonable efforts to clear the decks for the actual writing of the essay					
7	I made referencing easy for myself by properly noting all of my sources as I did the reading					
8	I showed someone a draft of my essay before I completed it					
9	I acted on feedback I received to make my essay better					
10	I wrote a summary/abstract that encapsulated my key points succinctly					
11	I checked my work over carefully for obvious mistakes, and I used a spellchecker					

Figure 5.5 Feedback form: on submitting your first essay on a course

 Photocopiable *Making Learning Happen* © Phil Race, 2014 (SAGE)

	Please tick one or more comments as appropriate	This is what I did	I would have liked to do this, but didn't manage it	I didn't think this necessary	This just was not possible for me	I'll do this next time	This did not apply in this case
1	I read the tutor's comments carefully						
2	I read my essay again to see how the tutor's comments applied						
3	I noted things I needed to do before the next assignment						
4	I looked back again at the assignment brief to see the extent to which my essay had complied with it						
5	I looked forward to the next assignment to see which tutor comments might apply to my preparation for the next one						
6	I followed up tutor advice on further reading						
7	I used the feedback to check up on the things I did best in my essay, so I can build on my strengths in my next essay						
8	I followed up tutor advice on my own writing practices						
9	I shared my feedback with one or more other students to see how the commentary on my work compared with theirs						
10	I considered aspects of my approach on which I would especially ask for feedback next time						
11	I asked my tutor for further clarification on comments which I didn't understand						
12	I identified any feedback comments which I felt were unjustified, so that I could find out more about them from my tutor in discussion						

Figure 5.6 Feedback form: reflecting on tutor feedback on your essay

 Photocopiable *Making Learning Happen* © Phil Race, 2014 (SAGE)

approaches to planning their work and making the most of your feedback. It works all the better if you can persuade learners to allow *you* to see copies of their reflections, so that you too can help them further to develop their approaches to assessed work, and improve how you design feedback for them in future.

DESIGNING FEEDBACK IN RESPONSE TO POOR WORK

This is the most delicate of feedback tasks. Suppose you're in a position of needing to write feedback comments to a learner whose *first* assignment you've just marked. It was a poor assignment. It would be considered a fail. Suppose, furthermore, that circumstances dictate that you have no alternative to giving this feedback in writing (or email) and you've got to put pen to paper or fingers to keyboard to compose a feedback missive to the learner concerned. Under normal circumstances, you would be wise to choose *not* to put this particular element of feedback into writing or print, and to see the learner face to face to handle this difficult situation with all the tact and sensitivity you could muster. But perhaps the learner concerned is away on a work placement, or perhaps there's just no way the two of you can get together for a face-to-face meeting in the immediate future and the feedback needs to be given sooner rather than later. Your choice of words can be critical.

At staff development workshops, I often charge participants with this difficult task, and ask them to compose a feedback letter or email dealing with the issue. I then ask them to swap letters so that they now have no idea whose they have in their hands. Next, I ask them to read aloud the letter or email they now have – but with a difference. I ask them to read it out in a sinister, threatening, menacing manner! This is to simulate how the well-intentioned language used in the document might come across to the learner concerned, who may already know the work was poor, may be having a 'bad day' and may be on the point of discontinuing their studies altogether.

It is surprising how threatening some quite ordinary words can be in this context. Words which are often followed by bad news include 'however', 'unfortunately' and even plain 'but'. There is, of course, no way that the use of these 'caution' words can be avoided, but it is worth reminding tutors that such words can cause learners' spirits to fall as they read feedback responses.

Then there's 'power language' which often creeps in. For example 'submit your next attempt' or 'resubmit your assignment after ...', and so on. The word 'submit' puts the tutor on a pedestal and the learner much lower down. 'Send me your next version' is so much milder somehow.

And there are the fatal phrases, possibly the worst imaginable of which is 'You've failed to grasp the basics of ...'. This position seems beyond all hope, when read out in a sufficiently sinister way! Surprisingly, some well-intentioned ploys to soften the blow of delivering feedback on poor work can also lead to disaster. Phrases such as 'You've obviously put a lot of effort into ...' or 'Clearly, you spend a lot of time on ...' bring their own dangers. In particular, what if they hadn't? What if they rushed the assignment off at the eleventh hour, and here they find the tutor responding, 'Obviously, you've spent a lot of time ...'? There is no quicker or more sure-fire way of losing credibility as a tutor! That learner will never trust you again.

BRINGING TOGETHER PEER FEEDBACK AND ASSESSMENT

Throughout this book, I have been saying how much students can learn by self-assessing and peer-assessing, and also how much they can gain using feedback from each other. In Chapter 1, I mentioned that learners using MOOCs often benefit a great deal from feedback from each other when required to peer-review each other's assignments, before they are allowed to gain a certificate of completion of the MOOC (even though they have not been tutor-assessed). Here is a way of applying all of this to a normal tutor-set assignment, with a conventional group of campus-based learners (see Figure 5.7)

Any of the steps can be adjusted to meet the circumstances of the assessed piece of work. For example, step 9 represents an optional 'bonus' for students who self-assess their work accurately, as a reward for the perspective they no doubt will have gained by reviewing 'x' other examples of fellow students' work. Step 10, involving students reflecting on their experience of the whole process, could optionally count towards the tutor assessment of their next assignment.

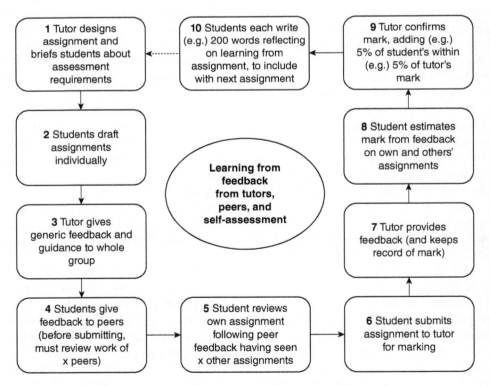

Figure 5.7   Learning from feedback from tutors, peers and self-assessment

An obvious question is: 'Won't students gain too many ideas from peers if they have to comment on other students' work before they submit their own work?' This could be a problem, but also could cause the overall standard of the work done by all students to improve dramatically – in other words more learning could happen as a result of this process. It can also be seen that the work of the tutor is reduced significantly, while students gain a great deal of feedback before submitting their work, and therefore need less tutor feedback later.

USING FEEDBACK TO MAKE LEARNING HAPPEN: 20 WAYS FORWARD FOR TUTORS

To summarize some of the main ideas in this chapter, here are 20 recommendations about feedback for tutors. You may well be able to add yet more to this list.

1 *Help learners to* want *feedback.* Spend time and energy helping learners to understand the importance of feedback and the value of spending some time after receiving work back to learn from the experience. Most learners don't do this at the moment, concentrating principally on the mark.

2 *Get the timing right.* Aim to get feedback on work back to learners very quickly, while they still care and while there is still time for them to do something with it. The longer learners have to wait to get work back, especially if they have moved into another semester by the time they receive their returned scripts, the less likely it is that they will do something constructive with the lecturer's handwritten comments. It could be useful to consider a policy not to give detailed written feedback to learners on work that is handed back at the end of the semester if that area of study is no longer being followed by the learner, and to concentrate on giving more incremental feedback throughout the semester.

3 *Provide learners with a list of feedback comments given to a similar assignment or essay prior to them submitting their own.* You can then ask learners, for example in a large-group session, to attempt to work out what sort of marks an essay with these kinds of comments might be awarded. This helps them to see the links between feedback comments and levels of achievement, and can encourage them to be more receptive to constructive but critical comments on their own future work.

4 *Make feedback interesting!* Learners are much more likely to study feedback properly if they find it stimulating to read and feel it is personal to them, and not just routine or mundane. It takes more time to make feedback interesting, but if it makes the difference between learners making good use of it or not, it is time well spent.

5 *Give at least* some *feedback straight away.* Explore the possibilities of giving learners at least *some* feedback at the time they hand in their work for marking. For example, a page or two of comments responding to 'frequently occurring

problems' with the assignment they are handing in, or illustrative details along the lines 'A good answer would include ...' can give learners some useful feedback while their work on the assignment is still fresh in their minds, and can keep them going until they receive the detailed and individual feedback on their own attempts in due course. Giving 'generic' feedback at the time of submission in this way can also reduce the time it takes to mark learners' work, as there is then no need to repeat on script after script the matters that have already been addressed by the generic feedback, and tutors can concentrate their time and energy on responding to the individual learner's work, and giving specific feedback on *their* strengths and weaknesses.

6 *Let learners have feedback comments on their assignments prior to them receiving the actual mark.* Encourage them to use the feedback comments to estimate what kind of mark they will receive. This can then be used as the basis of an individual or group dialogue on how marks or grades are worked out.

7 *Get learners to look back positively after receiving your feedback.* For example, ask them to revisit their work and identify what their most successful parts of the assignment were on the basis of having now read your feedback. Sometimes learners are so busy reading and feeling depressed by the negative comments that they fail to see that there are positive aspects too.

8 *Ask learners to respond selectively to your feedback on their assignments.* This can, for example, include asking them to complete sentences such as:

   o   'The part of the feedback that puzzled me most was ...'

   o   'The comment that rang most true for me was ...'

   o   'I don't get what you mean when you say ...'

   o   'I would welcome some advice on ...'.

9 *Ask learners to send you, confidentially, an email after they have received your feedback, focusing on their feelings.* In particular, this might help you to understand what emotional impact your feedback is having on individual learners. It can be useful to give them a menu of words and phrases to underline or ring, perhaps including: 'exhilarated', 'very pleased', 'miserable', 'shocked', 'surprised', 'encouraged', 'disappointed', 'helped', 'daunted', 'relieved', and others.

10 *Don't miss out on noticing the difference.* Comment positively where you can see that learners have incorporated action resulting from your advice given on their previous assignment. This will encourage them to see the learning and assessment processes as continuous.

11 *Make use of the speed and power of technology.* Explore the uses of computer-assisted formative assessment. While a number of universities, including Bedfordshire, Plymouth and the Open University, are using computer-assisted assessment summatively, many would argue that it is currently most powerfully used to support formative feedback, often automatically generated by

email. Learners seem to really like having the chance to find out how they are doing, and attempt tests several times in an environment where no one else is watching how they do. They may be more willing to maximize the benefits of learning through mistakes when their errors can be made in the comfort of privacy, and when they can get quick feedback on these before they have built them into their work. Of course, many computer-assisted assessment systems allow you to monitor what is going on across a cohort, enabling you to concentrate your energies either on learners who are repeatedly doing badly or those who are not engaging at all in the activity.

12 *Link feedback directly to the achievement of intended learning outcomes.* Explore ways in which formative assessment can be made integral to learning. Too often assessment is bolted on, but the more we can constructively align (Biggs and Tang, 2011) assignments with planned learning outcomes and the curriculum taught, the more learners are likely to perceive them as authentic and worth bothering with. Giving learners feedback specifically on the level of their achievement of learning outcomes helps them to develop the habit of making better use of the learning outcomes as targets, as they continue to study.

13 *Provide most feedback at the beginning.* Investigate how learning can be advanced in small steps using a 'scaffolding' approach. This means providing lots of support in the early stages which can then be progressively removed as learners become more confident in their own abilities.

14 *Use feedback to let learners know what style of work is expected of them.* Devote energy to helping learners understand what is required of them in terms of writing, that is, work with them to understand the various academic discourses that are employed within the institution, and help them to understand when writing needs to be personal and based on individual experience, such as in a reflective log, and when it needs to be formal and use academic conventions such as passive voice and third person, as in written reports and essays.

15 *Use feedback to help learners learn how best to use different kinds of source materials.* Help them also to understand that there are different kinds of approaches needed for reading, depending on whether they are reading for pleasure, for information, for understanding or reading around a topic. Help them to become active readers, with a pen and Post-its in hand, rather than passive readers, fitting the task in alongside television and other noisy distractions.

16 *Take care with the important words.* Ensure that the language you use when giving feedback to learners avoids destructive criticism of the person rather than the work being assessed. Boud (1995) talks about the disadvantages of using 'final language', that is, language that is judgemental to the point of leaving learners nowhere to go. Words like 'appalling', 'disastrous' and 'incompetent' fall into this area, but so do words like 'incomparable' and 'unimprovable' if they don't also help outstanding learners to develop ipsatively – i.e. build yet further on their already high achievements.

17 *When possible, use feedback in rehearsal contexts.* Consider providing opportunities for resubmissions of work as part of a planned programme. Learners often feel they could do better work once they have seen the formative feedback and would like the chance to have another go. Particularly at the early stages of a programme, consider offering them the chance to use formative feedback productively. Feedback often involves a change of orientation, not just the remediation of errors.

18 *Get learners* giving *feedback, not just receiving it.* Think about ways of getting learners to give each other formative feedback. The act of giving feedback often causes deeper thinking than just receiving feedback. Involve learners in their own and each other's assessment. Reflection is not a luxury; it is the best means available to help them really get inside the criteria and understand the often hidden 'rules of the game' of higher education. In particular, asking learners to review each other's draft material prior to submission can be really helpful for all learners, but particularly those who lack confidence about what kinds of things are expected of them.

19 *Cause learners to build on your feedback.* For example, ask them to include with their next assignment an indication of how they have incorporated your feedback from the last one into the present one.

20 *Encourage learners to analyse, systematically, all the feedback they get.* Explain how useful it is for them to identify recurring trends, for example similar comments given to them by different tutors. Above all, encourage learners to identify their strengths, as indicated by recurring feedback, so that they can aim to demonstrate these strengths again and again quite purposefully.

Finally, how best can you help your own students to make the most of feedback? You could give them the following suggestions, adapted from *How to Study* (Race, 2003) – or much better, fine-tune some of the ideas below with your own tips for your students.

  ## Tips for students: making the most of your feedback

Feedback is important. You'll get lots of feedback, and this can really deepen your learning. But you need to be *looking* for feedback to get the most from it. And you need to be *receptive* to it when you get it. The following tips can help you make the most of feedback.

Feedback in general

1   *Regard all feedback as valuable.* Whether feedback is in the form of praise or criticism, you will get a lot more out of it if you value it.

2 *Feedback from anyone is useful.* While it's understandable to regard the feedback you get from lecturers and tutors as authoritative, you can also get feedback all the time from fellow students, and other people around you.

3 *Don't shrug off positive feedback.* When you're complimented on your work, there's a temptation to try to ease any feeling of embarrassment by saying, 'We'll, it's not so special really'. The problem with doing this is that you then start to believe this. It's much better to allow yourself to swell with pride, at least for a little while. This helps you to accept the positive feedback, and to build upon it and do even better next time perhaps.

4 *Practise thanking people for their positive feedback.* Simply saying, 'Thanks, I'm glad you liked that' can be enough sometimes. When people are thanked for giving you praise or compliments, they're more likely to do so again, and this means more and better feedback for you.

5 *Don't get defensive when feedback is critical.* It's perfectly natural to try to protect yourself from the hurt of critical feedback, but the problem then is that this interferes with the flow of critical feedback to you. The more you can gently probe for even more feedback, the more useful the feedback turns out to be.

6 *Thank people for critical feedback too.* Even when you're not actually too pleased with the critical feedback you've just received, it can be useful to say something along the lines, 'Well, thanks for telling me about this, it should be useful for me in future'.

7 *Don't just wait for feedback, ask for it.* Don't lose any opportunities to press gently for even more feedback than you already have received. Ask questions, such as 'What do you think was the best thing I did here?' and 'What would have been the most useful change I should make next time I do something similar', and so on.

8 *Before you finish an assignment, look back at the feedback you've already received so far.* You can often polish up that assignment quite quickly, and avoid some of the things which caused you to lose marks last time.

Getting your marked work back

9 *Decide to regard it as an important feedback opportunity.* If you really want to learn from whatever feedback you get, you're much more likely to make the most of it.

10 *Acknowledge that when you get your work back with a grade, your feelings may run high.* It's not unknown for a student to take a marked assignment to a place outside, set fire to it and then stamp on it! That may indeed make people feel better, but it's a lost learning opportunity (and could be dangerous of course).

11 *Don't take too much notice of the mark or grade you're given.* There is, of course, nothing you can now do about whatever mark or grade you were given. The opportunity is to learn about why you got whatever mark or grade you were given. This can help tremendously with your next assignment.

12 *Don't become defensive.* It's all too easy to look at every critical comment as a personal affront. Remind yourself that any critical comments are about what you wrote, not about you as a human being. You can change what you write next time. You don't have to try to change who you are!

13 *If your mark wasn't good, find out exactly why.* We learn at least as much through getting things wrong as we do through getting them right. And even if your

(Continued)

(Continued)

mark was poor, look carefully for any clues regarding where you did in fact score the marks you got.

14   *Don't be too smug if your mark or grade is good.* Try to work out why your work scored well. What did you do that pleased your assessors? How best can you put such things to work again in your next assignment? And even if you did very well indeed, continue to look for what you might have done to make your work even better.

15   *Put it away for a while, then look at it again.* The real problem with feedback and marks together is that the marks cloud the picture. When your mind is full of thoughts about getting a high mark (or a low mark), you don't have room to really benefit from the feedback about your work. Once you've got used to whatever mark you were awarded, you will find you are much better able to look dispassionately at the feedback, and get maximum value from it.

16   *Don't rest on your laurels.* 'Pride comes before a fall', and so on. If you got a really high mark or grade this time, the chances are that you'll have to work really hard to improve on it – or even to equal it again. Indeed, the chances are that your next mark won't be quite so good. Then you'll be disappointed of course. But you can minimize that pain by learning as much as you can now about why you did well the first time.

17   *Analyse your mark or grade against the marking scheme.* Sometimes you'll have access to quite a lot of detail about how the marks were allocated for the assignment. See where your work scored well alongside particular assessment criteria. More importantly, look at where you didn't score well. Try to work out why you missed particular marks. This will be really useful for next time round.

18   *Try to look at the feedback fellow students received too.* In fact, it's sometimes easier for you to make sense of the feedback comments on other people's work – you're not too close to that work to have your judgement clouded by emotions. At the same time, fellow students may be able to give you useful insights into the real meaning of feedback comments written on your own work. Besides, looking at other people's marked assignments tells you yet more about the overall 'rules of the game' regarding getting good marks for assignments. The better you become acquainted with these rules, the more marks you can get next time – and indeed in exams too.

19   *Don't be afraid to seek clarification.* If you can't understand some of the feedback comments written on your work, find an appropriate time to ask about them. Be careful, however, not to come across as if asking for higher marks. And don't harangue your assessors in corridors or at the end of lectures. Don't make them feel as though their judgement is being challenged – that certainly doesn't help you to endear yourself to them! Make an appointment to see them, so that they have time to explain to you anything you need them to explain.

20   *Make yourself an action plan.* For each assignment you have marked, jot down three things you've learned to try to do again next time round, and three things to try to avoid in future. Then you can really let the assignment go, as a useful learning experience, and hang on to your learning, rather than that mark or grade. Now file that assignment, but keep your action plan.

Some of the resources in this chapter are available to print for your own use on the companion website. To access these, along with some video clips of the author, please visit: **www.sagepub.co.uk/makinglearninghappen**

CHAPTER 6

MAKING LECTURES INSPIRING

O━━ Key topics in this chapter

- Large groups
- Keeping students active
- Slides
- Online lectures
- Questions and answers
- Student behaviours
- Note-making, note-taking

HOW HAVE THINGS CHANGED IN THE LECTURE ROOM?

You may remember lectures quite differently from the way present-day students actually experience them. You may have been inspired in some lectures, bored stiff in others. You may have scribbled down pages of notes in each lecture, or just sat and thought. The lectures may have been the backbone of what you needed to learn, and what you needed to give back in exams or assignments. The course *was* the lectures, you may have thought. Here are some differences between the lecture context now and formerly.

- Now many – even most – students arrive at lectures without a pen, and without anything to write on. That just didn't happen in an earlier era of lectures.

- Many students now bring their laptops, tablets or smartphones to any lecture, and use them. They may use them really relevantly and productively if we've got them hooked on a topic, or they may (and do) use them frivolously if we haven't.

- Now, students expect that most of the content of a lecture will be made available to them electronically, including the slides lecturers use, and other supporting material which used to be given to them on paper, as handouts.

- Students now expect that if they miss a lecture, they can still download the slides and supporting resources, and of course, they do this.

- They may (as in the UK now) be paying (or borrowing) tuition fees, and have higher expectations of lectures than formerly. This, they think, is the tuition they're buying.

- They may be expecting the standard of many TED Talks they can quickly find on the web, and be expecting that their own lecturer's performance will continue to be available to them, recorded in this quality.

If in doubt that students don't want to use pens or pieces of paper in lectures nowadays, just look at some of the audience shots in TED Talks. And why, when resources such as TED Talks (and the lecture element of MOOCs) are free, easily available, and (mostly) quite excellent in quality, should today's students bother to get out of bed for a lecture, we may ask?

BRINGING LECTURES TO LIFE

What are lectures for? Long gone are the days where students came to lectures to boringly write notes to study and learn, and give back boringly in exams. In our digital age, the best content in the world is free, online – but there's so much of it. Many of the world's best lecturers in any subject can be watched free, online – often with wonderful visual backup. With today's free MOOCs, all this is available to anyone. So why do we need lectures in universities and colleges? Do we need them at all?

When we get it right, it's about *being* there. It is quite different being in the same room, at the same time, as fellow students, and indeed the lecturer. But the agenda is no longer just the subject content. It's now the processes that are important to students. The questions in their minds include:

- Why should I get out of bed for this lecture?
- What's really important amid all this subject content?
- Does what I already know about the topic count?
- What exactly am I going to be required to show?
- What does a good answer to an exam question look like?

- What does a good essay or report or dissertation or portfolio look like?
- How do the minds work of those who're going to assess my learning?
- How best do I get my own particular head around this stuff?
- What are the important questions and issues I should think about?
- Who's worth reading up on?
- When and how should I start getting my act together to show I've mastered this stuff?
- Why not just get this essay written and catch up on that lecture from a mate?

Countless students have already found that it's just no good copying the notes from someone who was there. They've only caught parts of it. It doesn't work just downloading the slides and handouts from the web. It's not even much good watching a podcast of the event, it's just not the same as being there, breathing the same air, sharing the same excitements (and frustrations) of a live lecture. The podcast might, however, be a good aide-memoire for someone who *was* there, giving reminders about the thoughts going on during the occasion, the un-asked questions, and so on. But you've got to be there in the first place for that to happen.

So what can we lecturers do? Don't 'lecture' for a start. Don't use up valuable time getting students to write down things we say or things we put on our slides. Instead, use every minute of the time addressing how human beings really learn.

- Arouse the *want* to learn – get them excited, curious, fascinated.
- Clarify what they *need* to learn, and what they need to become able to do with the subject.
- Keep them *doing* – asking questions, arguing with each other, probing and questioning, 'what *else?*', 'why *else?*', 'how *else?*', and so on.
- Help them find out where they're at, getting *feedback* from the fellow students beside them, behind them, in front of them – each student needs to know how he or she is doing right there and then.
- Get them *making sense* of the key aspects there and then, so that the learning has already been substantially started right there in the lecture room.
- Get them *talking to each other*, explaining things to each other, arguing with each other, helping them to get their heads around the subject.
- Above all, get them *making judgements* – making decisions, assessing their own thinking and each other's thinking, assessing your thinking, helping them to get their heads around how assessment works, long before their learning will be assessed. Now and then, give them material in lectures to assess – good and bad reports, good and bad essays, good and bad exam answers. More learning happens from assessing a *range* of examples – not just from seeing exemplars.

A successful lecture isn't a 'lecture' at all in the traditional sense. It's a busy event – everyone is busy. It's a noisy event, at times everyone is talking, arguing, probing, questioning, practising and above all *thinking*. Time flies, for them and for us. It's unmissable. If you weren't there, you've lost it. We need to use all the tricks in the book to make lectures work in the age of MOOCs.

Set yourself the challenge of watching how 20 colleagues do it, and taking on board from each two things that really worked with their students and avoiding two things that just didn't work. Trial and error rules, but it's less of a trial to learn a lot every week from others' errors. Watch the students' faces in other people's lectures. Watch their body language. Watch what works, and what doesn't. That's the most important learning *we* can all do in lectures.

WHY NOWADAYS HAVE LEARNERS IN LARGE GROUPS?

There are many reasons why large-group teaching remains important in post-compulsory education, but we need to bear in mind all the time the question 'What can *we* do for students that can't be achieved by a TED Talk or any other online lecture?' Among the reasons for striving to make lectures work effectively for students is that there are many more learners in our systems than before, and with more pressures on institutional finances, it is clearly cost-effective to try to work with them in large groups for at least some of the time. Also, learners *expect* lectures. But perhaps the most significant reasons for making good use of large-group teaching is to give whole cohorts of learners shared experiences, so that each learner feels part of the group and knows what is expected of them. Feedback from students on their experience of higher education (including that gathered annually since 2005 in the National Student Survey in the UK) shows that students want more contact with lecturers. Making the most of such contact in large-group contexts is a very significant way we can enhance students' perceptions of the quality of our higher education provision – when, of course, we succeed at making lectures inspiring.

What are the differences between the kinds of learning which happen best in a large group and those which go on in all the other facets of higher education, such as tutorials, seminars, laboratories or problem classes? In some subject disciplines, subject coverage is split carefully between large-group sessions and various kinds of small-group sessions. Probably the most important features of the learning which we should strive to engender in large groups are:

- giving students a sense of 'belonging' to a course or module cohort, and making the large-group experience so positive that they feel valued and cared for

- helping learners to see the big picture, including exactly where tutorials, seminars and other teaching–learning elements contribute to the overall context

- giving the whole group shared experiences – for example, developing attitudes and feelings towards the subject matter and the various sources and resources available to deepen the learning experience

- providing the overall information map – for example, using handouts, downloadable files from the intranet, reading lists, specific references, and so on

- helping learners to set their sights regarding the real meaning of the intended learning outcomes, what forms the expected evidence of achievement that these outcomes should take, and the ways in which learners' evidence of achievement will be assessed in due course

- sharing expectations about what learners are required to do on their own, so all members of the whole group are aware of the expected scope of reading around the subject they are intended to do

- providing an opportunity for clarification, so that collectively learners can have their questions answered

- helping learners to gain a real sense of identity in the cohort and to see the links between the different subject areas they are studying

- linking learners' experience of lectures to all the other things they can now access at any time – Ted Talks, online lectures, and all sorts of things in the digital world outside

- inspiring learners – arousing their curiosity and interest in a subject, and motivating them to do a lot of reading and studying – starting them off and keeping them going on making learning happen.

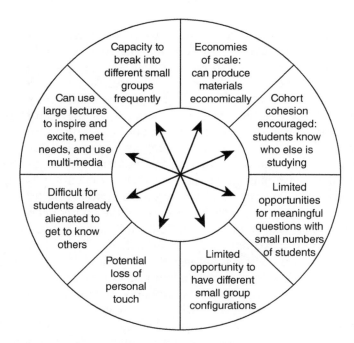

Figure 6.1 Upsides and downsides: teaching large groups

Figure 6.1 provides a way of thinking about the relative advantages and drawbacks to consider regarding large-group lectures and small-group seminars and tutorials. In practice, some tradeoffs are necessary in either context.

Tutorials, seminars and other small-group learning contexts are necessarily not identical learning experiences for different sub-groups of the whole cohort, so large-group sessions need to address all the things that *all* members of the whole group need to share, particularly explanations about the evidence of achievement students are required to meet to reach the targets specified in assessment criteria.

WHAT DO STUDENTS THINK OF LECTURES?

In the UK National Student Survey, the whole of the first section of the survey (the first four of 22 statements) links to large-group teaching. The section is called 'The teaching on my course', and students are asked to make judgements as follows: 'definitely agree', 'mostly agree', 'neither agree nor disagree', 'mostly disagree', 'definitely disagree' or 'not applicable' on each of the following statements:

1   Staff are good at explaining things.

2   Staff have made the subject interesting.

3   Staff are enthusiastic about what they are teaching.

4   The course is intellectually stimulating.

These statements apply not just to large-group teaching, but to all the other aspects of a course. However, I am sure that when most students make their judgements on statements 1 to 4 above in the survey, the first thing to cross their minds is the most public form of teaching – lectures. Where students are paying tuition fees for higher education, one of the first things that comes to their minds in the 'value for money' stakes is their experience in the lecture theatre. And perhaps the second thing to come to mind might be the responses to statements 1 to 4 that would be given by audience members at a good TED talk.

Back to our lectures. The first four National Student Survey statements link in turn to how well we have managed to address the factors underpinning successful learning. Students are likely to think we're good at explaining things if we have made it straightforward for them to make sense of difficult concepts and get their heads around fundamental principles. Students are likely to think we have made the subject interesting if we have kept them actively engaged in their learning, including in large-group contexts. Conversely, if we have bored them in lectures, we are unlikely to get a vote of confidence on statement 2.

In particular, large-group contexts are probably our most important occasions to demonstrate our enthusiasm about what we're teaching. If *we* look bored with what we're teaching, we can hardly expect to enthuse our students about it. It's not just enthusiasm about the subject matter we need – it's also enthusiasm about *students*. If we give the impression of being really pleased to be there with them

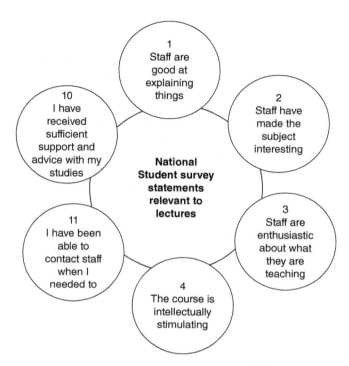

Figure 6.2 Six statements from the National Student Survey which link to lectures

in lectures, and we're really keen to ensure that they succeed, we're far more likely to get a vote of confidence with statement 3. Moreover, if we really show that we care that our students succeed, that vote of confidence will be enhanced. That's where helping students to get a real grip on what we're looking for as *evidence of achievement* of the learning outcomes comes in. Similarly, if we do everything in our power to help students *learn by assessing* right there in the lecture room, so that in due course they can prepare successfully for assessment, we're winning.

Statement 4 is rather more complex. What do we mean by 'intellectually stimulating'? Naturally, if we've got ourselves into the position of giving lectures on a topic, we might be expected to find it intellectually stimulating ourselves. But in the UK's National Student Survey, statement 4 is about whether *students* find the subjects intellectually stimulating. And this extends to 'what can we do to *be* intellectually stimulating?' – a much tougher nut to crack.

Furthermore, later in the survey, under the title 'Academic support', statements 10 and 11 are:

10 I have received sufficient support and advice with my studies.

11 I have been able to contact staff when I needed to.

When students respond to these statements, they are likely to think of their lecturers, and at least some of the support and advice students receive should link to large-group teaching. Students are also likely to think of whether their lecturers were sufficiently available for contact when needed, even though when groups are very large, it may be intended that they contact other staff (for example, teaching assistants and personal tutors) rather than lecturers for most things.

There is plenty of evidence nowadays that students are becoming more choosy regarding which lectures they attend – and yet the evidence also shows strong links between non-attendance at lectures and failure or drop-out. A student recently explained to me, 'We go to the first couple of lectures to see how they go, and if we don't think much of them we tend to skip the lectures and get the slides and other information from the web later, or from mates who were there, instead of turning up'. With lectures, we may not have any second chance to make a good first impression.

MAKING LEARNING HAPPEN IN LARGE GROUPS

There is no 'best' way of working effectively with a large group of learners. There is no best way of lecturing – though lecturing in the traditional sense is unlikely to be the best way of making learning happen, when the learning will in due course be measured and accredited. Furthermore, if all lecturers did the same things in lectures, it would be very boring for students. Indeed, the most common criticism students make about the lectures they find least useful is summed up in one dreaded word in their feedback to us – 'boring'!

There are as many ways of working excellently with large groups as there are skilled lecturers. Many of them do it successfully in their own ways, and others trying to imitate them just can't do it – it's a very personal thing, excellence in teaching large groups. We can, however, improve what we do in large groups through two main approaches:

- observing how many, many colleagues go about it, and noting things to try to emulate and, particularly, things to avoid doing ourselves

- paying attention to the *learning* which is happening in large-group contexts, and consciously addressing the factors underpinning successful learning outlined in Chapter 2 of this book.

In the discussion which follows, I will address each of these factors in turn.

1 Wanting to learn

What can we do to enhance the *want* to learn in large groups? Ideally, each large-group session should result in as many as possible of the group members going away fired up to continue their learning. Different lecturers achieve this in completely different ways. Probably the most important common factor is enthusiasm. If we seem bored with a subject, there's not much chance we will inspire others to go and learn more about it. But it's not just enthusiasm for the subject that matters. Learners are quick to pick up the vibrations of our enthusiasm for *themselves as people*. Lecturers who come across as really *liking* learners – and respecting them and treating them accordingly – do much to inspire learners to learn. If we enhance the *wanting to learn* dimension, attendance at large-group sessions improves, students look forward to our lectures, and try not to miss them.

One factor we can play with is students' *curiosity*. If they're curious about the topic, they want to learn it – they want to find out answers to the questions about the topic which are in their minds. It's therefore very useful to us to find out what questions students want to explore. Even with hundreds of learners in a lecture theatre, in just a few minutes we can ask everyone to jot down on a Post-it, 'What I really want to find out about is …'. We can count up the number of times the most popular questions occur and make slides containing these questions. We can then confidently proceed to address these, knowing that many members of the audience wanted to find out more about these aspects of the topic.

Another aspect worth addressing is the *learning incomes* of the students. Another Post-it scenario: ask everyone to jot down their response to the statement, 'The most important thing I already know about "x" is …'. Students often surprise themselves (and indeed surprise us too) with how much a large group collectively knows about a topic before we've even started a lecture on it. Students are more likely to come to a large-group session if they know that we'll take into account and build upon what they already know about the topic, rather than them having to sit there being told things they already know.

2 Ownership of the *need* to learn

How best can we clarify the need to learn in large groups – sharing the standards we expect regarding students' evidence of achievement, putting the intended learning outcomes to work? Large-group teaching contexts are our best shot at clarifying the need to learn, not least because it is the *fairest* context in which to give learners information about exactly what we expect of them. This is the context where it is fair to tell everyone at once about the assessment standards which underpin the achievement of the intended learning outcomes. Large-group sessions are occasions when we can give cues and clues about the sorts of exam questions which would be reasonable ways to measure learners' achievement of the intended outcomes – much better than giving such clues to only *some* of the learners in particular small-group tutorials or in response to individual questions privately. We can collect learners' individual enquiries about the standards expected of them from all sorts of contexts, but the best chance to clarify our expectations is when *all* the learners in a cohort are present. Indeed, if we make a habit of using large-group contexts to let learners into the fine detail of our expectations, large-group session attendance is improved.

It's useful to start each and every large-group session by going through the intended learning outcomes for that particular session. There are normally only three or four of these. It helps further to illustrate what kinds of evidence of achievement we're expecting students to furnish in due course, for assessment. It is also useful to remind students of what they should already be able to do as a result of past lectures. Where possible, arrange that the intended learning outcomes remain visible for the whole of the lecture – for example, by showing them on an overhead projector continuously, while doing other visual things on PowerPoint slides. This allows us to make it quite clear now and then through the session exactly which outcome we're addressing, and it helps students to keep the overall picture of the session in mind throughout.

3 Learning by doing in large groups

What do learners *do* in lectures? What would we *like* them to do? Which of the things they do have high learning pay-off? And which things have little to do with learning? You might like to browse down the list below, thinking of what your own students tend to do in lectures, and what you'd like them to be doing.

Table 6.1 Some things your learners may do in your lectures

Adding important points, in their notes, to what's on the slides	Making judgements
Admiring the cool, calm way you handle awkward questions	Making links with things they had learned previously
Answering each other's questions	Making mistakes in buzz group tasks and learning from them
Answering your questions	Making their own notes
Asking each other questions	Picking up cues about what's important
Asking you questions	Practising things
Being bored	Showing fellow learners how to do something
Chatting to the next learner	Summarizing what's being discussed
Copying down important things from the screen	Trying to sort out what's important and what's just background
Copying things down (or trying to) that you say	Tweeting and texting
Discussing things with each other	Waiting, and waiting for the whole thing to move on
Explaining things to fellow learners	Wanting to leave, but not daring to
Feeling embarrassed that they couldn't answer a question	Wanting to talk to their neighbour to check out whether they are the only one who can't see the point
Feeling the light dawning – and trying to capture it	
Fretting about their relationships	Watching you
Getting annoyed at the learner in front busy texting on a mobile	Wishing they'd brought a pen
	Wishing they'd kept up with the content of the last two lectures
Having misconceptions debunked	
Hearing a range of opinions	Working out what seems likely to be coming up in the exam
Highlighting things in any handouts available	
Itching to get to their books to get into the topic deeper	Writing down their own questions for later study
Jotting down their own answers to your questions	Writing down their own questions so that they can check them out later
Looking for clues about how to tackle the assignment	

You can probably add many things to this list. The thing to think about, however, is which of these learner actions really link to learning, and how can we make their experience of your lectures a good one?

What can we do in large groups?

As already said, there is no one best way of running a successful large-group teaching session – different people do it well in quite different ways. Asking workshop participants to identify the most important large-group teaching behaviours gives a wide range of responses, all of which have their place. But each works best for different people in different ways. Table 6.2 shows a list of such behaviours.

All these processes can be regarded as contributing to making learning happen in large groups. Note how many of these actions go well beyond just 'lecturing' or 'telling learners things'. The more different things we can include in any large-group session, the less likely it is that it will be found to be boring by learners.

Table 6.2 Some things teachers can do to make learning happen in large-group teaching sessions

Adapting the session to the actual needs of the group at that time	Getting feedback from learners
Asking learners questions	Getting learners to apply things from previous lectures
Asking learners to identify issues	Getting learners to do things with handouts
Being accessible and approachable	Getting learners to make individual learning plans
Being enthusiastic	
Being flexible	Giving learners feedback on their work
Building on learners' experience	Giving learners practical examples
Challenging learners' thinking	Giving value-added to people who bother to turn up
Developing learners' study skills	Initiating discussion
Doing a variety of things	Inspiring learners
Dropping hints about what to concentrate on	Listening to the learners
Encouraging feedback	Making it relevant to learners – personalizing it
Encouraging participation	Managing the time well
Encouraging them to ask questions	Orientating and guiding
Entertaining	Playing short video clips
Explaining concepts	Providing notes
Explaining outcomes/objectives	Quizzing learners
Facilitating learners working in groups	Relating the topic to assignments
Facilitating processing of material	Reviewing material they have previously learned

(Continued)

Table 6.2 *(Continued)*

Setting learners challenges	Signposting the intended learning
Setting the scene – placing the present subject into context	Stimulating interest
	Storytelling
Setting the scene about how learning should happen	Testing learners
	Using humour where appropriate
Showing internet materials	Using real examples
	Using visually attractive material

Some of these things you'll recognize only too well. You may indeed do many different things too. The point is that even if for much of the time you're standing, and talking, and listening, there are a lot of different ways you can cause learning to happen.

4 Learning through feedback in large groups

How best can we make use of large groups as a feedback-rich environment? Too often, the value of lectures as feedback-receiving opportunities is underused. We can give each and every learner in even the largest group feedback, but only if we have got them to do something – decision-making, problem-solving, and so on. Feedback only really works after action.

How not to do it (1)

- **Lecturer**: asks class a question. Waits seven seconds. Then answers own question.
- **Students**: sit there thinking, 'Just been asked another question. I'll hang on for seven seconds, then he'll answer it, and I'll write down the answer'.

I've seen somewhere a figure for how long the average lecturer waits after posing a question before proceeding to answer it – 1.8 seconds!

How not to do it (2)

- **Lecturer**: asks class a question. Waits seven seconds. Picks a student to try to answer the question.
- **Students**: sit there thinking, 'He's just asked another question. I'll keep my head down, avoid eye contact. With a bit of luck, he'll pick someone else to answer the question, and if they get it right, I'll write down their answer'.

How to do it

- **Lecturer**: asks class a question, showing it on a slide so students don't forget what was said. Then he or she says, 'Everyone jot down privately your own answer to the question'.

- **Most students**: jot down their answers (if they have pens with them – or on their laptops or smartphones).

- **Some students**: do nothing.

- **Lecturer**: 'Hands up anyone who is sitting *next to* someone who hasn't jotted down their answer'.

- **Many students raise hands**: but all students have now had the feedback of seeing others' answers.

- **Lecturer**: 'OK, nothing more happens until you've all jotted down your answer to the question'.

- **Remaining students**: shamed into jotting down their answers to the question.

- **Lecturer**: 'Many of you will have written down a good answer to this question. Volunteer to share your answer?' (Picks volunteer, who reads out answer.)

- **Lecturer**: 'Well done – that's great. How many of you wrote down a similar answer?'

- **Several students raise hands**: all students have received feedback now – those whose answers were correct and those whose were not.

We can get much more feedback to each member of a large group if we include buzz-group episodes, and get them arguing, debating, speculating, practising, explaining things to each other, and so on *during* the large-group session. It is worth remembering how valuable it is for each learner not just to receive feedback, but to give it to fellow learners. Both processes link strongly to making sense of what is being covered.

We can pave the way towards making optimum use of the feedback-rich environment of large groups by taking away the perceived pressure we often feel, that we must use the precious time to cover as much as possible of the syllabus content prescribed. We can make time to spend on feedback by using a VLE (Virtual Learning Environment) or handouts to provide learners with the information they need, rather than allowing them to simply gather it from us in a one-way process, or wasting their time merely copying down the information from our slides or from what we say. We can then get learners working individually or collectively *processing* the information in their handout materials, making sense of it as they proceed.

5 Making sense in large groups

How can we help learners to get their heads around things in large-group contexts? Ideally, we need to make learning happen *in* large groups, not just some time later when learners revise the contents of a session for exams or assignments. The more we succeed in making large-group sessions occasions where learners feel that they're making sense of the subject matter, the better the attendance will be – in all senses of the word. The example above of getting them to jot down their own answers to questions, then compare, then volunteer, helps to allow everyone in a large group to get feedback on their own thinking, helping them to make sense of the question and its answer. Helping learners to get their heads around ideas and concepts *during* large-group sessions is best done by making sure that there are plenty of learning-by-doing episodes during the session, each followed by feedback (from fellow learners and from us) so that each learner has the opportunity to find out how much making sense has so far occurred. Just as important, it's worth learners finding out which parts of the light haven't dawned *yet*.

Our best chance to help learners to make sense of things is when they have us with them, with all the extra dimensions of tone of voice, body language, eye contact, gesture, repetition, emphasis, and so on. Many of these things we can use in a lecture are not at all the same on a screen, for example in a lecture on a MOOC, or in a webinar. Few of the live dimensions of a lecture can be taken away by learners from the session itself, unless they have distilled these into their notes. And it is worth thinking about the power of pauses. A short silence can cause students to think, in a way they'd have missed out on if we'd just carried on talking. It has to feel like a purposeful silence of course, and not just where we're having a rest (even if we are). Pauses in speaking are something different from what happens when students sit and read something. It is indeed *possible* to pause and think while reading something, but it tends not to happen often enough.

We can cause further making sense to occur by setting tasks for learners to do between one session and the next, so that they engage in further learning by doing, practice, trial and error, and so on. This is made all the better if we can arrange that they get feedback as quickly as possible – for example, by encouraging them to do some of the tasks in small groups with discussion. Alternatively, we can, for example, issue a problems sheet (physically or online) at the end of the session, with a marking scheme and model answers made available, perhaps a few days later. If we're lucky, few learners will fall into the temptation of waiting for the model answers before they have a go at the problems. The feedback they get when they do their self-marking and compare their work to the model answers is much more rapid than if they had to wait until the next teaching session. We can put some pressure, where necessary, on learners to make sure that they actually *do* the between-sessions work by quizzing the whole group about the work in the opening minutes of the forthcoming session, choosing names at random to shame any learners who have not got round to the task. That said, we've got to be really careful not to shame any learners too much – otherwise next time they haven't done the task, they won't come to the lecture to avoid the risk of humiliation.

6 Learning through verbalizing orally – explaining

At first sight, we can be forgiven for thinking that the explaining is *our* job in large-group contexts. Indeed, we might feel under pressure to do most of the talking in such contexts. However, we can reverse the situation, allowing learners to deepen their learning, perhaps by explaining things to each other. For example, suppose you've just gone through a rather complex explanation of a difficult concept with a large lecture group. You might then ask, 'How many of you are still with me at this point? Raise your hand if you reckon you've made sense of what we've just been thinking about'. Suppose a third of the class raises their hand. You can now invite them to get into threes or fours, each cluster containing one student who has mastered the concept. Then ask that person in each group to spend a few minutes explaining the concept to those who haven't yet 'got it', until they have all made sense of it. This has enormous benefits for the 'explainers'. The act of explaining something about which the 'light has just dawned' is a very memorable activity, and the explainers retain it strongly. Those being explained to are also advantaged, as this time the concept is being explained by someone who remembers the light dawning. Lecturers may have known the concept so long that they can't remember the feeling of the light dawning.

'But what about using my precious time in this way?', lecturers may ask. 'It is well worth it in terms of students' learning pay-off', is my response. Students remember what *they do* in large groups much more than they might remember what *we say*. We can go further than this, and actively encourage learners to spend time out of the lecture context discussing the content with each other. Some institutions go as far as to have 'supplemental instruction' or 'peer teaching' provision, where, for example, third-year students are given the responsibility of supporting first-year students in chosen aspects of the curriculum. As before, the greatest value of this is to the 'explainers'. The third-year students develop a strong mastery of the fundamentals they are teaching to the first-year students, who in turn feel more relaxed learning difficult concepts from a fellow student than from a lecturer, and are more willing to ask questions as necessary until the 'making sense' has been achieved.

7 Learning through assessing – making informed judgements

This is one of the most powerful things we can do in large-group teaching contexts. Shortly, I will discuss the rise and fall of handouts in lectures, and their use becoming restricted to when they serve an important purpose. The example outlined below is one such case, where a whole large-group session can be used as follows.

1   Give everyone in the room three handouts on different colours of paper, for example of an essay or report or assignment, or examples of an answer to a past exam question. Make one of them an excellent example, one a poor example and one an intermediate one. Ensure that the three examples don't immediately *look* excellent, poor and intermediate, but that they need to be studied quite carefully before it becomes apparent which is which.

2   Ask everyone in the class to work independently for a few minutes, looking through the three examples, and deciding which is the excellent one, which is the poor one and which is the intermediate one.

3 Get the class to vote – for example, 'Hands up those who think the pink hand-out is the poor one', and so on.

4 Then get students into clusters, to work out *why* the yellow one is better than the blue one, and why the blue one is better than the pink one.

5 Ask different clusters for the *criteria* that distinguish the excellent one from the intermediate one, and so on, writing up these criteria (in the students' own words) on to a slide, board or chart.

6 Now show students a marking scheme for the piece of work they have been judging, and ask the clusters to apply the marking scheme to the three exam-ples. The students are now *making informed judgements* on the pieces of work they are examining. Moreover, they are making these judgements in the same ways that will be used for their own work in due course – they are get-ting their heads around the assessment culture in which they are studying.

7 Finally, remind the class about how the same sort of criteria will be used to judge the students' own work on a forthcoming assignment or exam answer.

These steps are summarized and illustrated in Figure 6.3.

A whole lecture period spent in this way has a really high learning pay-off, and the paper-based handouts help things to happen which could not have occurred without them. It is a way of using a whole-group session to:

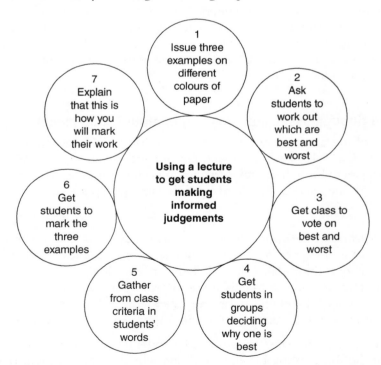

Figure 6.3 Using a lecture to deepen students' learning by making informed judgements

- show students details of the *evidence of achievement* which in due course will be expected of them

- illustrate what the related *learning outcomes* actually mean in practice, and how they link to forthcoming assessment

- help students to see the *standards* expected of them so that they take increased ownership of the need to achieve the learning outcomes and produce suitable evidence to demonstrate this

- allow students to experience the *assessment criteria* they will in turn be judged against, and to apply these criteria to examples of essays (or reports or exam answers, and so on) so that they get their heads around exactly how their own work will in due course be assessed.

In fact, there are few ways of achieving such a high amount of learning pay-off with a large group in a single lecture period. Just giving yet another lecture would only have achieved a fraction of that learning pay-off for the students. It can be argued that getting a class to make judgements in this kind of way is one of the best things to do in whole-group contexts. Furthermore, when students see that they find out in such a lecture a great deal of useful information about how their work will be assessed, their motivation increases, and they are far less likely to risk missing a lecture in case they should miss such valuable information relating to their future assessment. At the same time, they are still learning about the topic concerned, but in a much deeper way than if they were simply being told about it in 'lecture mode'.

Making learning happen by *not lecturing*!

You will have seen from the discussion so far in this chapter that large-group teaching–learning contexts can play a really vital part in making learning happen for our students – particularly if we don't fill these sessions with the sound of our voices merely *telling* students things. We can, as you've seen above, purposefully address in large-group contexts each and every one of the factors underpinning successful learning as outlined in Chapter 2. Lectures are no longer just to give students information – if that's all we want to do, we may as well give each of them a data stick full of information, or refer them to web sources, including lectures on MOOCs. Live lectures in our institutions are for helping students to get their heads around information together, and begin there and then the tasks of turning it into their own knowledge and linking it to what they already know.

This in no way detracts from the value of the old-fashioned sort of lecture as enlightenment or entertainment. Going to that sort of lecture for pure pleasure remains one of the attractions of the experience of university or college life, not least attending professorial inaugural lectures which can be entertaining as well as informative. But when there is the serious business of *learning*, followed by the even more serious business of *assessment*, we can argue that the primary purpose of a large-group session is that the students should leave the session with much more in their heads than when they entered the room, and that mere 'lecturing' has little part to play.

RESOURCE MATERIALS SUPPLEMENTING LECTURES

The rise and fall of handouts

Only three or four decades ago, the use of handouts in lectures was relatively rare. Learners in lectures needed to make notes if they were to take away from the lecture the content that had been covered by the lecturer. Typically, this meant that in an hour they could only acquire a few pages' worth of information. If they had just been furiously writing out all they could capture from the lecture, this information may have been mainly unprocessed when they took it away, but at least the task of going through it again and turning it into their own knowledge was manageable. Later, it became common for a great deal more information to be placed directly into learners' hands on paper, than they could ever have written down in a lecture. So it is was not uncommon for learners to receive several pages of information around a lecture – and printed pages could contain many more words (numbers, pictures, graphs, diagrams, and so on) than could be written or drawn by any learner in an hour.

Meanwhile, where formerly learners had needed to make their own notes from books in libraries, it became possible for them to make photocopies of the information they believed to be most relevant or important, and carry the information away with them. Cue-seeking learners were probably the best at deciding which extracts were important enough for them to make their own copies, and cue-oblivious learners ran the greatest risk of copying everything which *might* turn out to be relevant – postponing (often indefinitely) the task of getting down to making sense of the information and turning it into their own knowledge. However, nowadays students much prefer to get the material from libraries electronically, often without even going there and browsing the stocks, and download material on to their computers. This makes it even easier, of course, just to collect masses of material, and not get round to really using much of it for study.

For a while, handouts became increasingly important in the context of large-group teaching, and were important not only to learners, but as elements of the evidence used to assess the quality of post-compulsory education. More recently, however, the number of handouts issued has decreased dramatically, and unless there is a really good reason for learners to use something directly on paper during the lecture, they are rarely issued nowadays. Reasons for the demise of handouts include:

- Handouts were costly to produce, and groups are often much larger these days than they used to be.

- It was onerous for lecturers to organize the production of handouts in time for a given session, and tedious to carry around large bundles of these for big classes.

- It has become much easier to put up the equivalent of handout materials on an intranet or on the web, and they can be put there just before the lecture, with the request that students look at them as preparation, or even print them and bring copies to the lecture to annotate during the session (though students seem increasingly reluctant to do this, not least because of the costs and nuisance of printing).

- Lecturers can annotate the material made available electronically immediately after the lecture (usually quite quickly) before putting them up on the web, for example adjusting material which may have been pre-issued before a lecture to include issues which emerged during the actual session.

- Students can be impressed that a spontaneous discussion which took place in the lecture has been summarized shortly afterwards in the web-based material – 'I was part of this', they may think.

Nevertheless, the accompanying resource materials remain an important aspect of large-group teaching, even when no paper is involved. I have reflected the importance of resource materials by discussing their use in some detail below, linking them to the factors underpinning successful learning quite overtly.

While feedback may be considered to be the lifeblood of making learning happen in post-compulsory education, resources supplementing lectures can be thought of as the arteries controlling the flow of information to learners' hands. However, perhaps such resources are not an entirely successful means of getting the information processed in students' brains. Returning to Einstein's idea that 'learning is experience, everything else is just information', it is easy to see that the main danger associated with resources supplied electronically is that they give learners information which is not, in due course, processed by them to become their own knowledge.

Some problems with digital resources

- Some learners take the view, 'I don't need to go to the class, I can simply get the stuff from the web'. It is true that learners can get the *information* in this way, but with an element of good teaching, just having the information does not equate to actually *being there*. Learners who miss out on the tone of voice, body language, facial expression, emphasis, clarification and often *inspiration* of participating in a class are seriously disadvantaged. But frequently they do not realize this until too late, thinking that they've 'got it all' in their downloaded files. Indeed, in many an effective face-to-face session, a downloaded resource is more of an *adjunct* to the intended learning than a summary of it.

- 'I don't need to pay attention now. I've already got the information so I can sit back and switch off'. This can be the view of learners sitting in a class with their own copies of material safely in their possession. True, they may already have got the *information*, but they are then missing out on the best chance to turn that information into the beginnings of their own *making sense* of that information, using tone of voice and so on as cues and clues.

- 'What am I expected to *do* with this material – read it now, revise from it later, do things with it now and soon after now, just file it, collect stuff until I've got all of it and *then* do something with it ...?' This list is endless. In fact, all such reactions to resources can be regarded as study avoidance tactics – excuses for putting off doing some *real* learning until later.

Using digital resources to make learning happen in lectures

How, then, can we make best use of weblinks and electronic files for learners to view on-screen or print out for themselves, to maximize the associated learning pay-off learners derive from them?

1 Wanting to learn

For a start, if digital resources *look* interesting, there's more chance that they will be used and not just filed away. Making materials look interesting can be done in several ways, including:

- arousing curiosity, making the subject matter seem irresistible to study

- selecting or making materials which are *digestible* rather than dry and forbidding

- bringing visual learning into play, using images to capture diagrams, graphs, pictures, and so on to bring to life the ideas concerned

- selecting or developing *interactive* materials, which prompt learners to make decisions, choose options, add their own ideas and so on.

However, the most important way of ensuring that digital resources associated with lectures enhance learners' *want* to learn is to make sure that learners find them really *useful*. This can be partly achieved by paying attention to the content of the materials, and helping learners to feel that at least some of the work of acquiring the information involved has already been done for them. By narrowing down the subject content so that everything on the chosen resources can already be regarded as important, learners will be encouraged to invest time and energy following up the subject matters.

2 Taking ownership of the need to learn

Perhaps the most direct way that available resource materials can help learners to take ownership of their need to learn is linking them (prominently) to the relevant intended learning outcomes and, where necessary, translating these into language which learners can readily relate to. In other words, it is useful to give learners some guidance about what in due course they need to become able to *do* with the content of the resource materials – how learners will be expected to become able to *evidence* their achievement of the intended learning outcomes.

This does not assume that all the intended outcomes can be achieved just by studying the information using the prescribed or suggested resources. The intended outcomes can range outward and link to guidance about how best to approach each individual source. Rather than, for example, suggesting, 'Now read Chapter 4 of Smith and Jones', resource material is much more useful if it suggests, 'Consult Chapter 4, particularly sections 3 and 5, looking for answers to the following questions …'. In addition, including a self-assessment exercise will help learners to focus their work on the source so that they do indeed get the most important things out of the material. This sort of guidance can also include advice such as 'You don't need to bother with sections 2 or 7 unless you really want to – these are not directly relevant to your own particular intended learning outcomes relating to this source'.

3 Learning by doing

Throughout this book I have stressed the importance of learning by doing – particularly practice, repetition of relevant activities, and learning by trial and error. When resource materials are chosen or designed quite overtly as learning-by-doing devices, the chances of them just being filed away are dramatically reduced. Resources which contain several recommended tasks and exercises are likely to be used, not just stored. If it is made clear that the activities contained in a particular resource relate directly to the achievement of relevant aspects of the intended learning outcomes, learners are all the more likely to engage with the material. If it is also made very clear that *doing* these activities will relate well to the sorts of *doing* which will in due course be assessed (exam questions, assignments, essays, essay plans, and so on), learners become much more aware that they need to engage with the activities in resource materials accompanying a lecture.

Cue-seeking learners are in their element here, of course, but cue-conscious learners find this way of identifying what is important (and what isn't) useful too, and cue-oblivious learners are still able to benefit to the extent that the things they *do* using the resources are already designed to be relevant and important, saving them perhaps from spending too much time or energy going off on tangents, or straying too far away from the intended learning outcomes which will form the basis of their assessment further down the line.

4 Making sense of what is learned

There are several things we can do to choose and use resources which help learners to get their heads around ideas and concepts. As indicated above, we can design in relevant learning by doing, so that learners get the chance to apply their minds to the information and process it as part of the journey towards building their own knowledge using the resources. Also as noted above, careful use of intended learning outcomes can assist learners in finding out *what exactly* they should be trying to make sense of, and alerting them to the ways in which they will need to become able to demonstrate that they have made sense of the material addressed by the resources.

Moreover, study guides can be really useful, referencing a wide range of print-based and web-based sources and resources, helping learners to see exactly which parts of these sources are most relevant to them, and how they can use these sources to evidence their own achievement of the intended learning outcomes.

5 Learning through feedback

When the primary intention of resource material is to give learners feedback on things they have already done, they can be particularly useful in making learning happen. For example, when learners have struggled with something, a resource showing them how best to go about it may be eagerly used. However, one of the best ways of coupling learning by doing with feedback is to include in resource materials self-assessment exercises of one kind or another, where learners can have a go at a task or problem, then find elsewhere in the resource the means to judge their own efforts. In this way, they find out the extent to which they 'got it right', and, more importantly, they address the 'if not, why not?' question. Clearly, there are disadvantages in making the feedback *too* easy to find. If learners can see it at the same time as seeing the tasks themselves, the temptation for eyes to stray towards the answers remains great. Only the most conscientious learners will resist looking straight at the solutions. Other learners who skip having a go at the problems may *feel* that looking immediately at the solutions is good enough, but we all know that being able to do something is not the same as *feeling* that one can do it correctly.

6 Verbalizing orally, explaining, coaching, teaching

One of the dangers with resource materials linking to a lecture is that learners tend to study them in solitary silence. We can encourage learners to explain things to each other using resources, for example by setting group tasks based on the materials involved. We can encourage learners to coach each other in the deeper points of material addressed in resources, and we can start off such processes *during* lectures, so that learners get the message that this is a valuable thing to continue doing afterwards.

7 Making informed judgements

This is perhaps where well-chosen, or well-designed resource materials really reap the greatest rewards in terms of making learning happen. For example, when students are practising applying assessment criteria to material similar to work they will themselves do later, the process can achieve a high learning pay-off. It is again useful to start students off doing this kind of activity in the lecture room, to whet their appetites to continue doing the same sorts of things on their own – and, more importantly, in groups.

When should I make my presentation materials available to students?

Having explored resources accompanying lectures in general terms, the following discussion is about one particular variety of resource: presentation materials, for example PowerPoint slides. Many institutions now have policies to address students' special needs, often including the availability (in advance) of PowerPoint presentations and other resources. Learners nowadays (rightly) expect that slides they see during lectures, and weblinks to other materials used in the lecture, will be made available to them, and they also expect not to have to scribble down as much as possible of the information which appears on a screen during a lecture. Indeed, students often expect to be able to look at – and annotate – the materials they see on-screen during the actual lecture.

Some reservations about availability of presentation materials

- Learners are likely to switch off when they already have access to the materials being used during a lecture. They think, 'There's no real need to pay attention now. I can look at this stuff again anytime'.

- In practice, many learners never look at the presentation materials ever again! Students rarely file such materials in a systematic way.

- Too often, slides are effectively just information. Learning only happens when people process information, and do things with it, apply it, argue with it, extrapolate from it, compare and contrast it, and so on. Therefore it is very unsafe to assume that just because everyone has the information, all will have learned.

- Students *want* their own copies of the slides, but not everything that they want is good for them. This is partly because they seek the safety of ensuring that they get all the relevant information. While it is good to avoid them wasting time and energy simply copying down information from a screen in a lecture theatre, it remains important that they engage actively during lectures, and are getting their heads around information rather than just looking at it on the screen or on their own copy of what's on the screen.

- Making slides available in advance greatly restricts flexibility in presentations and lectures. When slides have been issued in advance, students may get dissatisfied when several slides are 'missed' in the session. It is good to keep the freedom to skip particular sections of a prepared presentation, and concentrate on the key issues, especially when time is taken to address questions and follow up the emergent interests or needs of the particular audience. It can therefore be better to issue the slides actually used after each lecture, giving you freedom to choose which slides to use during the event and allowing you to add slide sequences to address matters that arose in the lecture, for example questions from the audience.

- Making copies of the slides available tempts students to miss sessions. Many lecturers have now realized that attendance drops as students just download the slides and other resources, rather than coming to the lecture. The students who miss the lecture usually fare much worse in coursework assessment or exams, and merely give back the information which was in the slides or hand-outs, whereas those who were present learn a lot more through the actual discussion, where communication is aided by tone of voice, body language, eye contact, emphasis in speech, repetition of important points from different perspectives, and so on. At a good lecture, human communication is more important than just the images which may have appeared on a screen.

HOW CAN WE GET LEARNERS TO ASK US QUESTIONS IN LECTURES?

In many teaching–learning contexts, not least lectures and small-group sessions, one of the most productive ways of making learning happen is to cause learners to ask questions and provide answers to their questions. When they are working out what questions to ask, they are exploring their own *need* to learn, and at the same time they are often working on what they *want* to find out. Asking questions is one kind of *learning by doing*. Receiving answers to their own questions is, of course, *learning through feedback*, as is hearing answers to other people's questions. Ideally, all of these processes should help them to *make sense* of the topics which are the basis of the questions.

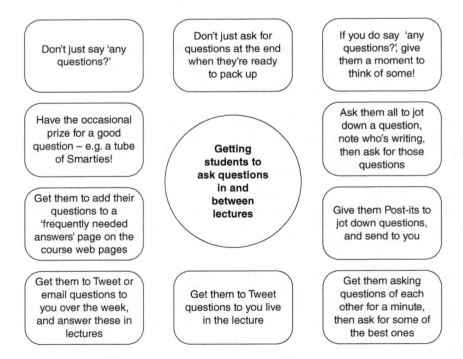

Figure 6.4   Some considerations on getting questions from students

While it is relatively easy to get learners to fire their questions at us in small groups or in one-to-one contexts, it is harder to achieve this with hundreds of learners at a time. One thing that can help is to ask everyone to jot down two or three questions. Give them a couple of minutes to do so. Then ask them to compare their questions with those of their immediate neighbours. Then ask the class for some of the questions. This way, there is more chance of you being asked the questions that are more widely owned, and are thus more important. It is also a way of getting everyone to think about at least some questions, so that even the learners who don't get answers to their questions during the session are still able to take the questions away with them. If you'd just got learners to *think* of some questions and call them out, many of the questions in their minds would have evaporated away very soon after the session. Figure 6.4 summarizes a few ways of eliciting question in and between lectures. However, there can be another problem – dominant learners. Read on.

HOW CAN WE AVOID A FEW STUDENTS DOMINATING QUESTIONING?

How can we enable all learners to get answers to their questions in large-group sessions without the sessions being monopolized by a few vociferous learners? Following on from my response to the previous question, it remains worthwhile trying to get all the learners to write down a question or two in the first instance. However, when you know that it will be the same learners who voice their questions, possibly because they are more confident than their course mates, some alternative tactics can come in handy.

For example, pass out Post-its so the whole group can have one each, and ask everyone to jot down one or two questions on their Post-it. Then ask for the Post-its to be passed to you and stick them on a flipchart, whiteboard, window or suitable wall. With really large groups, get the learners themselves to do this, it's quicker. You can then scan through the questions, picking off a Post-it at a time, and reading out the question so everyone knows what you're going to be answering. Then you can answer the question, filing the Post-it so you have an accurate record of which questions you have answered.

Normally it is worth concentrating on those questions which you can readily see to be relatively common ones, so that you are satisfying the needs of a reasonable cross-section of the large group. However, it is also worth taking away with you *all* the Post-its, so you can look through them in your own time. You can then create a FAQ (frequently asked questions) web page which you can post in a *frequently needed answers* bulletin on the web.

HOW CAN WE HELP LEARNERS TO BE HEARD IN LECTURES?

We've already explored some ways to get questions from individual learners, for example using Post-its. However, it's useful to be able to respond to spontaneous questions from learners too. When a learner asks a question, it's always worth trying to repeat the question back to the whole group before proceeding to answer it, as people behind the questioner may not have been able to hear the question when first posed. If the question is a long one, a complex one or an unclear one, it can be worth clarifying the question, for example by asking, 'Is your question really about …?', or suggesting, 'Let's break this question into three parts …' and then breaking it down into a logical sequence before continuing to answer it. Repeating the question back to the whole group also gives you a little longer to mentally rehearse how you're going to respond to it.

Sometimes, a dialogue happens between one particular learner and yourself. In such cases, if the room allows, it can improve things if you can move closer to the questioner, so that it is easier for you to interact well with this learner and so that they are better able to make sense of your responses to them. If, however, the dialogue becomes too protracted, it may be necessary to explain to the whole group, 'I think this is a matter for the two of us to explore outside this session', so that they don't feel that they are being ignored.

WHAT DO LEARNERS DO THAT HINDERS LEARNING?

We've already explored some learners' actions which hinder learning – coming in late and chatting inappropriately. There are many other things they may do which get in the way of their learning. These include:

- *Taking notes rather than making notes.* At one level, this is not a problem; if they're busy copying things down from the screen or board or writing down what you are saying to them, they're unlikely to be disruptive in other ways. However, *taking* notes is usually very passive; *making* notes is much better for learning. *Making* notes can include making their own summaries of what has been covered in the last few minutes, or annotating a handout with the main points that you have covered which are not already presented there, and so on. It is important to help learners to make notes by building in suitable time spans (e.g. two minutes) to give them an opportunity to do this. It can also be useful to allow another minute or two for them to compare the notes they made with each other and add further ideas to their own notes. 'Now steal your classmates' best ideas for a minute' is irresistible to many learners.

- *Just sitting passively.* This is all too easy. Unless we *cause* learners to be active in large-group sessions, many will just sit there waiting until they're told to do something. They may look as though they're listening – even quite attentively – but may have already found out that as long as they *look* as though they are there in spirit, they can switch off mentally! The answer is for us to continue to take control of what they do, so they have a variety of things to do and are less likely to sink into passivity. We can alternate between getting them to answer questions, discuss points with each other, make notes, solve problems, apply what they've just learned to a case study scenario, explain things to each other, make judgements on things we give them to assess, and so on. Students very rarely complain in evaluation feedback, 'I was kept too busy during lectures!' They much more often complain of being bored.

- *Going to sleep and snoring!* This is many lecturers' worst-case scenario of things going wrong in large groups. It has to be said that for things to get this far, they must have been passive for rather too long in the first place, and we need to look to what *we* have done – or not done – to cause them to slumber. That said, it is worth remembering that at least some learners in any large group will be in *need* of sleep. Some may have worked late or early shifts, and may be already deprived of sleep. Others may have enjoyed themselves into the early hours, to the same effect. Sitting still for a long time in a relatively warm comfortable environment, especially if the lights are dimmed for slides to be seen, fulfils fairly ideal conditions for human sleep! It does not help to make anyone who has nodded off feel seriously embarrassed – that may have the effect of causing them not to bother turning up at all next time they are tired and in danger of falling asleep. The kindest thing to do is perhaps to change the activity, for example getting *everyone* to discuss a point with their nearest neighbours – even if they have to wake up the odd neighbour in the process.

WHAT DO LECTURERS DO THAT HINDERS LEARNING?

Learners themselves can tell us a lot about this. The worst, and all too frequent, comments that learners make about unsatisfactory experiences of large-group teaching feature one word – 'boring'. Their feedback includes:

- droning on and on
- going right over our heads
- not looking at us – or ignoring us
- going too fast – or going too slow (this is a problem in any large group, with people learning at their own speeds, of course, and we need to try to vary the pace accordingly, with 'catch-up' time for the slower learners but also giving the faster ones something extra to think about so that they don't become bored)
- telling us things we already know
- not linking the topic to what *we* know about it
- doing things that seem irrelevant
- forgetting to explain *why* a particular topic will be useful
- failing to make things relevant to our own experience
- not responding to our questions or giving us the chance to ask them
- not giving us anything to do.

Some of this feedback warns us to sharpen up our own act, to make things as interesting as we can, checking regularly that the large group is 'with us' and keeping each and every member of the large group as active as we can. However, there are many well-intentioned lecturer actions which can hinder learning too. These include:

- going off on lengthy tangents to the main purpose of the session, sometimes out of a will to make a topic more interesting

- explaining things in detail when most of the group already need no further explanation

- presenting too much information without giving learners the chance to do something with the information

- sticking too closely to the agenda for the session when all the signs are that learners need a few minutes of rest from thinking about a difficult concept

- doing *anything* for too long at a time and failing to bring some variety to learners

- being too predictable!

It is helpful to us to continuously gather feedback from our learners about what they like about our large-group sessions and what they dislike. We can't please all of them all of the time, but the more we find out about their likes and dislikes, the better we can strike a balance. It is also really useful to sit in on colleagues' large-group sessions as often as possible. In someone else's lecture, whatever the topic, we can usually come out with two lists:

- things that seemed to work well for them, that I can try in my own large-group sessions

- things I noticed which didn't work and which I'll try to avoid in my sessions.

This can all be done quite informally and, where team teaching is the norm, lecturers find it very useful simply to learn informally from each other's approaches in this way. Many institutions nowadays have systems of peer observation (more detail in Chapter 8), and it is then useful to have direct feedback from different colleagues about how they find our individual approaches to large-group teaching.

HOW CAN WE INCREASE THE *TAKEAWAY* FROM LECTURES?

I've already referred to the differences between *making* notes and just *taking* notes. It can be useful to help learners themselves to take ownership of the need to capture much more than just the information which is covered in large-group sessions. Remind them that even just an hour or two after a lecture, especially if they have already been in two or three other lectures, much of the fine detail will have evaporated away. Suggest that learners consciously try to capture questions which go through their minds all the way through large-group sessions, and jot these questions down in their notes (perhaps in a different colour). These questions can include things they would have liked to have asked in the lecture but didn't, questions other learners asked, questions about things not yet understood, and so on. Even when questions are jotted down only to be followed by the answers becoming clear, it is valuable to have written down the question, and then perhaps ticked it or drawn an arrow to where the answer is now written down.

A wise and experienced colleague told me how he fell in with his institution's policies and put all his lecture materials and PowerPoint slides on the intranet. He did this a couple of weeks ahead of each lecture, for the sake of any learners with special needs. But two things happened:

- attendance fell off at his lectures
- exam performance in due course worsened dramatically.

He analysed this. The learners who *didn't* come to his lectures only gave him back in exam answers that which he'd given them in the materials and Power-Point slides, nothing more. The learners who *did* attend his lectures gave back much more, from the thinking which he got them to do *during* his lectures, and the reading around the subject that he inspired them to do *after* his lectures. Yet many colleagues continue to put up all of the information for learners in similar ways, and it is often now institutional policy to do so. We need to make sure that our best efforts to respond to learners with special needs do not end up disadvantaging many more learners. In fact, many institutional policies for learners with special needs are misguided. Those who know a lot about responding to special needs emphasize that each affected learner is an expert in his or her particular needs, and 'blanket' solutions are usually quite inappropriate. It is worth asking each affected student, 'How best can I help you?' and working forwards individually from their responses.

HOW CAN WE USE LECTURES TO BUILD APPROPRIATE STUDY SKILLS?

What kinds of briefing do learners need to help them understand how best to learn in large-group contexts? In particular, learners need guidance on what to do in lectures. Especially in first-year courses, they may feel strangely alone even in a packed lecture theatre, with no idea what they are expected to do. Write it all down? Hardly possible in a lecture full of slides and images and talk. Sit there and think about it? Try to look as intelligent as possible? Be quiet and 'good' and not interrupt by asking questions?

Learners need to be well briefed on the importance of intended learning outcomes as a framework for their learning and as the basis of a specifications framework laying down the standards of the evidence that they themselves need to become able to provide for their learning in the different kinds of assessment which will follow.

Left to themselves, learners often simply add any notes they make to any handouts they download, gathering together loads of information-bearing files or papers. Sometimes, it's only when revising for exams or tests that they return to these original materials and, unsurprisingly, it is then often not at all easy to make sense of the materials. All the *extra* impact of tone of voice, emphasis, body language, repetition, clarification, and so on has evaporated away from the information in the materials they may have saved. Learners often ask themselves, 'Was I actually *there* for this session? Did I copy the notes from someone who was there?'

We can advise learners how useful it is to follow up each large-group session within two or three days, to edit and improve any notes and resource materials while the memory of the session itself is still present. One way of helping learners to realize for themselves the importance of not losing the experience of large-group teaching is to get them to reflect on what they do after the average lecture. The self-assessment checklist shown below is one way of alerting learners to what we hope they will be doing after each lecture. Furthermore, if we can persuade learners to give us copies of filled-in self-assessment questionnaires of this kind, we too can find out a lot more about what they are actually doing after each large-group session. This may make our expectations rather more realistic.

SUMMING UP: MAKING LECTURES UNMISSABLE!

Giving learners information is only part of the business of designing a lecture, so we've got to make sure that lectures are learning experiences and not just information distribution events. In particular that *first* lecture in any series is a make or break occasion for many a learner. It's also make or break for us – there's no second chance to make a good first impression! In other words, we've got to try to make lectures unmissable! It's got to be worth *being* there. This chapter has been about making learning happen in large-group contexts – usually called lectures on timetables. We've seen that the act of *lecturing* is rarely the best way of making learning happen, and that we need to be thinking carefully about what learners are doing while sitting in lecture theatres or large classrooms. In this final section of the chapter, I would like to condense some of my main suggestions, linking them particularly to the context of starting off a lecture series. Every new lecturer's nightmare is getting a lecture series off to a bad start, and learner attendance falling off as the series goes on – or worse, lots of learners later failing the related exam and the blame coming back to the lecturer. This isn't confined to new lecturers. The following suggestions may help you to make your lectures unmissable.

Please tick one or more columns for each of the options below		This is what I did	I would have liked to do this, but didn't manage it	I didn't think this necessary	This just was not possible for me	I'll do this next time
1	I've looked through any notes I made during the lecture to check I understood everything					
2	I've downloaded the lecture slides, if available, and checked through them to remind me of the content of the lecture					
3	I've downloaded relevant resource materials and annotated them, adding extra comments and questions to help me to remember what seemed clear during the lecture					
4	I've jotted down questions where I don't yet understand something, for me to follow up later					
5	I've filed my notes and resources carefully where I can find them easily later					
6	I've followed up reading suggestions made by the lecturer					
7	I've noted down for revision purposes the three most important things from the lecture					
8	I've looked back on the course outline to see how this lecture fits into the programme as a whole					
9	I've looked forward on the course outline to see what will be coming up in the next lecture					
10	I've made sure that the intended learning outcomes for the lecture are included in or with my notes					
11	I've checked how well I reckon I've already achieved each of the intended learning outcomes, and marked these decisions against the outcomes for future reference					
12	I've asked my fellow learners for their reactions to what we learned in the lecture					
13	I've compared my notes with those of at least one fellow learner, and added in things I missed					
14	I've self-tested myself on what I remember from the lecture, and to find those parts that are in danger of slipping away again					

Figure 6.5 Student self-assessment checklist to use after a lecture

Photocopiable *Making Learning Happen* © Phil Race, 2014 (SAGE)

- *Start reasonably punctually.* When most of the group is there, get started. Remind learners of some of the things they should already know but that you will discuss in more depth. Alert them to some of the things you don't expect them to know yet too. Don't be unkind to people drifting in late – that won't encourage them to come to your next lecture if they are late again. Don't punish the people who are punctual by making them wait too long for their less punctual colleagues. Gently allow the people who are coming in late to feel that they may have missed something useful.

- *Make the most of the live occasion.* Learners may well do much of their later learning from materials they download relating to the lecture, but use tone of voice, gesture, facial expression, and so on to arouse their curiosity, so that they're looking for answers to the questions that are in their minds.

- *Don't put too much into the first lecture with a group.* It's better to get learners thinking deeply about a couple of important things than to tell them about dozens of things which future lectures will address. It's worth finding out all you can during the first lecture about what they already know. First impressions endure, so try to ensure that learners get a good first impression about the subject, and indeed about *you*.

- *Make good use of intended learning outcomes.* Near the start of the lecture, let learners in on what *they* should be able to do by the end of that particular lecture. Towards the end of the lecture, show the intended outcomes again, and check to what extent learners now feel that they have cracked the learning outcomes. Help them to *feel* the added value of having been there.

- *Always link lectures to assessment.* Give learners cues and clues about how this particular lecture counts when it comes to assessment. Whenever you say, 'You'll need today's material for exam questions like such-and-such' you'll notice learners' attention increasing, many jotting something down!

- *Make sure you can be seen and heard.* Use a microphone if it helps. Don't just say, 'Can you hear me at the back?' Ask someone in the back row a question and find out. And don't dim the lights to show your slides at the expense of learners no longer being able to see *you*. Remind yourself that low lighting for too long at a time is one of the components of the natural conditions to induce human sleep!

- *Don't keep slides up too long.* Learners will keep looking at the screen, even when that slide is quite finished with. Get them to look at *you* now and then. For example, when using PowerPoint, on most systems pressing B on the keyboard makes the screen go black. Pressing B again brings it back.

- *Don't just read out your slides.* Learners can read the slides themselves faster than you can talk. Talk *about* the slides. Explain now and then what's really important. This helps learners to prioritize the content of the lecture.

- *Ask plenty of questions.* Give learners the chance to answer them, and be encouraging even when answers aren't good. Celebrate what they know when possible. Get them to jot down answers first, so they are better armed to share their answers with each other, and with the whole class.

- *Avoid death by bullet point.* Make different slides *look* different. Include some charts or pictures where possible. If you're confident with technology, put in some very short video clips now and then, and link in to web-based material you want your learners to study in more detail – but don't be too dependent on the technology working every time – have plan B ready for when it doesn't work.

- *Try to make the learners like you.* Smile. Be human. Look at them. Respond to them. If they like you, they're more likely to come to your *next* lecture too. Remember that the feedback students will give on your course depends rather a lot on how much they actually like you.

- *Keep thinking of what learners are intended to be* doing *during the lecture.* Don't worry too much about what *you* will be doing, plan to get your learners' brains engaged. Get them making decisions, guessing causes of phenomena, applying ideas, solving problems, and so on. They'll learn more from what they *do* than from what you tell them.

- *Help learners to capture their learning.* For example, try to get learners to jot down *their* views and ideas, and not just try to write out yours. You can give them *your* ideas on a handout to download later on the intranet.

- *Give learners time to think.* Short silences can be very useful – and indeed welcome. From time to time, put a question up on the screen, and ask learners to ponder for (say) a minute or two.

- *Get learners talking to each other.* Purposeful talking is useful learning. Get them talking to each other now and then, arguing, debating, explaining. This is much better than just allowing chatting to break out because of boredom. Get learners to have a go at explaining something you've just introduced, reminding them this is good practice for answering questions later, for example in exams.

- *Be kind to learners' brains.* Concentration spans are measured in minutes, not hours. Break up each lecture into at least three parts, with something lighter in between the tougher parts.

- *Bring in some appropriate humour.* The odd funny slide, amusing anecdote or play on words can work wonders at restoring learners' concentration levels. Then follow up something funny with an important point, while you've still got their full attention.

- *But don't use humour if it's not working!* Watch their faces and respond accordingly. If they're liking the funny bits, keep putting them in, but if they're not, don't!

- *Flag up related sessions.* For example, if you're lecturing to a large group and learners will be going later into tutorial sessions to followup the content of the lecture, show learners some of the questions which will be covered in the tutorials. This will get them started on thinking about them.

- *Keep yourself tuned into WIIFM.* 'What's in it for me?' is a perfectly intelligent question for any learner to have in mind. Always make time to remind learners about *why* a topic is included and *how* it will help them in due course.

- *Don't be unkind to learners who missed your previous lecture.* They're here now. Giving them a bad time won't encourage them to come again. And at least *some* learners will have very good reasons for not having been able to be there last time – illness, crises, whatever. The more unmissable your lectures are, the more learners will try not to miss them whatever else is happening in their lives.

- *Don't overrun.* At least some of your learners are likely to have something else to go to after your lecture, and perhaps with not much of a margin for error. If you come to a good stopping place and there are 15 minutes left, do your closing bit and stop. Learners actually *like* lectures which finish early now and then.

- *Pave the way towards your next lecture.* After reviewing what learners should have got out of the present lecture, show, for example, a slide with three questions which will be covered in next week's instalment.

- *Don't just stop.* Bring your lecture to a definite close. Make a good final impression. Learners are more likely to follow up the lecture if they leave feeling it has been an important and interesting occasion, and well worth attending rather than just downloading the associated links and materials.

 Tips for students: getting the most from lectures

1 *You'll get a lot more from lectures if you do a little bit of thinking before you go in to class.* Think about what has been covered in sessions before and look in the course handbook to see how this week's work is likely to be assessed through assignments or exams. If the course documentation uses any specialist terms you haven't come across before, check these out before the class.

2 *Keep your course handbook on hand to see what areas your lectures are due to cover.* Remember that it is indeed your course. It's you who's going to have to learn the material, not your lecturers – they've already done it. So make sure you have all the details of what's on your agenda, and keep an eye on what's already been covered and what's still to come.

3 *Consider what the real purpose of lectures is nowadays.* Now there is so much material available on the web, including TED talks, open educational resources and learning packages, the lecture is seen by most lecturers as something more than just passing on information that you could have got anyway from a book or from the web. Lectures today are likely to be as much about making you think and posing you challenges as they are about simply delivering content. Your responsibility as a learner is to be active and engaged in lectures just as much as in any other area of your studies.

4   *Look really carefully at the intended learning outcomes.* Most course documents explain what students are required to learn in the form of such outcomes. They are often expressed as statements of what students will be expected to have become able to do at the end of a unit of study. Lecturers will often include the particular intended outcomes for each lecture – watch out for these and make sure you've got them to remind you later of what you're supposed to be aiming towards.

5   *Think about how you are going to retain information and your thoughts from the lectures.* Don't just take notes, make notes. Whether you make notes with pen and paper, on a laptop, on your phone or using Twitter, the notes you make in lectures are important resources for later study. Don't just rely on the presentation being available on the course VLE after class because it's your thoughts on what's being said that you need to retain. Take the view that you're only really learning if you're capturing important aspects of the lecture. So get your brain working, but don't just use it busily, use it wisely.

6   *Don't just switch off if you are given handouts in class or pointed to where the notes will be on the VLE for later use.* It's dangerously easy to think, 'Ah well, I've got all the slides, so I don't have to think hard about it now during the lecture – I can catch up later!' Actually, your time in class is particularly valuable as it's your best chance to interrogate the material, whether privately or by asking questions of the lecturer or peers.

7   *Resist the temptation to excessively multi-task.* It is possible to check your Facebook page and send texts and tweets in a lecture, but this is unlikely to improve your concentration unless you're focussed on the topic in hand. But don't be afraid to Google unfamiliar terminology and to check you've accurately recorded references.

8   *If you miss a lecture, remember that any notes provided by the lecturer are no substitute for having been there.* Use any available handouts or virtual copies of the slides and other resources to enable you to catch up on what you missed to fill at least some of the inevitable gaps in your understanding of the topic. But also try to talk to some people who were actually there, and get them to explain the main points to you, or check on the course VLE to see if there is ongoing discussion of the key topics.

9   *Make sure you do something to help you concentrate in the lecture, rather than just being a passive listener.* Don't be embarrassed to make notes even if folk around you are just sitting there doing nothing. If you find it helps you to jot down key points now and then, do it. Or maybe draw diagrams, tables or mind maps of what you are hearing and seeing, or use mind mapping software to record the ideas. It's your learning which will be assessed in due course, so make a good start on it right there and then in lectures. Think about what is really meant by what you see and hear, and capture the meaning. This keeps you alert, and helps to stop you becoming distracted from the class.

10 *Put things into your own words rather than just writing down or audio-recording what is said.* You need to think about what you're writing. Sometimes you will need to keep detailed notes, for example if you're expected to write down an exact definition or quotation. But for most of the time, what you should try to do is to capture for yourself the essence of what's being said and shown in lectures.

(Continued)

(Continued)

11   *Keep asking yourself: 'What am I expected to become able to do with this?'* When you're asking this, you can deliberately and consciously record your own thoughts so that they remind you of what seems to be expected of you.

12   *Watch out for cues you are being given by your lecturer.* Lecturers give all sorts of hints during any lecture by tone of voice, emphasis, body language and repetition. Sometimes they give these clues deliberately in order to get you thinking about how the material will be assessed or what kinds of approaches you should be taking to skills development or the acquisition of knowledge. Even more often, they do it subconsciously. Either way, you need to know what is really important, so that you can make sure you have a firm grip on such things when assessments loom up.

13   *Write down your own questions.* Every time there's something you can't quite understand, turn it into a short question and note it down. When you've captured these questions, you can find out the answers in your own time, looking them up or asking other people, or asking the lecturer. Or you could tweet questions to fellow attendees using a hashtag. If you haven't captured your questions in class, a few hours later you probably won't remember what they were, and then there's no chance at all of getting them answered.

14   *Note also your own reactions, feelings and thoughts.* Quite often in a lecture you'll 'see the light dawn' about something, but if you don't jot down something about what you are thinking, it might not happen again, even when you look back at your notes.

15   *At the end of the lecture, take action to help you retain information.* Whatever filing and recording system you use to keep track of what you are learning (whether paper notes, blogs or sections in your ePortfolio) keep these up to date so you can access them easily when you need to use them again for revision or to inform your professional practice.

Some of the resources in this chapter are available to print for your own use on the companion website. To access these, along with some video clips of the author, please visit: **www.sagepub.co.uk/makinglearninghappen**

CHAPTER 7

MAKING LEARNING HAPPEN IN SMALL GROUPS

Key topics in this chapter

- Less important than lectures?
- Why turn up?
- The chance to talk
- The chance to assess
- Personal tutoring
- No hiding place
- Employability and enterprise

SHORT MEASURE FOR SMALL-GROUP TEACHING?

This chapter has grown in this edition, not least with the inclusion of some thoughts about the value of small-group learning to address employability and enterprise, and with the addition of some considerations of personal tutoring, extending the discussion to one-to-one tutoring. Chapter 6 already included a wide range of ideas about turning large-group sessions into individual learning experiences for all present, *and* getting learners in large groups to work with each other in smaller groups. Many of the suggestions offered in Chapter 6 continue to apply to groups which are intentionally small, for example contexts including tutorials and seminars, particularly the comments on helping students to ask questions and on finding out what they already know. But as the discussion in this chapter shows, small-group contexts can be the sharp end of learning, not least because there is no hiding place in small groups. Indeed, it is worth reminding ourselves that in many parts of the world, higher education functioned for hundreds of years in what we would now regard as small-group teaching/learning contexts, and hundreds of learners in the presence of one teacher would have been hard to imagine for most of the history of higher education until relatively recently.

There are many disciplines where small-group work is at the heart of the curriculum. For example, where students spend a lot of their time in studios, laboratories, workshops, gyms and in field work, the nature of a course or module involves them working with each other, rather than sitting in a lecture theatre, or working online. However, in other disciplines, especially where there are very large groups in lectures, there has been a tendency to reduce or scrap follow-up tutorials or seminars, simply because of the difficulty of accommodating dozens of small-group sessions in the available accommodation, with the available staffing. One of the purposes of this chapter is to remind both tutors and students of the value of small-group sessions, to increase the quality of our provision of this kind of learning.

'But we can't fit in as much small-group teaching'

In times of resource and staffing constraints, managers are only too ready to take fright at the costs of providing small-group elements of courses and modules. 'There's lots of pressure on our timetables and teaching spaces', they explain. 'And in any case, nowadays we put all sorts of material online for students to work at in their own way, at their own pace, and wherever they choose to study', they further explain. However useful it is for learners to intensify their learning alone online, they are still often missing out on the further dimensions of learning which can develop in small-group contexts – the interaction, the discussion and the relative exposure of the 'no hiding place' context.

'But small-group stuff isn't taken seriously'

This is said just as often by learners and by tutors, and used as a justification for relegating small-group elements of the curriculum to online or resource-based independent learning. Lecturers complain that too many students just don't turn up for small groups, and students complain that too often their tutor doesn't turn up! Lecturers grumble that students who do turn up haven't done the expected preparation for a small-group session, and students grumble that lecturers don't seem to have planned anything particular when they do turn up! Students pick up the impression that the lecture programme is the backbone of the course or module, and that small-group learning is just the icing on the cake, and is 'missable'. And in the UK's National Student Survey, for example, some managers rationalise: 'there aren't any questions about small-group teaching, therefore it can't be as important a part of the intended student experience after all'. However, as we shall see, small-group experience has a lot to do with various other dimensions of the student experience as gleaned from such surveys, and (perhaps more importantly) the opportunity for students not just to deepen their learning but also to develop the skills and attributes which will make them employable.

Therefore, just as in the case of live lectures, where there are many things that couldn't have been gained nearly as well just by participating in a MOOC, I hope that the discussion in this chapter will convince you that there are many things to be gained from small-group learning experiences which simply could not have been achieved by any combination of lectures, and independent learning online.

WHY HAVE SMALL-GROUP LEARNING?

One answer to the question is that a great deal of normal human learning takes place in what can be regarded as small-group contexts – families and friends. For most people, that is how learning first happened. That's how we first learned to learn. Therefore, it should continue to be a natural part of any wider learning environment. Moreover, small-group contexts can be much more 'social' than studying alone – and more personal than large-group contexts such as lectures, where there is usually less room for social interchange. Furthermore, the student voice can be exercised much more readily in small-group contexts. We've already explored how valuable it is to learners to verbalise orally, as a way of deepening and clarifying their own thinking about any subject. But conversely, there may be no hiding place in a small group, in contrast to the relative ease of disappearing into the crowd in large-group lectures.

Small-group teaching does not always get an easy ride, however, not just in students' eyes, but also in the view of their lecturers, and sadly often managers of post-compulsory education institutions. 'Why do we persist in pretending that small-group teaching is as good as or better than other methods?' is the sort of question asked by those who don't like small-group teaching – or who are not very good at doing it. Indeed, when small-group teaching is done badly, it might be better if it had been abandoned. Sadly, too many learners continue to report unsatisfactory experiences of learning in small-group contexts. Perhaps it boils down to the fact that what we should really be trying to achieve in small groups is skilled facilitation of learning, rather than 'teaching', though I would argue that this should be a general maxim and by no means applies only to small groups.

Further light is thrown on the value of small-group work from cases where class sizes have increased (or staffing has decreased) to such an extent that small-group work (particularly tutorials and seminars) has had to be discontinued, and manifestations such as the following develop:

- increased drop-out and failure statistics because learners don't have enough opportunity to have help with their difficulties

- learners themselves remaining unaware of study problems they have, which would otherwise have come to the surface in tutorials or seminars

- more time being needed trying to help those learners who make appointments for one-to-one help with particular problems – often the same problem many times over

- more interruptions to the flow of large-group teaching, when it is no longer possible in a lecture to reply to a question: 'This is just the right sort of question to discuss in detail in your next tutorial – bring it along then and make sure that it is sorted out to your satisfaction'

- increased risk of learners succeeding satisfactorily in written assessment scenarios, but not having gained the level of mastery of the subject matter that comes from discussing it, arguing about it and explaining it to other people

- increased risk of lecturers remaining unaware of significant problems which learners were experiencing until too late – when the problems have turned into assessment failures.

WHERE IS THE REAL PAY-OFF FROM SMALL-GROUP LEARNING?

The real learning pay-off from small-group learning is linked to the following factors:

- increased opportunity for learners to ask us questions

- more time for us to spend answering specific questions

- more opportunity for learners to deepen their learning by verbalizing orally, explaining things to us and to each other, helping them to make sense of difficult parts of the subject matter

- more opportunity for in-depth discussion of things learners *want* to find out

- more opportunity for us to clarify to learners exactly what they should be aiming to achieve

- the opportunity for us to make ourselves approachable to learners and get to know them as individuals

- the chance to give high-quality feedback to individuals in the group, where eye contact, tone of voice, body language and emphasis can all clarify our feedback – much more than just written, printed or emailed comments ever can

- the chance for learners to learn from the feedback *others* are receiving

- the opportunity for learners to find out how their learning is going by comparing the level to which they are making sense of concepts and ideas with each other

- time for learners to look at past evidence of achievement – for example, portfolios, essays – and clarify what the learning outcomes mean in practice, and how their future work will be assessed

- the opportunity for learners to make informed judgements about their own work, and about each other's work, helping them to deepen their learning and find out more about the assessment culture surrounding them

- the opportunity for us to gain feedback about how their learning is progressing, allowing us to make adjustments where necessary to other teaching contexts, including large-group sessions.

Such is the scope of the pay-off in the points listed above, that we may ask whether post-compulsory education could possibly succeed without the contribution of small-group learning. Wise prospective students might well research the quantity and quality of small-group work when choosing a course or an institution.

WHAT *ELSE* ARE WE TRYING TO DO IN SMALL GROUPS?

Among the most significant reasons for using small-group teaching are the benefits learners acquire that lie beyond the curriculum as expressed through intended learning outcomes. The *emergent* learning outcomes associated with small-group work help learners to equip themselves with the skills and attitudes they will need for the next stages of their careers – and lives.

I've referred in earlier chapters to the National Student Survey used in the UK since 2005 to find out about the experience of final-year students. None of the statements in the questionnaire refers directly to small-group teaching and learning, but three of them (numbers 19–21) under the heading 'Personal development' have strong links:

19 The course has helped me to present myself with confidence.

20 My communication skills have improved.

21 As a result of the course, I feel confident to tackle unfamiliar problems.

Each one of these aspects of the student experience links to small-group learning contexts. This at least partly explains why the overall results of the survey tend to be better for smaller higher education institutions, where group size is likely to be lower in general, and where it may be argued staff and students get to know each other better.

Ideally, we should be using small-group teaching to achieve as many as possible of the things we wish to do to help learners to succeed, but which can't be directly incorporated into large-group teaching or resource-based learning online. This is why it can be so wasteful if small-group sessions just degenerate into a continuation of what we're doing in large-group contexts. Among the additional outcomes of successful small-group work are the following (which of course also link strongly to the 'personal development' agenda of the National Student Survey in the UK):

- the opportunity for learners to develop their confidence in speaking, presenting, arguing, discussing, debating, and so on, linking strongly to employability
- the opportunity for learners to practise and develop their oral communication skills, such as those they will need for job interviews or oral exams
- the chance for learners to learn a great deal from each other, adding to what they learn from us and online resources
- the chance for learners to develop and practise their interpersonal skills, learning how best to work collaboratively with different people, not least with *difficult* people
- the chance for learners to reflect together on how their learning is going and to find out more about how they stand compared to their peers
- the opportunity to get learners to deepen their own learning by verbalizing orally, explaining difficult ideas and concepts to each other.

DESIGNING LEARNING INTO SMALL-GROUP CONTEXTS

Deep learning is most likely to happen in small-group contexts when as many as possible of the seven factors underpinning successful learning are involved, in short when students:

- are motivated to the extent that they *want* to learn from the small-group setting
- have clear targets so they know what they *need* to be getting out of the session
- have plenty of opportunity for learning by doing, practice, trial and error and participation
- gain useful feedback from each other as well as from the tutor
- realize that they are making sense of the subject matter being addressed in the session
- get their heads around key concepts by explaining them to each other
- make informed judgements about their evidence of achievement of the learning outcomes, deepening their learning.

I will expand on the links between small-group settings and these factors below.

1 Wanting to learn

What can we do to help learners *want* to learn in small groups? The best we can do is to make small-group sessions so enjoyable that learners can't wait to come along to them! However, this is perhaps rather harder to achieve if the session is a problems class on applications of the second law of thermodynamics, or some other element of 'troublesome knowledge' in your own discipline.

It is a measure of the success of small-group teaching sessions if learners always feel that it is worth coming along and joining in, and that they leave with things they simply wouldn't have got if they'd missed the session – explanations, discussion, answers to their own questions, ideas and, particularly, the feeling that during the session they had made sense of parts of the subject matter. If they feel they've not got anything more than some extra information, the want to learn is hardly likely to be enhanced. We can easily gather feedback from learners, for example asking them to rate small-group sessions in terms of how much they feel them 'time well spent'. When learners feel that they have progressed their own learning faster as a result of participating in a small-group session than they would have done simply studying the topic on their own, they are likely to come to the sessions with greater expectations and increased willingness to take part actively.

2 Taking ownership of the need to learn

How best can we use small-group contexts to clarify the learning need and to help students take ownership of this need? Small-group sessions are ideal occasions to spend extra time clarifying the intended learning outcomes so that learners gain a greater awareness regarding what exactly we are, in due course, going to expect them to do to evidence their achievement of the outcomes. While we should be doing this in large-group contexts too, small-group sessions can allow us to let learners *get their hands on* examples of the kind of evidence we're looking for, such as portfolios, dissertations, past essays or assignments, and subject-specific artefacts such as drawings, photos, posters, and so on.

Small-group contexts are also an opportunity to gather learners' questions about how exactly assessment works, though for fairness it is best for us to *respond* to these questions in a large-group context so that particular small groups do not become advantaged regarding their insight into assessment expectations. We can use small-group sessions to get learners themselves applying assessment criteria to past work or their own work, and we can clarify for them how the criteria are used in practice.

3 Learning by doing in small groups

What actions do learners learn most from in small groups? Table 7.1 lists some actions we can help learners to do in small groups to maximize their learning pay-off. There are, of course, countless other subject-specific things we can get learners doing in small groups, but it is useful to ask learners from time to time exactly what they are finding works well for them in terms of learning pay-off.

Table 7.1 Some things we can get learners doing in small groups to maximize their learning pay-off

Agreeing solutions	Engaging	Remembering
Analysing	Explaining	Reviewing
Arguing	Guessing	Selecting
Assessing	Helping	Sharing
Connecting	Listening	Sketching
Debating	Note-making	Solving problems
Demonstrating	Observing others	Succeeding
Designing	Participating	Summarizing
Discussing	Questioning	Talking

4 Making sense of things in small groups

As mentioned throughout this book, *making sense* of ideas, concepts, theories, and so on has to be done by learners themselves – we can't do this for them. We can, however, strive to ensure that small-group contexts provide them with ideal environments for getting their heads around things, not least by allowing them to compare their own grasp on a subject with that of other group members, alerting them to exactly where the blocks may be, and encouraging them to feel good about the things they've mastered successfully. Additionally, small-group sessions can give learners *time* to get their heads around things – time they may not have found for themselves on their own. In particular, ways of helping learners to make sense of things in small groups link strongly to the remaining three factors underpinning successful learning – getting them to give and receive feedback in small groups, helping them to explain things to each other, and involving them in making informed judgements about their own and each other's work by using small-group contexts for self-assessment and peer assessment activities.

5 Making the most of feedback in small groups

How best can we maximize the feedback learners get from each other in small groups? Feedback is most useful when it is about something learners have just done. We can therefore give them tasks to do in small groups (and before the sessions), then get them reviewing each other's efforts and explaining what they think about them.

It is useful to discuss with learners how best to receive feedback from each other (and, indeed, from ourselves). For example, learners often need to be encouraged not just to shrug off positive comments or praise, but to allow themselves to *accept* such feedback, swell with pride about it and take on board exactly what they have done well, so that they can continue to build on their achievements. They also need to be helped to receive critical feedback well, not to become defensive and try to justify their actions, but to listen carefully to the feedback and see what they can learn from it so that mistakes or deficiencies can be useful learning experiences for them. Giving and receiving feedback is also excellent practice for future employment – and life in general.

6 Speaking: explaining, coaching and teaching in small groups

There is enormous potential for using small-group contexts to help students to learn by explaining things to each other, coaching each other, and even teaching each other. This is, of course, dependent on us as tutors refraining from doing all that explaining, coaching and teaching ourselves! There is a balance to be struck. Learners may indeed expect us to do most of the work in small groups, not least answering their questions and helping them to solve their problems with the subject concerned. We can, however, invite fellow learners to answer questions first, and only step in when we are really needed. We need to be honest with learners about our intention to help them get the most out of working with each other in small groups, to reduce any feeling that they are not getting full value out of us in the sessions. We may need to propose to learners how valuable it is to practise explaining difficult ideas to each other, as a precursor to them becoming able to explain them quickly and confidently in assessment contexts such as exam answers or coursework assignments.

In the case of seminars, where it is normal to ask one or more students to take the lead in presenting a particular topic which they have researched, we can strengthen the learning pay-off they derive from the exercise by suggesting that they not only *present* the topic, but do so in a way designed to help their audience to *learn* significantly as a result. This necessarily helps them to see their presentation from the point of view of the audience, improving the presentation, and better still perhaps, designing questions or exercises which will involve the audience. It is well established that students remember for a long time things that they prepared and presented in seminars – deep learning.

Moreover, when learners leave a small-group session feeling that it was well worth their time having been there, they are more likely to invest in such sessions more earnestly, not least doing any work we have suggested as preparation for their participation in the session. In addition, when learners get to know each other by explaining things to each other, they are much more likely to continue to make the most of working with each other outside the timetabled curriculum – all the more learning then happens without any additional effort on our part. So it is in our interest to help learners to become more dependent on learning from each other.

7 Learning by assessing in small groups

We can, as mentioned in Chapter 6, help our students to learn by assessing in large-group contexts, but we can often achieve this even better in small-group contexts where we can oversee how they apply assessment criteria to their own and each other's work. Where necessary we can explain exactly what the criteria really mean. For example, we can ask learners to bring along to small-group sessions work they have prepared, then ask them to exchange scripts, and mark the work of a fellow learner, talking them through the marking scheme, and helping them to make judgements on the quality of the work. This allows all present to:

- learn from things a fellow learner may have done better, and thereby become able to emulate the better performance in future work

- learn from mistakes a fellow learner may have made, and more consciously avoid making similar mistakes in future work

- get their heads around the finer detail regarding how their work may be assessed when exam answers or formal coursework are assessed by tutors – in other words, find out important detail about the assessment culture in which they are studying.

The last of these is particularly important. When learners realize that if they miss a small-group session, they are losing out on finding out valuable information about how assessment will work for them, they are less likely to choose to miss such a session in future. If it was just some *information* they would miss, they could copy that from those who were there, but if it was an important *experience* they would miss, they soon realize the importance of such small-group sessions.

FACTORS TO CONSIDER IN SMALL-GROUP LEARNING

In this part of the chapter, we explore answers to a number of frequently asked questions about small-group learning – see Figure 7.1.

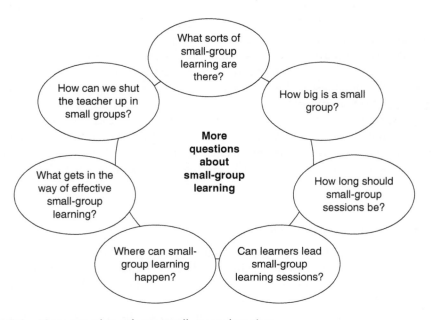

Figure 7.1 More questions about small-group learning

What sorts of small-group learning are there?

There are many contexts that can be thought of as small-group learning, not all involving tutors. *Tutorials* in some institutions are scheduled meetings between a tutor and a few learners, often used to follow up the content of lectures and to get learners applying what they are meant to do with theories and concepts. One problem is that learners don't necessarily know what is expected of them in tutorials. Sally Brown (2009) says of her first experiences of tutorials as a learner, 'I tried to be good, and sit quietly and listen to what the tutor had to say'. Few nowadays would regard that as 'good' behaviour. Tutorials are ideal occasions for learners to bring their own individual questions and problems and to seek help from the tutor. In some institutions, the word 'tutorial' is used to describe face-to-face meetings between a tutor and one learner at a time – we'll look in some detail later in this chapter at 'personal tutoring' which is often one-to-one, but which has purposes quite different from those of 'academic tutorials'. With increasing class sizes, however, it is not uncommon to find the term 'academic tutorial' used for subject-related work with groups of as many as 20 learners.

Seminars are often confused with tutorials. Learners often don't know what they're supposed to do in these sessions. The essential difference between a seminar and a tutorial in many tutors' minds is that in seminars, learners themselves contribute most of the content. For example, they prepare to talk as individuals or small groups about pre-allocated topics, then open the topics up for discussion.

Other kinds of small-group teaching include laboratory work, studio work, problems classes and practical work of various kinds where learners work independently or in twos and threes, with individual support from time to time from tutors.

Learners can, and do, work collaboratively in small groups without the presence of tutors. They often benefit from informal 'study syndicates', explaining things to each other, practising and gaining confidence in the things they will need to show evidence of their achievement in due course. Not all small-group collaboration nowadays is face-to-face. Learners often publish blogs and use social media to include discussions and comments about their learning. It can be useful for tutors to build this into a given face-to-face tutorial or seminar, for example by starting off a '#topic' thread on Twitter before a group session, encouraging students to post tweets during the session, and continue the thread after the event.

How big is a small group?

It all depends. In some subjects, a small group is no more than about four learners. However, seminar groups are often much bigger, for example a cohort of 300 learners may be broken into seminar groups of around 20. Problems classes in maths, science and engineering may be as large as 40. This increases the danger that they become a continuation of large-group teaching unless tutors take care to keep the focus on learner activity, for example by dividing the group up into fours or fives so that every learner has an opportunity to discuss things and gain feedback from peers. With group sizes of three to six or so, there is less chance of passenger or bystander behaviours, and it is fairly straightforward to get every-one to contribute. With larger groups, however, it becomes more difficult to keep everyone engaged.

How long should small-group sessions be?

In practice, the duration of small-group sessions is less important than how well the time is spent. A well-facilitated small group can achieve in as little as half an hour much more than a poorly facilitated group achieves in a couple of hours. The problem with short duration sessions is that the time can all too easily be eroded if it takes some minutes to get everyone there. Where small-group ses-sions last for an hour or two, it is important to build in a variety of processes and get learners involved in different tasks and activities. When small-group learning is working well, learners often comment that the time has flown by, even when the session lasts a day or half-day.

Can learners lead small-group learning sessions?

They *can*. Getting learners to lead sessions develops just the kind of confidence that the National Student Survey is looking for. Learners are helped to lead small-group sessions (seminars in particular) if they have clear, manageable briefings about what exactly is expected of them, sufficient time to prepare to take the lead and are not interrupted too often by tutors! It remains important that the task of leading sessions is not made too daunting for any shy or retiring learners, nor just given to the vociferous ones. Tutor interventions need to be restricted to when the learner leading a session really needs to be rescued or helped out – but even then it can be better to facilitate other learners coming to their aid.

Where can small-group learning happen?

Small-group sessions can occur just about anywhere. Small teaching rooms are often heavily timetabled in institutions, and it is all too common for a tutor and small group to be seen wandering the corridors looking for a suitable venue, particularly if a tutorial or seminar has had to be rescheduled. Libraries often contain small bookable rooms, which can be booked by students themselves to continue small-group work on their own. Small-group sessions often spill over into other areas, including lounges, dining areas and even the nearest comfortable pub (but we need to remember that if the group contains members whose reli-gion prohibits alcohol then this venue would be entirely inappropriate).

By common consent, small-group sessions on late Friday afternoons or early Monday mornings, for example, are often rescheduled, but this can add to the dif-ficulties of finding suitable space. In most institutions, staff are urged only to book rooms for sessions that definitely will take place, rather than make block bookings for a whole semester, even when some of the small-group sessions are going to happen in alternative places such as computer suites, laboratories or field visits.

How to make learners feel at home in small groups?

How can we ensure in small groups that learners don't feel marginalized, alienated and ignored? Using learners' names can help. The simplest and most effective way of getting to know learners' names in small groups is to give learners self-adhesive labels, ask them to write down what they prefer to be called, and stick the labels to their clothing. This has the advantage of revealing what they *really* want to be called – at least some of their chosen names will be different from those printed on a class list. Addressing learners by name makes a surprisingly big difference, especially when asking questions or giving feedback. When learners spend much of their contact time in very large groups, where they can easily feel just one of a crowd, small-group teaching can compensate, and has the additional benefit of helping them to get to know each other – always useful.

It is up to tutors to ensure that learners don't feel alienated in a small group. Where there is just one female learner in a group, or one male learner, care needs to be taken not to allow this to cause them to feel exposed in any way. Similarly, ethnic background differences need to be handled sensitively. The best way of checking that all is going well in small-group sessions is to have a sufficiently relaxed and informal atmosphere so that it is easy to keep asking, 'How are you finding these sessions?' and 'Is there anything we can do to improve these sessions for you?' and so on.

What gets in the way of effective small-group learning?

The principal factors getting in the way of effective small-group learning include:

- Learners not turning up, when they don't feel small-group contexts are as important as large-group sessions. This is often because learners think that all the important material will be linked to large-group sessions such as lectures, and we need to make it very clear to them all that, although most of the *information* may be aired in large-group sessions, the *making sense* of the information by applying it and practising with it is often best done in small groups, where there can be quick and individual feedback to all present, helping them to turn the information into their own knowledge.

- Tutors not taking small-group teaching as seriously as they take large-group teaching, and arriving for small-group sessions relatively unprepared.

- Learners being shy and embarrassed about being expected to join in discussions in small groups. However, as tutors we need to help them to gain the confidence to contribute actively, and it is important that they don't feel 'put down' if they get things wrong or don't communicate their ideas effectively at first.

- Small-group teaching being viewed in institutions as not very cost-effective compared to large-group teaching.

- Insufficient attention being paid by tutors to what is *best* covered by small-group work compared with what should be covered by large-group teaching.

- Learners not doing their part in preparing for small-group sessions.
- Failure to adjust group membership and composition when particular groups fail to work well together.
- Failure to clarify the intended learning outcomes for small-group sessions.
- Tutors continuing to teach in a non-participative way.
- Difficulties in finding suitable spaces and environments for small-group teaching.
- Dominant learners being allowed too much air time in discussions.
- Passive learners being allowed to remain passive. Human nature being what it is, it is easier to be passive in small-group learning situations than to take the risk of being active but wrong. The words 'passenger' and 'bystander' are often used to describe the behaviours that can lead learners to get nothing out of small-group work.
- Difficulties in achieving equity of the learning experience when a large group is divided into several small groups, and particularly when different group sessions are facilitated by different tutors.

As indicated in some elements of the list above, most of these factors can be addressed directly by tutors, provided they themselves are indeed convinced of the benefits for learners of small-group teaching contexts. There are, however, some institutional factors which can be harder to address. These include:

- costs associated with small-group provision, especially in times of financial restraint
- staff availability to cover small-group work
- difficulties finding sufficient suitable small-group learning venues when very large groups are split up into a lot of small ones
- timetabling difficulties: for example fitting in a dozen parallel sessions between two lectures in a series
- tutors who lack the experience or expertise in the subject matter, especially when other parallel sessions are being facilitated by the lecturer responsible for the associated large-group sessions
- tensions between research and teaching getting in the way of researchers putting enough time and effort into preparing for their small-group teaching work
- the institutional ethos regarding small-group teaching, if it is regarded as not very important or 'a bit of a luxury' or 'just the icing on the cake'
- lack of feedback from learners on their experience of small-group teaching when, as often happens, monitoring and evaluation tends to focus on large-group teaching.

How can we shut the teacher up in small groups?

Probably the most significant danger in most small-group learning contexts is that teachers just continue to teach, and learners are not involved as much as they should be. Sometimes the blame goes to the teacher, but often teachers continue to talk to fill the silence caused by learners *not* being ready, willing or able to contribute.

It takes a little nerve for a teacher to pose a question to a small group of learners and wait for them to answer it. Silence is threatening, and it's all too easy for teachers to go for the comfort of filling the silence. It can be better to wait a while, and if the silence is still continuing, to clarify the question, putting it into other words or breaking it down into more manageable sub-questions. One of the best ways to cause learners to participate is to give them a little time, individually or in twos or threes, to jot down notes in response to a question, *then* ask them to give their answers orally. Armed with some jottings, most learners feel more confident to speak. We also need to encourage learners to participate, particularly by not ridiculing their contributions when they are wrong, and always trying to find something positive to say in response to their efforts.

Which other tutor behaviours *damage* learning in small groups?

I've already mentioned that just continuing to teach (or lecture!) can damage the learning pay-off which might have resulted from small-group work. However, the most damaging tutor behaviour is not taking small-group teaching as seriously as large-group teaching. For example, it is relatively rare for a large-class session to be cancelled or postponed, but much more common for small-group sessions to be cancelled at short notice. This infuriates part-time learners who may have travelled to the institution just for the cancelled tutorial. Learners are quick to get the message that if small-group sessions are not valued by their tutors, the sessions can't be very important.

Another tutor behaviour that can easily damage small-group teaching is to put learners down. If they arrive late, for example (perhaps for unavoidable reasons), a sharp retort from a tutor can make them feel really bad about being there at all, and sometimes they don't return to small-group sessions again. More often, however, tutors demotivate learners by responding inappropriately to their comments and questions. This is likely to make learners less likely to participate and undermines the whole rationale of the less-formal communication between tutors and learners which small-group teaching should allow.

SMALL-GROUP LEARNING AND EMPLOYABILITY, ENTREPRENEURSHIP AND ENTERPRISE

'With the changing economy, no one has lifetime employment, but community colleges provide lifetime employability' (President Barack Obama, 2009). In the recession we have experienced in the last few years, it is encouraging that the importance of employability, and our role in trying to develop it, is recognized by such a world leader.

Part of the purpose of post-compulsory education in the grand scheme of things is to help learners become ready for what is likely to be one of the main features of the rest of their lives – getting a job and staying in employment. For the last two decades and more, there has been a lot of discussion about the balance we need to strike in our educational provision between deepening learners' knowledge and understanding of the subjects they are studying and developing the skills they will need for their careers, and indeed the rest of their lives. Many aspects of becoming more employable can be developed alongside the subject-related knowledge and skills which are the basis of the main intended learning outcomes of our provision, and indeed can be regarded as important 'intended learning outgoings', as mentioned in Chapter 3. Indeed, it is perfectly possible to formulate intended learning outcomes and outgoings for the whole field of 'becoming more employable', and to assess learners' evidence of achievement of the former alongside the subject-based curriculum. Because of the key role of interpersonal skills and oral communication skills, small-group learning remains our best chance to enhance employability.

How can we help learners to *show* that they are employable?

There are many good reasons for building into our curriculum opportunities for learners to evidence their employability. Employers themselves know better than to rely simply on academic results when choosing the right candidate for a post. They seek evidence of employability from letters of application, CVs and, above all, from interviews with job applicants.

Evidence of employability needs to arise from purposefully designed learning by doing activities, including plenty of opportunity to learn by trial and error in safe environments – mock interview panels, CV selection panels, and so on. Therefore, it is useful to think, when designing learning by doing towards the achievement of subject-based intended learning outcomes, to what extent the same activities can embrace the skills and attributes associated with employability. In particular, many of these activities lend themselves best to small-group learning contexts. These can give learners practice at evidencing their employability, and in contexts where it is not just seen as an add-on, but as a process directly linked to the mainstream curriculum. For example, getting learners to role-play interviewers and candidates in interview simulations, and capturing the process on video, can help learners to see themselves as future employers might see them, and learn by trial and error in a safe context. We can get learners to put together applications for fictitious posts, and allow them to learn by judging each other's applications as 'shortlisting committees', prior to using these applications as part of the basis for the interview simulations. They then learn a great deal about which aspects of an application may lead to good (or difficult) interview questions. The whole process develops their written and oral communication skills by practice, and trial and error, in a safe environment and can do a lot to help them to feel that they can succeed in making a good job of preparing to be seen to be employable.

Striking the balance between independence, collaboration and followership

There is much discussion of the importance of using post-compulsory education to develop learner autonomy and independence, but the ways that learning is driven by assessment often pushes us in the reverse direction towards conformity and uniformity. One aspect of employability which attracts a lot of attention is the development of leadership. However, particularly in the early stages of employment, perhaps an even more important set of skills and attributes to be identified are those linked to the concept of 'followership' – at any time there need to be more followers around than leaders, even when some perfectly capable leaders are present. Perhaps we also need to consider some attributes which can be thought of as more conformist, perhaps including the following:

- recognizing when *not* to air one's own views, in the interests of getting things done and promoting teamwork

- listening without giving one's disagreement away by body language, facial expression, and so on, when disagreement is not important – or, indeed, when it needs to be shelved for the purposes of the task in hand

- accepting action plans that are not quite as good as those in one's own mind, so that others continue with the increased momentum which comes from their sense of ownership of the action plan

- allowing others to do things which one could have done better to aid everyone's contribution to a task.

'To lead people, walk beside them ... As for the best leaders, the people do not notice their existence. The next best, the people honor and praise. The next, the people fear; and the next, the people hate ... When the best leader's work is done the people say, We did it ourselves!' (Lao Tzu, c. sixth century BC).

Beyond employability – enterprise and entrepreneurship

In recent years, several higher education institutions have addressed purposefully the development of enterprise skills and entrepreneurship qualities in students, alongside their subject-related studies. In times of recession, it is likely to be these qualities which are needed to move us back towards prosperity.

It is very clear that we can't develop these qualities *for* our students – only *they* can do this. This is similar to *making sense* in the context of their subject-related learning. It is also clear that developing enterprise skills and entrepreneurship qualities is not likely to be achieved in a 'conformist' environment. We need to allow students the time and space to learn these skills by trial and error (giving plenty of feedback) and, above all, by a great deal of interpersonal interaction – interaction with other students, with tutors and, more importantly perhaps, interaction with real-life entrepreneurs from outside the relatively conservative confines of higher education.

As ever, when learning is driven substantially by assessment, we face the challenging task of designing assessment processes and instruments which will serve as targets to students, so that they develop their enterprise and entrepreneurship qualities along the way. By their very nature, however, there are no 'right answers' to assess, and our traditional assessment methods are far from fit for purpose as means of measuring these qualities.

Perhaps if a future version of an instrument such as the National Student Survey should probe final-year students' experiences of the extent to which their courses helped them to develop enterprise and entrepreneurship, we would see much greater attention paid by institutions to providing students with the opportunity, time, space and feedback needed to achieve these qualities alongside their studies in higher education, and learning in small-group contexts would move towards centre-stage.

Learning to be enterprising

All seven of the factors underpinning successful learning discussed throughout this book can be considered to link strongly to developing learners' employability (and indeed can link to enterprise and entrepreneurship development too). In the section that follows, I will take the particular dimension of enterprise, and look at how the development of relevant skills and attributes in small-group learning contexts can link to the factors underpinning learning discussed throughout this book.

1 Wanting to become enterprising

When students want this, it's a very good start. This kind of attitude links closely to the sort of motivation employers value. Getting students to think consciously about their wish to become enterprising during their studies paves the way to them being conscious of their own driving forces in general, and helps them to remain more aware of what they desire in employment. This, in turn, helps them quickly to communicate their ambitions both to prospective employers at interview – helping to secure a job in the first place – and to their actual employers when in post – helping them perhaps to justify some training or development they would like, or indeed to secure promotion as 'someone who knows their own mind' and takes responsibility for their own progression.

2 Needing to become enterprising

Even when students don't *want* to become enterprising, we can do a lot to move them in the right direction by helping them take ownership of the *need* to do so. We can provide them with suitable targets, and help them to see how useful it will be for them to reach these targets. Working towards targets is necessary in the day-to-day life of being employed. Working towards other people's targets, in particular, is very important in the early stages of any post. Skills gained working out what intended learning outcomes actually boil down to in practice are usefully extended to breaking overall targets in employment into achievable, manageable steps. Enterprise and entrepreneurship could be regarded as including helping students to set new targets and plan how to reach them. Enterprise could also be regarded as linking to resilience in the context of steadfastly taking ownership of the need to reach 'imposed' targets.

3 Learning by being enterprising

Students learn by doing – practice, trial and error, repetition. We're good at getting students learning by doing, but perhaps not good enough yet at making that 'doing' link to enterprise. Any job can be regarded as an extension of practice, repetition, learning through mistakes, and so on. If we can help learners to be more conscious of the enterprise nature of their learning by doing, they are likely to remain so as they move into employment, and continue to be more willing and able to have a go at new problems, even when some trial and error will be involved.

4 Making sense of enterprise

This is about students getting their heads around the whole business of going about learning in enterprising ways. We can do a lot by helping learners become aware of how best they achieve enterprise, paving the way for them to become better at it during employment. The more conscious they are of what works best for them in getting their heads around new scenarios and concepts, the better they can take charge of understanding the employment contexts they find themselves in, and the less likely they are to rush into things, having only thought through the consequences at a superficial level.

5 Learning enterprise through feedback

Learning through feedback is perhaps the most important of the factors underpinning successful learning. We know, however, not least from the National Student Survey, that students remain dissatisfied with our efforts to give them feedback on their learning. So we need to make sure that they get more and better feedback, not only from us but also from each other. We need to help them become better 'receivers' of feedback, as well as becoming more focused on providing it. Employers value highly the skills of good listeners. However, receptive listeners are those who take feedback on board rapidly and easily, and adjust their actions accordingly. Similarly, the skills of giving feedback constructively are very important in work-based contexts, and employees who experience least difficulty in supervising other employees are all the more valued by employers. Resilience remains a vital dimension of enterprise, and links very strongly to becoming skilled at receiving feedback well, and giving it sensitively.

6 Developing enterprise through explaining, coaching and teaching

We know as teachers how much we deepen our own learning every time we teach, in particular the very first time we teach something. We can help our students develop enterprise qualities by getting them to explain things to each other, coaching each other and even teaching each other. Skills students gain through these processes are very close to the skills needed for employability, and vital for many particular kinds of job. We can do a great deal to develop students' communication and interpersonal skills by giving them time, space and reason to deepen their learning in these ways. Especially in the context of developing enterprise skills, this does sometimes mean that we as tutors should step back from the temptation to do most of the explaining, coaching and teaching, and realize that while it may be somewhat slower to allow learners to do this with each other, the end results are much more profound.

7 Learning enterprise through assessing – making informed judgements

Making informed judgements is one of the fastest ways of deepening learning. The pay-off resulting from involving learners in self-assessment and peer assessment of enterprise-related skills and attitudes has huge relevance to developing these skills quickly and deeply. People who have the ability to assess their own activities during the doing of them are likely to do a much better job. Practice gained through peer assessment not only develops judgement-related skills, but also the accompanying interpersonal and communication skills to convey these judgements effectively and sensitively to fellow employees in workplace environments.

Overall, learners who become skilled at learning enterprisingly, and good at consciously reflecting about their own learning, are in a strong position to continue to develop as enterprising individuals long after leaving education. Equipping learners to be able to get the most from their brains paves their way towards lifelong learning: employers value 'a good learner' possibly more than anything else. Therefore, when a primary purpose of higher education is to equip students for their future careers, there is nothing better we can do for them than help them to take conscious control of how they learn best, and to become well-practised in exercising key enterprise, communication and interpersonal skills during their time with us. We should design our curriculum intentionally as a vehicle for students to develop in these ways, and not just hope that this development will occur alongside the curriculum. Furthermore, we need to allow learners opportunities to 'step out of the box of higher education' and exercise their own minds in ways that prepare them to be enterprising and entrepreneurial. There is a great deal we can do to make enterprise happen for our students – and indeed for ourselves.

PERSONAL TUTORING

Students are often assigned a 'personal tutor' for the duration of a year of their course, or (better) for their entire time at an education institution. These tutors are normally expected to exercise a counselling or advisory role when necessary, with the wide agenda of anything that may be causing concern to their respective students. However, the success of personal tutorial support in higher education is, at best, patchy. Some tutors take it very seriously, get to know their students well, and remain well briefed on the progress of each student. For many students in higher education institutions, however, their personal tutor is just a name. A result of this situation is that for most students, the majority of personal tutoring happens in the context of the contact they have with academic staff in those teaching/learning situations where the staff–student ratio is low enough for advice and counselling to be available, and that often means in what are intended to be academic tutorials.

Everyone who is involved in tutorial work agrees that there is no clear dividing line between academic and personal tutorials. Academic tutorials may be subject-related, while personal tutorials are normally thought of in terms of development of the 'whole student', but either kind of tutorial is likely to spill over into the other domain. Personal tutoring fits closely into this chapter on small-group learning, as sometimes the interactions involve more than one student at a time. However, personal tutorials are usually regarded as one-to-one encounters between a student and a tutor, where the purpose is not to extend or deepen the academic under-standing of the subjects being studied, but to support the student's learning in a

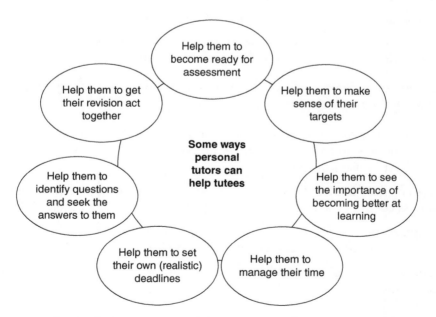

Figure 7.2 Some of the ways in which personal tutors can help tutees

much broader sense. The tutor may be one of the lecturers involved in the student's course, or may be a teaching assistant or research assistant with some tutorial duties.

This section examines what personal tutors can do to help their tutees succeed in making learning happen. Figure 7.2 summarizes some of the things discussed.

Specific responsibilities as a personal tutor

As long ago as 1992, David Jaques suggested some specific responsibilities of a personal tutor. Adapted from his work are the following:

- provide a personal contact for the student within what might otherwise feel like a large, impersonal institution
- liaise between the student and course tutors where appropriate
- offer advice or assistance when it is within your competence
- recognize when the assistance required is beyond your competence
- refer students, when necessary, to appropriate sources of specialist help and support
- help students review and reflect on their own progress and identify ways of improving it
- maintain an overview of students' progress and help them with any learning problems
- pick up from students informal feedback on the course
- help students in making choices regarding courses, modules or options
- participate in training events about the role of the personal tutor, the counselling service and the problems that students encounter.

Jaques also considered some of the broader considerations of the processes of personal tutoring, advising tutors to:

- acquaint yourself with the services that are available within your institution and to understand how the various processes and procedures that students may need to use function
- respect tutees' rights of confidentiality, to make this clear to them and to get permission from them if you need to speak to others about their difficulties
- recognize that some students may not get on with you and to accept and facilitate, if necessary, their seeing someone else
- respect any tutees' right not to seek or accept support or help, even though this might appear to be to their own disadvantage.

In the context of personal tutoring, in the next section I suggest a number of ways in which those charged with the role of personal tutor – and those who find themselves in this role even by default – can interact successfully with students individually or in small groups. In this section, I'm using the word 'tutee' rather than just student or learner, to emphasize that the role of personal tutor is at times quite different from that of a subject teacher (even when you may be both teacher and personal tutor at the same time).

Ten ways to help your tutees

1 Help your tutees to become ready for assessment

This is the sharp end of personal tutoring, not least because most forms of assessment involve winners and losers – and it is very uncomfortable to be a loser. Perhaps the most important attribute of excellent tutors is the ability to be perceived by students as helping them to put their best foot forward in the assessment battle. Even when tutors are going to be doing the assessment themselves, it is helpful for students to feel that everything possible is being done by their tutors to maximize their chances of succeeding at the assessment hurdle. Preparing for assessment should not degenerate into the 'guess what's in the tutor's mind' game – there should be no guesswork involved; students should have a clear idea of what their tutors are looking for. In particular, it helps when personal tutors strive to help students to make sense of what they have learned, so that they have turned it into their own knowledge and have a sense of ownership of their achievement well before the time when they are required to demonstrate evidence of their achievement of the learning outcomes.

2 Negotiate agreements with tutees

Some call these 'learning contracts', but there's something more positive about the word 'agreement' even when it boils down to a contract. The main advantage of learning agreements is that they help students to take ownership of the need to learn, and that because it is an agreement they feel they have played a part in working out the timescales involved, deciding what to learn, and how best to go about learning it, and at what level the learning needs to take place. The best ways of making it feel like an agreement to students is to ensure that they see that their tutors have their own parts to play in bringing the agreement to fruition.

3 Help your tutees to make sense of their targets

In particular, help your tutees to see exactly what is meant by the intended learning outcomes. It is all very well to use phrases such as 'demonstrate your understanding of …' but students need to know exactly how they are expected in due course to do this. They need to know what the evidence will look like when they have understood something to the level required, and what standards will be applied to this evidence. They need to understand the contexts in which this evidence will be generated – whether it is exams, coursework, practical work, independent work, and so on. If you can help your tutees to see clearly what they are trying to achieve, they are much more likely to succeed in achieving it.

4 Help your tutees to see the importance of becoming better at learning

Study skills are important, not just in the context of helping students to succeed in their present studies, but for life in general. At the heart of lifelong learning are well-honed study skills. Your tutees will continue to need to learn new things far beyond the years when they are involved in formal study, and the better they are able to take on new learning targets, and work systematically and purposefully towards achieving these targets, the better the quality of their future lives will be. Even when an element of learning has proved unsuccessful, there are usually useful study skills lessons to be gained from the experience. Study skills cannot be directly taught – they are (like just about everything else) learned by doing, practice, trial and error, and experience. As a personal tutor you can help your tutees to respond to the trial and error, and learn productively from each experience.

5 Help your tutees to manage their time

Time management is not only an essential study skill – it is a life skill. Probably the most important single element of time management is getting started on each task. Therefore you can help your tutees to get their learning underway, not least by pointing out that it is human nature to find work avoidance tactics which delay getting started, but which when recognized as such can be addressed head-on. A task that has only been started for five minutes is much more likely to be completed than a task that has not yet been started. Therefore, where possible, help by making sure that tasks get started in face-to-face contact time, even if only for those vital minutes that will allow your tutees to go away and continue them in their own time and at their own speed.

6 Help your tutees to set their own (realistic) deadlines

This goes hand-in-hand with formulating learning agreements. For most people, it is human nature to need deadlines. Any editor will confirm how important deadlines are in getting authors to complete articles or books – even when the deadlines are missed for good reasons. If there are no deadlines, many tasks falter in progress. Suggest to your tutees that they set their own deadlines for assignments and revision at least a week or two ahead of necessity. It is a great boost to their confidence to feel ahead of the game – and confidence breeds success.

7 Help your tutees to balance their act

An important addition to good time management is good task management. In other words, help students to prioritize their tasks. This involves making sure that the important ones get done, and the less important ones aren't given too much time. You can help your tutees to work out what exactly are the most important tasks, and to put these at the top of their agenda. You can also help by advising on sensible limits for the important tasks, so that they don't swallow up all of your students' available time and energy, leaving other important tasks unstarted. Help your tutees to see that it can be better to do an hour's worth on each of three tasks than to spend all three hours on one task, especially if all three tasks contribute to the assessment agenda.

8 Help your tutees to identify questions and seek the answers to them

'If I knew what the exam questions were going to be, I could easily prepare for the exam', many students say. But they *can* know what the questions are going to be. 'Any important piece of information can simply be regarded as the answer to a question' is a useful way of helping students to think in terms of questions rather than information. Once they know what a question is, they can find out the answer in any of the following ways:

- look it up in a book or handout
- look it up on the internet
- ask other students and see if they know the answer
- ask other people
- ask expert witnesses – their tutors.

Encourage students to make question banks of their own. In other words, get them to jot down all the questions which they might someday need to be able to answer, to demonstrate their learning. It is useful to start with the intended learning outcomes, and turn these into long lists of very short, sharp questions, so that students get the message that if they can answer lots of straightforward questions, they can in fact usually answer much more complex questions. It can be particularly useful to get students to make question banks in small groups, so that the range of questions is better, and to help them to learn from each other's questions. As a personal tutor you may be able to give valuable responses regarding which questions are the really important ones, to help to steer your tutees towards the main agendas of their learning.

9 Help your tutees to become better readers

Not all students come from households where walls are lined with bookshelves. Not all students devour books. Indeed, for many students, reading is not a particularly pleasurable activity, unless they are reading about something about which they are already passionate. You can help your tutees to realize that they don't have to devour books, but that all that may be needed is to use them successfully to find information from them. In other words, *information retrieval* (whether from books or websites) does not necessarily mean reading everything in sight, but homing in to what's important. This goes back to starting reading with questions in mind. If students read a page of text pre-armed with five questions, they are much more likely to get what is intended out of the page than if they just 'read' it. Help your tutees to become better at making good use of headings, sub-headings, contents pages and the indexes of books and journals. Help them to read in 'search and retrieve' mode, so they are looking for particular things and noting them down as they find them, rather than simply reading page after page vainly hoping that some of the information there will stick.

10 Help your tutees to get their revision act together

Most students regard revision for tests or exams as a bore. This is all too often because they have previously tackled the job in boring ways. They have tried to learn their subject materials in non-productive ways, and become disillusioned. A good start is for personal tutors to reinforce that revision is simply about systematically becoming better able to answer questions – that's what exams and tests actually measure. As with anything else, the best way to become better at something is to do it – and do it again – until it becomes second nature. Students who have practised answering a question seven times in a fortnight are very likely indeed to get it right the eighth time – in the test. Another way you can help your tutees with revision is by alerting them to what *not* to revise. There's no point spending a lot of time and energy on learning something that won't or can't be the basis of a sensible exam or test question. Similarly, anything that isn't directly related to an intended learning outcome is not on the revision agenda – if it were important it would have been there among those intended outcomes. You can remind your tutees that what is measured by tests and exams isn't what's in their heads – it's usually what comes out of their pens. In other words, it's their evidence of achievement of the intended learning outcomes that is the basis for assessment, and the best revision processes involve purposeful practice at evidencing that achievement.

TOWARDS BETTER SMALL-GROUP LEARNING

To summarize this chapter on small-group learning, I offer the following suggestions.

- *Be seen, by your students and your colleagues, to take small-group sessions seriously.* Learners will take cues from how important you treat small-group sessions. Be as punctual for small-group sessions as you are for lectures.

- *Don't just fill small-group sessions by continuing to lecture!* Avoid the temptation to fill a silence just by providing yet more information. Get the students doing something instead.

- *Link sessions to intended learning outcomes.* This helps learners to see that small-group sessions are at least as important as lectures. Sometimes it's worth flagging up a particular intended learning outcome in a lecture, then explaining that this one will be addressed *only* in related small-group teaching, but that evidence of achievement will still be assessed in the normal ways through coursework or exam questions.

- *Gather the emergent learning outcomes from small-group sessions.* Ask learners *what else* they learnt as a result of this seminar (or tutorial, or team meeting, and so on). Then flag up typical emergent outcomes in large-group sessions so that learners realize that the additional learning which accompanies small-group learning is important and relevant to them.

- *Address purposefully the factors underpinning successful learning.* In particular, make optimum use of small-group contexts to allow students to speak – *learning by explaining* – and to listen to each other.

- *Purposefully use small-group learning to help students to develop skills and attitudes relating to future employability.* In particular, help students to become more confident in their abilities to talk, explain, argue and defend.

- *Get students learning by assessing.* Use the time to allow students to *make informed judgements* on things they do themselves, and on other things you give them to rate, so that they *make sense* of important concepts and ideas, and deepen their grasp of the subject concerned.

- *Make small-group learning a personal experience for learners.* Help learners to get to know you better in small-group contexts and (more importantly) to get to know each other so that they can learn more from each other.

- *Ensure that learners feel it was worthwhile turning up for each small-group session.* If they can see the value of being present, they are less likely to choose to miss future sessions. Don't grumble to those who turn up about those who don't!

- *Take care with learners' feelings.* Remember the 'no hiding place' dimension. Some learners may be intimidated having so much more attention from someone as scholarly and important as *you* in a small-group context, and may be easily damaged by criticism. (Others won't be nearly so fragile, of course.)

- *Use small-group sessions to feed into large-group sessions.* For example, when important questions relating to assessment come up in small-group contexts, bring the questions to the attention of the whole group, rather than deal with them solely with the small group.

- *If you're also a personal tutor to some students, use this to tune in all the better to how students in general are handling their studies.* Use this experience to further enhance the value you bring to academic tutorials with students in general.

 Tips for students: getting the most from small-group learning

1 *Use small-group contexts to find out more about how tutors think.* Expect to find that different tutors think quite differently – that's human nature. The more you can tune in to the general ethos and academic climate of your institution, the better prepared you can become for showing yourself at your best, for example in assessments.

2 *Try not to miss small-group events.* When you miss a lecture you may be able to catch up on quite a lot of it from downloadable resources and from fellow students'

(Continued)

(Continued)

notes and comments, but with a small group there's little chance of really catching up on the processes involved in what those present actually achieved. It can also be a real headache if you miss group activity that leads to assessed tasks, as is increasingly the case in universities and colleges nowadays.

3 *The purpose and nature of lectures has changed.* Much information is now available online. Therefore tasks and activities you do in group work, and the interactions you have with tutors, and the learning opportunities you get from working with your peers (including peer assessment) are increasingly valuable as a means of helping you to feel part of your programme, and help you combat feelings of isolation or alienation.

4 *Group activities can be your best opportunities to develop skills and competences which evidence your employability.* Keep good records of capabilities you develop and practise, such as creative problem solving, leadership, team work, handling conflict, and so on. Collect together evidence of these skills, perhaps through an ePortfolio or a personal blog. This can give you extra things to talk about at job interviews, especially when they ask you for examples of how you have developed expertise in areas such as working in teams.

5 *When participating in group work, don't just be passive and go along with what others say and do.* Look for opportunities to offer ideas to solve problems and seek innovative solutions. There can be much more chance in group work for you to shine than there often is in formal contexts or assignments.

6 *Play fair with fellow students in terms of letting others contribute and taking turns at leading the group.* Don't regard the TV programme *The Apprentice* as providing a blueprint for good group behaviour in assessed tasks! The kinds of selfishness, self-aggrandisement and bragging as championed by the programme are not valued skills in the everyday world of employment.

7 *Use group work as a continuous monitor to find out how you're doing.* It's great to know when you're ahead of the game by comparing your thinking and achievements with fellow students, but equally useful to identify when you may need to do a bit of catching up. It's never as long as you think it will be until exams or other assessments test how well you're doing.

8 *Take care of colleagues who haven't really got to grips with the programme and may be feeling out of their depth.* Any help you can give them in terms of building confidence and skills development won't detract from the benefits you gain, indeed they will enhance what you get out of group work yourself. There's nothing like explaining something to someone to help you get your own head around it all the better.

9 *When staff ask you to reflect on your individual contribution to group activities, don't regard this as a tiresome chore.* Research shows that it's actually an excellent means of making sure that you benefit from these learning opportunities. Being caused to take stock of your learning and thinking helps to deepen your grasp of things, and skill in self-evaluation is regarded by many employers as a key capability.

10 *Make good use of all the technologies available to you, including the VLE or other media platforms used in your institution.* Don't just do what you're asked, for example recording outputs and outcomes on shared space in the VLE, but take opportunities to provide discussion space for you and your fellow students. Don't forget, however, that some media platforms may not be available to you

once you've left the institution, so back up things such as e-portfolio or blogging space, to other locations, which you can access after you've left and no longer have an institutional sign-in.

11 *Use Twitter productively.* Social media can enhance your experience of small-group work. For example, hashtags on Twitter can help you keep in contact with the students who are present at particular group work sessions as well as those who couldn't be there, and often tutors will join in.

12 *When working in groups, keep channels of communication open with tutors.* Clarify uncertainties about what you're supposed to be doing, and regularly check assessment requirements. It's all too easy to go off at a tangent, and to fail an assignment even though your group project is good, because you haven't satisfied college requirements.

13 *Think of group work with fellow students as an opportunity rather than a problem, as it is sometimes regarded.* Some you'll get on with well – others will try your patience. However, the more mixed your group is, the more you'll learn about working with people in general – always useful for future employment contexts.

14 *Make the most of the diversity you will often find within groups.* People from different cultures will bring alternative perspectives and may help you think in different ways by bringing international perspectives to some of the tasks you are tackling together. It's also great for employability to have developed cross-cultural capability. You won't always have opportunities to learn so fast about different cultures and perspectives, and international understanding is priceless.

15 *If you have real problems within group work, either because the group is dysfunctional or because of your own special needs, don't just let it fester.* Let the tutor know what is going on thereby providing a space for issues to be resolved. In some cases you may be told that sorting out inter-group conflicts is part of the task in hand, but in other cases an intervention may help to put things right before too much time has passed.

CHAPTER 8

LEARNING THROUGH OBSERVING AND REFLECTING

O— **Key topics in this chapter**

- Ways of reflecting
- The 'else' factor
- Reflective logs
- Handling feedback on teaching
- Self-reflective checklist
- Learning by observing others
- Word-constrained writing

This chapter is mainly about peer observation of teaching, but is also about reflecting. To be more precise, it's about using the reflecting which happens when purposefully observing someone else's teaching, to enhance your own teaching. And it's more about observation of *learning* as it happens well (and less well) in other people's classes than it is about watching how well they teach.

The term 'reflection' is widely used and discussed in post-compulsory education in the context of a broad range of professional development programmes, and peer observation of teaching is becoming ever more common and *powerful* in our attempts to make learning happen. Many institutions now have in place systems for the peer observation of teaching. These are often associated with the most public form of teaching – whole-class or large-group contexts. However, peer observation should not be restricted to the lecture room. There is much to be gained by observing teaching and learning in progress in each and every context in post-compulsory education, and also in extending observation to other aspects of higher education, as suggested by contributors in Gosling and Mason O'Connor (2009), not least assessment. Furthermore, learning from peers can happen in all sorts of useful ways, and is in no way restricted to just happening to sit in one of their teaching sessions. But there's one thing really special about observing – that's the luxury of having *time* to watch and reflect.

Sometimes, models of peer observation can be set up to be 'inspectorial', for example in many further education institutions in the UK, with observers making judgements on what they experience, resulting in grades or scores. In such schemes, observers are often armed with detailed checklists, and make judgements on a series of particular aspects of the event they observe. Inspectorial approaches are often favoured by those wearing quality assurance or quality management hats, in their belief that the data gathered would be reliable and valid, and would warrant consideration in appraisal and promotion contexts, or as a basis for targeted development where shortfalls were identified. There is, however, usually an overall judgement. Are these *informed* judgements? Too often, observation is carried out where there has not been sufficient (or indeed any) training or rehearsal in the processes involved. Too often in inspectorial models, no one observes the teaching of the observers – the observation isn't mutual. Sometimes they don't actually teach at all. Sometimes they are completely external, and may know little about the bigger picture surrounding the particular snapshots they take of teaching.

The resultant wording following on from such judgements can be problematic. How would you feel, for example, if the result of you being observed was that your teaching was 'satisfactory'? Damned with faint praise? It would be fine if the judgement were to be 'excellent' or 'outstanding', but all teaching–learning events can't be 'outstanding'. What about the rest? Words such as 'adequate' or 'satisfactory' may be perfectly acceptable descriptors of the standard of operation of a vacuum cleaner, but should hardly be applied to human endeavours (this reservation also applies to the use of such words in feedback to students about their work).

My own view is that inspectorial approaches to peer observation do not bring out the best in teaching, nor maximize the benefits that can be realized from collegial or informal approaches where the main results are discussion, feedback and, above all, reflection – particularly reflection by observers themselves being applied to developing their own teaching further. This indeed can justify the use of the term 'reflective observation' in this context. In this collegial approach to observation, observers gain a great deal of opportunity to see things they can emulate in their own approaches to teaching, as well as noticing things to strive to avoid in their own work. Gosling (2009: 9) usefully compares the characteristics of 'evaluation', 'development' and 'collaborative' models of peer observation, and prefers the word 'review' rather than 'observation'. It is this collaborative approach which I will expand upon in this chapter.

Later in this chapter, more detail is presented about the nuts and bolts of collegial approaches to the peer observation of teaching. First, we will think about the nature of the reflection that can accompany such processes. Then there is the wider picture of reflection, and the ways that reflection can help students deepen their learning. Finally there are the processes through which reflection can be evidenced – and even assessed.

REFLECTION AND THE FACTORS UNDERPINNING SUCCESSFUL LEARNING

As long ago as 1933, Dewey defined reflection as 'an active persistent and careful consideration of any belief or supposed form of knowledge in the light of the grounds that support it and the further conclusion to which it tends' (Dewey, 1933: 6). In many disciplines and professions, the term 'reflective practitioner' is in widespread use. The work of Donald Schön (1987) is well known in this area, and commentators have differentiated between 'reflection on action' (looking back reflectively at events and happenings) and 'reflection in action' (interrogating one's present actions in a reflective way and making adjustments). Both of these processes can be useful in thinking about teaching, and both can help to deepen learning.

In the context of using reflection as an aid to making learning happen (and making teaching work better), we can think of reflection as linking to all seven of the factors underpinning successful learning, as follows.

1 Wanting to improve our teaching by reflecting

The fact that we engage in reflection is one form of our own evidence for wanting to (continue to) learn. It implies an intention to improve by finding out more about what is going on in an element of learning. In our own teaching, we are too busy to be able to look closely at what is happening as shown on students' faces, and only pick up part of the messages which may be available to us. Sitting, however, in a colleague's class, we can take our time and watch the learning that is going on. To become *skilled* at capturing reflection depends on rehearsal and practice at doing so. We also need to help our students to reflect as part of their taking stock of their learning, so that they increasingly want to improve their learning. What we pick up ourselves watching others teach can help us to become better at linking reflection to students' motivation, and work towards them *wanting* to provide good evidence of reflecting on their learning experience. It's always good to be in students' shoes, and *feel* what it's like for them – there's nothing better than sitting with them in a colleague's session every now and then.

2 Taking ownership of the need to reflect

Engaging in the process of reflection shows at least some degree of willingness to find out more about what is going on. How well the need to learn is identified depends, of course, on the effectiveness of the reflection itself, and on how well it is used to analyse what is going on in the learning process. Well-designed opportunities for students to reflect on their learning can tell them (and us) a great deal about their perceptions of what they need to do to improve their learning, and help us to help them to learn successfully – in other words, to make learning happen.

3 Reflecting through doing – practice, trial and error, repetition, and so on

Reflecting is itself a form of doing, albeit usually quite a cognitive one. However, reflection can be intensified if it involves making informed judgements about one's own actions, or about other people's actions and then applying or internalizing the judgements to one's own context. It is important to ensure that reflecting is not just another thing we require students to do – or indeed just another thing we require ourselves to do. It is one of the most important things – and we could argue that learning is never complete without it.

4 Making sense by reflecting

Whether reflecting on our own practice or on observations of others' practice, reflection can be regarded as a natural part of the overall process of making sense of a situation, topic or context, helping us get our heads around it, deepening our awareness and understanding of the picture. Similarly, we need to help students not only to learn something to the extent that they can do things with it, but also to have increased their learning about themselves by reflecting on *how* they got to the stage of becoming able to demonstrate their evidence of achievement.

5 Reflecting using feedback on our teaching

Reflection can involve gathering and analysing feedback on one's own actions and rethinking how those actions can be improved and developed by taking on board things learned from the feedback. Similarly, giving feedback to others on their actions can be regarded as reflection on our observations of what they do, and can also link to thinking inwards into our own parallel actions. Although, in essence, reflection can be thought of as a private process, it becomes much better developed if it is discussed and shared, not least in helping to develop better approaches to the process by learning from the practice of others.

6 Reflecting by putting things into spoken words – coaching, explaining, teaching

When we're directly engaged in any of these processes, it can be argued that we are necessarily reflecting on what is being taught or explained. However, if we're actually reflecting on the processes of coaching, explaining or teaching as well as on the subject matter involved, the reflections are all the deeper, and help us further in the *making sense* both of the topic and of our attempts to communicate the topic.

7 Making informed judgements by reflecting

This is perhaps where some of the deepest forms of reflection occur – for example, when applying criteria to things we have done (reflection on action) or on things we are doing (reflection in action). In the context of peer observation of teaching, for example, we may be making informed judgements on others' actions, and on how well those actions are working in a given context, but we may also be reflecting on how we can apply our thinking to our own future actions in similar contexts.

REFLECTING MORE DEEPLY – THE 'ELSE' FACTOR

Reflecting on a given event or process may well involve us interrogating it using the normal question words of why, what, how, where, when, who, which, and so on. There is a danger, however, that the *evidence* of reflection degenerates into a mere 'reflective log' in a rather low-key, narrative mode, just *describing* what is happening rather than analysing or interrogating the event. Reflective logs are widely used as evidence of reflection, and are often an assessed element in professional development programmes (not least in the teaching profession), but can be tedious to compile and don't lend themselves to meaningful assessment when they are predominantly descriptive. However, if we start using 'else' to include and address questions such as:

- What *else* was going on?
- Why *else* might this have happened?
- Where *else* may this be useful?
- Who *else* may be affected by this?
- Where *else* may this work well?
- How *else* can this be achieved?
- Where *else* are our students learning?

the reflections become much deeper, and more useful. In most instances, the response to an 'else' question is deeper, more interesting and indeed more *reflective* than the response to the corresponding basic question underpinning it. A reflective log becomes much deeper if the straightforward questions are answered deliberately precisely (i.e. the relatively obvious is stated concisely) and the 'else' questions are answered more expansively. Moreover, evidence of reflection is further deepened by extending the 'else' questions along the following lines:

- What *else* happened?
- What *else else* happened?

and so on. The deeper the 'else' questions probe, the deeper the level of reflection that they elicit from us – and from our students.

PUTTING WORD LIMITS ON REFLECTION?

Here's a short case study for us to reflect upon. For several years until 2010 the website of Leeds Metropolitan University carried a series of 200-word reflections from staff and students. The process was initiated by a former vice-chancellor, who for six years provided a daily reflection for the site, the topic ranging widely around academia, sport, management, and beyond. The 'game' was for each reflection to be *exactly* 200 words, and in two paragraphs (fitting nicely on to a computer screen). Before long, a series of 200-word reflections appeared on the website daily, written by other people, under such umbrella headings as 'International', 'Sporting', 'Assessment', 'Partnerships', and so on. Many colleagues and students who wrote these reflections noted that whittling the piece down to exactly 200 words invariably improved the quality of the piece (just about always, in practice, it turned into a matter of shortening a longer piece, rather than looking for words to expand a shorter one – 200 words is quite a short bit of writing). In shortening a piece to 200 words, decisions had to be made along the following lines:

- There are three ideas in this paragraph but there is only room for two ideas – which is the weakest idea?

- Which words in this sentence are not pulling their weight? How can I adjust the sentence to make the point I want to make, but more concisely?

- How can I make the first impression striking enough to draw readers in to the rest of this short piece?

- I want to end such a short piece with a bang rather than a whimper – how can I best achieve this?

In other words, the final 200-word reflections involved quite a lot more *reflection* than if there had not been a tight word constraint.

Teaching staff soon saw the benefits of applying this principle to assessed coursework, setting students word-constrained tasks, such as:

- a 200-word reflection on a critical incident in their practice
- a 150-word summary of the main points a selected author said about a given topic
- a 300-word critique of the views of two authors on a given subject
- a 250-word proposal for a given course of action.

When assessing a pile of students' word-constrained work in such formats, several things increased the reliability, validity and authenticity of the assessment, not least:

- plagiarism is just about eliminated, as it would be very easy to spot it in a pile of one-pagers

- most students have necessarily drafted and redrafted their work to get it to the right length, and the work is therefore less rushed and more 'mature' as evidence of their thinking

- the task has been more *manageable* for students in terms of time spent than, for example, writing essays or reports
- the quality of thinking behind the writing is much higher – less description, more analysis, more *making sense*, and so on
- it takes far less time to assess a batch of 158 one-page reflections than 158 3,000-word essays, and the reliability and the manageability of the assessment have increased very significantly
- students writing in English as a second language may well be less disadvantaged writing short pieces than when writing extended essays
- students can do a greater number of high-level, concise formative tasks, ranging their thinking much more widely than if they had to do just a single, big, low-level summative task
- the quality of students' evidence of their thinking is higher than if they were free to word-spin at length.

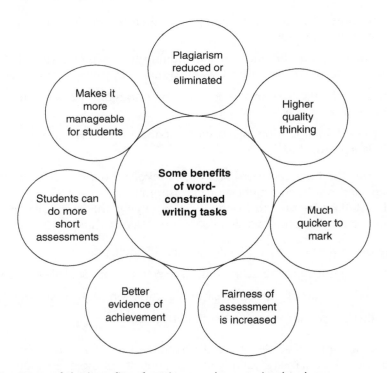

Figure 8.1 Some of the benefits of setting word-constrained tasks

When reflective logs are an assessed element of students' work, taking into account the factors mentioned above, free-ranging reflection, with the associated danger of word-spinning, seems far less attractive than focused, word-constrained reflection.

PEER OBSERVATION OF TEACHING: WHAT'S IN IT FOR ME?

Why should we undertake peer observation? What can we get out of having our teaching observed by our colleagues? As teachers in higher education, the benefits we can derive from peer observation include the following:

- opportunities, through both observing and being observed in our teaching sessions, to reflect on and review our teaching skills with the assistance of our colleagues

- time to *think* while we're sitting in someone else's class – there are few enough occasions in our busy lives where we really have this luxury

- identifying good practice, and needs which we can address, to ensure our ongoing personal and professional development

- helping to continue to learn from each other so that we develop shared understandings of best practices in relation not just to teaching, but to processes of assessment and feedback to students

- continuing opportunities to observe *students* as they learn in colleagues' teaching sessions, increasing our own awareness about how students learn well (and less well), allowing us to reflect on how we can enhance students' learning in our own sessions

- mutually beneficial learning experiences through both processes of observing colleagues and being observed ourselves

- getting to know a range of colleagues much better so that we have friends we can turn to when we are perplexed about difficult situations we may experience in our teaching

- learning new tricks from one another (Experienced colleagues learn much from new staff and they in turn can teach new colleagues old tricks!)

- identifying generic development needs to feed into ongoing and future staff development activities

- increased confidence of all involved, derived from feedback on being observed and from picking up good ideas while observing others' teaching

- noticing outstanding practice when we see it, so that this is more easily shared and built upon

- identifying commonly experienced problems and needs so that these can be made the basis of staff development opportunities

- focused 'learning conversations' between observees and observers, mutually helping everyone involved to continue to develop professional skills relating to teaching and learning.

With a list of benefits as powerful as that above, it is surprising that there is sometimes considerable resistance about peer observation. However, such resistance as there is can be considerably eased if it is accepted that it is really *learning* that is being observed, rather than just other people's teaching. In the next part of this chapter I will share details of how a framework for peer observation can be designed for *enhancement* rather than for judgements.

DESIGNING A FRAMEWORK FOR PEER OBSERVATION

Essentially, it is best when the processes of peer observation are entirely confidential between you and your observer. A reasonable expectation is that everyone who teaches should be observed at least twice per year – and should observe someone else teach at least twice per year. It is natural that feedback from peer observation will be valuable evidence to put forward for appraisal or other forms of performance review. Later in this chapter you can see an example of a pro forma that you can use as the basis for your observation. You can use it to plan with your observer at a pre-meeting, and review at a post-meeting, where the form is returned to you to keep.

Ten steps in a peer observation framework

Below are details of ten steps which may be used as the basis of a peer observation scheme. These guidelines are written with 'you' being the observee. You can easily turn around steps 1–8 when it's your turn to be the observer – which may well be *before* you go in as an observee. There is no better training for being observed than to have had a go at observing two or three colleagues first. The intended processes are as follows:

1 *You choose your own peer observers and agree with them that you will observe their teaching too.* Normally, the intention is you choose a different peer observer for each session that is reviewed, to optimize the sharing of experience. In selecting observers, you might ask colleagues from your own subject groups or similar, but could also consider approaching staff from different areas or departments. If at all possible, you observe your observer (or others) before you yourself are observed. In this way you gain experience of the overall process.

2 *You decide what sort of teaching/learning is going to be observed.* All forms of teaching can be considered for review, not just lecturing. It may be intended that one observation should be of a classroom-based session, and the other could be a further similar session, or a tutorial, a practice/work-based learning session or a review of learning materials, or whatever else you would like feedback upon. Ideally, the first session should take place in the earlier part of the academic year and the second at a later time. If you are teaching at a distance, virtual observation and review can be undertaken.

Furthermore, there is nothing to prevent you having an *assessment* event observed, where the process of assessment is designed primarily *as* learning for students.

3 *You meet to set the scene.* You arrange a brief pre-meeting with your chosen observer in advance of the session to be observed, to explain its context and objectives and to agree any particular focus for the observation. For lengthy sessions, for example teaching taking place in a studio or laboratory, you should negotiate the duration of the observation with your observer.

4 *You plan with your observer your feedback agenda.* At the pre-meeting you plan the date, time and duration of the observation, and you also plan ahead for a post-meeting after the observation so you can get feedback. Feedback should be constructive, focused, supportive and developmental. You choose with your observer a framework for the recording of appropriate observations for your session. Examples included later in this chapter show some possible frameworks for feedback, but these are only for illustration. The particular examples included in this chapter are designed primarily for observation of a classroom-based session. You (and your observer) can adapt these for other forms of teaching, as appropriate.

5 *You do your bit – your observation takes place.* Your observer uses the agreed agenda as a basis for recording observations and suggestions during your session, and prepares to bring this back to hand over to you at the post-meeting referred to above.

6 *The two of you meet for the post-meeting.* This might be immediately following the observed session or be planned deliberately to be a bit later, allowing both of you time to reflect informally on the session and the observation. During the feedback discussion, aspects of good practice and developmental needs are shared. It is your observer's role to assist you in the process of review and reflection with the aim of improving the quality of your teaching as well as highlighting good practice for wider dissemination. Remember you will be doing (or will already have done) exactly the same for your observer. Peer observation is a reciprocal process throughout.

7 *The two of you 'seal the deal' with your joint thoughts.* You could design a form along the lines of the example included later in this chapter for this purpose. Remember, no one else sees this form unless you choose to show it to them, so you can be frank and direct in your own comments about the session you taught. This makes it easier to revisit the form in future action planning.

8 *You send in the basic data of the observation.* After the post-meeting, you contact the person who oversees the overall process, simply supplying the date, location and nature of the observation session and the name of the observer, thereby recording that the observation has taken place. You are welcome to provide alongside the basic data any generic feedback points you would like to have disseminated more widely, and any training needs you have identified, to ensure relevant development opportunities can be provided.

9 *Reviewing managers do their bit.* At agreed points in the year, the reviewing managers collate a record of peer observations completed by staff. Records may include:

o   dates of observations, locations

o   names of persons observing

o   names of observees

o   nature of sessions (e.g. lectures, seminars, tutorials, practicals, and so on).

In addition, reviewing managers may compile and share an anonymous summary of general areas of good practice and development needs arising from the peer observations they oversee.

10 *Whoever is in charge of the overall scheme does their bit.* This could be producing an annual report on the implementation of peer observation of teaching for consideration by an appropriate committee.

WHAT MAY YOU LIKE YOUR OBSERVERS TO FOCUS ON?

Here are some broad areas which might be useful in particular observations, but you may well be able to think of additional aspects which will be more directly relevant to your own teaching, level and style.

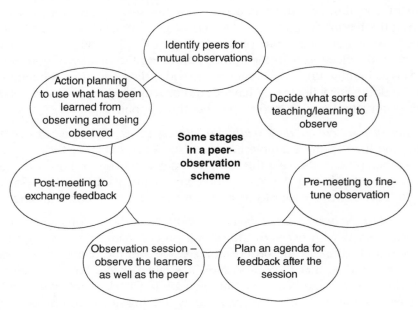

Figure 8.2   Some stages in a peer-observation scheme

- *How effectively you start your session*: how clearly you spell out the particular intended learning outcomes for the session, how well you link the session to what students should already know from previous sessions, and so on.

- *Questioning*: for example, the way you ask questions to the class, the way the students respond to your questions, how readily students ask you questions, how well you respond to their questions, and so on.

- *Student attention*: how well you seem to achieve students' attention, the length of time the students seem able to be attentive, what you do to regain their attention when it has wandered off, and so on.

- *Your talking*: how clear your voice is, how well students can hear you at the back of the room, how long you talk at a time, and so on.

- *How you deal with student mistakes and misunderstandings*: how well you avoid students who have made mistakes feeling embarrassed or uncomfortable, how well you make it felt that 'learning by getting things wrong at first' is a useful step towards learning things correctly, and so on.

- *Student activities in class*: the way you brief students about activities, the balance of individual and group activities, how long activities take and how you de-brief activities when they have been completed, and so on.

- *Student motivation*: how well you warm up students' interest in the topic, how you arouse their curiosity, how effectively you show them what they need to become able to do, how well students take ownership of the targets you set them, and so on.

- *Students 'making sense' of the topic*: the extent to which they seem to gain understanding during the session, how well they get their heads around complex ideas and concepts, and so on.

- *Students speaking, explaining and discussing*: how well from time to time you make use of the learning which is achieved when students put things into words orally, helping each other to master difficult ideas, and so on.

- *Students making informed judgements*: for example, where you get students to assess past examples of work, or peer-assess each other's work, or self-assess their own work, and so on.

- *Students using resources*: how effectively students make use of web-based materials or other resources you provide them with during the class.

- *Your own use of resources*: for example, how effectively you use PowerPoint or other media, how well you avoid reading out what is on your slides to the class, how effectively you link to online resources, how clearly visible your presentations are at different parts of the room, and so on.

- *Time management*: how well you make use of the time available for the session, how well you avoid rushing towards the end, how well you time tasks and activities, and so on.

- *How effectively you round off your session towards the end*: for example, summarizing the main points students should by now have mastered, reminding students about the targets associated with the intended learning outcomes, how well you come to the final part of the session (for example, avoiding students gathering together their materials ready to leave while you are still saying important things), and so on.

EXPERIENCES OF PEER OBSERVATION

What do you gain by being observed? Most importantly, you gain feedback both on your teaching and on how the students are responding to the way you teach. The following quotes from a range of staff in several institutions illustrate how beneficial peer observation can (and should) be.

- I have always found peer observation of teaching invaluable. I have learned a lot from watching other colleagues teaching. Consequently, I am able to be a better teacher with improved style of teaching and classroom practice. Likewise, others who had observed my teaching had commented how this experience had helped them. I have been teaching for 28 years and I continue to find each peer observation adding to my teaching skills.

- For me, peer observation of my teaching is an invaluable and constructive way of ascertaining the extent to which I am achieving my stated aims. The feedback from observers enables me to identify areas that require further thought and also highlights existing good practice.

- The reward for me is the discovery of new approaches and constructive feedback on what I think I am doing. We think we are self-aware but you can't replace the reality of other people's observation. What a learning experience!

- I think that part of the value of peer observation is that it is a great prompt for reflective practice. It is sometimes easy to get complacent about teaching situations and to do it as you have always done it because it seems to go OK, but setting up an observation makes you reflect on the session from beginning to end, thinking, 'What am I trying to do here?', 'Is what I normally do really the best way to do that?' and so on. Not wanting to show ourselves up [in front of the observer] is a great incentive to having a bit of a rethink!

EVEN GREATER BENEFITS TO OBSERVERS

What do you gain by being an observer? The short answer is 'probably even more than through being observed!' A good scheme of peer observation is designed so that everyone is an observer as often as they are observed. But of course it's easy enough to gain even more practice at being an observer, not least when attending conferences and staff development sessions. And if you're lucky enough to be involved in team-teaching, you get even more opportunity to learn by watching how others do things.

Here are some of the benefits you can gain from the opportunity to sit in others' classes and watch what happens. You may well be able to add to this list if you've already got some experience of watching how colleagues go about their teaching.

- *You see colleagues doing things that you can emulate.* Even very experienced observers comment that they continue to learn new things that they can take back and apply to their own teaching.

- *You find out what you can do with technology – and what not to do.* You may learn much from watching others use weblinks, social media, conferencing software or equipment unfamiliar to you. It's often really helpful to watch someone else in action before you try something new yourself.

- *You see other ways of going about teaching.* The more the better. In a small circle of colleagues you might only see a limited range of approaches to helping students to learn. When you widen that circle, you're likely to experience different approaches that you would not otherwise have met, some of which may well be worth trying out for yourself.

- *You may choose to observe colleagues who are renowned for their teaching.* This can feel a bit intimidating – 'However can I live up to how they approach it?' you might ask, and 'What will such an excellent teacher make of my attempts?' But it's still possible to selectively take away even just one or two of their techniques to try out for yourself. And when it's their turn to observe you, you may be surprised at how positive and reassuring they usually are. No one has been a 'renowned teacher' from day one, and they usually remember their relatively clumsy histories.

- *You get time out to watch and reflect.* For once, you don't have to say anything. You can watch, think, listen, reflect on your own teaching, and capture things in your notes to share later with your colleague. How often in your busy life do you get time to sit, watch and think for the best part of an hour?

- *You can be a student for a while.* It's really useful to sit being a student. For some, it's a long time since we were *real* students. Watching the students as we observe helps us think about how our students feel in our own sessions. You can share the joy and excitement when your colleague generates such emotions with the class. You can also share the tensions when things are going less well. You can *watch* the students in a way you can't manage in your own classes when you're busy teaching.

- *You may see things to avoid doing yourself!* When you see something going wrong in a session you're observing, you can make a note to yourself to avoid that in your own teaching, or prevent a problem from occurring as you watch one developing. You may or may not choose to share all these things with the colleague you're observing. If they know they've got a problem, they don't need you to tell them. They might, however, welcome some feedback on alternative approaches which may have prevented the problem occurring, but let them tell you first that it was indeed a problem.

- *You get to know more and more colleagues.* Peer observation, and the discussions which follow it, are an excellent way of finding new friends and allies. They make teaching in higher education far less lonely than it can be when confined to one's own classrooms. You'll have more people to turn to when you need help or advice. In particular, it's good to build bridges with colleagues in other faculties.

- *You get the luxury of leading a 'learning conversation' with your colleague about teaching and learning.* Such conversations are extremely valuable, and in busy lives where time is precious it is good to take time out from all those other things and talk about learning and teaching. After all, the main part of most of our jobs is to do with these things.

- *The process of giving feedback to colleagues on their teaching helps you become more receptive to feedback on your own teaching.* For example, if something has gone really well, you will want to make sure that they know it has gone well so that they can build on it and repeat it. Or if something hasn't quite worked, you'll want to help them find ways of making it work better next time. In either case, you'll be choosing how best to be a supportive colleague to the person whose teaching you observed. All this pays dividends when it's your turn to be receptive to your own observers.

- *Being an observer is the best possible preparation for getting the most out of being observed.* Someone's got to go first, and in any reciprocal peer observation it could be you who is first to be observed. But when it's your turn to observe, it will still make future observation occasions all the more productive.

SOME NUTS AND BOLTS OF A PEER OBSERVATION SCHEME

Let's flesh out the discussion above, regarding the rationale of having peer observation and the benefits which can accrue from it, with some of the finer detail of peer observation. The discussion which follows suggests how to go about designing the pre-meeting, the observation itself, the post-meeting and some examples of the paperwork which might be used to make it all work in practice.

Preparing to be observed

It's best to have the pre-meeting within a few days of the observation, rather than trying to squeeze it in ten minutes before the observation itself. This gives your observer more time to tune in to the nature of the session, and what you're planning to gain from the observation. The pre-meeting can address, for example, some of the following questions and issues:

- *What's the background?* For example, is this your fifth lecture in a series of ten, or a seminar following up a particular lecture, or a practical session based on previous lectures, and so on?

- *How do you feel about being observed on this occasion?* You may be very used to the experience, or it could be new and a bit scary for you. It can be worth sharing your feelings with your observer – you'll often get a lot of reassurance.

- *How long is the session to be observed?* If it's a long session, is observation just going to be for part of your session?

- *How is this particular group of students shaping up to date?* Any difficulties with them? Any particular strengths or characteristics that the observer could find useful to know?

- *What are the particular learning outcomes for the session?* For example, what exactly are the students intended to get out of the session? How (very briefly) do these outcomes fit into the bigger picture of their studies?

- *What, in particular, do you want to find out from the observation?* For example, are you trying out something new and would like feedback on how it works? Are you having some difficulties with this class and would like feedback on what seems to be happening to help you address these difficulties?

- *What pro forma would you like to be used by the observer during the observation?* Have you one of your own you'd prefer to be used? Is there one that's widely used in your own subject area or faculty? Would you like to rough out a specific one for this observation? If there's a particular form you'd like to be used to capture the observations, it is really useful to have this ready at the pre-meeting to give to your observer.

- *What do you want your observer to do at the session?* For example, 'be one of the students', 'sit in a particular place', and so on.

- *Will you explain to the students why someone else is in the room?* If so, how will you do this? At the time, or in advance?

- *Observing what exactly?* Do you want your observer to watch what your students are doing rather than just what you are doing?

- *What else might you want to find out as a result of the observation?* What *don't* you want to find out? For example, are there things you know already about your teaching in this particular context and would prefer not to be told?!

The observation event

There's a lot to be gained by both parties. Perhaps the most useful starting place is the form you choose to use at the session. An example of the sort of document which the observer might use during the observation is shown below. This form is quite detailed and may well need to be shortened to suit a particular observation

Name of lecturer		Name of observer	
Date of lecture		Time of lecture	
Venue		Topic of lecture	
Date of report		Approx no. of students	

Aspects of the lecture	Responses, comments and suggestions
First impressions made by the lecturer	
How the intended outcomes of the lecture were made clear to students at the beginning of the lecture	
How this particular lecture was put into context regarding previous and forthcoming lectures	
How intended evidence of achievement of the learning outcomes was clarified to students during the lecture	
How the intended learning outcomes were revisited towards the end of the lecture	
How the lecturer checked the extent to which the students felt they had achieved the intended learning outcomes	
The general tone and style of the presentation	
How visual aids were used to enhance students' learning	
How student diversity (ethnic origin, disability, learning needs) was catered for during this particular lecture	
How body language was used to enhance communication at the lecture	
Tone of voice, clarity of diction, audibility, and so on	

What students seemed to be doing during the lecture	
The extent to which students were kept actively learning during the lecture	
How students seemed to be using any handout materials during the lecture	
How students' questions were invited and handled during the lecture	
How well use was made of the available space as a learning environment	
How links were made between the content of the lecture and how this would be assessed	
Comments about the close of the lecture	
Any further overall comments and suggestions	
Further specific things on which the lecturer asked for feedback at the pre-meeting: 1 2 3	
The extent to which a lecture was the most appropriate format to help students to achieve the learning outcomes	
Action planning comments by observer, for example, things to consider in own teaching	

Figure 8.3   Example of an observation pro forma

 Photocopiable *Making Learning Happen* © Phil Race, 2014 (SAGE)

context. My intention of including this example is to alert you to other things you might want to include in the agenda for an observation, or indeed to get you thinking about further things you might want to add. This form is quite specific to the lecture as the observation event, but can be adapted readily for other teaching/learning contexts, such as tutorials, problems classes, practical sessions, and so on.

A shorter alternative observation format

A much more basic example than the one above can also be very effective in practice (see below). It is simply a log of the event observed, with the timescale down the left-hand side, a concise summary of what was happening in the next column, and observations and comments in the right-hand column.

The post-meeting

Why is a post-meeting really useful? The main purposes of the post-meeting are as follows:

- to enable you to gain feedback from your observer
- to enable you to receive your observer's notes and store them for your own information and use
- to enable your observer to explain things included in these notes
- to enable you to explain to your observer any things which need elaboration
- to complete, jointly, a summary record of the observation.

Why is it best to have this as a face-to-face meeting rather than an email exchange or a paper-trail afterwards? After all, feedback can be dropped in your pigeon hole, sent via email, put through your letter box or given by phone. But there's something about a face-to-face meeting, not least that you can both sign the documentation as a record for your own files. Most important, however, is that when you are face to face with your observer you've got tone of voice, eye

Time	What was happening	Observations and comments

Figure 8.4 Example of a simpler observation pro forma

contact, the chance to question and answer until you know exactly what your observer means, the chance to clarify things, the opportunity to explain why you did what you did instead of what your observer might have thought you might have done, and so on. The language of written feedback can sometimes look formal and cold on paper, but face-to-face explanation and discussion can be so much more natural and informal – that's often where the real learning and development takes place. 'Just like with students', you may be thinking.

What comes out of the post-meeting?

The post-meeting usually takes a bit longer than the pre-meeting so it's best to allow for between 30 minutes and an hour. You also need to allow a few minutes to jointly draft a short, agreed record of the meeting, following on from your observer's comments. This record is based on your observer's feedback and your own thoughts about the session, and can be used in connection with appraisal if you choose to do so. You may also wish to quote directly from your observer's comments in an appraisal. A possible format is presented below to illustrate how you could design what suits you best.

BEYOND PEER OBSERVATION

Good teachers reflect all the time, both during teaching and afterwards. However, a problem with reflecting is that unless some *record* of reflection is made at the time, one's best ideas can just evaporate away. It can be useful to design your own reflection template, and to spend say five minutes after particular

Teaching observation joint notes	
Observee:	Observer:
Signature:	Signature:
Date of observation:	Date of these notes:
Observee: summary of main thoughts (e.g. what you got out of the observation, feedback from your observer and discussion)	**Observer: summary comments** (e.g. what impressed you about what you observed, things you may take back and put into your own teaching practice)
Agreed action points and any other matters arising	

Figure 8.5   Example of a formal record of an observation

teaching sessions jotting down your responses to various questions. You can then keep a file of your completed questionnaires. The actual questionnaire you use should develop over time as you find out more about what is most worthwhile to reflect upon. Indeed, as you find that you've developed your practice further as a result of reflecting frequently, some questions may no longer be needed.

To end this chapter on observation and reflection, let's look at how you can do something on your own, in addition to the peer observation discussed already. This also goes right back to the factors underpinning successful learning, and in particular making informed judgements, by interrogating examples of your own teaching against various criteria, and planning what else you might do next time you run a similar event. There follows quite a long reflective checklist for a teaching element (see Figure 8.6), which you may shorten or lengthen according to the nature of your own teaching, and the amount of time and energy you feel able to devote to such reflections. Ideally, it is worth using such a checklist regularly rather than rarely, so you can continually fine-tune the checklist to keep pace with the developing quality of your teaching.

What might you use as a starting point for designing your own reflective checklist? The following checklist is far too long to use as it stands, but is presented as food for thought. You can select those elements that you think will be worthwhile in the context of your own teaching and that will inspire you, or you can create better questions that are more relevant to your own discipline area. You may notice that some of the questions are about your own performance, while others are about the students themselves. It's worth reflecting about both sides of the picture.

Jotting down your thoughts as reflections on a session can sometimes be a relief! If you've had a session where things didn't go well, and it continues to prey on your mind, making a short, reflective analysis of the session can be a way of getting it out of your system, helping you to identify particular issues that you can address another time. This is better than the whole session continuing to creep into your thoughts. It takes rather more self-discipline to make the time to reflect on a session which went splendidly – but the time is well spent as it may help you identify the features which made it go really well. You can then actively replicate them, rather than just hoping it will happen again.

In the checklist below, the order of the questions is not important. You'll notice that the questions are written in the first person, using 'I', 'my', and so on. This is meant to help the process become your reflection, and not an interrogation of your practice by someone else questioning you. In most cases, the main thrust of each checklist question is presented in bold print, with supplementary probing or deepening questions in plain print. It is worth spending a minute or two to record the basic details of the session – what sort of teaching/learning session it was, the date, time, number of students, topic taught, and so on. This prevents such things gradually becoming mixed up in our minds as time elapses.

Main facts about the particular session

Date:	Topic of session:
Place:	Time:
Nature of session: lecture, tutorial, etc.?	Number of students:
Overall, how I feel this session went: One of my very best. Fine. OK. Could have been better. Not at all happy about this one!	

Checklist questions to capture my reflections	*My responses, reflections and planning ideas*
What is the thing about this session that is at the top of my mind at this moment?	
What did I like most about the way this session went? Why is this?	
What *else* worked really well at this session?	
What worked *least* well at this particular session? Why was this? What can I do in future sessions to minimize the chance that similar things will happen again?	
What surprised me most at this particular session? Why was this unexpected? What would I now do, with hindsight, to address this, if it were to happen again at a future session?	
How well do I now think that I *started* this particular session? Have I learned anything about how best to start this particular kind of session? How may I now fine-tune the beginning of a future similar session?	
How effectively did I explain the intended learning outcomes to students? Which of these outcomes seemed to be most important to them? With hindsight, can I adjust the intended learning outcomes to be more relevant to future students at similar sessions?	
How well did the students seem to take ownership of the *need* to work towards achieving the outcomes? Could the students see 'what's in it for me' regarding putting effort into the subject?	
Did I let the students know what, in due course, they needed to do with the topic? How clearly did I explain to the students what exactly they would need to work towards to show they had achieved the learning outcomes?	

(Continued)

(Continued)

Questions	
To what extent did the students seem to *want* to learn the topic? Is there anything I need to do to help them to increase their want to learn next time?	
How much did the students know already about this topic, on average? Was this more than I expected or less than I expected? How would I adjust the content of a future session to fine-tune it better to what the students are likely to know already? How can I find out what they already know?	
What was the best thing about the teaching room at this particular session? Why did this really help the session? What can I do to try to ensure that this kind of venue feature will be put to good use in future sessions?	
What was the worst thing about the teaching room at this particular session? What can I do in future to minimize the risk of similar things spoiling a session?	
To what extent did I manage to get the students *learning by doing* during this session? Was this enough? If not, how could I have built in more student activity?	
Overall, how did the students behave at this session? Am I happy with this?	
Was there something I did at this session that I wished I hadn't done? If 'yes', what was this? What else could I have tried?	
What was my own best moment at this particular session? Why do I feel good about this particular aspect? What can I do to lead to more such moments at future sessions?	
What did the most 'difficult' student do at this particular session? What can I do to address such behaviours at future sessions, if they occur again?	
To what extent did teaching this session help me to *make sense* of the topic better? What was the most important thing I learned about the topic?	
How much feedback did the students get on their learning during this session? How much of this feedback was from each other rather than just from me?	
Did I manage to include opportunities for students to deepen their learning by *explaining things to each other* during the session? Could I do more of this next time?	

Questions		
To what extent did I manage to help students to deepen their learning of the topic by making informed judgements during the session? (e.g. on their own work, or on things I gave them to judge).		
What, with hindsight, would I now miss out of the session? Why would I now choose to miss this out of similar sessions in future?		
What else, with hindsight, do I wish I had been able to include in this particular session? How best can I make time to include something along these lines in future similar sessions?		
How well do I think I closed the session? Did I end it with a whimper or a bang?! Was I rushed towards the end of the session, trying to get through everything on my agenda? What would I do next time round, with hindsight, to make sure that a future similar session ended really positively?		
What do I feel about the feedback I have received from students at this session? What will be the most important thing that I will do differently next time as a result of this feedback? What will be the most important thing I will do in exactly the same way because of this feedback?		
What was the most hurtful comment or grading in students' feedback? Why do I find this hurtful? Was it justified? Is it really important considering the feedback as a whole? Would it be useful for me to do something different next time round to address this particular aspect of critical feedback?		
What was the most pleasing comment or grading I received in students' feedback? Why does this please me so much? Will it be possible for me to get further similar feedback in future, and how will I adjust a future session to do so?		
How well did students feel that they had achieved the intended learning outcomes at the end of the session? Which outcomes had they achieved best? Were any of the intended outcomes less important than others? How would it be useful, with hindsight, to adjust the intended learning outcomes for a similar session next time round?		
What is the most important thing I have learned about teaching sessions of this kind from this particular experience? How will I put this learning to good use at future sessions?		
Any further thoughts?		
Date completed:		

Figure 8.6   Example of a self-reflective checklist

CONCLUSIONS

This chapter is intended to help you to find out more about your teaching and about the nature of reflection so that you are better equipped to make learning happen effectively, efficiently and enjoyably with your own students. Einstein is reported to have said, 'It is simply madness to keep doing the same things and expect different results'. Reflecting on our teaching, watching others teach and learning from their teaching, and being observed and getting feedback on our teaching from observers are three of the best tools we have for improving our performance. They allow us to go on to try *different* things to make our teaching even better, and to further enhance the learning experience of our students.

The chapter ends with some tips relating to observing others' teaching, having your teaching observed, and drawing out feedback from those who have been observing what happens in your sessions. This time, the tips are for you, and I haven't included a set of parallel tips for students, because exactly the same tips can be modified for students, preferably *by* students themselves, for example in contexts where they are observing each other giving presentations.

 Tips for you, and your students: peer observation

1 *Think about why you might want to get involved in peer observation.* Research shows it's a really positive practice for both the observer and the observee and can help you reflect on what comprises teaching. In some institutions, it is a contractual expectation. Whatever your reasons, you can get more out of it by being clear about your rationale.

2 *Listen to and value feedback from your colleagues.* We all try to gather feedback from students and adjust our teaching accordingly, but feedback from colleagues can be even more useful, as they can bring their own expertise and share different approaches in a collaborative way, learning from what you do particularly well, expanding your repertoire, helping you to get better at what you do and, at your request, helping to identify any problems and remediate them.

3 *When you're observing, keep watching the learners to see what they are doing.* When you are actually teaching, you can only do this to a limited extent. Reflecting on how learners react to what your colleague is doing can help you to think deeply about how your own learners react to things you do. Watch out for things that really work with learners, and things which lose them.

4 *Make observing and being observed a normal part of life, rather than a special occasion.* This implies doing it regularly and informally. When teaching observation is a familiar part of our routine, it is much less scary when visitors from outside are in our classrooms, for example during inspections or when a professional body is checking up on how teaching is actually working.

5 *Being observed can be really good practice for conferences.* Getting feedback on teaching can help you think about what works really well for you so when it comes to conference presentations you can play to your strengths and be all the more confident, thereby helping increase your reputation in your field.

6 Make good use of opportunities to learn how best to observe and be observed, for example within PG Certs in HE, or in staff development programmes. Using different techniques for observing and being observed will help you find the ones that are most comfortable (or indeed most challenging) for you. Regular observations can help you become accustomed to the experience of other people watching your teaching performance, and can build your confidence at handling such situations.

7 *When observing colleagues new to teaching, don't go in too hard too early.* The nature and level of detail of the feedback on observation should match experience levels. While experienced colleagues may request and welcome robust critique as part of a process of continuous self-improvement, colleagues just starting out can have their confidence badly undermined by heavy-handed criticism. When pairing for observation purposes with a new colleague, it may help to let them watch you first and ask them for their comments in a structured and non-judgemental way, which will reassure them that you will adopt a similar approach when you do your observation.

8 *Remind yourself that in everyday teaching, students do see you in action, but don't really observe you.* Having a peer in observing you can help you think about some of the things that students might now comment on. While it is possible that some students might pass comment on your teaching approaches (keep away from Rate My Prof, for example, unless you are feeling very strong!) your students are more likely to be focused on their own needs rather than your performance. So when you're alerted by the person observing you of aspects of your teaching that could benefit from being changed, don't assume that students will necessarily be thinking along the same lines.

9 *Observation is a good defence against 'getting into a rut'.* When anyone has been teaching a particular topic for a considerable time, it is entirely possible to go onto autopilot and teach unreflectively, thereby being less aware of what actual learning is happening during your teaching sessions. Teaching observation can act as a powerful aid to re-energizing your teaching approaches.

10 *Make the most of team teaching opportunities where you can be watched and watch others teach informally.* You are likely to benefit as much from these occasions as from scheduled teaching observation sessions. When, for example in team teaching contexts, you are regularly in the position of watching how your colleagues approach particular topics or skills development, a considerable amount of automatic staff development occurs as you learn from each other's diverse approaches. For example, you could see how they use digital technologies with which you may be unfamiliar.

11 *Getting feedback on your teaching need not be a lengthy process.* If you have a chat in advance and ask your observer to concentrate on two or three aspects of what you are doing (for example, 'Can you concentrate on how I ask and answer questions? Could you keep a watching brief on how well students are picking up unfamiliar concepts?'), these can form the basis of a short post-observation debrief. Getting such thoughtful comments on your teaching can be just about the most powerful staff development you can get.

12 *When you've observed someone else teach, always focus on the most successful aspects first.* Help to put the colleague you have observed at ease by talking initially about the most successful aspects of the session, which is likely to make them more open to any comments you might have about potential improvements.

(Continued)

(Continued)

It may well be even better to ask them to start talking about the session first, as we often are aware of shortcomings ourselves ('I really got the timing wrong in that session and had to hurry at the end'), which then opens up the possibility of productive dialogue without you having to sound negative.

13 *Try to offer more positive than negative remarks at the outset.* If colleagues have to listen to a lot of negative remarks, they may turn off from the process or become hostile and then fail to listen to your constructive suggestions. Even when there is much to comment on adversely, it is important to give sufficient good news early on to help them remain receptive.

14 *When you are being observed, treat it almost as free consultancy.* Teaching can in some ways be a private and lonely task and it isn't always possible to make realistic judgements about how you are doing without a fairly neutral sounding board. Observations can provide real opportunities to have an informed educational conversation about a really important aspect of your professional life.

15 *Practise gently drawing out feedback from your observers if they are inexperienced at doing it.* Gain skills in getting your observer to clarify their thinking and expand on it when necessary. You might ask: 'Thinking about the session you've watched as a whole, can you identify the points in the class where I best held the students' attention and where I lost them?', 'Are there any aspects of my teaching you would suggest I try to change?', 'What do you consider the best thing about the way I am handling such-and-such?' and so on.

16 *Be prepared to receive positive feedback without shrugging it off.* In many cultures, there can be a sense of embarrassment about receiving praise without self-deprecation. This can lead to failing to take on board what your colleagues really value about what you do. It is important to acknowledge it, and thank the people who commend your practices, before entering discussions about potential enhancements. The majority of people who have had their teaching observed are delighted with the feedback they receive, and often surprised at how positive it was.

17 *Regard any criticism you receive as useful feedback.* Avoid the temptation to justify your position, or to make excuses for things that were found to be sub-optimal. When critical feedback is felt to have been openly received and noted, the observer tends to be much more satisfied that their job has been done effectively and is likely to continue to be a source of information that can be helpful to you.

18 If you receive criticism that you feel is unjustified, listen to it, probe the reasons behind it and park your negative feelings until you have a chance to think it through further in private. Chances are that there is an element of truth in what you are hearing, and even if this is not the case, you are unlikely to change the mind of your observer by arguing back on the spot.

Some of the resources in this chapter are available to print for your own use on the companion website. To access these, along with some video clips of the author, please visit: **www.sagepub.co.uk/makinglearninghappen**

CHAPTER 9

WHAT CAN I DO WHEN ...?

This chapter contains a selection of answers to frequently occurring problems. A few of these are adapted from suggestions which proved popular in editions of *In at the Deep End* which I wrote for Leeds Metropolitan University in 2006, and revised in 2009, but most are entirely new. I sought difficult questions from a number of web lists, including those of the National Teaching Fellows in the UK, the members of the All Ireland Society for Higher Education (AISHE), the mailing list of the Higher Education Research and Development Society of Australasia (HERDSA), and the members of the Staff and Educational Development Association (SEDA). Additional useful questions came from reviewers of the second edition. From over 200 questions, I've chosen here to try to provide some answers to the most commonly occurring ones.

> ## What can I do when I'm feeling very nervous?

You're not alone. Even many very experienced lecturers are quite nervous, especially with a new group, or with a subject they don't know particularly well. Some tactics that can help include:

- Smile! You'll notice that at least some of the students will smile back – this immediately makes you feel better.

- Have good prompts available. It's reassuring to have a list of your slides, for example, so that you won't be nervous about losing your place in the lecture.

- If all the students have copies of a handout, ask them to study a short section of it for two minutes. For a while, just about all eyes are off you.

- Ad-lib an explanation of the importance of a point you've just recently been making. Sometimes the very fact that you're making a spontaneous addition is relaxing in its own right.

- Bring in your students. For example, ask them a question along the lines: 'How many of you have already come across ...?' or 'How many of you have never yet heard of ...?'

- Don't be afraid to pause for a short while, and take a deep (quiet) breath.

- Act courageous even when you feel ghastly. Stage performers do this all the time, and it works.

What can I do when I forget where I am in my lecture?

This happens to most lecturers now and then, so don't feel that there's something wrong with you if it happens to you. Your choices include:

- Give your students something to do for a couple of minutes. For example, have a slide or overhead already prepared for such an eventuality. Make the activity seem a perfectly natural step for your students, for example by saying: 'Now would be a really good time for you to think for a minute or two about ...' and then put up your task briefing. While the students are doing the task, you've got time to sort out where *you* are and get ready to resume your lecture after debriefing students' work on the short task.

- Minimize the chance of losing where you are by having a print-out of your slides so that you can quickly *see* what you've done and what you were talking about.

- Ask students to jot down the two most important things they've learned so far from your lecture. Then ask them to compare with those sitting close to them. Then ask for volunteers to tell you what they chose as these things. This often helps you to regain a feel for exactly what has been happening in *their* minds up to the point at which you lost your way.

- If you're very confident, you could say: 'Oops, I've lost it! Anyone like to remind me what I was going to say next?' At least then, you'll have the full attention of your students for a moment – and they normally respond well to you just being human.

What can I do when I don't know the answer to a student's question?

A common nightmare. You'll feel less concerned about this as you gain experience, but the following tactics can take away some of the worries you may have about this.

- Give yourself time to think. Repeat the question to everyone, as other students may not have heard the question. Sometimes this extra time is enough to give you a chance to think of how you may respond.

- Don't try to make an answer up! If it turns out to be wrong, or if you get stuck in the process, you will soon have the full attention of all the students – not what you really want at this stage!

- Say, 'This is a really good question. How many of *you* can respond to this?' and look for volunteers. Quite often, there will be someone there who is willing answer it.

- Break it down into smaller parts. Then start by responding to one of the parts where you *do* have something to say. If it's a question that your students don't actually *need* to know an answer to, say so. 'Interesting, but not actually needed for your course', and so on.

- Admit that at this point you don't have an answer to the question, but you will find one by the time of the next lecture. Invite the student who asked the question to jot it down on a Post-it, with their email address, so that you know *exactly* what the question was and can respond to the questioner directly as soon as you've located an answer. But don't forget to share the answer with the whole group at the next lecture too.

What can I do when students repeatedly come in late and disrupt my lecture?

This is a balancing act. There will usually be *some* students who arrive late, but sometimes the problem becomes more significant in certain time slots and at particular times in a module.

- Don't keep the punctual students waiting until they're fed up. Start the session with something that will be useful or interesting to them.

- Don't gradually get more and more annoyed with latecomers! The *next* student to arrive may have a very good reason for being late.

- Resist the temptation to be sarcastic (e.g. 'How good of you to join us today'). Mostly, students who come in late don't actually enjoy being late, and if they get a rough ride from you, next time they're late they may well decide not to risk coming in at all.

- If the late-coming is noisy (loud doors, shoes on floors, and so on), pause until it will be possible for everyone to hear you properly again. The students themselves will get tired of having to wait for latecomers, and will often show their own disapproval, sparing you the need to do so.

- If necessary, agree some ground rules with the whole group. For example, if quite a lot of the students have had to come from another session at the other end of the campus, negotiate to start promptly five minutes *after* the normal time.

- Build in a little 'warm-up' time at the start of each lecture. In other words, start doing something useful with the students (for example, reminding them of three important points from last week, or quizzing them gently).

What can I do when the technology lets me down?

For example, your PowerPoint slides disappear, or freeze! The thing *not* to do is to struggle for ages, with a mouse, a remote control, a keyboard, or any other piece of technology – *with the undivided attention of the whole group!* Alternatives include:

- Smile, rather than sweat! Even if inside you're quite tense about it, it's best to give the impression of being cool about it.

- Give your students a discussion task to do – something to talk about to those sitting next to them, for example a decision to reach, a problem to solve, and so on. It's a good idea *always* to have such a task ready and waiting. Then when they're all busy and eyes are off you, you can try to rescue the technology.

- Ask for help. 'Anyone know how to fix this please?' quite often brings a competent volunteer from the floor. Sometimes, you can ring up technical support, but it remains advisable to give the students something else to do until help materializes.

- Recognize when the problem is terminal – for example, when the bulb has failed in a ceiling-mounted data projector.

- Improvise a quiz. This can be good revision, particularly if you are really on top of the subject matter (but don't try this if you don't know the material well).

- If it's towards the end of a session, wind up. Remind your students of the intended learning outcomes, and promise to cover anything important that remains outstanding on a future occasion or to put the relevant slides on to the web. Your students won't mind you stopping early!

What can I do when attendance drops off during a series of lectures?

It could be, of course, that your students are getting bored – or tired – or are busy trying to catch up ready for someone else's assignment deadline. Whatever the cause of absentee-ism, one or more of the following tactics may help:

- Don't wait an inordinate time for more students to appear. Those who came punctually deserve to be getting some value, so get started even if the audience is sparse.

- Don't take it out on the students who *do* attend. Make it well worth their while coming to the lectures.

- Probe the causes. For example, if students are taking handouts for their absent friends, only bring enough handouts for those who do attend, and send a message to those who have missed the handout to come and collect it from you at a given time, and ask them why they missed the session.

- Find ways outside the lecture room to ask a few students why they missed a particular session. However, don't rail on them and tell them how unwise they are being – keep to fact-finding until you know more about what's going on.

- Link each and every lecture firmly to the assessment agenda. Students don't like to miss, for example, clarification of what a typical exam question could reasonably ask of them.

- Include some activities for students in groups in some lectures, with a small proportion of the coursework marks allocated to participation in the lectures. Students don't like to miss any opportunity to gain marks.

- Try for added value. Make sure that the students who do turn up feel that it's been well worth doing so. Give them a useful and enjoyable learning experience – and things they would have missed if they had not turned up.

What can I do when students do not attend lectures but get the notes from the VLE?

This is a problem which is increasing rapidly in scale. The following tactics may help:

- Remind the students that what is on the VLE is essentially *information* not knowledge, and is only part of the story. Explain to the class that one of the purposes of the lectures is to help them to *navigate* all of that information, so that they can make sense of it all much faster and more efficiently.

- Include in every lecture some details relating to how students' mastery of what's on the VLE will in due course be assessed. Ensure that students know that they need to come to lectures to find out what they are going to be expected to show for their studies using the information on the VLE.

- Include things for students to *do* in lectures, which get them making sense of concepts and ideas, and making judgements to deepen their learning. Make it clear to students that coming to lectures will help them to get their heads around topics much faster than just reading all about it on the VLE.

What can I do if I get very critical comments from students in the annual feedback?

We *all* get very critical comments sometimes, and often we've earned them! But it's easy to get things out of perspective when it comes to critical comments, and one or more of the following tactics may help you in such a position.

- Don't let one or two savage comments prey on your mind unduly. If the overall comments are favourable on the whole, it could be the case that a few students really didn't like you very much, and much as we all wish to be liked, we can't achieve that all the time with everyone.

- Work out whether the criticism is justified. If it is, think of what you could do next time round to address the criticism and the issue behind it.

- Balance the picture by searching out the favourable comments you attracted at the same time. Think of how you can build on these, and get more of these next time.

- Take opportunities to find out more about the teaching of any colleagues who attracted more favourable comments than you did. Watching others teach regularly is an excellent opportunity to learn from others. There may be things you can emulate.

What can I do if I'm near the end but have only got through half my material?

This can happen to any of us. Any number of good things can cause this, not least going into detail answering important questions which arose during the session. It's only really a problem if you've got no more lectures coming up. General tactics which may help include the following.

- Don't overrun. That would annoy whoever is booked into the room next, and many of the students may have other places to go at the scheduled close of your session.

- Come to a sensible stopping place at the scheduled time, and re-plan your next session to pick up the ground which wasn't covered, and if necessary to delete something less important from that session.

- Alternatively, set the students a task which gets *them* to explore some of the ground you are not able to cover, and pick this up next time.

- In any case, it's probably only *you* who knows that you've only got through half of your material – the students only know what *was* covered.

- If it *was* your only lecture with the group, spend the last few minutes explaining that you will issue a self-study resource package on paper or on the web in a week or two, to enable your students to find out even more about the topic than you were able to cover in just one lecture with them. There's no need to tell them that you only got through half of your material!

What can I do if students are sitting like puddings and not responding?

One distinguished and experienced teacher recalls how he explained to the class that he was bored with their lack of response, and was going to have a short sleep, and lay down at the front of the room for half a minute, after which the class continued with much more gusto! Less risky tactics include:

- Remind yourself that this is human nature – it's easier to sit like a pudding and not respond than to think about something or actually do something. Think of what *you* do in a lecture, if you're not enthralled by it. It's probably time to give your students something to do, for example ...

- Ask all of the students to jot something down. For example, 'See if you can jot down three things that could cause ...'. Then get them to compare notes with their neighbours, and ask for some of the things thought of by students who you can see have something to say about it.

- Amuse them for a moment or two. It's useful to have a hidden action button at the bottom of each slide which can link you to a 'fun' menu – little video clips, cartoons, witty puns, and so on. Students (and staff) are often easier to engage after a little light heartedness.

- Look for links between the topic of the lecture and contemporary issues, and cross-refer your material, inviting discussion.

What can I do if students are texting or checking Facebook online in my lecture?

This is just about the most common 'What can I do when ...?' question posed nowadays. We can't turn the clock back – students *will have* laptops and smartphones with them in lectures, and they *will* have them turned on, even when requested not to do so. Many students live life with one eye on the laptop or smartphone screen, and one ear with an earpiece in it, and the other eye/ear on the rest of the world, whether watching TV, or in pubs and clubs. We're not going to succeed in getting them all to switch these things off in our lectures. Tactics for dealing with this situation include:

- Set out your own ground rules and ask your students to abide by them.

- Don't threaten them that you'll ask them to leave unless they stop doing these things. It would just take one student to *refuse* to leave to give you a much more serious problem with the class.

- As best as you can, ignore those students you notice doing these things. If they're totally captivated by your lecture, they'll stop doing such things. Try to be more captivating!

- Now and then, give them something to *do* with these devices. For example, in groups see what the most important three things you can find on the web about 'x' is. Then quiz the class about what they've found. This can get them using gadgets in a more productive activity. Or ask them to Tweet questions to a #classdate list, which you can respond to if there's time, or save to answer at later sessions.

What can I do when students have not done the necessary preparation before their small-group sessions?

This is a really common 'What can I do when ...?' question! Here are some thoughts:

- Don't give those who have not prepared a hard time. If you do, next time they haven't prepared, they will probably choose not to come at all – that is worse in the long run.

- Try to capitalize on the work of those who *have* prepared. For example, divide the small group into threes, and ask each trio to find answers to half-a-dozen questions based on their preparation, if you think that each trio is likely to have at least one member who has done some preparation. It will actually do the students who did prepare some good, explaining what they found to the others.

- Where possible, have handout material available so that the small group can do some further preparation at the start of the session (including those who have and have not done the advance work) and build on this.

- Next time, try to make the prepared work more engaging!

What can I do to encourage online participation in a discussion?

This is a common question. Here are some thoughts:

- Make participation count. For example, tell the class that some of their coursework marks will arise from the extent and quality of contributions to the discussion. In practice, this is not actually difficult to estimate (albeit rather roughly), for example all five marks for really good contribution, exactly zero for no contribution, and somewhere between for at least some contribution. Students don't like to risk losing even the odd mark or two.

- Use email to give positive, short, encouraging responses to those who do participate. Help them to feel that their efforts are worthwhile.

- In the nicest possible way, cool off the odd student who contributes too much, in case they put others off joining in. 'Great stuff, Tasmin, but could you ease off now and let some of the others catch up?'

- Report some of the main findings of those who did participate to the whole group at a lecture. Gently allow those who didn't participate to feel that they missed something useful.

- Make the discussion irresistible! Choose something suitable, and get a real debate going in a lecture, then say, 'We'll continue this online'.

What can I do to ensure all the students in the group feel confident to ask questions or join in the discussion?

It's not surprising that some students are shy, especially in their first year, and in large groups. They don't want to say anything that may make them look or feel stupid. Some international students may also feel uncomfortable about 'putting themselves forward' as they may see it, or about the level of their spoken English. The following ways of helping them join in with more confidence may help you to get them all contributing:

- Use the old adage, 'Better to look silly for a moment than to remain ignorant for a lifetime – please do ask me questions'.

- Never make a student who does ask a question feel silly.

- Accept that at least some students will remain very shy, and will be unlikely to feel confident enough to ask questions. Sometimes it may be because they are learning in a second language, and are embarrassed that they aren't yet as fluent as students around them.

- Get them all to jot down a question or two, for example on Post-its, and then share their questions with their near neighbours, then invite students to ask *someone else's* question.

- For greater 'comfort of anonymity' in a big group, ask students to write questions on Post-its and send the Post-its down to you.

- Use a question box to collect queries, and reply via the course web page.

- Suggest that students email you with *short* questions, and then answer some of them in the next whole-class session.

What can I do to inspire students (and myself) when I'm getting bored with delivering the same content year after year?

Boredom is as infectious as enthusiasm. If we radiate boredom with a topic, students will catch it. The following tactics may help you increase your enthusiasm for the content which is currently beginning to bore you.

- Remind yourself that the content may be the same, but the students are different. They will already know different things this year, and will have at least some different problems with the content.

- Avoid just turning up with the same notes and slides as you used last time. Give yourself some time to do some editing of your materials, getting rid of the most boring bits and putting new ideas in. Perhaps even frighten yourself by deleting the old material and starting again from scratch.

- Try doing things differently yourself. Invent new in-lecture tasks for the students to do to get their heads around the content.

- Do a bit of web searching, looking for two or three recent sources you hadn't known about, and build them into your lecture. There is always new information out there!

- Try to make sure that you've got at least some different content to work with, rather than just the same old workload.

- Start some team teaching going with the sections you're getting bored with – you may find that watching someone else handling these gives you new ideas and increases your own enthusiasm.

What can I do to stop the mobile phones that keep going off in my lecture?

The short answer is probably 'You can't!' However, the following tactics may reduce the occurrence of the problem.

- Say to the class at the start of a lecture, 'Please leave your mobile phones *on* if you really need to be contacted, for example if you've got a seriously ill relative, or child, or a crisis in the family, and so on. I want you all to be relaxed enough to give your attention to the lecture, so remain possible to be contacted if needed. If your phone *does* go off, please slip out quietly and deal with the emergency'. Alternatively, 'Please set your phone to "silent" and do not answer it in class'. One result of this is that when someone's phone does go off, everyone wants to know what the emergency is, and students whose phones ring for no important reason are now quite embarrassed.
- Make sure *your* mobile phone doesn't go off! (Sadly, this is an occasion when I don't practise what I preach – I never remember to switch mine off, and when it does go off several members of my audience switch theirs off!).
- Alternatively, arrange that your mobile phone *does* go off, and pretend to have a seemingly long discussion with the (non-existent) caller, explaining that you're actually in the middle of giving a lecture just now, and so on! Sometimes, this makes the point you're wanting to get across.
- Stop the whole session and allow the student concerned to answer the call. It's quite uncomfortable answering a call with a large number of people listening in!

What can I do when a student asks 'Will this be in the exam?'

A natural enough request. The following tactics can help.

- Always say 'Yes, it certainly could be' – if the answer was to have been 'no', students might well ask why they should be bothering to learn it.
- Expand a little on what exactly students should expect to become able to do, to illustrate the evidence of their achievement of the learning outcomes which will relate to the topic.
- Avoid students having to ask the question by regularly reminding the class of the sort of things that you are expecting from them in the exam and any other modes of assessment.

- When something is not suitable to be in the exam, for example when a student asks a question about the topic which is off-target, it's sometimes worth responding along the lines, 'This is very interesting, but you don't need this in the context of this particular course'.

- If the question arises *too* frequently, you might reply, 'Ah yes, that would be a *good* idea' and be seen to make a note to yourself.

What can I do when a student challenges my mark for an assignment?

This is sometimes a tricky situation, and one which needs to be handled sensitively, especially if the challenge occurs in a public context, such as in a large-group session. The following tactics can help.

- Provide detailed explanations of how marks are awarded from the outset, ideally during the briefing for the assignment.

- Don't take offence. There might have been a problem with your marking of the assignment. More likely, the student may have a blind spot, and not yet see why marks had been lost in the answer submitted to you.

- Publish the marking scheme and assessment criteria in any case, written in language where students can see exactly how the marking has been done, so that it's less likely that any student will challenge your mark.

- Don't give the impression to all present that marks are not negotiable. Arrange a one-to-one session with the student concerned.

- At the one-to-one session, work through the marking scheme and assessment criteria with the student concerned, and (usually) show that the original mark was justified.

- Allow it to gradually become apparent to the whole group that you remain willing to renegotiate marks if there is a genuine case to be made, but that in practice it's extremely rare for a student to emerge with a better mark as a result of the process, and that sometimes they emerge with lower marks.

What can I do when all the students sit at the back and the front half of the room is empty?

This is a very common occurrence. It is human nature – just watch lecturers themselves at conferences! But most human beings do not at all like being told where to go. One or more of the following tactics may be useful.

- Sometimes you can nip this in the bud by placing 'reserved' cards on back seats or using 'do not cross this line' ribbon for the back rows.

- Encourage students to sit in the central block rather than at the sides so you can at least see them all.

- Don't try to make the students move forwards. They actually resent quite strongly being made to sit elsewhere, and it just takes one or more to refuse to move, and you've lost some authority.

- There could be some students who really do feel most comfortable at the back – not least anyone who might have to leave the room relatively suddenly, for example due to a panic attack which could be triggered by them being hemmed in, in the middle of a row.

- Put out any handouts only on the seats you wish them to use.

- Offer a few 'prizes' for the first half-dozen students to come and sit in the front row – an extra handout, for example.

- Show a start-up slide with very small print on it, for example a shot of a newspaper cutting about the topic. This can cause students entering the room to move to where they can see the screen rather better (but don't continue to show small print to the class thereafter).

- Just continue as though you don't mind at all where they sit. If the atmosphere of the class becomes warmer and friendlier, they may well gravitate towards you on future occasions.

- Set a group activity for the students, and indicate that group A is here, group B here, etc., including locations at the front and back of the room. This can get at least some of them nearer to you.

- See if you can rearrange the session to a smaller room. The chances are that there will be a colleague with a large class who would like the larger room.

What can I do when asked at the last minute to cover a session for a colleague who has not turned up?

Just about anything is better than simply cancelling a session – some students may have travelled a long way for it, and students remember cancellations when evaluation comes round. Being asked to cover a session is in fact sometimes a useful opportunity for you to illustrate how professional you are. It's worth always finding a way to meet the request, not least to enhance your reputation of being dependable and flexible. It also makes it more likely that someone will return the favour if you need to miss one of your sessions due to illness or an emergency. One or more of the following tactics may help.

- Don't berate your absent colleague in front of the students (or to anyone else). It could be the case that the absence was quite unavoidable.

- Don't apologise for being there. It's better to say, 'I'm really pleased to have the chance to see you all today, but I'm sorry Dr Jones can't be here'.

- If you have teaching sessions with the class concerned, you may be able to substitute one of your own sessions for the last-minute session, and make one of your future classes available to the colleague who did not turn up.

- If you really do need to try to cover your colleague's topic, you could run a revision session based on what the class had already covered, for example getting the class to generate questions about the topic on Post-its, then facilitating a quiz of two or three teams of students, with a prize for the winning team.

- If it's a topic you know something about, you could give a session putting your own slant on the topic, keeping notes to pass on to your colleague to indicate what you have covered.

What can I do when I don't have a powerful voice, but don't like to be stuck behind the lectern near a microphone?

Lecturers need to be seen and heard. Ways of ensuring the latter include the following:

- See if you can get a radio mic. This normally allows you to walk around the room quite a lot, so long as you don't cause feedback loops by getting into the path of the linked loudspeakers. Using a microphone is good inclusive practice anyway, as hearing-impaired students will benefit if there is an audio loop in the room (and you may well not know that anyone has hearing difficulties, if they haven't declared them). Do, however, remember to switch the radio mic off as soon as you've finished. Few things are more amusing to audiences than to hear the private discussions (and worse!) of someone who's forgotten to switch one off.

- Encourage the students to sit close enough to hear you. Admit that your voice is relatively quiet.

- Get some voice projection training. You may be amazed how much better you can project by due attention to breathing and stance.

- If you use a particular room often, find out more about its acoustics. Sometimes there are places from which a quiet voice projects better.

- Don't try to be louder than is comfortable for you – you may injure your voice, making the problem worse.

- Don't try to compete with students talking. Wait until it is quiet enough for you to be heard. Students' peer pressure usually causes them to stop talking if it is clear you are waiting for silence.

What can I do when I realize that I no longer understand the next point I'm about to teach?

This can be rather scary. Here are some thoughts:

- Celebrate! Understanding dawns a little at a time, and we never stop deepening our understanding of something.
- As soon as you've done your best to explain the point to the students, get them explaining it to each other. Ask them, 'What was the thing that helped you most to make sense of this idea?' and find out whether they've come up with better ways of explaining it than yours turned out to be.
- Point out to students that this is a tricky concept, 'One day you've got it, and then it can slip away. Keep regaining it for the next few days until it's less likely to slip'.
- Take time before your next session with the group to have a good rethink about the point concerned, and see if there's another better way you can get the point across to them.

What can I do when no one seems to be taking any notes?

Nowadays, lots of students may arrive without pens or paper, but with their laptops and smartphones. It's useful to have spare pens and paper (a good supply of Post-its will do) to give out. Perhaps the question should be, 'Is it important that students take notes, or are there better things I can get my students to do during the lecture?' There are plenty of *other* things that are *good* for students to do during lectures. These include the following:

- Jotting down their own thoughts and ideas in response to a question posed orally or on-screen.
- Comparing their ideas with the ideas of those sitting next to them.
- Making a mind-map about what they've been hearing about for the last ten minutes.
- Writing down questions they need answered about the topic.

What can I do when nobody seems to listen at the end of my lecture because they are busy packing up?

A very common problem. It only takes one student to make packing up noises and it spreads like wildfire. Try one or more of the following.

- End with something really important, such as a short explanation of the sort of exam question which could be based on what has been covered in the lecture.
- Make the close of the lecture so interesting that no one thinks of packing up.

- Avoid saying 'and finally ...' too early, which is often the cue students take to start packing up.

- Avoid saying 'Right now, are there any questions?' This is widely interpreted by students as time to pack up. In any case, it's much better to seek questions in the middle of the lecture, or even at the very beginning.

- Some lecturers get away with ending each lecture with a joke or anecdote, and if this is engaging enough it prevents students from starting to pack up, or at least means those who do pack up are not missing anything important.

- Prepare yourself to close the lecture a few minutes before the students will begin to pack up. Continuing while they are packing up won't be of value to them in any case, so you may as well make the lecture that bit shorter.

What can I do when someone responds to my question with a totally wrong answer?

This is bound to happen from time to time, especially if you're successful at getting most students to contribute to answering your questions. The following tactics may help.

- Don't make the student giving the wrong answer look foolish. Thank them for their contribution, try to find something positive in what was said, then say, 'Anyone got a different answer for this question?' and make it clear gently that the next answer is better (if, of course, it is better).

- Try to avoid picking the student who gave the totally wrong answer, when several students are offering to answer your next question.

- When a student gives a really good answer, be generous with your praise, for example, 'Well done, that's great'.

What can I do if students are talking in my lecture?

Many lecturers get upset by this, and clearly if students can't hear you over each other's chatter, the situation becomes untenable.

- Don't just carry on trying to ignore it. That often makes the problem get worse. Pause, looking at the people who are talking until they stop – or until the other students shut them up for you.

- Don't necessarily assume they're just being rude. Sometimes, one will have asked another to explain or repeat something that has been missed. Sometimes they could be translating what you say into another language for each other.

- Acknowledge that you may have been talking for too long yourself, and give them something to talk about with near neighbours. In other words, *legitimize* their talking for a few minutes, and let them get the need to talk out of their system.

- Note any persistent talkers but resist the temptation to confront them in front of the whole group. Instead, find a time to talk to them on their own, and explore how they're finding your lectures.

- Don't ask an offender to leave! If they actually *refuse* to leave, you'll have a much more difficult problem to deal with. Never issue a threat that you would not be able to implement in practice.

What can I do when I come to the end and there are still 15 minutes to go?

Possibilities include:

- Say, 'This is a good place to stop this particular session' and revisit the intended learning outcomes for a moment or two, then wind up. Your students will not be terminally disappointed!

- Have with you a revision activity – for example, a set of short, sharp quiz questions on your lectures to date with the group – and give them a quick-fire quiz until the time has been used up.

- Give out Post-its and ask students to write any questions they would like to ask about the subject on them, and pass the Post-its down to you. Choose which questions to answer to the whole group until the time is used up.

- Put up a slide of a past exam question on the topic you've been covering, and explain to students a little about what was expected in answers to that question.

- Ask the students to write down the two most important things they now know, that they didn't know when the lecture started. Then get them to compare with their neighbours, and invite volunteers to read out a few such things.

- Give a brief overview of what's coming next – for example, showing the students the intended learning outcomes for the next couple of lectures.

What can I do when students don't turn up for my small-group sessions?

In practice, there's little mileage in trying to force students to turn up to any element in their programmes, and when students don't regard small-group teaching as particularly important, the problem of absenteeism increases. However, a combination of one or more of the following tactics can improve things sometimes.

- When the students who *are* present come away with something they would not have wanted to miss (be it handouts, the light dawning, tasks they found valuable doing, and so on), the word can get around and attendance can improve.

- If your institution has student liaison officers, or other staff who support the student experience, ask them to help you check up on absentees.

- Track down some regular absentees and ask them 'What's wrong?' Sometimes there could be a timetable clash you didn't know about, or travel difficulties relating to a particular time slot. Sometimes, of course, the answer can be, 'I didn't find the sessions helpful' and we may need to probe gently into 'Why not exactly?' and remain ready to listen to the responses.

- Keep the assessment agenda on the table. When students can see that each small-group session has a bearing on helping them become ready for future exam questions, or helps them see what's being looked for in coursework assignments, students are less likely to miss them.

- Include at least *some* coursework mark for participation. Don't just include it for *attendance*, however, or the odd student may come along but not join in!

What can I do when students refuse to do a task?

This is an awkward one. If *all* the students won't start your task, it's worse. The following tactics can help.

- Make sure the task briefing is really clear. Explain again exactly what you want them to do. It can be useful to say, 'What it really means is ...' and then put it into straightforward language.

- Show the task on a slide or overhead, or give it out as a handout. Sometimes, students can get the gist of a task better if they can see it and hear it at the same time.

- Try to find the block. For example, ask students, 'Which part of the task are you having problems with?' and see if clarifying that part helps them to get started.

- Break the task into smaller parts. Ask students to do only the first part now, and then explain the later stages one by one when they're properly under way.

- Ask them to work in twos or threes to start with. You can then go round any pairs who still seem reluctant to start the task, and find out more about what could be stopping them.

- Set a precise deadline for the first part of the task. Sometimes this is enough to get them started.

- Resist the temptation to keep talking. Give them some time when there's really nothing more going on, and it's clear that you expect them to get stuck into the task. A few seconds of solemn silence may seem interminable to you, but the resistance to getting started with the task may be fading away.

What can I do when one student dominates a group?

This is a frequent occurrence. Sometimes the causes are innocent enough – enthusiasm, knowing a lot about the topic, and so on. One or more of the following tactics may help you to balance things out.

- Set appropriate ground rules at the start of small-group work. It can be useful to say a little about leadership and followership – making the point that in many small-group situations in real life, too many leaders can militate against success and that everyone needs to be able to be a good follower for at least some of the time.

- Rearrange group membership regularly. This means that the domineering student moves on and doesn't dominate other students for too long.

- Intervene gently. For example, after the domineering student comes to a pause, ask: 'Would someone else now like to add to this please?'

- Have a quiet word. Do this with the domineering student outside the group context, giving suggestions about 'air time' and allowing everyone's views to be heard, for example.

- Change the dynamic. Appoint the domineering student as chairperson for a particular activity, with the brief not to make any input on that task, but to coordinate everyone else's thinking.

- Don't fight it too hard. Recognize that domineering is a common human trait and that domineering people often reach distinguished positions in the world around us and may be developing relevant skills in small-group contexts.

What can I do when a new colleague asks for suggestions regarding how long it should take to prepare a lecture?

How long does it take to prepare a lecture? 'All my life so far' is one answer! The problem boils down to what the most important things to do are exactly in order to prepare for a lecture. The following tactics may help you give good advice to a colleague asking this question.

- Remember that a one-hour lecture is really only about 40 minutes in terms of the real teaching/learning time. Five minutes are needed for settling in, explaining the intended outcomes, and so on. At least five minutes at the end are needed for summarizing, pointing the way forward to the next lecture, reminding students about what *they* need to be able to do in due course with the topic in exams or coursework assignments, and so on.

- Don't try to find all the information in the world on the topic of each lecture! Your students can only get their heads around a relatively small amount in 40 minutes.

- Work out at least two things that the students will *do* during the lecture. For example, what decisions can they be given to make? What can you get them to do in buzz groups? What can you get them arguing about?

- If you will have easy and reliable internet access, it's worth finding two or three relevant sites to dip into, for example with a couple of minutes of video to illustrate an important point, and so on.

- Point out that any class will already know some things about the topic, and that it's useful to build students' confidence by valuing what they already know, and giving them the chance to show what they know.

- Suggest to your colleague that if everything had been covered ten minutes ahead of schedule, it won't be the greatest disappointment in the lives of the students present if it is announced 'That's about all for today, thank you'.

- Remind your new colleague that the same lecture next time round will feel a lot more comfortable on the basis of experience of that first one, and that it's better to get the student activity side of the lecture going well rather than over-preparing topic-related content.

What can I do when senior colleagues ignore procedures relating to deadlines for submission of work, allowing their students to make late submissions, and so painting me in a bad light in students' eyes when I'm firm with deadlines?

This is a tricky one. Ideally, procedures (good or bad) should be adhered to uniformly. Some ways out of this dilemma are suggested below.

- Explain to your students that you want to make sure they get quick and useful feedback on their submitted work, and that you have prepared a discussion sheet which you will issue immediately after the deadline has passed, so that they get quick feedback on submission, to keep them going until they get their marked work back. Remind the class that this of course will make any late submissions invalid.

- Point out to students that you've got their best interests in mind. You don't want them to be struggling with backlogs in your subject when the time comes for them to be getting their act together ready for important assessments such as exams, and that firm deadlines for coursework will help them to keep to schedule.

- Try not to give any impression that you're critical of those colleagues who aren't following agreed procedures. Students are very quick to pick up on disagreements or conflicts among teaching staff! Simply explain if necessary that you're responsible for your parts of their curriculum, and you want to make it all go smoothly for them.

> **What can I do when a student has absolutely no interest and continues to sidetrack me during the lecture?**

This is relatively rare – the students with no interest aren't usually present! When it does happen, however, here are some things to try – and some to avoid:

- Don't ask the student to leave. What if he or she refused to leave? That would turn the situation into a drama – much more interesting for the class than the lecture!
- Continue to respond politely, but very briefly, to each sidetracking episode.
- Allow peer pressure to come to bear. If the other students get irritated by the constant sidetracking, they will usually cause the sidetracker to desist.
- Consider the possibility that this student is reflecting a wider boredom with what's happening. Bring more activity into the session – or some fun.
- It can be useful to have a quiet word with the student concerned, but not in the lecture. You may sometimes be able to find out more about what the student is interested in, and sometimes steer the content a tiny bit in that particular direction, smiling encouragingly at the person concerned.

> **What can I do when a student who has missed a necessary previous lecture continues to interrupt my continuation lecture?**

This happens quite often. One or more of the following tactics can help:

- Politely remind the student that such-and-such was addressed in the previous lecture, and that the resources referred to are indeed on the VLE (or in the handout used on that occasion, and so on).
- Sometimes you will be able to respond to the whole group along the lines that 'this is a very important question. How many of you remember the answer to this?' and illustrate to the student who posed the question that fellow students have already 'got it'.
- Allow peer pressure to work. Other students who were there will quite quickly lose patience with someone who is holding them up.
- Suggest to the class that 'question time' will be held in the last ten minutes of the lecture, and it would be really helpful for all questions to be held over until then.

What can I do if I am running late for a lecture?

With the best will in the world, we're sometimes unavoidably late for a lecture we're giving. This goes against all of our efforts to help the students be punctual and avoid the disruption of late-comers. When you know you're going to be late, one or more of the following tactics may help – but try to avoid this situation altogether – it's a bad example for students.

- Think of something you're going to get the class to do, once you get there, so that you can catch your breath and calm yourself down. A buzz-group task – for example, a choice to make between options – can give you a couple of minutes to recover.

- See if there's any way you can get a message to the lecture venue so that, for example, an announcement can be made – 'Dr Jones's lecture this morning will begin at 10.20' – and a slide can be projected onto the screen to the same effect. This gives students the chance to go for a break themselves, or at least sit chatting without getting increasingly annoyed at you.

- Remember to apologise to the students you've kept waiting. Don't feel you have to tell them exactly why you're late (unless they will find it amusing or very human).

What can I do if students who haven't bothered to attend revision sessions ask me for extra help to catch up?

This can be very irritating. It can also make us feel that we should put ourselves out to help any student in need of help. It is probably best to try to avoid this sort of situation occurring, for example as follows:

- Explain well in advance that there will be revision classes, and that in these all sorts of things will be discussed and explained relating to the standard and nature of forthcoming exams.

- Further explain that things to do with assessment will *only* be explained in whole-class meetings, and will not be discussed with individuals or small groups at other times. Explain that this is to make it fair for all students, and to ensure that no students get 'advantaged' by separate discussions about revision or assessment.

- Keep reminding the whole class to bring all questions and issues for discussion to the scheduled revision sessions and, if they wish, to email you in advance about things they would like to ask, or explanations they would like from you.

- Explain that you will indeed continue to be willing to see the occasional student individually, if they still can't make sense of something after trying their best during the appropriate 'questions and revision' session, but that you have not the time to do so for students who didn't participate in that session, and that it would in any case be at a time when you had very little time left due to all the other commitments in your job.

> ## What can I do when several students ask to leave early?

There will often be the occasional student who apologises in advance for needing to leave a particular lecture early, but it becomes a problem if too many students are doing this. The danger is setting a precedent, so that more and more students ask to leave early, especially if you're saddled with a lecture at an unpopular time, for example Friday afternoons. Ways of handling the situation, but avoiding escalation, include the following:

- Never refuse. If some students want to leave early for whatever reason, and you say 'no', you will not have much of their attention towards the end of the session anyway.
- Find out whether the timing of the session needs to be adjusted in the long term. For example, if there's something regular that several students want to get away for, it could be worth shortening the session each time, or finding a better time slot altogether.
- Always make it worthwhile for the students who don't leave early to stay. For example, towards the end of each lecture give some useful revision advice, or illustrate what would get students good marks for an old exam question on the topic of the session.
- Have something for students to follow up at the very end of the session, for example explanations or tasks based on material on the web.

> ## What can I do when a student says my material has no possible relevance to their future jobs?

A tricky one. Here are some possibilities:

- Try to increase, broadly, the sense of 'relevance to future jobs' regarding the material you're covering, so that students become aware of a wide range of real-world contexts where the material will prove helpful.

- Answer the student concerned along the lines that 'the material is relevant to many of the group' and accept that there will be exceptions.

- Find other answers to the question 'what's in it for me?' regarding this particular material, for example – 'well, this could indeed come up in your exam, and you want a good qualification to get that job, don't you?'

- Check out honestly whether that particular bit of material may be best missed out altogether in future.

What can I do when some students have finished making notes on something I've shown but other students are still copying it down slowly?

This begs the question, do you really want them to be spending valuable time in your lecture copying things down from what you show them? Ways of avoiding the problem include the following:

- Explain that your slides will be available on the VLE after the lecture, and that you will often move on relatively quickly from one slide to another, and students should aim to make quick headline notes only.

- Get your students to do plenty of *other* things during the lecture apart from merely copying down information from your slides. Get them thinking of causes of things, making decisions, explaining things to each other – anything but routine copying.

- Suggest to students that they should *make* notes, not just *take* notes. In other words, they should be writing down their own individual thoughts and ideas, rather than just copying down things you show them.

What can I do when students ignore regulations and eat in class?

This can be disconcerting, but is probably not serious enough to make an issue of. One or more of the following tactics may help.

- Remember that the occasional student may be diabetic, and may *need* to eat. It is best just to continue the class as if nothing was amiss, then have a quiet word with the student later, for example to see if there is a reason for them contravening the regulations.

- Try not to take it as a personal affront or sign of disrespect. There may well be other students who find it irritating, and you can often leave this sort of problem to sort itself out without any intervention.

- See if colleagues are experiencing the same problem. If it's a common problem, it could be raised at a departmental meeting and agreement reached on a policy.

What can I do if I'm double booked for a room and have nowhere to take my class?

This is the sort of occasion when students will remember what you did. It's important to be seen to behave really professionally.

- If there's someone else preparing to teach in the room, check with them calmly that you have in fact been double booked. Don't argue with them, especially if their students are already in place.
- If you're already in place, avoid becoming territorial. Neither of you may be to blame, and their need may be greater than yours – for example, if they've got a larger group of students to accommodate.
- Take your students to somewhere not in the way, i.e. not blocking a corridor, and put a Post-it or paper note on the door of the original room saying, for example, 'Class moved to lobby on ground floor'. Wait there until all of your students have gathered, then try for a short while to find an alternative venue.
- If nowhere can be found, brief the students carefully for a reading or research task to do between now and the next session. Make sure that the next session isn't double booked too, and remember to spend a few minutes quizzing the students about the reading they did, so that they feel their efforts are valued.

What do I do when I see on my slide that I have made a mistake?

This is, of course, exactly when most of us *do* see our mistakes – up there on the big screen, with dozens of other pairs of eyes looking at it. When we checked through it previously, we saw what we meant – not what we wrote. The following tactics could help.

- Routinely say to students, 'There's £1 for the first person to alert me to mistakes on my slides – spelling, factual, whatever'. Always have a few £1 coins ready! Students then tell us our mistakes with some enthusiasm, but we also increase their concentration levels regarding what's on our slides.
- Alternatively, quickly say to the class, 'What's wrong with this slide?' Let them find the mistake, as if it were a deliberate ploy.
- Alternately, when they spot the mistake before you do, thank them, and move on.

What can I do when students don't get on with each other?

This is more likely to be a problem in small-group contexts than in lectures. The following tactics can help:

- Re-arrange group membership now and then. This can be done randomly, but check that particular pairs of students who didn't seem to be getting on are then moved apart into different groups.

- Give them all a task to start on their own. Sometimes if all of the students have already invested some energy in thinking through the topic before the actual group work begins, differences between students are pushed further into the background.

- Make the first part an individual written task. For example, give out Post-its, and ask everyone to jot down a single idea relevant to the task. Then when everyone is armed with at least one idea, the chances of students not getting on with each other can be reduced.

- Go closer to the people who don't seem to be getting on. Sometimes, your proximity will cause them to bury any differences – for the moment at least. You may also then get the chance to work out what exactly has been causing the confrontation between the students concerned.

- Watch out for the occasional 'difficult student'. When the same person doesn't get on in group work contexts with different individuals, it can be worth having a quiet word. Just sometimes, you'll find the odd student who really doesn't function well in group contexts.

What can I do when I have a 'senior moment' during a lecture?

This happens at any age, at any time, and in any place. Don't worry about it! You can pick and choose from the following options, and you probably have even better tactics of your own for this occurrence.

- Probably the only person who knows you're having a 'senior moment' is you – that is, unless you do things which make it clear to everyone that this is happening. So at least at first, try not to show that anything is wrong.

- Often, going on to your next slide will mean you can carry on as normal, without anyone noticing that your concentration had lapsed. Usually within a short while, whatever it was that 'escaped you' temporarily will filter back into your mind, and when necessary you can go back and cover the missing point if it was important enough to do so.

- Give the students something to do – for example, 'Right, now think back over the last few minutes, and jot down in a few words what you think is the most important point we've covered'. Then, 'OK, spend a minute comparing what you reckon the most important point was with your neighbour'. Then, 'OK (pointing to someone who's clearly being discussing with their neighbour) what did *you* think it was?' More often than not, this will remind you of whatever was going on before your 'senior moment' (but probably it will have come back to you anyway while the students were chatting to each other).

What can I do if I have lost my energy for teaching and have become overly self-critical?

This can be quite frightening. It can happen if your job has moved on to other things (managing, researching, committee work, you name it) and you do not have as much time for teaching. It can also happen if you've been teaching the same part of the curriculum for a long time, and have perhaps got bored yourself with the content. It can also feel worse if there are dynamic new colleagues around who seem to be getting all the best feedback from students. One or more of the following suggestions may help. However, just about all of us lose our energy now and then.

- Being self-critical can be useful, but not when one is *too* self-critical. There will always be 'better' ways to do anything (lectures, small-group sessions, designing assessment, and so on) but what we need to do is to do *good* things as often as possible, not *perfect* things.

- Ask yourself whether perhaps you're trying to do too much. In a lecture, for example, we can gradually drift into trying to go deeper and deeper every time we repeat a topic, and end up going too deep, or too fast for the students. The main thing is that they are getting what they need to achieve the related intended learning outcomes – it's not good for them to exceed this too much.

- Sometimes, moving to a new topic helps. When one has taught something many times, the challenge can fade, and a new challenge inspires us more.

- A bit of peer-observing can help. For a start, it gives you some time just to think, and you can often notice something in your colleague's teaching that inspires you to try out something a bit different in your own work. You may also soon be less critical of your own teaching too.

What can I do if my mentor is not helpful?

Mentors can be brilliant and inspiring. They can be life-saving, especially when we're new to teaching. But some of them are much better than others. If you're not getting the most from your mentor, try the following:

- You may be able to change your mentor – but that's probably not the best thing to do (hurt feelings, awkward silences, and so on). It's a bit like when students want to change their personal tutor – neither side comes out well if this becomes an issue.

- It is often possible to get at least some support from someone else. After all, there's no reason why an appointed mentor should be the only human being to give helpful advice. In practice, it's often really useful to find people in other disciplines or parts of the institution to talk to. Fellow participants on a staff development programme are often ideal. It's sometimes much easier to talk to someone you only see now and then, than to someone who has a prescribed role such as a mentor.

- Fellow mentees can be really helpful. Most people new to teaching are all too happy to share their experiences – good ones and bad ones.

- Support and advice does not have to come from a particular person. There is loads of literature with helpful tips. Use online discussion lists. Work out what you really need help with, and find 'frequently asked questions' online.

- Above all, try not to resent the great support other colleagues seem to be getting from their super mentors. We all have to grow out of dependence on mentoring – you may just have to do this rather sooner than you would have preferred.

> ## What can I do to improve and vary my questioning skills so that students provide more detailed and sustained responses?

Questioning skills are important, and are learned by practice. It is indeed useful if we're able to get students to make sustained and detailed responses. The following tactics may help you to achieve this.

- It can make quite a difference when students can both *see* and *hear* a question. It's useful to have important questions on a slide (or whiteboard, or whatever) so they can see them, but also to *speak* the question so they can *hear* which words may be most important.

- In lectures or small groups, try getting students to individually jot down responses to questions, rather than answer orally straightaway. Also, give them time to jot, time to think. Giving out Post-its helps – a small, non-threatening space to jot down an answer. You can soon judge when to move on, just by watching students' faces and pens. Then get students to share responses informally for a minute or so, before asking someone to share their response with the whole group. They are more prepared to do so by now, and usually more confident to go into depth.

- 'Elsify'. Ask students, for example, the question 'why ...?'. Then take answers orally. When the first respondent gives an answer, thank them for it, then ask 'Anyone know why else ...?' And so on. Keep using *'else'*: 'what *else* ...?', 'when *else* ...?', 'who *else* ...?', 'where *else* ...?', 'how *else* ...?', and so on.

- Ask students to note down *three* factors causing a particular phenomenon. Then ask different students for just one of these. Turn it into a game to see how many good answers the group has come up with. If you'd just asked for *one* factor in the first place, the responses would have been much more limited.

- Where appropriate, try case study type questions. On a slide, for example, have a short scenario, then add questions such as, 'What do you think would be the *best* thing to do?' and also 'What do you think would be the *worst* thing to do?', giving students time to think about both before starting to draw out answers from them.

- Get students themselves to nominate the next respondent. For example, start with a volunteer, then thank them for their response, and suggest, 'Now pick someone else', and so on. Students then don't feel it's *you* who is picking them, and most students don't want *not* to have anything to say if one of their fellow students picks them, so most get more ready to answer.

What can I do about one or more difficult, uncooperative colleagues?

This question must have perplexed just about everyone who has ever taught in post-compulsory education (and every other field of human endeavour). Whole books and websites abound with responses. But just sometimes, such a question can dominate one's whole life – if we let it. In such circumstances, one or more of the following responses might be helpful:

- This may be largely about feelings. You're in charge of your feelings, and no one can *make* you feel anything.

- Is this person making you *do* something you don't want to, or *stopping* you doing something you do want to? If not, just stay out of their way and get on with your job.

- Identify what exactly it is about them that really bugs you. This could be a multiple-choice question with hundreds of options, including, 'They're paid more than me and do their job much less well', 'They get in the way of me doing my job well', 'They won't even listen to me', 'They're just *wrong*'.

- Next, identify what exactly you'd like to do about it, *but can't*. Your response might be a long and gruesome one, but at least that's now out of the way. You can now move on.

- Think now of *your* students in *your* classes. The most important thing is to be doing as good a job as *you* can with your students.

What can I do when teaching isn't my main job?

'What can I do to make a reasonable job of the teaching I'm given to do, alongside all the other things on my plate? Have I got to keep up to date with all that's happening in teaching, learning and assessment as well?' you may be asking. Lots of people do *some* teaching alongside research. Even more people do *some* teaching alongside other jobs, or partial retirement. The following suggestions may help you make a *good* job of those curriculum elements you happen to teach.

- Remind yourself that your teaching is important for students. Remember that though teaching may only be a small part of your agenda, the learning which your students do with you counts a lot for them. It will no doubt be assessed, and may influence the qualifications they're heading towards.

- Do everything you can to link your part of the curriculum to things students will need in the overall picture of their studies. Make things as relevant as possible to the other things your students are learning from other people.

- Talk to your students, and find out how they are finding 'your' parts. They will often have useful suggestions for ways you can tune in further to their perspectives on learning.

- Take every chance to observe other people teaching the same kinds of students. Even if you only do a small amount of teaching, you can always pick up useful things to try out while watching others teach – and also things to avoid in your own teaching!

- Even if you're under pressure in other parts of your life (research, other jobs, and so on), use teaching as a chance to relax from all these other things. Just focus on the task in hand when you're teaching – that is to help make learning happen for your students.

- Don't over-prepare. It's dangerously easy to prepare so much that you can't get through it all on the day. It is much better to leave yourself room to manoeuvre, so that when you're teaching you have time to respond to students' questions, and to find out what they already know and move ahead from that position.

REFERENCES

Anderson, D. and Race, P. (2002) *Effective Online Learning: The Trainer's Toolkit*. Ely: Fenman.

Ausubel, D.P. (1968) *Educational Psychology: A Cognitive View*. London: Holt, Rinehart and Winston.

Bandura, A. (1997) *Self-efficacy: The Exercise of Control*. New York: Freeman.

Bates, A.W. (1995) *Technology, Open Learning and Distance Education*. London: RoutledgeFalmer.

Bates, A.W. (2002) *National Strategies for e-Learning in Post-secondary Education and Training*. New York: UNESCO.

Biggs, J. and Tang, C. (2011) *Teaching for Quality Learning at University: What the Student Does* (4th edn). Maidenhead: Open University Press/SRHE.

Blackwell, R. and McLean, M. (1996) 'Peer observation of teaching and staff development', *Higher Education Quarterly*, 50(2): 156–71.

Bloom, B.S., Engelhart, M.D., Furst, E.J., Hill., W.H. and Krathwohl, D.R. (1956) *Taxonomy of Educational Objectives: Cognitive Domain*. New York: McKay.

Boud, D. (1995) *Enhancing Learning through Self-assessment*. London: Routledge.

Boud, D. and Associates (2010) *Assessment 2020: Seven Propositions for Assessment Reform in Higher Education*. Sydney: Australian Learning and Teaching Council.

Bowl, M. (2003) *Non-traditional Entrants to Higher Education: 'They Talk about People Like Me'*. Stoke-on-Trent: Trentham Books.

Boyd, P. (2009) 'University of Cumbria: peer review of teaching, learning and assessment', in D. Gosling and K. Mason O'Connor (eds), *Beyond the Peer Observation of Teaching*. London: SEDA Publications. pp.29–35.

Brown, S. (2009) *Assessing First Year Students Effectively – Right from the Start*. Keynote at First Year Learning and Assessment Project Conference: Leeds Metropolitan University, 16 June.

Brown, S. and Knight, P. (1994) *Assessing Learners in Higher Education*. London: Kogan Page.

Brown, S. and Race, P. (2002) *Lecturing: A Practical Guide*. London: Routledge.

Brown, S., Jones, G. and Rawnsley, S. (eds) (1993) *Observing Teaching*. SEDA Paper 79 (a collection of articles on good practice, with example forms). London: SEDA Publications.

Bryson, B. (2004) *A Short History of Nearly Everything*. London: Black Swan.

Burge, E.J. and Haughey, M. (eds) (2001) *Using Learning Technologies: International Perspectives on Practice*. London: RoutledgeFalmer.

Claxton, G. (1998) *Hare Brain, Tortoise Mind*. London: Fourth Estate.

Claxton, J., Mathers, J. and Wetherell-Terry, D. (2004) 'Benefits of a 3-way collaborative learning system: action learning, continuous editing and peer assessment'. Paper presented at the BEST conference 'Reflection on teaching: the impact on learning', Edinburgh.

Coffield, F., Moseley, D., Hall, E. and Ecclestone, K. (2004) *Learning Styles and Pedagogy in Post-16 Learning: A Systematic and Critical Review*. London: Learning and Skills Research Centre. (For a shorter review, see also Coffield, F., Moseley, D., Hall, E. and Ecclestone, K. (2004) *Should We Be Using Learning Styles? What Research Has to Say to Practice*. London: Learning and Skills Research Centre.)

Coiffait, L. (ed.) (2011) *Blue Skies: New Thinking about the Future of Higher Education*. London: Pearson Centre for Policy and Education. Available at: http://pearsonblueskies.com/ (accessed 2 December 2013).

Cotton, D. (2004) 'Essentials of training design. Part 5: adult learning theories and design', *Training Journal*, May: 22–7.

Cottrell, S. (2013) *The Study Skills Handbook* (4th edn). Basingstoke: Palgrave-MacMillan.

Coursera (2013) 'Terms of use: honor code'. Available at: www.coursera.org/about/terms (accessed 12 December 2013).

Curry, L. (1990) 'A critique of the research on learning styles', *Educational Leadership*, 48(2): 50–6.

Denton, S. and Brown, S. (eds) (2009) *A Practical Guide to University and College Management: Beyond Bureaucracy*. London: Routledge.

Dewey, J. (1933) *How We Think*. New York: Dover.

Dweck, C. (2013) 'Do you trust in your ability to grow?' (interview, 27 September). Available at: http://nilofermerchant.com/2013/09/27/do-you-trust-in-your-ability-to-grow/ (accessed 2 December 2013).

Educause (2012) 'What campus leaders need to know about MOOCs'. Available at: www.educause.edu/library/resources/what-campus-leaders-need-know-about-moocs (accessed 2 December 2013).

Entwistle, N. (2009) *Teaching for Understanding at University*. London: Palgrave-Macmillan.

Financial Times Lexicon (2013) 'Definition of small private online course SPOC'. Available at: http://lexicon.ft.com/Term?term=small-private-online-course-SPOC (accessed 2 December 2013).

Fleming, N. (2001–13) VARK®: a guide to learning styles. Available at: www.vark-learn.com/english/index.asp (accessed December 2009).

Flint, N.R. and Johnson, B. (2011) *Towards Fairer University Assessment – Recognizing the Concerns of Students*. London: Routledge.

Gardner, H. (1993) *Frames of Mind: The Theory of Multiple Intelligences*. New York: Basic Books.

Gardner, H. and Hatch, T. (1989) 'Multiple intelligences go to school: educational implications of the theory of multiple intelligences', *Educational Researcher*, 18(8): 4–9.

Gibbs, G. (2010) *Using Assessment to Support Student Learning*. Leeds: Leeds Met Press.

Gibbs, G. and Simpson, C. (2002) 'Does your assessment support your students' learning?' Milton Keynes: Open University. Available at: http://citeseerx.ist.psu.edu/viewdoc/download?doi=10.1.1.201.2281&rep=rep1&type=pdf (accessed 11 April 2014).

Godfrey, J. (2013a) *How to Use Your Reading in Your Essays* (2nd edn). Basingstoke: Palgrave-MacMillan.

Godfrey, J. (2013b) *The Student Phrase Book: Vocabulary for Writing at University*. Basingstoke: Palgrave-MacMillan.

Goral, T. (2013) 'SPOCs may provide what MOOCs can't: the acronym may be new, but the SPOC concept isn't'. Available at: http://iamstem.ucdavis.edu/2013/07/06/spocs-may-provide-what-moocs-cant/ (accessed 2 December 2013).

Gosling, D. (2009) 'A new approach to peer review of teaching', in D. Gosling and K. Mason O'Connor (eds), *Beyond the Peer Observation of Teaching*. London: SEDA Publications. pp.7–15.

Gosling, D. and Mason O'Connor, K. (eds) (2009) *Beyond the Peer Observation of Teaching*. London: SEDA Publications.

Greetham, B. (2013) *How to Write Better Essays* (3rd edn). Basingstoke: Palgrave-MacMillan.

Hall, M. (2013) Vice-chancellor's blog (University of Salford). Available at: www.corporate.salford.ac.uk/leadership-management/martin-hall/blog/2013/03/my-mooc/ (accessed 2 December 2013).

Hammersley-Fletcher, L. and Orsmond, P. (2004) 'Evaluating our peers: is peer observation a meaningful process?', *Studies in Higher Education*, 29(4): 489–503.

Harper, S., Gray, S., North, S., Brown, S. with Ashton, K. (2009) 'Getting the most from staff', in S. Denton and S. Brown (eds), *A Practical Guide to University and College Management: Beyond Bureaucracy*. London: Routledge. pp.246–335.

Hativa, N. (2000) *Teaching for Effective Learning in Higher Education*. Dordrecht, Boston, MA and London: Kluwer Academic.

Hodgkinson, M. (1994) 'Peer observation of teaching performance by action enquiry', *Quality Assurance in Education*, 2(2): 26–31.

Honey, P. and Mumford, A. (1982) *The Manual of Learning Styles*. Maidenhead: Peter Honey Publications.

Hounsell, D. (2008) 'The trouble with feedback: new challenges, emerging strategies', *Interchange*, Spring. Available at: www.docs.hss.ed.ac.uk/iad/Learning_teaching/Academic_teaching/Resources/Interchange/spring2008.pdf (accessed 2 December 2013).

Hunt, D. and Chalmers, L. (eds) (2012) *University Teaching in Focus: A Learning-centred Approach*. Australia: ACER Press, and London: Routledge.

Jaques, D. (1992) *Being a personal tutor: further induction pack III*. Oxford: Oxford Polytechnic.

JISC (2004) *Designing for Learning: An Update on the Pedagogy Strand of the JISC eLearning Programme*. Bristol: JISC.

Joughin, G. (2010) *A Short Guide to Oral Assessment*. Leeds: Leeds Met Press.

Knight, P. and Yorke, M. (2003) *Assessment, Learning and Employability*. Maidenhead: SRHE/Open University Press.

Kolb, D. (1984) *Experiential Learning: Experience as the Source of Learning and Development*. Englewood Cliffs, NJ: Prentice-Hall.

Kolb, D.A. (1999) *The Kolb Learning Style Inventory*, Version 3. Boston: Hay Group.

Krathwohl, D.R. (2002) 'A Revision of Bloom's Taxonomy: An Overview', *Theory into Practice*, 41, 4 (Ohio State University).

Laurillard, D. (2001) *Rethinking University Teaching: A Framework for the Effective Use of Educational Technology* (2nd edn). London: RoutledgeFalmer.

Lindsay, R. (2004) Book review, *Studies in Higher Education*, 29(2): 279–86.

Meyer, J.H.F. and Land, R. (2003) 'Threshold concepts and troublesome knowledge 1 – linkages to ways of thinking and practising within the disciplines', in C. Rust (ed.), *Improving Student Learning – Ten Years On*. Oxford: OCSLD.

Miller, C.M.L. and Parlett, M. (1974) *Up to the Mark: A Study of the Examinations Game*, Monograph 21. London: SRHE.

Nicol, D.J. and MacFarlane-Dick, D. (2006) 'Formative assessment and self-regulated learning: a model and seven principles of good feedback practice', *Studies in Higher Education*, 31(2): 199–218.

Overbye, D. (1991) *Lonely Hearts of the Cosmos: The Scientific Quest for the Secret of the Universe*. London: Macmillan.

Peelo, M. (2002) 'Setting the scene', in M. Peelo and T. Wareham (eds), *Failing Students in Higher Education*. Buckingham: SRHE/Open University Press.

Peelo, M. and Wareham, T. (eds) (2002) *Failing Students in Higher Education*. Buckingham: Society for Research into Higher Education/Open University Press.

Pellegrino, J., Chudowsky, N. and Glaser, R. (eds) (2003) *Knowing What Students Know: The Science and Design of Educational Assessment*. Washington, DC: National Academy Press.

Petty, G. (2009) *Evidence-based Teaching: A Practical Approach* (2nd edn). Cheltenham: NelsonThornes.

Pratt, J.R. (2002) 'The manager's role in creating a blended learning environment', *Home Health Care Management & Practice*, 15(1): 76–9.

Price, M., Rust, C., O'Donovan, B. and Handley, K. (2012) *Assessment Literacy: The Foundation for Improving Student Learning*. Oxford: ASKe, Oxford Centre for Staff and Learning Development, Oxford Brookes University.

QAA (2013) *The UK Quality Code for Higher Education*. Gloucester: The Quality Assurance Association for Higher Education. Available at: http://www.qaa.ac.uk/assuringstandardsandquality/quality-code/Pages/default.aspx (last accessed 5 February 2014).

Race, P. (2003) *How to Study*. Oxford: Blackwell.

Race, P. (2005) *500 Tips on Open and Online Learning*. London: Routledge.

Race, P. (2006) *The Lecturer's Toolkit* (3rd edn). London: Routledge.

Race, P. (2007) *How to Get a Good Degree* (2nd edn). Maidenhead: Open University Press.

Race, P. (2009) *In at the Deep End* (2nd edn). Leeds: Leeds Metropolitan University Press.

Race, P. (2010) *Making Learning Happen* (2nd edn). London: Sage.

Race, P. and Pickford, R. (2007) *Making Teaching Work*. London: Sage.

Reynolds, M. (1997) 'Learning styles: a critique', *Management Learning*, 28(2): 115–33.

Robinson, A. and Udall, M. (2003) 'Developing the independent learner: the Mexican hat approach', conference proceedings of the 3rd International Symposium on Engineering Education, Southampton.

Sadler, D.R. (1989) 'Formative assessment and the design of instructional systems', *Instructional Science*, 18: 119–44.

Sadler, D.R. (1998) 'Formative assessment: revisiting the territory', *Assessment in Education: Principles, Policy and Practice*, 5: 77–84.

Sadler, D.R. (2003) 'How criteria-based grading misses the point', Presentation to the Effective Teaching and Learning Conference, Griffith University, Australia.

Sadler, D.R. (2005) 'Interpretations of criteria-based assessment and grading in higher education', *Assessment and Evaluation in Higher Education*, 30: 175–94.

Sadler, D.R. (2007) 'Perils in the meticulous specification of goals and assessment criteria', *Assessment in Education: Principles, Policy and Practice*, 14: 387–92.

Sadler, D.R. (2009a) 'Grade integrity and the representation of academic achievement', *Studies in Higher Education*, 34(7): 807–26.

Sadler, D.R. (2009b) 'Indeterminacy in the use of preset criteria for assessment and grading', *Assessment and Evaluation in Higher Education*, 34(2): 159–79.

Sadler, D.R. (2010) 'Beyond feedback: developing student capability in complex appraisal', *Assessment and Evaluation in Higher Education*, 35(5): 535–50.

Salmon, G. (2002) *E-tivities: The Key to Active Online Learning*. London: RoutledgeFalmer.

Salmon, G. (2004) *E-moderating: The Key to Teaching and Learning Online* (2nd edn). London: RoutledgeFalmer.

Sambell, K., McDowell, L. and Montgomery, C. (2013) *Assessment for Learning in Higher Education*. London: Routledge.

Schön, D. (1987) *Educating the Reflective Practitioner*. San Francisco: Jossey-Bass.

Smithers, R. (2004) 'Degree grading system faces axe', *The Guardian*, 4 November.

Soundsgood (2010) Available at: https://sites.google.com/site/soundsgooduk/ (accessed 2 December 2013).

Sparrow, B., Liu, J. and Wegner, D.M. (2011) 'Google effects on memory: cognitive consequences of having information at our fingertips', *Sciencexpress*. Available at: www.wjh.harvard.edu/~wegner/pdfs/science.1207745.full.pdf (accessed 2 December 2013).

Stowell, N. (2001) 'Equity, justice and standards: assessment decision making in higher education', paper presented at the SRHE Annual Conference, University of Cambridge (*mimeo*).

Waldrop, M.M. (2013) 'Massive Open Online Courses, aka MOOCs, transform higher education and science', *Scientific American*, 13 March. Available at: www.scientificamerican.com/article.cfm?id=massive-open-online-courses-transform-higher-education-and-science (accessed 2 December 2013).

Wierstra, R.F.A. and de Jong, J.A. (2002) 'A scaling theoretical evaluation of Kolb's Learning Style Inventory-2', in M. Valcke and D. Gombeir (eds), *Learning Styles: Reliability and Validity*. Proceedings of the 7th Annual European Learning Styles Information Network Conference, 26–28 June, Ghent: University of Ghent, pp. 431–40.

Yorke, M. (2002) 'Academic failure: a retrospective view from non-completing students', in M. Peelo and T. Wareham (eds), *Failing Students in Higher Education*. Buckingham: SRHE/Open University Press.

SEVEN FACTORS UNDERPINNING SUCCESSFUL LEARNING: PRINCIPAL LINKS

INDEX